Ancient Texts
for the Study
of the Hebrew Bible

Ancient Texts
for the Study
of the Hebrew Bible

A Guide to the
Background Literature

KENTON L. SPARKS

HENDRICKSON
PUBLISHERS

© 2005 by Hendrickson Publishers, Inc.
P. O. Box 3473
Peabody, Massachusetts 01961-3473

ISBN 1-56563-407-1

Printed in the United States of America

Second Printing — March 2006

Cover Art: The cover photo is of a statue of a hero taming a lion (possibly Gilgamesh, the legendary king of Uruk). From the palace of Sargon II (722–705 B.C.E.), Khorsabad. The colossal statues of genii protected the entrance to the throne room. The statue is located in the Louvre, Paris, France.

Photo Credit: Erich Lessing/Art Resource, NY. Used with permission.

Library of Congress Cataloging-in-Publication Data

Sparks, Kenton L.
   Ancient texts for the study of the Hebrew Bible : a guide to the background literature / Kenton L. Sparks.
      p. cm.
   Includes bibliographical references and indexes.
   ISBN 1-56563-407-1 (alk. paper)
   1. Middle Eastern literature—Relation to the Old Testament. 2. Bible. O.T.—Extra-canonical parallels. 3. Bible. O.T.—Criticism, Form. I. Title.
   BS1184.S63 2005
   221.9′5—dc22
                                        2005010365

To John Van Seters

Contents

Preface

Early in my graduate study at the University of North Carolina, I found myself wishing for an introductory survey of the comparative literature that was valuable for readers of the Hebrew Bible. At that time, in 1990, my search for such a book yielded only one survey volume, and it was too brief—and sometimes too influenced by theological fundamentalism—to be of use for serious biblical research. Meanwhile, my appreciation for the comparative value of Near Eastern literature was stirred again and again by my studies with John Van Seters and Jack Sasson, two scholars who, in their respective ways, have made extensive use of Near Eastern materials when reading the Hebrew Bible. Not long after I completed my terminal degree, I approached John Kutsko, then of Hendrickson Publishers, with a proposal to write the book that I had wished for during my graduate work.

This project was originally conceived to fill two roles for readers of the Hebrew Bible: to introduce important comparative texts from the ancient Near East, and to outline the import of these ancient texts for the study of Israelite literature. As most projects do, this one has taken much longer, and become much larger, than originally planned. The project has morphed into two different books, each addressing one side of the comparative equation. This book provides an overview and introduction to the comparative Near Eastern literature, and the second volume—now in an advanced state of preparation—will examine the Hebrew Bible in this comparative literary context. For this reason, insofar as possible, I have refrained from campaigning for my unique generic judgments about the Hebrew Bible in the present volume. The generic parallels that I have highlighted are of a general nature, and should be self-evident to most scholars, regardless of their theoretical stripe. If there is a clear exception to this rule, it would be in the discussion of love poetry, where I offer a preliminary suggestion for how one ought to read the Hebrew Song of Songs.

I would like to offer a few cautions, directions, and explanations to readers of this volume. First, although the presentation of so many texts might create the impression that this survey of the Near Eastern literature is "complete," it should be remembered that "complete" is a relative term, particularly in this case. I have indeed attempted to include the most important comparative exemplars from the ancient Near East, but many thousands of texts have been unearthed from Mesopotamia, Anatolia, Egypt, Syria, and Palestine, and only a small fraction of these are actually treated in the chapters that follow. In this regard, we should note that Giovanni Pettinato reports that some 300,000 unpublished cuneiform tablets are presently stashed in the basement of the National Museum in Baghdad, Iraq, and this only adds to the thousands of unpublished texts presently housed in museums all over the world.

Second, I would caution readers against the illusion that reading a single chapter, such as the chapter on "History and Historiography," adequately introduces the genre. As I have studied the various genres, it has become more and more apparent that genres are like religions—"to know one is to know none." So, for instance, ancient historiography cannot be appreciated apart from a good grounding in myths, novels, folktales, genealogies, king lists, and archives, among others. It is by acquiring good familiarity with the full range of ancient literature that we begin to appreciate any one genre very well.

Third, readers should be aware that the entries in this volume vary significantly with respect to the materials that they cover. Some entries treat a single ancient text that was written at one historical point in time, while other entries cover a whole range of related texts from a long historical period. Such differences are dictated mainly by pragmatic concerns.

Fourth, in a related matter, I would point out that the order of the chapters in the book, as well as the arrangement of the individual entries in each chapter, follow a certain logic that is not immediately visible to readers. The chapter order gives priority to those genres that provide basic conceptual features for understanding the others. So, for instance, I find that a background in archives and libraries (ch. 1) and in scribal wisdom (ch. 2) is basic for appreciating the other genres in the volume. Scribal wisdom then leads organically into discussions of hymns, prayers, laments, love poetry, omens, apocalyptic, and priestly wisdom, thus accounting roughly for the order of the first seven chapters. At the same time, there was logic working in another direction. Because historiography tends to draw upon many types of source material, it was important to cover the narrative and chronographic genres that are used by historians before looking at historiography itself. This is why tales, epics, myths, and genealogies/king lists are where they are in the book. As for the arrangement within the chapters, the tendency is to move from Mesopotamia, to Egypt, and then to Syria/Palestine and Hatti. This is primarily because the vast majority of comparative exemplars come from Mesopotamia and Egypt. However, when one of the represented civilizations was much more important than the others regarding the genre in question (e.g., Egypt and novellas; Hatti and treaties), then I began with that civilization. This said, it is clear that chronology is also an important factor in the arrangement of the materials.

Fifth, the references and bibliographies in the volume require a word of explanation. Sources are cited using only the author's last name. When necessary, a page number accompanies the reference [e.g., (Lambert, 253)], and a date of publication is also provided when more than one work is cited for that author [e.g., (Lambert 1984, 253)]. If the reader wishes to consult the complete bibliographic reference, he/she should first consult the bibliography for the entry in question. If the source does not appear there, the reader should consult the general bibliography at the end of the chapter and then, this failing, the list of abbreviations and basic sources provided at the beginning of the volume.

Sixth, readers should be aware that some of the translations in this volume have been "modernized," a necessity given that many of the translations—such as those in *ANET*—are older and followed punctuation conventions that are different than in our own day.

Seventh, I should provide a word of explanation for certain variations in the "tone" of this volume, given that the book vacillates to some extent between bookish and less bookish sorts of discourse. I have always envisioned this project as a tool for both the initiated and the uninitiated, but this decision has required that my rhetoric take a simpler turn in certain instances, particularly in the theoretical introduction. Although the rhetoric of the introduction may seem sophomoric at times when judged from an informed scholarly perspective, I believe that it offers theoretical insights that will be valuable even for seasoned biblical scholars. One result of this rhetorical effort is that the book serves not only as a resource volume for scholars and graduate students but also as a textbook. I presently use it at Eastern University in a three-semester-hour class entitled, "The Genres of the Hebrew Bible," where students read it alongside the primary sources from the ancient Near East and Hebrew Bible. Each week of class requires reading a chapter of this book as background (for Monday class), selected readings from primary Near Eastern sources (for Wednesday), and then appropriate readings from the Bible (for Friday). I have found that the sixteen chapters fit nicely into standard sixteen-week semesters, but this format will obviously need to be adjusted for the vagaries of different institutional calendars. The overall responses from students, and the pedagogical effects, have been very positive. I find that students come away from the class with a better sense of the Hebrew Bible than they might receive in standard introductions to the corpus.

In the interest of improving future editions of this book, I would invite those who use it to contact me for any of the following purposes: (1) To inform me of important resources or publications that I may have overlooked; (2) To inform me of new resources and publications; (3) To point out substantive errors that appear in any of the book's entries; (4) To point out where my treatment of a text (or texts) seems to leave out or unduly neglect important interpretive issues; or (5) To alert me to interesting parallels between the Hebrew Bible and ANE that have been overlooked. Any comments along these lines will be deeply appreciated and thoughtfully considered.

Several important publications have reached me too late to incorporate into my discussions and bibliographies. These include the following: J. Black, G. Cunningham, E. Robson, and G. Zólyomi, *The Literature of Ancient Sumer* (Oxford: University Press, 2005), F. W. Dobbs-Allsopp, J. J. M. Roberts, C. L. Seow, and R. E. Whitaker, *Hebrew Inscriptions: Texts from the Biblical Period of the Monarchy with Concordance* (New Haven; London: Yale, 2004), and B. R. Foster, *Before the Muses: An Anthology of Akkadian Literature* (3d ed.; Bethesda, MD: CDL Press, 2005). All of these volumes are very nicely done and should be duly noted by readers.

Many colleagues and friends have contributed to the work in these pages, either by helping me with its substance or by encouraging me to stay the course. Special thanks goes to John Kutsko, who originally accepted the proposal at Hendrickson and has remained interested in my work even after accepting his new position at Abingdon Press. After John's departure, Hendrickson was very fortunate to acquire the expertise of my editor, Allan Emery. Allan is not only an excellent editor but also a top-notch scholar in his own right; much of what is good about this book can be traced back to his academic competence and careful eye. Other scholars who rendered assistance to me include James Allen (Metropolitan Museum), Jan Assmann (Heidelberg), Robert Biggs (Chicago), Stephanie Dalley (Oxford), Jim Eisenbraun (Eisenbrauns Publishers), Peter Enns (Westminster Theological Seminary), Walter Farber (Chicago), Dan Fleming (New York), Andrew George (London), Steven Grosby (Clemson), Bill Hallo (Yale), Ben Haring (Leiden), James Hoffmeier (Trinity International University), Harry Hoffner (Chicago), John Huddlestun (College of Charleston), Shlomo Izre'el (Tel Aviv), Janet Johnson (Chicago), Alasdair Livingstone (Birmingham), Tremper Longman (Westmont), David Lorton (Baltimore), Martti Nissinen (Helsinki), Simo Parpola (Helsinki), Stephen Quirke (London), Chris Rollston (Emmanuel School of Religion), Benjamin Sass (Tel Aviv), Itamar Singer (Tel Aviv), Theo van den Hout (Chicago), Andy Vaughn (Gustavus Adolphus College), David Wright (Brandeis), Lawson Younger (Trinity International University), Jim Watts (Syracuse), Moshe Weinfeld (Jerusalem), and my four electronic colleagues on the ANE list, Liz Fried (Michigan), Victor Hurowitz (Ben Gurion), Raz Kletter (Israel Antiquities Authority), and Bob Whiting (Helsinki). I should also like to single out two fine graduate students, Andrea Kucharek (Heidelberg) and Mary Frances Wogec (Berkeley), who lent me their expertise even during the last busy stages of their respective dissertations. Academia will soon hear more from both of them.

It goes without saying that my former advisors at the University of North Carolina, Jack Sasson (now at Vanderbilt) and John Van Seters (now at Wilfred Laurier), were constant sources of insight and encouragement. As my Doktor-Vater, John has been particularly helpful in a thousand ways along the way; I dedicate this volume to him as a modest gesture of appreciation for his assistance and friendship.

The institutional debts that I have accrued are also great. Providence Baptist Church (Raleigh, N.C.), my former academic and ministry home, provided extensive financial support for my research and granted time and stipends for study in the States and in Europe. These investments were only one small part of Pastor David Horner's wide-ranging vision to develop the intellectual lives of his pastoral team. As for the nuts and bolts of the actual work on this volume, no one at Providence was more important than my administrative assistant, Beverly Benfield; her leadership skills lightened my administrative load, and her industrious spirit yielded the thousands of photocopies—of countless articles and out of print monographs—that I needed to consult for this volume. No less valuable has been the support of my present institutional home, Eastern University. The administration has regularly provided financial support and course reductions, as well as funding for my research assistants, Steve Krening and Sara Schlapping, who are chiefly responsible for the indexes in this volume. As for the Eastern library staff, it is second to none when it comes to negotiating through the vagaries of the Inter-Library Loan cyberworld. This counts especially for Ellen Mergner and Jonathan Beasley. Faculty colleagues at Eastern have also contributed to this book in enumerable ways. Those who have read and commented on parts of the manuscript include Steve Boyer (Theology), Phil Cary (Philosophy), Chris Hall (Theology), Dwight Peterson (New Testament), Margaret Peterson (Theology), and my colleague in Hebrew Bible, Ray Van Leeuwen.

Closer to home, I reserve special words of thanks for friends and family, who remind me again and again that true joy is found not merely in learning but in living. Here I think fondly of my close friend Leo Sandgren (University of Florida), of my parents, Morris and Jean, and of my brother Kelly and his family. Of course, my deepest sense of gratitude is felt toward those who have paid the greatest price for this volume, my wife Cheryl, and daughters Emily and Cara. Should any readers happen to benefit from this volume, the debt owed is not to me but to them, and to the one who alone knows all that is true: Soli Deo Gloria!

Note on the Second Printing

This second printing of ATSHB (as the book has come to be known) has allowed me to correct several infelicities in the first printing and to make two substantive changes, one regarding the practice of circumcision in ancient Egypt (p. 203) and another regarding the location of Izbet Ṣarṭah (p. 465). I have the opportunity as well to note the discovery of new abecedary at Tell Zayit, where excavations are being directed by Ron Tappy of Pittsburgh Theological Seminary. This inscription dates to the Iron I period and is comparable to texts treated on pp. 450-51 and 465 of this volume.

Bibliographically, I would like to alert readers to the following new and promising sources for the study of ANE texts: J. P. Allen, *The Ancient Egyptian Pyramid Texts* (Atlanta, 2005); R. J. Dumbrill, *The Archaeomusicology of the Ancient Near East* (London, 2005); U. Koch, *Secrets of Extispicy: The Chapter Multābiltu of the Babylonian Extispicy Series and Niṣirti bārûti Texts mainly from Aššurbanipal's Library* (Münster, 2005); J. L. Miller, *Studies in the Origins, Development and Interpretation of the Kizzuwatna Rituals* (Wiesbaden, 2004); N. C. Strudwick, *Texts from the Pyramid Age* (Atlanta, 2005); B. Sass, *The Alphabet at the Turn of the Millennium: The West Semitic Alphabet ca.1150-850 BC* (Tel Aviv, 2005); E. Reiner and D. Pingree, *Babylonian Planetary Omens: Part Four* (Groningen, 2005); and J. J. A. van Dijk and M. J. Geller, *Ur III incantations from the Frau Professor Hilprecht-Collection, Jena* (Wiesbaden, 2003).

Abbreviations

General Abbreviations

AKL	Assyrian king lists
Amen.	The Instructions of Amenemope
ANE	Ancient Near East
BD	Book of the Dead
BKL	Babylonian king lists
ca.	circa
cf.	*confer*, compare
ch(s).	chapter(s)
CT	Coffin Texts
DC	Demotic Chronicle
ed(s).	editor(s), edited by
e.g.	*exempli gratia*, for example
Eng.	English
enl.	enlarged
esp.	especially
et al.	*et alii*, and others
etc.	*et cetera*, and the rest
exp.	expanded
Gr.	Greek
i.e.	*id est*, that is
Ki.	Kish
LKL	Lagaš King List
MT	Masoretic Text to abbrev.
n.p.	no place; no publisher
no(s).	number(s)
NS	New Series
OB	Old Babylonian
p(p).	page(s)

P.	Papyrus
pl(s).	plural; plate(s)
PT	Pyramid Texts
rev.	revised (by)
SB	Standard Babylonian
SKL	Sumerian King List
TC	Turin Canon
trans.	translator, translated by
v(v).	verse(s)
vol(s).	volume(s)

Sigla for Collections and Provenances

AeIN	Aegyptisk Inventar-Nummer, Egyptian collection of the Ny Carlsberg Glyptotek, Copenhagen, Denmark
AIS	Aramaic Inscriptions from Sefire, I–III
AO	collections of the Department des antiquités orientales, Musée du Louvre
Bab	field numbers of tablets excavated at Babylon
BE	Babylonian Expedition of the University of Pennsylvania (Philadelphia)
BIN	Babylonian inscriptions in the collection of James B. Nies
BM	collections of the British Museum, London
CBS	catalogue of the Babylonian Section, University of Pennsylvania Museum of Archaeology and Anthropology
CTUPOI	cuneiform texts from the Ur III period in the Oriental Institute
EA	El-Amarna tablets. According to the edition of J. A. Knudtzon, *Die el-Amarna-Tafeln.* Leipzig: J. C. Hinrichs, 1908–1915. Reprint, Aalen, Germany: O. Zeller, 1964. Continued in A. F. Rainey, *El-Amarna Tablets, 359–379.* 2d revised ed. Kevelaer, Germany: Butzon & Bercker, 1978
Emar	Emar texts. According to the edition of D. Arnaud, *Recherches au pays d'Aštata.* 4 vols. *Emar* 6. Paris: Éditions Recherche sur les Civilisations, 1985–1987
HL	Hammurabi's Laws (Code of Hammurabi)
JE	Journal d'Entrée, Cairo Museum, Cairo, Egypt
M	Mari texts
O	Oriental (ancient). Inventory for the oriental collection of the Museum of Brussels
RIH	Ras Ibn Hani
RS	Ras Shamra: museum siglum of the Louvre and Damascus (Ras Shamra)

TIM	texts in the Iraq Museum
U	find siglum, Ur (London/Philadelphia/Baghdad)
UCLM	tablets in the collection of the Robert H. Lowie Museum of Anthropology of the University of California, Berkeley
UIOM	tablets in the collections of the University of Illinois Oriental Museum
VAT	tablets of the Vorderasiatische Abteilung, Staatliche Museen, Berlin
W	field numbers of tablets excavated at Warka
YBC	tablets in the Yale Babylonian Collection, New Haven

Secondary Sources

AAA	*Annals of Archaeology and Anthropology*
AASOR	Annual of the American Schools of Oriental Research
AAT	Ägypten und Altes Testament
AbB	Altbabylonische Briefe in Umschrift und Übersetzung
ABD	*Anchor Bible Dictionary*. Edited by D. N. Freedman. 6 vols. New York: Doubleday, 1992
AbrN	*Abr-Nahrain*
AcAntHung	*Acta antiqua Academiae scientiarum hungaricae*
ActSum	*Acta sumerologica*
AEL	*Ancient Egyptian Literature*. M. Lichtheim. 3 vols. Berkeley: University of California Press, 1971–1980
ÄF	Ägyptologische Forschungen
AfK	*Archiv für Keilschriftforschung*
AfO	*Archiv für Orientforschung*
AfOB	Archiv für Orientforschung: Beiheft
ÄgAbh	Ägyptologische Abhandlungen
AHI	*Ancient Hebrew Inscriptions: Corpus and Concordance*. G. I. Davies. Cambridge: Cambridge University Press, 1991
AJA	*American Journal of Archaeology*
AJSL	*American Journal of Semitic Languages and Literature*
AKPAW	Abhandlungen der königlich Preussischen Akademie der Wissenschaften
ALANE	*Archives and Libraries in the Ancient Near East: 1500–300 B.C.* O. Pedersén. Bethesda, Md.: CDL Press, 1998
ALASP	Abhandlungen zur Literatur Alt-Syren-Palästinas und Mesopotamiens
AMD	Ancient Magic and Divination
AnBib	*Analecta biblica*
AncSoc	*Ancient Society*

ANET	*Ancient Near Eastern Texts Relating to the Old Testament.* Edited by J. B. Pritchard. 3d ed. Princeton: Princeton University Press, 1969
AnOr	Analecta orientalia
AnSt	*Anatolian Studies*
AO	*Der Alte Orient*
AOAT	Alter Orient und Altes Testament
AoF	*Altorientalische Forschungen*
AOS	American Oriental Series
ARAB	*Ancient Records of Assyria and Babylonia.* Daniel David Luckenbill. 2 vols. Chicago: University of Chicago Press, 1926–1927
ARM	Archives royales de Mari
ARMT	Archives royales de Mari, transcrite et traduite
AS	Assyriological Studies
ASAE	*Annales du service des antiquités de l'Egypte*
ASOR	American Schools of Oriental Research
ASTI	*Annual of the Swedish Theological Institute*
AThR	*Anglican Theological Review*
Atiqot	ᶜAtiqot
AuOr	*Aula orientalis*
AuOrSup	Aula Orientalis Supplementa
AUSS	*Andrews University Seminary Studies*
BA	*Biblical Archaeologist*
BAeg	Bibliotheca aegyptiaca
BaghM	*Baghdader Mitteilungen*
BaghMB	Baghdader Mitteilungen: Beihefte
BAR	*Biblical Archaeology Review*
BASOR	*Bulletin of the American Schools of Oriental Research*
BASP	*Bulletin of the American Society of Papyrologists*
BBVO	Berliner Beiträge zum Vorderen Orient
BdE	Bibliothèque d'étude
BEATAJ	Beiträge zur Erforschung des Alten Testaments und des antiken Judentum
Bib	*Biblica*
BibOr	Biblica et orientalia
BIFAO	*Bulletin de l'Institut français d'archéologie orientale*
BJRL	*Bulletin of the John Rylands University Library of Manchester*
BJS	Brown Judaic Studies
BM²	*Before the Muses: An Anthology of Akkadian Literature.* B. R. Foster. 2d ed. Potomac, Md.: CDL Press, 1996
BM³	*Before the Muses: An Anthology of Akkadian Literature.* B. R. Foster. 3d ed. Bethesda, Md.: CDL Press, 2005
BMECCJ	Bulletin of the Middle Eastern Culture Center in Japan
BMes	Bibliotheca mesopotamica

BN	*Biblische Notizen*
BO	*Bibliotheca orientalis*
BoSt	Boghazköi-Studien
BR	*Biblical Research*
BRev	*Bible Review*
BSac	*Bibliotheca sacra*
BTB	*Biblical Theology Bulletin*
BWANT	Beiträge zur Wissenschaft vom Alten und Neuen Testament
BZ	*Biblische Zeitschrift*
BZAW	Beihefte zur Zeitschrift für die alttestamentliche Wissenschaft
CahRB	Cahiers de la Revue biblique
CAI	*A Corpus of Ammonite Inscriptions*. W. E. Auffrecht. Ancient Near Eastern Texts and Studies 4. Lewiston, N.Y.: Mellen, 1989
CANE	*Civilizations of the Ancient Near East*. Edited by J. Sasson. 4 vols. New York: Scribner, 1995
CBQ	*Catholic Biblical Quarterly*
CBQMS	Catholic Biblical Quarterly Monograph Series
CHLI	*Corpus of Hieroglyphic Luwian Inscriptions*. J. D. Hawkins and H. Çambel. 2 vols. in 4. New York: de Gruyter, 1999–2000
CHSTB	Corpus der hurritischen Sprachdenkmäler, 1: Die Texte aus Boğazköy
CJT	*Canadian Journal of Theology*
CM	Cuneiform Monographs
ConBOT	Coniectanea biblica: Old Testament Series
COS	*The Context of Scripture*. Edited by W. W. Hallo. 3 vols. Leiden: Brill, 1997–2002
CRAI	*Comptes rendus de l'Académie des inscriptions et belles-lettres*
CT	*Cuneiform Texts from Babylonian Tablets in the British Museum*. London: Trustees of the British Museum, 1896–
CTH	*Catalogue des textes hittites*. E. Laroche. Paris: Klincksieck, 1971
CTM	Calwer theologische Monographien, Reihe A, Bibelwissenschaft
CTU	*The Cuneiform Alphabetic Texts from Ugarit, Ras Ibn Hani, and Other Places*. Edited by M. Dietrich, O. Loretz, and J. Sanmartín. Münster: Ugarit, 1995
DE	*Discussions in Egyptology*
DFIFAO	Documents de fouilles publiées par les membres de l'Institut français d'archéologie orientale du Caire
DJD	Discoveries in the Judaean Desert
DMOA	Documenta et monumenta Orientis antiqui
DNP	*Der neue Pauly: Enzyklopädie der Antike*. Edited by H. Cancik and H. Schneider. 16 vols. in 19. Stuttgart: J. B. Metzler, 1996–2003

DNWSI	*Dictionary of the North-West Semitic Inscriptions.* J. Hoftijzer and K. Jongeling. 2 vols. Leiden: Brill, 1995
EncJud	*Encyclopaedia Judaica.* 16 vols. Jerusalem, 1972
ER	*The Encyclopedia of Religion.* Edited by M. Eliade. 16 vols. New York, 1987
ERE	*Encyclopaedia of Religion and Ethics.* Edited by J. Hastings. 13 vols. New York: C. Scribner's Sons, 1908–1927. Reprint, 7 vols., 1951
ErIsr	*Eretz-Israel*
EvQ	*Evangelical Quarterly*
FAT	Forschungen zum Alten Testament
FM	Florilegium marianum
GM	*Gottinger Miszellen*
GOA	Gottinger Orientforschungen, 4 Reihe, Ägypten
HAE	*Handbuch der althebräischen Epigrafik.* J. Renz and W. Röllig. Darmstadt: Wissenschaftliche Buchgesellschaft, 1995–
HAR	*Hebrew Annual Review* .
HS	*Hebrew Studies*
HSCP	*Harvard Studies in Classical Philology*
HSM	Harvard Semitic Monographs
HSS	Harvard Semitic Studies
HTR	*Harvard Theological Review*
HTS	Harvard Theological Studies
HUCA	*Hebrew Union College Annual*
HUCASup	Hebrew Union College Annual Supplements
IDBSup	*Interpreter's Dictionary of the Bible: Supplementary Volume.* Edited by K. Crim. Nashville: Abingdon, 1976
IEJ	*Israel Exploration Journal*
Int	*Interpretation*
IstMitt	*Istanbuler Mitteilungen*
ITQ	*Irish Theological Quarterly*
JA	*Journal asiatique*
JAAR	*Journal of the American Academy of Religion*
JANES	*Journal of the Ancient Near Eastern Society* (Jewish Theological Seminary, New York, NY)
JAOS	*Journal of the American Oriental Society*
JARCE	*Journal of the American Research Center in Egypt*
JBL	*Journal of Biblical Literature*
JCS	*Journal of Cuneiform Studies*
JEA	*Journal of Egyptian Archaeology*
JEOL	*Jaarbericht van het Vooraziatisch-Egyptisch Gezelschap (Genootschap) Ex oriente lux*
JESHO	*Journal of the Economic and Social History of the Orient*
JETS	*Journal of the Evangelical Theological Society*
JNES	*Journal of Near Eastern Studies*

JNSL	*Journal of Northwest Semitic Languages*
JQR	*Jewish Quarterly Review*
JSOR	*Journal of the Society of Oriental Research*
JSOT	*Journal for the Study of the Old Testament*
JSOTSup	Journal for the Study of the Old Testament: Supplement Series
JSPSup	Journal for the Study of the Pseudepigrapha: Supplement Series
JSS	*Journal of Semitic Studies*
JSSEA	*Journal of the Society for the Study of Egyptian Antiquities*
JSSSup	Journal of Semitic Studies: Supplement
JTS	*Journal of Theological Studies*
KAI	*Kanaanäische und aramäische Inschriften.* H. Donner and W. Röllig. 3d ed. 3 vols. [texts 1–279]. Wiesbaden: Harrassowitz, 1971–1976; 5th ed. Vols. 1– [texts 1–320]. Wiesbaden: Harrassowitz, 2002–
KAR	*Keilschrifttexte aus Assur religiösen Inhalts.* Edited by E. Ebeling. 2 vols. Leipzig, 1919–1923
KBo	Keilschrifttexte aus Boghazköi
KTU	*Die keilalphabetischen Texte aus Ugarit.* Edited by M. Dietrich, O. Loretz, and J. Sanmartín. AOAT 24/1. Kevelaer, Germany: Butzon & Bercker, 1976. 2d enlarged ed. of *KTU: The Cuneiform Alphabetic Texts from Ugarit, Ras Ibn Hani, and Other Places.* Edited by M. Dietrich, O. Loretz, and J. Sanmartín. Münster: Ugarit, 1995 (= *CTU*)
KUB	Keilschrifturkunden aus Boghazköi. Vols. 1–13. Berlin: Akademie-Verlag, 1921–1925
KUB	Keilschrifturkunden aus Boghazköi. Vols. 14–. Berlin: Akademie-Verlag, 1926–
KZ	*Zeitschrift für Vergleichende Sprachforschung (Kuhns Zeitschrift)*
LÄ	*Lexikon der Ägyptologie.* Edited by W. Helck, E. Otto, and W. Westendorf. Wiesbaden: Harrassowitz, 1972–
LAE	*The Literature of Ancient Egypt: An Anthology of Stories, Instructions, Stelae, Autobiographies, and Poetry.* W. K. Simpson, R. K. Ritner, V. A. Tobin, and E. F. Wente Jr. 3d ed. New Haven; London: Yale, 2003
LAPO	Littératures anciennes du Proche-Orient
LAS	*Letters from Assyrian Scholars to the Kings Esarhaddon and Assurbanipal.* S. Parpola. 2 vols. Kevelaer, Germany: Butzon & Bercker, 1970–1983
LCL	Loeb Classical Library
LKA	*Literarische Keilschrifttexten aus Assur.* E. Ebeling. Berlin: Akademie, 1953
MAD	Materials for the Assyrian Dictionary

MAOG	Mitteilungen der Altorientalischen Gesellschaft
MARI	*Mari: Annales de recherches interdisciplinaires*
MC	Mesopotamian Civilizations
MDAI	*Mitteilungen des Deutschen archäologischen Instituts*
MDAIK	*Mitteilungen des Deutschen archäologischen Instituts, Abteilung Kairo*
MDOG	*Mitteilungen der Deutschen Orient-Gesellschaft*
MelT	*Melita theologica*
MIOF	*Mitteilungen des Instituts für Orientforschung*
MVAG	Mitteilungen der Vorderasiatisch-ägyptischen Gesellschaft. Vols. 1–44. 1896–1939
NABU	*Nouvelles assyriologiques breves et utilitaires*
NCB	New Century Bible
NPEPP	*The New Princeton Encyclopedia of Poetry and Poetics.* Edited by A. Preminger and T. V. F. Brogan. Princeton, N.J.: Princeton University Press, 1993
Numen	Numen: International Review for the History of Religions
OBO	Orbis biblicus et orientalis
OCD	*Oxford Classical Dictionary.* Edited by S. Hornblower and A. Spawforth. 3d ed. Oxford: Oxford University Press, 1996
OEANE	*The Oxford Encyclopedia of Archaeology in the Near East.* Edited by E. M. Meyers. 5 vols. New York: Oxford University Press, 1997
OIP	Oriental Institute Publications
OLA	Orientalia lovaniensia analecta
OLP	*Orientalia lovaniensia periodica*
OLZ	*Orientalistische Literaturzeitung*
OMRO	*Oudheidkundige Mededelingen in het Rijksmuseum van Oudheiden te Leiden*
OPBIAA	Occasional Publications of the British Institute of Archaeology at Ankara
OPSNKF	Occasional Publications of the Samuel Noah Kramer Fund
Or	*Orientalia* (NS)
OrAnt	*Oriens antiquus*
OTL	Old Testament Library
OTP	*Old Testament Pseudepigrapha.* Edited by J. H. Charlesworth. 2 vols. New York: Doubleday, 1983–1985
OTS	Old Testament Studies
OtSt	*Oudtestamentische Studiën*
PA	Probleme der Ägyptologie
PAAJR	*Proceedings of the American Academy of Jewish Research*
PBS	Publications of the Babylonian Section
PCBRHEAM	Publications du Comité belge de recherches historiques, épigraphiques, et archéologiques en Mésopotamie
PEQ	*Palestine Exploration Quarterly*

PSBA	*Proceedings of the Society of Biblical Archaeology*
PW	*Paulys Realencyclopädie der classischen Altertumswissenschaft.* A. F. Pauly. New edition G. Wissowa. 49 vols. Munich: A. Druckenmüller, 1980
QS	Quaderni di semitistica
RA	*Revue d'assyriologie et d'archéologie orientale*
RAI	Rencontre assyriologique internationale
RB	*Revue biblique*
RdE	*Revue d'égyptologie*
REg	*Revue d'égyptologie*
REG	*Revue des études grecques*
RHA	*Revue hittite et asianique*
RHR	*Revue de l'histoire des religions*
RIDA	*Revue internationale des droits de l'antiquité*
RIMA	The Royal Inscriptions of Mesopotamia, Assyrian Periods
RlA	*Reallexikon der Assyriologie.* Edited by Erich Ebeling et al. Berlin: de Gruyter, 1928–
RSO	*Revista degli studi orientali*
SAA	State Archives of Assyria
SAAB	*State Archives of Assyria Bulletin*
SAALT	State Archives of Assyria Literary Texts
SAAS	State Archives of Assyria Studies
SAHG	*Sumerische und akkadische Hymnen und Gebete.* A. Falkenstein and W. von Soden. Zurich: Artemis, 1953
SAK	*Studien zur altägyptischen Kultur*
SANE	Sources from the Ancient Near East
SANT	Studien zum Alten und Neuen Testaments
SAOC	Studies in Ancient Oriental Civilizations
SBAW	Sitzungsberichte der bayerischen Akademie der Wissenschaften
SBLABS	Society of Biblical Literature Archaeology and Biblical Studies
SBLDS	Society of Biblical Literature Dissertation Series
SBLMS	Society of Biblical Literature Monograph Series
SBLRBS	Society of Biblical Literature Resources for Biblical Study
SBLSymS	Society of Biblical Literature Symposium Series
SBLWAW	Society of Biblical Literature Writings from the Ancient World
SBS	Stuttgarter Bibelstudien
SCCNH	Studies on the Civilization and Culture of Nuzi and the Hurrians
ScrHier	Scripta hierosolymitana
SEL	*Studi epigrafici e linguistici*
Sem	*Semitica*
SemeiaSt	Semeia Studies
SJLA	Studies in Judaism in Late Antiquity

SKPAW	Sitzungsberichte der königlich Preussischen Akademie der Wissenschaften
SÖAW	Sitzungen der österreichischen Akademie der Wissenschaften in Wien
SSEA	Society for the Study of Egyptian Antiquities
SSI	*Textbook of Syrian Semitic Inscriptions.* J. C. L. Gibson, 3 vols. Oxford: Clarendon, 1971–1982
SSN	Studia semitica neerlandica
ST	*Studia theologica*
StBoT	Studien für den Boğazköy-Texten
StudOr	*Studia orientalia*
SubBi	Subsidia biblica
Sumer	*Sumer: A Journal of Archaeology and History in Iraq*
TA	*Tel Aviv*
TAPA	*Transactions of the American Philological Association*
TCL	Textes cunéiformes. Musée du Louvre
TCS	Texts from Cuneiform Sources
TH	Texte der Hethiter
TLZ	*Theologische Literaturzeitung*
TSTS	Toronto Semitic Texts and Studies
TUAT	*Texte aus der Umwelt des Alten Testaments.* Edited by Otto Kaiser. Gütersloh, Germany: G. Mohn, 1984–
TWAT	*Theologische Wörterbuch zum Alten Testament.* Edited by G. J. Botterweck, H. Ringgren, and H. J. Fabry. Stuttgart: W. Kohlhammer, 1970–
TynBul	*Tyndale Bulletin*
UBL	*Ugaritisch-biblische Literatur*
UET	Ur Excavations: Texts
UF	*Ugarit-Forschungen*
UNHAII	Utigaven van het Nederlands Historisch-Archaeologisch Instituut te Istanbul
Urk	Urkunden des ägyptischen Altertums. 8 vols. Edited by K. Sethe, H. W. Helck, H. Schäffer, H. Grapow, O. Firchow. Leipzig: Hinrichs; Berlin: Akademie, 1903–57
VAB	Vorderasiatische Bibliothek. Lepizig, 1907–
VT	*Vetus Testamentum*
VTSup	Supplements to Vetus Testamentum
WHJP	World History of the Jewish People
WMANT	Wissenschaftliche Monographien zum Alten und Neuen Testament
WO	*Die Welt des Orients*
WTJ	*Westminster Theological Journal*
WVDOG	Wissenschaftliche Veröffentlichungen der deutschen Orientgesellschaft
YNER	Yale Near Eastern Researches

YOS	Yale Oriental Series, Babylonian Texts
ZA	*Zeitschrift für Assyriologie*
ZABR	*Zeitschrift für altorientalische und biblische Rechtgeschichte*
ZAH	*Zeitschrift für Althebräistik*
ZÄS	*Zeitschrift für ägyptische Sprache und Altertumskunde*
ZAW	*Zeitschrift für die alttestamentliche Wissenschaft*
ZDMGSup	Zeitschrift der deutschen morgenländischen Gesellschaft: Supplementbände
ZDPV	*Zeitschrift des deutschen Palästina-Vereins*
ZPE	*Zeitschrift für Papyrologie und Epigraphik*
ZTK	*Zeitschrift für Theologie und Kirche*

List of Tables

Archaeological Period in Palestine	Mesopotamia	
Early Bronze 3100–2100	Sumerian Dynasties 3100–2400 B.C.E.	
	Old Akkadian Period 2400–2100	
Middle Bronze 2100–1500	Ur-III Dynasty (Neo-Sumerian) 2100–2000	
	Old Babylonian Period 2000–1600	Old Assyrian Period 2000–1750
Late Bronze 1500–1200	Middle Babylonian Period, 1600–1200 -Kassites, 1600–1150	
Iron I 1200–900		Middle Assyrian Period 1250–900
Iron II 900–600	Neo-Babylonian Period 750–539	Neo-Assyrian Period 900–609
Iron III 600–330	Persian Period 539–330	
Hellenistic Period 330–	Greek Period (Seleucids from 323) 330–	

Egypt	Syria-Palestine	Anatolia
Early Dynastic and Old Kingdom (Dynasties 1–6) 3000–2150		
	Ebla, 2500–2300	
First Intermediate Period (D. 7–11) 2150–2050	Amorites, 2100–1700	
Middle Kingdom (D. 11–14) 2050–1650	Yamkhad, 1850–1550 Mari, 1800–1750	
		Hittite Old Kingdom 1750–1550
Second Intermediate Period—the Hyksos (D. 15–17) 1650–1550	Alalakh, 1650–1450 Mitanni, 1620–1350	
New Kingdom (D. 18–20) 1550–1100		Hittite Middle Kingdom 1550–1380
	Ugarit, 1350–1200	Hittite New Kingdom 1380–1200
Late Period/Third Intermediate Period (D. 21–26) 1100–525	Sea Peoples, c. 1200 United Monarchy, Israel 1000–925	Neo-Hittite States (in southeast Anatolia and north Syria) 1200–700
	Divided Hebrew Kingdoms -Israel, 925–722 -Judah, 925–586	
Persian Period 525–330	Persian Period 538–330	Persian Period 545–350
Greek Period (Ptolemies from 323) c. 330–	Greek Period, 330– -Ptolemies, 323–198 -Seleucids, 198–	Greek Period 330–

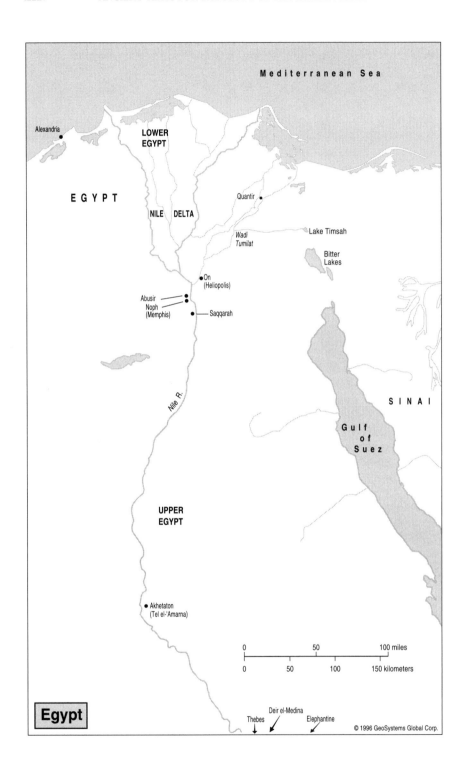

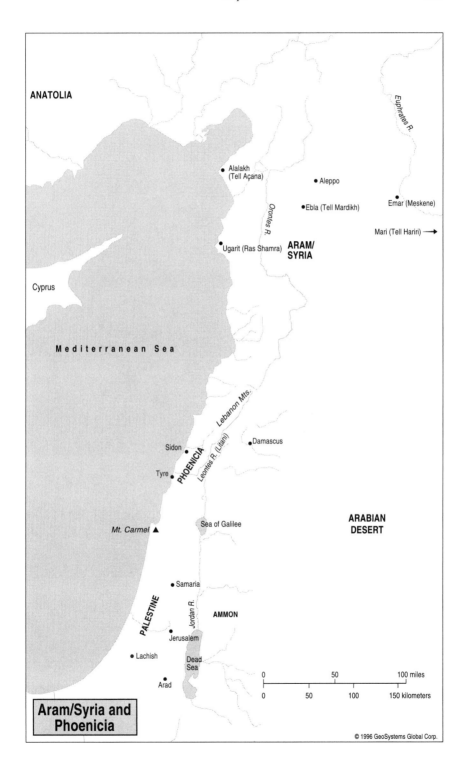

ANATOLIA

Euphrates R.

Alalakh
(Tell Açana)

Aleppo

Ebla (Tell Mardikh)

Emar (Meskene)

Mari (Tell Hariri) →

Orontes R.

Ugarit (Ras Shamra)

ARAM/
SYRIA

Cyprus

Mediterranean Sea

Lebanon Mts.

Sidon

PHOENICIA

Leontes R. (Litani)

Damascus

Tyre

Mt. Carmel ▲

Sea of Galilee

ARABIAN
DESERT

Samaria

PALESTINE

Jordan R.

AMMON

Jerusalem

Lachish

Dead
Sea

Arad

0		50		100 miles
0	50	100		150 kilometers

Aram/Syria and
Phoenicia

© 1996 GeoSystems Global Corp.

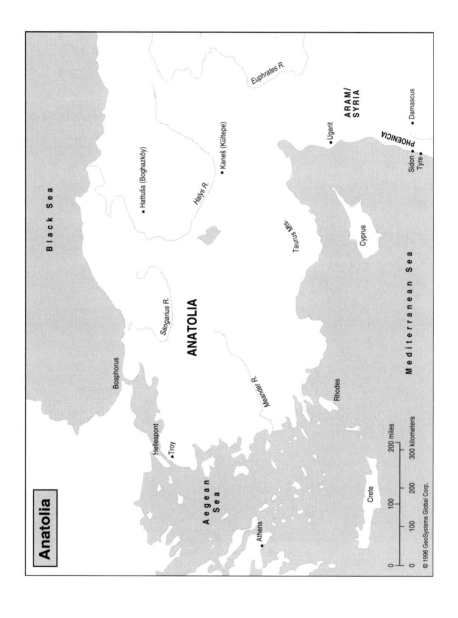

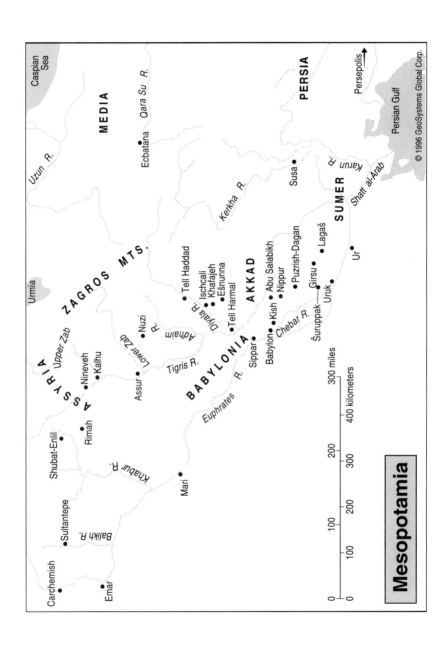

Introduction

In its modern translations, the Bible superficially appears to be a single, homogeneous work of literature. Each copy bears a single title page, preface, and table of contents, and the pages are continuously paginated in the same typeface. Concordances and indexes sometimes fill out this very harmonious impression. However, a careful reading of the Bible reveals the true complexity and diversity that lies behind these signs of homogeneity and coherence. Biblical literature was written over a period of some one thousand years by many authors, in three languages and to differing audiences. Genesis, Daniel, and Romans are not chapters of a single story so much as different kinds of literature addressing different people and circumstances. Although it may be true that these differing books reveal an underlying theological unity, as some Jews and Christians claim, a good reading of the texts should also account for their diversity. One factor that has made the uniqueness and diversity of the biblical books yet more visible is the discovery of documents from the ancient Near East that are similar to those in the Hebrew Bible. For readers who may be unfamiliar with the comparative study of biblical and Near Eastern literature, we can cite a familiar and well-traveled example from the history of biblical interpretation.

During the first half of the seventeenth century, James Ussher (1581–1656) served as the Church of Ireland's archbishop of Armagh. Although he was the first scholar to carefully distinguish St. Ignatius's seven authentic letters from the later spurious letters, he is perhaps better known for his attempt to produce a comprehensive synthesis of all biblical, classical, and scientific chronologies. The results were published in his *Annales Veteris et Novi Testamenti* and *Chronologia sacra*, which concluded, among other things, that the creation of the world took place on October 22, 4004 B.C.E. (see Finegan; Barr; Hughes). From our modern perspective, Ussher's work may seem rather naïve, for it now appears that the cosmos is quite a bit older—by conservative estimates, at least ten billion years old. But the bishop can hardly be blamed for his errant conclusions because, in the absence of modern astronomical data, his primary source for early chronology was the Hebrew Bible, especially the book of Genesis. But as we shall see, the book of Genesis is not the sort of material one should consult for accurate historical chronologies C.E.

Let us take, for example, the genealogy of Genesis 5 (for more on this text, see 11.1). This text enumerates ten generations of pre-flood patriarchs (from Adam to Noah) and provides chronological data about the first nine, including their ages when they first became fathers, the number of years they lived after this, and their ages at death. The life spans of these patriarchs are particularly long, with Methuselah—the oldest man in the Bible—living 969 years. In this respect, the biblical genealogy is unusual because neither Near Eastern genealogies nor the genealogies studied by anthropologists normally include chronological information. How is this anomaly to be explained? Although Near Eastern genealogies do not provide chronological data, Near Eastern king lists regularly do. For instance, there is a Sumerian King List that is very similar to the Genesis genealogy. It too provides a list of pre-flood heroes and grants them very long life spans, even longer than in Genesis (see table 0.1).

Table 0.1

Genealogy from Genesis 5				The Sumerian King List	
Name	Ages at birth of first son, remaining years, and total			Name	Length of reign
Adam	130	800	930	Alulim	28,800
Seth	105	807	912	Alagar	36,000
Enosh	90	815	905	EnmenluAnna	43,200
Kenan	70	840	910	EnmengalAnna	28,800
Mahalalel	65	830	895	Dumuzi	36,000
Jared	162	800	962	EnsipaziAnna	28,800
Enoch	65	300	365	Enmeduranki	21,000
Methuselah	187	782	969	Ubar-Tutu	18,600
Lamech	182	595	777		
Noah	500	450	—		

Another similarity between the biblical and the Mesopotamian texts concerns the seventh person in the primeval list. The Mesopotamian king lists often stress the special importance of the seventh king (in this case Enmeduranki) as well as his wise advisor (often Utuabzu), who did not die but "ascended into heaven." Genesis 5 describes the seventh patriarch in a similar way: "Enoch walked with God; then he was no more, for God took him." This evidence suggests that the author of Genesis 5 modified a Hebrew genealogy so that it mimicked the older Mesopotamian king lists. The correctness of this reading is further confirmed by the chronological information provided by Genesis 5. The final digit of the genealogy's chronological numbers is 0, 2, 5, or 7 in all cases but one (twenty-eight out of twenty-nine; see table). The probability of random data like this is on the order of 4.50 × 10⁻¹¹, meaning, of course, that these numbers are not chronological in the usual sense. In fact, as we will see in 11.1, a comparison of these numbers with the Near Eastern evidence suggests that in both cases—the Bible and Mesopotamia—the numbers were derived from, or influenced by, astronomical or mathematical figures. In sum, Archbishop Ussher's use of the Genesis chronology did not work because his biblical source was not chronological in the sense that he had assumed. Our comparison of this genealogy with the Near Eastern king lists reveals that the bishop's quest to begin his modern chronology with creation was doomed from the start.

This is only one example in which our appreciation for ancient Hebrew texts is enhanced by recognizing them as coming from a class of similar ancient texts. Theorists call these groups of similar texts *genres* (adjective form, *generic*). The primary purpose of this volume is to help us understand and appreciate the generic character of the Hebrew Bible by comparing it to similar texts written by Israel's ancient neighbors. Naturally, this effort requires that we understand something about both comparison and genre, so this will be our first task.

The Essentials of Comparison

Childhood is a time of awakening and exploration. During this early phase of life, we instinctively and unconsciously begin to form ideas about how the world works and about how we fit into it. This path to understanding is paved with trial and error. The result is a tacit set of ideas about the shape of reality and the patterns that govern our existence. One of the essential ingredients in this tacit developmental process is comparison. Comparison allows us to form implicit models of the world by verifying in a repetitious way the regular patterns of experience. Once embraced, these patterns permit us to move confidently from familiar situations to new contexts that are similar. Our concept of the world is reinforced when this transaction is successful, whereas failure forces us to rethink and improve our conceptual patterns. Hence, comparison is a process that accounts for both similarities and differences. In this way, human beings give shape to the world we live in, although it is perhaps equally true to say that the world shapes and molds us.

As anyone with small children will know, the lenses through which children see the world are concrete and rigid. Once they are warned to avoid the hot stove, they find it disturbing when adults or older siblings break the rules. Naturally, maturity brings in its wake an awareness of life's complexity, along with an ability to appreciate how the rules of engagement apply in subtly different situations. Among the most important transitions in this intellectual process is a shift from concrete to abstract reasoning. This shift allows us to expand the tacit and unconscious process of learning into a more explicit and intentional activity. Scholarship represents humanity's most explicit and serious pursuit of understanding. Although every scholarly discipline has its very technical and complicated aspects, at one level the task of all scholarship is fundamentally the same: it includes deliberate acts of comparison. As we have seen, comparison serves the straightforward role of either confirming the accuracy of our assumptions or challenging their validity. It is a twofold process that helps us uncover the patterns in life and also to test those patterns to determine where they fit and where they do not. Implied by this act of testing is that the results of comparison are always tentative and subject to review. As J. Z. Smith has concluded, "That comparison has, at times, led us astray there can be no doubt; that comparison remains *the* method of scholarship is likewise beyond question."

Let's consider comparison in a little more detail. Comparison can be done from a variety of perspectives. For instance, from a sociological perspective, comparison observes the similarities and differences between cultures. From a psychological perspective, it explores the uniqueness of individuals and also the similarities human beings share with each another. Comparison from an historical perspective examines data from temporally distant contexts. This allows us to compare a culture with itself (as in a comparison of ninth-century Israel with eighth-century Israel) or even to compare individuals with themselves (as in a comparison of the earlier phenomenological Martin Heidegger with the later, more "poetic" Heidegger). But in the end, whether done from a cultural, psychological, or historical perspective—or from some other viewpoint—the ultimate aim of comparison is to understand our world better by identifying and explaining similarities and differences. How do scholars explain similarities and differences?

As we have seen in the genealogy example at the beginning of this chapter, I have suggested that the biblical genealogy in Genesis 5 is similar to the Mesopotamian king lists, which in turn implies that we can use the patterns from the king lists to help us read the genealogy. On what basis do I affirm the significance of this similarity? One of the most common explanations for similarity—and the one I would cite in this case—is *cultural diffusion* (Smart). Cultural diffusion posits that the similarities we observe are due to the transfer of ideas or practices from one culture to another, either directly or indirectly. This is an attractive option when the similarities are between neighboring cultures, as in the case of Israel and the ancient Near East. At least four basic types of diffusion are distinguishable: *direct connection* (A is dependent upon B), a *mediated connection* (A knows about B from source C), a *common source* (A and B utilized a common source, C), and a *common tradition* (A and B have no immediate connections but participate in a common tradition; see Malul). Whenever researchers cite diffusion to explain cultural similarities, they also accept the burden to provide a reasonable explanation for where, when, how, and in what direction the influence may have occurred. The explanation should give particular attention not only to similarities but also to differences because no two societies are in all respects alike, which implies that traditions will always be modified as they pass from one culture to another (Hallo 1990). For instance, my reading of Genesis 5 above assumes that the diffusion of traits from the Mesopotamian king lists into Israel also entailed a transition from the king list genre to a genealogy.

Another, more basic explanation for cultural similarity appeals to our common humanity. The work of religion scholar R. Otto provides a good example. In *The Idea of the Holy*, Otto explained that the universal experience of human religion is prompted by our innate awareness of, and experience with, "the holy." We are not religious because our culture borrowed the concept from another culture; we are religious because holiness and our response to it are inherent in the human condition. Because this intercultural similarity presupposes a common phenomenon in different human contexts, it is often referred to as a *phenomenological* similarity (sometimes also called *typological*).

When researchers conclude that a similarity is significant and meaningful on the basis of either diffusion or phenomenology, a strenuous debate often ensues because other scholars disagree with this conclusion. Disputes of this sort are to be expected not only because similarities can be deceiving (as is aptly illustrated by C. Geertz's popular illustration that good scholarship must distinguish between "a blink" and "a wink") but also because no two scholars conduct their research with precisely the same viewpoints and assumptions. The most common reason for criticizing a comparison is either that it fails to include elements that should have been considered or that it includes elements too different to be useful (the "apples and oranges" maxim applies here). In other words, good comparisons include successful classification. Classification is central to comparison because choices must be made about what should be included in, and excluded from, our comparative considerations. These choices are necessary because even the best minds cannot manage the practically infinite world of our experience without dissecting it into finite pieces and cross sections.

Although this description of comparison and classification applies to all types of intellectual endeavors, here we are concerned not merely with comparison but, more specifically, with the interpretive problems of the Hebrew Bible. These interpretive problems entail a particular kind of comparison: the comparison of literary genres from ancient Israel with similar types of literature from the ancient Near East. Though a detailed discussion of modern generic theory is prerequisite for this comparative task, we should first examine the somewhat older discipline that studies biblical genres: form criticism.

Form Criticism and the Hebrew Bible

As we have said, comparisons always include classification, and in the case of biblical studies, the methodology that has focused on classifying and comparing literary genres is called form criticism, a discipline developed especially by the German scholar H. Gunkel (1862–1932). Gunkel sought to identify the genres of texts and traditions in the Bible on the basis of three criteria: *mood, form,* and *Sitz im Leben* (see Buss). Mood referred to the internal dispositions of the author; form, to the structure of the discourse; and *Sitz im Leben,* to the "life setting," or context, that produced the genre (*Gattung*). Although Gunkel's original interest was in the oral genres from which he believed the biblical texts developed, Old Testament scholars eventually extended his approach to include written traditions as well. Although Gunkel's attention to form and genre initiated a great leap forward in biblical studies, theoretical deficiencies in his view of genre have created certain problems. Gunkel presumed that each piece of literature belonged to only one genre, that each genre stemmed from one unique *Sitz im Leben,* and that the relationship between form and context was essentially inflexible. This inflexible approach to genre was a consequence of Gunkel's theoretical belief in *generic realism.* Generic realism posits that texts are uniquely and intrinsically related to the generic categories in which we place them. For instance, when realists say that the book of Deuteronomy is a lawbook, they mean that there is an ontologically fixed category called "lawbook" and that Deuteronomy fits into that genre and none else. The fallacy inherent in this approach to generic classification can be illustrated by an example from the animal kingdom.

Ostriches can be classified in a number of different ways. We can call them "animals," "warm-blooded," "birds," and "long-legged" at the same time without occasioning any sort of contradiction. Of course, these four classifications accomplish somewhat different purposes. By excluding rocks and sand, the first category focuses our attention on the features that are intrinsic to life itself. The second classification excludes cold-blooded species such as reptiles, thereby facilitating a thoughtful consideration of the similarities and differences between birds and mammals. The third classification takes a more restrictive step that separates birds from mammalians, and the last example—"long-legged animals"— creates a somewhat bizarre cross section of species that includes not only ostriches but also giraffes and octopi. Although any one of these classifications could be useful, the criteria applied and the results they bear are obviously very flexible. Birds and reptiles are of precisely the same "genre" in the first instance, but not at all in the second, third, or fourth. Each classification represents a different but legitimate way of slicing up the comparative pie. *Ab uno disce omnes* ("From one example learn about all") applies here: there is a flexible and partially arbitrary character to all classifications, and this counts for literary genres as well as for animal life. The theory that generic categories are essentially taxonomic inventions is called *generic nominalism,* which contrasts with the *generic realism* of traditional form criticism (although readers versed in philosophy should note that one can be a philosophical realist while adhering at the same time to a nominalist view of genre).

If generic nominalism is preferable to generic realism, as I am suggesting, what are the negative consequences of generic realism, and how does nominalism allay them? One unfortunate consequence of generic realism is the persistence of debates about the definitions of certain biblical genres. For instance, although Old Testament scholars generally agree that there are several books in the Hebrew Bible that fall into a category called "wisdom literature" (e.g., Proverbs), there is an ongoing discussion about what wisdom literature is and about what texts fit, or do not fit, into this category. Although some of this discussion has been healthy and valuable, much of the debate has been fueled by the subtle assumption that wisdom literature is a thing that already exists, that the task of scholarship is merely to correctly identify it by isolating its salient features from the wisdom texts. Generic nominalism helps to diffuse these needless debates by averring that there may be many legitimate ways to define wisdom literature. As a result, our intellectual energies can be productively focused on more important matters.

Another negative consequence of generic realism is discernible in form criticism's use of three basic criteria to identify texts generically (mood, form, *Sitz im Leben*). So long as one believed that genres were rigid ontological categories, these criteria provided more than enough data for us to identify them. Generic nominalism reminds us, however, that there are many other criteria that may be useful for classifying texts. Not only does this summon us to thoughtfully consider a broader range of generic features in our comparative deliberations; it also invites us to consider several different genres with respect to a single text. For example, the book of Deuteronomy is no longer understood merely as a lawbook but also as an ancient treaty, a book of rituals, a history book, and a series of religious speeches. Nominalism does not force us to choose between all of these helpful alternatives.

During the last few decades, biblical scholars have become increasingly aware of the problems inherent in traditional form criticism (Buss; Knierim; Sweeney/Ben Zvi), but their critiques of form criticism often perpetuate some of the misconceptions present in Gunkel's old formulation of the genre question (see, however, the insightful comments of Longman and Van Leeuwen in Sweeney/Ben Zvi). Some scholars have attempted to solve the difficulties by introducing yet another "criticism," in this case rhetorical criticism, which gives careful attention to the unique and distinctive features in each biblical text (see Muilenburg; Trible). This approach imagines that form and rhetorical criticisms are discrete but complementary ventures, where one attends to the similarities between texts (form criticism) while the other attends to textual uniqueness (rhetorical criticism). As the two disciplines are practiced, this often is the case. However, I believe that a good theory of genre needs to explain how textual similarities and differences fit into a single conception of the text.

Using the terminology of the present volume, I would say that form and rhetorical critics generally fail to grasp three related but distinct dimensions of genre: the *generic matrix, intrinsic genre,* and *analytical genre*. I will discuss these three interrelated aspects of genre in the following section. But, we should note before moving on that the limitations of form and rhetorical criticisms have not prevented their adherents from making important and lasting contributions to the study of ancient Hebrew texts and traditions. Here our aim is to improve on what form and rhetorical critics already do with some success.

An Introduction to Generic Theory

Theoretical discussions of genre go back as far as the Greeks, and in modern times genre has been a perennial topic of debate in literary circles and among folklorists. These scholarly deliberations are rather complex, making it impossible in this venue to raise all of the questions being posed, let alone address the possible solutions. But this needn't prevent us from appreciating the basic generic issues and from adopting a working theory of genre. After all, the simple fact that we are able to read implies some competency in matters of literature and genre. Here our aim is to describe more explicitly what we already do as readers, because focused reflection on the act of reading will help us do it better. Foundational to any explicit description of reading is an appreciation of generic theory, which is the primary concern in this section of our discussion.

Genre is an essential ingredient in communication because it establishes the ground rules shared by authors and readers. Just as the rules of grammar dictate how we correctly form and understand a sentence, so too the rules of genre dictate how we form and understand literature. In the words of P. Ricouer, genre functions "to mediate between speaker and hearer by establishing a common *dynamics* capable of ruling both the production of discourse as a work of a certain kind and its interpretation according to rules provided by the genre." In essence, we are able to understand the utterances and writings of others because their speech and literature adhere to verbal patterns that we recognize. While this definition of genre seems straightforward, it also raises important questions. If genre plays such a controlling role in the production of a literary work, and if it in essence "forces" an author to follow certain patterns within narrow limits, how does it come about that texts are unique, and how is it possible for genres to change or for new sets of generic traits to develop? Doesn't uniqueness and change imply a deviation from the accepted generic pattern?

New genres are created according to two primary patterns, *generic assimilation* and *generic extension* (cf. Hirsch). Let's return to our genealogy from Genesis as an example. Generic assimilation combines existing genres into newer ones. In the case of Genesis 5, the features of king lists and genealogies were combined to produce a new and unusual kind of text. As this new combination illustrates, assimilation commonly brings together smaller generic units or traits into a larger "host" text, whose genre is often referred to as the dominant genre (in this case, a genealogy). In the Hebrew Bible this pattern comes to the foreground especially in the Hebrew Pentateuch, which nests many different genres—itineraries, genealogies, legends, myths, treaties, laws, and ritual texts—into what appears otherwise a historical narrative framework.

Generic extension, on the other hand, arises when an existing genre is used in a new context or for a different purpose. This too can be illustrated by our genealogy from Genesis 5. Scholars are fairly certain that the list of names in Genesis 5 was derived from genealogies in Genesis 4. When the author of Genesis 5 attempted to mimic the Mesopotamian king lists, he took up the genealogical list of names from Genesis 4 and then added chronological information so that his new genealogy looked more like a king list. This process generically extended the genealogy in Genesis 4 to make it serve a new purpose. At its core, generic extension is a process of metaphor in which an author moves from one genre to another on the basis of analogy. In this case, the key analogy that connected the genealogies and king lists was that both were lists of names. The two basic categories of generic development—generic assimilation and extension—can be further subdivided and refined, as A. Fowler has done in *Kinds of Literature.*

Because of the human capacity to recognize relationships between things known and things new through analogy, an author can successfully exploit the liberties of generic assimilation and extension so long as readers can manage the metaphorical leaps. The authorial error of extending metaphors too far is generally precluded by this fact: if an author can draw the initial analogical or metaphorical relationships, then it is likely that competent readers within the author's literary community can take the same metaphorical steps. But how, specifically, do readers accomplish this?

The reading of any text, particularly one that is generically unfamiliar, begins with *heuristic genre* (Hirsch). Heuristic genre is an imaginative conjecture in which readers make an educated guess about how a text ought to be read. The guess is not a leap in the dark because it begins with assumptions based on the generic traits and elements that readers already recognize. If this initial guess misses, the result is an uneasy feeling that the text does not cohere and that it has not been understood. In such cases, we often read the text several times, each time postulating anew how the piece's elements might function together as a unit and within a context. The process is an intuitive one that, if successful, results in a sensation that the text has been understood. In sum, by an imaginative and intuitive process, human beings are able to make sense of what is generically new through a metaphorical process that connects it with what they already know.

In the case of ancient documents, which are linguistically, culturally, and historically remote from modern readers, our ability to make these imaginative and intuitive leaps is especially challenged. Nevertheless, scholars have enjoyed relative success in their efforts to read and understand ancient texts. In some instances, modern scholars can actually best the ancient scribes, as is the case on one tablet where we can eavesdrop on a Neo-Assyrian scholar as he misreads an older Babylonian text (Livingstone; cf. Al-Fouadi).

Modern success in reading ancient texts is the consequence of a fundamental reality. Because all readers and writers are shaped by a common human experience in the same world, the fact that one of us can generate a text implies, it would seem, that it is feasible for someone else to understand it. Although some theorists are resistant to this image of humanity's "psychic unity," the very act of reading and translating ancient texts presumes that a profound connection binds together human beings from very diverse cultural and linguistic backgrounds (see Grosby). This assumption has been reinforced by recent studies in language, which suggest that each language employs a rather limited number of elementary structures (Chomsky) and that all languages may share common foundations (so linguistic typologists; see Shibatani and Bynon). In sum, scholarly success in reading ancient documents stems from our common humanity and from our innate capacity to make sense of new things through analogy and metaphor.

More about Genre: The Generic Matrix, Intrinsic Genre, and Analytical Genres

Like a fingerprint, each instance of verbal discourse is unique because it bears the marks of the distinctive *generic matrix* that produced it. The generic matrix is the sum total of all determinants and contingencies that result in the production of a verbal utterance or a written text; it is context in the widest possible sense. Although in any given text this contextual matrix is partially shared by other instances of discourse, its matrix is ultimately unique because no two contexts are in all respects alike. If each text is a product and part of a unique context, it follows that each text is its own type, its own genre. Theorists refer to the unique genre of any text as its *intrinsic genre* (i.e., *sui generis,* "one of a kind"), but we must be clear at this point: intrinsic genre is more than the textual inscription itself. For instance, if a bank president writes a legal affidavit claiming, "I did not falsify our financial statements," the inscription will be the same whether she is telling the truth or lying. There are, obviously, profound generic differences, however, between lies and truth telling, and this generic distinction rests not in the inscription itself but rather in the contextual matrix that produced the inscription. Intrinsic genre imbibes of this generic matrix and accounts for the noninscriptional aspects of a text (and in oral discourse, it accounts for the nonlocutionary [unspoken] aspects of our locutionary [spoken] actions).

At first glance, it seems that the intrinsic uniqueness of each text would create problems for readers, since this implies that every text is in some sense new to us. Although there is some truth in this observation, many of the interpretive problems implied by this scenario are resolved because the text is similar enough to other text types that we recognize. But in more difficult cases—such as in ancient texts—we must deliberately compare problem texts with others in the hope that this will help us understand what is unclear. This grouping of similar texts creates an *analytical genre,* a class of texts that serve our comparative purposes by helping us adjust our generic expectations, which may be either broadened or narrowed, depending on the situation. Comparisons of this sort can be done intraculturally (by comparing the Greek historians Thucydides and Herodotus) or interculturally (by comparing the Greek Herodotus with the Hebrew Chronicler). In this comparative endeavor, two basic analytical errors can occur.

First, we can mistakenly believe that two texts are similar in ways they are not. Let us return to our example from the genealogy in Genesis 5. Archbishop Ussher made the mistake of assuming that the chronological information in the genealogy was of the same sort found in modern historical chronologies. As a result, he produced a quite faulty chronology of early human history. The bishop's generic error was to fit Genesis 5 into an analytical genre (in this case, modern chronology) that was inappropriate. As a result of this category error, he read the genealogy in a manner ill suited to the text. In proverbial terms, this type of comparative mistake assumes that "apples *are* oranges." The second error that we can make in generic comparison is to adopt analytical categories that are not very useful. For instance, if I am interested in how ancient historians wrote their histories, it is not very helpful to adopt as my analytical genre "all written texts." This category is in one sense too broad (because it includes too many kinds of texts), and it is in another sense too narrow (because it leaves out oral histories that might be relevant for comparative purposes). Therefore, although there are many legitimate ways to classify texts, not all of these classifications are equally helpful.

Readers should also be alerted to an important implication of analytical genre, namely, that generic classification is always an exercise in circular reasoning because we cannot derive a generic definition—such as "myth"—without presupposing already what myths are and what texts fit the category. This is only one symptom of what scholars call the hermeneutical circle, the interpretive path that our thought takes as we attempt to make sense of the parts in light of the whole and of the whole in light of the various parts. In the final analysis, all interpretation, including the interpretation of texts, entails some level of circularity. Consequently, the analytical generic categories adopted in this volume are matters of judgment rather than science. Readers are encouraged to examine critically the classification schemes adopted here and to propose for themselves, where necessary, new and more valuable taxonomies.

To summarize, generic matrix, intrinsic genre, and analytical genre represent three theoretically discrete aspects of genre that are interrelated and mutually important for the study of texts. The relationships between these can be illustrated spatially by saying that generic matrix lies *behind* the text, analytical genre *in front of* the text, and intrinsic genre *between* the two but organically related to both (see Vanstiphout).

Defending the Analytical Generic Approach

At its core, this volume presupposes the value of analytical genres, which intentionally use generic categories—usually modern generic categories—to identify texts from the ancient Near East that can in turn be compared with texts from the Hebrew Bible. Two important theoretical challenges have been raised against such a use of analytical generic categories. First, some scholars aver that the use of modern generic categories illegitimately neglects *ethnic genres* (Ben-Amos). Ethnic genres are the indigenous labels used by a culture to name and describe its verbal discourse. The resulting classification of genres may be very simple or rather complex. Among the Nigerian Yoruba there are only two classes of stories, "true" and "false," whereas in other cultures we find many classes of stories: epics, legends, tales, histories, and myths, among others (Bascom). The ethnic genres of ancient Israel are visible explicitly in its generic terminology (e.g., *mashal* = "proverb") and implicitly in collections of similar texts, such as the Psalms. According to advocates of ethnic genre, analytical approaches do us an interpretive disservice because they obscure native generic traditions by imposing upon them modern generic categories. In certain respects, the objection raised by these scholars is altogether legitimate. Good readings of ancient texts should indeed pay close attention to ethnic generic categories. There are, however, other important theoretical considerations.

The primary problem created by an exclusive use of ethnic genres is that the generic labels used in common practice never reflect the full range of actual genres used. Just as we unconsciously follow the grammatical rules of syntax, voice, and mood to make a sentence, likewise in every culture we adhere to various generic patterns without recognizing them or naming them. This suggests that the scholarly effort to classify and understand subtle generic elements through analytical categories is both useful and legitimate. Moreover, we should remember that ethnic genres are, in the end, the analytical genres used by native culture.

Another challenge against analytical generic approaches has appeared among literary critics, such as B. Croce (1866–1952), who are interested in critically evaluating the unique qualities of individual texts. In their eyes, generic classification is an aesthetic blunder because it groups together otherwise unique texts and, in doing so, obscures the artistic and creative distinctiveness of each literary work. Although most scholars share Croce's concern for the uniqueness of literary works, I would argue that Croce is incorrect to aver that analytical genres necessarily involve a denial of literary uniqueness. There is no reason we cannot give attention to both intrinsic and analytical aspects of genre.

Generic Traits and Analytical Genre

Ancient Israelite scribes were formally educated and informally inculturated into the setting that produced the Hebrew Bible. As a result, they were implicitly or explicitly aware of how genres generally worked in their context, both in terms of the composition of texts and in terms of reading them. It follows that modern readers who want to understand these ancient authors should pursue an understanding of the social, historical, linguistic, and literary world in which they lived. The ideal result of this pursuit is what N. Chomsky has called literary competence (see Barton), a familiarity with the ancient context that approximates, albeit feebly at times, that of the Israelite scribes.

First and foremost in our pursuit of literary competence is the reading and comparison of texts *within the Hebrew Bible itself.* For example, there are hundreds of prophetic oracles recorded in the Hebrew corpus, and these provide a wealth of material from which to infer the generic patterns that appear in Israelite prophecy; the same can be said for the Hebrew psalms. In such cases, biblical scholars might legitimately explore the biblical genres without considering in much detail the ancient Near Eastern evidence (e.g., see Westermann's study of prophetic speech forms). The need for considering extrabiblical literature is more acute when the Bible presents us with very few exemplars of a given genre. For instance, although the Bible includes a wide assortment of prophetic oracles and psalms, it contains very few prophetic books (e.g., Isaiah) and only one collection of liturgical literature (the Psalms). In such cases, a good understanding of the biblical genres is enhanced by—and even dependent upon—our comparison of the texts with similar Near Eastern exemplars. Our objective in this portion of our discussion is to list some of the more important traits that can be used to define analytical generic categories for comparison. Although for convenience I will explicitly note only eight traits for consideration, it is theoretically important to emphasize that this is not merely an expansion of Gunkel's three criteria—mood, form, and *Sitz im Leben*—to a larger number. Rather, these eight could be multiplied ad infinitum if we listed every legitimate criterion for making generic distinctions.

1. Content and Theme

One of the most common and useful criteria employed to form analytical generic categories is content. Let's return to our example from Genesis 5. Our comparison of the Genesis genealogy with the Mesopotamian king lists was prompted by their similar elements. Both texts included a list of names belonging to men who lived before the great flood, ostensibly arranged in chronological order and with chronological information. As this case illustrates, comparison often begins with obvious prima facie similarities and then pursues a more detailed assessment of similarities and differences. The history of biblical scholarship is replete with comparisons, based on content, of biblical and Near Eastern texts. The pessimism of Qoheleth has prompted comparisons with the pessimistic Gilgamesh Epic, the erotic themes of Song of Songs have been compared to the Egyptian love songs, and Judean sorrow in the book of Lamentations has been appraised by reading it alongside the Mesopotamian laments. Countless other examples could be cited.

2. Language

Closely related to, and overlapping with, a text's content are its linguistic and stylistic features. For example, Sumerian scribes often quoted the speech of women in a distinctive Emesal dialect, Greek epics were composed in a Homeric dialect, and Hebrew poetry reflects linguistic features that distinguish it from Hebrew prose (Edzard; Davies). Some ancient Mesopotamian texts, especially incantations, were preserved and recited exclusively in Sumerian long after the spoken tongue had disappeared. This practice followed from the belief that ritual incantations were effective only when they rehearsed the ancient Sumerian traditions with precision. As these examples show, the language of a text is often closely related to the generic traditions in which it stands. It follows that careful consideration of a text's linguistic features can yield important insights into the conventions employed by its author, which in turn helps us read the text better. Language can also be generically useful because it might indicate something about the historical or social context in which the text was written.

3. Context *(Sitz im Leben)*

Because the generic matrix that produces a text is practically, if not theoretically, infinite, discussions of context normally have in mind only a thin but significant slice of this generic matrix. In biblical studies, the technical term commonly used to refer to this slice of context is *Sitz im Leben* (literally, "setting in life"). Context is an important consideration in reading texts because verbal discourse has meaning only with reference to a context that makes it intelligible. Consider, for instance, the following inscription from a silver bowl recovered in Egypt (*COS* 2.51B: 175–76):

> Ḥarbek son of Pausiri offered to Hanilat the goddess.

What sense can we make of this inscription? Many readers initially find the text somewhat obscure, but two contextual matters help to clear the mist. First, the text was found at a shrine where worshippers regularly left gifts for the goddess Hanilat. And second, we know from other sources that the ancients often presented libations (drink offerings) to their deities. We can surmise from this evidence that the bowl originally contained a liquid offering of beer or wine and that Ḥarbek placed the bowl in the temple to secure the favor of the goddess. Apart from this contextual background, our prospects for reading the text adequately would not be very good.

In such cases, an appreciation for a text's *Sitz im Leben* is an indispensable aspect of generic competence. But this attention to context must necessarily avoid the old idea of H. Gunkel that each text has one—and only one—setting in which it was used. For it is now clear that different settings can produce similar generic forms and that the selfsame text can be used in a variety of settings (Parkinson).

4. Function

Context and *Sitz im Leben* sometimes direct our attention to other valuable comparative evidence. For instance, in matters of war, both Israelites and Mesopotamians sought the deity's approval before pursuing military campaigns, but they did so in somewhat different ways. In Mesopotamia this often included a ritual process called extispicy, in which the entrails of a sacrificial animal were thought to deliver a message from the deity (see ch. 6). The message was detected by diviners, who interpreted the viscera (often the liver) by consulting a catalogue of previous observations made by other diviners. This interpretation was then presented to the king in a written report. In contrast, Hebrew kings normally consulted prophets rather than diviners before battle, and the prophet's message was sometimes delivered in person. Although prophecy and divination clearly served similar functions in times of potential war, the two practices produced quite different literary genres:

> **Hebrew Prophecy:** [Query] And when he had come to the king, the king said to him, "Micaiah, shall we go to Ramothgilead to battle, or shall we forbear?" [Answer]

And he answered him, "Go up and triumph; the LORD will give it into the hand of the king." (1 Kgs 22:15)

Mesopotamian Omen Report: [Query] If the men and army of Assurbanipal king of Assyria, march against Šamaš-šumu-ukin, will he fall into their hands? [Answer]. . . The strength and "well being" are present [in the liver]. The "path" on the left of the gall bladder is long and reaches the place of the "base of the throne" . . . There is a design in the middle of the surface of the "finger" which penetrates from right to left . . . Favorable. (from Starr, 266–67)

The perception that prophecy and divination are similar implicitly creates an analytical genre, in this instance a genre that scholars call "intermediary texts" because they communicate the divine will through a human mediator (here through a prophet or diviner; see Wilson). In this case, our generic category is based on the common function of the texts, which suggests that the appreciation of a given text is enhanced not only by comparing it with similar types of literature but also by recognizing how it compares with quite different texts that may serve the same kind of function (Parker). As much as is feasible, in this volume our discussions of each generic category will consider functionally equivalent genres as well as texts that are similar in terms of form and content.

If very different texts can serve quite similar functions, it is equally true that very similar texts can serve profoundly different functions. Although the stories in tales and histories are so similar that it can be difficult to tell them apart, the former is generally more suited to amusement than the latter. Apart from this distinction, we might errantly interpret a playful and entertaining campfire story as a serious depiction of the past. Good readers can become more sensitive to the functions of texts by adopting categories that make functional distinctions more explicit. Some of the functional categories represented in this volume include, but are not limited to, the following (adapted from Bascom; Fowler; Longman 1996): *amusement, apology/propaganda, doxology* (praise), *catharsis* (expression of emotion), *instruction* (didactic), *institutional legitimation* (promotion of the authenticity and authority of religious, political, and social institutions), *institutional and social critique, intellectual satisfaction,* and *social cohesion* (promotion of the social order). Obviously, these categories are not mutually exclusive and could easily be subdivided (hence creating more functional types) or simplified (hence creating fewer functional types). An example of the latter strategy appears in the popular and influential work of W. W. Hallo. Hallo has suggested that Near Eastern texts fall into three primary functional genres: canonical, monumental, and archival (Hallo 1980). The canonical texts were those from the ongoing scribal tradition that were regularly studied, taught, copied, and recopied by the scribes. Monumental texts were of a commemorative nature and included royal inscriptions, boundary stones, and other texts that might be displayed in the public forum. By contrast, the archival texts were records preserved for utilitarian purposes. This category included letters, receipts, legal contracts, and other documents that the ancients preserved to serve the political, economic, and religious needs of the community. Insofar as we are pursuing a useful purview of textual function, we should attend carefully to those taxonomies that recognize many functional categories (such as Longman 1996) as well as to those that recognize only a few (such as Hallo).

5. Form and Structure

Although in biblical studies the word *form* is frequently used as a synonym for genre, here I use the term with reference to a text's structure and format. Consider, for instance, this Latin text:

Artium Magister:

Arma virumque cano, Trojae qui primus ab oris Italiam fato profugus Lavinaque venit litora—multum ille et terris jactatus et alto vi superum, saevae memorem Junonis ob iram, multa quoque et bello passus, dum conderet urbem inferretque deos Latio—genus unde Latinum Albanique patres atque altae moenia Romae.

Musa, mihi causas memora, quo numine laeso quidve dolens regina deum tot volvere casus insignem pietate virum, tot adire labores impulerit. Tantaene animis caelestibus irae?

Malis avibus,
Docendo Discimus

What is the genre of this text? Although most readers will not know Latin, they will undoubtedly suppose that the text is a short letter, with "Artium Magister" and "Docendo Discimus" being the receiver and sender, respectively. In reality, however, the first name means "Master of Arts," the second means "We learn by teaching," and the closing remark, "malis avibus," means "under unfavorable signs." The main body of this "letter" is actually an extract from the opening lines of a Latin epic, the *Aeneid*. The pastiche nevertheless appears to be a letter because of its formal arrangement, suggesting that form is a dimension of genre that stands somewhat apart from content. In the ancient Near East, as in every milieu, the formal layout of a text can provide useful signals to the generic conventions its author employed. For example, poetic texts were sometimes arranged to highlight their meter and versification, and ancient chronicles often used rulings (dividing lines) to separate one historical period from another. In these instances and many others, spacing, column arrangement, and separating lines provided visible signs of a text's generic character. Other formal characteristics may not be so pronounced as lines and columns, but they are still important. For instance, the discourse in ancient treaties often followed a clear structural pattern, even when no conspicuous lines or spaces were used to mark off the various parts of the treaty. Nevertheless, the formal order of the treaty elements remained generically important.

Biblical form critics have long used the structures of texts to classify them generically. Early form critics, following Gunkel, were especially interested in using form to identify the smaller preliterary oral units ("form-critical units") that they believed gave rise to the larger literary works in the Hebrew Bible. Biblical scholarship has become increasingly skeptical about our ability to identify oral materials in the Bible, and many scholars now believe that orality played a rather modest role in the origins of the biblical text (Kirkpatrick). Nevertheless, attention to form has allowed scholars to recognize that parts of the Hebrew Bible, such as the Pentateuch, are composed of many different generic units—some oral, other written—that existed before their incorporation into the biblical text. For this reason, interpreters who are interested in the tradition history and composition of a text will need to take account of these originally independent units.

6. The Material Attributes of Texts

It is obvious that all texts are inscribed on objects, but it is perhaps less obvious that the physical properties of these objects can provide important generic clues for interpreters. Hammurabi's famous law code furnishes a good example (see ch. 13). Our copies of the laws appear on diverse materials, in some cases on large stone stelae and in other cases on clay tablets. Although the contents of the tablet and stela versions are nearly identical, it is clear that their material properties point to different functions. Stela copies were erected in public forums as propaganda for the king whereas Mesopotamian scribes used the tablet copies to facilitate their academic research. This implies that a text's physical features stand alongside content as a useful indicator of genre. The physical traits that are relevant for generic classification vary widely, including such items as the ink colors used on papyrus, illustrations in the text, the shape and size of the text, and the colors and types of stones used for inscriptions. All of these material attributes and many others can provide useful indices for our generic considerations.

7. Mode of Composition and Reception

As we have seen, Gunkel and the biblical form critics have long recognized that a text's genre is related to *mood*, to the internal dispositions and motivations of the text's author. Nevertheless, in actual practice, this issue has generally been neglected by form critics and so needs to be highlighted here. What was the author trying to do when he composed his text, and how did he prosecute his literary effort? How was this tradition then appropriated by readers and passed on to others? These are questions of *modality*, the controlling thoughts, purposes, and processes that regulate the text's composition by the author and its reception by readers or hearers (Fowler). Our first task regarding generic modality will be to appreciate the role of modality in the composition of a text, and then we'll tackle the problem of modality in reading texts.

Recent studies in language have emphasized that writing is a *speech act,* that is, something that human beings seek to accomplish using words (Austin; Searle; see Vanhoozer, 208–14). This means that good interpretation includes an effort to determine what an author or speaker is trying to accomplish with a given utterance. Suppose that I am asked, "Would you like a cup of coffee?" and I respond, "That would keep me awake." Have I said "yes" or "no"? The answer depends a great deal on whether I am on a late-night drive in the car or in my pajamas before bedtime. In these two cases, the *locutionary act* is the same, but the *illocutionary act*—what I am trying to accomplish and communicate—is different. The cues that help us make such modal distinctions are obviously not in the text or utterance itself but rather in the interplay between the utterance and its context. Hence, generic distinctions never rest in the words alone but depend on all sorts of other matters external to the words (or text).

This brings us to modality and the reader. Theoretically speaking, if we are interested in what an author had to say, the best reading of any text is one that adopts a modal posture similar to the author's mode of composition. This ideal is, of course, never fully achieved because differences between modes of composition and reception are inevitable. In more extreme cases, such as mistaking sarcasm for candor, the interpretive consequences of modal confusion can be considerable. Once again, Archbishop Ussher provides an illustration. The bishop presumed that the author of Genesis 5 produced his genealogy using modern chronographic modes of composition when, in fact, it appears that the Hebrew author was toying with astronomical and mathematical figures. Ussher's mode of reception did not match the author's mode of composition, and this resulted in an innocent but significant misunderstanding of what the genealogy was offering readers.

Not all modal rifts between author and reader are accidental, however. In some cases, an author may adopt one modal posture while supposing that his readers will mistakenly assume a different posture. A good example is the use of *vaticinium ex eventu* (prophecy after the fact) by many ancient authors. The writers pretended to predict events before they had occurred when, in fact, the prophecies were composed *after* the events they predict. This had the obvious effect of enhancing the prophet's reputation or message because readers interpreted the prophecies as accurate predictions of the future. Such intentional rifts between author and reader can be characterized as *generic ruses*. Generic ruses dupe the reader into believing that the author is doing something generically that he is not doing. The key issue in such cases is the disparity between the author's illocutionary mode of composition (e.g., pseudoprophecy) and the locutionary impression he gives to readers (e.g., that this is genuine prediction). My use of the term *ruse*, with its potentially playful overtones, is intentional, for it is not at all clear that generic ruses constitute mendacious and tendentious acts against readers (early Christian defenses of the "pious ruse" spring to mind; see John Chrysostom, *Treatise on the Priesthood* 1.6–8, and Augustine's letters to Saint Jerome [Letter 82]). Where we are tempted to impugn the motives of an author in this matter, I would reserve the term *generic deception* as a subspecies of generic ruse.

In sum, good interpretation must consider the modal traits of a composition, and this includes thoughtful reflection on the locutionary and illocutionary aspects of the text as well as on a host of other features that determine how an author did his work.

8. Genre and Tradition

Ancient texts were not protected by copyrights. As a result, scribes felt the liberty to borrow and modify texts in ways that would perhaps make modern readers uncomfortable. The resulting modifications could be minor or profound. Biblical scholars have developed several discrete but related methodologies that identify and explain the changes that texts and traditions undergo during transmission. *Textual criticism* identifies intentional and unintentional changes to the text. *Redaction criticism* looks for evidence of a more thoroughgoing editorial process that subjects the text to significant thematic and ideological changes. *Source* and *form criticisms* identify units within the text that previously existed as separate traditions. In the case of source criticism (sometimes called literary criticism), the focus is usually on lengthy written sources used by an author whereas form critics often focus on the shorter (often oral) traditions taken up by the text's author. All of these critical endeavors are closely related to the more general task of *tradition history*, which explores the historical transmission and development of a given tradition. Some German scholars have further divided the duties of tradition history into two different tasks, *Traditionsgeschichte* (which traces the history of a tradition's content) and *Überlieferungsgeschichte* (which traces the history of this content as it is transmitted in the same form or genre; see Knierim 1985, 146–48). For my purposes in this chapter, these interpretive strategies address important aspects of what is a more global interpretive challenge, namely, the traditional nature of literary genres.

Tradition is the recurrence of structures of conduct and patterns of belief over several generations (Shils). It is passed on from one generation to the next through performance and through oral and/or written verbal discourse. Although tradition by definition is stable and resilient, it also reflects patterns of change. Some changes are forced upon society by external or internal circumstances. For instance, although sacrifices were the centerpiece of Israelite and Jewish ritual practice for many centuries, the destruction of the temple and its altar in 70 C.E. prompted drastic changes in tradition. Rituals that previously included sacrifice—such as the Passover seder—were reconfigured to account for the problem. In general, Judaism was compelled to identify theologically sound replacements for sacrifice, which it found in prayer and good deeds. Tradition is also altered by innovation, when charismatic and insightful individuals (or communities) suggest new strategies for living that they find more helpful or appropriate. For instance, although biblical law required all Jews to attend the Jerusalem Passover on an annual basis, in early Judaism this requirement was applied only to Jews *in Palestine*. This innovative reading of the law solved a problem for Diaspora Jews, who lived too far from Jerusalem to make annual trips to Judea practical (Sanders, 130). Finally, it is perhaps helpful to remember that tradition is sometimes altered accidentally, as Plutarch long ago illustrated: "At Athens Lysimache, the priestess of Athene Polias, when asked for a drink by the mule drivers who transported the sacred vessels, replied, 'No, for I fear it will get into the ritual'" (Plutarch, *De vitioso pudore* 534C).

To review, there are two primary forces at work in the process of tradition, one for preserving it and another for its modification. The result is often conflict and competition between those vying to protect tradition and those seeking to amend it. Because tradition is generally respected because of its supposed antiquity, the battleground between these communities often centers on history. Traditionalists appeal to the antiquity of their viewpoint, and reformers often present their modifications of tradition as very old. The desire to modify tradition in this way does not always reflect tendentious motives on the part of reformers, who may legitimately believe that the past must have been as they suggest it was. The strong momentum of tradition in ancient societies, however, generally precluded radical changes to long-standing social patterns. Barring extreme circumstances, social change and the generic changes that went along with it were slow, but also inevitable.

Ancient Near Eastern literature reflects both a healthy respect for tradition and obvious tendencies to revise and reformulate these inherited traditions. Scholars now generally recognize that many ancient works, the Hebrew Bible among them, have undergone a number of changes and revisions over the course of their transmission history (e.g., Kramer; Tigay 1982). The evidence for this viewpoint will be everywhere visible in the chapters that follow.

Tradition processes of this sort raise an important question for generic study. How can we speak of a text's genre when the work in question is not that of a single individual but rather of several authors or editors who composed it over a sometimes lengthy period of time? Our first observation is that an author may compose a text with awareness that others will later edit it. For instance, it may be a necessary feature of functioning law codes that they are routinely edited and updated to account for changing circumstances, so that one can conceive of legal codes being generated with a full awareness that later revisions would be necessary and even welcomed. If this is so, then one trait of some law codes—and of other genres—may be that they are diachronically envisioned and generated categories of literature.

On the other hand, not all authors of redacted works would welcome this editorial activity, which raises more explicitly an important question that is already implied by our law code example. If substantive changes are made to the text of a literary work, is its genre altered? The short answer is "yes," since every change to a text alters its intrinsic genre in some way. But in terms of analytical genre, the answer to this question depends on the extent and type of the editorial work. For instance, many scholars believe that the book of Deuteronomy originated as a law code and that it was later recast in the form of a treaty (Mayes). If this is true, it suggests that Deuteronomy began as a legal text and then *became* a treaty text. Although this suggests that editorial work can alter the broad analytical genre of a text, it also presupposes that any number of changes can be made to a literary work before its generic history is entirely concealed from careful readers.

Although editorial activity was frequent in ancient literature, it is not always easy to identify revisions because revisers tended to follow the generic patterns of the edited work. For this reason, revisions are discernible in three primary cases: (1) the editor intentionally hints at his presence in the text; (2) the editor adheres to the genre's pattern but diverges markedly from the viewpoint of the original text and so creates obvious tensions; (3) the editor fails to follow the generic pattern that is established already within the edited work. Editorial revision sometimes alters a text's meaning and generic character in profound ways. Although some biblical scholars do not view this editorial history as an important aspect of interpretation, particularly those advocating certain strains of modern literary criticism (Barton, 121–39), here it is presumed that a serious effort to reconstruct this redactional process helps us appreciate a work's generic character as well as its meaning and significance. We should always be interested in the final form of an edited text, but to ignore its editorial history is to taste a very thin slice of literature, culture, and history.

Conclusions

Scholarly discussions of literature, philosophy, generic theory, and the comparative process are obviously very complex. On virtually every important issue—from the nature of reading, to human nature, to interpretation, to genre—one finds a broad range of perspectives that can differ markedly. My effort to provide theoretical underpinnings for our generic discussion has attempted to acknowledge the relative value of the various perspectives so that the insights of form critics, literary theorists, nominalists, and others are appreciated even as they are criticized. This somewhat eclectic posture is perhaps not theoretically rigorous, but then again, on issues as mysterious as interpretation, provisional and heuristic postures are perhaps preferable to more comprehensive theories. I hope that the theoretical presuppositions outlined here will provide readers with an adequate, if provisional, basis for considering the generic character of Hebrew and Near Eastern literature. It is to this task that we now turn.

Select Bibliography

R. D. ABRAHAMS, "The Complex Relations of Simple Forms," in *Folklore Genres* (ed. D. Ben-Amos; Austin: University of Texas, 1976), 193–213; A.-H. AL-FOUADI, "Lexical Text from Dhiba'i," in *Kramer Anniversary Volume: Cuneiform Studies in Honor of Samuel Noah Kramer* (ed. B. L. Eichler; AOAT 25; Kevelaer, Germany: Butzon & Bercker, 1976), 1–11; J. L. AUSTIN, *How to Do Things with Words* (2d ed.; Cambridge: Harvard University Press, 1975); J. BARR, "Why the World Was Created in 4004 B.C.: Archbishop Ussher and Biblical Chronology," *BJRL* 67 (1985): 575–608; J. BARTON, "Form Criticism," *ABD* 2:838–41; IDEM, *Reading the Old Testament* (rev. and enlarged ed.; Louisville: Westminster John Knox, 1996); W. R. BASCOM, "Four Functions of Folklore," in *The Study of Folklore* (ed. A. Dundes; Englewood Cliffs, N.J.: Prentice-Hall, 1965), 279–98; T. O. BEEBEE, *The Ideology of Genre: A Comparative Study of Generic Instability* (University Park: Pennsylvania

State University Press, 1994); D. BEN-AMOS, "Analytical Categories and Ethnic Genres," in *Folklore Genres* (ed. D. Ben-Amos; Austin: University of Texas, 1976), 215–42; A. BERLIN, "A Search for a New Biblical Hermeneutics," in *The Study of the Ancient Near East in the Twenty-First Century: The William Foxwell Albright Centennial Conference* (ed. J. S. Cooper and G. M. Schwartz; Winona Lake, Ind.: Eisenbrauns, 1996), 195–207; R. S. BRIGGS, *Words in Action—Speech Act Theory and Biblical Interpretation: Toward a Hermeneutic of Self-Involvement* (Edinburgh: T&T Clark, 2001); M. J. BUSS, *Biblical Form Criticism in Its Context* (JSOTSup 274; Sheffield, England: Sheffield Academic Press, 1999); D. M. CARR, *Reading the Fractures of Genesis* (Louisville: Westminster John Knox, 1996); N. CHOMSKY, *The Chomsky Reader* (New York: Pantheon, 1987); R. COHEN, "History and Genre," *New Literary History* 17 (1986): 203–18; J. L. CRENSHAW, *Education in Ancient Israel* (New York: Doubleday, 1998); R. S. CRANE, *The Language of Criticism and the Structure of Poetry* (Toronto: University of Toronto Press, 1953); B. CROCE, *Aesthetic as Science of Expression and General Linguistic* (trans. D. Ainslie; 2d ed.; London: Peter Owen, 1953); J. CULLER, "Structuralism," *NPEPP* 1215–22; A. M. DAVIES, "Greek language," *OCD* 653–56; G. L. DILLON, *Constructing Texts: Elements of a Theory of Composition and Style* (Bloomington: Indiana University Press, 1981); D. DUFF, ed., *Modern Genre Theory* (Harlow: Longman, 2000); T. EAGLETON, *Literary Theory: An Introduction* (2d ed.; Minneapolis: University of Minnesota, 1996); D. O. EDZARD, "The Sumerian Language," *CANE* 4:2107–16; J. FINEGAN, *Handbook of Biblical Chronology* (rev. ed.; Peabody, Mass.: Hendrickson, 1998), 401–5; A. FOWLER, *Kinds of Literature: An Introduction to the Theory of Genres and Modes* (Cambridge: Harvard University Press, 1982); F. GARBER, "Genre," *NPEPP* 456–59; C. GEERTZ, "The Growth of Culture and the Evolution of the Mind," in *The Interpretation of Cultures* (New York: Basic Books, 1973), 55–83; IDEM, "Religion as a Cultural System," in *Reader in Comparative Religion* (ed. W. A. Lessa; New York: Harper & Row, 1965), 204–16; M. GERHART, "Generic Studies: Their Renewed Importance in Religious and Literary Interpretation," *JAAR* 45 (1977): 309–25; W. R. GOLDSCHMIDT, *Comparative Functionalism: An Essay in Anthropological Theory* (Berkeley: University of California Press, 1966); J. GOODY, *The Interface between the Written and the Oral* (New York: Cambridge University Press, 1987); S. GROSBY, *Biblical Ideas of Nationality: Ancient and Modern* (Winona Lake, Ind.: Eisenbrauns, 2002); V. HALL JR., *A Short History of Literary Criticism* (New York: New York University Press, 1963); W. W. HALLO, "Compare and Contrast: The Contextual Approach to Biblical Literature," in *The Bible in the Light of Cuneiform Literature* (ed. W. W. Hallo, B. W. Jones, and G. L. Mattingly; Scripture in Context 3; Lewiston, N.Y.: Mellen, 1990), 1–30; IDEM, "The Expansion of Cuneiform Literature," *PAAJR* 46–47 (1980): 307–322; J. H. HAYES, ed., *Old Testament Form Criticism* (San Antonio, Tex.: Trinity University Press, 1974); K. W. HEMPFER, *Gattungstheorie: Information und Synthese* (Uni-Taschenbücher 133; Munich: Wilhelm Fink, 1963); E. D. HIRSCH JR., *Validity in Interpretation* (New Haven: Yale University Press, 1967); J. HUGHES, *Secrets of Times: Myth and History in Biblical Chronology* (JSOTSup 66; Sheffield, England: Sheffield Academic Press, 1990); O. KEEL, *The Symbolism of the Biblical World*

(New York: Seabury, 1978); P. G. KIRKPATRICK, *The Old Testament and Folklore Study* (JSOTSup 62; Sheffield, England: Sheffield Academic Press, 1988); R. KNIERIM, "Criticism of Literary Features, Form, Tradition, and Redaction," in *The Hebrew Bible and Its Modern Interpreters* (ed. D. A. Knight and G. M. Tucker; Philadelphia: Fortress; Decatur: Scholars, 1985), 123–65; IDEM, "Old Testament Form Criticism Reconsidered," *Int* 27 (1973): 435–48; K. KOCH, *The Growth of the Biblical Tradition: The Form Critical Method* (New York: Scribners, 1969); S. N. KRAMER, "BM 96927: A Prime Example of Ancient Scribal Redaction," in *Lingering over Words: Studies in Ancient Near Eastern Literature in Honor of William L. Moran* (ed. Tz. Abusch et al.; HSS 37; Atlanta: Scholars Press, 1990), 251–69; B. LANDSBERGER, "Die Eigenbegrifflichkeit der Babylonischen Welt," *Islamica* 2 (1926): 355–72; M. T. LARSEN, "The Babel/Bible Controversy and Its Aftermath," *CANE* 1:95–106; C. LÉVI-STRAUSS, *The Savage Mind* (Chicago: University of Chicago Press, 1966); A. LIVINGSTONE, "The Case of Hemerologies: Official Cult, Learned Formulation, and Popular Practice," in *Official Cult and Popular Religion in the Ancient Near East* (ed. E. Matsushima; Heidelberg: Universitätsverlag C. Winter, 1993), 97–113; T. LONGMAN III, *Fictional Akkadian Autobiography: A Generic and Comparative Study* (Winona Lake, Ind.: Eisenbrauns, 1991); IDEM, "Form Criticism, Recent Developments in Genre Theory, and the Evangelical," *WTJ* 47 (1985): 46–67; IDEM, "Literary Approaches to Biblical Interpretation," in *Foundations of Contemporary Interpretation* (ed. M. Silva; Grand Rapids: Zondervan, 1996), 91–192; M. MALUL, *The Comparative Method in Ancient Near Eastern and Biblical Legal Studies* (AOAT 227; Neukirchen-Vluyn: Neukirchener Verlag, 1990); A. D. H. MAYES, *Deuteronomy* (NCB; Grand Rapids: Eerdmans, 1979), 29–55; J. MUILENBURG, "Form Criticism and Beyond," *JBL* 88 (1969): 1–18; K. MÜLLER-DYES, *Literarische Gattungen: Lyrik, Epik, Dramatik* (Freiberg in Breisgau: Herder, 1978); E. NICHOLSON, *The Pentateuch in the Twentieth Century: The Legacy of Julius Wellhausen* (Oxford: Clarendon, 1998); S. NIDITCH, *Oral World and Written Word: Ancient Israelite Literature* (Library of Ancient Israel; Louisville: Westminster John Knox, 1996); W. ONG, *Orality and Literacy: the Technologizing of the Word* (New York: Routledge, 1988); R. OTTO, *The Idea of the Holy* (New York: Oxford University Press, 1958); S. B. PARKER, "Some Methodological Principles in Ugaritic Philology," *Maarav* 2 (1980): 7–41; R. B. PARKINSON, "Types of Literature in the Middle Kingdom," in *Ancient Egyptian Literature: History and Forms* (ed. A. Loprieno; PA 10; New York: Brill, 1996), 297–312; B. PECKHAM, "Writing and Editing," in *Fortunate the Eyes That See: Essays in Honor of David Noel Freedman* (ed. A. B. Beck et al.; Grand Rapids: Eerdmans, 1995), 364–83; P. RICOEUR, "The Hermeneutical Function of Distanciation," *Philosophy Today* 17 (1973): 129–41; B. ROEST and H. L. J. VANSTIPHOUT, eds., *Aspects of Genre and Type in Pre-modern Literary Cultures* (COMERS/ICOG Communications 1; Groningen, Neth.: Styx, 1999); J. W. ROGERSON, *Anthropology and the Old Testament* (Atlanta: John Knox, 1979); A. ROSMARIN, *The Power of Genre* (Minneapolis: University of Minnesota Press, 1985); S. SANDMEL, "Parallelomania," *JBL* 81 (1962): 1–13; E. P. SANDERS, *Judaism: Practice and Belief, 63 B.C.E.–66 C.E.* (Philadelphia: Trinity Press, 1992); D. B. SANDY and R. L. GIESE JR.,

Cracking Old Testament Codes: A Guide to Interpreting the Literary Genres of the Old Testament (Nashville: Broadman, 1995); A. SCHLOTT, *Schrift und Schreiber im Alten Ägypten* (Beck's Archäologische Bibliothek; Munich: C. H. Beck, 1989); J. SEARLE, *Speech Acts: An Essay in the Philosophy of Language* (Cambridge: Cambridge University Press, 1969); E. J. SHARPE, *Comparative Religion: A History* (2d ed.; LaSalle, Ill.: Open Court, 1986); M. SHIBATANI and T. BYNON, eds. *Approaches to Language Typology* (Oxford: Clarendon, 1995); E. SHILS, "Tradition," *Comparative Studies in Society and History* 13 (1971): 122–59; M. SILVA, *God, Language, and Scripture: Reading the Bible in the Light of General Linguistics* (Foundations of Contemporary Interpretation 4; Grand Rapids: Zondervan, 1990); J. L. SKA, *Our Fathers Have Told Us: Introduction to the Analysis of Hebrew Narratives* (SubBi 13; Rome: Editrice Pontificio Istituto Biblico, 1990); I. STARR, *Queries to the Sungod: Divination and Politics in Sargonid Assyria* (SAA 4; Helsinki: Helsinki University Press, 1990); N. SMART, "Comparative-Historical Method," *ER* 3:571–74; J. Z. SMITH, *Map Is Not Territory: Studies in the History of Religions* (SJLA 23; Leiden: E. J. Brill, 1978); J. SWEEK, "The Monuments, the Babel-Bibel Streit, and Responses to Historical Criticism," in *The Pitcher Is Broken: Memorial Essays for Gösta W. Ahlström* (ed. S. W. Holloway and L. K. Handy; JSOTSup 190; Sheffield, England: Sheffield Academic Press, 1995), 401–19; M. A. SWEENEY and E. BEN ZVI, eds., *The Changing Face of Form Criticism for the Twenty-First Century* (Grand Rapids: Eerdmans, 2003); S. TALMON, "The Comparative Method in Biblical Interpretation—Principles and Problems," in *Congress Volume: Göttingen* (VTSup 29; Leiden: E. J. Brill, 1978), 320–56; A. TAYLOR, "Folklore and the Student of Literature," in *The Study of Folklore* (ed. A. Dundes; Englewood Cliffs, N.J.: Prentice-Hall, 1965), 34–42; J. H. TIGAY, *The Evolution of the Gilgamesh Epic* (Philadelphia: University of Pennsylvania Press, 1982); IDEM, "On Evaluating Claims of Literary Borrowing," in *The Tablet and the Scroll: Near Eastern Studies in Honor of William W. Hallo* (ed. M. E. Cohen, D. C. Snell, and D. B. Weisberg; Bethesda, Md.: CDL Press, 1993), 250–55; J. H. TIGAY, ed., *Empirical Models for Biblical Criticism* (Philadelphia: University of Pennsylvania Press, 1985); T. TODOROV, *Genres in Discourse* (Cambridge: Cambridge University Press, 1990); P. TRIBLE, *Rhetorical Criticism: Context, Method, and the Book of Jonah* (Philadelphia: Fortress, 1994); G. M. TUCKER, *Form Criticism of the Old Testament* (Philadelphia: Fortress, 1971); F. L. UTLEY, "Oral Genres as a Bridge to Written Literature," in *Folklore Genres* (ed. D. Ben-Amos; Austin: University of Texas Press, 1976), 3–15; K. J. VANHOOZER, *Is There a Meaning in This Text?* (Grand Rapids: Zondervan, 1998); H. L. J. VANSTIPHOUT, "Some Thoughts on Genre in Mesopotamian Literature," in *Keilschriftliche Literaturen: Ausgewählte Vorträge der XXXII. Rencontre assyriologique internationale* (ed. K. Hecker and W. Sommerfeld; BBVO 6; Berlin: Dietrich Reimer, 1986), 1–11; J. H. WALTON, *Ancient Israelite Literature in Its Cultural Context* (Grand Rapids: Zondervan, 1989); C. WESTERMANN, *Basic Forms of Prophetic Speech* (Louisville: Westminster John Knox, 1991); R. WELLEK and A. WARREN, *Theory of Literature* (3d rev. ed.; London: Jonathan Cape, 1966); R. R. WILSON, *Prophecy and Society in Ancient Israel* (Philadelphia: Fortress, 1980), 21–98.

CHAPTER ONE

Near Eastern Archives and Libraries

Introduction

Modern editions of the Hebrew Bible are conveniently available because scribes copied and preserved the text from the time of its composition until the advent of Gutenberg's printing press in the fifteenth century C.E. This phenomenon is quite exceptional; the vast majority of ancient Near Eastern texts were long ago forgotten, buried beneath many feet of earth and rubble. When nineteenth- and twentieth-century archaeologists began to unearth these texts, it did not take long to recognize that some of them were quite similar to those in the Hebrew Bible. This naturally generated an interest in comparing biblical and Near Eastern literature. Our access to the Near Eastern texts has been facilitated by the ancient tendency to collect them in libraries and archives. Originally, the archival and library materials were composed on a variety of materials, including not only clay tablets—probably the medium most familiar to modern readers—but also "wax boards" (wax-covered wooden or ivory tablets), wood, ostraca (pottery shards), metal, stone, parchment (animal skins), and papyrus. Many of these materials are perishable, and those that are not—stone, metal, and ostraca—were not commonly used. Fortunately, thousands of texts were composed on clay tablets in ancient Mesopotamia, Syria, Anatolia, Egypt, and the Levant. These tablets were preserved because they were deliberately hardened by kiln or sunshine or, as sometimes happened, because they were baked inadvertently when invaders burned the buildings that held them.

Many of the ancient archives and libraries were housed in public buildings such as palaces and temples while others were stored in private collections. It is conceptually helpful to distinguish the libraries from the archives, although we should stress that both could be kept at the same site. Ancient libraries, like their modern counterparts, made the cultural resources found in canonical texts (scientific, literary, religious, and historical texts) more easily accessible to scholars for reading, consultation, and research. Archives, on the other hand, were administrative sites where various types of official records were stored, such as receipts, inventories, loan and business contracts, diplomatic texts, legal records, marriage and adoption contracts, astrological reports, oracle queries, census reports, tribute lists, royal grants, treaties, letters, and all manner of other documentation. A further distinction can be made between *storage* archives and *functional* archives. The former included records that were unlikely to be consulted on a regular basis whereas the latter made texts conveniently accessible. Modern examples of each could include birth records (storage archives) and medical records (functional archives). It is worth noting that some archival records served only temporary purposes and so were quickly discarded. For instance, in Mesopotamia, it appears that temporary records were usually written on horizontally-oriented tablets (the *u'iltu* format used in temporary copies of contracts) while permanent archival records were written in a vertical-column format called *ṭuppu* (see Parpola 1997, liii; Radner). A good collection of English translations of archival documents is available in *COS 3.*

O. Pedersén is producing an exhaustive study of Near Eastern libraries and archives. He has already prepared a monograph (*ALANE*) that covers the period from 1500 to 300 B.C.E., and a second volume covering the earlier period is under way. Pedersén's first volume can be provisionally regarded as representative of the earlier contexts it does not discuss. According to Pedersén, a total of 253 libraries and archives from the period between 1500 and 300 B.C.E. have been unearthed from fifty different cities. These finds include 28 libraries, 198 archives, and 27 library/archive collections. About half of the collections were found in public buildings (127), the other half in private homes (126). The private collections—which included both archives and libraries—were owned by priests, scribes, diviners, exorcists, temple singers, businessmen, and public officials. Private archives were generally the property of businessmen, containing records of their business transactions, and the private libraries normally belonged to the professional classes, especially those connected to the temples or palace.

By far the largest and most important library recovered from the ancient world is that of King Assurbanipal of Assyria (669–c. 627). This collection from Tell Kuyunjik (the ancient citadel of Nineveh) is our primary source of both Assyrian and Babylonian literature. We owe its existence to Assurbanipal's literary obsessions, which inspired him to learn cuneiform and undertake the promethean task of collecting all known Mesopotamian literature into a single library. Although he did not succeed in acquiring all ancient literature, we are fortunate that he came as close as one reasonably could. This also means, however, that our understanding of Mesopotamian culture and tradition is somewhat skewed because we are overly dependent upon literature from a single location and time frame.

Most of the archives were relatively small (less than one hundred texts) and covered a period of no more than fifty years, that is, about one lifetime. Rarely were archives maintained for one hundred years or more, and rarely did they exceed one thousand documents. The administrative chanceries of temples and other public buildings generated the largest archives, in one case about thirty thousand texts (Sippar's Neo-Babylonian temple of Šamaš). Although most of the major archives were unearthed in Mesopotamia, Egypt also produced large archives and libraries, but most of the Egyptian texts were inscribed on perishable materials. Telling examples come from several Egyptian temples—most notably the Horus temple at Edfu—where the empty library chambers are inscribed with lists of the books that they once contained (see Burkard; Wessetzky; Sauneron). The literary samples that survive from earlier in Egyptian history include the exceptional papyri from dry regions and tombs and the nonperishable texts, such as ostraca. Still, our corpus of Egyptian papyri is significant—especially from the later periods—and appears meager only when compared with the archives and libraries of the cuneiform cultures (for a good survey of the Egyptian papyrological sources, see *LÄ* 4:667–899).

Table 1.1

Important Archival and Library Finds from the Ancient Near East

Location/Date	Before 2000	2000–1500	1500–1000	1000–300
Mesopotamia	Uruk, Ur, Nippur, Puzrish-Dagan	Assur, Kish	Assur, Babylon, Nippur, Nuzi	Assur, Babylon, Kalḫu, Sippar, Nineveh, Uruk, Nippur
Syria-Palestine	Ebla	Mari, Alalakh	Emar, Alalakh	
Anatolia		Kaneš (Kültepe)	Ḫattuša	
Egypt	Abusir	Deir el-Medina, Saqqara	Akhetaton (Amarna)	Elephantine

Modern name in parentheses ( ); all dates B.C.E.

The summaries below cover some of the more important libraries and archives from the ancient Near East, but readers should note that there were scores of ancient archives and libraries containing many thousands of texts. The sketch of the archives presented here is therefore admittedly selective; studies listed in the general bibliography at the conclusion of this chapter provide a more complete introduction to the ancient Near Eastern archives. There are also many closely related entries elsewhere in this volume, especially the Israelite archives (from Samaria, Arad, and Lachish) treated in chapter 15. Before we turn to the entries on archives and libraries, several pertinent introductory issues need to be discussed: languages, writing, literacy, schools, and canonicity.

Language and Writing in the Ancient Near East

The texts discussed in this volume come from five major centers of ancient civilization: Mesopotamia, Syria-Palestine, Egypt, Asia Minor, and Greece. The earliest written "texts" were small symbols inscribed on clay tokens and tablets from Mesopotamia. These inscribed tokens, dating to as early as about 4000 B.C.E., were generally used for economic purposes, such as inventories and transfers of goods (see Schmandt-Besserat; Nissen et al.). Sumerian, the earliest written language, seems to have developed from this ancient token system (Walker; Kaltner/McKenzie). Sumerian civilization emerged as a series of independent city-states in southern Mesopotamia during the second half of the fourth millennium and continued on until about 1900 B.C.E. Although the Sumerian people themselves are little understood, scholars have been reasonably successful in translating their literary texts, which first appeared in the third millennium B.C.E. The Sumerian language employed a system of signs that represented both concepts (ideograms) and syllabic values (syllabograms). For instance, the sign *PA* could represent the concept "twig" or the phoneme "pa." The signs were composed by impressing a stylus upon clay tablets (or other media), thus producing a variety of wedge-shaped patterns that scholars call *cuneiform* (from the Latin for "wedge-shaped"). Although Sumerian texts were composed during the Classical Sumerian period (ca. 2500 B.C.E.) and the so-called Sumerian Renaissance (Ur III, ca. 2000–1900 B.C.E.), most of our copies come from the Old Babylonian period (ca. 1800–1600 B.C.E.), when Akkadian speakers studied Sumerian as a foreign language (for more on Sumerian, see Diakonoff; Edzard).

During the last half of the second millennium, a new culture, the Semites, began to exert influence in Mesopotamia. The Semites continued to study and copy Sumerian texts (see Hallo), but they also adapted its cuneiform script to their own language, which modern scholars call Akkadian (see Huehnergard). Alongside the old Sumerian ideograms, which now took on Akkadian meanings (e.g., the Sumerian *LUGAL* = the Akkadian *šarru* = "king"), the Semites created an elaborate system of syllabic signs by which words could be phonetically represented (e.g., the Akkadian *šarrum* = *šar* + *rum*). This system was more flexible than the Sumerian ideograms and somewhat easier to learn and employ. Its phonetic nature allowed other cultures in the region—for example, those of the Hittites, Hurrians, Elamites, and Urartians—to adapt the script to their own languages. But this script was not as efficient as the alphabetic writing systems that would develop in Syria-Palestine. Akkadian was widely used by the Assyrian and Babylonian civilizations, but the writing and copying of Akkadian texts outlasted the heyday of both, with the latest Akkadian text dating to the first century of our era (see Sachs).

Between 2000 and 1000 B.C.E. a number of Semitic tongues related to Akkadian developed in Syria and Palestine. Scholars describe these languages as West Semitic, in contrast to the East Semitic dialects of Akkadian. The West Semitic tongues included Amorite, Ugaritic, Canaanite, Aramaic, Phoenician, Ammonite, Moabite, Edomite, and Hebrew, among others. The earliest substantial literary texts from this language family come from Ugarit (fourteenth–thirteenth century B.C.E.), a city-state located on the eastern shore of the Mediterranean Sea (modern Syria). Although Ugaritic scribes knew Akkadian well, they also adapted its cuneiform medium to produce their own thirty-character alphabetic system.

This system, which they used to write texts in their native tongue, was an obvious improvement over the several hundred syllabic signs needed to write Akkadian. But a cuneiform alphabet was still quite cumbersome and eventually gave way to the more cursive alphabetic scripts that began to develop in the region (Naveh; Whitt). The Hebrew Bible, together with various Phoenician, Ammonite, Moabite, and Aramaic texts, was composed in such an alphabetic script. Hebrew itself appears to have emerged between the twelfth and tenth centuries B.C.E., although the Bible generally reflects somewhat later dialects from the first millennium B.C.E. (Sáenz-Badillos). Modern Arabic and Modern Hebrew, still spoken in the Near East, are also Semitic languages and share many similarities with the ancient Hebrew tongue. Modern dialects of Aramaic are also spoken in some quarters, although these are quickly disappearing.

The Egyptian language is a distant relative of these Semitic tongues, but this relationship is only visible to scholars with expertise in historical linguistics (for an overview, see Loprieno). Egyptian texts first appeared at about the same time that Sumerian was appearing in Mesopotamia (ca. 3000 B.C.E.). The earliest texts were composed in a pictographic script that scholars call hieroglyphics, which, like Sumerian, combined phonetic and logographic features in what was essentially a consonantal script. Hieroglyphs were developed primarily for lapidary purposes (writing on stone) and so were especially suited for monumental texts, the last example dating to 394 C.E. (James, 82). Although pictographic hieroglyphs were also used in some canonical texts (most notably in funerary literature), canonical and archival texts were more commonly written in cursive scripts known as *hieratic* and *demotic*. Hieratic, essentially a direct cursive rendering of the hieroglyphs, appeared about 2600 B.C.E. and was used until the third century B.C.E. It gradually gave way to the other cursive form, demotic, a shorthand rendition of the hieroglyphs, used from the seventh century B.C.E. until the fifth century C.E. Modern Coptic, a language preserved in the Christian communities of Egypt, is the direct but distant successor of these ancient Egyptian dialects (see Behlmer).

Hittite was the administrative language of Hatti, the Hittite empire that flourished in ancient Anatolia (modern Turkey) during the second half of the second millennium B.C.E. (see Melchert). The language differs from both the Semitic and the Egyptian tongues because of its Indo-European origins, a heritage that it shares with modern Western European languages (such as English and German) and with some modern Asiatic languages (e.g., Farsi and Hindi). During the second millennium B.C.E., the Hittites adopted the Mesopotamian cuneiform system, in which most of our Hittite texts were written. The vast majority of these clay tablets were discovered in the ancient Hittite capital of Ḫattuša, near what is now the modern city of Boğazköy in central Turkey. The dialects of these texts include Old Hittite (ca. 1550–1450 B.C.E.), Middle Hittite (ca. 1450–1400 B.C.E.), and Neo-Hittite (ca. 1400–1220 B.C.E.). Several other languages appear in the Hittite corpus, mostly in the ritual texts and in royal inscriptions (see Gragg; Melchert). One of these, called Hattic, was the language of the region before the Indo-European Hittites arrived. Other languages from the Hittite theater include

the Tigris and Habur Rivers. Hurrian was written in cuneiform and appears especially in Hittite rituals and ceremonies that originated in Kizzuwatna (southeastern Anatolia). Palaic was written using cuneiform, and Luwian was composed in
both cuneiform (on tablets) and hieroglyphic (in royal inscriptions) scripts.

   Ancient Greek dialects share their Indo-European origins with the Hittite
language. The Greeks, however, like the West Semites, wrote their texts in alphabetic scripts that they seem to have borrowed and adapted from the Semitic-
speaking Phoenicians. Greek texts will be cited sparingly in this volume, but they
are particularly important in our comparative discussions of ancient historiography and law.

   Ancient texts can leave misleading impressions about the languages spoken
in antiquity because the oral and literary worlds sometimes used different languages. Sumerian was written long after the spoken tongue had disappeared, and
Amorite (a West Semitic tongue) was widely spoken during the Old Babylonian
period even as scribes copied and composed Sumerian and Akkadian texts.
Somewhat later, the foreign Kassite dynasties that ruled Babylon (ca. 1600–1200
B.C.E.) spoke their native language even as they were meticulously editing older
Sumerian and Akkadian texts and writing new Akkadian texts. A similar pattern
appears during the Neo-Babylonian period (seventh–sixth century B.C.E.), when
the Chaldean rulers of Babylon spoke Aramaic but wrote texts in Akkadian. Indeed, during the first millennium B.C.E., Aramaic gradually became the lingua
franca of the Near East, used in diplomacy from Persia in the East to Egypt in the
West (Kaufman). This aramaization began full-force with the Neo-Assyrians,
who in the ninth century initiated policies of assimilation and integration that
included the imposition of the Aramaic language and script (see Tadmor;
Zadok). By the end of the seventh century, Aramaic was spoken all over Mesopotamia. Unfortunately, Aramaic documents were usually written on perishable
materials such as papyrus and leather, so few texts have survived from this early
period. The emergence of Aramaic during the first millennium accounts for
the language's prominence in Jewish history and tradition, and this circumstance may also explain another phenomenon. It is commonly recognized that
the authors of the Hebrew Bible were familiar with many Mesopotamian traditions. Although it is possible that some Israelite scribes read Akkadian, it is more
sensible to imagine that the Mesopotamian traditions were mediated to Israel
through oral or written Aramaic, especially during the exile and afterwards (cf.
2 Kgs 18:26).

Scribes, Scholars, Literacy, and Canonicity

   Scribal education was particularly arduous in the ancient world because
most of the ancient writing systems were very complex. Although many people in
the upper levels of society perhaps had some facility with the languages, years of
professional training were required for any real mastery of them (Parpola 1997).
For this reason, true literacy was not widespread in the major cultural centers of

the upper levels of society perhaps had some facility with the languages, years of professional training were required for any real mastery of them (Parpola 1997). For this reason, true literacy was not widespread in the major cultural centers of Mesopotamia, Syria, Egypt, and Anatolia. In most cases, perhaps 2 percent or less of the population was fully literate (Young). Scribes were trained through apprenticeships, in private schools, and in palace or temple schools. During the Sumerian and Old Babylonian periods, Mesopotamian education was centered in various academies known as "tablet houses" (É.DUB.BA), but scribal education was gradually disseminated into a variety of additional private and public institutions after about 1600 B.C.E. (Landsberger). In Egypt education was provided in the temple-sponsored "House of Life" as well as in court schools (Olivier; Gardiner).

There are important similarities between all of these ancient schools, but the scribes that they produced varied in expertise and filled many different roles. Some scribes were primarily "functional scribes," whose role was to copy, read, and write texts for the institutions in which they served. Ancient administrative centers in temples and palaces were probably well stocked with these scribes. Other scribes, sometimes called "professional scribes," were trained to serve specialized roles as priests, diviners, exorcists, doctors, pharmacists, and so forth. These scribes were, naturally, well versed in their own lore, but there is good evidence that they studied a broad range of other texts and traditions (Parpola 1983). Closely related to the professional scribes were the "scholastic scribes," who represented the ancient equivalent of our modern intellectual tradition. These sages generally worked within the sphere of the palace or temple, for it was here that their expertise was tapped to aid in the administration of political, social, and religious order. Scribal sages were particularly active in creating, compiling, preserving, and transmitting ancient canonical tradition. Functional and professional scribes, however, also played key roles in this canonical process; this suggests that the role distinctions highlighted here can easily be pressed too far. Role differentiation was not as pronounced in the ancient world as in modern, complex societies (Visicato).

Smaller states such as Israel could not support extensive scribal and scholastic infrastructures like those in Egypt and Mesopotamia. Indeed, some recent scholarship has suggested that for most of Israel's history its political and economic apparatus was too small to support a class of scribes and formal scribal schools (P. R. Davies; Jamieson-Drake; Lemche). Given that the earliest reference to formal Jewish schools comes from the second century B.C.E. (Ben Sira's school in Sir 51:23), is it reasonable to assume that schools existed earlier, during the preexilic period? A comparison of Israelite literature with the literature from another Levantine city, Ugarit, is instructive here. Ugarit, a city of eight thousand, ruled a kingdom of thirty-three thousand inhabitants (see Yon). The city appears to have had schools of some sort (Mack-Fisher), and its scholars were familiar with foreign literature (see Richardson) and produced an important corpus of local literary texts. By comparison, preexilic Jerusalem reached populations as high as twenty-five thousand, ruling over a territory and population much larger than Ugarit (see King); thus, on a comparative basis, Judean society was of an adequate size to support schools and scholarship on some scale. Granted, Ugarit was an important trade center and was certainly a more cosmopolitan city than Jerusalem, but the large corpus of Hebrew literature produced in ancient Israel supports the conclusion—perhaps even demands it—that instructional institutions such as schools existed in ancient Israel (Lemaire; Crenshaw; G. I. Davies). Furthermore, if we may judge from the Ugaritic literature, Israelite scribes not only were versed in their native literature but also were familiar with some of the canonical literature from Egypt and Mesopotamia. The caveat here is that Israelite schools would have been relatively small institutions located only in the most important political and cultural centers of the north and south, especially Samaria and Jerusalem. Present evidence makes it unlikely that there was a complex educational system throughout monarchic Judah, as Lemaire would have us believe.

I have pointed out that Israelite and Ugaritic scribes were familiar with the Near Eastern canonical traditions. What were these canonical traditions? Each center of Near Eastern culture possessed its own body of scientific, literary, religious, and historical traditions that was produced and formally perpetuated by its scribal scholars. Centuries of copying and revising these texts often produced very long documents. The Egyptians solved this problem by using long papyrus scrolls, an option not available to those using clay tablets. The usual Mesopotamian solution was to connect a series of related tablets using numbers and "catch lines," in which the last line of one tablet was repeated on the first line of the next tablet to mark the proper order of the series. The development of writing boards connected by hinges also solved this problem. By the Neo-Assyrian period, it appears that Mesopotamian scholars described their traditions using three native terms: *iškaru* (the official canonical series), *ahû* (external to the official series but authoritative and important), and *ša pî ummānī* (the oral tradition of the sages) (on these three categories, see Lieberman; Rochberg-Halton; Parpola 1993; Farber). We should remember, however, that descriptions such as this should not be pressed too far because Mesopotamia's canonical traditions changed from period to period, constantly altered by shifts of political power and by the various migrations that disrupted Mesopotamian culture from time to time. The situation was quite different in Egypt, where libraries reflect three and a half millennia of almost uninterrupted canonical tradition (Redford).

Our use of canonical terminology to describe Egyptian and Mesopotamian literature must be qualified, for it does not imply a closed corpus of sacred literature such as we have in the Hebrew canon. Rather, in the hands of modern scholars, canon terminology is put to two related usages. *Canonical* sometimes describes texts that were commonly transmitted by scribes and preserved in ancient libraries. In this sense, *canonical* refers to texts that were traditional. The other common use of the word *canon* refers more specifically to standard editions of the ancient texts. By *standard edition,* we mean that at certain points—especially during the first millennium—Mesopotamian texts that had previously been edited and revised for many centuries were finally given a fixed form. From that point forward, scribes who copied these texts did so with the goal of preserving the readings found in their *Vorlage* (source text). Although these notions of canon do not correspond precisely to the concept of Hebrew canonical literature, there is a significant overlap between the two; the Hebrew texts became religiously authoritative precisely because they were preserved as a part of the Israelite scribal tradition, and Near Eastern texts were preserved because they were deemed valuable and, in some sense, authoritative (Leiman). If we can judge from the literature of Israel's Near Eastern counterparts, we may presume that many pieces of Hebrew literature underwent a lengthy process of growth and revision before finally reaching their fixed canonical shape.

Although Israelite society could not match the size and complexity of the Egyptian and Mesopotamian cultural centers, its use of an alphabetic script was a potentially decisive advantage in matters of literacy. Competent use of hieroglyphics or cuneiform required many years of study, but reading and writing with a twenty-two-letter Hebrew alphabet was theoretically within the reach of most every Israelite commoner (Millard 1972; 1985). For some time, largely on the basis of the supposedly widespread literacy in Athenian Greece, it has been commonly assumed that literacy was quite high in Israel in comparison with its Near Eastern neighbors. Recent studies of literacy in ancient Greece have concluded, however, that literacy there was quite limited (Harris; Thomas). Consequently, it is now commonly supposed that in Israel, as elsewhere in the ancient world, the mostly illiterate population was dependent upon the services of a rather small corps of professional scribes when it came to reading and writing texts (Haran).

Our overview of the archival and library materials begins with regions close to Israel (Syria-Palestine) and then goes on to consider the finds from Mesopotamia, Egypt, Anatolia, and Persia.

1.1. Syria-Palestine

Alalakh (Tell Açana). More than five hundred texts from the eighteenth–seventeenth and fifteenth centuries B.C.E. were discovered at this site. Taken together, the sources give us a fairly good picture of society and economic life at these two junctures in the city's history. Most exemplars were administrative records, but a few treaty texts were discovered, as were several literary texts (hymns, omens, and incantations). Perhaps the best known of these texts is the statue inscription of King Idrimi, which is discussed in 9.1.3. Nearly all of the texts are in Akkadian, but the dialect reflects influences from Hurrian and West Semitic tongues. Texts from Alalakh are designated with an "AT" prefix (e.g., AT 457).

Texts and translations: D. J. WISEMAN, *The Alalakh Tablets* (OPBIAA 2; London: British Institute of Archaeology, 1953); IDEM, "Supplementary Copies of the Alalakh Tablets," *JCS* 8 (1954): 1–30. *Bibliography:* ALANE 33–37; E. GAAL, *Alalaḫ VII: Social Structure and Economic Life in the 18–17th Centuries B.C.* (Budapest: ELTE, 1972); E. L. GREENSTEIN, "Alalakh Texts," *OEANE* 1:59–61; R. S. HESS, "The Bible and Alalakh," in *Mesopotamia and the Bible* (ed. Chavalas and Younger), 209–21; IDEM, "A Preliminary List of the Published

Alalakh Texts," *UF* 20 (1988): 69–87; D. L. STEIN, "Alalakh," *OEANE* 1:55–59; L. WOOLLEY, *Alalakh: An Account of the Excavations at Tell Atchana in the Hatay, 1937–1949* (Oxford: Society of Antiquaries, 1955).

Ebla (Tell Mardikh). This ancient city was located in Northern Syria, about 100 km east of the Mediterranean Sea and 60 km south of Aleppo. There is an on-going debate about whether its Eblaite language should be viewed as essentially East Semitic (like the later Akkadian of Mesopotamia) or West Semitic (like the tongues spoken in Syria/Palestine). Most scholars favor the former view. Ebla's central palace archive dates to the 24th century B.C.E. and has yielded about 3,000 documents (from 15,000 tablets and fragments) covering a period of some 40 to 50 years. Most of the texts are administrative, but several lexical lists, ritual texts, hymns, letters, royal decrees and treaties were also unearthed. Texts from Ebla are designated with a "TM" (Tell Mardikh) prefix, followed by the year, find location, and text number for that year (e.g., TM 74.G.120).

Texts and translations: See the following series: Archivi reali di Ebla: Testi (Rome: Missione Archeologica Italiana in Siria, 1981–); Materiali epigrafici di Ebla (Naples: Istituto Universitario Orientale, 1979–) (see esp. G. PETTINATO, *Catalogo dei testi cuneiformi di Tell Mardikh-Ebla* [Naples: Istituto Universitario Orientale, 1979]). ***Bibliography:*** A. ARCHI, "The Archives of Ebla," in *Cuneiform Archives and Libraries* (ed. Veenhof), 72–86; IDEM, "Ebla Texts," *OEANE* 2:184–86; S. G. BELD, W. W. HALLO, and P. MICHAL-OWSKI, *The Tablets of Ebla: Concordance and Bibliography* (Winona Lake, Ind.: Eisenbrauns, 1984); C. H. GORDON, G. A. RENDSBURG, and N. H. WINTER, *Eblaitica: Essays on the Ebla Archives and Eblaite Language* (4 vols.; Winona Lake, Ind.: Eisenbrauns, 1987–2002); P. MATTHIAE, "The Archives of the Royal Palace G of Ebla: Distribution and Arrangement of the Tablets according to the Archaeological Evidence," in *Cuneiform Archives and Libraries* (ed. Veenhof), 53–71; IDEM, "Ebla," *OEANE* 2:180–82; G. PETTINATO, *The Archives of Ebla: An Empire Inscribed in Clay* (Garden City, N.Y.: Doubleday, 1981).

Emar (Meskene). Large portions of this ancient site are now submerged under the el-Assad lake, created when the Tabqa dam was built on the Euphrates in Syria. Excavations at the site before the dam's completion yielded more than eight hundred texts dating to between the late fourteenth and early twelfth centuries B.C.E. Archival texts, mainly economic texts and contracts, made up about half of the find, but the remainder included lexical texts, literary texts, and a large corpus of ritual tablets and fragments that attest to previously unknown rites and festivals observed in the city. The vast majority of the texts were written in Akkadian, but Hittite, Hurrian, and Sumerian exemplars are included as well. Students of the Hebrew Bible will be particularly interested in the ritual texts discovered in the library of the city's chief diviner, which reflect some similarities with Hebrew ritual (see 5.4; 5.5; 5.6). Because Emar was under Hittite authority during this period, the materials provide us with helpful images of life in the Hittite provinces. Texts from Emar are designated with an "Msk" (Meskene) prefix (e.g., Msk 731035), although they are also commonly referenced from Arnaud's standard collection (e.g., *Emar* 446).

Text and translation: D. ARNAUD, *Recherches au pays d'Aštata* (4 vols; *Emar* 6; Paris: Éditions Recherche sur les Civilisations, 1985–1987). *Bibliography:* M. W. CHAVALAS, ed., *Emar: The History, Religion, and Culture of a Syrian Town in the Late Bronze Age* (Bethesda, Md.: CDL Press, 1996); P. Y. HOSIKISSON, "Emar as an Empirical Model of the Transmission of Canon," in *The Biblical Canon in Comparative Perspective* (ed. K. L. Younger Jr., W. W. Hallo, and B. F. Batto; Lewiston, N.Y.: Mellen, 1991), 21–32; J. HUEHNERGARD, "Emar Texts," *OEANE* 2:239–40; J.-C. MARGUERON and M. SIGRIST, "Emar," *OEANE* 2:236–39.

Mari (Tell Hariri). Excavations at Tell Hariri in Syria began in 1934. More than twenty thousand documents have been unearthed, and modest numbers of texts continue to appear. With a few exceptions, these texts date to the reigns of the last kings of Mari, Yasmaḫ-Addu and Zimri-Lim (eighteenth century B.C.E.). Archival and administrative texts consitute nearly the entire collection, and although the absence of canonical texts has been a disappointment for scholars, the archives nevertheless provide important sources for reconstructing the city's history and for enlightening our perspectives on the Hebrew Bible. The most important comparative sources include the prophetic letters, vital for the study of Hebrew prophecy (see ch. 6), and the many sources that reflect tribal life within Mari and on its immediate periphery. Many scholars believe that the mix of tribal and urban life at Mari sheds comparative light on the emergence of urban Israel from its tribal origins. The only true literary text from Mari is the unpublished Epic of Zimri-Lim (see 9.1.3). Texts from Mari are designated in a somewhat arbitrary fashion, being prefixed with "A" from A.1 to A.4700 and then largely with "M," although there are also some "B" and "TH" prefixes. An explanation for the development of these sigla is found in ARMT 23, iii–iv.

Texts and translations: See the the series Archives royales de Mari (Paris: various publishers, 1950–); Florilegium marianum (Paris: SEPOA, 1992–); *Mari: Annales de recherche interdisciplinaires* (Paris: Éditions Recherche sur les Civilisations, 1982–). See also the annotated translation of Mari letters in J.-M. DURAND, *Les documents épistolaires du palais de Mari* (3 vols.; Littératures anciennes du Proche-Orient 16–18; Paris: Cerf, 1997). *Translation:* W. HEIMPEL, *Letters to the King of Mari: A New Translation, with Historical Introduction, Notes, and Commentary* (MC 12; Winona Lake, Ind.: Eisenbrauns, 2003). *Bibliography:* D. CHARPIN, "La fin des archives dans le palais de Mari," *RA* 89 (1995): 29–40; J. M. DURAND, "Réalités amorrites et traditions bibliques," *RA* 92 (1998): 3–39; D. E. FLEMING, "Mari and the Possibilities of Biblical Memory," *RA* 92 (1998): 41–78; M.-H. GATES, "The Palace of Zimri-Lim at Mari," *BA* 47 (1984): 70–87; M. GUICHARD, "Mari Texts," *OEANE* 3:419–21; J.-G. HEINTZ et al., *Bibliographie de Mari: Archéologie et textes* (Wiesbaden: Harrassowitz, 1990); A. LEMAIRE, "Mari, the Bible, and the Northwest Semitic World," *BA* 47 (1984): 101–8; A. MALAMAT, *Mari and the Bible: A Collection of Studies* (Jerusalem: Hebrew University Press, 1975); IDEM, *Mari and the Early Israelite Experience* (Oxford: Oxford University Press, 1989); J.-C. MARGUERON, "Mari," *OEANE* 3:413–16; V. H. MATTHEWS, "Syria to the Early Second Millennium," in *Mesopotamia and the Bible* (ed. Chavalas and Younger), 168–90; D. PARDEE and J. T. GLASS, "The Mari Archives: Literary Sources for the History Of Palestine and Syria," *BA* 47 (1984): 88–99; J. M. SASSON, "About 'Mari and the Bible,'" *RA* 92 (1998): 97–123; IDEM, "Some Comments on

Archive Keeping at Mari," *Iraq* 34 (1972): 55–57; G. D. YOUNG, *Mari in Retrospect: Fifty Years of Mari and Mari Studies* (Winona Lake, Ind.: Eisenbrauns, 1992).

Shubat-Enlil (Tell Leilan). Also known in antiquity as Shekna, Shubat-Enlil is located in the eastern half of the upper Habur plain, where it was the capital of the land Apum. Apart from some older seals and seal impressions, the primary textual evidence comes from several Old Babylonian archives belonging mainly to the last three kings of Leilan, who reigned just before the city was destroyed by Samsuiluna of Babylon in 1728 B.C.E. Over 800 administrative texts and letters have been found at the site, as well as a treaty text (see ch. 14) and a copy of the Sumerian King List (see 11.1). A complete edition of the letters and treaties by J. Eidem is in an advanced state of preparation.

Texts and translations: J. EIDEM, "Tell Leilan Archives 1987," *RA* 85 (1991): 109–35; C. VINCENTE, *The 1987 Tell Leilan Tablets Dated by the Limmu of Habil-kinu* (PhD diss., Yale University, 1991). *Bibliography:* J. EIDEM, "Les archives paléo-babyloniennes de Tell Leilan," *Les Dossiers d'Archéologie* 155 (1990): 50–53; IDEM, "Tell Leilan Tablets 1987: A Preliminary Report," *Annals archéologiques arabes syriennes* 38–39 (1989): 20–40; H. WEISS, "Leilan, Tell," *OEANE* 3:341–47; R. M. WHITING, "The Tell Leilan Tablets: A Preliminary Report," *AJA* 94 (1990): 568–79.

Ugarit (Ras Shamra). This city was the capital of an ancient kingdom on the Mediterranean coast of what is now Syria, where it was entombed in the mound of Ras Shamra until excavations began in 1929. Since that time, archaeologists digging at Ras Shamra and nearby Ras Ibn Hani have unearthed nearly fifteen hundred texts, most of them in Ugaritic or Akkadian, although Sumerian, Hittite, and Hurrian exemplars are known as well. The find locations included several palace archives, private archives, private libraries, and especially the library of the high priest on the acropolis, from which most of the important Ugaritic literary texts have come (see van Soldt). According to figures from 1994, these texts fall into the following generic categories: (1) lists and business documents, 767; (2) unclassified, 217; (3) literary and religious texts, 161; (4) letters, 72; (5) labels, 63; (6) unreadable texts, 30; (7) school texts and abecedaries, 22; (8) treaties, 9. Ugaritic texts have greatly illumined our perspective on Hebrew language and poetry and on various dimensions of Israelite myth, ritual, and culture.

　　Ugaritic scholars refer to Ras Shamra texts using either a publication number in *KTU* and *CTU* (the new edition of *KTU*) or a realia number that takes the form "RS NN.nn," where "RS" stands for Ras Shamra, "NN" for the number of the archaeological season, and "nn" for the individual find number (texts from the nearby site of Ras Ibn Hani are designated with an "RIH" prefix). Season numbers began with RS 1 in 1929—the first season at Ugarit—and continued to follow this convention until 1975, when the RS number was changed to the actual year of the season (e.g., all 1975 texts are referred to with "RS 1975.nn"). Because tablets are often fragmentary, a single text such as *KTU* 1.4 may be represented by more than one RS realia number (in this case, RS 2.008, 3.341, and 3.347).

Text and translation: M. DIETRICH, O. LORETZ, and J. SANMARTIN, *The Cuneiform Alphabetic Texts from Ugarit, Ras Ibn Hani, and Other Places* (Münster: Ugarit, 1995) (transliterated texts only). *Translation: COS* 3.45: 89–114. *Bibliography:* P. BORDREUIL, *Une bibliothèque au sud de la ville* (Ras Shamra-Ougarit VIII; Paris: Éditions Recherche sur le Civilisations, 1991); A. BOUNNI and J. LAGARCE, "Ras Ibn Hani," *OEANE* 4:411–13; J.-L. CUNCHILLOS, *Bibliographie*, vol. 2 of *La trouvaille épigraphique de l'Ougarit* (Paris: Éditions Recherche sur les Civilisations, 1990); P. L DAY, "Ugaritic," in *Beyond Babel* (ed. Kaltner and McKenzie), 223–41; L. R. FISHER, ed., *Ras Shamra Parallels: The Texts from Ugarit and the Hebrew Bible* (2 vols.; Rome: Biblical Institute Press, 1972–1975); A. L. KRISTENSEN, "Ugaritic Epistolary Formulas: A Comparative Study of the Ugaritic Epistolary Formulas in the Context of the Contemporary Akkadian Formulas in the Letters from Ugarit and Amarna," *UF* 9 (1977): 143–58; S. LACKENBACHER, "La correspondance internationale dans les archives d'Ugarit," *RA* 89 (1995): 67–76; D. PARDEE, "Ugaritic," *OEANE* 5:262–64; IDEM, "Ugaritic Inscriptions," *OEANE* 5:264–66; W. T. PITARD, "Voices from the Dust: The Tablets from Ugarit and the Bible," in *Mesopotamia and the Bible* (ed. Chavalas and Younger), 251–75; RICHARDSON, "The Less Inspired Scriptures"; W. VAN SOLDT, "The Written Sources," in *Handbook of Ugaritic Studies* (ed. Watson and Wyatt), 28–75; W. G. E. WATSON and N. WYATT, eds., *Handbook of Ugaritic Studies* (Leiden: Brill, 1999); YON, "Ugarit," 255–62.

1.2. Mesopotamia

Abu Salabikh. The ancient name of this site is not known, but its date (fourth and third millennia) and location in southern Iraq, between the Euphrates and Tigris Rivers, favor identification with Eresh. About five hundred Sumerian texts were unearthed from the site, among them copies of the Kesh Temple Hymn (see 3.1.1), the Instructions of Shuruppak (see 2.1.1), and the early Sumerian proverbs (see 2.1.1).

Texts and translations: B. ALSTER, "Early Dynastic Proverbs and Other Contributions to the Study of Literary Texts from Abū Ṣalābīkh," *AfO* 38–39 (1991–1992): 1–51; R. D. BIGGS, *Inscriptions from Tell Abū Ṣālābīkh* (OIP 99; Chicago: University of Chicago Press, 1974). *Bibliography:* M. KREBERNIK, "Die Texte aus Fāra und Abū Ṣābaliḫ," in J. Bauer, R. K. Englund, and M. Krebernik, *Mesopotamien: Späturuk-Zeit und Frühdynastische Zeit* (OBO 160/1; Freiburg, Switz.: Universitätsverlag, 1998), 237–427; J. N. POSTGATE, "Abu Salabikh," *OEANE* 1:9–10.

Assur. This city lay on the west bank of the Tigris River in what is now northern Iraq. From the beginning of the second millennium B.C.E. until early in the first millennium, it was the religious and administrative capital of Assyria. When the Neo-Assyrian Empire emerged, the capital was moved several times, first to Kalḫu/Nimrud (by Aššurnaṣirpal II, 883–859 B.C.E.), then to Dur Sharrukin/Khorsabad (by Sargon II, 721–705 B.C.E.), and finally to Nineveh/Kuyunjik (by Sennacherib, 704–681 B.C.E.). Meanwhile Assur continued to be an important city. Fifty-three archives and libraries have been unearthed in Assur, fourteen dating to the Middle Assyrian period and the remainder to the Neo-Assyrian period.

These finds have yielded more than four thousand texts, most in stashes of less than fifty documents, although two large libraries were discovered (of three hundred and eight hundred texts, respectively). Also discovered at Assur is our only Aramaic letter from the Neo-Assyrian period, in which an Assyrian officer stationed in Babylon reports that rebellion is brewing in the south (Lindenberger). The best source of texts and studies is the State Archives of Assyria series, published by the Neo-Assyrian Text Corpus Project, University of Helsinki, Finland.

Bibliography: ALANE 81–88, 132–43; W. ANDRAE, *Das wiedererstandene Assur* (ed. B. Hrouda; 2d ed.; Munich: Beck, 1977); R. W. LAMPRICHS, "Aššur," *OEANE* 1:225–28; J. M. LINDENBERGER, *Ancient Aramaic and Hebrew Letters* (2d ed.; SBLWAW 14; Atlanta: Scholars Press, 2003), 17–23; O. PEDERSÉN, *Archives and Libraries in the City of Assur* (2 vols.; Uppsala: Uppsala University Press, 1985–1986); IDEM, "The Libraries in the City of Assur," in *Keilschriftliche Literaturen: Ausgewählte Vorträge der XXXII. Rencontre assyriologique internationale* (ed. K. Hecker and W. Sommerfeld; BBVO 6; Berlin: Dietrich Reimer, 1986), 143–47.

Babylon. This famous site lies on the Euphrates River about fifty-five miles southwest of modern Baghdad, Iraq. Babylon, the on-again, off-again capital of independent Babylon, was an important cultural and religious center through most of ancient history. Scholars have unearthed thousands of Sumerian and Akkadian texts there, distributed among numerous archives and libraries that date from the Old Babylonian period (see Pedersén 2005) down to the Parthian era. Groundwater has prevented extensive digging in the older layers of the city, so we are more informed about the Neo-Babylonian and Persian periods of the city's history. Nevertheless, fragmentary remains of private archives and libraries were discovered in Old Babylonian levels of the city, as were several smaller private libraries and archives from the Middle Babylonian period. German excavations in the Neo-Babylonian and Persian levels, conducted in 1899–1917, unearthed small private libraries containing literary texts as well as much larger archives in private, palace, and temple contexts. The largest find from this late period was an archive of three thousand to four thousand tablets belonging to the influential Egibi family, its contents dating to 602–482 B.C.E. The documents were found still sealed in their storage jars. The next largest find included fifteen hundred school tablets that were used as fill in the construction of the temple of Nabu, god of scribal arts. These texts were leftovers from scribal training, which apparently took place in the temple of the scribes' patron deity. A third large find, the Kasr archive, included about 950 Persian-era legal and business documents. These are particularly interesting because they bear Aramaic summary notations alongside the cuneiform text. Tablets discovered during the extensive German excavations bear the prefix "Bab" followed by the text number, but many texts from Babylon were acquired in uncontrolled conditions. These texts are generally known by their museum number designations, of which there are many.

Texts and translations: H. D. BAKER, *The Archive of the Nappahu Family* (AfO Beiheft 30; Vienna: Institut für Orientalistik, 2004); A. CAVIGNEAUX, *Textes scolaires du temple de*

Nabû ša ḫarê (Texts from Babylon 1; Baghdad: Republic of Iraq, Ministry of Culture and Information, State Organization of Antiquities and Heritage, 1981); the series Wissenschaftliche Veröffentlichung der Deutschen Orient-Gesellschaft, vols. 1, 2, 4, 15, 32, 47, 48, 54, 55, 59, 62; H. KLENGEL, *Altbabylonische Texte aus Babylon* (Vorderasiatische Schriftdenkmäler der Staatlichen Museen zu Berlin, N.F. 6; Berlin: Akademie-Verlag, 1983; IDEM, "Spät-altbabylonische Briefe aus Babylon (VS 22, 83–92)," *AoF* 10 (1983): 42–63; IDEM, "Altbabylonische Texte aus Babylon: Eine Nachlese zu VS 22," *AoF* 11 (1984): 92–109. *Bibliography:* K. ABRAHAM, *Business and Politics under the Persian Empire: The Financial Dealings of Marduk-naṣir-apli of the House of Egibi (521–487 B.C.E.)* (Bethesda, Md.: CDL Press, 2004); *ALANE* 107–12, 183–91; E. KLENGEL-BRANDT, "Babylon," *OEANE* 1:251–56; R. KOLDEWEY, *Das wieder erstehende Babylon* (ed. B. Hrouda; 5th ed. rev. and enlarged; Munich: Beck, 1990); O. PEDERSÉN, *Archive und Bibliotheken in Babylon: Die Tontafeln der Grabung Robert Koldewey 1899–1917* (ADOG 25; Saarbrücken: Saarbrücker Druckerei und Verlag, 2005); M. W. STOLPER, "The Kasr Archive," in *Centre and Periphery: Proceedings of the Groningen 1986 Achaemenid History Workshop* (ed. H. Sancisi-Weerdenburg and A. Kuhrt; Achaemenid History 4; Leiden: Nederlands Instituut voor het Nabije Oosten, 1990), 195–205.

Ešnunna (Tell Asmar), Ischcali and the Lower Diyala Region. The sites treated in this entry were located in the Diyala river basin near the river's confluence with the Tigris, not far from modern Baghdad. From an archival perspective, the most important of the cities in this region was Ešnunna, but texts were also found at Ischcali (ancient Neribtum), Khafajeh (ancient Tutub), Tell Harmal (ancient Šaduppum), and in the Hamrin district, where archaeological salvage operations were done before the Hamrin Dam project covered the sites with water (note especially Tell Haddad). Over 1500 texts were discovered at Ešnunna, about 300 from the Ur III period and the remainder from the Old Babylonian era (Whiting). There is archival continuity between the Ur III and Old Babylonian periods. Letters, cylinder seals, and administrative texts make up the bulk of the collection. Somewhat less than 700 texts were found in Ischcali, and a few more at Khafajeh (see Greengus). The Ischcali texts include letters, legal documents, school texts, and many administrative records, as well as our oldest Akkadian treaty text. Most of the texts from Khafajeh are muster rolls for military conscription. Tell Harmal has yielded, among other things, copies of the Laws of Ešnunna (see 13.2) and an interesting fragment of the Gilgamesh Epic (see 9.1.1). An additional copy of the Laws of Ešnunna was discovered in the Hamrin Dam area at Tell Haddad.

Texts and translations: H. FRANKFORT, S. LLOYD and Th. JACOBSEN, *The Gimilsin Temple and the Palace of the Rulers at Tell Asmar* (OIP 43; Chicago: University of Chicago Press, 1940); S. GREENGUS, *Old Babylonian Tablets from Ischali and Vicinity* (Istanbul: Nederlands Historisch-Archaeologisch Instituut, 1979); R. HARRIS, "The Archive of the Sin Temple in Khafajah (Tutub)," *JCS* 9 (1955): 31–88, 91–120; R. M. WHITING, *Old Babylonian Letters from Tell Asmar* (AS 22; Chicago: Oriental Institute of the University of Chicago, 1987). *Bibliography:* E. AUERBACH, "Eshnunna," *OEANE* 2.261–65; D. P. HANSEN, "Khafajeh," *OEANE* 3:288–90; M. ROAF, "Hamrin Dam Salvage Project," *OEANE* 2:471–74; I. THUESEN, "Diyala," *OEANE* 2:163–66.

Girsu (Telloh) and Lagaš (al-Hiba). Girsu, the capital of the Sumerian city-state of Lagaš, was a twin city with the nearby town of Lagaš. Forty thousand texts and fragments were found there, dating to the time of the Akkad dynasty and the Ur III period. Nearly all of these texts were administrative documents from the temple archives. Numerous royal inscriptions were also found in the area.

Bibliography: J. BAUER and D. P. HANSEN, "Lagaš," *RlA* 6:419–30; A. FALKENSTEIN and R. OPIFICIUS, "Girsu," *RlA* 3:385–401; R. J. MATTHEWS, "Girsu and Lagash," *OEANE* 2:406–9.

Ḫuzirina (Sultantepe). This site in southern Turkey has yielded a small but important library containing four hundred tablets that belonged to a family of *šangu*-priests. The collection is surprisingly comprehensive from a generic point of view, including incantations, rituals, omens, medical texts, prayers, hymns, lexical texts, god lists, epics, myths, wisdom literature, astrological texts, and even a letter that was fictionally attributed to the epic hero Gilgamesh, king of Uruk (see Gurney 1957; Kraus). The texts are Neo-Assyrian, dating to the late eighth and seventh centuries B.C.E.

Texts and translations: O. R. GURNEY, "The Sultantepe Tablets," *AnSt* 2 (1952): 25–35; 3 (1953): 15–27; 4 (1954): 65–100; 5 (1955): 93–114; 6 (1956): 145–64; 7 (1957): 127–36; 10 (1960): 105–31; O. R. GURNEY and J. J. FINKELSTEIN, *The Sultantepe Tablets* (2 vols.; OPBIAA 3, 7; London: British Institute of Archaeology at Ankara, 1957–1964); W. G. LAMBERT, "The Sultantepe Tablets, VIII: Shalmaneser in Ararat," *AnSt* 11 (1961): 143–58. ***Bibliography:*** *ALANE* 178–79; F. R. KRAUS, "Der Brief des Gilgameš," *AnSt* 30 (1980): 109–21; W. G. LAMBERT, "The Sultantepe Tablets," *RA* 53 (1959): 119–138; S. LLOYD, "Sultantepe (Part II)," *AnSt* 4 (1954): 101–10; S. LLOYD and N. GÖKÇE, "Sultantepe," *AnSt* 3 (1953): 27–51.

Kalḫu (Nimrud). Aššurnaṣirpal II (883–859 B.C.E.) moved the Neo-Assyrian capital from Assur to this site during the ninth century B.C.E. More than one thousand documents have been recovered at Nimrud, mostly archival texts but also a few literary texts. These texts date considerably later than Aššurnaṣirpal, many of them coming from the period just before Sargon II moved the Assyrian capital to Dur-Šarrukin, or from later periods. A large palace in the city's southeast quarter is called Fort Shalmaneser because it was constructed by Shalmaneser III as a location for reviewing his troops. The biblical writers not only knew the city's ancient name (Calah; see Gen 10:11–12) but also provided the basis for its modern name, Nimrud (see Gen 10:8–9).

Bibliography: *ALANE* 143–54; J. CURTIS, "Nimrud," *OEANE* 4:141–44; W. W. HALLO, "The Rise and Fall of Kalah," *JAOS* 88 (1968): 772–75; M. E. L. MALLOWAN, *Nimrud and Its Remains* (2 vols.; New York: Dodd, Mead & Co., 1966).

Nineveh. This city lay on the eastern bank of the Tigris River, in what is now the city of Mosul in Northern Iraq. It was made the capital of the Neo-Assyrian Empire by Sennacherib (704–681 B.C.E.), but Nineveh owes its special literary prominence to Assurbanipal, who assembled a large library at Tell Kuyunjik, the ancient palace mound of Nineveh. Approximately thirty thousand tablets or fragments of tablets have been unearthed at the site, with these yielding an estimated five thousand literary texts and many more archival documents. The literary exemplars include omens, incantations, medical texts, lexical texts, epics, prayers, hymns, myths, historical texts, and wisdom texts; the archival sources include letters, reports, and queries from the royal archives. It is noteworthy that archaeologists discovered 450 clay bullae in one room of Assurbanipal's palace. Scholars surmise that these were probably used to seal papyrus documents written in Aramaic, which reminds us that many Mesopotamian documents have not been preserved and that Aramaic was emerging as the lingua franca during the first millennium B.C.E. The texts from Kuyunjik are housed in the British Museum in London and bear the prefix siglum "K" (e.g., K 622). The best source of texts, translations, and studies is the State Archives of Assyria series, published by the Neo-Assyrian Text Corpus Project, University of Helsinki, Finland.

Bibliography: ALANE 158–65; L. ARKSEY, "The Library of Assurbanipal, King of the World," *Wilson Library Bulletin* (June 1977): 833–40; S. J. LIEBERMAN, "Canonical and Official Cuneiform Texts"; PARPOLA, "Assyrian Library Records"; D. STRONACH and K. CODELLA, "Nineveh," *OEANE* 4:144–48.

Nippur. This site lies about 110 miles southwest of Babylon in the center of the floodplain between the Euphrates and Tigris Rivers. Occupation began as early as the sixth millennium B.C.E. and continued, with a few breaks, until 800 C.E. During the Old Babylonian period, the southeastern portion of the city, known to modern scholars as Tablet Hill, served as a scribal quarter. Thousands of tablets were discovered there, including almost all the important Sumerian literary texts known to modern scholars. Archaeologists have also unearthed a large archive from the Kassite period and smaller archives from the Neo-Babylonian period. One of Nippur's best-known archives is a 730-tablet Persian-era collection belonging to the Muraŝû family, merchant bankers with vast commercial and agricultural interests during the Achaemenid period. The texts refer to Jews who owned houses and land, suggesting that a large concentration of Jews in the city were living in relative prosperity. These sources provide good evidence for the assimilation of Jews to Mesopotamian culture following the Babylonian exile. Texts discovered at Nippur are identified by scholars with the siglum "Ni."

Bibliography: ALANE 112–16, 198–201; L. B. BREGSTEIN and T. J. SCHNEIDER, "Nippur Bibliography," in *Nippur at the Centennial: Papers Read at the 35e Rencontre assyriologique internationale* (ed. M. deJ. Ellis; OPSNKF 14; Philadelphia: University Museum, 1992), 337–57 (bibliography of primary publications of Nippur texts); M. D. COOGAN, "Life in the Diaspora: Jews at Nippur in the Fifth Century B.C.," *BA* 37 (1974): 6–12; V. DONBAZ and M. W. STOLPER, *Istanbul Muraš û Texts* (Istanbul: Nederlands Historisch-Archaeologisch Instituut te Istanbul, 1997); J. A. FRANKE, "Nippur," *ABD* 4:1119–1122; S. N. KRAMER, *Sumerische literarische Texte aus Nippur* (2 vols; Berlin, Akademie-Verlag, 1961–67); M. W. STOLPER, *Entrepreneurs and Empire: The Muraŝû Archive, the Muraŝû Firm, and Persian Rule in Babylonia* (Leiden: Nederlands Historisch-Archaeologisch Instituut te Istanbul,

1985); IDEM, "Fifth Century Nippur: Texts of the Murašûs and from Their Surroundings," *JCS* 53 (2001): 83–132; IDEM, "Murashu, Archive of," *ABD* 4:927–28; R. ZADOK, *The Jews in Babylonia in the Chaldean and Achaemenian Periods in the Light of the Babylonian Sources* (Haifa: University of Haifa Press, 1979); R. L. ZETTLER, "Nippur," *OEANE* 4:148–52.

Nuzi. About 3,500 fifteenth-and fourteenth-century archival texts have been unearthed at this site in northeastern Iraq, in antiquity a provincial administrative center in the land of Arraphe. Among the finds are a number of family archives, composed of letters, loans, deeds, adoptions, contracts, and other legal and economic documentation. Social customs reflected in the family archives were initially interpreted as parallels to the patriarchal narratives and were cited as evidence for the antiquity and historicity of the patriarchal traditions. The studies of Thompson and Van Seters, however, eventually demonstrated that the parallels were often imaginary and that the patriarchal customs fit just as easily—perhaps better—in the first-millennium context. Although the Nuzi texts were written in Akkadian, their dialect reflects Hurrian influences and identifies the city as a Hurrian-speaking site. Many of the pertinent texts and studies are published in the series Civilization and Culture of Nuzi and the Hurrians and in the series Studies on the Civilization and Culture of Nuzi and the Hurrians. Other important sources are cited in the bibliography.

Texts and translations: See below Harvard Semitic Museum, *Excavations at Nuzi: Conducted by the Semitic Museum and the Fogg Art Museum of Harvard University, with the Cooperation of the American School of Oriental Research at Bagdad* (HSS 5, 9, 10, 13–16, 19; Cambridge: Harvard University Press, 1929–1962); *Joint Expedition [of the American School of Oriental Research in Bagdad] with the Iraq Museum at Nuzi* (6 vols.; Paris: P. Guenther, 1927–1931 [vols. 1–3]; Philadelphia: For the American Schools of Oriental Research by the University of Pennsylvania Press, 1934 [vols. 4–5]; New Haven: American School of Oriental Research, 1939 [vol. 6]). *Bibliography:* ALANE 15–28; M. DIETRICH, O. LORETZ, and W. MAYER, *Nuzi-Bibliographie* (AOAT Sonderreihe 11; Kevelaer, Germany: Butzon & Bercker, 1972); B. L. EICHLER, "Another Look at the Nuzi Sistership Contracts," in *Essays on the Ancient Near East in Memory of J. J. Finkelstein* (ed. M. deJ. Ellis; Hamden, Conn.: Archon Books, 1977), 45–59; IDEM, "Nuzi and the Bible: A Retrospective," in *DUMUE2–DUB-BA-A: Studies in Honor of Åke W. Sjoberg* (ed. H. Behrens, D. T. Loding, and M. Roth; OPSNKF 11; Philadelphia: University Museum, 1989), 117–19; J. FINCKE, *Die Orts-und Gewässernamen der Nuzi-Texte* (Répertoire Géographique des Textes Cunéiformes 10; Wiesbaden: Harrassowitz, 1993); C. H. GORDON, "Biblical Customs and the Nuzu Tablets," *BA* 3 (1940) 1–12; S. GREENGUS, "Sisterhood Adoption at Nuzi and the 'Wife-Sister' in Genesis," *HUCA* 46 (1975): 5–31; K. GROSZ, *The Archive of the Wullu Family* (CNI Publications 5; Copenhagen: Carsten Niebuhr Institute of Ancient Near Eastern Studies, University of Copenhagen, Museum Tusculanum Press, 1988); B. LION, "La fin de site de Nuzi et la distribution chronologique des archives," *RA* 89 (1995): 77–88; B. LION and D. STEIN, *The Pula-ğali Family Archives* (SCCNH 11; Bethesda, Md.: CDL Press, 2001); M. A. MORRISON, "Nuzi," *ABD* 4:1156–62; C. F. MYER JR., "Sample Interpretation from Extra-biblical Sources: The Nuzi Material and the Patriarchal Narratives," in *Biblical Interpretation* (ed. F. F. Kearley et al.; Grand Rapids: Baker, 1986), 168–80; P. NEGRI-SCAFA, "Scribes locaux et scribes itinerants dans le royaume d'Arrapḫa," in *La circulation des biens, des personnes, et des idées dans le Proche-Orient ancien: Actes de la XXXVIIIe Rencontre assyriologique internationale* (ed. D. Charpin and F. Joannès; Paris: Éditions Recherche sur les Civilisations, 1992), 235–40; D. I. OWEN and G. WILHELM, eds., *Nuzi at Seventy-Five* (SCCNH 10; Bethesda, Md.: CDL Press, 1999); D. L. STEIN, "Nuzi," *OEANE* 4:171–75; IDEM, *Das Archiv des Šilwa-Teššup* (2 vols.; Wiesbaden: Harrassowitz, 1993); A. TAGGAR-COHEN, "Law and Family in the Book of Numbers: The Levites and the Tidennutu Documents from Nuzi," *VT* 48 (1998): 74–94; T. L. THOMPSON, *Historicity of the Patriarchal Narratives: The Quest for the Historical Abraham* (BZAW 133; Berlin: de Gruyter, 1974); K. VAN DER TOORN, "Gods and Ancestors in Emar and Nuzi," *ZA* 84 (1994): 38–59; J. VAN SETERS, *Abraham in History and Tradition* (New Haven: Yale University Press, 1975).

Puzrish-Dagan (Drehem). A huge administrative archive dating to the Ur III period (2100–2000 B.C.E.) was discovered at this site in the floodplain between the Euphrates and Tigris Rivers. Its thirty thousand texts are indispensable primary sources for the study of the socioeconomic, political, and religious history of the Ur III period.

Texts and translations: M. HILGERT, *Drehem Administrative Documents from the Reign of Šulgi* (OIP 115; CTUPOI 1; Chicago: Oriental Institute of the University of Chicago, 1998); IDEM, *Drehem Administrative Documents from the Reign of Amar-Suena* (OIP 121; CTUPOI 2; Chicago: Oriental Institute of the University of Chicago, 2003); S. T. KANG, *Sumerian Economic Texts from the Drehem Archive* (Sumerian and Akkadian Cuneiform Texts in the Collection of the World Heritage Museum of the University of Illinois 1; Urbana: University of Illinois Press, 1972); M. SIGRIST, *The Administration at Drehem: Neo-Sumerian Texts from the Royal Ontario Museum* (Bethesda, Md.: CDL Press, 1995); F. YIL-DIZ, *Die Puzriš-Dagan-Texte der Istanbuler archäologischer Museen* (Stuttgart: Steiner, 1988). ***Bibliography:*** M. SIGRIST, *Drehem* (Bethesda, Md.: CDL Press, 1992).

Rimah (Tell al-Rimah). This site in northern Iraq lies between the Tigris and Habur Rivers. Occupation of the site goes back to prehistoric times, but our cache of textual materials dates to the Old Babylonian period. More than 300 texts were unearthed at al-Rimah, mostly letters and economic texts, but also a few seal inscriptions. Identification of the site with an ancient city is not yet certain, but it appears to be either Karana or Qaṭṭara.

Text and translation: S. DALLEY, C. B. F. WALKER, and J. D. HAWKINS, *The Old Babylonian Tablets from Tell al Rimah* (London: British School of Archaeology in Iraq, 1976). ***Bibliography:*** S. DALLEY, "Rimah, Tell er-," *OEANE* 4:428–30.

Sippar (Abu Habbah). Located on the Euphrates River between modern Baghdad and ancient Babylon, Sippar's long history ran from the fourth millennium B.C.E. until the Parthian period (ca. 100 C.E.). The city was religiously significant for the Mesopotamians because it was the home of the god Šamaš, who was housed at his temple, Ebabbar. Some evidence of the temple archives and libraries from the Old Babylonian period were unearthed at Sippar (see Weitemeyer 1955), but the most impressive finds were from the Neo-Babylonian era. These included more than thirty thousand tablets from the archive in the temple of Šamaš and eight hundred texts in a library associated with the temple of Šamaš's consort, Aya. The library was discovered intact, still stacked in the niches of the library wall. Most of the library texts are yet to be published, but it is reported that many of the classical Akkadian and bilingual Sumerian-Akkadian works are represented in the corpus. Textual realia from Sippar are designated using the prefix "Si."

Text catalogues: British Museum, Department of Western Asiatic Antiquities, *Catalogue of the Babylonian Tablets in the British Museum* (London: Trustees of the British Museum, 1961–), vols. 6–8. *Bibliography: ALANE* 193–97; W. AL-JADIR and Z. R. ABDULLAH, "Preliminary Reports on the Baghdad University Excavations at Sippar (Abu Habba), 1978–1983," *Sumer* 39 (1983): 97–122; A. C. V. M. BONGENAAR, *The Neo-Babylonian Ebabbar Temple at Sippar: Its Administration and Its Prosopography* (Istanbul: Nederlands Historisch-Archeologisch Instituut te Istanbul, 1997); G. COLBOW, "Samsu'iluna-zeitliche Abrollungen aus nordbabylonischen Archiven ausserhalb Sippars," *RA* 89 (1995): 149–89; H. GASCHE and C. JANSSEN, "Sippar," *OEANE* 5:47–49; R. HARRIS, *Ancient Sippar: A Demographic Study of an Old-Babylonian City (1894–1595 B.C.)* (Leiden: Nederlands Historisch-Archaeologisch Instituut te Istanbul, 1975); M. JURSA, *Die Landwirtschaft in Sippar in neubabylonischer Zeit* (AfOB 25; Vienna: Eingentümer & Verleger, Institut für Orientalistik der Universität Wien, 1995); J. MACGINNIS, *Letter Orders from Sippar and the Administration of the Ebabbara in the Late-Babylonian Period* (Poznan: Bonami, 1995).

Šuruppak (Tell Fara). This site is located about halfway between modern Baghdad and the Persian Gulf on a former riverbed of the Euphrates. About eight hundred Sumerian texts were unearthed there, mainly school texts and economic documents. The exemplars date to the third millennium B.C.E.

Texts and translations: A. DEIMEL, *Die Inschriften von Fara* (3 vols.; Leipzig: Hinrichs, 1922–1925); S. N. KRAMER, "New Tablets from Fara," *JAOS* 52 (1932): 110–32. *Bibliography:* M. KREBERNIK, "Die Texte aus Fāra und Abū Ṣābaliḫ," in *Mesopotamien: Spāturuk-Zeit und Frühdynastische Zeit* (ed. J. Bauer, R. K. Englund, and M. Krebernik; OBO 160/1; Freiburg, Switz.: Universitätsverlag, 1998), 237–427; H. P. MARTIN, "Fara," *OEANE* 2:301–3.

Ur (Tell el-Muqayyar). Archaeologists have determined that Ur was inhabited from as early as the fifth millennium to as late as the middle of the first millennium B.C.E.; the city reached its zenith between 2100 and 2000 B.C.E., when it served as the capital of the Ur III Empire in lower Mesopotamia. Private and public archives were discovered there, nested in levels associated with the Ur III period, the Middle Babylonian period, and the Neo-Babylonian era. Libraries dating to the Isin-Larsa and Neo-Babylonian periods were also found. The site is perhaps best known for its archaic cemetery, which contained two thousand graves and sixteen royal tombs, in which deceased Sumerian kings were apparently buried with an entourage of sacrificed people (i.e., human sacrifice). Texts from Ur are usually designated with the siglum "U," e.g., U 7745.

The biblical account of Abraham's purchase at Machpelah in Gen 23 is strikingly similar to Neo-Babylonian dialogue contracts unearthed at Ur and

Uruk, contracts that were used around 700–500 B.C.E. for transferring property and other possessions. The Babylonian contract pattern is reflected in Ephron's quoted offer (v. 15), in the third-person description of Abraham's acceptance (v. 16), in the payment clause (v. 16), and in the transfer clause, which includes a description of the property (v. 17–18).

Texts and translations: The series Ur Excavations and the series Ur Excavation Texts (19 vols.; Philadelphia: Published for the trustees of the two museums [the British Museum and the Museum of the University of Pennsylvania], 1927–1976). *Bibliography: ALANE* 116–18, 201–4; J. A. BRINKMAN, "Ur: 'The Kassite Period and the Period of Assyrian Kings,'" *Or* 38 (1969): 310–48; S. POLLOCK, "Ur," *OEANE* 5:288–91; G. ROUX, "The Great Enigma of the Cemetery at Ur," in J. BOTTÉRO, *Everyday Life in Ancient Mesopotamia* (Baltimore: Johns Hopkins University Press, 1992), 24–40; G. M. TUCKER, "The Legal Background to Genesis 23," *JBL* 85 (1966): 77–84.

Uruk (Warka). This site in southern Iraq is the source of our oldest cuneiform texts, which were composed in a primitive pictographic script during the late fourth and early third millennia (Uruk levels IV and III, c. 3300–2900 B.C.E.). About 85 percent of these early texts were economic, and the remaining exemplars were lexical lists containing the correct signs for various officials, commodities, and animals. Similar texts dating to about the same period were found at Jemdet Nasr. From the Neo-Babylonian and early Persian periods, Uruk has provided us with archives and libraries connected with Ištar's temples, containing more than ten thousand texts, including at least 250 standard literary texts. Early Hellenistic and Seleucid-era archives and libraries from the temple of Anu were also discovered, yielding some literary texts as well as bullae that once sealed Greek or Aramaic papyri. A small but significant find was the private library of a Babylonian exorcist, a few hundred texts from the early Greek period that included exorcistic rituals, incantations, medical texts, lexical lists, omens, astronomical and astrological texts, myths, and hymns. The biblical sources remember Uruk by the name of Erech (Gen 10:10; Ezra 4:9), reflecting a familiarity with the large city that Uruk became during the first millennium B.C.E.

Texts and translations: The series Ausgrabungen der Deutschen Forschungsgemeinschaft in Uruk-Warka (Leipzig: Harrassowitz, 1936–); *Ausgrabungen in Uruk-Warka, Endberichte* (Mainz am Rhein: P. von Zabern, 1987–). *Bibliography: ALANE* 204–13; R. M. BOEHMER, "Uruk-Warka," *OEANE* 5:294–98; WALKER, *Cuneiform,* 7–15.

1.3. Egypt

Because the Egyptians often wrote on perishable papyri, most of the texts once housed in their archives and libraries have vanished from history. We are fortunate that the Egyptians also inscribed texts on more durable materials, the most prominent examples being the many tomb, palace, and stela inscriptions they left for us. Remnants from libraries, archives, and schools have also been found, not only on ostraca, stone, and clay tablets but also in the occasional stashes of papyri that have survived because they were stored in protected areas that were not subject to moisture from the Nile and it inundations. Our primary sources of Egyptian texts have been the two major necropolis areas around Thebes and Memphis, where royal tombs and temples were built to service the needs of the deceased. The key site in the Theban area is Deir el-Medina, and the primary sites in the Memphis area are Abusir and Saqqara. Important text collections have also been found at Akhetaton (Amarna) and Elephantine, but the key finds at these two sites were not Egyptian texts but, rather, Akkadian and Aramaic texts, respectively. Good surveys of the Egyptian archives and texts are found in Quirke and Tait. Another volume, *Textes et langages de l'Egypte pharaonique* (see under title in general bibliography), not only provides an excellent overview of Egyptian literature but also valuable descriptions of the most important Egyptian museum collections at Berlin, Boston, Brooklyn, Brussels, Cairo, Leiden, London, Moscow, New York, Paris, St. Petersburg (Leningrad), Turin, Vienna, and several other museums in Italy.

Abusir. Named for a nearby modern Egyptian village, this site was part of the large Memphite necropolis in lower Egypt. It has yielded two small but important archives. The first stash of three hundred papyrus fragments was discovered in the funerary temple of Pharaoh Neferirkare (2446–2426 B.C.E.). Although it was discovered at the beginning of the twentieth century, the texts were not published until 1976 (see Posener-Kriéger). A Czechoslovak team, which made further valuable finds at Abusir, discovered papyrus fragments of varied length in the unfinished pyramid of King Raneferef (2419–2416 B.C.E.). Both archives preserve texts dealing with the administration of the respective mortuary temples and their cults.

Text and translation: P. POSENER-KRIÉGER, *Les archives du temple funéraire de Néferirkarê-Kakaï (les papyrus d'Abousir): Traduction et commentaire* (BdE 65; Cairo: Institut Français d'Archéologie Orientale du Caire, 1976). *Bibliography:* M. BARTA and J. KREJCI, *Abusir and Saqqara in the Year 2000* (Prague: Academy of Sciences of the Czech Republic, Oriental Institute, 2000); P. POSENER-KRIÉGER, *État d'avancement de la publications des archives d'Abu-Sir* (Göttingen: Vandenhoeck & Ruprecht, 1965); M. VERNER, *The Excavations of the Czechoslovak Institute of Egyptology at Abusir* (Prague: Charles University Press, 1977–).

Akhetaton (El-Amarna). Tell el-Amarna is located on the Nile about 185 miles south of Cairo. There we find the ruins of an ancient city founded by Amenophis IV (Akhenaten), a pharaoh best know for his "heretical" doctrine that Egyptians should worship only Aton, the sun disk. An archive of 380 tablets was discovered at the site, most of them Akkadian letters addressed to Amenophis III (1391–1353) or to his son Akhenaten (1353–1335). Some of the letters were from powerful kings in the region—from Babylon, Assyria, Hatti, and Mitanni—but the vast majority of the texts were from Egypt's vassals in Canaan and in the wider Levant. Because the Canaanite dialects of the writers influenced the Akkadian in these texts, the Amarna letters are an important source for reconstructing the history of Canaanite languages. At the same time, the texts also provide a valuable window into the fourteenth-century world of Syria-Palestine, just a few centuries before Israel would emerge in the region. The texts mention the city of Jerusalem, and some scholars have taken a particular interest in the *ḫapiru*, a class of social outlaws who were wreaking havoc in Syro-Palestine at the time. It is supposed that there may be some connection between these *ḫapiru* and the biblical Hebrews. In addition to the letters, a small corpus of Akkadian literary texts was also discovered at the site (see Izre'el). Amarna sources are identified with the siglum "EA" followed by the text number, but one must be careful to distinguish another common use of this code, in which "EA" refers to "Egyptian Antiquities" in the British Museum.

Texts and translations: S. IZRE'EL, *The Amarna Scholarly Tablets* (CM 9; Groningen, Neth.: Styx, 1997); J. A. KNUDTZON, *Die El-Amarna-Tafeln* (2 vols.; Vorderasiatische Bibliotek 1–2; Leipzig: Hinrichs, 1907–1915); A. F. RAINEY, *El Amarna tablets 359–379* (2d ed. rev.; AOAT 8; Kevelaer, Germany: Butzon & Bercker, 1978). *Translations:* ANET 483–90; COS 3.92: 237–42; W. L. MORAN, *The Amarna Letters* (Baltimore: Johns Hopkins University Press, 1992). *Bibliography:* E. F. CAMPBELL, *The Chronology of the Amarna Letters* (Baltimore: Johns Hopkins Press, 1964); R. COHEN and R. WESTBROOK, "Introduction: The Amarna System," in *Amarna Diplomacy* (ed. R. Cohen and R. Westbrook; Baltimore: Johns Hopkins University Press, 2000), 1–12; Y. GOREN, I. FINKELSTEIN, and N. NA'AMAN, eds., *Inscribed in Clay: Provenance Study of the Amarna Tablets and Other Ancient Near Eastern Texts* (Emery and Claire Yass Publications in Archaeology; Monograph Series of the Institute of Archaeology 23; Tel Aviv: Tel Aviv University Press, 2004); R. S. HESS, *Amarna Personal Names* (Dissertation Series, American Schools of Oriental Research 9; Winona Lake, Ind.: Eisenbrauns, 1993); M. LIVERANI, "A Seasonal Pattern for the Amarna Letters," in *Lingering over Words: Studies in Ancient Near Eastern Literature in Honor of William L. Moran* (ed. Tz. Abusch, J. Huehnergard, and P. Steinkeller; Atlanta: Scholars Press, 1990), 337–48; W. L. MORAN, *Amarna Studies: Collected Writings* (ed. J. Huehnergard and S. Izre'el; Winona Lake, Ind.: Eisenbrauns, 2003); IDEM, "The Syrian Scribe of the Jerusalem Amarna Letters," in *Unity and Diversity: Essays in the History, Literature, and Religion of the Ancient Near East* (ed. H. Goedicke and J. J. M. Roberts; Baltimore: Johns Hopkins University Press, 1975), 146–66; D. B. REDFORD, *Egypt, Canaan, and Israel in Ancient Times* (Princeton: Princeton University Press, 1992), 192–213.

Deir el-Medina. This site was home to a community of supervisors, foremen, and workmen (and their families), whose task was to build the great tombs of the Egyptian pharaohs in a necropolis near Thebes in Upper Egypt. More than ten thousand texts have already been found at the site, and scholars are certain that many more remain. The texts generally date to the New Kingdom, but later texts were found as well. Some exemplars are on papyrus, but most were inscribed on ostraca or on flakes of limestone. Many of the texts are of the archival sort, inscribed with letters, notes, records, and other kinds of evidence that inform us about life in the community and about administrative aspects of pyramid construction. Scribes and scribal students at Deir el-Medina also left behind a corpus of literary texts, including numerous wisdom texts, tales, and myths. The most frequently copied work appears to have been the Satire on the Trades (see 2.2.1), a text that was commonly used in the Egyptian scribal curriculum. Portions of a private library belonging to a fellow named Qenherkhepshef have also been found; these yielded numerous important papyri, including myths, tales, love songs, a book for interpreting dreams, hymns, several incantation texts, wisdom texts, an offering ritual for Amenhotep I, and even a list of aphrodisiacs. Most of these papyri come from one of nineteen Chester Beatty papyri found at Deir el-Medina (see Gardiner 1935; Koenig; Pestman). A Late Ramesside letter from Elephantine refers to such a collection of papyri purportedly stored in a tomb at Deir el-Medina. It is possible that the letter refers precisely to these Chester Beatty papyri.

Readers should also note the Ramesseum papyri, discovered in the nearby mortuary temple of Rameses II (see Helck; Gardiner 1955). This important collection of papyri was resting in a wooden box in a Middle Kingdom tomb shaft over which the Ramesseum was built. The collection includes magical, medical, and literary texts that date to the time of Amenophis III (1391–1353 B.C.E.).

Texts, translations, and catalogues: J. CERNÝ, *Ostraca hiératiques* (2 vols.; Catalogue général des antiquités égyptiennes du Musée du Caire, nos. 25501–25832; Cairo: Institut Français d'Archéologie Orientale, 1930–1935); J. CERNÝ and A. H. GARDINER, *Hieratic Ostraca* (Oxford: Oxford University Press, 1957–); J. CERNÝ, G. POSENER, and Y. KOENIG, *Papyrus hiératiques de Deir el-Médineh* (2 vols.; DFIFAO 8, 22; Cairo: Institut Français d'Archéologie Orientale, 1978–1986); J. CERNÝ, S. SAUNERON, and P. GRANDET, *Catalogue des ostraca hiératiques non littéraires de Deîr el-Médînêh* (DFIFAO 3–7, 13, 14, 39, 41; Cairo: Institut Français d'Archéologie Orientale, 1935–); A. H. GARDINER, *Hieratic Papyri in the British Museum, Third Series: Chester Beatty Gift* (2 vols.; London: British Museum, 1935); IDEM, *The Ramesseum Papyri* (Oxford: Oxford University Press, 1955); G. POSENER and A. GASSE, *Catalogue des ostraca hiératiques littéraires de Deir el Médineh* (DFIFAO 1, 18, 20, 25; Cairo: Institut Français d'Archéologie Orientale, 1938–). *Translation:* WENTE, *Letters from Ancient Egypt*, 132–70 (letters only). *Bibliography:* J. CERNÝ, *A Community of Workmen at Thebes in the Ramesside Period* (Cairo: Institut Français d'Archéologie Orientale, 1973); R. J. DEMARÉE and A. EGBERTS, eds., *Deir el-Medina in the Third Millennium AD: A Tribute to Jac. J. Janssen* (Leiden: Nederlands Instituut voor het Nabije Oosten, 2000); R. J. DEMARÉE and JAC. J. JANSSEN, *Gleanings from Deir El-Medîna* (Leiden: Nederlands Instituut voor het Nabije Oosten, 1982); M. GUTGESELL, *Die Datierung der Ostraka und Papyri aus Deir el-Medineh und ihre ökonomische Interpretation* (2 vols.; Hildesheim: Gerstenberg, 1983–2002); W. HELCK, "Papyri Ramesseum I," *LÄ* 4:726–27; Y. KOENIG, "Notes sur la découverte des Papyrus Chester Beatty," *BIFAO* 81 (1982): 41–43; P. W. PESTMAN, "Who Were the Owners, in the 'Community of Workmen,' of the Chester Beatty Papyri," in *Deir el-Medina in the Third Millennium AD: A Tribute to Jac. J. Janssen* (ed. R. J. Demarée and A. Egberts; Leiden: Nederlands Instituut voor het Nabije Oosten, 2000), 155–72; R. VENTURA, *Living in a City of the Dead: A Selection of Topographical and Administrative Terms in the Documents of the Theban Necropolis* (OBO 69; Freiburg, Switz.: Universitätsverlag, 1986); S. WIMMER, *Hieratische Paläographie der nicht-literarischen Ostraka der 19. und 20. Dynastie* (2 vols.; AAT 28; Wiesbaden: Harrassowitz, 1995).

The Elephantine Archive and Related Texts. This ancient town was located on an island in the Nile River opposite modern Aswan, in the extreme south of Egypt near the first cataract of the Nile. Elephantine was the town's Greek name. Textual finds at the site included Egyptian, Aramaic, and Greek papyri. Thousands of Late period Egyptian papyrus fragments were discovered at Elephantine (see Quirke), but it is the Aramaic material that is of direct interest for biblical scholarship and Jewish history. Several Aramaic Jewish archives were found at Elephantine, belonging to members of a Jewish military colony stationed there by the Persians (although the colony itself may date back to the Assyrian period). One of the archives was communal and the other two belonged to individual families. The small family archives spanned two to three generations and included legal documents as well as business and family contracts. The communal archive was associated with Jedaniah, who was a priest—probably high priest—of the Elephantine Jewish community. In addition to contracts, legal documents, and administrative texts, this communal archive included a corpus of very interesting letters bearing dates between 419 and 407 B.C.E. (see Lindenberger, 61–79). One of these came from Hananyah, a Jewish Persian administrator who may have been the brother of Nehemiah (cf. Neh 1:2; 7:2). His letter, written in the authority of King Darius, instructed the Jewish community at Elephantine to follow Passover regulations approved by the Jerusalem temple. Some of these regulations were found in the Hebrew scriptures, but others appear to reflect oral law. Also in the archive was a series of letters that trace the deteriorating relationship between Jews and local Egyptian priests of the god Khnum, who had a temple nearby. This conflict came to a head when Arshama, the Persian satrap of Egypt, took an extended leave in the East. In his absence, the Egyptians bribed the sitting Persian governor and destroyed the Jewish temple at Elephantine. Three further letters record the community's request to rebuild the temple, as well as the Persian response from Arshama: the temple could be rebuilt, but only meal and incense offerings could be made there. This policy was in keeping with traditional Jewish law, which forbade flesh offerings at all sites but the Jerusalem temple. Consequently, this stipulation reveals the profound influence that the Jerusalem temple exerted on Persia's Jewish policies in Egypt and perhaps elsewhere. Also included in Jedaniah's community archive was a copy of one literary text, The Story and Proverbs of Ahiqar (see 2.3), and a papyrus copy of Darius I's Bisitun inscription (see Greenfield and Porten and 12.4). Several older letters written on ostraca were also discovered at Elephantine, dating to ca. 475 B.C.E. (Lindenberger, 41–59). One of the letters refers to Sabbath observance in Egypt, another mentions the obscure *marzeaḥ* institution (see Amos 6:7; Jer 16:5), and in another a friend requests, "Let me know when you will be celebrating the Passover." This may suggest that the Passover date was not yet fixed in Jewish tradition, but it is perhaps more likely that religious observance at Elephantine was idiosyncratic.

Three collections of Aramaic documents are closely related to the Jewish texts from Elephantine. The first is a parcel of twelve letters belonging to Arshama, the Persian satrap of Egypt mentioned in the previous paragraph (Lindenberger, 81–106). Most of these letters have to do with Arshama's business dealings in his far-flung network of private estates, scattered about the empire from Egypt to Mesopotamia. Arshama's letters were acquired on the antiquities market, so, apart from their fifth-century date, little is known of their provenance.

The second relevant Aramaic collection is a stash of sixth-century private letters discovered at Hermopolis, a site about midway between the Nile Delta and Elephantine (Lindenberger, 25–36). These letters concerning family commercial activities were destined for recipients in the Elephantine area; the fact that they were found at Hermopolis, still tied together and sealed, suggests that the courier never delivered this mail. A third set of letters, in the Civic Museum of Padua, Italy, address the business concerns of Jewish families living in Elephantine (Lindenberger, 36–38). Although the provenance of these fifth-century texts is unknown, Elephantine would obviously be the most likely location.

Texts and translations: J. C. GREENFIELD and B. PORTEN, *The Bisitun Inscription of Darius the Great: Aramaic Version* (Corpus inscriptionum iranicarum, Part I: Inscriptions of Ancient Iran; London: Lund Humphries, 1982); J. M. LINDENBERGER, *Ancient Aramaic and Hebrew Letters* (2d ed.; SBLWAW 14; Atlanta: Scholars Press, 2003), 25–106 (partial); E. LÜDDECKENS, *Ägyptische Handschriften* (4 vols.; Verzeichnis der orientalischen Handschriften in Deutschland 19; Wiesbaden: Steiner, 1971–1994), vol. 2 (demotic Egyptian papyri); B. PORTEN and A. YARDENI, *Textbook of Aramaic Documents from Ancient Egypt* (4 vols.; Winona Lake, Ind.: Eisenbrauns, 1986–1999) (Aramaic papyri); O. RUBENSOHN, *Elephantine-Papyri* (Berlin: Weidmann, 1907) (Greek papyri). *Translations:* ANET 491–92; COS 3.46–54: 116–34, 3.59–81: 141–98; 3.87: 207–17. *Bibliography:* ALANE 204–13; F. M. FALES, "Aramaic Letters and Neo-Assyrian Letters: Philological and Methodological Notes," *JAOS* 107 (1987): 451–69; J. A. FITZMYER, "Some Notes on Aramaic Epistolography," *JBL* 93 (1974): 201–25; W. KAISER, "Elephantine," *OEANE* 2:234–36; B. PORTEN, *Archives from Elephantine: The Life of an Ancient Jewish Military Colony* (Berkeley: University of California Press, 1968); IDEM, "The Elephantine Papyri," *ABD* 2:445–55.

Saqqara. This site on the southern end of the Nile Delta, just west of Memphis, was the largest and most important necropolis in ancient Egypt. Numerous school texts dating to the Nineteenth and Twentieth Dynasties were either discovered there or probably came from there, including model letters, hymns, codes of behavior, and other genres. These exemplars constitute a majority of the school texts that Egyptologists call the Late Egyptian Miscellanies (see Gardiner; Caminos). There is a body of important literary manuscripts linked by the contents and by names of the copyists to each other and to the Saqqara necropolis. It is not known whether these manuscripts came from a single burial or from some other context, but the texts date to about 1200 C.E. Exemplars in the collection include a copy of the Satirical Instruction Letter (P.Anastasi 1), didactic excerpts and hymns (P.Anastasi 3–6), a copy of the hymn to the Nile inundation (P.Anastasi 7), two formal letters (P.Anastasi 8–9), our only copy of the Tale of Two Brothers (P.D'Orbiney) together with the Instructions of Amenemhet and the Tale of the Quarrel of Seqenenra Taa and Apepi (P.Sallier 1), the Instructions of Amenemhet, the Instructions of Khety, and the hymn to the Nile inundation (P.Sallier 2), a copy of the Battle of Qadesh (P.Sallier 3), and a copy of the so-called Calendar of Lucky and Unlucky Days, with additional school miscellanies on the reverse (P.Sallier 4). Many demotic papyri from much later periods were also found at Saqqara (see Depauw).

Texts and translations: R. A. CAMINOS, *Late-Egyptian Miscellanies* (London: Oxford University Press, 1954); A. H. GARDINER, *Late-Egyptian Miscellanies* (BAeg 1; Brussels: Fondation Égyptologique Reine Élisabeth, 1937). *Translations: ANET* 258–59; *COS* 3.2–5: 9–17; WENTE, *Letters from Ancient Egypt. Bibliography:* M. DEPAUW, *A Companion to Demotic Studies* (Papyrologica bruxellensia 28; Brussels: Fondation Égyptologique Reine Élisabeth, 1997), 85–121; Z. HAWASS, "Saqqara," *OEANE* 4:478–81.

1.4. Anatolia

Ḫattuša (Boğazköy) and Other Hittite Sites. Located about ninety miles east of Ankara in northeastern Turkey, Ḫattuša was the capital of the Hittite Empire during most of the second millennium (ca. 1750–1200 B.C.E.). Archives and libraries at the site have yielded more than thirty thousand texts, the vast majority written in Hittite. Other languages represented in the corpus include Akkadian, Sumerian, Luwian, Palaic, Hattic, and Hurrian. All of the major Near Eastern generic categories are represented in the finds, including historical texts, administrative texts, laws, myths, prayers, rituals, festivals, omens, and lexical texts. Two other sites have yielded significant numbers of Hittite texts. Preliminary reports confirm that about three thousand tablets and fragments have been discovered at Šapinuwa (Ortaköy), a city located about thirty-five miles northeast of Ḫattuša (see Süel). These texts have not yet been published. Several hundred tablets were also discovered at Tapigga (Masat Höyük), about 70 miles east of Ḫattuša (see *ALANE*). The Tapigga texts include mainly archival records and letters. Hittite texts have been published in a number of different texts and series, including especially Texte der Hethiter; Keilschrifttexte aus Boghazköi; Studien zu der Boğazköy-Texten; and Keilschrifturkunden aus Boghazköi. Research in the Hittite corpus has profited especially from Laroche's exhaustive catalogue of the Hittite texts, which is now being updated in a Web-based edition (see the "Hittite Home Page," http://www.asor.org/HITTITE/HittiteHP.html).

Text and translation: E. LAROCHE, *Catalogue des textes hittites* (Paris: Éditions Klinckcksieck, 1971; updated on-line ed., "Catalog of Hittite Texts (CTH)," http://www.asor.org/HITTITE/CTHHP.html). *Translations COS* 3.13–40: 43–72. *Bibliography: ALANE* 44–57; *Ancient Libraries in Anatolia: The 24th Annual Conference Libraries and Education in the Networked Information Environment (June 2–5 2003, Ankara)* (Ankara: METU, 2003); G. BECKMAN, "Mesopotamian and Mesopotamian Learning at Hattusha," *JCS* 35 (1983): 91–114; H. G. GÜTERBOCK, "Boğazköy," *OEANE* 1:333–35; A. SÜEL, "Ortaköy: Eine hethitische Stadt mit hethitischen und hurritischen Tontafelentdeckungen," in *Hittite and Other Anatolian and Near Eastern Studies in Honour of Sedat Alp* (ed. H. Otten et al.; Ankara: Türk tarih Kurumu Basımevi, 1992), 487–92.

Kaneš (Kültepe). More than fifteen thousand Akkadian tablets and tablet fragments have been discovered at this site in modern Turkey, in ancient Cappadocia. Although a few texts were found in the city's citadel, the vast majority of the tablets were recovered from the city's commercial quarter (*kārum*). Between 2000 and 1800 B.C.E., an Old Assyrian trading colony dominated the *kārum* of Kaneš, and it is to these Assyrian merchants that we owe the archives. Nearly all of the recovered documents related to economic trade, but several literary texts were also discovered.

Texts and translations: E. BILGIÇ, ed., *Ankara Kültepe Tabletleri* (Türk Tarih Kurumu Yayinlari 6/33; Ankara: Türk Tarih Kurumu Basımevi, 1990–); K. R. VEENHOF and E. KLENGEL-BRANDT, *Altassyrische Tontafeln aus Kültepe: Texte und Siegelabrollungen* (Berlin: G. Mann, 1992). *Bibliography:* M. T. LARSEN, *Old Assyrian Caravan Procedures* (UNHAII 22; Istanbul: Nederlands Historisch-Archaeologisch Instituut in het Nabije Oosten, 1967); IDEM, *The Old Assyrian City-State and Its Colonies* (Mesopotamia 4; Copenhagen: Akademisk Forlag, 1976); T. ÖZGÜÇ, "Kaneš," *OEANE* 3:266–68; IDEM, *Kültepe-Kaniş: New Researches at the Center of the Assyrian Trade Colonies* (Ankara: Türk Tarih Kurumu Basımevi, 1959); IDEM, *Kültepe-Kaniş II: New Researches at the Trading Center of the Ancient Near East* (Ankara: Türk Tarih Kurumu Basımevi, 1983); K. R. VEENHOF, "Kanesh: An Assyrian Colony in Anatolia," *CANE* 2:859–71; IDEM, "Kültepe Texts," *OEANE* 3:308–10.

1.5. Persia

Persepolis. Thousands of Elamite tablets dating to the late sixth and early fifth centuries B.C.E. have been unearthed in an archive at this site, one of three Achaemenid-era Persian capitals (along with Susa and Ecbatana). These tablets are administrative records of food and commodity transfers. A smaller find in the area of the royal treasury yielded more than two hundred tablets and evidence that Aramaic texts on papyri, skins, and other perishable materials were once stored there.

Texts and translations: R. A. BOWMAN, *Aramaic Ritual Texts from Persepolis* (OIP 91; Chicago: University of Chicago Press, 1970); G. G. CAMERON, *Persepolis Treasury Texts* (OIP 65; Chicago: University of Chicago Press, 1948); R. T. HALLOCK, *Persepolis Fortification Texts* (OIP 92; Chicago: University of Chicago Press, 1969). *Bibliography: ALANE* 216–19; D. STRONACH and K. CODELLA, "Persepolis," *OEANE* 4:273–77.

General Bibliography

H. BEHLMER, "Ancient Egyptian Survivals in Coptic Literature: An Overview," in *Ancient Egyptian Literature: History and Forms* (ed. A. Loprieto; PA 10; New York: Brill, 1996), 567–90; J. A. BLACK and W. J. TAIT, "Archives and Libraries in the Ancient Near East," *CANE* 4:2197–2209; G. BURKARD, "Bibliotheken im alten Ägypten," *Bibliothek: Forschung und Praxis* 4 (1980): 79–115; C. CASTEL, "Contexte archéologique et statut des documents: Les Textes retrouvés dans les maisons mésopotamiennes du Ier millénaire av. J.-C.," *RA* 89 (1995): 109–37;

M. W. CHAVALAS and K. L. YOUNGER JR., eds. *Mesopotamia and the Bible: Comparative Explorations* (Grand Rapids: Baker, 2002); M. CIVIL, "From the Epistolary of the Edubba," in *Wisdom, Gods, and Literature: Studies in Assyriology in Honour of W. G. Lambert* (ed. A. R. George and I. L. Finkel; Winona Lake, Ind.: Eisenbrauns, 2000), 105–18; IDEM, "Lexicography," in *Sumerological Studies in Honor of Thorkild Jacobsen on His Seventieth Birthday* (AS 20; Chicago: University of Chicago Press, 1975), 123–57; J. L. CRENSHAW, *Education in Ancient Israel: Across the Deadening Silence* (New York: Doubleday, 1998); G. I. DAVIES, "Were There Schools in Ancient Israel?" in *Wisdom in Ancient Israel: Essays in Honour of J. A. Emerton* (ed. J. Day, R. P. Gordon, and H. G. M. Williamson; Cambridge: Cambridge University Press, 1995), 199–211; P. R. DAVIES, *Scribes and Schools: The Canonization of the Hebrew Scriptures* (Louisville: Westminster John Knox, 1998), 74–88; I. M. DIAKONOFF, "Ancient Writing and Ancient Written Language: Pitfalls and Peculiarities in the Study of Sumerian," in *Sumerological Studies in Honor of Thorkild Jacobsen on His Seventieth Birthday* (AS 20; Chicago: University of Chicago Press, 1975), 99–121; D. O. EDZARD, "The Sumerian Language," *CANE* 4:2107–16; R. S. ELLIS, *A Bibliography of Mesopotamian Archaeological Sites* (Wiesbaden: Harrassowitz, 1972); X. FAIVRE, "Le recyclage des tablettes cuneiforms," *RA* 89 (1995): 57–66; W. FARBER, "'Forerunners' and 'Standard Versions': A Few Thoughts about Terminology," in *The Tablet and the Scroll: Near Eastern Studies in Honor of William W. Hallo* (ed. M. E. Cohen, D. C. Snell, and D. B. Weisberg; Bethesda, Md.: CDL Press, 1993), 95–97; A. H. GARDINER, "The House of Life," *JEA* 24 (1938): 157–79; G. B. GRAGG, "Less-Understood Languages of Ancient Western Asia," *CANE* 4:2161–79; H. G. GÜTERBOCK, "Resurrecting the Hittites," *CANE* 4:2765–77; W. W. HALLO, "Bilingualism and the Beginnings of Translation," in *Texts, Temples, and Traditions: A Tribute to Menahem Haran* (ed. M. V. Fox et al.; Winona Lake, Ind.: Eisenbrauns, 1996), 345–57; M. HARAN, "On the Diffusion of Literacy and Schools in Ancient Israel," in *Congress Volume: Jerusalem, 1986* (VTSup 40; New York: Brill, 1988), 81–95; W. V. HARRIS, *Ancient Literacy* (Cambridge: Harvard University Press, 1989); J. HUEHNERGARD, "Semitic Languages," *CANE* 4:2117–34; T. G. H. JAMES, *Introduction to Ancient Egypt* (New York: Harper & Row, 1979); D. W. JAMIESON-DRAKE, *Scribes and Schools in Monarchic Judah: A Socio-archaeological Approach* (JSOTSup 109; Sheffield, England: Almond, 1991); F. JOANNÈS, "L'extinction des archives cuneiforms dans la seconde partie de l'époque perse," *RA* 89 (1995): 139–47; J. KALTNER and S. L. MCKENZIE, *Beyond Babel: A Handbook for Biblical Hebrew and Related Languages* (Atlanta: Scholars Press, 2002); S. KAUFMAN, *The Akkadian Influences on Aramaic* (Chicago: University of Chicago Press, 1974); P. J. KING, "Jerusalem," *ABD* 3:747–66; B. LAFONT, "La chute des rois d'Ur et la fin des archives dans les grands centres administratifs de leur empire," *RA* 89 (1995): 2–13; B. LANDSBERGER, "Scribal Concepts of Education," in *City Invincible: A Symposium on Urbanization and Cultural Development in the Ancient Near East* (ed. C. H. Kraeling and R. M. Adams; Chicago: University of Chicago Press, 1960), 94–123; S. Z. LEIMAN, *The Canonization of the Hebrew Scripture: The Talmudic and Midrashic Evidence* (2d ed.; New Haven: Connecticut Academy of Arts and Sciences, 1991); A. LEMAIRE,

Les écoles et la formation de la Bible dans l'ancien Israël (OBO 39; Göttingen: Vandenhoeck & Ruprecht, 1981); N. P. LEMCHE, *Prelude to Israel's Past: Background and Beginnings of Israelite History and Identity* (Peabody, Mass.: Hendrickson, 1998), 66–69; S. J. LIEBERMAN, "Canonical and Official Cuneiform Texts: Towards an Understanding of Assurbanipal's Personal Tablet Collection," in *Lingering over Words: Studies in Ancient Near Eastern Literature in Honor of William L. Moran* (ed. Tz. Abusch, J. Huehnergard, and P. Steinkeller; Atlanta: Scholars Press, 1990), 305–36; A. LOPRIENO, "Ancient Egyptian and Other Afroasiatic Languages," *CANE* 4:2135–50; L. R. MACK-FISHER, "A Survey and Reading Guide to the Didactic Literature of Ugarit," in *The Sage in Israel and the Ancient Near East* (ed. J. G. Gammie and L. G. Perdue; Winona Lake, Ind.: Eisenbrauns, 1990), 67–80; H. G. MELCHERT, "Indo-European Languages of Anatolia," *CANE* 4:2151–59; A. R. MILLARD, "The Practice of Writing in Ancient Israel," *BA* 35 (1972): 98–111; IDEM, "An Assessment of the Evidence for Writing in Ancient Israel," in *Biblical Archaeology Today: Proceedings of the International Congress on Biblical Archaeology, April 1984* (Jerusalem: Israel Exploration Society, 1985), 301–12; J. NAVEH, *Early History of the Alphabet: An Introduction to West Semitic Epigraphy and Paleography* (2d rev. ed.; Jerusalem: Magnes Press, 1987); H. J. NISSEN, P. DAMEROW, and R. K. ENGLUND, *Archaic Bookkeeping: Early Writing and Techniques of Economic Administration in the Ancient Near East* (Chicago: University of Chicago Press, 1993); J. P. J. OLIVIER, "Schools and Wisdom Literature," *JNSL* 4 (1975): 49–60; S. PARPOLA, "Assyrian Library Records," *JNES* 42 (1983): 1–30; IDEM, *Assyrian Prophecies* (SAA 9; Helsinki: Helsinki University Press, 1997); IDEM, *Letters from Assyrian and Babylonian Scholars* (SAA 10; Helsinki: Helsinki University Press, 1993), no. 8; IDEM, "The Man without a Scribe and the Question of Literacy in the Assyrian Empire," in *Ana šadî Labnāni lū allik: Beiträge zu altorientalischen und mittelassyrischen Kulteren, Festschrift für Wolfgang Röllig* (ed. B. Pongratz-Leisten et al.; AOAT 247; Neukirchen-Vluyn: Neukirchener Verlag, 1997), 315–24; L. E. PEARCE, "The Scribes and Scholars of Ancient Mesopotamia," *CANE* 4:2265–78; IDEM, "Statements of Purpose: Why the Scribes Wrote," in *The Tablet and Scroll: Near Eastern Studies in Honor of William W. Hallo* (ed. M. E. Cohen, D. C. Snel, and D. B. Weisberg; Bethesda, Md.: CDL Press, 1993), 185–93; O. PEDERSÉN, *Archives and Libraries in the Ancient Near East: 1500–300 B.C.* (Bethesda, Md.: CDL Press, 1998); IDEM, "Use of Writing among the Assyrians," in *Assyrien im Wandel der Zeiten: XXXIXe Rencontre assyriologique internationale* (ed. H. Waetzoldt and H. Hauptmann; Heidelberg: Heidelberger Orientverlag, 1997), 139–52; E. POSNER, *Archives in the Ancient World* (Cambridge: Harvard University Press, 1972); S. G. QUIRKE, "Archive," in *Ancient Egyptian Literature: History and Forms* (ed. A. Loprieno; PA 10; New York: Brill, 1996), 379–401; K. RADNER, "The Relations between Form and Content of Neo-Assyrian Texts," in *Nineveh, 612 BC: The Glory and Fall of the Assyrian Empire. Catalogue of the 10th Anniversary Exhibition of the Neo-Assyrian Text Corpus Project* (ed. R. Mattila; Helsinki: Helsinki University Press, 1995), 63–77; D. B. REDFORD, "Scribe and Speaker," in *Writings and Speech in Israelite and Ancient Near Eastern Prophecy* (ed. E. Ben Zvi and M. H. Floyd; Atlanta: SBL, 2000),

145–218; M. E. J. RICHARDSON, "The Less Inspired Scriptures," in *Ugarit and the Bible* (ed. G. J. Brooke, A. H. W. Curtis, and J. F. Healey; Münster: Ugarit, 1994), 276–291; F. ROCHBERG-HALTON, "Canonicity in Cuneiform Texts," *JCS* 36 (1984): 127–44; A. SACHS, "The Latest Datable Cuneiform Tablets," in *Kramer Anniversary Volume: Cuneiform Studies in Honor of Samuel Noah Kramer* (ed. B. L. Eichler; AOAT 25; Kevelaer, Germany: Butzon & Bercker, 1976), 379–98; A. SÁNZ-BADILLOS, *A History of the Hebrew Language* (Cambridge: Cambridge University Press, 1993); S. SAUNERON, *The Priests of Ancient Egypt* (Ithaca, N.Y.: Cornell University Press, 2000), 132–36; D. SCHMANDT-BESSERAT, "Record Keeping before Writing," *CANE* 4:2097–2106; E. SCHOTT, "Bücher und Bibliotheken im alten Ägypten," *GM* 25 (1977): 73–80; H. TADMOR, "The Aramaization of Assyria: Aspects of Western Impact," in *Mesopotamien und seine Nachbarn—politische und kulturelle Wechselbeziehungen im alten Vorderasien vom 4. bis 1. Jahrtausend v. Chr.: XXV. Rencontre assyriologique internationale* (ed. H.-J. Nissen and J. Renger; 2 vols.; BBVO 1; Berlin: Dietrich Reimer, 1982), 2:449–69; W. J. TAIT, "Demotic Literature: Forms and Genres," in *Ancient Egyptian Literature: History and Forms* (ed. A. Loprieno; PA 10; New York: Brill, 1996), 175–87; *Textes et langages de l'Egypte pharaonique, cent cinquante années de recherches, 1822–1972: Hommage à Jean-François Champollion* (Cairo: Institut Français d'Archéologie Orientale du Caire, 1972); R. THOMAS, *Oral Tradition and Written Record in Classical Athens* (Cambridge: Cambridge University Press, 1989); H. L. J. VANSTIPHOUT, "Memory and Literacy in Ancient Western Asia," *CANE* 4:2181–96; K. R. VEENHOF, ed., *Cuneiform Archives and Libraries: Papers Read at the 30e Rencontre assyriologique internationale* (UNHAII 57; [Istanbul]: Nederlands Historisch-Archaeologisch Instituut te Istanbul, 1986); IDEM, "Libraries and Archives," *OEANE* 3:351–57; H. TE VELDE, "Scribes and Literacy in Ancient Egypt," in *Scripta signa vocis (Hospers Festschrift)* (ed. H. L. J. Vanstiphout; Groningen, Neth.: Egbert Forsten, 1986), 253–64; G. VISICATO, *The Power and the Writing: The Early Scribes of Mesopotamia* (Bethesda, Md.: CDL Press, 2000); C. B. F. WALKER, *Cuneiform* (Berkeley: University of California Press, 1987); M. WEITEMEYER, "Archive and Library Technique in Ancient Mesopotamia," *Libri* 6 (1956): 217–38; IDEM, *Babylonske og assyriske arkiver og biblioteker* (Copenhagen: Branner og Korchs, 1955); E. F. WENTE, *Letters from Ancient Egypt* (SBLWAW 1; Atlanta: Scholars Press, 1990); IDEM, "The Scribes of Ancient Egypt," *CANE* 4:2211–21; V. WESSETZKY, "Die Bücherliste des Temples von Edfu und Imhotep," *GM* 83 (1984): 85–89; W. D. WHITT, "The Story of the Semitic Alphabet," *CANE* 4:2379–97; R. D. WOODARD, ed., *The Cambridge Encyclopedia of the World's Ancient Languages* (Cambridge: Cambridge University Press, 2004); M. YON, "Ugarit," *OEANE* 5:255–64; I. M. YOUNG, "Israelite Literacy: Interpreting the Evidence" *VT* 48 (1998): 239–53, 408–22; R. ZADOK, "The Ethnolinguistic Composition of Assyria Proper in the 9th–7th Centuries BC," in *Assyrien im Wandel der Zeiten: XXXIXe Rencontre assyriologique internationale* (ed. H. Waetzoldt and H. Hauptmann; Heidelberg: Heidelberger Orientverlag, 1997), 209–16.

CHAPTER TWO

Wisdom Literature

Introduction

Biblical scholars first coined "Wisdom" as a literary category to describe Hebrew books in which ḥokmah ("wisdom") and its cognates were common. The resulting corpus included not only Proverbs, Job, Qoheleth, and certain of the Psalms but also similar Jewish apocryphal works, such as the Wisdom of Ben Sira, sometimes called Sirach or Ecclesiasticus. On these apocryphal works, see the companion volume to this book (Evans). When scholars discovered Near Eastern texts that were very similar to these Hebrew and Jewish works, it became clear that wisdom was an international rather than strictly Israelite/Jewish phenomenon. Over the years scholars have attempted to refine their definitions of wisdom, and there is now a prominent tendency to define wisdom not in terms of wisdom terminology, or even in terms of wisdom themes, but as a corpus of literature produced by ancient scribal scholars. This approach offers a taxonomic advantage because it provides a good explanation for why biblical and Near Eastern wisdom texts are so similar, namely, that the texts were composed by scholars engaged in an active intercultural exchange of literature and ideas. At the same time, however, it has become increasingly clear that there are problems with almost any definition of wisdom. Modern scholars now believe that many other Hebrew texts reflect wisdom themes and concerns, which is a natural consequence of the fact that, in the end, *all* ancient literary texts were written by scribal scholars. Moreover, it is becoming increasingly clear that the phenomenon of practical wisdom as understood by the ancients was always much broader than scribal wisdom alone; wise men and women included builders of houses, craftsmen, farmers, makers of fine clothes, and other practitioners, who did not write texts but were nonetheless skilled in their respective arts.

The discussion below introduces us first to Mesopotamian wisdom and then moves on to the wisdom of Egypt, Hatti, and the West Semitic world. Presupposed in this discussion is a distinction between standard and speculative wisdom that needs to be spelled out. *Standard wisdom* refers to texts that optimistically assume predictable patterns in reality, so that wise followers of the pattern reap good results and those deviating from it face trouble. In technical terminology, this pattern is commonly referred to as *retributive theology.* By way of contrast, *speculative wisdom* refers to texts that either implicitly or explicitly questioned the validity of standard retributive wisdom. Scholars sometimes refer to these two perspectives as optimistic and pessimistic wisdom.

2.1. Mesopotamian Wisdom

According to early Mesopotamian tradition, the proper order of all things divine and human was dependent upon the ME (a plural Sumerian term, rendered *parṣū* in Akkadian), those powers and properties of the gods that enabled civilized human life. Human success was achieved by living in harmony with the pattern (GIŠ-HUR) determined by the ME, and failure was the expected result in the absence of these divine resources. In Mesopotamian tradition, these fundamental patterns for civilization were transmitted from the gods to humanity when the god Enki/Ea revealed his wisdom to pre-flood sages called the *apkallū*, who were in turn succeeded by a series of post-flood scholars known as *ummānū* (see Bolle). These primeval *ummānū* were then followed by a class of human *ummānū*, so that, according to the Mesopotamian understanding, the wisdom tradition followed a line from Enki, to the *apkallū*, to the heroic *ummānū*, to the human *ummānū* of historical time (although we should note that omen wisdom traditionally took a somewhat different path, being revealed by the gods Šamaš and Adad to Enmeduranki, an early king of Sippar [see Lambert 1967]). Even during the historical period itself, it seems that the *ummānū* were theologically committed to the idea that the gods were involved in their work. This idea was explicitly stated by one *ummānu,* who credited the gods for his new edition of the medical-omens series SA.GIG: "In the reign of Adad-apla-iddina, King of Babylon, Esagil-kīn-apli . . . the sage of King Hammurabi, *ummānu* of Sin, Lisi and Nanai, a prominent citizen of Borsippa . . . through the incisive intelligence that Ea and Asalluḫi/Marduk had bestowed upon him, deliberated with himself, and produced the authorized editions for SA.GIG, from head to foot" (see Finkel).

What kinds of texts did this wisdom tradition create? One distinguishing trait of the Mesopotamian scribal tradition was its penchant for collecting and preserving information in lists—modern scholars call this *list science*—and this exercise generated a large corpus of lists covering almost everything imaginable that was divine or natural. The scribes also produced numerous texts that are more similar to biblical wisdom, including not only proverbs and instructions but also educational literature and speculative wisdom. The most important of these texts are described below.

2.1.1. Standard Mesopotamian Wisdom

Sumerian Proverb Collections. The Sumerians began to collect proverbs in the middle of the third millennium B.C.E.; twenty-eight collections are known to modern scholars (the numbering system used below follows that of Alster). We possess early collections from Tell Abū Ṣalābīkh and Tell Fara (the so-called Early Dynastic Proverbs; see Alster 1991–1992; Biggs; Deimel), but our best collections stem from the Old Babylonian period, when the texts were used eight hundred years after their composition to train scribes for whom Sumerian was a foreign language. The Old Babylonian collections are of three types: full compositions (master copies by competent scholars), school tablets (sometimes containing two columns, one by the teacher and the other by the student), and excerpts. The most common rationale for the collections was subject matter, the content arranged in list form using horizontal rulings to separate each saying. The collections included both practical wisdom and scribal court wisdom: "Tell a lie, (and) then tell the truth, it will be counted as a lie" (2.70); "Before the fire has gone out, write your exercise tablet" (3.132); "A palace is a huge river; its interior is a goring ox" (2.154). Many sayings featured animals, whose behavior illustrated the best and worst of human behavior. The collections included a variety of saying forms (precepts, maxims, apothegms, adages, bywords, taunts, compliments, and wishes/greetings) as well as short tales, parables, and poems (on these forms, see Gordon). Of these genres, the two that appear most commonly in the Bible and other Near Eastern texts are the precepts (rules concerning moral conduct) and the maxims (rules dealing with the practical side of life). Because the scribal proverbs sometimes comment on palace life in a critical or satirical way, some scholars infer that Sumerian scribal communities—and the later schools of Mesopotamia—enjoyed some degree of ideological independence from the palace itself.

Texts and translations: B. ALSTER, "Early Dynastic Proverbs and Other Contributions to the Study of Literary Texts from Abū Ṣalābīkh," *AfO* 38–39 (1991–1992): 1–51; IDEM, *Proverbs of Ancient Sumer: The World's Earliest Proverb Collection* (2 vols.; Bethesda, Md.: CDL Press, 1997); R. D. BIGGS, *Inscriptions from Tell Abu Salabikh* (OIP 99; Chicago: University of Chicago Press, 1974); A. DEIMEL, *Inschriften von Fara* (3 vols.; WVDOG 40, 43, 45 Leipzig: Hinrichs, 1922). *Translation: COS* 1.174: 563–68. *Bibliography:* B. ALSTER, "Literary Aspects of Sumerian and Akkadian Proverbs," in *Mesopotamian Poetic Language: Sumerian and Akkadian* (ed. M. E. Vogelzang and H. L. J. Vanstiphout; CM 6; Groningen, Neth.: Styx, 1996), 1–21; E. I. GORDON, *Sumerian Proverbs: Glimpses of Everyday Life in Ancient Mesopotamia* (Philadelphia: University Museum, University of Pennsylvania, 1959); N. VELDHUIS, "Sumerian Proverbs in Their Curricular Context," *JAOS* 120 (2000): 383–99.

The Instructions of Shuruppak. We possess good copies of this text from the classical Sumerian (ca. 2500 B.C.E.) and Old Babylonian periods (ca. 1800 B.C.E.), as well as a later but very fragmentary Akkadian translation (ca. 1100). The original Sumerian version adopted Shuruppak as its author because he was the eponymous royal ancestor of the pre-flood city of Shuruppak (Tell Fara). This claim was obviously fictional and reflects a common practice in ancient wisdom whereby a text's authority was enhanced by attributing it to a famous sage or personality of the past. Later revisions of the text made Shuruppak the father of Ziusudra, the Sumerian flood hero. This change reinforced the text's authority by a further implication, namely, that Ziusudra alone had survived the flood because he alone had obeyed his father's instructions. So, by two acts of fiction (Shuruppak, then Ziusudra) this proverbial collection was cast as a path to wisdom and blessings.

Shurappak's poetic instructions are more carefully structured than the other Sumerian proverb collections: (1) introduction, (2) frame story, (3) first instruction list, (4) frame story, (5) second instruction list, (6) frame story, (7) third instruction list, (8) conclusion. Three types of sayings predominate in the instructions: prohibitions ("Do not [do this or that]"), positive commands ("You shall do [this or that]"), and sayings that are best regarded as conventional proverbs. In spite of the clear structure in the text as a whole, the proverbs and instructions appear to be randomly arranged. This differs from the topical rationale used to arrange other Sumerian proverb collections but is reminiscent of sections of the biblical Proverbs. The text's central theme was the contrast between chaotic foolishness and the ordered society produced by wise living. The proper pattern for this social order, according to Shuruppak, was found in the wisdom of Utu (god of justice), whose knowledge was as old as the stars of heaven. A comparison of the Sumerian and Old Babylonian versions reveals a pattern of revision in the instructions, most notably that the Old Babylonian text added a series of contrasts that pitted temporal values against enduring values, foolishness against wisdom, wickedness against prayer, and native against foreign. The later versions also expanded the Sumerian edition's contrast between civilization and barbarism.

Texts and translations: B. ALSTER, *The Instructions of Shuruppak: A Sumerian Proverb Collection* (Mesopotamia 2; Copenhagen: Akademisk Forlag, 1974); IDEM, "Additional Fragments of the Instructions of Shuruppak," *AO* 5 (1987): 199–206. *Translations: ANET* 594–95 (partial); *COS* 1.176: 569–70. *Bibliography:* B. ALSTER, *Studies in Sumerian Proverbs* (Mesopotamia 3; Copenhagen: Akademisk Forlag, 1975); M. CIVIL, "Notes on the Instructions of Šuruppak," *JNES* 43 (1984): 281–98; see also the bibliography for the previous entry, "Sumerian Proverb Collections."

The Instructions of Urninurta. This Sumerian text describes the divine election of Urninurta (1923–1896 B.C.E.) as king and then provides a religious treatise on retributive theology. Its instructions are presented as divinely revealed to Urninurta, but it is not clear whether the text was composed to illustrate Urninurta's piety, to provide wisdom to his subjects, or both.

Text, translation, and comments: B. ALSTER, "The Instructions of Urninurta and Related Compositions," *Or* 60 (1991): 141–57. *Translation: COS* 1.177: 570. *Bibliography:* B. ALSTER, "Corrections to 'The Instructions of Urninurta and Related Compositions,'" *NABU* 1992.83.

The Counsels of Wisdom. Although later Mesopotamian scribes continued to copy, study, and translate Sumerian proverbs, very few Akkadian literary proverbs were composed (see the bibliography). Akkadian scribes, however, did produce several collections of instructional admonitions, among them the Counsels of Wisdom, which contains 150 lines of topically organized maxims. Each section of the text is introduced with a lead instruction (e.g., "Do not frequent a law court. Do not loiter where there is a dispute") followed by a list of related maxims (e.g., "Should it be a [legal] dispute of your own, extinguish the flame"; "Do not return evil to the man who disputes with you [at law])." Topics covered in the text include legal advice, proper and improper speech, choosing companions, sex and marriage, kindness to the needy, conduct in friendships, and religious piety.

Text and translation: LAMBERT, *Babylonian Wisdom Literature,* 96–117 (Counsels of Wisdom), 213–82 (Akkadian and bilingual proverbs). *Translations:* ANET 426–27, 595–96 (Counsels of Wisdom), 425–26, 593–94 (Akkadian proverbs); BM 1.326–29 (Counsels of Wisdom), 1.336–47 (Akkadian proverbs). *Bibliography:* McKANE, *Proverbs,* 153–56; see also bibliography above for "Sumerian Proverb Collections."

Advice to a Prince. This Akkadian text admonished the future king to practice justice, heed the counsel of his advisers, and protect the rights of citizens in the cities of Sippar, Nippur, and Babylon. Its author warned that oppression of these cities would anger the gods and prompt them to abandon their temples and the king. The interest in these three cities and the emphasis on scholarly advice is easily explained. Scholars in these three cities were considered the chief recipients of omen lore from the gods, so we can surmise that the author was a scholar who wrote to protect the privileges of his own class (Lambert 1967). This would explain an interesting feature in these royal instructions, namely, that they mimic the casuistic forms of omen literature: "[If] the king does not heed justice, [then] his people will be thrown into chaos, and his land will be devastated." Just as the omens portended good or evil, so too the king's behavior dictated his future for better or worse. Although the text was probably written to address a Babylonian king who reigned sometime between 1000 and 700 B.C.E. (perhaps Nabû-šuma-iškun; see Cole), citations of the text in Neo-Assyrian letters and astral omens suggest that it became popular among court scribes. There is some evidence that the author wanted to present this text as a composition of the god Ea (Hurowitz; cf. the Erra Myth in 10.1.2).

Text and translation: LAMBERT, *Babylonian Wisdom Literature,* 110–15. *Bibliography:* F. M. T. BÖHL, *Der babylonische Fürstenspiegel* (Leipzig: Harrassowitz, 1937); G. E. BRYCE, "Omen-Wisdom in Ancient Israel," *JBL* 94 (1975): 19–37; S. W. COLE, "The Crimes and Sacrileges of Nabû-šuma-iškun," *ZA* 84 (1994), 220–52; V. A. HUROWITZ, "Advice to a Prince: A Message from Ea," *SAAB* 12 (1998): 39–53; LAMBERT, "Enmeduranki and Related Matters"; E. REINER, "The Babylonian Fürstenspiegel in Practice," in *Societies and Languages of the Ancient Near East: Studies in Honour of I. M. Diakonoff* (Warminster, England: Aris & Phillips, 1982), 320–23; J. J. A. VAN DIJK, *La sagesse suméro-accadienne* (Leiden: Brill, 1953), 112–18.

2.1.2. Mesopotamian Speculative Wisdom

The Dialogue of Šube'awilum and His Father. This author's skeptical sentiments are well illustrated by his thrice-repeated refrain: "Rules were formulated by Enki, regulations were laid down at the command of the gods, from days of old there has been vanity." In this instance and at other points in the dialogue, the vanity of human existence is lamented because life is "but the twinkling of an eye" and death is "the lot of mankind" (cf. the Gilgamesh Epic). Unlike the Akkadian dialogues (see below), theodicy was not the issue in this text; the problem was death itself and its implications. The author's pessimistic appraisal of this matter apparently intrigued ancient scholars, who copied, translated, and studied the text for at least fourteen hundred years in places as diverse as Nippur, Emar, Ugarit, Hatti, and Assur (our copies include the original Sumerian as well as Akkadian and Hittite translations). The Nippur fragments are our oldest exemplars, and those from Assurbanipal's Neo-Assyrian library the latest (seventh century B.C.E.). On the basis of the Nippur fragments (ca. 1800–1600), scholars surmise that the text was composed sometime around 2000 B.C.E. M. Dietrich and G. Keydana have completed a new edition that accounts for all of the major copies.

Texts and translations: M. DIETRICH and G. KEYDANA, "Die Dialog Šūpē-amēli und seinem 'Vater,'" *UF* 23 (1991): 323–74; IDEM, "Proverb Collections of Šūpē-amēli from Ugarit, Emar, and Boğazköy," in *Verse in Ancient Near Eastern Prose* (ed. J. C. de Moor and W. G. E. Watson; AOAT 43; Kevelaer, Germany: Butzon & Bercker, 1993), 52–62. *Translation:* BM² 1.330–34. *Bibliography:* W. G. LAMBERT, "Some New Babylonian Wisdom Literature," in *Wisdom in Ancient Israel* (ed. Day), 30–42.

A Man and His God, the "Sumerian Job." This Sumerian text is the earliest Mesopotamian exemplar to explore the problem of pious suffering. Although its protagonist proclaims his innocence, the bulk of his monologue is a penitential lament that leads to restoration and healing by the god. So, unlike Job, in this text resolution was reached when the sufferer embraced conservative orthodoxy ("Never has a sinless child been born") and confessed his sins committed in ignorance: "I, the young man, shall publicly declare my sins before you!" Hence, the poetic monologue does not challenge traditional retributive theology so much as it explains why life seems to deviate from this pattern. The text's viewpoint is retrospective, since it not only ends but also begins with an optimistic charge: "Let man utter constantly the exaltedness of his god." Weinfeld has noted that the structure and viewpoint of this piece (praise–lament–restoration–praise) parallels closely the biblical thanksgiving psalms (e.g., Ps 34).

Text and translation: S. N. KRAMER, "Man and His God: A Sumerian Variation on the 'Job' Motif," in *Wisdom in Israel and in the Ancient Near East Presented to Professor Harold Henry Rowley* (ed. M. Noth; VTSup 3; Leiden: Brill, 1955), i–iv, 170–81. *Translations:* ANET 589–91; COS 1.179: 573–75. *Bibliography:* J. KLEIN, "'Personal God' and Individual Prayer in Sumerian Religion," in *Vorträge gehalten auf der 28. Rencontre assyriologique internationale* (ed. H. Hunger and H. Hirsch; AfOB 19; Horn, Austria: F. Berger, 1982), 295–306;

G. L. MATTINGLY, "The Pious Sufferer: Mesopotamia's Traditional Theodicy and Job's Counselors"; WEINFELD, "Job and Its Mesopotamian Parallels—a Typological Analysis."

Dialogue between a Man and His God. This fragmentary Akkadian text from the Louvre (AO 4462) dates to the Old Babylonian period. It relates the conversation of a suffering man with his god, in which the god responded with this admonition: "Your disease is under control, let your heart not be despondent. . . . You must never, till the end of time, forget your god, your creator, now that you are favored." The text concludes with the sufferer speaking the words "May your servant's supplication reach your heart," but it is not clear how this supplication relates to the text itself. The original editor interpreted the sufferer as a Job-like "righteous sufferer" (Nougayrol), but this is not at all clear (Lambert 1987).

Texts and translations: W. G. LAMBERT, "A Further Attempt at the Babylonian 'Man and His God,'" in *Language, Literature, and History: Philological and Historical Studies Presented to Erica Reiner* (AOS 67; New Haven: American Oriental Society, 1987), 187–202; J. NOUGAYROL, "Une version ancienne du 'juste souffrant,'" *RB* 59 (1952): 239–50. *Translation:* *BM²* 1.78–80. *Bibliography:* LAMBERT, *Babylonian Wisdom Literature*, 10–11; W. VON SODEN, "Zu einigen altbabylonischen Dichtungen," *Or* 26 (1957): 306–20; WEINFELD, "Job and Its Mesopotamian Parallels—a Typological Analysis."

Ludlul Bēl Nēmeqi, the "Babylonian Job." This Akkadian text from the Kassite period (fourteenth–twelfth century B.C.E.) is generically and thematically similar to the Sumerian Job (see above). It is a four-tablet poetic monologue, entitled *Ludlul Bēl Nēmeqi* ("I Will Praise the Lord of Wisdom"), that begins and ends with praise for the god Marduk. The chief protagonist of the text was a prosperous public figure named Šubši-mešrê-Šakkan, who appealed to the gods for help when he lost his post, wealth, family, and health. Despite intense suffering, Šubši-mešrê-Šakkan praised Marduk—and encouraged other sufferers to do the same—because his appeals to Marduk were eventually answered when the god sent an exorcist to expel the demons that oppressed him. This outcome suggests that the text was not a philosophical treatise on theodicy so much as a work of propaganda on behalf of Marduk, the chief Babylonian god and patron deity of exorcists and diviners (Moran). The meaning of the name Šubši-mešrê-Šakkan embodies the text's theology: "May Esagil [Marduk's temple] declare the righteous pure." As in the case of the Sumerian Job text, the structure and viewpoint of this piece (praise–lament–restoration–praise) parallels closely the biblical thanksgiving psalms, such as Ps 34 (see Weinfeld).

Texts and translations: LAMBERT, *Babylonian Wisdom Literature*, 21–62; D. J. WISEMAN, "A New Text of the Babylonian Poem of the Righteous Sufferer," *AnSt* 30 (1980): 101–7. *Translations:* *ANET* 596–600; *COS* 1.153: 486–92. *Bibliography:* J. BOTTÉRO, *Le Problème du Mal en Mésopotamie ancienne: Prologue à une étude du 'Juste souffrant,'* (L'Arbresle: Centre Thomas More, 1977); MATTINGLY, "The Pious Sufferer: Mesopotamia's Traditional Theodicy and Job's Counselors"; W. L. MORAN, "The Babylonian Job," in W. L. Moran, *The Most Magic Word* (ed. R. S. Hendel; CBQMS 35; Washington: Catholic Biblical Association, 2002), 182–200; H.-P. MÜLLER, "Keilschriftliche Parallelen zum biblischen Hiobbuch:

Möglichkeit und Grenze des Vergleichs," in *Mythos–Kerygma–Wahrheit: Gesammelte Aufsätze zum Alten Testament in seiner Umwelt und zur Biblischen Theologie*, 136–51; W. VON SODEN, "Das Fragen nach der Gerechtigkeit Gottes im alten Orient," *MDOG* 96 (1965): 41–59; WEINFELD, "Job and Its Mesopotamian Parallels—a Typological Analysis."

The Babylonian Theodicy. This dialogue between a human sufferer and a sage openly challenged the retributive orthodoxy of Mesopotamia, making it thematically and generically closer to the biblical book of Job than to either the Sumerian or Babylonian "Job" texts listed above. As in Job, this sufferer is accused of arrogance and blasphemy, is abandoned by his friends, and strongly avers his own innocence. Both this text and the book of Job stress the great gulf between divine and human wisdom. The dialogue concludes when the sufferer's sage friend finally accepts the conclusion that the very gods who are responsible for maintaining justice have created men with evil inclinations that thwart justice. In the face of this theological contradiction, the sufferer can only plea that the gods will protect him. The dialogue is cast in the form of an acrostic poem, whose twenty-seven 11–line stanzas spell out a-na-ku sa-ag-gi-il-ki-[i-na-am-u]b-bi-ib ma-áš-ma-šu ka-ri-bu ša i-li ú šar-ri, "I, Saggil-kinam-ubbib, the incantation priest, am adorant of the god and the king." This author, also known as Esagil-kīn-apli, was the famous chief scholar (*ummānu*) of kings Nebuchadnezzar I and Adad-apla-iddina during the twelfth and eleventh centuries (see Finkel). A Seleucid-era commentary on the Babylonian Theodicy was discovered at Sippar (see Labat), and fragments of a text that is similar to the Theodicy have been published in Lambert, 90–91.

Text and translation: LAMBERT, *Babylonian Wisdom Literature*, 63–91. *Translations:* *ANET* 601–4; *COS* 1.154: 492–95. *Bibliography:* FINKEL, "Adad-apla-iddina, Esagil-kīn-apli, and the Series SA.GIG"; R. LABAT, *Commentaires assyro-babyloniens sur les présages* (Bordeaux: Imprimerie-Librairie de l'Université, 1933), 102–9, 122–25; MATTINGLY, "The Pious Sufferer: Mesopotamia's Traditional Theodicy and Job's Counselors"; MÜLLER, "Keilschriftliche Parallelen zum biblischen Hiobbuch: Möglichkeit und Grenze des Vergleichs," in *Mythos–Kerygma–Wahrheit: Gesammelte Aufsätze zum Alten Testament in seiner Umwelt und zur Biblischen Theologie*, 136–51; VAN DER TOORN, "The Ancient Near Eastern Literary Dialogue as a Vehicle of Critical Reflection"; WEINFELD, "Job and Its Mesopotamian Parallels—a Typological Analysis."

The Dialogue of Pessimism. This dialogue, composed near the beginning of the first millennium B.C.E., is more cynical than the similar Babylonian Theodicy. Here a master and slave engage in a sarcastic discussion from which they conclude that life's activities are pure vanity. In successive rounds, the master announces his intention to engage in an activity. After his wise slave concurs, the master decides not to take the action, to which the slave responds with words of agreement. Among the master's possible courses of action are chariot drives, the pleasures of dining, having a family, leading a revolution, sex, worshipping god, becoming a money lender, and undertaking public benefits for his country. Particularly striking is the text's impiety. When the master decides not to sacrifice to the gods, the slave responds, "Do not sacrifice, sir, do not sacrifice. You can teach your god to run after you like a dog." Equally telling is the slave's response to the master's decision not to undertake a public benefit for his country: "Do not perform, sir, do not perform. Go up on the ancient ruin heaps and walk about; See the skulls high and low. Which is the malefactor, and which is the benefactor?" The text concludes with the master asking his slave what is worth doing; the slave avers that death is the only suitable end for this meaningless life.

Modern scholars originally interpreted the dialogue as a serious philosophical composition until Speiser argued that it was humorous and sarcastic. Lambert has suggested in retrospect that there is some truth in both of these views; the dialogue's author has proffered a serious message in sarcastic and humorous tones. Whoever the author was, the uniqueness of his impiety marks him as an unusual, if not extraordinary, person. There are obvious similarities between the views of life espoused in this text and those expressed by Qoheleth in the Hebrew Bible. The two works differ primarily in their conclusions, with Qoheleth affirming that life's transient joys are an end in themselves whereas the Dialogue rejects life's transience in favor of death. The fact that Qoheleth seems to have known the pessimistic Gilgamesh Epic (see 9.1.1 below) makes it more likely that he was also familiar with the Dialogue of Pessimism.

Text and translation: LAMBERT, *Babylonian Wisdom Literature,* 139–49. *Translations:* ANET 600–601; COS 1.155: 495–96. *Bibliography:* J. BOTTÉRO, *Mesopotamia: Writing, Reasoning, and the Gods* (Chicago: University of Chicago Press, 1992), 251–67; E. A. SPEISER, "The Case of the Obliging Servant [Dialogue of Pessimism]," *JCS* 8 (1954): 98–105.

2.1.3. Other Mesopotamian Wisdom Texts

A Sumerian Riddle Collection. The Hebrew term "riddle" (*ḥîdâ*) appears in a list of wisdom speech forms along with proverbs, sayings, and parables (Prov 1:6). Although no corpus of wisdom riddles is preserved in the Hebrew canon, certain Hebrew proverbs have riddle-like qualities (e.g., Prov 11:22; see Alter), and riddle collections from the Ancient Near East, such as this Sumerian exemplar, provide hints of what the Hebrew riddles must have been like. Modern scholars surmise that the riddles were valued as tests of the ancient scribe's intellectual ability.

Text and translation: B. ALSTER, "A Sumerian Riddle Collection," *JNES* 35 (1976): 263–67. *Bibliography:* J. L. CRENSHAW, "Riddles," *ABD* 5:721–23; R. ALTER, *The Art of Biblical Poetry* (New York: Basic Books, 1985), 175–79.

Contest Literature. Contest or dispute poems first appeared during the Sumerian period, but Akkadian exemplars are known as well. Disputants in the texts could be animals (e.g., Disputation between the Bird and the Fish [Sumerian]), plants (e.g, Disputation between the Tamarisk and the Palm [Akkadian]), or inanimate objects (e.g., Disputation between the Hoe and the Plow [Akkadian]). The usual form of the dispute fables was as follows: (1) a mythological introduction providing the origins of the disputants; (2) the dispute between the contestants; and (3) a judgment scene where the gods pronounced the victor. The texts were copied in

Old Babylonian schools, but the Sumerian exemplars explicitly refer to the royal courts, where the disputations provided entertainment on festive occasions.

Texts, translations, and studies: B. ALSTER, "Sumerian Literary Dialogues and Debates and Their Place in Ancient Near Eastern Literature," in *Living Waters: Scandinavian Orientalistic Studies Presented to Professor Dr. Frede Løkkegaard* (Copenhagen: Museum Tusculanum Press, 1990), 1–16; B. ALSTER and H. L. J. VANSTIPHOUT, "Lahar and Ashnan: Presentation and Analysis of a Sumerian Disputation," *ActSum* 9 (1987): 1–43; M. S. BRUNNER, "The Fable of the *Babylonian Tree*," *JNES* 39 (1980): 191–202, 291–302; S. DENNING-BOLLE, "Wisdom and Dialogue in the Ancient Near East," *Numen* 34 (1987): 214–34; E. EBELING, *Die babylonische Fabel und ihre Bedeutung für die Literaturgeschichte* (MAOG 2.3; Leipzig: Eduard Pfeiffer, 1927); G. GRAGG, "The Fable of the Heron and the Turtle," *AfO* 24 (1974): 51–72; LAMBERT, *Babylonian Wisdom Literature*, 150–212; G. J. REININK and H. L. J. VANSTIPHOUT, eds., *Dispute Poems and Dialogues in the Ancient and Mediaeval Near East* (OLA 42; Leuven: Peeters, 1991); H. L. J. VANSTIPHOUT, "The Importance of the Tale of the Fox," *ActSum* 10 (1988): 191–227; IDEM, "The Mesopotamian Debate Poems: A General Presentation," *ActSum* 12 (1990): 271–318; 14 (1992): 339–67; IDEM, "On the Sumerian Disputation between the Hoe and the Plough," *AuOr* 2 (1984): 239–51. *Other translations:* ANET 410–11, 592–93 (partial); COS 1.178: 571–73, 1.180–83: 575–88.

Sumerian School Dialogues. Another wisdom genre, the Sumerian school dialogues, shared the jocular and entertaining character of the disputations. These dialogues, which satirically pitted experienced older scribes against hapless younger scribes, poked fun at both the young upstart scribes and at the educational establishment in general.

Texts, translations, and studies: COS 1.184–186: 588–93; W. H. P. RÖMER, "Aus einem Schulstreitgespräch in sumerischer Sprache," *UF* 20 (1988): 233–45; H. L. J. VANSTIPHOUT, "Remarks on 'Supervisor and Scribe' (or Dialogue 4, or Eduba C)," *NABU* 1996.1.

The Sumerian Farmer's Almanac. This text from Nippur, purportedly written by the god Ninurta himself, provided a one-year calendar of farming operations from plowing to harvest. Evidently, just as mantic wisdom was normally traced back to the god Enki, so too was agricultural wisdom traced back to Ninurta. Although the function of this tablet is not transparent, it probably summarized basic agricultural wisdom for didactic purposes. The Israelite Gezer Calendar (see 15.1) is perhaps a comparable text.

Text and translation: M. CIVIL, *The Farmer's Instructions: A Sumerian Agricultural Manual* (AuOrSup 5; Barcelona: Editorial AUSA, 1994). *Bibliography:* P. WALCOT, "Hesiod and the Didactic Literature of the Near East," *REG* 75 (1962): 14–26.

2.2. Egyptian Wisdom

Like their Mesopotamian counterparts, Egyptian sages filled a variety of roles, serving as advisers, counselors, magicians, physicians, diplomats, government officials, architects, and even as court entertainers (see R. J. Williams in

Gammie/Perdue, 95–98). Although this broad range of duties produced a variety of genres that might be reasonably called wisdom literature, four Egyptian wisdom genres are of primary importance for purposes of comparison with the Hebrew Bible: instructions, admonitions, pessimistic dialogues, and pessimistic songs. Central to Egypt's wisdom ideology was *ma'at*, the primordial harmony of order, truth, and justice set down by the creator god at the beginning of the world. Those who lived in adherence with *ma'at* were promised a blessed life and a pleasant afterlife, whereas failure and death awaited all others. Although most of the wisdom texts examined in this chapter explained how one could live in accordance with *ma'at* and reap its rewards, in the more pessimistic exemplars the principles of *ma'at* were openly questioned.

2.2.1. Standard Egyptian Wisdom: The Instructions

These texts bear the title *sboyet*, which, like the Hebrew term *mûsār*, carries the dual meaning of "teaching" and "discipline" (see Shupak, 31–34). The purpose of the instructions, generally speaking, was to teach readers how to live according to *ma'at*. Although the Egyptian instructions include many traditional maxims, they differ from proverbial collections in that they typically offer not mere sentence wisdom but rather poetic discourses. Those familiar with the Hebrew proverbs will already recognize this distinction, since Prov 1–9 is composed of wisdom discourses whereas Prov 10–22 contains mostly proverbial sentence wisdom. The oldest exemplars of the Egyptian instructions date to the Old Kingdom, and new texts were being composed as late as the Hellenistic and Roman periods. In at least one case (the Instructions of Amenemhet), the same text was being copied and studied for a period of some fifteen hundred years.

Instructions of Hardjedef (Old Kingdom). According to Egyptian tradition, eight ancient wise men attained immortality because of the instructions they wrote. These were usually enumerated in pairs of two as Hardjedef and Imhotep, Neferti and Kheti, Ptahemdjehuti and Khakheperresonbu, and Ptahhotep and Kairsu (Fox). Several of these figures appear in other Egyptian wisdom texts, but in this fragmentary exemplar we meet the first of these sages, Hardjedef (or Djedefhor), the son of Pharaoh Cheops (Fourth Dynasty). The text, first identified on a scribal-exercise ostracon, contained words of advice that Hardjedef ostensibly penned for his son Awetibre, but the text is too fragmentary to venture much of a description. Did Hardjedef actually pen these instructions? Egyptian tradition fictionally credited Hardjedef with the composition of a Harper's Song (see 2.2.2) and with a role in the fictional tale of P.Westcar (see 8.1), prompting modern scholars to doubt Hardjedef's role in the instructions. Although we cannot answer this authorship question categorically, the obvious pseudonymity of later Egyptian instructions is perhaps instructive.

Text and translation: W. HELCK, *Die Lehre des Djedefhor und die Lehre eines Vaters an seinen Sohn* (Wiesbaden: Harrassowitz, 1984). **Translation:** *LAE* 127–28. **Bibliography:**

G. POSENER, "Le Début de l'Enseignement de Hardjedef (Recherches Littéraires IV)," *RdE* 9 (1952): 109–20.

The Instructions of Ptahhotep (Old Kingdom). Our oldest complete exemplar of Egypt's instructional genre is this text, in which an Old Kingdom vizier distilled wisdom for his son. Like later exemplars, these instructions were framed by a prologue and epilogue. The prologue introduced the author and his intention to provide words of wisdom, and the longer epilogue (more than 150 lines) admonished the son to heed this wisdom. The instructions themselves were essentially thirty-seven wisdom speeches, each introduced casuistically (e.g., "If you are a man who leads . . .") and containing a series of related commands (e.g., "Listen calmly to the speech of one who pleads") and wise statements (e.g., "Not all one pleads for can be granted, But a good hearing soothes the heart"). Topics covered in the text range from human relationships to basic virtues (kindness, generosity, justice, honesty, self-control, etc.). According to the epilogue, the son who wisely accepted these instructions would be rewarded with long life and success. Because the text's language reflects influences from Middle Egyptian, it was probably composed near the end of the Old Kingdom, long after Ptahhotep would have lived. For this reason it is suspected that these instructions were composed pseudonymously and attributed to Ptahhotep. But written by Ptahhotep or not, the text became a source of wisdom for many later generations. Attached to our principle manuscript of Ptahhotep's wisdom is the only known fragment of another instruction text, the Teaching of Kagemni (see Gardiner; Parkinson, 290–93).

Texts and translations: BUDGE, *Facsimiles of Egyptian Hieratic Papyri in the British Museum*, pls. xxxiv–xxxviii; G. JÉQUIER, *Le Papyrus Prisse et ses variants* (Paris: Geuthner, 1911). *Translations:* AEL 1:61–80; ANET 412–14; LAE 129–48; PARKINSON, *The Tale of Sinuhe and Other Ancient Egyptian Poems: 1940–1640 BC*, 246–72. *Bibliography:* BRUNNER, "Zitate aus Lebenslehren"; C. CANNUYER, "L'obèse de Ptahhotep et de Samuel," *ZÄS* 113 (1986): 92–102; C. R. FONTAINE, "A Modern Look at Ancient Wisdom: The Instruction of Ptahhotep Revisited," *BA* 44 (1981): 155–60; A. H. GARDINER, "The Instruction Addressed to Kagemni and His Brethren," *JEA* 32 (1946): 71–74; MCKANE, *Proverbs*, 51–65, 75–82; R. B. PARKINSON, "'Homosexual' Desire and Middle Kingdom Literature," *JEA* 81 (1995), 57–76; L. TROY, "Good and Bad Women: Maxim 18/284–288 of the Instructions of Ptahhotep," *GM* 80 (1984): 77–81.

The Instructions of Merikare (First Intermediate Period). Although purportedly composed by Pharaoh Khety for his son Merikare, this text was more likely the work of Merikare himself and served as a gift to honor his deceased father and as an expression of Merikare's own political policies. In this respect, the text is essentially a royal instruction, a treatise on kingship that covers such topics as the threat of rebellion, justice in the royal courts and society, troop conscription, and religious duties. Khety also explains how his son might duplicate his father's accomplishments, concluding these directives with remarks on divine retribution and with a hymn to the creator god. The text is arranged in sections of two, three, or four sentences that are joined using various types of poetic parallelism. As in

the earlier Instructions of Ptahhotep, imperative forms predominate. New Kingdom editions of the text were organized by adding topical rubrics, but in some
cases it is difficult to understand the logic behind these subtitles.

Texts and translations: W. GOLÉNISCHEFF, *Les papyrus hiératiques nos. 1115, 1116A, et
1116B de l'Ermitage imperial à St-Petersbourg* (Saint Petersburg: Manufacture des papiers
de l'état, 1916), pls. ix–xiv; HELCK, *Die Lehre für König Merikare;* J. F. QUACK, *Studien
zur Lehre für Merikare* (GOA 23; Wiesbaden: Harrassowitz, 1992). *Translations: AEL*
1:97–109; *ANET* 414–18; *COS* 1.35: 61–66; *LAE* 152–65; PARKINSON, *The Tale of Sinuhe
and Other Ancient Egyptian Poems,* 212–34. *Bibliography:* E. BLUMENTHAL, "Die Lehre für
König Merikare," *ZÄS* 107 (1980): 5–41; HELCK, *Die Lehre für König Merikare;* MCKANE,
Proverbs, 67–82; A. SCHARFF, *Der historische Abschnitt der Lehre für König Merikarê* (Munich: Verlag der Bayerischen Akademie der Wissenschaften, 1936).

Instructions of Amenemhet (Middle Kingdom). Whereas the older Instructions
to Merikare encouraged the new king to surround himself with trustworthy advisors, the Middle Kingdom Instructions of Amenemhet warned, to the contrary,
that even close advisors pose a threat to royalty. This counsel rested upon good
grounds, for Amenemhet himself had been assassinated in a rebellious coup attempt. Amenemhet delivered his instruction to his son Sesostris after the rebellion, so that his instructions are not only pseudonymous, like those of Ptahhotep
and Merikare, but also posthumous. After a brief introduction, Amenemhet provides his account of the tragic coup and then advises Sesostris how to succeed
while avoiding the same fate. As in the earlier instructions, imperative forms predominate in this advice. Unfortunately, the text's conclusion is missing.

Texts and translations: F. L. GRIFFITH, "The Millingen Papyrus," *ZÄS* 34 (1896): 35–51;
W. HELCK, *Der Text der "Lehre Amenemhets I. für seinen Sohn"* (2d ed.; Wiesbaden: Harrassowitz, 1986). *Translations: AEL* 1:135–39; *ANET* 418–19; *COS* 1.36: 66–68; *LAE*
166–71; PARKINSON, *The Tale of Sinuhe and Other Ancient Egyptian Poems,* 203–11. *Bibliography:* R. ANTHES, "The Legal Aspect of the Instruction of Amenemhet," *JNES* 16
(1957): 176–190; BRUNNER, "Zitate aus Lebenslehren"; J. L. FOSTER, "The Conclusion to
The Testament of Ammenemes, King of Egypt," *JEA* 67 (1981): 35–47; H. GOEDICKE, *Studies
in "The Instruction of King Amenemhet I for his Son"* (Varia aegyptiaca: Supplement 2; San
Antonio, Tex.: Van Siclen, 1988); R. GUNDLACH, "Ägyptische Weisheit in der politischen
'Lebenslehre' König Amenemhet I," in *"Jedes Ding hat seine Zeit . . ."—Studien zur
israelitischen und altorientalischen Weisheit: Diethelm Michel zum 65 Geburtstag* (ed. A. A.
Diesel et al.; BZAW 241; Berlin: de Gruyter, 1996), 91–105; MCKANE, *Proverbs,* 82–86; C.
A. THÉRIAULT, *"The Instruction of Amenemhat* as Propaganda," *JARCE* 30 (1993): 151–60.

The Teaching of Dua-khety, or Satire on the Trades (Middle Kingdom). Here
Dua-khety addressed his son Pepi as the young aristocrat was preparing to train
in a school for elite scribes. The text is often called Satire on the Trades because it
humorously extols the advantages of a scribal career over the toil of alternative
professions such as carpentry, gardening, and farming. Conventional words of
advice follow this sarcastic introduction in a text that was obviously composed
to encourage devotion to a rigorous program of scribal education. The scribal

career is similarly celebrated in P.Lansing (see below), but Lansing does not include instructions.

Text and translation: W. HELCK, *Die Lehre des Dw3-Ḥtjj* (Wiesbaden: O. Harrassowitz, 1970). *Translations:* AEL 1:184–92; ANET 432–34; COS 1.48: 122–25; LAE 431–37; PARKINSON, *The Tale of Sinuhe and Other Ancient Egyptian Poems,* 273–83. *Bibliography:* B. COUROYER, "Un égyptianisme dans Ben Sira IV, 11," *RB* 82 (1975): 206–17; J. E. HOCH, "The Teaching of Dua-Kheti: A New Look at the Satire of the Trades," *JSSEA* 21–22 (1991–1992): 88–100; MCKANE, *Proverbs,* 86–91; A. PIANKOFF, "Quelques passages des 'Instructions de Douaf' sur une tablette du Musée du Louvre," *REg* 1 (1933): 51–74; C. A. ROLLSTON, "Ben Sira 38:24–39:11 and the Egyptian Satire of the Trades: A Reconsideration *JBL* 120 (2001): 131–39; B. VAN DE WALLE, *L'humour dans la littérature et dans l'art de l'ancienne Égypte* (Leiden: Nederlands Instituut voor het Nabije Oosten, 1969), 11.

The Loyalist Instruction (Middle Kingdom). The first half of this text was discovered on a mortuary stela (see *AEL*), but scholars later recognized it as a part of a longer wisdom composition, which Posener was able to reconstruct on the basis of a Ramesside-era papyrus and several fragmentary copies. The first half of the text espouses profound loyalty to the king ("Praise the king within your bodies. . . . The man he favors will be lord of provisions; his adversary will be a nobody. . . . You should be free from disloyal action!"); the second half offers words of wisdom for success in the royal courts. The author was both a priest and a vizier to Pharaoh, perhaps Montuhotep, the historical vizier of Senwosret I. The fragmentary text known as the Teaching of a Man for His Son includes a similar combination of loyalist teachings and court wisdom (see Fischer-Elfert).

Texts and translations: H. W. FISCHER-ELFERT, *Die Lehre eines Mannes für seinen Sohn: Eine Etappe auf dem "Gottesweg" des loyalen und solidarischen Beamten des Mittleren Reiches* (2 vols.; ÄgAbh 60; Wiesbaden: Harrassowitz, 1999) (Teaching of a Man for His Son); G. POSENER, *L'enseignement loyaliste: Sagesse égyptienne du Moyen Empire* (Hautes études orientales 5; Geneva: Droz, 1976) (Loyalist Instruction). *Translations:* AEL 1:125–29 (partial); LAE 172–74; PARKINSON, *The Tale of Sinuhe and Other Ancient Egyptian Poems,* 235–45. *Bibliography:* A. LOPRIENO, "Loyalistic Instructions," in *Ancient Egyptian Literature: History and Forms* (ed. A. Loprieno; PA 10; New York: Brill, 1996), 403–14; G. POSENER, *Littérature et politique dans l'Égypte de la XIIe dynastie* (Bibliothèque de l'École des hautes études 307; Paris: Champion, 1956), 117–28; W. K. SIMPSON, "Mentuhotep, Vizier of Sesostris I, Patron of Art and Architecture," *MDAI* 47 (1991): 331–40.

Papyrus Lansing (New Kingdom). Although ostensibly an "instruction in letter-writing" written by the royal scribe Nebmare-nakht for his apprentice Wenemdiamun, this text does not contain standard instructions so much as exhortations for his student to pursue a scribal education. To this end the text praises the scribal profession and critiques other professions, and it shames the student into diligent compliance by describing him as conceited, dense, and lazy. Our copy of the text is carelessly written and contains many errors; this is no surprise given that it was certainly composed for use in scribal curricula.

Texts and translations: A. M. BLACKMAN and T. E. PEET, "Papyrus Lansing: A Translation with Notes," *JEA* 11 (1925): 284–98; BUDGE, *Facsimiles of Egyptian Hieratic Papyri in the British Museum, Second Series,* pls. 15–30; A. ERMAN and H. O. LANGE, *Papyrus Lansing: Eine ägyptische Schulhandschrift der 20. Dynastie* (Copenhagen: Høst & Søn, 1925). ***Translation:*** *AEL* 2:168–75. ***Bibliography:*** MCKANE, *Proverbs,* 86–91.

The Instructions of Any (New Kingdom). Whereas earlier Egyptian instructions were addressed to the aristocratic sons of the royal and gentry classes, the New Kingdom instructions of Any reflect a democratization of the genre, being composed by a middle-class scribe for a middle-class audience. Here a preoccupation with success in the royal court is replaced by more practical advice about marriage, the threat of strange women, religious piety, temperance in the use of alcohol, establishment of a household, care for aged parents, and compassion for the poor. Other unique features stand alongside this new middle-class tone. The conditional "if" clauses, so common in the older instructions, give way almost entirely to positive and negative commands in which the vetitive ("Do not . . .") predominates slightly. And unlike the older instructions, Any's teachings conclude with a dialogue between Any and his son Khonshotep, in which the son argues that he is ill suited to follow his father's footsteps into government service. Naturally, the father has the last word in this debate, but a sensitive reading of the text reveals that the debate is literary and artificial: its father-son rhetoric, so common in earlier Egyptian instructions, was pedagogically composed to address not only Any's son but also other father-son and student-teacher relationships.

Text and translation: E. SUYS, *La sagesse d'Ani: Texte, traduction, et commentaire* (AnOr 11; Rome: Pontificio Istituto Biblico, 1935). ***Translations:*** *AEL* 2:135–46; *ANET* 420–21; *COS* 1.46: 110–15. ***Bibliography:*** MCKANE, *Proverbs,* 92–102; A. VOLTEN, *Studien zum Weisheitsbuch des Anii* (Copenhagen: Levin & Munksgaard, Ejnar Munksgaard, 1937).

The Instructions of Amenemope (New Kingdom). Perhaps the best known of the New Kingdom instructions are Amenemope's teachings for his son, primarily because this text apparently influenced the author of Prov 22:17–23:14. Although Amenemope was composed during the twelfth century B.C.E., it was copied and studied down into the Late period, providing ample opportunity for contacts between this text and Israelite wisdom. The best copy is a complete twenty-seven-page hieratic papyrus from the British Museum (Papyrus 10474). Amenemope's instructions differ from earlier exemplars in both form and content. In terms of form, the text is arranged in lines that reflect its poetic character. These lines are related to each other through parallelism and other poetic devices and are arranged into thirty numbered "chapters," each containing ten to forty thematically related lines. In terms of content, unlike earlier instructions, Amenemope no longer motivates his son by straightforward promises of wealth and achievement but rather through a concern for developing his inner qualities and virtues. According to Lichtheim (*AEL* 2:146–7), two key themes shaped this depiction of virtue: the contrast between the silent man of wisdom and the heated intemperate man, and the choice between honesty and duplicity. The author pursued this twofold agenda with generous doses of negative commands, such as "Do not force yourself to greet a heated man, for then you injure your own heart" and "Do not move the markers on the borders of fields." With this and similar advice, the middle-class Amenemope promises to help his son succeed as a government official; this suggests that his book was a guide for would-be government functionaries.

Formal and material similarities between the Instructions of Amenemope and the wisdom collection in Prov 22:17–24:22 have convinced most scholars that this Egyptian text directly influenced the biblical author. Each text describes its teaching as "thirty sayings" (cf. Prov 22:20; Amen. XXVII. 7), and, as Table 2.1 shows, there are many parallels between the two exemplars (note that the parallels are in the first half of the collection, 22:17–23:14; table from Helmbold).

Table 2.1

Prov 22:17	Amen. III. 9–10
Prov 22:18	Amen. III. 11–16
Prov 22:20	Amen. XXVII. 7–10
Prov 22:21	Amen. I. 5–6
Prov 22:22	Amen. IV. 4–5
Prov 22:24	Amen. XI. 13–14
Prov 22:25	Amen. XI. 15–18; XIII. 8–9
Prov 22:28	Amen. VII. 12–13
Prov 22:29	Amen. XXVII. 16–17
Prov 23:1–3	Amen. XXIII. 13–18
Prov 23:4–5	Amen. IX. 14–X. 5
Prov 23:6–7	Amen. XIV. 5–10
Prov 23:8	Amen. XIV. 17–18
Prov 23:9	Amen. XXII. 11–12
Prov 23:10–11	Amen. VII. 12–19; VIII. 9–10

Text and translation: BUDGE, *Facsimiles of Egyptian Hieratic Papyri in the British Museum, Second Series,* 9–18, 41–51, pls. 1–14. ***Translations:*** *AEL* 2:146–63; *ANET* 421–25; *COS* 1.47: 115–22; *LAE* 223–43. ***Bibliography:*** BRUNNER, "Zitate aus Lebenslehren"; J. A. EMERTON, "The Teaching of Amenemope and Proverbs xxii 17–xxiv 22: Further Reflections on a Long-standing Problem," *VT* 51 (2001): 431–465; A. K. HELMBOLD, "The Relationship of Proverbs and Amenemope," in *The Law and the Prophets: Old Testament Studies Prepared in Honor of Oswald Thompson Allis* (ed. J. H. Skilton; Nutley, N.J.: Presbyterian and Reformed, 1974), 348–59; MCKANE, *Proverbs,* 102–117; P. OVERLAND, "Structure in The Wisdom of Amenemope and Proverbs," in *"Go to the Land I Will Show You": Studies in Honor of Dwight W. Young* (ed. J. E. Coleson and V. H. Matthews; Winona Lake, Ind.: Eisenbrauns, 1996), 275–91; D. RÖMHELD, *Wege der Weisheit: Die Lehren Amenemopes und Proverbien 22:17–24:22* (Berlin: de Gruyter, 1989); J. RUFFLE, "The Teaching of Amenemope and Its Connection with the Book of Proverbs," *TynBul* 28 (1977): 29–69; H. C. WASHINGTON, *Wealth and Poverty in the Instruction of Amenemope and the Hebrew Proverbs* (SBLDS 142; Atlanta: Scholars Press, 1994).

Instructions of Ankhsheshonqy (Egyptian Late Period). Although this demotic text purports to be a composition from the Twenty-Second Dynasty (ca. 945–715

B.C.E.), it was actually composed several centuries later, during the second century
B.C.E. According to the text's narrative prologue, Ankhsheshonqy was a priest of Re
who was incarcerated after being unjustly accused in a plot against Pharaoh. This
circumstance explains why our protagonist was forced to fulfill the paternal duty to
educate his son through a written text. Ankhsheshonqy's instructions differ from
those found in earlier exemplars. Whereas the older instructions were generally poetic, polystichic (with "multiple lines"), and joined into topically related groups,
the wisdom of Ankhsheshonqy is cast in monostichic ("one-lined") prose with
maxims that are either randomly distributed or arranged according to form. The
text is also unusual because it is very long (several hundred maxims) and because it
includes not only instructions ("Do not be stingy," 12.18) and statements ("Good
fortune turns away destruction by a great god," 14.17) but also proverbial sayings
("The friend of a fool is a fool; the friend of a wise man is a wise man," 13.6). The
international flavor of Ankhsheshonqy is visible in numerous instances: the combination of narrative with wisdom sayings mimics the earlier Proverbs of Ahiqar; the
monostichic form of Ankhsheshonqy reflects Hellenistic influence; the author's agricultural advice was modeled after Hesiod's Works and Days; and seven of
Ankhsheshonqy's proverbs are "international proverbs" found also in foreign texts
(e.g., "He who was bitten of the bite of a snake is afraid of a coil of rope," 14.14, is
found in both Hebrew midrashim and in Greek proverb collections; see Lichtheim). The influence of these foreign sources and ideologies probably explains why
Ankhsheshonqy lacks traditional expressions of Egyptian moral order (*ma'at*). The
same can be said for the next collection of late instructions.

Text and translation: S. R. K. GLANVILLE, *The Instructions of 'Onchsheshonqy (British Museum Papyrus 10508)* (vol. 2 of *Catalogue of Demotic Papyri in the British Museum;* London: British Museum, 1955). *Translations: AEL* 3:159–84; *LAE* 497–529. *Bibliography:*
LICHTHEIM, *Late Egyptian Wisdom Literature in the International Context;* MCKANE, *Proverbs,* 117–50; P. WALCOT, "Hesiod and the Instructions of 'Onchsheshonqy," *JNES* 21
(1962): 215–19.

Papyrus Insinger (Egyptian Late Period). Papyrus Insinger is a demotic text
even longer than the already lengthy Instructions of Ankhsheshonqy. Although
Insinger dates to the first century C.E., the composition itself is somewhat older,
perhaps as old as the Ptolemaic period. The text was arranged into numbered
"instructions" (i.e., chapters), each accompanied by a topical heading that more
or less described the maxims in the section. A total of twenty-five sections were
originally included, but sections 1–5 and part of 6 are lacking. This division into
chapters is comparable to the thirty chapters in the Instructions of Amenemope.
Foundational for Insinger's maxims is a comparison between the pious wise man
and the impious fool, wherein the wise man is one who understands and manages
himself properly with respect to gluttony, women, sex, friendship, humility,
greed, anxiety, anger, retaliation, moderation, and self-control, among other
things. Some of these themes, such as moderation and self-control, reflect the influence of Hellenistic ideas, as does Insinger's emphasis on "fate." Although in
many respects Insinger is reminiscent of standard retributive theology, each

chapter ends with a confession that wise living does not guarantee success. This is the first overt expression of pessimism in the Egyptian instructions. The Hellenistic flavor of Insinger is comparable to that found in Jewish wisdom from the same period, such as Sirach and especially the Wisdom of Solomon (for a discussion of these texts, see Evans).

Text and translation: F. LEXA, *Papyrus Insinger* (2 vols; Paris: P. Geuthner, 1926). *Translation:* AEL 3:184–217. *Bibliography:* LICHTHEIM, *Late Egyptian Wisdom Literature in the International Context*, 107–232.

Table 2.2

Major Egyptian Instruction Texts

Old Kingdom (2650–2135 B.C.E., Dynasties 3–8)
> (Instruction of Hardjedef)
> (Instruction for Kagemni)
> Instruction of Ptahhotep

First Intermediate Period (2135–2040 B.C.E., Dynasties 9–11)
> Instructions to Merikare

Middle Kingdom (2040–1650 B.C.E., Dynasties 11–14)
> Instruction of Amenemhet
> Instruction of Dua-khety, or Satire on the Trades
> Loyalist Teaching
> (Instruction of a Man for his Son)

New Kingdom (1550–1080 B.C.E., Dynasties 18–20)
> Instruction of Any
> Instructions of Amenemope
> Papyrus Lansing, or the Instruction of Nebmare-nakht
> (Instruction of Amennakhte)

Late and Demotic Periods (After 1080 B.C.E., Dynasties 21–31)
> Instructions of Ankhsheshonqy
> Papyrus Insinger

Dates reflect the presumed period of composition rather than the provenance of the manuscripts. Fragmentary texts are in parentheses. Translations of these fragmentary texts, along with publication data, are found in *LAE.*

2.2.2. Speculative Egyptian Wisdom

The Complaints of Khakheperre-Sonb. This Egyptian priest depicted his homeland in social disarray, as a place where "the land is in calamity, mourning in

25

every place, towns and districts in woe, and everyone alike is wronged." The text was in fact composed, however, during an orderly and prosperous phase of the Egyptian Middle Kingdom. For this reason it is commonly supposed that the author's complaints are hyperbolic political criticisms or perhaps academic exercises that explored the tensions between order and chaos. This topos may have originated during Egypt's troublesome First Intermediate Period, but this is not certain. It is also possible that the text reflects the actual personal sufferings of the priest, which took on larger, more cosmic dimensions in his view than in ours.

Text and translation: A. H. GARDINER, *The Admonitions of an Egyptian Sage* (Leipzig: J. C. Hinrichs, 1909), 95–110. *Translations:* AEL 1:145–49; COS 1.44: 104–6; LAE 211–13; PARKINSON, *The Tale of Sinuhe and Other Ancient Egyptian Poems,* 144–50. *Bibliography:* J.-L. CHAPPAZ, "Un manifeste littéraire du Moyen Empire—les Lamentations de Kha-khéper-ré-seneb," *Bulletin de la Société d'égyptologie de Genève* 2 (1979): 3–12; G. E. KADISH, "British Museum Writing Board 5645: The Complaints of Kha-kheper-Rē'-senebu," JEA 59 (1973): 77–90; B. OCKINGA, "The Burden of Kha'kheperrē'sonbu," JEA 69 (1983): 88–95; R. B. PARKINSON, "*Khakheperreseneb* and Traditional Belles Lettres," in *Studies in Honor of William Kelly Simpson* (2 vols.; ed. P. Der Manuelian; Boston: Museum of Fine Arts, 1996), 2:647–654.

The Admonitions of Ipuwer. Like the author of the Complaints of Khakheperre-Sonb, here a scribe seems to explore the motif of social and political distress. The literary nature of this topos does not necessarily preclude other purposes for the text, however, because the same distress motif was employed in The Prophecy of Neferti to extol the virtues of Pharaoh Amenemhet I (see 7.2). If Ipuwer also ends by describing an anonymous savior king—as some Egyptologists contend—then the Admonitions of Ipuwer may well have provided political propaganda for this unnamed pharaoh, who would save Egypt from its social and political upheavals.

Texts and translations: A. H. GARDINER, *The Admonitions of an Egyptian Sage* (Leipzig: J. C. Hinrichs, 1909); W. HELCK, *Die "Admonitions": Pap. Leiden I 344 recto* (Kleine Ägyptische Texte 11; Wiesbaden: Harrassowitz, 1995). *Translations:* AEL 1:149–63; ANET 441–44; COS 1.42: 93–98; LAE 188–210; PARKINSON, *The Tale of Sinuhe and Other Ancient Egyptian Poems,* 166–99. *Bibliography:* W. BARTA, "Das Gespräch des Ipuwer mit dem Schöpfergott," SAK 1 (1974): 19–33; R. O. FAULKNER, "The Admonitions of an Egyptian Sage," JEA 51 (1965): 53–62; IDEM, "Notes on 'The Admonitions of an Egyptian Sage,'" JEA 50 (1964): 24–36; M. GILULA, "Does God Exist?" in *Studies Presented to Hans Jakob Polotsky* (ed. D. W. Young; East Gloucester, Mass.: Pirtle & Polson, 1981), 390–400; J. VAN SETERS, "A Date for the 'Admonitions' in the Second Intermediate Period," JEA 50 (1964): 13–23; R. J. WILLIAMS, "The Sages of Ancient Egypt in the Light of Recent Scholarship," JAOS 101 (1981): 1–20.

The Harper's Songs. Although Egypt's instructional genres first reflected pessimism during the Hellenistic era (P.Insinger), Egyptians questioned the principles of *ma'at* in much earlier periods in texts known as the Harper's Songs, monumental texts inscribed on the tomb walls or mortuary stelae of the deceased. The genre takes its name from the depictions of harpists that appear alongside the inscriptions. Early songs from the Middle Kingdom provided orthodox reflections

on the blessing of death and the reward of the afterlife, but the genre took a pessimistic turn when the tomb inscription of King Intef (Middle Kingdom) cast
doubt on the afterlife and satirized the traditional practice of tomb building. This
cynicism deeply influenced later Harper's Songs from the New Kingdom, which
either rejected Intef's pessimism as impious or preserved its skepticism in diluted
form. Papyrus copies of Intef show that by the New Kingdom this cynical and
imaginative monumental inscription was fitting snugly into Egypt's scribal tradition, but the text's presence on a New Kingdom tomb demonstrates that it continued in use as an inscriptional genre.

Texts and translations: BUDGE, *Facsimiles of Egyptian Hieratic Papyri in the British Museum,* xiv–xlvi, 23–24; A. HOLWERDA and P. BOESER, *Beschreibung der aegyptischen Samm-
ung des niederländischen Reichsmuseums der Altertümer in Leiden* (14 vols.; Haag: Nijhoff,
1905–1932), 4, pl. 6. *Translations:* AEL 1:194–97; ANET 467; COS 1.30–31: 48–50, 2.13:
64–66; LAE 332–33. *Bibliography:* M. LICHTHEIM, "The Songs of the Harpers," JNES 4
(1945): 178–212.

The Dispute of a Man with His Ba. The skepticism of the Harper's Songs may
have inspired the Dispute of a Man with his Ba (roughly equivalent to "soul"),
another text that voices pessimism about the afterlife. The protagonist longs for
death because it offers relief from life's inherent difficulties, but his *ba* disagrees,
threatening to part ways with him at death. This threat prompts the man's eloquent speeches, which finally convince his *ba* that traditional views of a blessed
afterlife are correct. Nevertheless, this disputation text, like the pessimistic
Harper's Songs, openly challenged the principle of *ma'at* and traditional Egyptian optimism regarding the afterlife. Thus, in Egypt as in Mesopotamia, there
were scribes who reflected upon traditional retributive theologies and found
them wanting, albeit in different ways.

Texts and translations: W. BARTA, *Das Gespräch eines Mannes mit seinem Ba (Papyrus
Berlin 3024)* (Münchner ägyptologische Studien 18; Berlin: Hessling, 1969); R. O. FAULK-
NER, "The Man Who was Tired of Life," JEA 42 (1956): 21–40; H. GOEDICKE, *The Report
about the Dispute of a Man with His Ba* (Baltimore: Johns Hopkins University Press, 1970).
Translations: AEL 1:163–69; ANET 405–7; LAE 178–87; PARKINSON, *The Tale of Sinuhe
and Other Ancient Egyptian Poems,* 151–65. *Bibliography:* E. BRUNNER-TRAUT, "Der
Lebensmüde und sein Ba," ZÄS 94 (1967): 6–15; H. JACOBSOHN, *Das Gespräch eines
Lebensmüden mit seinem Ba* (Zurich: C. G. Jung-Institut Zürich, 1952); V. A. TOBIN, "A Reassessment of the *Lebensmüde,*" BO 48 (1991): 341–63; VAN DER TOORN, "The Ancient
Near Eastern Literary Dialogue as a Vehicle of Critical Reflection"; P. J. WILLIAMS, "Reflections on *Lebensmüde,*" JEA 48 (1962): 49–56.

2.3. West Semitic and Hittite Wisdom

Ugaritic Wisdom. Ugarit's wisdom corpus was composed mainly of traditions
borrowed from Mesopotamia. Among these were copies of the Dialogue of Šube'-
awilum (RS 22.439; bilingual Akkadian and Hittite; see above), a fragmentary
collection of admonitions (RS 15.10; bilingual Akkadian and Hittite), several

fragmentary collections of proverbs (RS 25.130; 23.34+494+363; 25.434; biligual
Sumerian and Akkadian), and a pessimistic but fragmentary text similar to
Ludlul Bēl Nēmeqi (RS 25.460; see above). Native Ugaritic wisdom included
mostly school texts and astronomical, magical, and professional literature, but
nothing in the Ugaritic corpus stands generically close to biblical wisdom. For a
complete survey of the relevant materials, see Mack-Fisher.

Texts and translations: LAMBERT, *Babylonian Wisdom Literature,* 116 (RS 15.10); J. NOU-
GAYROL, *Textes accadiens et hourites des archives est, ouest, et centrales* (vol. 3 of *Le palais
royal d'Ugarit;* ed. C. F. A. Schaeffer; Mission de Ras Shamra 6; Paris: Imprimerie
Nationale, 1955–), 311–24, pl. cvi (RS 15.10); J. NOUGAYROL and E. LAROCHE, eds.,
Ugaritica V (ed. C. F. A. Schaeffer; Ugaritica 5; Paris: Imprimerie Nationale, 1968), 264–73
(RS 25.460), 273–90, 779–84 (RS 22.439), 291–300 (RS 25.130; 23.34+494+363; 25.434).
Bibliography: J. GRAY, "The Book of Job in the Context of Near Eastern Religion," *ZAW* 82
(1970): 251–69; J. KHANIJIAN, "Wisdom," in *Ras Shamra Parallels* (ed. Fisher), 2:371–400;
L. R. MACK-FISHER, "The Didactic Literature of Ugarit," in *The Sage in Israel and the An-
cient Near East* (ed. J. G. Gammie and L. G. Perdue; Winona Lake, Ind.: Eisenbrauns, 1990),
67–80; MÜLLER, "Keilschriftliche Parallelen zum biblischen Hiobbuch: Möglichkeit und
Grenze des Vergleichs," in *Mythos–Kerygma–Wahrheit: Gesammelte Aufsätze zum Alten
Testament in seiner Umwelt und zur Biblischen Theologie,* 136–51; D. E. SMITH, "Wisdom
Genres in RS 22.439," in *Ras Shamra Parallels* (ed. Fisher), 2:215–47.

The Aramaic Proverbs of Ahiqar. Our earliest Aramaic copy of this text was discovered in Upper Egypt on a papyrus from the fifth century B.C.E., but it is likely
that the proverbial collection is somewhat older. The papyrus includes two generic
segments: a story that introduces the reader to Ahiqar and a collection of proverbs.
Although this creates an impression that Ahiqar composed the whole piece himself,
scholars are reasonably sure that the same author did not write the proverbs and
the tale because the Aramaic dialect of the proverbs is older than that of the story.
This suggests that the tale was probably not the work of Ahiqar but was secondarily
attached to the proverb collection, perhaps in an attempt to enhance the text's authority by associating it with a well-known sage of the past. Although some scholars have argued that the proverbs originated in Mesopotamia, the language and
religious outlook of its maxims favor a context in northern Syria, where an Aramean king perhaps sponsored the text's compilation. The probable objective of the
composition was to produce didactic materials for functionaries in the royal court,
a purpose that is reflected in its combination of courtly scribal wisdom and popular folk wisdom. Because the papyrus is fragmentary, the precise number and order
of the original entries is unknown. The sixty preserved sayings are diverse in form
and content, including not only formal proverbs but also instructions, fables, and
numerical sayings. The author sometimes attempted to join together similar sayings on the basis of genre (e.g., animal fables in §§35–36), theme (e.g., self-control
in §§14–16), or formal structure (e.g., §§29–30). Although The Proverbs of Ahiqar
differ substantially from Mesopotamian wisdom, their features are similar to the
Hebrew wisdom of Proverbs in numerous respects. Similarities between the two
traditions include individual sayings as well as form-critical affinities, such as in-

structions on discipline (cf. Ahiqar 81–82; Prov 23:13–14) and numerical sayings (Ahiqar 92–93; Prov 6:16–19). Other similarities include the following: both Ahiqar and Proverbs address their pupil as "my son," personify wisdom as a female, contrast the "righteous" with the wicked, and include animal proverbs. Granted, some of these themes and motifs appear in Mesopotamian and Egyptian wisdom as well, but the unique combination of traits shared by Ahiqar and Proverbs suggests that West Semitic wisdom was a tradition in its own right, influenced by, but not entirely dependent upon, the Mesopotamian and Egyptian traditions to the east and west.

Text and translation: J. M. LINDENBERGER, *The Aramaic Proverbs of Ahiqar* (Baltimore: Johns Hopkins University Press, 1983). *Translations: ANET* 427–30; J. M. LINDENBERGER, "Ahiqar," *OTP* 2:479–507. *Bibliography:* J. C. GREENFIELD, "The Wisdom of Ahiqar," in *Wisdom in Ancient Israel* (ed. Day), 43–52; P. GRELOT, "Les proverbes araméens d'Ahiqar," *RB* 68 (1961): 178–194; MCKANE, *Proverbs,* 156–82; M. WEIGLE, "Compositional Strategies in the Aramaic sayings of Ahikar: Columns 6–8," in *World of the Aramaeans: Studies in Language and Literature in Honour of Paul-Eugène Dion* (ed. P. M. Michèle Daviau, J. W. Wevers, and M. Weigle; 3 vols.; JSOTSup 324–326; Sheffield, England: Sheffield Academic Press, 2001), 3:22–82.

Hittite Instruction and Protocol Manuals. Wisdom genres are poorly attested in our corpus of Hittite literature. Except for a few proverbs scattered about the literature, only one collection of Hittite sayings and wisdom parables has been discovered (see *COS* 1.80–82: 215–17; cf. Beckman). Better attested is a genre known as "instruction texts," but these are quite different from the Egyptian instructions. Hittite kings commonly published instruction manuals for those serving in various institutions of the empire. The manuals prescribed the behaviors and practices that the central government deemed important in each context. Because these instructions were not pedagogical in the academic sense, they are perhaps generically closer to civil and ceremonial laws (see chs. 5 and 13) than to the wisdom corpus per se. Among the most important Hittite instructions are those for princes and lords (von Schuler [= *CTH* 255]), for the royal guard (Güterbock/van den Hout; *COS* 1.85 [= *CTH* 262]), for border garrisons (Goetze; von Schuler; *COS* 1.84 [= *CTH* 261]), for palace personnel (*KUB* 13.3; *ANET* 207 [= *CTH* 265]), and for priests/temple officials (*COS* 1.83 [= *CTH* 264]). For more on the instructions for priests and temple officials, see 5.7. A complete list of the sixteen other instructional texts, plus fragments, is found in *CTH* 251–67.

Texts and translations: J. FRIEDRICH, "Reinheitsvorschriften für den hethitischen König," *MVOG* 4 (1928): 46–58; A. GOETZE, "The Beginning of the Hittite Instructions for the Commander of the Border Guards," *JCS* 14 (1960): 69–73; H. G. GÜTERBOCK and T. P. J. VAN DEN HOUT, *The Hittite Instruction for the Royal Bodyguard* (AS 24; Chicago: Oriental Institute of the University of Chicago, 1991); *KUB* 13.3 [= *CTH* 265]; E. VON SCHULER, *Hethitische Dienstanweisungen für höhere Hof-und Staatsbeamte* (AfOB 10; Graz: Im Selbstverlage des Harausgebers, 1957). *Translations: COS* 1.83–85: 217–30; *ANET* 207–11. *Bibliography:* R. H. BEAL, *The Organization of the Hittite Military* (TH 20; Heidelberg: Carl Winter, 1992); G. M. BECKMAN, "Proverbs and Proverbial Allusions in Hittite," *JNES*

45 (1985): 19–30; A. GOETZE, review of E. von Schuler, *Hethitische Dienstanweisungen für höhere Hof-und Staatsbeamte, JCS* 13 (1959): 65–70; H. A. HOFFNER, "The *Arzana* House," in *Anatolian Studies Presented to Hans Gustav Güterbock on the Occasion of his 65th Birthday* (ed. K. Bittel et al.; Istanbul: Nederlands Historisch-Archaeologisch Institut in het Nabije Oosten, 1974), 113–22.

Concluding Observations

1. The Context and Scope of Ancient Wisdom. Generally speaking, the ancients recognized that a distinct class of scribal scholars lived in their midst, "wise" men—and sometimes women—who served in the royal courts, in the temples, and, on occasion, in private contexts. These scholars composed texts that are quite comparable to biblical wisdom, but they also produced a large corpus of other genres (lists, riddles, magical lore, omen literature, etc.) that were distinctly different from Hebrew and Judaic wisdom. The absence of these genres from ancient Israelite literature is significant, but it cannot be taken as sure evidence that Israelite scribes were unfamiliar with them; it may only indicate that, for some reason, none of these genres found a place in the Hebrew canon. On a related matter, it cannot be emphasized enough that Near Eastern wisdom was a broader literary and cultural phenomenon than is implied by the notion of "scribal wisdom." Many of the proverbs and instructions in the wisdom corpus originated in the oral lore of common people, and more important, the ancients associated wisdom not only with the scribal arts but also with other kinds of skill and craft. It is the nature of textual evidence that it provides a window into the world of scribal wisdom rather than into the nonscribal wisdom lore of antiquity (a notable exception would be the Sumerian Farmer's Almanac).

2. Wisdom and Intellectual Freedom. Although ancient scholarship generally subsisted within the context of the palace or temple, there is some evidence that scribal wisdom occasionally moved about with more freedom than this might imply. Such freedom is reflected in the pessimistic appraisals of standard retributive theology and in the subtle instances where scribes satirically turned their pens against the palace and establishment (e.g., the Sumerian proverbs). On the other hand, in most cases the ancient scholar worked closely with the royal courts, so it would be too strong to assert that intellectual freedom was a nonnegotiable feature of ancient wisdom, as some scholars have asserted.

3. The International Flavor of Wisdom. One of the clearest features in our ancient wisdom corpus is its international scope. Some proverbs, instructions, and dialogues were read and copied throughout the ancient world (e.g., the Dialogue of Šube'awilum), and there are numerous instances in which one author seems to have been familiar with the work of another. The West Semitic Proverbs of Ahiqar are a good example of the confluence between traditions, for they not only reflect influences from Egypt and Mesopotamia but also seem to have inspired the work of a later Egyptian author in the Instructions of Ankhsheshonqy. Amenemope's influence on Prov 22–24 provides another example of this vibrant intertextuality.

4. **Persistence of the Wisdom Tradition.** The textual evidence confirms that wisdom texts were often studied and copied for rather long periods, in several cases for more than a millennium (e.g., the Instructions of Shuruppak, the Instructions of Amenemope, and the Dialogue of Šube'awilum). Long-lived traditions of this sort made possible a rich exchange of wisdom lore in the ancient Near East and provide a ready explanation for the similar features that appear in the texts that stem from diverse cultural and historical contexts.

5. **Ancient Wisdom and Authorship.** The wisdom texts provide us with a welcome glimpse into ancient concepts of authorship. Although many Near Eastern texts were anonymous works, wisdom texts provide a notable exception because they were often attributed to famous figures of the past, usually kings or sages. In some cases these authorial attributions may have been accurate (e.g., the Instructions of Amenemope), but in many instances we can surmise that they were pseudonyms, either because the authorial attributions are prima facie inventions (the Instructions of Shuruppak) or because the texts were written after their ostensible authors would have lived (see the Egyptian instructions). Jewish apocryphal wisdom provides examples of both genuine and pseudonymous wisdom, since scholars are willing to accept Ben Sira's (Sirach's) role in the book that bears his name while it is equally clear that the Wisdom of Solomon was not the work of the Israelite king (on these two works, see Evans). Where pseudonyms were used in ancient wisdom, it is often unclear whether these fictions were inherited by the text's author, proffered by the text's author, or invented by later scribes. Nevertheless, pseudonymity makes it quite plain that the scholars who wrote and edited ancient wisdom were often more concerned with disseminating their work than with making a name for themselves. At any rate, this comparative evidence squares nicely with the modern view that Qoheleth, Song of Songs, the Wisdom of Solomon and parts of Proverbs were pseudonymously attributed to Solomon.

6. **The Editorial Shaping of Wisdom.** Careful readings of ancient wisdom reveal the compositional techniques employed by wisdom authors as well as the editorial rationales followed by later editors of the texts. For the sake of brevity, let us focus our attention mainly on the instructional and proverbial genres. Regarding the composition of these texts, the authors often framed their wisdom collections with narratives or hortatory introductions

in order to infuse the text with authority or to inspire the reader's interest. Although the collections themselves were sometimes pulled together in a haphazard way, in many cases there is evidence of deliberate arrangement based on theme, form, or some other criterion. Later editors sometimes re-shaped the material in an organizational way (e.g., the rubrics added to late copies of the Instructions of Merikare), but in some cases editors were more heavy-handed. Such was in the case in the Instructions of Shuruppak, when Old Babylonian scribes made Shuruppak into the father of the flood hero and expanded the thematic content covered by the original text.

7. The Functions of Wisdom Literature. The texts in our wisdom corpus served a variety of functional purposes, including instruction, scribal training, en-tertainment, philosophical reflection, and propaganda. Let us consider each in turn.

a. Instruction. Much of our wisdom corpus was composed to perpetuate in-structions for successful living within the closely related royal, reli-gious, and scribal contexts of antiquity. In the case of Egypt, a certain democratization is visible in its instructional genre as the focus of the texts gradually shifted from Old Kingdom royalty to the middle classes of the New Kingdom, but even here we must assume that the texts influenced only a small portion of the population in any direct way, mainly those of means and privileged position. Foundational for all of these Near Eastern instructional texts was some concept of re-tributive theology in which wise living bred life's success, but as we have seen and will see, the retributive systems differed somewhat from culture to culture (see below).

b. Scribal Training and Entertainment. Some instructional texts were em-ployed in scribal curriculums either to inspire perseverance during the course of study (e.g., Satire on the Trades), or to improve rhetori-cal and analytical skills (e.g., contest literature, dialogues, riddles), or to teach foreign languages (e.g., Sumerian proverbs in the Old Baby-lonian schools). These scribal exemplars sometimes displayed a good deal of functional elasticity. Before the Sumerian proverbs and con-test literature were adopted as instruments for linguistic instruction, the former perpetuated Sumerian wisdom and the latter entertained kings and dignitaries in the royal courts.

c. Philosophical Reflection. While the sages composed instructional texts that were steeped in conventional wisdom, some of the ancient schol-ars—it is hard to know how many—also contemplated the limita-tions of standard wisdom. The result was a corpus of speculative or pessimistic texts that questioned the validity of retributive orthodoxy and even the value of life itself. It appears that these works were sometimes immensely popular among the scribes (e.g., the Dialogue of Šube'awilum and the Egyptian Harper's Songs); this attests to the perennial existential questions that the texts addressed. We should not be surprised, in light of this comparative evidence, to find that two pessimistic wisdom books are preserved in our Hebrew canon (Job and Qoheleth).

  d. Political and Religious Propaganda. Several of the wisdom texts in our corpus were as much works of propaganda as of instruction. The Instructions of Merikare provided propaganda for his political policies, Advice to a Prince was composed to protect the rights of scribes and citizens in Sippar, Nippur, and Babylon, and *Ludlul Bēl Nēmeqi* provided religious propaganda for the cult of Marduk (or for incantation priests employing Marduk's power). In such cases, our generic assessments do not require that we choose between "wisdom" and "propaganda"; in some situations, more than one generic label applies.

8. Retributive Theology and Speculative Wisdom. Retributive theology provided the ideological framework for optimistic wisdom in all of its permutations, from the Mesopotamian concept of ME to the Egyptian notions of *ma'at.* Generic expressions of this theology differed, however, for in Mesopotamia the proverbial genres dominated whereas in Egypt instructional discourses were the rule. Differences in the respective belief systems also produced different kinds of pessimism in Mesopotamia and Egypt. Because the afterlife was not central to Mesopotamian theology, its pessimism focused on life's injustices and on the futility implied by death itself. In Egypt things were quite different because the afterlife was fundamental to its concept of *ma'at.* Consequently, Egyptian pessimism appears prominently in tomb inscriptions that questioned long-standing dogmas of the hereafter (i.e., the Harper's Songs). Egyptian sages also composed pessimistic dialogues similar to those in Mesopotamia, but in Mesopotamia the dialogue was the primary genre of skepticism. The appearance of dialogues in both cultures is probably not a result of diffusion because the dialogues appeared rather early in both Egypt and Mesopotamia. There was, after all, no genre so natural for pessimistic reflection as a debate between the pessimistic and optimistic viewpoints.

9. Ancient Wisdom and the Hebrew Wisdom Genres. The three major wisdom sources of the Hebrew Bible—Proverbs, Job, and Qoheleth—each find good comparative exemplars in the Near Eastern corpus. Scholars have long recognized that Proverbs contains not only conventional proverbs, such as appear in Mesopotamian wisdom and Ahiqar, but also longer poetic compositions that resemble—some would say mimic—Egyptian instructions. Job is thematically and formally similar to the Mesopotamian dialogues about righteous suffering, although Israel's monotheism made the problem of human suffering more poignant. The active presence of the deity in Job also distinguishes the book from its Near Eastern counterparts. As for Qoheleth, its reflections on life's brevity and futility parallel closely prominent themes in Mesopotamian pessimism and also in some Egyptian pessimism. The framing techniques employed in Job and Qoheleth, which place the body of their content within a narrative (so Job) or discourse framework (so Qoheleth), also imitate Near Eastern literary patterns. Wisdom's international character undoubtedly accounts for many of these generic similarities.

General Bibliography

R. G. ALBERTSON, "Job and Ancient Near Eastern Wisdom Literature," in *More Essays on the Comparative Method* (ed. W. W. Hallo, J. C. Moyer, and L. Perdue; Scripture in Context 2; Winona Lake, Ind.: Eisenbrauns, 1983), 213–30; J. ASSMANN, *Ma'at: Gerechtigkeit und Unsterblichkeit im alten Ägypten* (Munich: Beck, 1990); S. D. BOLLE, *Wisdom in Akkadian Literature: Expression, Instruction, Dialogue* (Leiden: Ex Oriente Lux, 1992); H. BRUNNER, "Zitate aus Lebenslehren," *Studien zu altägyptischen Lebenslehren* (ed. E. Hornung and O. Keel; OBO 28; Freiburg, Switz.: Universitätsverlag, 1979), 105–71; G. E. BRYCE, *A Legacy of Wisdom: The Egyptian Contribution to the Wisdom of Israel* (Lewisburg, Pa.: Bucknell University Press, 1979); G. BUCCELLATI, "Wisdom and Not: The Case of Mesopotamia," *JAOS* 101 (1981): 35–47; E. A. W. BUDGE, *Facsimiles of Egyptian Hieratic Papyri in the British Museum* (London: British Museum, 1910); IDEM, *Facsimiles of Egyptian Hieratic Papyri in the British Museum, Second Series* (London: British Museum, 1923); J. DAY, ed., *Wisdom in Ancient Israel: Essays in Honour of J. A. Emerton* (Cambridge: Cambridge University Press, 1995); C. A. EVANS, *Ancient Texts for New Testament Studies* ([rev. ed. of *A Guide to Nonbiblical Texts for New Testament Interpretation;* Peabody, Mass.: Hendrickson Publishers, 1992] Peabody, Mass.: Hendrickson Publishers, forthcoming); I. L. FINKEL, "Adad-apla-iddina, Esagil-kīn-apli, and the Series SA.GIG," in *A Scientific Humanist: Studies in Memory of Abraham Sachs* (ed. E. Leichty, M. deJ. Ellis, and P. Gerardi; OPSNKF 9; Philadelphia: University Museum, 1988), 143–59; L. R. FISHER, *Ras Shamra Parallels: The Texts from Ugarit and the Hebrew Bible* (3 vols.; AnOr 50; Rome: Pontifical Biblical Institute, 1975–1981); M. FOX, "Two Decades of Research in Egyptian Wisdom Literature," *ZÄS* 107 (1980): 120–35; J. G. GAMMIE and L. G. PERDUE, *The Sage in Israel and the Ancient Near East* (Winona Lake, Ind.: Eisenbrauns, 1990); B. GEMSER, "The Instructions of 'Onchsheshonqy and Biblical Wisdom Literature," in *Congress Volume: Oxford, 1959* (VTSup 7; Leiden: Brill, 1960), 102–28; W. HELCK, *Die Lehre für König Merikare* (Wiesbaden: Harrassowitz, 1977); E. HORNUNG and O. KEEL, eds., *Studien zu altägyptischen Lebenslehren* (OBO 28; Freiburg, Switz.: Universitätsverlag, 1979); K. A. KITCHEN, "Basic Literary

Forms and Formulations of Ancient Instructional Writings in Egypt and Western Asia," in *Studien zu altägyptischen Lebenslehren* (ed. E. Hornung and O. Keel; OBO 28; Freiburg Switz.: Universitätsverlag, 1979), 235–52; IDEM, "Proverbs and Wisdom Books of the Ancient Near East: The Factual History of a Literary Form," *TynBul* 28 (1977): 69–114; IDEM, "Studies in Egyptian Wisdom Literature, I: The Instruction by a Man for His Son," *OrAnt* 8 (1969): 189–208; IDEM, "Studies in Egyptian Wisdom Literature, II: Counsels of Discretion (O. Michaelides 16)," *OrAnt* 9 (1970): 203–10; S. N. KRAMER, "Sumerian Wisdom Literature: A Preliminary Survey," *BASOR* 122 (1951): 29–31; W. G. LAMBERT, *Babylonian Wisdom Literature* (Oxford: Oxford University Press, 1960); IDEM, "Enmeduranki and Related Matters," *JCS* 21 (1967): 126–138; M. LICHTHEIM, "Didactic Literature," in *Ancient Egyptian Literature: History and Forms* (ed. A. Loprieno; PA 10; New York: Brill, 1996), 243–62; IDEM, *Late Egyptian Wisdom Literature in the International Context: A Study of Demotic Instructions* (OBO 52; Göttingen: Vandenhoeck & Ruprecht, 1983); IDEM, *Maat in Egyptian Autobiographies and Related Studies* (Freiburg, Switz.: Universitätsverlag, 1992); G. L. MATTINGLY, "The Pious Sufferer: Mesopotamia's Traditional Theodicy and Job's Counselors," in *The Bible in the Light of Cuneiform Literature* (ed. W. W. Hallo, B. W. Jones, and G. L. Mattingly; Scripture in Context 3; Lewiston, N.Y.: Mellen, 1990), 305–48; W. McKANE, "International Wisdom," in *Proverbs*, 51–208; IDEM, *Proverbs: A New Approach* (Philadelphia: Westminster, 1970); H.-P. MÜLLER, *Mythos-Kerygma-Wahrheit: Gesammelte Aufsätze zum Alten Testament in seiner Umwelt und zur Biblischen Theologie* (BZAW 200; Berlin: de Gruyter, 1991); J. P. J. OLIVIER, "Schools and Wisdom Literature," *JNSL* 4 (1975): 49–60; R. B. PARKINSON, *The Tale of Sinuhe and Other Ancient Egyptian Poems: 1940–1640 BC* (Oxford: Clarendon, 1997); L. G. PERDUE, B. B. SCOTT, and W. J. WISEMAN, *In Search of Wisdom: Essays in Memory of John G. Gammie* (Louisville: Westminster John Knox, 1990); *Les sagesses du Proche-Orient ancien* (Paris: Presses Universitaires de France, 1963); N. SHUPAK, *Where Can Wisdom Be Found? The Sages Language in the Bible and in Ancient Egyptian Literature* (Göttingen: Vandenhoeck & Ruprecht, 1993); K. VAN DER TOORN, "The Ancient Near Eastern Literary Dialogue as a Vehicle of Critical Reflection," in *Dispute Poems and Dialogues in the Ancient and Mediaeval Near East* (ed. G. J. Reinink and H. L. J. Vanstiphout; OLA 42; Leuven: Peeters, 1991), 59–75; J. J. A. VAN DIJK, *La sagesse suméro-accadienne* (Leiden: Brill, 1953); B. K. WALTKE, "The Book of Proverbs and Ancient Wisdom Literature," *BSac* 136 (1979): 221–38; M. WEINFELD, "Job and Its Mesopotamian Parallels—a Typological Analysis," in *Text and Context: Old Testament and Semitic Studies for F. C. Fensham* (ed. W. Claassen; JSOTSup 48; Sheffield, England: JSOT Press, 1988), 217–26; R. J. WILLIAMS, "The Functions of the Sage in the Egyptian Royal Court," in *The Sage in Israel and the Ancient Near East* (ed. J. G. Gammie and L. G. Perdue; Winona Lake, Ind.: Eisenbrauns, 1990), 95–98; IDEM, "The Sages of Ancient Egypt in the Light of Recent Scholarship," *JAOS* 101 (1981): 1–20; IDEM, "Theodicy in the Ancient Near East," *CJT* 2 (1956): 14–26; E. WÜRTHWEIN, "Egyptian Wisdom and the Old Testament," in *Studies in Ancient Israelite Wisdom* (ed. J. L. Crenshaw; New York: KTAV, 1976), 113–33.

CHAPTER THREE

Hymns, Prayers, and Laments

Introduction

The religious dimensions of life in the ancient Near East are no more visible than in the literary forms through which the ancients spoke to their gods. Three closely related genres fall within the purview of this discussion: hymns, prayers, and laments. The importance of these genres is illustrated by their sheer volume; the relevant Near Eastern evidence includes thousands of texts from diverse periods and contexts, including praise hymns, songs for dying gods, laments over destroyed temples and cities, prayers for healing or protection, and a number of other text types. Religious affections—and religious frustrations—abound in these texts. In most cases, the exemplars were musical compositions, recited by priests and singers to the accompaniment of instruments such as the harp, drum, and tambourine. Particularly interesting are the earliest attempts to write musical scores, which are unfortunately little understood by modern scholars (see Kilmer 1974). At any rate, it is clear that these texts themselves provide a one-dimensional window into what was a mulidimensional aesthetic experience of color, music, dancing, wailing, and ritual. Although there is no way to compensate entirely for the historical and cultural distance that separates us from these ancient rites, modern scholars have been surprisingly successful in their efforts to reconstruct the musical world of antiquity. The reader can explore their successes through the musicology bibliography at the end of this chapter.

Because of the close theological relationship between god and king in antiquity, the ancients addressed hymns and prayers not only to the gods but also to deceased and even living kings. In the Sumerian period, and especially in Egypt, these kings were actually viewed as divine, but even in periods where this was not so, the divine election of the king was enough to make him an object of veneration. The prominence of kings in these texts is not surprising given that most of the texts were state-sponsored compositions, destined for use in the royal courts and in the state-supported temple cults. Private individuals are thus poorly represented in our corpus of ancient hymns, prayers, and laments.

The genres covered in this chapter cannot be fully appreciated apart from the closely related discussions of ritual and cult in chapter 5. This illustrates yet again that our generic categories are artificial and heuristic taxonomies whose boundaries must be crossed again and again if we hope to appreciate ancient literature in all of its variety.

3.1. Mesopotamian Hymns, Prayers, and Laments

Mesopotamia's hymn, prayer, and lament traditions hark back to ancient times and hence were composed mostly in the venerable Sumerian language. Some of these texts were written in the standard dialect of Sumerian, while others—especially the laments—were composed in *Emesel* (literally, "thin"), apparently a "feminine" dialect used in texts that were sung by women or by male liturgical priests called the GALA (Akkadian, *kalû*). The GALA were probably castrates. According to one myth, the wise god Enki created them in order to soothe the troubled goddess Inanna (see Kramer 1981). The remaining corps of professional cult musicians were known by the terms NAR (Akkadian, *nâru*) and, less often, *zammāru* (Akkadian for "singer").

Our modern attempts to classify the Mesopotamian genres covered in this chapter are eased by the ancient tendency to place generic labels in the superscripts or subscripts of the texts. The labels sometimes corresponded to musical instrumentation used with the piece, such as the BALAG (harp song), TIGI (bass drum song), and ERŠEMMA (tambourine laments), while others related to the format or purpose of the text, such as the BALBALE (antiphonal recitation?), ERŠAHUNGA (lament for appeasing the heart) and ŠUILLA (incantation prayers offered with uplifted hands). Modern scholars are not always sure what to make of these terms, which is not suprising given that the ancients sometimes used the labels rather loosely and imprecisely.

Our earliest Mesopotamian lyric compositions were written in Sumerian. Some of these genres disappeared after the Old Babylonian period (when the texts were used to teach Sumerian), and others continued in use until the end of the first millennium B.C.E. The advent of Akkadian during the second millennium introduced not only bilingual Sumerian and Akkadian versions of some songs but also new Akkadian compositions and genres. Our Akkadian copies come mainly from the Neo-Assyrian period and later, but many of these represent or resemble older traditions.

3.1.1. Sumerian and Akkadian Hymns from Mesopotamia

Sumerian Hymns to Gods, Goddesses, and Their Temples. The Sumerian hymn tradition included texts with a divine focus and texts directed toward the king. Although this entry concerns hymns of the first type, the divine hymns often extolled the king as well, primarily because of his important role as patron of the temples and cults. Sumerian hymns flattered the deity with long lists of epithets and lavished praise on their sacred cities and temples. The hymns were composed for recitation at the induction of the deity's cult statue and during major festivals and processions of the statue (Hallo) whereas the hymns for temples were probably used during the refurbishing of temples (Falkenstein and von Soden). In matters of authorship, several exemplars are interesting. The Kesh Temple Hymn (third millenium B.C.E.) purports to have been dictated by the god Enlil and written down by the scribal goddess Nidaba. Also noteworthy are the hymnic compositions of Enḫeduanna, daughter of Sargon of Akkad (ca. 2300 B.C.E.) and priestess at the temple of Nanna in Ur (and also, it would seem, at the temple of Inanna in Uruk). So far as we know, she was the first female theologian and poet in the ancient world. In addition to her own composition, the great hymn for Inanna, she was also responsible for compiling a complete edition of the temple hymns from Sumer and Akkad (see Sjöberg and Bergmann).

When Enḫeduanna collected the temple hymns—forty-two texts in all—she shaped each composition so as to create a standard form, ending each hymn with a rubric akin to "the house of DN in GN" (e.g., "[hymn of] the house of Enki in Eridu"). In some cases the temple hymns in this collection were placed in groups of related songs (e.g., hymns 2–6, 8–9, 20–23), but it is not clear whether these smaller collections were inherited by Enḫeduanna or were in fact products of her editorial work. The collection as a whole shows no signs of a coherent overall structure, apart from the fact that it is introduced by a hymn for the wise god Enki and concluded by a temple hymn that omitted the musical refrain found in all others. In certain respects, Enḫeduanna's collection of temple hymns is comparable to the Hebrew Psalter not only because the Psalter is a hymn collection but also because it contains psalms that praise the temple site in Zion/Jerusalem (see Pss 48, 87, 122, and 137).

Selected texts and translations (Temple Hymns): R. D. BIGGS, "An Archaic Sumerian version of the Kesh Temple Hymn from Tell Abu Salabikh," *ZA* 61 (1971): 193–207; G. B. GRAGG, "The Keš Temple Hymn," in *The Collection of the Sumerian Temple Hymns* (ed. Å. W. Sjöberg, E. Bergmann, and G. B. Gragg; TCS 3; New York: J. J. Augustin, 1969), 155–88; S. N. KRAMER, "Hymn to the Ekur," *RSO* 32 (1957): 95–102; Å. W. SJÖBERG and E. BERGMANN, "The Collection of the Sumerian Temple Hymns," in *The Collection of the Sumerian Temple Hymns* (ed. Å. W. Sjöberg, E. Bergmann, and G. B. Gragg; TCS 3; New York: J. J. Augustin, 1969), 3–154. *Selected translations: ANET* 582–83; *COS* 1.162: 526–31; 1.163: 531–32; *SAHG* #29–32. *Bibliography:* M. E. COHEN, "The Incantation-Hymn: Incantation or Hymn?" *JAOS* 95 (1975): 592–611; HALLO, "The Cultic Setting of Sumerian Poetry"; J. G. WESTENHOLZ, "Enḫeduanna, En-Priestess, Hen of Nanna, Spouse of Nanna."

Selected texts and translations (Hymns for Gods and Goddesses): A. FALKENSTEIN, *Sumerische Götterlieder* (Heidelberg: Carl Winter Universitäts Verlag, 1959), 5–79; W. W. HALLO and J. J. A. VAN DIJK, *The Exaltation of Inanna* (New Haven: Yale University Press, 1968); W. HEIMPEL, "The Nanshe Hymn," *JCS* 33 (1981): 65–139; W. H. P. RÖMER, "Eine sumerische Hymne mit Selbstlob Innanas," *Or* 38 (1969): 97–114; Å. W. SJÖBERG, "In-nin shà-gur4-ra: A Hymn to the Goddess Inanna by the En-Priestess Enheduanna," *ZA* 65 (1975): 161–253; J. G. WESTENHOLZ, "Enḫeduanna, En-Priestess, Hen of Nanna, Spouse of Nanna." *Selected translations:* ANET 573–82; *COS* 1.160: 518–22, 1.162–3: 526–32; B. DE SHONG MEADOR, *Inanna, Lady of Largest Heart: Poems of the High Priestess Enheduanna* (Austin: University of Texas, 2000); JACOBSEN, *The Harps That Once,* 101–42; *SAHG* #1–15. *Bibliography:* See bibliographic entries under temple hymns (above).

Sumerian Royal Hymns. Scribes from early Mesopotamia composed two closely related types of praise hymns for their kings: hymns to honor the king and prayer hymns in which the king praised the gods and goddesses while appealing for their favor. A primary theme in both text types was the king's divine election to his office, but the two genres were used in different contexts. The prayer hymns contain liturgical rubrics and so were probably used in the cult whereas the royal praise hymns bear no liturgical marks and hence were used in ceremonies of the royal court. A good example of the praise hymn is Šulgi G, in which a poet or theologian from Nippur described Šulgi's miraculous conception and birth by an EN priestess of Ekur (see Klein 1987). It is likely that this hymn was composed for the king's coronation (Klein 1991). Although most of the royal hymns were canonical compositions, a few were monumental inscriptions (e.g., Gudea's temple building hymns). Exemplars come from as early as Gudea and include texts from Ur III, the Isin/Larsa period and the First Dynasty of Babylon. Numerous texts have been unearthed, but many of these are fragmentary. Biblical scholars have noted that there are some close parallels between the Sumerian royal hymns and the royal hymns in the Hebrew Psalter (see Weinfeld). The Psalter contains hymns from the king to God (Ps 21) as well as hymns addressed to the king himself (Ps 72).

Selected texts and translations: B. ALSTER and C. B. F. WALKER, "Some Literary Texts in the British Museum," in *DUMU-E²-DUB-BA-A: Studies in Honor of Åke W. Sjöberg* (ed. H. Behrens, D. T. Loding, and M. Roth; OPSNKF 11; Philadelphia: University Museum, 1989), 1–19; G. R. CASTELLINO, *Two Šulgi Hymns (BC)* (Studi semitici 42; Rome: Istituto di Studi del Vicino Oriente, Università, 1972); J. VAN DIJK, "L'hymne à Marduk avec intercesson pour le roi Abi'eshuh," *MIOF* 12 (1966–1967): 57–74; E. FLÜCKIGER-HAWKER, *Urnamma of Ur in Sumerian Literary Tradition* (OBO 166; Göttingen: Vandenhoeck & Ruprecht, 1999), 93–182; C. J. GADD, "Rim-Sin Approaches the Grand Entrance," *Iraq* 22 (1960): 157–165; J. KLEIN, "The Birth of a Crownprince in the Temple: A Neo-Sumerian Literary Topos," in *La femme dans le Proche-Orient antique: Compte rendu de la XXXIIIe Rencontre assyriologique internationale* (ed. J.-M. Durand; Paris: Éditions Recherche sur les Civilisations, 1987), 97–106; IDEM, "Building and Dedication Hymns in Sumerian Literature," *ActSum* 11 (1989): 27–67; IDEM, "The Coronation and Consecration of Shulgi in the Ekur (Shulgi G)," in *Ah, Assyria* (ed. Cogan and Eph'al), 292–313; IDEM, *The Royal Hymns of Shulgi, King of Ur: Man's Quest for Immortal Fame* (Philadelphia: American Philosophical Society, 1981); IDEM, *Three Šulgi Hymns: Sumerian Royal Hymns Glorifying King Šulgi of Ur* (Ramat Gan, Israel: Bar-Ilan University Press, 1981); D. REISMAN, "A 'Royal' Hymn of Išbi-erra to the Goddess Nisaba," in *Kramer Anniversary Volume: Cuneiform Studies in Honor of Samuel Noah Kramer* (ed. B. L. Eichler; AOAT 25; Kevelaer, Germany: Butzon & Bercker, 1976), 357–65; W. H. P. RÖMER, *Sumerische 'Königshymnen' der Isin-Zeit* (Leiden: Brill, 1965); Å. W. SJÖBERG, "A Blessing of King Urninurta," in *Essays on the Ancient Near East in Memory of Jacob Joel Finkelstein* (ed. M. deJ. Ellis; Hamden, Conn.: Archon Books, 1977), 189–195; IDEM, "Hymns to Meslamtaea, Lugalgirra, and Nanna-Suen in Honour of

King Ibbisuen (Ibbsîn) of Ur," *Orientalia suecana* 19–20 (1970–1971): 19–20, 140–178; IDEM, "Prayers for King Hammurabi of Babylon," in *Ex orbe religionum: Studia Geo Widengren . . . oblata* (ed. J. Bergman, K. Drynjeff, and H. Ringgren; 2 vols.; Brill: Leiden 1972), 2:58–72; IDEM, "Two Prayers for King Samsuiluna of Babylon," *JAOS* 93 (1973): 544–547; H. STEIBLE, *Rimsîn, mein König: Drei kultische Texte aus Ur mit der Schluss-doxologie* ᵈri-im-ᵈsîn *lugal-mu* (Freiburger altorientalische Studien 1; Wiesbaden: Franz Steiner, 1975); H. L. J. VANSTIPHOUT, "Lipit-Eštar's Praise in the Edubba," *JCS* 30 (1978): 33–53; E. J. WILSON, *The Cylinders of Gudea: Transliteration, Translation, and Index* (AOAT 244; Neukirchen-Vluyn: Neukirchener Verlag, 1996). *Selected translations:* ANET 583–86; COS 1.172: 552–553; JACOBSEN, *The Harps That Once,* 386–444 (cylinders of Gudea); SAHG #16–28. **Bibliography:** J. KLEIN, "Shulgi of Ur: King of a Neo-Sumerian Empire," *CANE* 2:843–57; IDEM, "Šulgi and Išmedagan: Originality and Dependence in Sumerian Royal Hymnology," in *Bar-Ilan Studies in Assyriology Dedicated to Pinḥas Artzi* (ed. J. Klein and A. Skaist; Ramat Gan, Israel: Bar-Ilan University Press, 1990), 65–136; T. J. H. KRISPIJN, "Beiträge zur altorientalischen Musikforschung, 1: Šulgi und Musik," *Akkadica* 70 (1990): 1–27; P. MICHALOWSKI, "Divine Heroes and Historical Representation: From Gilgamesh to Shulgi," *Bulletin of the Canadian Society for Mesopotamian Studies* 16 (1988): 19–23; M. WEINFELD, "Sumerian Literature and the Book of Psalms," *Beth Miqra* 19 (1974): 8–24, 136–60 (Hebrew).

Akkadian Hymns to Gods, Goddesses, and Their Temples. Like the earlier Sumerian hymns, these were performed in the temple cult as well as during festivals and processions of the divine statue. Our corpus of Akkadian hymns includes numerous Assyrian and Babylonian texts, and if we may judge from Mesopotamian incipit lists, many more were extant in antiquity. Certain Akkadian hymns have attracted a good deal of scholarly attention, especially the great hymns to Marduk and Šamaš. Exemplars of the Marduk hymn date to the mid–first millennium, but the existence of Akkadian-Sumerian (Emesal) bilingual copies suggests that it is somewhat older. The hymn's frequent refrain, "Be appeased," suggests that the song's purpose was to calm the deity after his return from the lengthy New Year festival (see 5.5). As for the Šamaš hymn, this first-millennium text praised Šamaš while espousing values of justice and equity through proverbial maxims. For this reason the Šamaš hymn—like a fragmentary song for Ninurta—has been dubbed a "precept hymn" and hence is comparable to the Hebrew wisdom psalms (e.g., Pss 1, 37, 49, 73, 112, 127, 128, 133). Unevenness in the Šamaš and Queen of Nippur hymns suggests that both were products of somewhat complex literary processes. This evidence fits Lambert's suggestion that some of the Mesopotamian hymns, such as the great Šamaš hymn, are better viewed as literature than as straightforward liturgical texts (Lambert 1960). The discovery of ancient commenataries on the Mesopotamian hymns reinforces the validity of this suggestion (Lambert 1999).

Like the Mesopotamian hymn corpus, the Hebrew Psalter includes many hymns to the Israelite deity as well as several psalms that praise his temple in Zion/Jerusalem, such as Pss 48, 87, 122, and 137.

Selected texts and translations: LAMBERT, *Babylonian Wisdom Literature* (Oxford: Oxford University Press, 1960), 118–20 (Precept Hymn to Ninurta), 121–38 (Precept Hymn to

Šamaš); IDEM, "The Hymn to the Queen of Nippur," in *Zikir Šumim: Assyriological Studies Presented to F. R. Kraus* (ed. G. Van Driel; Leiden: Brill, 1982), 173–218 (Hymn to the Queen of Nippur [i.e., Ištar]); W. VON SODEN, "Altbabylonische Dialektdichtungen," *ZA* 44 (1930): 30–44 (OB Hymn to Nanna); F. THUREAU-DANGUIN, "Un hymne à Ištar," *RA* 22 (1925): 169–77 (OB Hymn to Ištar); F. H. WEISSBACH, *Babylonische Miscellen* (Leipzig: J. C. Hinrichs, 1903), 13 (Hymn to Marduk). **Selected translations:** *ANET* 383, 385–90; *BM²* 1.68–74, 77; 2.495–502, 531–39, 573–75, 584, 596–99, 608–9, 612–15, 619–20, 654–56, 753; 886; *COS* 1.117: 418–19; *SAHG* #1–2, 4, 9–10, 45; SEUX, *Hymnes et prières aux dieux de Babylonie et d'Assyrie*, 39–136. **Bibliography:** P.-A. BEAULIEU, "Divine Hymns as Royal Inscriptions," *NABU* 1993.84; G. R. CASTELLINO, "The Šamaš Hymn: A Note on Its Structure," in *Kramer Anniversary Volume: Cuneiform Studies in Honor of Samuel Noah Kramer* (ed. B. L. Eichler; AOAT 25; Kevelaer, Germany: Butzon & Bercker, 1976), 71–74; W. G. LAMBERT, "Marduk's Address to the Demons," in *Mesopotamian Magic: Textual, Historical, and Interpretative Perspectives* (ed. Tz. Abusch and K. van der Toorn; AMD 1; Groningen, Neth.: Styx, 1999), 291–96; IDEM, "Three Literary Prayers of the Babylonians," *AfO* 19 (1959–1960): 47–66.

Akkadian Royal Hymns. The Akkadian royal hymns exist in two permutations: hymns honoring the king and prayer hymns in which the king praised the gods and goddesses while appealing for their favor. Both types also appear in our corpus of Sumerian royal hymns, but the old Sumerian texts were unknown to these first-millennium Akkadian authors and hence did not inspire their compositions. The occasions for which the hymns were composed varied, but several were offered when the king suffered from ill health. All of the texts are poetic, but the metrical schemes used in the poetry vary from text to text. The Marduk hymn is particularly unique because it includes an acrostic that reads, "I am Assurbanipal, who has called out to you: Give me life, Marduk, and I will sing your praises!" As this acrostic suggests, the petitionary dimension of the hymns was sometimes quite prominent. The same can be said for Ps 72, our only Israelite royal hymn. Although the psalm's focus is on the qualities of the king, it also addresses God with petitions and praise. For an Israelite hymn in which the king himself addresses the deity, see Ps 21.

Selected texts and translations: LIVINGSTONE, *Court Poetry and Literary Miscellanea*, 4–20. **Selected translations:** *ANET* 386–87; *BM²* 1.231–39; 2.699–711; *COS* 1.139: 470–71; 1.141: 472–73; 1.143: 474; 1.144: 475; *SAHG* #5–6, 8, 11, 14; SEUX, *Hymnes et prières aux dieux de Babylonie et d'Assyrie*, 489–530. **Bibliography:** BRUG, "Biblical Acrostics and Their Relationhip to Other Ancient Near Eastern Acrostics"; F. M. FALES, "New Assyrian Letters from the Kuyunjik Collection," *AfO* 27 (1980): 136–53, no. 46; V. A. HUROWITZ, "Joel's Locust Plague in Light of Sargon II's Hymn to Nanaya," *JBL* 112 (1993): 597–603.

Akkadian Hymns to Cities. Like the Sumerians before them, the Akkadians' scribal culture honored their chief cities with poetry and song. Our major exemplars come from the Neo-Assyrian period and address the cities of Arbela, Uruk, Assur, and Babylon, but these texts differ somewhat. The Arbela hymn is cast in vocative tones ("Arbela, O Arbela"), but the Uruk psalm offers first-person praise for the city and its temples ("Uruk: I love Uruk"). The Assur text is actually a prayer for the city

("Bring prosperity among them!"), but the Babylon hymn is a prayer for the king who restored the city. Livingstone has suggested that these city hymns may have been inspired by the older Sumerian tradition of praise songs for cities and temples, but he points out that there is no concrete evidence for this. Hence, these texts may represent a native Assyrian development. The Hebrew Bible contains several psalms that praise Zion and Jerusalem, including Pss 48, 87, 122, and 137.

Selected texts and translations: LIVINGSTONE, *Court Poetry and Literary Miscellanea,* xxi–xxvi, 20–26 (Arbela, Uruk, Assur); S. A. STRONG, "On Some Babylonian and Assyrian Alliterative Texts," *PSBA* 17 (1895): 131–151, esp. 133–35 (Babylon). *Selected translation:* *BM²* 2.723, 754–56.

3.1.2. Mesopotamian Prayers and Laments

In this section we face two generic distinctions that are theoretically useful but pragmatically difficult to follow. The first distinction is between prayers and laments. Although one might conceivably lament without praying or pray without lamenting, in the ancient Near East these two phenomena often appeared together. Consequently, it is sensible to treat these two overlapping types under a single heading. The second generic distinction is between communal and individual prayers/laments. It is clear enough that the Mesopotamians composed some laments for communal uses and others to address individual needs, but this distinction was not always rigorously preserved. Since laments such as the ERŠAHUNGAs were used both communally and individually, it is difficult to treat the communal and individual genres as entirely discrete categories. Readers should also note that the prayer incantations, which appear in the following section, are closely related to the hymns and prayers treated in this segment.

Our summary of the Mesopotamian prayers and laments is roughly chronological insofar as the vagaries of generic classification allow. It therefore begins with the Sumerian compositions and then moves on to consider the Akkadian exemplars. These Mesopotamian texts are particularly important comparative sources for the study of the Hebrew Bible because, although the fact is often overlooked, the laments make up a large portion of the Psalter and, when added to the book of Lamentations itself, they constitute the bulk of Israel's lyric corpus.

Dumuzi Laments. According to Mesopotamian theology, the seasonal cycles of the year corresponded to a pattern of death and resurrection in the life of the god Dumuzi (for the relevant mythology, see 4.1). The lamentation songs at hand were recited to commemorate his death: "The slain wild bull lives no more! The slain wild bull lives no more! Dumuzi, the slain wild bull, lives no more! The slain wild bull lives no more!" (Jacobsen 1987, 47). As we can see, the Dumuzi laments were, like many Sumerian poems, repetitious. During the pertinent rites, cultic priestesses stood in for Dumuzi's spouse and sister—Inanna and Geshtinanna—and wailed the loss of their loved one. We may infer that the purpose of the lament was not only to comfort Inanna, a fertility goddess upon whom no one wished discontent, but also to prepare the way for Dumuzi's later return to the land of the living. Since the myths that relate to Dumuzi's death overlap considerably in form and content with the Dumuzi laments, it is difficult and even artificial to distinguish between the two genres (e.g., In the Desert by the Early Grass). For this reason, the reader is directed to chapter 4 for the closely related Dumuzi myths and love songs. Because Dumuzi was a fertility deity, the identities of many local fertility gods coalesced around him. He was also known as Ama-ushumgalanna, Damu, Ningishzida, Ishtaran, Alla and by a host of other names. In later periods, Dumuzi was mourned under the name Tammuz, as we see in the Akkadian texts (Lambert; Livingstone) and also in the Hebrew Bible (Ezek 8:14).

One of the Akkadian texts, published by Lambert, appears to be something other than a cultic lament. Although it features the wailings of Ištar over the death of her husband, Tammuz, her grief is multiplied by the destruction of the couple's patron city, Uruk. The narrator tells us that Ištar's brothers and brothers-in-law were killed, that pregnant women were ripped apart, and that the city lay in ruins. These descriptions are clearly images of a military campaign against Uruk. Since this text dates to the first millennium and since Uruk is known to have suffered under the hands of Babylon during that period, Lambert surmises—no doubt correctly—that this unique text was published in Uruk as a piece of political propaganda against its Babylonian overlords. For a text that probably reflects the same political and historical context, see the Uruk Prophecy in 7.1.

Texts and translations: B. ALSTER, "A Dumuzi Lament in Late Copies," *ActSum* 7 (1985): 1–9; E. CHIERA, *Sumerian Epics and Myths* (Cuneiform Series 3; Chicago: University of Chicago Press, 1964), no. 91 (= Recognition); *CT* 15, nos. 18, 20–21 (= The Wild Bull Who Has Lain Down; Vain Appeal); W. G. LAMBERT, "A Neo-Babylonian Tammuz Lament," in *Studies in Literature from the Ancient Near East: Dedicated to Samuel Noah Kramer* (ed. J. M. Sasson; AOS 65; New Haven: American Oriental Society, 1984), 211–15 (Akkadian Tammuz Lament); LIVINGSTONE, *Court Poetry and Literary Miscellanea*, 39–41 (Akkadian Tammuz Lament); H. RADAU, *Sumerian Hymns and Prayers to God Dumu-zi* (Babylonian Expedition of the University of Pennsylvania, Series A: Cuneiform Texts 30, part 1; Munich: n.p., 1913), vol. 30, no. 1 ("My Heart Plays a Reed Pipe"); H. ZIMMERN, *Sumerische Kultlieder aus altbabylonischer Zeit* (2 vols; Leipzig: Hinrichs, 1912–1913), vol. 1, nos. 26, 27, 45 (In the Desert by the Early Grass). *Translations: COS* 1.118: 419–20; JACOBSEN, *The Harps That Once*, 47–84; IDEM, *The Treasures of Darkness: A History of Mesopotamian Religion* (New Haven: Yale University Press, 1987), 47–73. *Bibliography:* B. ALSTER, "Geshtinanna as Singer and the Chorus of Uruk and Zabalam: UET VI/1 22," *JCS* 37 (1985): 219–228; IDEM, "The Mythology of Mourning," *ActSum* 5 (1983): 1–16; IDEM, "Tammuz," *DDD* 828–34; HALLO, "Lamentations and Prayers in Sumer and Akkad"; T. JACOBSEN, *Toward the Image of Tammuz and Other Essays on Mesopotamian History and Culture* (HSS 21; Cambridge: Harvard University Press, 1970); T. G. PINCHES, "Assyriological Gleanings—II," *PSBA* 23 (1901): 188–210.

Laments for Deceased Kings. Common sense tells us that the ancients would have lamented the passing of their kings, particularly if the king's dynasty remained intact. Although we do not have many copies of such texts, there is a Sumerian exemplar that suitably represents what must have been more common than the evidence suggests. The lament mourns the passing of Ur-Nammu, first king of the Ur III dynasty (c. 2112–2095). The text relates the divine decree of An and Enlil that Ur-Nammu would die, and then, in powerful poetic verse, it describes the subsequent mourning of the gods and of Ur-Nammu's mother. Ur-Nammu's illness is depicted vividly: "The wise shepherd no longer gives orders in battle and combat. The king, Sumer's advocate, lies sick. His hands that used to grasp cannot grasp any more, he lies sick." Equally vivid is the cataclysmic imagery used to describe his death and its aftermath: "The wise one lay down; silence descended. The land became demolished like a mountain; like a cypress forest it was stripped, its appearance changed." After Ur-Nammu's death, the text reports the king's descent into the netherworld, where, after offering sacrifices to the underworld deities, he was granted a throne and was placed in authority over "all the soldiers who had been killed by weapons, and all the men who had been found guilty were given into the king's hands . . . so with Gilgamesh, his beloved brother, he will issue the judgments of the netherworld and render the decisions of the netherworld." Nevertheless, after this reward, Ur-Nammu ends the text with a lament over the family, nation, and world that he lost.

In addition to the explicit evidence of the Ur-Nammu lament, there is also circumstantial evidence for the practice of lamenting royal deaths. During the annual rite of sacred marriage, the early deified kings of Mesopotamia (ca. 2250–1750) normally represented Dumuzi in the rituals (see previous entry and 4.1). For this reason, it is commonly assumed—though by no means proved—that the Dumuzi laments were recited to commemorate the deaths of these kings. The closest biblical exemplar to the Ur-Nammu lament is David's lament over the deaths of Saul and Jonathan (1 Sam 1:17–27). This lament was supposedly preserved in the "Book of Jashar." There is also mention in 2 Chron 35:25 of a lament for king Josiah, which the author describes as one from a collection of similar laments. Readers should note as well the nineteen tumuli (man-made mounds) that lie to the east of Jerusalem. These sites may well mark where ancient Judeans gathered to lament the deaths of their kings between the tenth and seventh centuries B.C.E. (see Barkay). For related comments regarding Israelite and Near Eastern cults of the dead, see 5.9.

Text and translation: E. FLÜCKIGER-HAWKER, *Urnamma of Ur in Sumerian Literary Tradition* (OBO 166; Freiburg, Switz.: Universitätsverlag, 1999), 93–182, pls. 1–13. **Bibliography:** G. BARKAY, "Mounds of Mystery: Where the Kings of Judah Were Lamented," *BAR* 29, no. 3 (2003): 32–39, 66, 68; W. W. HALLO, "The Death of Kings: Traditional Historiography in Contextual Perspective," in *Ah, Assyria* (ed. Cogan and Eph'al), 148–65; IDEM, "Lamentations and Prayers in Sumer and Akkad"; S. N. KRAMER, "The Death of Ur-Nammu and His Descent to the Netherworld," *JCS* 21 (1967): 104–122; IDEM, "The Death of Ur-Nammu," in *Near Eastern Studies Dedicated to H. I. H. Prince Takahito Mikasa on the Occasion of His Seventy-Fifth Birthday* (ed. M. Mori, H. Ogawa, and M. Yoshikawa; Wiesbaden: Harrassowitz, 1991), 193–214.

Sumerian and Akkadian City/Temple Laments. The collapse of the Ur III (or Neo-Sumerian) dynasty resulted in extensive destruction to the major cities and temples in southern Mesopotamia. One result was a series of cultic songs that lamented the devastation and appealed to the gods for restoration, but it is not clear when these laments were composed. Although the texts give the impression that they were written by eyewitnesses, it is clear that several of them were composed fifty or more years later, when the temples were being rebuilt. Evidently, the ancients attributed the destruction to divine anger and so surmised that rebuilding the temples might anger the deities still more either because the rebuilding effort might be viewed as an act of human defiance or, more likely, because the temple remains had to be razed for reconstruction. The city laments were a liturgical effort to appease these deities. Because the rites were performed only during the period of destruction and/or reconstruction, the texts listed here disappeared from the Mesopotamian canonical tradition after the Old Babylonian period, when they were used to teach Sumerian (but note related comments in the following entry on BALAG laments). Three of the five most important exemplars were composed in the main dialect of Sumerian (for Uruk, Eridu, and Sumer/Ur), the other two in Emesal (for Ur and Nippur). A closely related text laments the fate of Ibbi-Sin, the last king of Ur, who was led away into captivity.

The theological and generic precursors of the Sumerian city laments appear to have been the Fall of Lagash (see Cooper) and the Curse of Akkad (see 9.1.2), and the city laments themselves seem to have inspired the still later BALAG laments. Akkadian city laments are known but unusual. We possess one such lament from the Old Babylonian period (see Gadd/Kramer; BM^2 1.94), but it was probably based on a Sumerian prototype. Obvious comparative exemplars from ancient Israel would include the book of Lamentations and Pss 74, 79, 89, and 137, but these city laments were not composed to appease God's wrath by mourning with him. On this point the Israelite and Mesopotamian city laments differ markedly.

Texts and translations: J. S. COOPER, *Presargonic Inscriptions* (Sumerian and Akkadian Royal Inscriptions 1; New Haven: AOS, 1986), 78–79 (Fall of Lagash); C. J. GADD and S. N. KRAMER, *Literary and Religious Texts* (2 vols.; UET 6; London: British Museum and of the University Museum, University of Pennsylvania, 1963–1966), 2:403 (Akkadian); M. W. GREEN, "The Eridu Lament," *JCS* 30 (1978): 127–67 (Eridu Lament); IDEM, "The Uruk Lament," *JAOS* 104 (1984): 253–79 (Uruk Lament); S. N. KRAMER, *Lamentation over the Destruction of Ur* (Assyriological Studies 12; Chicago: University of Chicago, 1940) (Ur Lament); S. LANGDON, *Historical and Religious Texts from the Temple Library of Nippur* (Munich: R. Merkel, 1914), no. 3 (Lament for Ibbi-Sin); P. MICHALOWSKI, *The Lamentation over the Destruction of Sumer and Ur* (MC 2; Winona Lake, Ind.: Eisenbrauns, 1989) (Sumer/Ur Lament); W. H. Ph. RÖMER, *Die Klage über die Zerstörung von Ur* (AOAT 309; Münster: Ugarit-Verlag, 2004) (Ur Lament); S. TINNEY, *The Nippur Lament* (OPSNKF 16; Philadelphia: University Of Pennsylvania Museum, 1996) (Nippur Lament). *Translations:* ANET 455–63 (Ur Lament), 611–19 (Sumer/Ur Lament); BM^2 1.94 (Akkadian example); COS 1.166: 535–39 (Ur Lament); SAHG #36–38. *Bibliography:* A. FALKENSTEIN, "Die Ibbisìn-Klage," *WO* 5 (1950): 377–84; FERRIS, *The Genre of Communal Lament in the Bible and the Ancient Near East,* 21–25, 28–38, 48; GWALTNEY, "The Biblical Book of Lamentations in the Context of Near Eastern Literature"; HALLO, "Lamentations and Prayers in Sumer and Akkad"; S. N. KRAMER, "Lamentation over the Destruction of Nippur," *ActSum* 13 (1991): 1–26; IDEM, "The Weeping Goddess: Sumerian Prototypes of the *mater dolorosa,*" *BA* 46

(1983): 69–80; T. F. MCDANIEL, "The Alleged Sumerian Influence upon Lamentations," *VT* 18 (1968): 198–209; H. L. J. VANSTIPHOUT, "The Death of an Era: The Great Mortality in the Sumerian City Laments," in *Death in Mesopotamia: Papers read at the XXVIe Rencontre assyriologique internationale* (Mesopotamia 8; Copenhagen: Akademisk Forlag, 1980), 83–89; N. WASSERMAN, "A Forgotten Old-Babylonian Lament Over a City's Destruction: UET 6/2,403 and Its Possible Literary Context," *ErIsr* 27 (2003): 126–32 [Hebrew].

Sumerian *BALAG* Laments. The Sumerian city laments mentioned in the previous entry were used for only a short time and did not outlast the Old Babylonian period. There is good evidence, however, that the genre was adapted to produce the congregational laments known as BALAGs ("harp songs"), which were regularly sung in the Mesopotamian temple cults by GALA priests. The purpose of these laments was to appease divine anger, especially when temples or temple paraphernalia were undergoing demolition in preparation for refurbishment or reconstruction; the genre was also used in the regular cult as part of an ongoing vigil against divine anger. Long lists of destroyed cities and temples appear in the texts, as do lists of gods and goddesses who were angered or saddened by the devastation. Our earliest copies of the BALAGs come from the Old Babylonian period, with all others coming from the Neo-Assyrian period or later. Substantial variation is visible in the Old Babylonian manuscripts, but the texts seem to have become standardized sometime before 1100 B.C.E. (Cohen). Distinctive changes occurred to the BALAG tradition during this long period of development. In the case of one city lament series, ABBA HULUHHA (see Kutscher), the song was originally used as a BALAG over Nippur (see OB copies) before it was adapted in a much expanded first-millennium form to address not only Nippur but also Babylon. Expansions in the first-millennium copies are in part the result of longer temple, god, and epithet lists, but the addition of short ERŠEMMA laments to conclusion of each BALAG also made the texts longer. The BALAGs were divided into stanzas using the word KIRUGU ("genuflect"?), but this term, like the Hebrew word *selâ* in the Psalms, is little understood by scholars. Interlinear Akkadian translations of the Sumerian BALAGs began to appear already during the Middle Assyrian period (ca. 1200 B.C.E.) and became the rule during the first millennium. Dated colophons indicate that our latest BALAG exemplars come from the second century B.C.E. (from Uruk in 165 B.C.E. and from Babylon dated to 112 B.C.E.).

During the Neo-Assyrian period, scribes who were assembling Assurbanipal's library organized the BALAGs into a tablet series (see Cohen). The first half of the series contained laments addressed to male deities (collected under the rubric "BALAGs of the god Enlil"), and the second half included laments for female deities (collected under the rubric "BALAGs of the goddess Inanna"). There is evidence that each half of the collection was submitted to still further editorial arrangement, but the compositional methods used by the scribes are not always clear. It is difficult to know in some cases whether the scribes followed editorial rationales that escape us or whether, in fact, they followed no rationale at all. At any rate, it does not appear that the Neo-Assyrian series arrangement became standard because later copies of the BALAGs lack the series catch-lines.

Scholars have long noted that the Hebrew book of Lamentations is similar in certain respects to the Sumerian laments. If the Sumerian city and temple laments influenced the composition of Lamentations, as some scholars aver, the influence obviously could not have come directly from the famous city laments of the Ur III period. More likely is that the influence would have been felt during the Babylonian exile and afterward, when the Jews had continuous contact with Mesopotamians who were copying and singing city and temple BALAGs. Moreover, as we saw in the previous entry, we have discovered at least one Akkadian city lament that dates to the Seleucid period (see Gadd/Kramer in the previous entry; *BM²* 1.94).

Texts and translations: COHEN, *The Canonical Lamentations of Ancient Mesopotamia;* R. KUTSCHER, *Oh Angry Sea (a-ab-ba hu-luh-ha): The History of a Sumerian Congregational Lament* (New Haven: Yale University Press, 1975); G. A. REISNER, *Sumerisch-babylonische Hymnen nach Thontafeln griechischer Zeit* (Berlin: Spemann, 1896), text 29. *Bibliography:* ALSTER, "Edin-na ú-sag-á: Reconstruction, History, and Interpretation of a Sumerian Cultic Lament," in *Keilschriftliche Literaturen: Ausgewählte Vorträge der XXXII. Rencontre assyriologique internationale* (ed. K. Hecker and W. Sommerfeld; BBVO 6; Berlin: Dietrich Reimer, 1986), 19–31; J. A. BLACK, "Sumerian *Balag* Compositions," *BO* 44 (1987): 36–79; F. W. DOBBS-ALLSOPP, *Weep, O Daughter of Zion: A Study of the City-Lament Genre in the Hebrew Bible* (BibOr 44; Rome: Editrice Pontificio Istituto Biblico, 1993); FERRIS, *The Genre of Communal Lament in the Bible and the Ancient Near East,* esp. 17, 37–43, 50; GWALTNEY, "The Biblical Book of Lamentations in the Context of Near Eastern Literature"; HALLO, "The Cultic Setting of Sumerian Poetry"; IDEM, "Lamentations and Prayers in Sumer and Akkad"; T. F. MCDANIEL, "The Alleged Sumerian Influence upon Lamentations," *VT* 18 (1968): 198–209.

Sumerian ERŠEMMA Laments. Like the BALAGs, these tambourine (ŠEM-drum) laments were used to appease divine anger during temple demolition and in the regular cult. Our primary exemplars come from the Old Babylonian period and from the first millennium B.C.E., all of them including three features: (1) the Emesal dialect; (2) concern for deities rather than kings; and (3) an introductory list of divine epithets, cities, and buildings. A few texts used mythological stories to explain the occasion of divine distress, so that these texts are narratives as well as hymns. Whereas our early texts have only one structural unit, many of the first-millennium exemplars include two or even three units that accentuate the theme of "appeasing the heart" of the god. This development occurred when the first-millennium ERŠEMMAs were appended to BALAG laments. In some cases we now possess both OB and first-millennium copies of the same ERŠEMMA, revealing not only formal but also theological changes. In Cohen's ERŠEMMA no. 1, for instance, the first-millennium version removed references to some southern cities that were prominent during the second millennium, and it replaced them with northern cities of the first millennium. Ancient catalogues mention almost two hundred ERŠEMMA incipits, but far fewer are extant. Cohen's standard publication includes thirty-two of the best-preserved examples.

Texts and translations: M. E. COHEN, *Sumerian Hymnology: The Eršemma* (HUCASup 2; Cincinnati: Hebrew Union College, 1981). *Bibliography:* HALLO, "Lamentations and Prayers in Sumer and Akkad"; S. N. KRAMER, "Two British Museum Iršemma Catalogues," *StudOr* 46 (1975): 141–66; W. G. LAMBERT, "The Converse Tablet: A Litany with Musical Instructions," in *Near Eastern Studies in Honor of William Foxwell Albright* (ed. H. Goedicke; Baltimore: Johns Hopkins University Press, 1971), 335–53; see also the bibliography for BALAG laments in the previous entry.

Sumerian ŠUILLA Prayers. Because the generic rubric ŠUILLA referred to the ritual gesture of "raising the hand" rather than to a text's thematic content, the corpus of ŠUILLAs includes a wide variety of text types in both Sumerian and Akkadian (Cooper 1988). Here our interest is in the Sumerian exemplars. The two Sumerian varieties include Emesal hymns and standard-dialect ritual incantations. The hymnic texts are similar to the ERŠEMMAs and appear in Old Babylonian catalogues of the lamentation priests' liturgy (the *kalû*), but the incantations were part of the repertoire of the exorcist priests (the *āšipu*). The later Akkadian ŠUILLAs, which will be discussed below, are nonliturgical incantations and hence are similar only to the second type of Sumerian ŠUILLA.

Texts and translations: J. S. COOPER, "A Sumerian Šu-íl-la from Nimrud with a Prayer for Sin-šar-iškun," *Iraq* 32 (1970): 51–67; IDEM, "Warrior, Devastating Deluge, Destroyer of Hostile Lands." *Translations:* ANET 385–86, 389–90; SAHG 222–25. *Bibliography:* DALGLISH, *Psalm Fifty-One,* 41–51; FERRIS, *The Genre of Communal Lament in the Bible and the Ancient Near East,* 65–67; HALLO, "Lamentations and Prayers in Sumer and Akkad."

Sumerian and Akkadian Letter Prayers. Mesopotamian worshippers sometimes attempted to establish a tangible presence before the gods by placing in the temple a votive object or statue of themselves inscribed with prayers for prosperity, long life, or healing. A less expensive alternative was to inscribe the prayer on a tablet and deposit it before the deity, thus producing a "letter prayer." Sumerian letter prayers appeared early in Mesopotamian history. In one instance, King Sin-iddinam of Larsa fashioned a statue of his dead father, Nur-Adad, and placed it in the temple along with two letter prayers. The letters petitioned Nur-Adad to intercede with the god Utu on behalf of Sin-iddinam's cause (see Hallo 1976). Because the early Sumerian kings were divinized, some of the letter petitions addressed not only the gods but also deceased and even living kings (Hallo 1980–1981; 1991). The closest Hebrew parallels to the Sumerian letter prayers are found in the prayer of Hezekiah (Isa 38; see Hallo 1976) and in several psalms. Particularly interesting are the Davidic *miktām* psalms (see Pss 16, 56–60), which may well have originated as royal inscriptions (note that the Septuagint translates *miktām* as *stēlographia,* i.e., "stela inscription"). If so, the *miktām* psalms would provide an explicit example of royal prayers that were inscribed for God to see (see Ginsberg; see also "Zakkur Inscription" in 15.2).

Our letter prayer exemplars also include bilingual and Akkadian prayers of both private and royal individuals, these coming from the Old Babylonian and Neo-Assyrian periods. Some of the Neo-Assyrian texts appear as parts of the Assyrian Annals (e.g., Sargon's letter to Assur), and others appear on tablets (the letter prayers of Sennacherib [see Na'aman] and Esarhaddon [Borger 1956]). The Neo-Assyrian letters differ in style and tone from the Sumerian types. They are essentially texts that enumerate royal accomplishments in order to secure divine pleasure. We learn from the Neo-Assyrian evidence that the gods could not only receive letters but also respond to them. For these letters *from* the gods, see 6.1.2.

In conclusion, we should note that some of the Sumerian letter prayers were scribal exercises rather than authentic prayers. For a relatively complete catalogue of the most important texts in the genre, see R. Borger, "Gottesbrief," *RlA* 3:575–76.

Texts and translations: B. BÖCK, "'Wenn du zu Nintinuga gesprochen hast': Untersuchungen zu Aufbau, Inhalt, Sitz-im-Leben, und Funktion sumerischer Gottesbriefe," *AoF* 23 (1996): 3–23 (Sumerian); R. BORGER, *Ein Brief Sin-idinnams von Larsa an den Sonnengott sowie Bemerkungen über "Joins" und das "Joinen"* (Nachrichten der Akademie der Wissenschaften in Göttingen 1: Philologische-historische Klasse 1991.2; Göttingen: Vandenhoeck & Ruprecht, 1991) (Sumerian); IDEM, *Die Inschriften Asarhaddons, Königs von Assyrien* (AfOB 9; Graz: Im Selbstverlage des Herausgebers, 1956), 102–7 (Neo-Assyrian); D. CHARPIN and J.-M. DURAND, "La prise du pouvoir par Zimri-Lim," *MARI* 4 (1985): 293–343, esp. pp. 339–42 (Royal OB); J.-M. DURAND, "Échange de lettres avec les dieux," in *Archives épistolaires de Mari* (ARM 26; Paris: Recherche sur les Civilisations, 1988–), vol. 1, part 1, pp. 413–19, nos. 191, 193 (Royal OB); W. W. HALLO, "The Royal Correspondence of Larsa, I: A Sumerian Prototype for the Prayer of Hezekiah?" in *Kramer Anniversary Volume: Cuneiform Studies in Honor of Samuel Noah Kramer* (ed. B. L. Eichler; AOAT 25; Kevelaer, Germany: Butzon & Bercker, 1976), 209–24 (Sumerian); IDEM, "The Royal Correspondence of Larsa, II: The Appeal to Utu," in *Zikir Šumim: Assyriological Studies Presented to F. R. Kraus* (ed. G. Van Driel; Leiden: Brill, 1982), 95–109 (Sumerian); IDEM, "The Royal Correspondence of Larsa, III: The Princess and the Plea," in *Marchands, diplomates, et empereurs: Études sur la civilisation mésopotamienne offertes à Paul Garelli* (ed. D. Charpin and F. Joannès; Paris: Éditions Recherche sur les Civilisations, 1991), 377–88 (Sumerian); F. R. KRAUS, "Ein altbabylonischer Privatbrief an eine Gottheit," *RA* 65 (1971): 27–36 (Private OB); IDEM, "Eine neue Probe akkadischer Literatur: Brief eines Bittstellers an eine Gottheit," *JAOS* 103 (1983): 205–9 (Private OB); L. D. LEVINE, "Observations on 'Sargon's Letter to the Gods,'" *ErIsr* 27 (2003): 111–119; L. DE MEYER, "Une letter d'Ur-Utu galamah à une divinité," in *Reflets des deux fleuves: Volume mélanges offerts à André Finet* (ed. M. Lebeau and P. Talon; Leuven: Peeters, 1989), 41–43 (Private OB); N. NA'AMAN, "Sennacherib's 'Letter to God' on His Campaign to Jerusalem," *BASOR* 214 (1974): 25–39 (Neo-Assyrian); M. STOL, *Letters from Yale* (AbB 9; Leiden: Brill, 1981), no. 141 (Private OB); W. H. VAN SOLDT, *Letters in the British Museum* (AbB 12; Leiden: Brill, 1990), no. 99 (Private OB); C. B. F. WALKER and S. N. KRAMER, "Cuneiform Tablets in the Collection of Lord Binning," *Iraq* 44 (1982): 71–86 (Sumerian). *Translations:* ANET 382; BM² 1.155–59; COS 1.164, 532–34, 1.165: 534. *Bibliography:* R. BORGER, "Gottesbrief," *RlA* 3:575–76; H. L. GINSBERG, "Psalms and Inscriptions of Petition and Acknowledgment," in *Louis Ginzberg Jubilee Volume* (New York: American Academy for Jewish Research, 1945), 159–71; HALLO, "The Cultic Setting of Sumerian Poetry"; IDEM, "Individual Prayer in Sumerian: The Continuity of a Tradition," *JAOS* 88 (1968): 71–89; IDEM, "Lamentations and Prayers in Sumer and Akkad"; IDEM, "Letters, Prayers, and Letter-Prayers," in *Proceedings of the Seventh World Congress of Jewish Studies* (4 vols.; Jerusalem: Magnes Press,

Hebrew University, 1980–1981), 2:17–27; J. KLEIN, " 'Personal God' and Individual Prayer in Sumerian Religion," in *Vorträge gehalten auf der 28. Rencontre assyriologique internationale in Wien, 6.–10. Juli 1981* (ed. H. Hunger and H. Hirsch; AfOB 19; Horn, Austria: F. Berger, 1982): 295–306; E. LEICHTY, "Esarhaddon's 'Letter to the Gods,'" in *Ah, Assyria* (ed. Cogan and Eph'al), 52–57; P. MICHALOWSKI, "Königsbriefe," *RlA* 6:51–59; A. L. OPPENHEIM, *Ancient Mesopotamia* (rev. ed.; Chicago: University of Chicago Press, 1977), 279–80.

The Sumerian ERŠAHUNGA *Laments (and related Akkadian Penitential Prayers).* Literally "laments for appeasing the heart," these individual prayers are the literary progeny of the Sumerian letter prayers. It was long believed that the ERŠAHUNGAs first appeared during the Kassite period, but we now have a single Old Babylonian exemplar. During the Neo-Assyrian period, from which most of our exemplars come, the ERŠAHUNGAs were recited during temple liturgies or during various apotropaic rituals (see Maul, 26–27). Evidence suggests that the king generally recited the prayer, but it is quite possible that private individuals sometimes used the laments, particularly in earlier periods. The usual four-part format of the ERŠAHUNGA included (1) a hymnic introduction, (2) a lament, (3) a penitential prayer, and (4) concluding expressions of thanks to the deity. Like most of our Sumerian laments, these were composed in Emesal, but they were spoken rather than sung and normally sported Akkadian interlinear translations. In terms of content and structure, the ERŠAHUNGA is very similar to the Hebrew lament psalms (Dalglish). For Akkadian penitential prayers that are similar to these Sumerian texts, see *ANET* 383–85; *BM²* 2.503–20, 525–30; 549–50, 585–87; *COS* 1.114: 416–17; *SAHG* #13, 18, 43, 61, 65; Seux, *Hymnes et prières aux dieux de Babylonie et d'Assyrie,* 169–201.

Texts and translations: S. LANGDON, *Babylonian Penitential Psalms* (Paris: P. Geuthner, 1927); S. M. MAUL, *"Herzberuhigungsklagen": Die sumerisch-akkadischen Eršahunga-Gebete* (Wiesbaden: Harrassowitz, 1976). *Translations:* *ANET* 391–92; *BM²* 2.560–61, 629–30, 670–72 (Akkadian portions of bilinguals); *SAHG* 45 (Sumerian); SEUX, *Hymnes et prières aux dieux de Babylonie et d'Assyrie,* 139–168. *Bibliography:* COHEN, *The Canonical Lamentations of Ancient Mesopotamia;* COOPER, "Warrior, Devastating Deluge, Destroyer of Hostile Lands"; DALGLISH, *Psalm Fifty-One,* 21–35; FERRIS, *The Genre of Communal Lament in the Bible and the Ancient Near East,* 67–69; HALLO, "Lamentations and Prayers in Sumer and Akkad"; P. MICHALOWSKI, "On the Early History of the Ersahunga Prayer," *JCS* 39 (1987): 37–48.

Sumerian and Akkadian Elegies for Private Individuals. Although we have numerous laments that commemorate the deaths of gods and kings, elegies for private individuals are rare in the Mesopotamian corpus. Our primary exemplars of this type include two Sumerian elegies (Kramer; Sjöberg) and one Akkadian text (Livingstone). The Sumerian texts are attributed to a certain Lu-dingira, whose elegies memorialize his deceased father (Nannaya) and wife (Nawirtum). The lament for his father narrates the story of Nannaya's death, mourns his passing, offers prayers that Nannaya would experience comfort in the underworld and receive regular offerings, and closes with a plea that the gods would grant Nannaya's descendants—including Lu-dingira, no doubt—long and happy lives. The lament for his wife Nawirtum includes a similar ending: prayers that her sin might be released (so that guilt did not fall on Lu-dingira) and a request that the gods might bless Lu-dingira and his children. Lu-dingira is also credited with a touching message sent to his living mother (see 4.1). All of the Lu-dingira texts were found in, and associated with, the city of Nippur.

Our Akkadian exemplar (see Livingstone) is an elegy that dates to a millennium after the Old Babylonian Lu-dingira texts. This unusual poetic dialogue recounts the last days of a woman who died after childbirth. Although both her husband and a goddess speak in the dialogue, most of the text is the dead woman's own account of the events. The text was probably composed to honor her and provides a rare glimpse into the funerary literature of nonroyal persons.

Texts and translations: S. N. KRAMER, *Two Elegies on a Pushkin Museum Tablet: A New Sumerian Literary Genre* (Moscow: Oriental Literature Publishing House, 1960, in Russian and English); LIVINGSTONE, *Court Poetry and Literary Miscellanea*, 37–39; Å. W. SJÖBERG, "The First Pushkin Museum Elegy and New Texts," *JAOS* 103 (1983): 315–320. *Translations:* BM² 2.890; COS 1.119: 420–21. *Bibliography:* M. CIVIL, *The Farmer's Instructions: A Sumerian Agricultural Manual* (AuOrSup 5; Barcelona: Editorial AUSA, 1994), 89; E. REINER, "An Assyrian Elegy," in *Your Thwarts in Pieces, Your Mooring Rope Cut: Poetry from Babylonia and Assyria* (Michigan Studies in the Humanities 5; Ann Arbor: Horace H. Rackham School of Graduate Studies at the University of Michigan, 1985), 85–93.

Akkadian Royal Prayers. Most of our royal prayers come from the building inscriptions of the Neo-Assyrian and Neo-Babylonian periods. Because building projects were considered works on behalf of the gods, this was a suitable venue for seeking divine favor. Our most interesting tablet exemplars are Neo-Assyrian and should be associated with the reign of King Assurbanipal. Some of these were appended as colophons to texts copied for his library (e.g., BM² 2.714), and others were genuine literary texts. For more detail on Assurbanipal's literary prayers, see the next three entries. The Hebrew Psalter explicitly identifies several psalms as royal prayers (Pss 20, 61, and 72), but it is likely that many of the anonymous prayers in the collection also originated as royal compositions.

Texts and translations: S. LANGDON, *Die neubabylonischen Königsinschriften* (VAB 4; Leipzig: Hinrichs, 1912) (dated and partial collection of Neo-Babylonian exemplars). For additional texts and publication information, see bibliographies in the following translations. *Translations:* ANET 317; BM² 1.240–48, 2.212–13, 604–6, 687–99, 714, 724–44; SAHG 12, 15, 17, 24–39, 68, 71; SEUX, *Hymnes et prières aux dieux de Babylonie et d'Assyrie,* 489–530. *Bibliography:* P. R. BERGER, *Die neubabylonischen Königsinschriften: Königsinschriften des ausgehenden babylonischen Reiches (626–539 a. Chr.)* (AOAT 4.1; Neukirchen-Vluyn: Neukirchener Verlag, 1973); H. HUNGER, *Babylonische und assyrische Kolophone* (AOAT 2; Neukirchen-Vluyn: Neukirchener Verlag, 1968); S. LIEBERMAN, "Canonical Official Cuneiform Texts: Towards an Understanding of Assurbanipal's Personal Tablet Collection," in *Lingering over Words: Studies in Ancient Near Eastern Literature in Honor of William L. Moran* (ed. Tz. Abusch et al.; Atlanta: Scholars Press, 1990), 305–36. See also the bibliography for the three entries that follow.

Akkadian Coronation Prayers. We have copies of two Assyrian prayers that were used during coronation rituals for the king. The older exemplar (see Müller) dates from around the time of Tukulti-Ninuta I (thirteenth century B.C.E.). It is a New Year's coronation rite, but we are not sure whether the rite was observed annually or only upon the king's ascension to the throne. As the text begins, the king is just entering the temple of Assur, where he distributes gifts of gold and silver to the priests. The high priest then crowns the king and prays for him. The god Assur is petitioned to establish the king's throne, to bless his dynasty, and to grant the king "commanding, hearing, and obedience—truth and peace." The second coronation prayer was apparently composed for Assurbanipal's coronation ceremony (ca. 668 B.C.E.), although it is likely that the prayer was recited in the royal court on other occasions as well (see Livingstone). The first portion of the text asserts the divine election of the king and pronounces blessings upon him. A single ruling separates this section of the text from its conclusion, which voices curses against the king's conspirator. Evidence suggests that the hymnist drew portions of his material directly from an older Babylonian coronation composition as well as from long-standing oral traditions (cf. Mayer; Livingstone). The Hebrew Psalter preserves an Israelite coronation prayer, which appears in Ps 2. Other royal psalms include Pss 18, 20, 21, 45, 61, 63, 72, and 78.

Texts and translations: LIVINGSTONE, *Court Poetry and Literary Miscellanea*, 26–27; K. F. MÜLLER, *Das assyrische Ritual, Teil I: Texte zum assyrischen Königsritual* (MVAG 41.3; Leipzig: J. C. Hinrichs, 1937). *Translations:* BM² 1.247; 2.697–99; COS 1.140: 472; 1.142: 473–74; SEUX, *Hymnes et prières aux dieux de Babylonie et d'Assyrie*, 110–13. *Bibliography:* M. DIETRICH, "Das Ritual für die Krönung des Assurbanipal (VAT 13831)," in *Textarbeit— Studien zu Texten und ihrer Rezeption aus dem Alten Testament und der Umwelt Israels: Festschrift für Peter Weimar zur Vollendung seines 60. Lebensjahres* (ed. K. Kiesow and T. Meurer; Münster: Ugarit, 2003), 127–56; LIVINGSTONE, *Court Poetry and Literary Miscellanea*, xxiii–xxiv; W. R. MAYER, "Ein Mythos von der Erschaffung des Menschen und des Königs," *Or* 56 (1987): 55–68; E. WEIDNER, "Assurbânipal in Assur," *AfO* 13 (1939–1941): 204–18.

A Righteous Sufferer's Prayer to Nabû. In this prayer a sufferer declares his righteousness and then appeals to the god Nabû for forgiveness, restoration, and deliverance from his "ill wishers." The lucid description of suffering is reminiscent of the wisdom text known as *Ludlul Bēl Nēmeqi* (see 2.1.2), but this text is a genuine prayer. It is likely that the protagonist was an Assyrian king, probably Assurbanipal (Livingstone).

Text and translation: LIVINGSTONE, *Court Poetry and Literary Miscellanea*, xxvi, 30–32. *Translation:* BM² 2.604–6. *Bibliography:* K. DELLER, "Neuassyrisches aus Sultantepe," *Or* 34 (1965): 457–77; W. G. LAMBERT, "The Sultantepe Tablets: A Review Article," *RA* (1959): 119–37.

Assurbanipal's Dialogue with Nabû. This unusual text narrates a dialogue between the Neo-Assyrian king Assurbanipal and the god Nabû. The king prayerfully declares his faithfulness to the god, and the deity responds with promises of deliverance from the king's troubles. The dialogue concludes with Nabû's vow that Assurbanipal's "ill-wishers . . . will be squashed before your feet like insects." It is likely that the text was recited in the royal courts to encourage the king. In certain respects, the text is comparable to the Neo-Assyrian prophecies discussed in 6.1.2.

Text and translation: LIVINGSTONE, *Court Poetry and Literary Miscellanea,* xxvi, 33–35. *Translations: BM²* 2.712–13; *COS* 1.145: 475–76; *SAHG* #39.

A Royal Prayer at the Divine Meal. Scholars have unearthed several copies of an Assyrian prayer that was recited when the king provided a meal for the god. Brief excerpts illustrate its content: "He who made this repast, who provided food and drink to the gods, grant that he administer far and wide forevermore. May he exercise the high priesthood, kingship, and universal dominion. May he attain a ripe old age. . . . May Assur bless the one who provided this repast." One of our copies inserts the name of a seventh-century king (Assur-etil-ilani), but the prayer itself is older.

Texts and translations: E. EBELING, "Kultische Texte aus Assur," *Or* 24 (1955): 1–15; R. FRANKENA, *Takultu: Fe sacrale maaltijd in het Assyrische ritueel: Met een overzicht over de in Assur vereerde goden* (Leiden: Brill, 1954); J.-J. GLASSNER, "Mahlzeit, A: Mesopotamien," *RlA* 7:259–67.

*Divination Prayers (*Ikribus*).* Before undertaking acts of divination, Mesopotamian *bārû* priests customarily requested favorable omens from the gods. Because extispicy was among the most widely practiced types of divination, most of these *ikribū* (prayers) addressed the chief gods of extispicy, Adad and Šamaš. The prayers featured legal imagery in which the query put before the gods was envisioned as a case and the divine response was understood as its verdict. Because the chief gods of extispicy slept at night, the practice of evening divination required that diviners address their *ikribū* to nocturnal deities. Our most important *ikribu* exemplars come from the Old Babylonian period and from the Neo-Assyrian period. In one text, the diviner cleanses his mouth and body using cedar resin before approaching the deity for divination (see YBC 5023 in Goetze). This practice is comparable to the cleansing of Isaiah's lips during his prophetic call (Isa 6). For more on ancient divination, see chapter 6, below.

Selected texts and translations: J. VAN DIJK, A. GOETZE, and M. I. HUSSEY, *Early Mesopotamian Incantations and Rituals* (YOS 11; New Haven: Yale University Press, 1985); G. DOSSIN, "Prières aux 'Dieux de la Nuit' (AO 6769)," *RA* 32 (1935): 179–87; A. GOETZE, "An Old Babylonian Prayer of the Divination Priest," *JCS* 22 (1968): 25–29; W. HOROWITZ and N. WASSERMAN, "Another Old Babylonian Prayer to the Gods of the Night," *JCS* 48 (1996): 57–59; L. DE MEYER, "Deux prières *ikribu* du temps d'Ammī-ṣaduqa," in *Zikir Šumim: Assyriological Studies Presented to F. R. Kraus* (ed. G. Van Driel; Leiden: Brill, 1982), 271–78; J. NOUGAYROL, "Textes hépatoscopiques d'époque ancienne conservés au Musée du Louvre," *RA* 38 (1941): 67–88; W. VON SODEN, "Schwer zugängliche russische Veröffentlichungen altbabylonischer Texte," *ZA* 43 (1936): 305–8; I. STARR, *The Rituals of the Diviner*

(BMes 12; Malibu, Calif.: Undena, 1983); H. ZIMMERN, *Beiträge zur Kenntnis der Babylonischen Religion* (2 vols.; Leipzig: J. C. Hinrichs, 1896–1901), vol. 2, nos. 1–25, 75–101. *Translations:* ANET 390–91; *BM²* 1.148–52, 2.621–22, 661–66; *COS* 1.115: 417; 1.116: 417–18; *SAHG* #20–23; SEUX, *Hymnes et prières aux dieux de Babylonie et d'Assyrie,* 467–86. **Bibliography:** A. L. OPPENHEIM, "A New Prayer to the 'Gods of the Night,'" *AnBib* 12 (1959): 282–301. For related materials, see 6.1.1.

3.1.3. Mesopotamian Incantation Prayers

Assyriologists commonly distinguish two types of Mesopotamian incantation, the prayer incantations (German, *Gebetsbeschwörung*) and the magical incantation (*Beschwörung*). Both types were uttered in association with rituals, but the penitential and petitionary elements were not so strong in the magical type. This chapter treats only the *Gebetsbeschwörungen.* For more on the magical incantations, see chapter 5 (esp. 5.8).

The Sumerian *KI.ᵈUTU.KAM* Incantations. This ritual series includes "prayers to the rising sun" (the god Šamaš) that were recited by incantation priests in various ritual contexts, especially expiation rituals such as the *namburbû* (= Sum. NAM.BÚR.BI) and *Bīt Rimki* (see 5.8). The deity is praised and words of thanksgiving are offered or promised by the priest. A primary purpose of the prayer was to legitimize the incantation priest, but intercession on behalf of the sufferer was also included. The *KI.ᵈUTU.KAM* prayers were added to the magical Sumerian incantations during the Kassite period, apparently to enhance the effectiveness of the older incantations. Akkadian translations were often included in the texts. For additional prayers of the incantation priests, see *BM²* 2.546, 568–70, 610–11, 623; *SAHG* 59, 69, 78; SEUX, *Hymnes et prières aux dieux de Babylonie et d'Assyrie,* 239–66.

Text and translation: LANGDON, *Babylonian Penitential Psalms,* 11–12, 44–60 (samples). *Translations:* *BM²* 2.660, 648–49 (Akkadian); *SAHG* 42–43 (Sumerian); P. SCHOLLMEYER, *Sumerisch-babylonische Hymnen und Gebete an Samas* (Paderborn: Schöningh, 1912), nos. 1, 2, 4–5, 7; SEUX, *Hymnes et prières aux dieux de Babylonie et d'Assyrie,* 215–37. **Bibliography:** DALGLISH, *Psalm Fifty-One,* 36–42.

The Sumerian *DINGER.ŠA.DIB.BA* Incantations. Literally, "prayers for the reconciliation of the angry god," these Sumerian texts—often preserved with Akkadian translations—are thematically similar to the Sumerian ERŠAHUNGAs and the Akkadian ŠUILLAs, sharing with both a threefold format of address/praise, prayer/lament, and thanksgiving. The chief distinction of the DINGER.ŠA.DIB.BA texts is their exclusive focus on appeasing the deity, which is only one of several important themes in the ŠUILLAs. DINGER.ŠA.DIB.BAs were used in conjunction with private rituals and also in a variety of more elaborate rites, such as *Bīt Rimki* and *Šurpu* (see 5.8.1). Several of the DINGER.ŠA.DIB.BA prayers are private petitions addressed to "personal gods," that is, family gods who were supposed to act as protectors and intercessors for the family and all individuals in it. The religious importance of such a concept is easy to explain given the great gulf that separated the average Mesopotamian from the gods and goddesses worshipped in the national temple cults. Some biblical scholars believe that the patriarchal "God of the fathers," mentioned in Genesis, reflects the Near Eastern concept of a personal god (see Gen 31:5, 42; 32:9). For more on the Mesopotamian concept of personal gods and its relationship to ancient Israel, see the studies of Albertz, van der Toorn, and Vorländer.

The structure and content of the DINGER.ŠA.DIB.BA is very similar to that of the Hebrew penitential psalms (e.g., Ps 51). It is likely that this similarity can be attributed to either direct or indirect Mesopotamian influence on the Israelite psalmists (see Dalglish).

Text and translation: W. G. LAMBERT, "DINGER.ŠÀ.DIB.BA Incantations," *JNES* 33 (1974): 267–322. *Translations: BM²* 2.630–31; 2.627–28; *SAHG* #19, 79, 80; SEUX, *Hymnes et prières aux dieux de Babylonie et d'Assyrie,* 203–11. *Bibliography:* R. ALBERTZ, *Persönliche Frömmigkeit und offizielle Religion* (CTM 9; Stuttgart: Calwer, 1978); DALGLISH, *Psalm Fifty-One,* 51–55; K. VAN DER TOORN, *Family Religion in Babylonia, Ugarit, and Israel: Continuity and Changes in the Forms of Religious Life* (Studies in the History and Culture of the Ancient Near East 7; New York: Brill, 1996); IDEM, "Gods and Ancestors in Emar and Nuzi," *ZA* 84 (1994): 38–59; IDEM, "Ilib and the 'God of the Father,'" *UF* 25 (1993): 379–87; H. VORLÄNDER, *Mein Gott: Die Vorstellungen vom persönlichen Gott im Alten Orient und im Alten Testament* (AOAT 23; Neukirchen-Vluyn: Neukirchener Verlag, 1975).

Akkadian ŠUILLA *Prayers.* This Akkadian genre came to the fore during the Kassite period (ca. 1500–1200). Its rubric, ŠUILLA, described the ritual gesture of "raising the hand," which was used in antiquity in two closely related types of individual prayers: penitential psalms and laments. Both prayer types exhibit a three-part form that includes address/praise, prayer/lament, and thanksgiving (or perhaps a vow to offer thanks when the prayer was answered). The tablets often include prescriptions for an accompanying ritual (e.g., "You will perform the rite either in a cultic setting or with an incense burner"). ŠUILLA prayers have come down to us in series collections, as parts of other ritual series (e.g, *Bīt Rimki*), as excerpts used in other ritual procedures (e.g, *namburbû,* medical rituals), and in small collections whose purpose is not entirely clear. Some exemplars were apparently transmitted as works of edifying religious literature (Dalglish, 42). We should note that there are numerous similar texts that do not bear the ŠUILLA rubric. The Akkadian ŠUILLAs are nonliturgical and so should be carefully distinguished from the earlier and poorly attested liturgical Sumerian ŠUILLAs.

The gesture of raising the hand in worship appears in some Hebrew psalms (Ps 28:2; 44:20; 63:4; 68:31; 88:9; 134:2; 141:2; 143:6), and the basic three-part structure of the Akkadian ŠUILLAs is also reflected in the individual laments of the Hebrew Bible. According to Dalglish, these similarities are probably the result of Mesopotamian influence on the biblical psalmists.

Texts and translations: E. EBELING, *Die akkadische Gebetsserie "Handerhebung"* (Berlin: Akademie, 1953); L. W. KING, *Babylonian Magic and Sorcery* (London: Luzac, 1896);

O. LORETZ and W. R. MAYER, *Šu-ila-Gebete: Suppl. zu L. W. King, Babylonian Magic and Sorcery* (AOAT 34; Kevelaer, Germany: Butzon & Bercker, 1978). *Translations: BM²* 2.540–48, 556–59, 576–77, 580–81, 593–95, 601–4, 617–18, 640, 624, 651, 667–68; *SAHG* #40–44, 48–54, 60, 62, 76–77; SEUX, *Hymnes et prières aux dieux de Babylonie et d'Assyrie*, 269–346. *Bibliography:* TZ. ABUSCH, "The Form and Meaning of a Babylonian Prayer to Marduk," *JAOS* 103 (1983): 3–15; DALGLISH, *Psalm Fifty-One*, 41–51; FERRIS, *The Genre of Communal Lament in the Bible and the Ancient Near East*, 65–67; HALLO, "Lamentations and Prayers in Sumer and Akkad"; W. G. KUNSTMANN, *Die babylonische Gebetsbeschwörung* (Leipzig: Hinrichs, 1932); W. MAYER, *Untersuchungen zur Formensprache der babylonischen Gebetsbeschwörungen* (Studia Pohl. Series Maior 5; Rome: Pontifical Biblical Institute, 1976).

An Incantation Prayer to Deceased Ancestors. The Mesopotamians believed that the ghosts of the dead could influence life among the living, especially by exerting their influence in the spirit world. This tablet records a man's prayer to his family ghosts in which he requests that they represent his case in the divine tribunal before the gods. As he offered the prayer he also offered funerary offerings, in this case "cool water" poured through a drinking pipe near the grave. The tablet itself was probably deposited there as well. We do not know the difficulties that prompted this prayer and offering, but we know the man's plea: "May I, your servant, live in well-being. . . . Revive me, let me sound your praises!"

Text and translation: E. EBELING, *Tod und Leben nach den Vorstellungen der Babylonier* (Berlin: de Gruyter, 1931), 131–32 (= *KAR* 227). *Translations: BM²* 2.562–63; SEUX, *Hymnes et prières aux dieux de Babylonie et d'Assyrie*, 431–32. *Bibliography:* M. BAYLISS, "The Cult of Dead Kin in Assyria and Babylonia," *Iraq* 35 (1973): 115–25; J. BOTTÉRO, *Mesopotamia: Writing, Reasoning, and the Gods* (Chicago: University of Chicago Press, 1992), 268–86; J. COOPER, "The Fate of Mankind: Death and Afterlife in Ancient Mesopotamia," in *Death and Afterlife: Perspectives of World Religions* (ed. H. Obayashi; New York: Praeger, 1992), 20–33; W. MAYER, *Untersuchungen zur Formensprache der babylonischen Gebetsbeschwörungen* (Studia Pohl: Series Maior 5; Rome: Pontifical Biblical Institute, 1976).

3.2. Egyptian Hymns, Prayers, and Laments

The Egyptians produced a large corpus of poetic hymns and prayers. Many of these are preserved in funerary genres, such as the Pyramid Texts, the Coffin Texts, and the Book of the Dead (cf. 5.9.1), but it appears that some of the funerary texts were used also in the regular temple cults and in noncultic contexts. Alongside these funerary exemplars are a significant number of nonfunerary hymns and prayers, which appear mainly in papyrus manuscripts, votive inscriptions, and temple inscriptions. Because the Egyptians' religious attention was focused mainly on solar worship and on the afterlife, many of their hymns and prayers addressed either the sun god (variously known as Amun-Re, Re, Atum, or Aten) or the god of the afterworld (Osiris). The pharaoh was a deity in his own right and received his share of praise and adoration.

For purposes of completeness, some Egyptian hymns and prayers may appear in more than one of the entries listed below.

Cult Hymns and Prayers to the Gods. The primary objective of Egyptian temple worship was to benefit Egyptian society by achieving an intimate nexus between the gods (especially the sun god) and their emissary, the king (who was often represented in the cult by priestly surrogates). Hymns and prayers served a vital role in this endeavor because their verbal and aesthetic qualities created a sacred setting for the divine presence. In order to accentuate the sacrality of the temple, the hymns offered vivid descriptions of the divine form but were reticent to speak of the human realm. In this respect, Egyptian worship was distinguished from its Mesopotamian and Hebrew counterparts (Assmann, 7). Sacred time was measured out ritually, with hymns and prayers marking the sun god's daily passage through the heavens. The solar day was divided into three basic periods: sunrise, noon, and sunset. These periods provided the central themes for entire hymns (e.g., hymns to the rising sun) and also for individual strophes in the hymnic poetry. As in Mesopotamia, Egyptian hymns often included litanies of epithets and honorific descriptions of the gods. This was in part from a desire to please the gods, but it also arose from the syncretistic tendencies in Egyptian religion. As various deities coalesced into single divine figures, the many names and epithets came to be focalized in the one god. Some of these temple hymns were also used in the funerary cults (see below). For related exemplars, see the following entry, "Hymns and Prayers to Aten."

Texts and translations: Text publications are listed in the translations of Assmann and Foster. *Translations: AEL* 2:86–89, 3:107–21; *ANET* 367–68; Assmann, *Ägyptische Hymnen und Gebete*, #1–26, 89, 113–31, 143–46, 201–12; *COS* 1.27: 43–44; Foster, *Hymns, Prayers, and Songs,* #30, 32. *Bibliography:* H. te Velde, "Theology, Priests, and Worship in Ancient Egypt," *CANE* 3:1731–49; see also the bibliography under the following entry.

Hymns and Prayers to Aten. Pharaoh Amenhotep IV (fourteenth century B.C.E.) has often been called the first monotheist because he turned from Egypt's standard polytheism to an exclusive worship of Aten, the solar disk and benevolent creator of all things. The king's devotion was so sincere that he built three new temples to Aten, changed his name to Akenaten, and set up his residence in a new city called Akhetaton (modern Tell el-Amarna; see 1.3). Akenaton's program naturally offended many Egyptians (not least the priests of rejected cults), and when he died, his temples were destroyed and the traditional cults restored. Nevertheless, several of the old Aten temple hymns were preserved in the tomb inscriptions of Aten devotees from Amarna. These texts differ from earlier funerary hymns because only Aten is mentioned and because traditional formulations for attaining a blessed afterlife do not appear. In a few cases the hymns address not only Aten but also king Akenaten, thus reflecting the close relationship between god and Pharaoh in Amarna theology. The longest of the Aten hymns is very similar to Ps 104, prompting many scholars to postulate a direct influence of the

Egyptian text upon the later Hebrew Psalmist. Several centuries separate the two exemplars, however, and it is difficult to imagine a potential path through which the influence would have come. The Aten hymns are, of course, more similar to other Egyptian solar hymns than to Ps 104.

Texts and translations: A. DE BUCK, *Egyptian Reading Book* (Leiden: Nederlands Instituut voor het Nabije Oosten, 1963), 113–15; N. DE GARIS DAVIES, *The Rock Tombs of el Amarna* (6 vols.; Boston: Egypt Exploration Fund, 1903–1908), 4:26–29; 6:17–19, 28–31; M. SAND-MAN, *Texts from the Time of Akhenaton* (BAeg 8; Brussels: Fondation Égyptologique Reine Élisabeth, 1938). *Translations:* AEL 2:89–100; ANET 369–71; ASSMANN, *Ägyptische Hymnen und Gebete,* #90–95; K. H. BERHARDT, "Amenophis IV und Ps 104," *Mitteilungen des Instituts für Orientforschung* 15 (1969): 193–205; COS 1.28: 44–46, 2:14: 66–67; P.-E. DION, "YHWH as Storm-god and Sun-god: The Double Legacy of Egypt and Canaan as Reflected in Psalm 104," *ZAW* 103 (1991): 143–71; FOSTER, *Hymns, Prayers, and Songs,* #45; LAE 278–83. *Bibliography:* AUFFRET, *Hymnes d'Égypte et d'Israel,* 133–310; J. L. FOSTER, "The Hymn to Aten: Akhenaton Worships the Sole God," *CANE* 3:1751–61.

Funerary Hymns and Prayers to the Gods. Egyptian funerary hymns and prayers served two primary purposes. The first purpose, filled by the Pyramid Texts, Coffin Texts, and Book of the Dead, was to enlist divine assistance for the passage from death to a blessed afterlife. In these texts the deceased are often identified closely with the god Osiris, apparently because that deity's reanimation after death—as portrayed in his myths and rites—prefigured that possibility for the dead (see the Osiris/Horus myths in 10.2 and the Osirian laments below, in this section). The sun god (often Re) was also prominent in the funerary hymns, in part because he visited his light and warmth upon the blessed dead each evening and in part because, according to some theologies, the dead could blissfully join Re's retinue during his daily circuit through the heavens and underworld. A second purpose of the funerary hymns was to secure divine help in the quest for food and drink offerings in the hereafter. Hymns and prayers of this type appear on many funerary stelae. In terms of form and content, these texts are very similar to the temple cult hymns, but there is an important generic distinction. While the temple hymns were pronounced by the priests on behalf of the community, funerary hymns were ostensibly spoken by the deceased individual on his or her own behalf.

Texts and translations: See "Pyramid Texts, Coffin Texts, and Book of the Dead" in 5.9.1; see also the sources listed in the translations of Assmann and Foster. *Translations:* AEL 1:32–48, 202–4; 2:81–86, 119–32; ASSMANN, *Ägyptische Hymnen und Gebete,* #27–112, 213–25; COS 1.26: 41–43; FOSTER, *Hymns, Prayers, and Songs,* #1–31, 34–45, 47–50, 69. *Bibliography:* J. ASSMANN, *Egyptian Solar Religion: Re, Amun, and the Crisis of Polytheism* (London: Kegan Paul, 1995); CAMINOS, *Late Egyptian Miscellanies,* 321–23; J. L. FOSTER, "Some Observations of Pyramid Texts 273–274, the So-Called 'Cannibal Hymn,'" *JSSEA* 9 (1978): 51–63; B. E. SHAFER, *Religion in Ancient Egypt: Gods, Myths, and Personal Practice* (Ithaca, N.Y.: Cornell University Press, 1991). See also related entries on Egyptian funerary literature in 5.9.1.

Literary Hymns and Prayers. The best of Egypt's hymnic literature is probably found in P.Leiden I 350 (ca. 1200 B.C.E.), a collection of hymns to Amun-Re that was composed not only for the speaker and his god but also for readers and audiences. So far as we know, these hymns were not used in the temple or funerary cults, so it is likely that the collection was regarded as a work of literature rather than as a cultic text. We may surmise that the hymns provided readers with an aesthetic literary experience and served as the grist for devotional and theological reflection. The text is divided into eight hundred units, each marked by an acrostic device in which the poem begins and ends with a wordplay on the phonetic value of the chapter (e.g., in English, stanza 12 might begin with "won," stanza 2 with "to," etc.; see Brug). Similar literary hymns are translated in Assman (#132–42) and Foster (#33). In some cases, such as P.Boulaq 18 (Foster #31), it is very difficult to determine whether a given hymn should be considered a literary compositon, a temple hymn, or both.

Papyrus Leiden I 350 recto and perhaps P.Leiden I 344 verso (see Zandee) are as close as the Egyptians came to assembling a Hebrew "psalter," but these texts were single, coherent compositions rather than anthologies of disparate hymns and prayers from different times and places. Thus, there are no anthologies of hymns from Egypt that are comparable to the Hebrew Psalter.

Texts and translations: A. MARIETTE, *Les papyrus égyptiens du Musée Boulaq* (3 vols.; Paris: Franck, 1871–1876), vol. 2, pls. xi–xiii (P.Boulaq 18); J. ZANDEE, *De Hymnen aan Amon van Papyrus Leiden I 350, recto* (Leiden: Het Rijksmuseum van Oudheden, 1947) (P.Leiden I 350); IDEM, *Der Amunhymnus des Papyrus Leiden I 334, verso* (3 vols.; Collections of the National Museum of Antiquities at Leiden 7; Leiden: Rijksmuseum, 1992) (P.Leiden I 344). *Translations:* ANET 365–67, 369, 371–72; ASSMANN, *Ägyptische Hymnen und Gebete,* #87–88, 132–42, 242; COS 1.16: 23–26, 1.25: 37–40; FOSTER, *Hymns, Prayers, and Songs,* #31, 33. *Bibliography:* J. ASSMANN, "Kulturelle und literarische Texte," in *Ancient Egyptian Literature: History and Forms* (ed. A. Loprieno; PA 10; New York: Brill, 1996), 59–82; BRUG, "Biblical Acrostics and Their Relationship to Other Ancient Near Eastern Acrostics."

Egyptian Letter Prayers. Like their Mesopotamian counterparts, the Egyptians sometimes addressed their gods by depositing letters in the temple. Letters of this sort were unusual during the New Kingdom, but the genre became much more common during the Persian and Ptolemaic periods. One of the New Kingdom letters explains the difficulty of getting the letter to the god (Wente, #355): "When I was looking for you [i.e., the god] to tell you some affairs of mine, you happened to be concealed in your holy of holies. . . . Now as I was waiting, I encountered Hori, this scribe of the Temple . . . and he said to me, 'I have access.' So I am sending him in to you." In this case, the purpose of the letter was to invite the god out for a public procession, during which the god could judge the petitioner's case and pronounce a verdict by divine oracle (see Egyptian bark oracles in 6.2). A second New Kingdom letter was a votive prayer that promised offerings of beer and bread to Amon-Re in exchange for divine blessings and success (Wente, no. 354). There are some Egyptian letters whose status as letter prayers is uncertain (e.g., Wente, no. 337).

Texts and translations: J. BARNS, "The Nevill Papyrus: A Late Ramesside Letter to an Oracle," *JEA* 35 (1949): 69–71 (= Wente, no. 355); J. CERNÝ and A. H. GARDINER, *Hieratic Ostraca, vol. 1* (Oxford: Griffith Institute, 1957), 50 (= Wente, no. 354); W. SPIEGELBERG, "Briefe der 21. Dynastie aus El-Hibe," *ZÄS* 53 (1917): 13–14, pls. 5–6 (= Wente, no. 337). *Translations:* WENTE, *Letters from Ancient Egypt,* nos. 337, 354, 355.

Hymns and Prayers to Kings and Dignitaries. The Egyptians attributed divinity to all their pharaohs, both living and dead, and they also divinized certain famous deceased individuals, such as Imhotep, vizier and architect of Pharaoh Djoser. As divine humans, these figures naturally became the focus of Egyptian hymns and prayers. Some of these hymns were literary compositions—recited perhaps in the royal courts—and others were used in the temple cults and on formal occasions. These royal hymns offered flattering litanies to the king, heightening the song's sacredness by avoiding references to the concerns and trappings of everyday human life. Prayers to the pharaoh were similarly thick with adulation. Royal hymns and prayers also appear in Egyptian narrative tales, most notably in the Tale of Sinuhe (see 8.1).

Texts and translations: A. H. GARDINER, *Late-Egyptian Miscellanies* (BAeg 1; Brussels: Fondation Égyptologique Reine Élisabeth, 1937); S. SAUNERON, "Un Hymne à Imouthès," *BIFAO* 63 (1965): 73–87; K. SETHE, *Ägyptische Lesestücke* (Leipzig: Hinrichs, 1928), 65–67 (for additional texts, see references in the translations of Assmann and Foster). *Translations:* AEL 1:198–210, 225–26; 3:104–7; ASSMANN, *Ägyptische Hymnen und Gebete,* #226–41; CAMINOS, *Late Egyptian Miscellanies,* 40–47, 101–4, 153–54; FOSTER, *Hymns, Prayers, and Songs,* #56–66; LAE 301–6. *Bibliography:* R. J. LEPROHON, "Royal Ideology and State Administration in Pharaonic Egypt," *CANE* 1:273–87; D. B. O'CONNOR and D. P. SILVERMAN, eds., *Ancient Egyptian Kingship: New Investigations* (PA 9; New York: E. J. Brill, 1995); B. G. TRIGGER, *Ancient Egypt: A Social History* (New York: Cambridge University Press, 1983); D. WILDUNG, *Imhotep und Amenhotep: Gottwerdung im alten Ägypten* (Münchner ägyptologische Studien 36; Munich: Deutscher Kunstverlag, 1977).

Hymns to the Nile. The Nile River, the source of all life in Egypt, was personified and worshipped as the god Hapy. Hapy did not enjoy a regular temple liturgy, but hymns were offered to him on special occasions. Our most important Nile hymn appears to be a literary composition rather than a liturgical text.

Texts and translations: G. POSENER and A. GASSE, *Catalogue des ostraca hiératiques littéraires de Deir el Médineh* (DFIFAO 1, 18, 20, 25; Cairo: Institut Français d'Archéologie Orientale, 1938–), 20: pls. 81–84a; D. VAN DER PLAS, *L'hymn à la crue du Nil* (2 vols.; Leiden: Nederlands Instituut voor het Nabije Oosten, 1986). *Translations:* AEL 1:204–10; ASSMANN, *Ägyptische Hymnen und Gebete,* #242; FOSTER, *Hymns, Prayers, and Songs,* #51, 52. *Bibliography:* M.-A. BONHÊME, "Les eaux rituelles en Égypte pharaonique," *Archéo-Nil* 5 (May 1995): 129–39.

Individual Prayers. Our corpus of individual Egyptian prayers appears on votive stelae, literary papyri, and scribal exercises. Some of these prayers include features that are reminisicent of the Hebrew Psalms. The votive stela of Neb-Re (*AEL*

2:105) parallels the Israelite votive prayers and thanksgiving psalms (Ps 30, 34, 66; see Auffret for other parallels), and the Prayer to Re-Harakhti (P.Anastasi 2; see *COS* 1.29) includes pious expressions of dependence on the god, such as appear in Pss 42, 43, and 84. Regarding the prayers preserved in scribal exercises, although some of these address the sun god, most of the petitions are directed toward the god Thoth. Since Thoth was the patron deity of scribes, we can surmise that these prayers were more than scribal exercises.

Texts and translations: A. ERMAN, *Denksteine aus der thebanischen Gräberstadt* (offprint; SKPAW 49; Berlin: Verlag der Königlich Preussischen Akademie der Wissenschaften, 1911), 1086–1110; A. H. GARDINER, *Late-Egyptian Miscellanies* (BAeg 1; Brussels: Fondation Égyptologique Reine Élisabeth, 1937). *Translations:* AEL 2:15–21, 104–14, 184 (in a love poem); ANET 379–81; ASSMANN, *Ägyptische Hymnen und Gebete*, #147–200; CAMINOS, *Late Egyptian Miscellanies*, 56–63, 321–23; FOSTER, *Hymns, Prayers, and Songs*, #46, 54–55, 67, 69–73; LAE 284–88. *Bibliography:* AUFFRET, *Hymnes d'Égypte et d'Israel*, 19–132; B. GUNN, "The Religion of the Poor in Ancient Egypt," *JEA* 3 (1916): 81–94.

Letters to the Dead. Like many in the ancient world, the Egyptians believed that the dead could influence life among the living. It is no surprise, then, that we have recovered fifteen letters sent by relatives to their deceased loved ones. Insofar as the letters addressed those in the spirit world, it is appropriate to call them prayers. We should not take the letters for expressions of intimate relationship. Without exception, they were prompted by difficulties that, it was thought, the deceased could help alleviate. In one exemplar, a troubled mother asked her husband to muster up a posse of deceased relatives to defend her and her son against those seeking to take his inheritance. In this case the text was composed on linen and then placed near the husband's tomb, but most of our exemplars were inscribed on bowls that were used for funerary offerings. The rationale seems to have been that the dead, needing food and drink, would not fail to notice such letters. How did the dead assist the living? It appears that the dead could represent the living in the tribunals of the "great god," where cases could be adjudicated and redress provided (see O'Donoghue). Most of the Egyptian letters to the dead date to between the Old Kingdom and the First Intermediate period, although some exemplars date to as late as the New Kingdom.

Texts and translations: J. CERNÝ and A. H. GARDINER, *Hieratic Ostraca* (Oxford: Griffith Institute, 1957–), vol. 1, pls. 80–80a; A. H. GARDINER, "A New Letter to the Dead," *JEA* 16 (1930): 19–22; A. H. GARDINER and K. SETHE, *Egyptian Letters to the Dead: Mainly from the Old and Middle Kingdoms* (London: Egyptian Exploration Society, 1928); A. PIANKOFF and J. J. CLÈRE, "A Letter to the Dead on a Bowl in the Louvre," *JEA* 20 (1934): 157–69; W. K. SIMPSON, "The Letter to the Dead from the Tomb of Meru (N 3737) at Nag' ed-Deir," *JEA* 52 (1966): 39–52; IDEM, "A Late Old Kingdom Letter to the Dead from Nag' ed-Deir N 3500," *JEA* 56 (1972): 58–62; E. F. WENTE, "A Misplaced Letter to the Dead," *OLP* 6–7 (1975–1976): 595–600. *Translation:* WENTE, *Letters from Ancient Egypt*, 210–19. *Bibliography:* H. GOEDICKE, "The Letter to the Dead, Nag' ed-Deir N 3500," *JEA* 58 (1972): 95–98; M. O'DONOGHUE, "The 'Letters to the Dead' and Ancient Egyptian Religion," *Bulletin of the Australian Centre for Egyptology* 10 (1999): 87–104; S. QUIRKE, "Letter to the

Dead," in *Mummies and Magic: The Funerary Arts of Ancient Egypt* (ed. S. D'Auria, P. Lacovara, and C. H. Roehrig; Boston: Museum of Fine Arts, 1988), 106–7.

Egyptian Laments. Our earliest Egyptian laments appear in mortuary texts. These include Coffin Texts 51–59, 73–74 (see 5.9.1), spell 172 from the Book of the Dead (see 5.9.1), and numerous "widow's laments" that were inscribed on private tombs dating to the New Kingdom (see Lüddeckens). From the theological standpoint, the most important cultic laments in ancient Egypt were songs recited in the rites of Osiris. We shall consider these Osirian laments in more detail.

The background of the Osirian rites is provided by the myth of the god's death at the hands of his brother Seth (see 10.2). Two women who represented his wife, Isis, and her sister Nephthys sang the ritual laments over Osiris's death. Their songs were essentially widow's laments, such as we see in the New Kingdom tomb inscriptions mentioned above. The women grieved the god's death and then implored Osiris to rise again. The ritual took place in the Hall of Embalming, a small chapel found in several Late period Egyptian temples where the Osiris rites were celebrated annually. The rite's purpose was to promote the healing of the god's torn body and to protect the corpse from his foes (Seth and his companions) until it could be properly mummified and protected. The laments were only part, often a small part, of a longer temple liturgy for the god. Our primary exemplars of the Osirian liturgy date to the fourth and second centuries B.C.E., but inscriptional evidence suggests that the Osirian rites originated long before these texts, probably no later than the Middle Kingdom (Faulkner 1936). Substantial variation must have appeared in the liturgy over such a long period, but we have no way of knowing the degree of modification. Our primary exemplars of the Osirian laments include a long text known as the Songs (see Faulkner 1933), shorter texts often called the Lamentations (see de Horrack; Faulkner 1934; see also the similar text published by von Lieven), and several other exemplars known as *Sakhu* IV (Goyon, 1967), *Sar asha* (unpublished; see Kaplony-Heckel), and the Great Decree (Goyon 1999). There are also several closely related texts that have been named the *Stundenwachen*, which were Osirian rites inscribed at the temples of Edfu, Dendera, and Philae (see Junker). In one instance, a copy of an Osirian lament (in this case, the Lamentations) was found in a private tomb, written on a papyrus alongside the Book of the Dead (P.Berlin 3008). This demonstrates that the Osirian laments were sometimes adapted to the funerary service of a private person, an adaptation that reflects the traditional association of every dead person with Osiris.

Several other Egyptian texts have some thematic connection to the lament genre. These texts include the Admonitions of Ipuwer (see 2.2.2), the Prophecy of Neferti (see 7.2), the Tale of the Eloquent Peasant (see 8.1), and a fragmentary Middle Kingdom papyrus that has been variously dubbed the "teaching," "discourse," or "lament" of Sasobek (see BM EA 10754 in Gardiner). To date, no comprehensive study of the Egyptian lament genre has appeared. This desideratum will be partly addressed in the forthcoming Heidelberg dissertation of A. Kucharek, which is being prepared under the direction of J. Assmann. Kucharek's dissertation will focus on the Late period Osirian laments.

Texts and translations: R. O. FAULKNER, "The Lamentations of Isis and Nephthys," in *Mélanges Maspero* (Mémoires publiés par les membres de l'Institut Français d'archéologie Orientale du Caire 66.1; Cairo: Institut Français d'Archéologie Orientale, 1934–), vol. 1, fasc. 1, 337–48 (Lamentations); IDEM, *The Papyrus Bremner-Rhind (British Museum no. 10188)* (BAeg 3; Brussels: Fondation Égyptologique Reine Élisabeth, 1933) (Songs); IDEM, "The Bremner-Rhind Papyrus—I," *JEA* 22 (1936): 121–40 (Songs); A. H. GARDINER, *The Ramesseum Papyri* (Oxford: Oxford University Press, 1955); J. C. GOYON, "Le cérémonial de glorification d'Osiris du papyrus du Louvre I. 3079 (colonnes 110 à 112)," *BIFAO* 65 (1967): 89–156 (*Sakhu IV*); IDEM, *Le papyrus d'Imouthès, fils de Psintaês, au Metropolitan Museum of Art de New-York (Papyrus MMA 35.9.21)* (New York: Metropolitan Museum of Art, 1999), 17–47, pls. I–XVI (Great Decree); P.-J. DE HORRACK, "Les Lamentations d'Isis et de Nephthys d'après un manuscrit hiératique de Musée royal de Berlin," in *Oeuvres diverses* (ed. G. Maspero; Bibliothèque égyptologique 17; Paris: Leroux, 1907), 33–53 (Lamentations); H. JUNKER, *Die Stundenwachen in den Osirismysterien: Nach den inschriften von Dendera, Edfu, und Philae* (Vienna: A. Hölder, 1910) (*Stundenwachen*); A. VON LIEVEN, "Musical Notation in Roman Period Egypt," in *Studien zur Musikarchäologie* (ed. E. Hickmann, A. D. Kilmer, and R. Eichmann; Orient-Archäologie 10; Rahden, Germany: M. Leidorf, 2000–), 3:497–510 (P.Carlsberg 589). *Translations:* AEL 3:116–121 (Lamentations); E. LÜDDECKENS, "Untersuchungen über religiösen Gehalt, Sprache, und Form der ägyptischen Totenklagen," *MDAIK* 11 (1943): 63–72 (Widow Laments). *Bibliography:* G. BURKARD, *Spätzeitliche Osiris-Liturgien im Corpus der Asasif-Papyri* (AAT 31; Wiesbaden: Harrassowitz, 1995); U. KAPLONY-HECKEL, *Ägyptische Handschriften* (ed. E. Lüddeckens; 4 vols.; Verzeichnis der orientalischen Handschriften in Deutschland 19; Stuttgart: F. Steiner, 1971–1994), 3:31, no. 42.

Papyrus Amherst 63, with an Israelite Psalm in Egypt. This unusual text from Upper Egypt dates to the fourth–third century B.C.E. and was written in Aramaic using an Egyptian demotic script. It contains a liturgy for the New Year's festival of Aramaic-speaking exiles in the region. Part of the liturgy includes the Tale of Sarbanapal and Sarmuge, which is treated in 9.1.3. The greater part of the papyrus is composed of rituals and laments associated especially with the goddess Marah but also with a number of other gods from Mesopotamia, Egypt, and the regions in between. Also wrapped into the ritual is a version of at least one, and perhaps two, Hebrew psalms known from the Hebrew Psalter. The first is a syncretistic version of Ps 20 that appears in column 11 of the papyrus. Although the text mentions the city of Bethel and the god Yahweh (here, Yaho), in this Aramaic liturgy the Israelite deity has coalesced with the Egyptian god Horus as Horus-Yaho. If Rösel is correct, the papyrus also includes allusions to Ps 75 in column 12, but the parallels are not as clear as in the case of Ps 20.

How did a Hebrew psalm come to be in this text? It is fairly clear that the traditions in the text reflect strong influences from Mesopotamia, the Assyrian province of Samaria in Palestine (including Bethel), and Egypt. The best explanation for this pattern is that Aramaic speakers in the east were conquered by Assyria and deported to the Assyrian province of Samaria. The exiles soon adopted native Israelite traditions and combined them with their own, just as we are told in 2 Kgs 17:33. Eventually some of these peoples then migrated to Egypt, as the papyrus specifically indicates: "I come up from Judah, my brother has been brought from Samaria, and now a man is bringing up my sister from Jerusalem." This has obvious and interesting implications for the nature of hymnic traditions, but it also indicates something more specific about Ps 20. In this Aramaic version of the psalm, Yahweh is identified as the "bull of Bethel." This suggests that Ps 20 may have originated as a northern psalm at the bull cult in Bethel before it was transmitted to Jerusalem and underwent a process of "zionization."

Text and translation: R. A. BOWMAN, "An Aramaic Religious Text in Demotic Script," *JNES* 3 (1944): 219–31. *Translation: COS* 1.99: 309–27. *Bibliography:* K. KOENEN, *Bethel: Geschichte, Kult, und Theologie* (OBO 192; Freiburg, Switz.: Universitätsverlag, 2003), 76–79; F. NIMS and R. C. STEINER, "A Paganized Version of Psalm 20:2–6 from the Aramic Text in Demotic Script," *JAOS* 103 (1983): 261–74; M. RÖSEL, "Israels Psalmen in Ägypten? Papyrus Amherst 63 und die Psalmen XX und LXXV," *VT* 50 (2000): 81–99; R. C. STEINER, "The Aramaic Text in Demotic Script: The Liturgy of a New Year's Festival Imported from Bethel to Syene by Exiles from Rash," *JAOS* 111 (1991): 362–63; IDEM, "Papyrus Amherst 63: A New Source for the Language, Literature, Religion, and History of the Arameans," in *Studia aramaica—New Sources and New Approaches: Papers Delivered at the London Conference of the Institute of Jewish Studies, University College, London, 26th–28th June 1991* (ed. M. J. Geller, J. C. Greenfield, and M. P. Weitzman; JSSSup 4; Oxford; New York: Oxford University Press, 1995), 199–207; M. WEINFELD, "The Pagan Version of Psalm 20:2–6— Vicissitudes of a Psalmodic Creation in Israel and Its Neighbors," in *Nahman Avigad Volume* (ed. B. Mazar and Y. Yadin; *ErIsr* 18; Jerusalem: Hebrew University, 1985), 130–40.

3.3. Hittite Prayers and Hymns

Although the Hittites must have used liturgical hymns in their temple cults, the surviving hymns appear only in conjuction with prayers to the gods. All of these exemplars were official texts, sanctioned and preserved by the Hittite state apparatus for repeated use in the temple liturgies. In every case but one, the prayers are royal petitions, the only exception being the prayer of Kantuzilli, a priest who was also a royal prince (see Singer, 30). The Hittites characterized their prayers as *arkuwar*, a judicial plea directed to the divine court of justice. The prayers requested one or more gods to hear the plea and to take it before the divine tribunal. In principle the intercessor could be any of the gods, but requests most often were presented to the deities who presided over the tribunal, that is, the storm and solar deities (which existed in various local manifestations). Petitioners usually confessed their sins or, in the absence of conscious sin, requested that the gods reveal the source of their guilt through dreams, prophets, or divination. Petitioners also attempted to sway the gods in their direction by averring innocence on the basis of ignorance, by citing the frailty of human beings, by noting their faithfulness to the gods, and by promising praise and sacrifice if their prayers were answered.

Two other elements in the Hittite prayers were the *mugawar* and the *walliyatar*. *Mugawar* was an "invocation" or "entreaty" that took the form of a ritual offering. Some texts include this rite or mention a separate *mugawar* tablet that contained it, but we gather that rituals accompanied all prayers even where they are not mentioned in the texts. As for *walliyater*, this was a hymn of praise included in the prayer. Hittite prayers normally included all three of the basic elements—*arkuwar*, *mugawar*, and *walliyater*—but rarely are all three preserved in our fragmentary copies.

For a complete list of the Hittite hymns and prayers, see *CTH* 370–89. The standard collection of texts and translations is Lebrun (in French), and the best English anthology is now Singer. The discussion below will refer to the texts by using Singer's numerations (prayers 1–24).

Early Hittite Prayers. Although they are preserved in texts from the Middle and Late Hittite periods, several Hittite prayers can be dated to the Old period on the basis of their language and religious outlook (Singer, nos. 1–3). Terminology in these early texts parallels the Hittite ritual texts, in one case including detailed prescriptions for sacrificial rituals (Singer, no. 3). Because the ritual participants are referred to anonymously as "priest," "king," and "queen," the texts were clearly canonical prescriptions that could be reused on appropriate occasions. The prayers were uttered by the high priest, who requested protection or help for the king and queen. Petitions were directed to the two primary deities of ancient Anatolia: the storm god and the sun goddess. In one exemplar, the Hittites attempted to sway the sun goddess by offering sacrifices and petitions to her entourage (Singer, no. 1).

As we have noted, our copies of the early Hittite prayers date to well after their composition and hence reflect influences from later theological viewpoints. For instance, the prayer to the sun goddess Arinna also mentions the sun god (Singer, no. 3), who did not appear in the Hittite tradition before the Middle Kingdom. Later editors of the text apparently added this reference to the male deity.

Texts and translations: A. ARCHI, "Eine Anrufung der Sonnengöttin von Arinna," in *Documentum Asiae Minoris antiquae: Festschrift für Heinrich Otten zum 75. Geburtstag* (ed. E. Neu and C. Rüster; Wiesbaden: Harrassowitz, 1988), 5–31 (prayer 3); LEBRUN, *Hymnes et prières hittites*, 83–91, 361–62, 392–96 (prayers 1–3). *Translation:* SINGER, *Hittite Prayers*, 21–28. *Bibliography:* J. FRIEDRICH, "Ein hethitisches Gebet an die Sonnengöttin der Erde," *RSO* 32 (1957): 217–24; H. G. GÜTERBOCK, "Some Aspects of Hittite Prayers," in *The Frontiers of Human Knowledge* (ed. T. R. Segerstedt; Uppsala: Uppsala University Press, 1978), 125–39.

Personal Prayers of the Middle Hittite Kingdom. As the Hittites expanded their territory during the Middle Kingdom, they increasingly came in contact with influences from the east. Two subsequent and important developments took place in the Hittite prayers (see Singer, Hittite Prayers, 13–14, 30–46). First, the Hittites adopted important elements of Mesopotamia's religious tradition, especially aspects of its solar religion associated with the god Šamaš. As a result, the Hittites not only copied and studied Mesopotamian hymns to Šamaš but also adapted these hymns for the worship of their native sun goddess. A second development in the prayers apparently resulted from Hurrian influence. A new genre of Hurrian and Hittite personal prayer appeared in which the petitioners were no longer anonymous but were mentioned in the texts by name. One of these texts, the prayer of the priest Kantuzzili, is our only nonroyal Hittite prayer. It was also the first Hittite prayer, so far as we know, to be based on a Mesopomian solar hymn. Like the earlier Hittite prayers, the personal prayers were preserved on tablets as model prayers for later use. As a result, Kantuzzili's personal prayer survives in two later anonymous versions: the Prayer of the King and the Prayer of a Mortal. In the second text, it is not clear whether "mortal" should be interpreted as a humble reference to the king or as a reference to private individuals. The former possibility seems more likely because the Hittite kings sometimes referred to themselves as "mortals" in their prayers.

Texts and translations: V. HAAS, *Die Serien itkahi und itkalzi des AZU-Priesters: Rituale für Tašmišarri und Tatuepa sowie weitere Texte mit Bezug auf Tašmišarri*(Texte aus Boğazköy 1; Rome: Multigrafica Editrice, 1984), 215–32 (prayer 6); LEBRUN, *Hymnes et prières hittites,* 92–164 (prayers 4–5, 7). *Translations: ANET* 399–401; SINGER, *Hittite Prayers,* 29–46. *Bibliography:* H. G. GÜTERBOCK, "The Composition of Hittite Prayers to the Sun," *JAOS* 78 (1958): 237–45; M. MARAZZI and H. NOWICKI, "Vorarbeiten zu den hethitischen Gebeten," *OrAnt* 17 (1978): 257–78; I. SINGER, "Kantuzili the Priest and the Birth of Hittite Personal Prayer," in *Silva anatolica: Anatolian Studies Presented to Maciej Popko on the Occasion of His 65th Birthday* (ed. P. Taracha; Warsaw: AGADE, 2002), 301–13; G. WILHELM, "Zur hurritischen Gebetsliteratur," in *Ernten, was man sät: Festschrift für Klaus Koch zu seinem 65. Geburtstag* (ed. D. R. Daniels, U. Glessmer, and M. Rösel; Neukirchen-Vluyn: Neukirchener Verlag, 1991), 37–47.

The Prayers of King Muršili II. During the reign of Suppiluliuma I (1380–1340 B.C.E.) a violent plague erupted in Hatti that continued to decimate its population for over two decades. Preserved in the archive of ancient Hatti is a series of prayers, known as the Plague Prayers, in which King Muršili II (1339–1306 B.C.E.) petitioned the gods to lift this plague from his people (Singer, nos. 8–14). The prayers were addressed to the sun goddess, the storm god, and, in some cases, the entire assembly of the gods. The form of the prayers varies somewhat. Two exemplars (Singer, nos. 8–9) clearly preserve all three prayer elements, the *mugawar* (ritual invocation), *walliyater* (hymn), and *arkuwar* (prayer). Text no. 8 is particularly interesting from an intertextual point of view. Its hymn to the sun goddess was adapted directly from a Mesopotamian hymn to Šamaš. The author adapted the hymn by eliminating all masculine elements found in his *Vorlage,* save at one point where he inadvertently preserved a reference to "my lord." For the prayer itself, that author modernized an earlier Hittite prayer to the sun goddess (Singer, no. 7).

Because of the plague's dire consequences, Muršili was preoccupied with determining the plague's causes in order that they might be addressed. Court scribes and diviners combed the archives looking for evidence and eventually discovered tablets that reflected two apparent sins of Muršili's father, Suppiluliuma: his neglect of sacrifices for the Mala cult (the deity of the Euphrates River) and especially his breach of a treaty with Egypt. This second explanation for the plague seemed particularly fitting, since the plague originated among the Egyptian prisoners Suppiluliuma brought back to Hatti. After confirming by divination that these were indeed the causes of the plague, Muršili undertook rituals to repair his father's broken oath regarding Egypt, and then he made plans to travel to the Euphrates to observe the neglected ritual for Mala. On the basis of these actions, Muršili appealed to the storm god for forgiveness and removal of the plague (Singer, no. 11).

Some scholars believe that Muršili's Plague Prayers can be ordered chronologically on the basis of certain theological developments in the king's understanding of collective guilt (Güterbock; Houwink ten Cate). In this line of thought, Muršili's early prayers pin the blame on his forefathers and emphatically insist that he is innocent, whereas the later prayers concede that the "father's sin comes upon his son." Not all scholars are convinced that this evolutionary scheme works so well (see Singer's critique). A biblical parallel to Muršili's Plague Prayers is found in 2 Sam 21:1: "Now there was a famine in the days of David for three years, year after year. And David inquired of the LORD. The LORD said, 'There is blood-guilt on Saul and on his house, because he put the Gibeonites to death.'"

We possess a few Muršili prayers that address issues of a more personal nature (Singer, nos. 15–18). Two of these are entreaties for the healing of his very sick wife, Gassuliyawiya (nos. 15–16). In prayer 15 the king refers to a substitution ritual similar to the Hittite ritual installation of a substitute king (see 5.8.3), in which a beautiful young woman was sent to the god with offerings and sacrifices. The king asked the god to accept these offerings and to accept the woman as a substitute for his wife (we do not know the fate of the woman). The prayer concluded with a promise: "Accept, O god, this offering in good spirit and turn again in favor of Gassuliyawiya. . . . Then it will come to pass that in the future Gassuliyawiya will constantly praise you, O god, and she will constantly invoke only your name." Unfortunately, Gassuliyawiya died. Through divination Muršili pinned the blame for her death on his "evil" stepmother, who had apparently cursed his spouse before the gods. After gaining divine approval, Muršili subsequently removed his stepmother from her office as high priestess. Later difficulties caused Muršili to have second thoughts about the banishment of his stepmother, so he composed two exculpatory prayers in which he averred his innocence in the matter, pointing out that her banishment was done with divine sanction and that his stepmother was an evil and guilty woman (Singer, nos. 17–18).

Texts and translations: F. CORNELIUS, "Ein hethitischer Hexenprozess," *RIDA* 22 (1975): 27–45 (prayers 17–18); LEBRUN, *Hymnes et prières hittites*, 165–71, 180–255 (prayers 8–16). *Translations: ANET* 394–96; *COS* 1.60: 156–60 (partial); SINGER, *Hittite Prayers*, 47–79. *Bibliography:* A. GOETZE, "Die Pestgebete des Muršiliš," *Kleinasiatische Forschungen* 1 (1929): 161–251; O. R. GURNEY, "Hittite Prayers of Mursili II," *AAA* 27 (1940): 1–167; H. G. GÜTERBOCK, "Mursili's Account of Suppiluliuma's Dealings with Egypt," *RHA* 66 (1960): 57–63; H. A. HOFFNER JR., "A Prayer of Muršili II about His Stepmother," *JAOS* 103 (1983): 187–92; P. H. J. HOUWINK TEN CATE, "Hittite Royal Prayers," *Numen* 16

(1969): 81–98; A. MALAMAT, "Doctrines of Causality in Hittite and Biblical Historiography: A Parallel," *VT* 5 (1955): 1–12.

Other Hittite Prayers. From the period after Muršili II we posses two prayers of Muwatalli II (nos. 19–20), two prayers concerning Hattušili III (nos. 21–22), a prayer of Tudhaliya IV (no. 24), and various fragments of prayers addressed to the storm god of Nerik (no. 23). From this corpus Muwatalli's prayers are the most innovative. Although his prayers drew upon earlier traditions, they address only male deities rather than the traditional sun goddesses, and the shift of focus drifts to the deities in the south of Anatolia. Moreover, a strong Hurrian-Luwian influence is discernable not only in the gods that are petitioned but also in the language of the prayers. These developments are connected with Muwatalli's decision to move his capital from Ḫattuša in the north to Tarhuntassa in the south, apparently because it was determined that the gods had been angered by Hatti's neglect of the southern cultic centers. One of the Muwatalli prescriptive prayer texts includes directions for the king to offer his own extempore prayers: "When he finishes breaking the thick breads, the things which are in His majesty's heart, he makes them into a plea to the gods" (see no. 20).

  Prayers composed after Muwatalli return to the traditional focus on the sun goddess. One of these is an exculpatory prayer in which Hattušili lists the sins of his forefathers and requests that the goddess not hold him culpable for them (no. 21). In another text, Tudhaliya openly confesses his sinful neglect of the sun goddess's cult. After promising to set things right, he asks for her to bless his army with success in battle (no. 24). Similar Israelite prayers for military success appear in Pss 44 and 60.

Text and translation: LEBRUN, *Hymnes et prières hittites,* 256–361. *Translations: ANET* 393–94, 397–99; SINGER, *Hittite Prayers,* 80–110. *Bibliography:* P. H. J. HOUWINK TEN CATE, "Muwattalis' 'Prayer to Be Spoken in an Emergency': An Essay in Textual Criticism," *JNES* 27 (1968): 204–8; P. H. J. HOUWINK TEN CATE and F. JOSEPHSON, "Muwattalis' Prayer to the Storm-God of Kummanni (KBo XI 1)," *RHA* 25 (1967): 101–40; I. SINGER, *Muwatalli's Prayer to the Assembly of Gods through the Storm-God of Lightening* (Atlanta: Scholars Press, 1996).

3.4. Ugaritic Hymns and Prayers

Ugaritic Hymns and Prayers. In certain respects, no Near Eastern texts are so close to the biblical psalms as the literary texts from Ugarit. Ugaritic texts were written in a West Semitic language that was closely related to Hebrew, and their poetic parallelism is very much like the parallelism of Israelite hymns and prayers. Nevertheless, a vital generic link between the texts is missing. In spite of the fact that Ugaritic literature frequently mentions rituals and prayers to the gods, most of the texts that we have from Ugarit are neither hymns nor prayers. Two notable exceptions are *KTU* 1.119 and *KTU* 1.123, of which the first text is probably the most important. The tablet is a ritual prescription for driving

Ugarit's enemies away during a siege of the city (see Miller). The text prescribes a series of rites and sacrifices in laconic prose, then it concludes with a poetic votive prayer to Baal: "O Baal, If you will drive the strong one from our gates / the warrior from our walls; a bull, O Baal, we shall consecrate / a vow, O Baal, we shall fulfill. . . . To the sanctuary of Baal we shall go up / the paths of the house of Baal we shall traverse" (cf. the votive conclusions of Pss 51, 56, 61, 79). After the prayer, the text closes with these confident words: "Baal has heard your prayer. He will drive the strong one from your gates, the warrior from you walls." As for *KTU* 1.123, it appears to be a petition for well-being directed to a long list of gods, but we cannot tell whose prayer it was nor for whom it was offered. Margulis has suggested that another text, *KTU* 1.108, includes a fragmentary hymn related to the little understood cult of the Rephaim, but this no longer seems to be the case (cf. Margulis; Pardee).

Text and translation: D. PARDEE, *Ritual and Cult at Ugarit* (SBLWAW 10; Atlanta: Society of Biblical Literature, 2002), 50–53, 149–50 (*KTU* 1.119), 150–53 (*KTU* 1.123), 195–210 (*KTU* 1.108). ***Translation:*** COS 1.88: 283–85 (*KTU* 1.119). ***Bibliography:*** B. MARGULIS, "A Ugaritic Psalm (RŠ 24.252)," *JBL* 89 (1970): 292–304; P. D. MILLER JR., "Prayer and Sacrifice in Ugarit and Israel," in *Text and Context: Old Testament and Semitic Studies for F. C. Fensham* (ed. W. T. Classen; Sheffield, England: JSOT Press, 1988), 139–55.

Concluding Observations

Ancient Israelite hymns, prayers, and laments are found primarily in Lamentations and in the Hebrew Psalms. When adjudged using modern generic categories, these materials display a wide range of literary forms, including praise hymns for the deity, communal prayers and laments, individual prayers and laments, laments over Jerusalem and its temple, royal psalms and hymns, penitential prayers of various kinds, didactic wisdom psalms, historical hymns, blessings and curses, pilgrimage songs, victory songs, and even a royal wedding song. The Hebrew hymns, prayers, and laments are better appreciated when viewed against the backdrop of the ancient Near Eastern world.

1. **The *Sitze im Leben* of Hymns, Prayers, and Laments.** It is common for scholars to assign particular contexts and functions to ancient lyrical texts on the basis of distinctions between "cultic" and "noncultic," "individual" and "communal," "official" and "popular," and so on. Such observations are useful and important insofar as they work, but classifications of this sort must always be tempered by an awareness of the generic complexity of these texts. Because of their very religious and emotive character, hymns, prayers, and laments were more susceptible than other genres to generic extension and adaptation. For instance, the Osirian cultic laments were easily adapted as private funerary texts, the Mesopotamian laments for temple construction were eventually used in ongoing vigils against divine anger,

and Ps 20—originally a Hebrew text from Yahweh's temple at Bethel—
shows up, in a much convoluted form, as part of a long New Year rite used
by Aramaic speakers in Egypt (see P.Amherst 63). Consequently, when we
come to the Hebrew Psalms, we must imagine that many of our modern
designations—such as "individual lament"—will not reflect all actual uses
of the text in antiquity. Individual laments of the Psalter were also used in
communal contexts, as the conclusion of Ps 69 suggests (see vv. 34–36). The
same observations apply to ancient generic designations, such as the super-
script in Ps 92 that identifies the text as a "Sabbath" psalm. Nothing in the
psalm ties it unambiguously to a Sabbath context, so we should imagine
that the song was not composed for the Sabbath so much as it became a
Sabbath song. Similar kinds of generic variation no doubt accompanied the
use of many other texts in the Psalter.

One contextual feature that comes to the fore in the Near Eastern corpus is
the concurrence of prayers and laments with ritual sacrifices and offerings.
Ritual offerings were an important part of the Hittite prayers, and many of
the private prayers from Mesopotamia specifically mention cultic offerings
of incense and other items. The calendars of Mesopotamian liturgies published long ago by Langdon reflect this as well (Langdon 1925–1926). Although the prayers and laments in the Hebrew Psalter do not often refer to
these rites explicitly, there are numerous psalms that connect petitions with
votive offerings by either promising offerings in exchange for answered
prayer (Pss 51, 54, 56, 61, 65, 67, 79) or by fulfilling vows after divine blessings (Pss 30, 66).We also have good evidence from the Mishnah that, at
least after the exile, the Jews recited several psalms during the daily sacrifices at the temple (Pss 24, 48, 81, 82, 92, 93, 94; see Trudinger).

Although this evidence makes it obvious that the national cults of ancient
Israel and Judah would have offered hymns and prayers in conjunction
with their sacrifices, it also seems wise to suppose that sacrifices and offerings accompanied individual and private uses of the psalms in some—perhaps most—cases. This observation counts not only for the recitation of
psalms by individuals in the temple but also for uses of the psalms in private contexts away from Israel's national cult centers, such as Jerusalem
and Bethel.

2. Generic Variety in the Hymns, Prayers, and Laments. A comparison of Israel's
lyrical genres with literature from the ancient Near East makes two points
clear. First, nearly all of the genres found in the Psalter and in Lamentations
have counterparts of some sort in the Near Eastern tradition. In some cases
these similarities turn out to be of a general sort, but in others they are particularly striking. The Sumerian DINGER.ŠA.DIB.BAs and ERŠAHUNGAs and
the Akkadian ŠUILLAs share a three-part format of address/praise, prayer/

lament, and thanksgiving that appears also in many Israelite laments and penitential prayers. It is commonly believed that this similarity arose because of Mesopotamian influence on Israelite authors. The letter prayers and votive texts from Mesopotamia and Egypt present another interesting parallel. These texts, usually deposited in temples, were either vows made in conjunction with requests for divine help or fulfillments of the vows themselves. Texts of this kind certainly appear in the Psalter (see above), and one cannot help but assume that some of the psalms—perhaps many of them—originated as individual or communal votive inscriptions. This judgment is reinforced by the Davidic *miktām* psalms (Pss 16, 57–60), which seem to derive from prayer inscriptions. There are, however, a few Hebrew texts for which we do not find precise corresponding types in the Near East, the most notable examples being Israel's historical psalms (e.g., Pss 106, 107), whose relative uniqueness perhaps parallels Israel's unique tendency to compose national histories (see ch. 12).

The second point that is clear from our comparative deliberations is that among the Near Eastern hymns, prayers, and laments are numerous generic types for which we do not have corresponding texts in the biblical corpus. Those responsible for the present form of the Psalter did not worship Israelite kings (Egypt, Ur III), did not lament dead gods (Dumuzi, Osiris), wrote no letters to deceased relatives (Mesopotamia, Egypt), offered no divination prayers (Mesopotamia), and did not sing hymns and recite prayers in order to secure a blessed afterlife (the Egyptian funerary texts). Do these differences mean that ancient Israel did not use these generic types? During the postexilic period, when the Hebrew Psalter was probably assembled, it seems likely that most Jews would have rejected the religious practices just mentioned as well as any related literary genres. In the earlier periods of Israelite history, however—particularly during the exilic and preexilic periods—the biblical sources aver, no doubt correctly, that religious belief and practice in Israel was quite diverse. Consequently, although the Psalter provides a partial window into the world of preexilic Judaism, it would be hazardous to assume that the book provides us with a complete picture of liturgical and religious life in preexilic and exilic Israel.

3. The Canonical Process in Ancient Hymns, Prayers, and Laments. Although the Hittite prayer of Kantuzzili originated as an individual petition, later readers recognized its cultic utility and rewrote the text so that it could be more easily used by others. In this new garb, the text was preserved in the Hittite canonical tradition as the Prayer of the King and as the Prayer of a Mortal. As this case illustrates, the canonicity of ancient lyrical texts was generally the result of usage. In Mesopotamia, prayers and laments that were regularly used in communal liturgies and in private ritual settings were perpetuated as scribes copied and recopied the text over the years.

These texts often took on fixed canonical forms, and in some cases, the scribes attempted to compile collections of the texts by listing them on catalogue tablets or by joining them together in ritual series. Somewhat different was the canonical phenomenon in Neo-Assyria, where scribes assembled an anthology of Sumerian BALAG laments in order to preserve the texts and make them accessible for study. In this instance, the Neo-Assyrians were not motivated by theological and liturgical concerns so much as by an interest in preserving tradition. It is easy to imagine that these two motives—liturgical usage and a desire to preserve tradition—may have played significant roles in the composition and assembly of the Hebrew Psalter.

4. The Compilation of Hymnic Anthologies. To what extent does the Near Eastern evidence enlighten our understanding of the development of the Hebrew Psalter? Hymn anthologies did not exist in ancient Egypt or in ancient Hatti. The closest Near Eastern exemplars to the Hebrew Psalter are the Mesopotamian liturgical anthologies, especially Enḫeduanna's collection of temple hymns and the Neo-Assyrian BALAG anthology. These two collections were not assembled in a haphazard way but reflect instead certain rationales that governed their overall shape. This observation reinforces the recent judgment of some biblical scholars who believe that the individual psalms of the Psalter were carefully arranged to create large-scale editorial structures in the book. The Hebrew and Mesopotamian anthologists were also similar in their tendency to identify the genres of their hymns using rubrics, such as TIGI, BALAG, and BALBALE in Mesopotamia, and *mizmôr, tefillâ, maśkîl,* and *šiggāyôn* in Israel. In the context of these similarities, two key differences distinguish the Mesopotamian anthologies from their Hebrew counterpart. First, if biblical scholars are right, then the detailed structural features of the Hebrew Psalter far outstrip the level of organization that appears in the Mesopotamian collections. This features in the Psalter may be related to the second difference between the texts. Whereas the Psalter brought together a wide variety of generic types into a single anthology, the Mesopotamian anthologies tended to include only texts of a single generic type (e.g., BALAGs). This suggests that, as anthologies go, the Hebrew Psalter reflects a more comprehensive effort, which attempted to include all of Judaism's most important hymns and prayers in a single corpus.

5. Lyrical Texts as Literature. There is good evidence that several hymns and prayers from Mesopotamia and Egypt were copied and studied because of their perceived aesthetic and religious value. The most notable examples are the great Šamaš hymn from Mesopotamia, the Akkadian ŠUILLA prayers, and Egypt's literary hymns and prayers (such as P.Leiden I 350). We may surmise from this evidence that Israel's hymns and prayers also served as sources of devotional and intellectual reflection in addition to—or perhaps instead of—whatever liturgical role these Hebrew psalms may have served.

6. The Cultural Diffusion of Lyrical Generic Traits. Hymns and prayers frequently crossed the cultural membranes that separated one ancient society from another. Nowhere is this more obvious than in Hatti, where Hittite scribes essentially lifted their solar hymns and prayers directly from Mesopotamian exemplars. We have already noted that Israelite songwriters seem to have been influenced by Mesopotamian scribal conventions, particularly in the cases of the Hebrew laments and penitential prayers. The most convincing case for foreign influences on Israelite hymnology, however, is Ps 104, which seems to be an Israelite version of a hymn to the Egyptian god Aton. The considerable time span between the Aton Hymn and Ps 104 makes it difficult to imagine how the influence may have come about, but the path of influence from Egypt to Israel, whatever it was, could not have been more surprising than the odd path from Israel to Egypt followed by Ps 20. This Hebrew psalm originated in the Israelite cult at Bethel and then appeared several centuries later in Egypt (P.Amherst 63).

7. Theological Adaptation in Lyrical Literature. Many of the hymns, prayers, and laments were used over long periods of time. Because these texts were religious in nature, it was frequently necessary to adapt them to changes in theological perspective. In Cohen's ERŠEMMA no. 1, for instance, the first-millennium version removed references to some southern cities found in the older versions and replaced them with northern cities that were prominent during the first millennium. Similarly, the Hittites adapted Mesopotamian hymns for use in their worship of the sun goddess, and the Egyptian king, Akenaton, adapted older solar hymns for the cult for Aton. Although many other examples of this phenomenon could be cited, perhaps the most fitting illustration of the phenomenon comes from the Hebrew Bible itself. As we have seen, Ps 20 seems to have originated as a liturgical hymn for Yahweh at Bethel. The hymn was eventually taken south to Judah and west to Egypt, resulting in two very different versions of the hymn. In the Aramaic version from Egypt, Yahweh was combined with the Egyptian deity Horus to create Horus-Yaho, whereas in Judah the text was "zionized," so that it praised Yahweh of Jerusalem rather than Yahweh, the bull of Bethel.

8. City and Temple Laments. Israelite laments over the destruction of Jerusalem and its temple appear in the book of Lamentations and to a lesser extent in the Psalter. The devastation experienced by Judah during the early sixth century, which prompted most, if not all, of these compositions, is comparable to the obliteration of the Ur III civilization (ca. the twenty-first century B.C.E.), which triggered ritual mourning for Ur's many cities and temples. The Israelite laments differ, however, from their Mesopotamian counterparts in two key features. First, the Israelite laments are, from an aesthetic standpoint, better pieces of literature than the long and repetitious litanies found in the Mesopotamian city laments. Second, it is not at all clear that the Hebrew city and temple laments were recited in order to appease God's anger during the razing and refurbishment of the Jerusalem temple, nor does it appear that the Hebrew laments were used in an ongoing vigil against divine wrath, as was the case with the Sumerian BALAGs. Jews in Palestine seem to have worshiped at the temple site after the building's destruction (see Jer 41:5), so it is possible that some of our Hebrew laments were composed and recited in such a context. The exiles in Babylon, however, would have had good reasons to mourn Jerusalsm and its temple as well.

9. A Note on Biblical Prose Prayer. The Hebrew narratives from Genesis to Chronicles contain ninety-seven prose prayers, which may be divided between the prayers of laypeople (thirty-eight) and those uttered by kings or prophets (fifty-nine). Because these prayers were not composed as liturgical texts like the Psalms, they might reflect more accurately the common extempore prayers spoken by people in everyday life. The standard discussion of these prayers is found in Greenberg.

General Bibliography

G. A. ANDERSON, "The Praise of God as a Cultic Event," in *Priesthood and Cult in Ancient Israel* (ed. G. A. Anderson and S. M. Olyan; JSOTSup 125; Sheffield, England: Sheffield Academic Press, 1991); J. ASSMANN, *Ägyptische Hymnen und Gebete* (2d ed.; OBO Sonderband; Freiburg, Switz.: Universitätsverlag, 1999); P. AUFFRET, *Hymnes d'Égypte et d'Israel* (OBO 34; Friburg, Switz.: Éditions Universitaires, 1981); A. BARUQ and F. DAUMAS, *Hymnes et prières de l'Égypte ancienne* (Paris: Cerf, 1980); J. BEGRICH, "Die Vertrauensäusserungen im israelitischen Klageliede des Einzelnen und in seinem babylonischen Gegenstück," *ZAW* 64 (1925): 221–60; A. M. BLACKMAN, "The Psalms in the Light of Egyptian Research," in *The Psalmists: Essays on Their Religious Experience and Teaching, Their Social Background, and Their Place in the Development of Hebrew Psalmody* (ed. D. C. Simpson; London: Oxford University Press, H. Milford, 1926), 177–97; J. BOTTÉRO, *Mythes et rites de Babylone* (Paris: Champion, 1985); J. F. BRUG, "Biblical Acrostics and Their Relationhip to Other Ancient Near Eastern Acrostics," in *The Bible in the Light of Cuneiform Literature* (ed. W. W. Hallo, B. W. Jones, and G. L. Mattingly; Scripture in Context 3; Lewiston, N.Y.: Mellen, 1990), 283–304; W. BURKERT and F. STOLZ, *Hymnen der Alten Welt im Kulturvergleich* (OBO 131; Freiburg, Switz.: Universitätsverlag, 1994); R. A. CAMINOS, *Late Egyptian Miscellanies* (London: Oxford University Press, 1954); A. CAVIGNEAUX, "Mesopotamian Lamentations," *JAOS* 113 (1993): 251–57; M. CLAGETT, *Ancient Egyptian Science:*

A Source Book (3 vols. in 4; Philadelphia: American Philosophical Society, 1989–1999); M. E. COHEN, *The Canonical Lamentations of Ancient Mesopotamia* (2 vols.; Potomac, Md.: Capital Decisions, 1988); IDEM, *Sumerian Hymnology: The Eršemma* (HUCASup 2; Cincinnati: Hebrew Union College, 1981); J. S. COOPER, "Warrior, Devastating Deluge, Destroyer of Hostile Lands: A Sumerian Šuila to Marduk," in *A Scientific Humanist: Studies in Memory of Abraham Sachs* (ed. E. Leichty, M. deJ. Ellis, and P. Gerardi; OPSNKF 9; Philadelphia: University Museum, 1988), 83–93; P. C. CRAIGIE, "The Comparison of Hebrew Poetry: Psalm 104 in the Light of Egyptian and Ugaritic Poetry," *Semitics* 4 (1974): 10–21; E. R. DAGLISH, *Psalm Fifty-One in the Light of Ancient Near Eastern Patternism* (Leiden: Brill, 1962); F. W. DOBBS-ALLSOPP, *Weep O Daughter of Zion: A Study of the City-Lament Genre in the Hebrew Bible* (Rome: Editrice Pontificio Istituto Biblico, 1993); G. R. DRIVER, "The Psalms in the Light of Babylonian Research," in *The Psalmists: Essays on Their Religious Experience and Teaching, Their Social Background, and Their Place in the Development of Hebrew Psalmody* (ed. D. C. Simpson; London: Oxford University Press, H. Milford, 1926), 109–75; E. EBELING, *Ein Hymnen-Katalog aus Assur* (Berlin: Im Selbstverlage des Herausgebers, 1923); A. FALKENSTEIN and W. VON SODEN, *Sumerische und akkadische Hymnen und Gebete* (Zurich: Artemis, 1953); C. L. FEINBERG, "Parallels to the Psalms in Near Eastern Literature," *BibSac* 104 (1947): 290–97; P. W. FERRIS JR., *The Genre of Communal Lament in the Bible and the Ancient Near East* (SBLDS 127; Atlanta: Scholars Press, 1992); B. R. FOSTER, *Before the Muses: An Anthology of Akkadian Literature* (2d ed.; Potomac, Md.: CDL Press, 1996); J. L. FOSTER, *Hymns, Prayers, and Songs: An Anthology of Ancient Egyptian Lyric Poetry* (SBLWAW 8; Atlanta: Scholars Press, 1995); M. GREENBERG, *Biblical Prose Prayer: As a Window to the Popular Religion of Ancient Israel* (Berkeley: University of California Press, 1983); W. C. GWALTNEY, "The Biblical Book of Lamentations in the Context of Near Eastern Literature," in *More Essays on the Comparative Method* (ed. W. W. Hallo, J. C. Moyer, and L. Perdue; Scripture in Context 2; Winona Lake, Ind.: Eisenbrauns, 1983), 191–211; W. W. HALLO, "The Cultic Setting of Sumerian Poetry," in *Actes de la XVIIe Rencontre assyriologique internationale* (ed. A. Finet; Ham-sur-Heure, Belgium: Comité Belge de Recherches en Mésopotamie, 1970), 116–34; IDEM, "Lamentations and Prayers in Sumer and Akkad," *CANE* 3:1871–81; T. JACOBSEN, *The Harps That Once . . . Sumerian Poetry in Translation* (New Haven: Yale University Press, 1987); S. N. KRAMER, "BM 29616: The Fashioning of the *Gala*," *ActSum* 3 (1981): 1–11; IDEM, "Poets and Psalmists: Goddesses and Theologians," in *The Legacy of Sumer* (ed. D. S. Besserat; BMes 4; Malibu, Calif.: Undena, 1976), 3–21; W. G. LAMBERT, "A Catalogue of Texts and Authors," *JCS* 16 (1962): 59–77; S. LANGDON, *Babylonian Penitential Psalms* (Paris: Paul Geuthner, 1927); IDEM, "Calendars of Liturgies and Prayers," *AJSL* 42 (1925–1926): 110–27; R. LEBRUN, *Hymnes et prières hittites* (Louvain-la-Neuve, Belgium: Centre d'Histoire des Religions, 1980); A. LIVINGSTONE, *Court Poetry and Literary Miscellanea* (SAA 3; Helsinki: Helsinki University Press, 1989); O. LORETZ, "Der altorientalische rechtliche Hintergrund der biblischen 'Klage des Einzelnen,'" in *Textarbeit: Studien zu Texten und ihrer Rezeption aus dem Alten Testament und der*

Umwelt Israels: Festschrift für Peter Weimar (ed. K. Kiesow and T. Meurer; AOAT 294; Münster: Ugarit, 2003), 285–310; L. MANNICHE, *Music and Musicians in Ancient Egypt* (London: British Museum Press, 1991); N. NICOLSKY, *Spuren magischer Formeln in den Psalmen* (BZAW 46; Giessen, Germany: Töppelmann, 1927); R. T. O'CALLAGHAN, "Echoes of Canaanite Literature in the Psalms," *VT* 4 (1954): 164–76; E. OTTO, "Psalm 2 in neuassyrischer Zeit: Assyrische Motive in der judäischen Königsidealogie," in *Textarbeit: Studien zu Texten und ihrer Rezeption aus dem Alten Testament und der Umwelt Israels: Festschrift für Peter Weimar* (ed. K. Kiesow and T. Meurer; AOAT 294; Münster: Ugarit, 2003), 335–39; X. H. T. PHAM, *Mourning in the Ancient Near East and the Hebrew Bible* (JSOTSup 302; Sheffield, England: Sheffield Academic Press, 1999); W. H. P. RÖMER, *Hymnen und Klagelieder in sumerischer Sprache* (AOAT 276; Münster: Ugarit, 2001); W. H. P. RÖMER, K. HECKER, and O. KAISER, *Lieder und Gebete, 1* (part 5 of *Religiöse Texte*, vol. 2 of *Texte aus der Umwelt des Alten Testaments;* ed. Otto Kaiser; Gütersloh: Gerd Mohn, 1989); J. M. SASSON, ed., *Studies in Literature from the Ancient Near East: Dedicated to Samuel Noah Kramer* (AOS 65; New Haven: American Oriental Society, 1984); M.-J. SEUX, *Hymnes et prières aux dieux de Babylonie et d'Assyrie* (Paris: Cerf, 1976); A. SHAFFER, "From the Bookshelf of a Professional Wailer," in *The Tablet and the Scroll: Near Eastern Studies in Honor of William W. Hallo* (ed. M. E. Cohen et al.; Bethesda, Md.: CDL Press, 1993), 209–10; I. SINGER, *Hittite Prayers* (SBLWAW 11; Atlanta: Society of Biblical Literature, 2002); F. STUMMER, "Die Psalmengattungen im Lichte der altorientalischen Hymnenliteratur," *JSOR* 8 (1924): 123–34; IDEM, *Sumerisch-akkadische Parallelen zum Aufbau altestamentlicher Psalmen* (Paderborn: Schöningh, 1922); F. THUREAU-DANGIN, *Rituels accadiens* (Osnabrück, Germany: Otto Zeller, 1975); P. L. TRUDINGER, *The Psalms of the Tamid Service: A Liturgical Text from the Second Temple* (Leiden: Brill, 2003); E. WENTE, *Letters from Ancient Egypt* (SBLWAW 1; Atlanta: Scholars Press, 1990); J. G. WESTENHOLZ, "Enḫeduanna, En-Priestess, Hen of Nanna, Spouse of Nanna," in DUMU-E2-DUB-BA-A: *Studies in Honor of Åke W. Sjöberg* (ed. H. Behrens, D. T. Loding, and M. Roth; OPSNKF 11; Philadelphia: University Museum, 1989), 539–56; G. WIDENGREN, *The Accadian and Hebrew Psalms of Lamentation as Religious Documents: A Comparative Study* (Uppsala: Almquist & Wiksells, 1936); H. ZIMMERN, "Zu den 'Keilschrifttexten aus Assur religiösen Inhalts,'" *ZA* 30 (1915–1916): 184–229.

Near Eastern Musicology Bibliography

D. ANDERSON, "Music and Dance in Pharaonic Egypt," *CANE* 4:2555–68; IDEM, *Musical Instruments* (vol. 3 of *Catalogue of Egyptian Antiquities in the British Museum;* London: British Museum, 1976); J. ARNDT-JEAMART, "Zur Konstruktion und Stimmung von Saiten-instrumenten nach den musikalischen Keilschrifttexten," *Or* 61 (1992): 425–47; H. AVENARY, "The Discrepancy between Iconographic and Literary Presentations of Ancient Eastern Musical Instruments,"

Orbis musicae 3–4 (1973–1974): 121–27; IDEM, "Flutes for a Bride or a Dead Man: The Symbolism of the Flute according to Hebrew Sources," *Orbis musicae* 1 (1971): 11–24; N. AVIGAD, "The King's Daughter and the Lyre," *IEJ* 28 (1978): 146–51; Y. AVISHUR, "KRKR in Biblical Hebrew and in Ugaritic," *VT* 26 (1976): 257–61; R. D. BARNETT, "New Facts about Musical Instruments from Ur," *Iraq* 31 (1969): 96–103; B. BAYER, "The Hazor Conch-Horn," *Tatzlil* 3 (1953): 140–42; IDEM, *Material Relics of Music in Ancient Palestine and Its Environs* (Tel Aviv: Israel Music Institute, 1963); IDEM, "Music: Biblical Period; Second Temple Period," *EncJud* 12:559–66; R. D. BIGGS, "The Sumerian Harp," *American Harp Journal* 1 (1968): 6–12; F. BÖHL, "Eine altbabylonische Plakette mit der Darstellung eines kultischen Tanzes," *JEOL* 8 (1942): 725–28; J. BRAUN, "Iron Age Seals from Ancient Israel Pertinent to Music," *Orbis musicae* 10 (1991): 11–26; IDEM, *Music in Ancient Israel/Palestine: Archaeological, Written, and Comparative Sources* (Grand Rapids: Eerdmans, 2002); IDEM, "Musical Instruments," *OEANE* 4:70–79; J. F. BRUG, "Biblical Acrostics and Their Relationhip to Other Ancient Near Eastern Acrostics," in *The Bible in the Light of Cuneiform Literature* (ed. W. W. Hallo, B. W. Jones, and G. L. Mattingly; Scripture in Context 3; Lewiston, N.Y.: Mellen, 1990), 283–304; E. BRUNNER-TRAUT, *Der Tanz im alten Ägypten nach bildlichen und inschriftlichen Zeugnissen* (New York: J. J. Augustin, 1992); A. CAUBET, "La musique à Ougarit," *CRAI* 4 (1987): 731–54; IDEM, "La musique à Ougarit: Nouveaux témoignages matériels," *UBL* 12 (1996): 9–31; M. K. CERNY, "Some Musicological Remarks on the Old Mesopotamian Music and Its Terminology," *Archív orientálni* 62 (1994): 17–26; M. COGAN and I. EPH'AL, eds., *Ah, Assyria . . . Studies in Assyrian History and Ancient Near Eastern Historiography Presented to Hayim Tadmor* (ScrHier 33; Jerusalem: Magnes Press, 1991); D. COLLON and A. D. KILMER, "The Lute in Ancient Mesopotamia," *Music and Civilisation* (British Museum Yearbook 4; London: British Museum, 1980), 13–28; R. L. CROCKER, "Mesopotamian Tonal Systems," *Iraq* 59 (1997): 189–202; IDEM, "Remarks on the Tuning Text UET VII 74 (U. 7/80)," *Or* 47 (1978): 99–104; R. L. CROCKER and A. D. KILMER, "The Fragmentary Music Text from Nippur," *Iraq* 46 (1984): 81–85; M. DUCHESNE-GUILLEMIN, "A Hurrian Musical Score from Ugarit: The Discovery of Mesopotamian Music," *Sources from the Ancient Near East* 2 (1984) 63–94; IDEM, "Music in ancient Mesopotamia and Egypt," *World Archaeology* 12 (1981): 287–97 and plates; R. J. DUMBRILL, *The Musicology and Organology of the Ancient Near East* (London: Green Press, 1998); H. G. FARMER, "The Music of Ancient Egypt" and "The Music of Ancient Mesopotamia," in *The New Oxford History of Music* (ed. J. A. Westrup et al.; Oxford: Oxford University Press, 1957), 1:255–82, 228–56; H. FISCHER, "The Trumpet in Ancient Egypt," in *Pyramid Studies and Other Essays Presented to I. E. S. Edwards* (ed. J. R. Baines et al.; Occasional Publications 7; London: Egypt Exploration Society, 1988), 103–9; O. R. GURNEY, "Babylonian Music Again," *Iraq* 56 (1994): 101–6; IDEM, "An Old Babylonian Treatise on the Tuning of the Harp," *Iraq* 30 (1968): 229–33; O. R. GURNEY and B. LAWERGREN, "Ancient Mesopotamian Terminology for Harps and Soundholes," in *The Archaeology of Early Music Cultures: Third International Meeting of the ICTM Study Group on Music Archaeology* (Bonn: Verlag für systematische

Musikwissenschaft, 1988), 175–88; O. R. GURNEY and M. WEST, "Mesopotamian Tonal Systems: A Reply," *Iraq* 60 (1998): 223–27; H. G. GÜTERBOCK, "Musical Notation in Ugarit," *RA* 64 (1970): 45–52; I. H. JONES, "Music and Musical Instruments," *ABD* 4:934–39; A. D. KILMER, "The Cult Song with Music from Ancient Ugarit: Another Interpretation," *RA* 68 (1974): 69–82; IDEM, "The Discovery of an Ancient Mesopotamian Theory of Music," *Proceedings of the American Philosophical Society* 115 (1971): 131–49; IDEM, "Music and Dance in Ancient Western Asia," *CANE* 4:2601–13; IDEM, "A Music Tablet from Sippar(?): BM 65217+ 66616," *Iraq* 46 (1984): 69–80; IDEM, "The Musical Instruments from Ur and Ancient Mesopotamian Music," *Expedition* 402 (1998): 12–19; IDEM, "The Strings of Musical Instruments: Their Names, Numbers, and Significance," in *Studies in Honor of Benno Landsberger on His Seventy-Fifth Birthday, April 21, 1965* (ed. H. G. Güterbock and T. Jacobsen; AS 16; Chicago: University of Chicago, 1965), 261–68; IDEM, "World's Oldest Musical Notation Deciphered on Cuneiform Tablet," *BAR* 6, no. 5 (1980): 14–25; A. D. KILMER and M. CIVIL, "Old Babylonian Musical Instructions Relating to Hymnody," *JCS* 38 (1986): 94–98; A. D. KILMER and S. TINNEY, "Old Babylonian Music Instruction Texts," *JCS* 48 (1996): 49–56; M. KOITABASHI, "Music in the Texts of Ugarit," *UF* 30 (1998): 363–90; J. KUCKERTZ, "Das Skalensystem der altmesopotamischen Musik," *BaghM* 24 (1993): 185–91; L. MANNICHE, *Music and Musicians in Ancient Egypt* (London: British Museum, 1991); IDEM, *Musical Instruments from the Tomb of Tutankhamun* (Tutankhamun's Tomb Series 6; Oxford: Griffith Institute, 1976); S. DE MARTINO, "Music, Dance, and Processions in Hittite Anatolia," *CANE* 4:2661–69; W. MAYER, *Untersuchungen zur Formensprache der babylonischen Gebetsbeschwörungen* (Studia Pohl: Series Maior 5; Rome: Pontifical Biblical Institute, 1976); R. ROSZKOWSKA, "Musical Terminology in Hittite Cuneiform Texts," *Orientalia varsoviensia* 1 (1987): 23–30; G. SELZ, "The Holy Drum, the Spear, and the Harp," in *Sumerian Gods and Their Representations* (ed. I. L. Finkel and M. J. Geller; Groningen, Neth.: Styx, 1997), 167–213; M. L. WEST, "The Babylonian Musical Notation and the Hurrian Melodic Texts," *Music and Letters* 75 (1993–1994): 161–79; D. WULSTAN, "Music from Ancient Ugarit," *RA* 68 (1974): 125–28; IDEM, "The Tuning of the Babylonian Harp," *Iraq* 30 (1968): 215–28; C. ZIEGLER, *Catalogue des instruments de musique égyptiens au Musée du Louvre, département des Antiquités égyptiennes* (Paris: Réunion des Musées Nationaux, 1979).

CHAPTER FOUR

Love Poetry (and Related Texts)

Introduction

Although love songs represent only a small portion of the Hebrew canon, this modest corpus of amorous poetry—most of it in Song of Songs—has presented perennial problems for both ancient and modern interpreters. These hermeneutical difficulties extend beyond Song of Songs itself to other smaller compositions, such as the Song of the Vineyard in Isa 5:1–7 (see Willis). It is widely agreed that our attempts to traverse this hermeneutical impasse have benefited greatly from comparisons of Song of Songs with Near Eastern literature. The most important step forward has been the comparative insight that traditional Jewish and Christian readings of the Song, which interpret it as an allegory about God's love for his people, fail to do justice to the book's highly erotic love poetry. On the other hand, comparative approaches have also spawned a variety of new and, in certain respects, incompatible readings of the Song. These new interpretations regard the Song as a cultic celebration of sacred marriage, as a love drama, as a love incantation, or even as a collection of unrelated secular love poems. Each of these options finds its counterpart in the Near Eastern literature.

4.1. Mesopotamian Love Poetry

An ancient catalogue of Mesopotamian songs and hymns survives that originally listed about 400 songs, of which 275 entries legibly remain (*KAR* 158; see Ebeling; Black). Of these 275 incipits, about 40 percent are Sumerian titles and the rest are Akkadian. Fifty-five of the texts are love songs, but so far scholars have recovered only four of these songs, three in Sumerian and one in Akkadian. Scholars have discovered a number of other love songs not found in the catalogue, but when all of these texts are taken together, they constitute only a handful in comparison with the many love songs that the Mesopotamians obviously produced. The entries in this section cover all of the important Mesopotamian parallels to the Hebrew Song of Songs, including not only the love songs but also the myths associated with Dumuzi and Inanna. The myths are included not only because they sometimes approach being love songs themselves but also because the Dummuzi/Inanna love songs proper cannot be appreciated apart from this mythological background.

Dumuzi-Inanna Myths and Love Songs. We possess a large corpus of Sumerian materials that feature the relationship between Dumuzi and Inanna, who together formed a divine couple associated with love and fertility. Inanna was a goddess in her own right—the most important in Mesopotamian tradition—and Dumuzi was a primeval Mesopotamian king who, as the deified shepherd king, attracted Inanna's amorous attention. Because of his connections with fertility, many similar fertility deities coalesced around the image of Dumuzi, so that he was also known as Ama-ushumgal-anna, as Damu, and by other names. The Inanna/Dumuzi traditions carried over into the Akkadian period, where the pair was known by the names Ištar and Tammuz. The corpus associated with Dumuzi/Tammuz and Inanna/Ištar falls out into four groups of texts: (1) songs about the love and marriage of Dumuzi and Inanna; (2) myths about the death of Dumuzi, especially the Descent of Inanna into the Netherworld (the Akkadian version is the Descent of Ištar); (3) lamentations expressing sadness over the death of Dumuzi; and (4) medical rituals and incantations in which one or both deities were called upon to aid in healing. In certain respects the texts defy this fourfold classification, since love lyrics often appear not only in the love songs but also in the myths and laments.

Two key religious institutions stood behind these texts. The first institution was the rite of sacred marriage, in which a Mesopotamian king played the role of Dumuzi as he ritually copulated with a high priestess standing in for Inanna. There is an ongoing debate about whether the king and priestess actually engaged in sexual intercourse (so most scholars) or whether they did so only metaphorically (see Cooper; Steinkeller; cf. Sweet's theory that there was no ritual at all). At any rate, most scholars would say that this cultic act, practiced mainly during the Ur III and Isin periods, was believed to bring fertility and prosperity to the kingdom. Sacred marriage rites may have been observed in Mesopotamia after this period as well (see the installation rites for the high priestess at Emar, 5.6), but it is not clear whether the later kings actually had relations with the priestesses or whether the act was carried out only symbolically. The second religious institution related to Dumuzi/Inanna pivots on the myth of the dying and rising god, in which the annual seasonal cycle was associated with the death and resurrection of Dumuzi/Tammuz. It is easy to see how the text types listed above relate to these two institutions. The myths and laments were associated with the death of Dumuzi, and the love songs commemorated his resurrection and the renewal of his marriage. Less obvious is the connection between Dumuzi/Ištar and the medical rites and incantations, but it is not much of a stretch to imagine why the sick saw in Dumuzi's annual resurrection a hope in the power of renewal and restoration. The present entry covers the Dumuzi/Inanna myths and love songs. For the laments and incantations, see 3.1.2 and 5.8.1, respectively.

(1) Myths of Inanna and Dumuzi. The primary myth is the Descent of Inanna, which relates how Inanna's unsuccessful attempt to take over the underworld from her sister Ereshkigal resulted in Inanna's imprisonment there. By the wisdom of Enki, Inanna was eventually freed, but the netherworld required a surrogate to take her place. When Inanna discovered that her husband, Dumuzi, had not been mourning her absence, she selected him as the substitute. In the end it was decided that Dumuzi and his sister Geshtinanna would alternate six-month stays in the underworld. The Descent of Inanna is extant in two editions, a long Sumerian text and an abbreviated Akkadian exemplar that would be difficult to understand unless one knew the Sumerian version (see the Descent of Ištar). In the Akkadian version the chief characters became Ištar, Ea, and Tammuz rather than Inanna, Enki, and Dumuzi. Mesopotamian tradition attributed the seasonal patterns to Dumuzi's annual death and resurrection; his death was ritually observed through laments, and his resurrection was ritually celebrated using love songs in the annual rite of sacred marriage. Other related myths include the stories of Dumuzi's death (In the Desert by the Early Grass; His Heart Was Filled with Tears; How You Walk About; In the Desert, My Dumuzi), a story of his sexual infidelity (Unfaithfulness), and a poetic tale about Dumuzi's competition with a shepherd named Enkimdu for the hand of Inanna (the Shepherd and the Farmer; see Sefati, 324–43). Also extant is an idiosyncratic text in which Dumuzi ascends to the heavens and takes his place as a star in the sky (Kramer 1984).

(2) Dumuzi-Inanna Love Songs. These poems include vivid descriptions of the couple and their mutual courting and marriage. Hence, the songs are not merely collections but reflect some degree of narrative progress. The texts are often cast as dialogues that include Inanna and Dumuzi as well as their friends and relatives. Transitions between the speakers are sometimes visible in the Sumerian language itself, since Inanna's speech is often cast in the feminine Emesal dialect whereas Dumuzi's speech is written in the standard Emegir dialect. Regarding their courtship, it is fairly accurate to describe Inanna's pursuit of Dumuzi as aggressive, in contrast to the more reserved and passive Dumuzi (see Sefati). The female point of view predominates in this highly erotic poetry (Alster 1993), whose sexual explicitness ranges from "praise of the vulva" to metaphorical images of sex as "ploughing the garden." According to the ethnic labels used by the ancient scholars, most of the Dumuzi/Inanna poems were BABALE songs, although a few were identified as ŠIRNABŠUB, KUNGAR, or TIGI songs. Two additional points made by Alster are worth noting (Alster 1993). First, because the female point of view is more common in the love poems, it is possible—perhaps even likely—that women composed some of these songs. Second, because Dumuzi and Inanna are multivalent figures who can stand for any couple, it is very sensible to presume that these texts were sometimes used in ordinary marriage ceremonies quite apart from their usual cultic usage. A case in point is the OB Manchester Tablet from Nippur, which combines various Sumerian love songs into a single text, so that "the composition leaves us with the impression of

a conglomerate or a compilation of short songs of various origins" (Alster 1992). Although the songs on the tablet feature Dumuzi and Inanna, Alster notes that the text makes a "very realistic impression" and that it would "hardly make sense if this were exclusively to be understood as a sacred ritual."

Texts and translations: B. ALSTER, *Dumuzi's Dream: Aspects of Oral Poetry in a Sumerian Myth* (Copenhagen: Akademisk Forlag, 1972) (His Heart Was Filled with Tears; or, the Death of Dumuzi; or, Dumuzi's Dream); IDEM, "The Manchester Tammuz," *ActSum* 14 (1992): 1–46; R. BORGER, *Babylonisch-assyrische Lesestücke* (2d ed.; Rome: Pontificium Institutum Biblicum, 1979) (Descent of Ištar); T. JACOBSEN, "The Myth of Inanna and Bilulu" in *Toward the Image of Tammuz and Other Essays on Mesopotamian History and Culture* (ed. W. L. Moran; HSS 21; Cambridge: Harvard University Press, 1970), 52–71 (In the Desert, My Dumuzi); S. N. KRAMER, "BM 88318: The Ascension of Dumuzi to Heaven," *Recueil de travaux et communications de l'Association des études du Proche-Orient ancien* 2 (1984): 5–9 (Dumuzi's Ascension); IDEM, "The Death of Dumuzi: A New Sumerian Version," *AnSt* 30 (1980): 5–13 (How You Walk About); IDEM, " 'Inanna's Descent to the Nether World' Continued and Revised," *JCS* 5 (1951): 1–17 (Descent of Inanna); S. LANGDON, *Babylonian Liturgies* (Paris: P. Geuthner, 1913), no. 194 (Unfaithfulness); Y. SEFATI, *Love Songs in Sumerian Literature: Critical Edition of the Dumuzi-Inanna Songs* (Ramat Gan, Israel: Bar-Ilan University Press, 1998) (collection of Dumuzi/Inanna love songs); W. R. SLADEK, *Inanna's Descent to the Netherworld* (Ann Arbor: University Microfilms, 1974) (Descent of Inanna); H. ZIMMERN, *Sumerische Kultlieder aus altbabylonischer Zeit* (2 vols.; Leipzig: Hinrichs, 1912–1913), nos. 26, 27, 45 (In the Desert by the Early Grass). ***Translations:*** ANET 41–42 (The Shepherd and the Farmer), 52–57 (Descent of Inanna), 106–8 (Descent of Ištar), 637–45 (Inanna/Dumuzi Myths and Love Songs); COS 1.108: 381–84 (Descent of Ištar), 1.169: 540–43 (Dumuzi-Inanna Songs); S. DALLEY, *Myths from Mesopotamia* (Oxford: Oxford University Press, 1989), 154–62 (Descent of Ištar); JACOBSEN, *The Harps That Once,* 1–84, 205–32 (Inanna/Dumuzi Myths and Love Songs); S. N. KRAMER, *The Sumerians: Their History, Culture, and Character* (Chicago: University of Chicago Press, 1963), 156–60. ***Bibliography:*** B. ALSTER, "Inanna Repenting: The Conclusion of Inanna's Descent," *ActSum* 18 (1996): 1–18; IDEM, "Marriage and Love in the Sumerian Love Songs: With Some Notes on the Manchester Tammuz," in *The Tablet and the Scroll: Near Eastern Studies in Honor of William W. Hallo* (ed. M. E. Cohen et al.; Bethesda, Md.: CDL Press, 1993), 15–27; IDEM, "The Mythology of Mourning," *ActSum* 5 (1983): 1–16; IDEM, "The Sumerian Love Song SRT 31," *Studia iranica, mesopotamica, et anatolica* 1 (1999): 1–11; IDEM, "Sumerian Love Songs," *RA* 79 (1985): 127–59; J. S. COOPER, "Sacred Marriage and Popular Cult in Early Mesopotamia," in *Official Cult and Popular Religion in the Ancient Near East* (ed. E. Matsushima; Heidelberg; Universitäts-verlag C. Winter, 1993), 81–93; M. M. FRITZ, ". . . *und weinten um Tammuz*": *Die Götter Dumuzi-Ama'ushumgal'anna und Damu* (AOAT 307; Münster: Ugarit, 2004); T. JACOB-SEN, *Toward the Image of Tammuz and Other Essays on Mesopotamian History and Culture* (ed. W. L. Moran; Cambridge: Harvard University Press, 1970); D. KATZ, "How Dumuzi Became Inanna's Victim: On the Formation of 'Inanna's Descent,'" *ActSum* 18 (1996): 93–102; A. D. KILMER, "How Was Queen Ereshkigal Tricked? A New Interpretation of the Descent of Ishtar," *UF* 3 (1971): 299–309; S. N. KRAMER, "The Biblical 'Song of Songs' and the Sumerian Love Songs," *Expedition* 5 (1962): 25–31; IDEM, "Cuneiform Studies and the History of Literature: The Sumerian Sacred Marriage Texts," *Proceedings of the American Philosophical Society* 107 (1963): 485–527; IDEM, "The Dumuzi-Inanna Sacred Marriage Rite: Origin, Development, Character," in *Actes de la XVIIe Rencontre assyriologique* internationale (ed. A. Finet; Ham-sur-Heure, Belgium: Comité Belge de Recherches en Mésopotamie, 1970), 135–59; IDEM, *The Sacred Marriage Rite: Aspects of Faith, Myth, and Ritual in Ancient Sumer* (Bloomington: Indiana University Press, 1969); IDEM, "Sumerian Literature and the British Museum: The Promise of the Future," *Proceedings of the American Philosophical Society* 124 (1980): 299–310; P. LAPINKIVI, *The Sumerian Sacred Marriage in the Light of Comparative Evidence* (SAAS 15; Helsinki: Helsinki University Press, 2004); D. REISMAN, "Iddin-Dagan's Sacred Marriage Hymn," *JCS* 25 (1973): 185–202; Y. SEFATI, "An Oath of Chastity in a Sumerian Love Song (SRT 31)?" in *Bar-Ilan Studies in Assyriology* (ed. J. Klein and A. Skaist; Ramat Gan, Israel: Bar-Ilan University, Institute of Assyriology 1990), 45–63; P. STEINKELLER, "On Rulers, Priests, and Sacred Marriage: Tracing the Evolution of Early Sumerian Kingship," in *Priests and Officials in the Ancient Near East* (ed. K. Watanabe; Heidelberg: Universitätsverlag C. Winter, 1999), 103–37; R. F. G. SWEET, "A New Look at the 'Sacred Marriage' in Ancient Mesopotamia," in *Corolla torontonensis: Studies in Honor of Ronald Morton Smith* (ed. E. Robbins and S. Sandahl; Toronto: TSAR, 1994), 85–104.

Sumerian Royal Love Songs. In addition to the Dumuzi-Inanna love songs, the Sumerians also composed a series of royal love songs about the king and his beloved. These songs were apparently used in sacred marriage rites, as the king in question filled the role of Dumuzi. Evidence for this appears in the love songs of Šulgi, king of Ur, and Iddin-Dagan, king of Isin. From these two texts (Šulgi X and Iddi-Dagan A), we discover that the sacred marriage rituals began on New Year's Eve at the king's palace and continued into the following day at the temple of the goddess. Similar royal love songs include the love song of an anonymous king (text D1 in Sefati) and three important exemplars associated with King Shu-Suen, who reigned during the Ur III period. In the first of Shu-Suen's songs (Shu-Suen A), a priestess representing the goddess Baba invites the king to observe the sacred marriage rite with her. In Shu-Suen B, the king's beloved describes his physical attributes and expresses her longing for him, concluding with a metaphorical request for sexual union. Shu-Suen C is a very short text that expresses the beloved's affection for Shu-Suen. It also includes brief comments by the beloved's friends, just as we see in Song of Songs.

Texts and translations: J. KLEIN, *Three Šulgi Hymns: Sumerian Royal Hymns Glorifying King Šulgi of Ur* (Ramat Gan, Israel: Bar-Ilan University Press, 1981), 124–66 (Šulgi X); S. N. KRAMER, "Inanna and Šulgi: A Sumerian Fertility Song," *Iraq* 31 (1969): 18–23 (Šulgi Z, fragmentary); D. REISMAN, "Iddin-Dagan's Sacred Marriage Hymn," *JCS* 25 (1973): 185–202 (Iddin-Dagan A); Y. SEFATI, *Love Songs in Sumerian Literature: Critical Edition of the Dumuzi-Inanna Songs* (Ramat Gan, Israel: Bar-Ilan University Press, 1998) (D1 and Shu-Suen texts A, B, C). *Translations:* ANET 640–41, 644–45; COS 1.173: 554–59 (Iddin-Dagan A); JACOBSEN, *The Harps That Once,* 85–98 (partial). *Bibliography:* See the entry just above.

Lu-dingira's Message to His Mother. This Sumerian literary text is known from five Old Babylonian copies and from two trilingual tablets—Hittite, Sumerian, and Akkadian—that were discovered at Boğazköy and Ugarit (see Civil [Sumerian]; Nougayrol/Laroche [trilinguals]). According to the text, Lu-dingira planned to send a message to his mother in Nippur, but the messenger needed a description so that she could be properly recognized. Lu-dingira responded to this request with a list of five "signs" that characterized his mother. The first sign roughly parallels the description of the valiant woman in Prov 31:10–31, but the remaining descriptions are couched in somewhat erotic imagery: "My mother is rain from heaven, water from the finest seed. . . . A harvest of plenty. . . . A garden of delight, full of joy. . . . A watered pine, adorned with pine cones. . . . A spring flower, a first fruit." In Song of Songs 5:8–16, a similar description of the lover was occasioned when the young woman asked the "daughters of Jerusalem" to deliver a message to him.

Texts and translations: M. ÇIG and S. N. KRAMER, "The Ideal Mother: A Sumerian Portrait," *Belleten* 40 (1976): 413–21; M. CIVIL, "The 'Message of Lú-dinger-ra to His Mother' and a Group of Akkado-Hittite 'Proverbs,'" *JNES* 23 (1964): 1–11; J. NOUGAYROL and E. LAROCHE, eds., *Ugaritica V* (ed. C. F. A. Schaeffer; Ugaritica 5; Paris: Imprimerie Nationale, 1968), 310–19, 443–44 [no. 169]. *Bibliography:* J. S. COOPER, "New Cuneiform Parallels to the Song of Songs," *JBL* 90 (1971): 157–62.

An Old Akkadian Love Charm. This magical text from the late third millennium (MAD 5.8 [see Gelb]) enabled a man to secure the love of a woman he desired. It invokes the wisdom of Enki (god of magical lore) and the powers of two love goddesses: "I have seized your mouth for love making! By Ištar and Išara I conjure you: May you find no release from me till your neck and his neck lie close beside!" Some scholars suspect that Song of Songs, or parts of it, reflects a similar kind of love magic (Cooper; cf. Sasson).

Texts and translations: I. J. GELB, *Sargonic Texts in the Ashmolean Museum, Oxford* (MAD 5; Chicago: University of Chicago Press, 1970), 7–12 [no. 8]; J. WESTENHOLZ and A. WESTENHOLZ, "Help for Rejected Suitors: The Old Akkadian Love Incantation MAD V 8," *Or* 46 (1977): 198–219. *Translation: BM²* 1.59–60. *Bibliography:* W. G. LAMBERT, "Devotion: The Languages of Religion and Love," in *Figurative Language in the Ancient Near East* (ed. M. Mindlin, M. J. Geller, and J. E. Wansbrough; London: School of Oriental and African Studies, University of London, 1987), 25–39; J. M. SASSON, "A Further Parallel to the Song of Songs?" *ZAW* 85 (1973): 359–60.

Love Lyrics of Rim-Sin. This poetic Akkadian dialogue was apparently used during the sacred marriage rite as Rim-Sin, king of Larsa (ca. 1822–1763 B.C.E.), ritually copulated with a priestess during New Year festivities. Cultic singers frequently interrupt the dialogue with encouragement for the two lovers. In a few instances, the speech of the lovers is more soliloquy than dialogue, since their words are directed toward the audience and not their partner. In other cases, the dialogue is direct and explicit: "Let us perform lovers' task, never sleep all night. Let both of us on the bed be in the joyful mood for lovemaking. . . . Burn out your desire on top of me!"

Text: J. VAN DIJK, A. GOETZE, and M. I. HUSSEY, *Early Mesopotamian Incantations and Rituals* (YOS 11; New Haven: Yale University Press, 1985), no. 24. *Translation: BM²* 1.101–2.

Love Lyrics of Nanay and Muati. This fragmentary Old Babylonian tablet appears to be a dialogue between the goddess of love Nanay and a little-understood male deity, Muati. The text concludes with a prayer on behalf of Abiešuh, king of Babylon about 1711–1684 B.C.E. A similar and more complete text from the Neo-Assyrian period appears in the love lyrics of Nabû and Tašmetu (see below).

Text and translation: W. G. LAMBERT, "Divine Love Lyrics from the Reign of Abiešuh," *MIOF* 12 (1966): 41–57. *Translation: BM²* 1.99–100.

Akkadian Love Song Ki. 1063. This Old Babylonian text from ancient Kish is quite fragmentarily preserved, but its explicit sexual content is clear: "Reach forth with your left hand and stroke our vulva. Play with our breasts. Enter, I have opened my thighs" (notice the so-called plural of ecstasy; see Paul 1997). Given the fragmentary state of the text, it is impossible to determine whether the original tablet included a monologue or dialogue or whether the text was a religious or secular composition. According to the editor, however, the text's tone suggests a secular rather than cultic setting.

Text and translation: J. G. WESTENHOLZ, "A Forgotten Love Song," in *Language, Literature, and History: Philological and Historical Studies Presented to Erica Reiner* (ed. F. Rochberg-Halton; AOS 67; New Haven: American Oriental Society, 1987), 415–25.

The Love Poem of a Persistent Woman. Here we have a dialogue between a woman in love and the man who resisted her amorous advances. Because of the woman's persistence, the man eventually rejected "the other woman" and embraced this persistent woman as his "one and only" lover. The text is playful and entertaining, and its theme of rejection is vaguely reminiscent of the frustrations sometimes expressed by the young woman in Song of Songs (e.g., chs. 5, 8). Our copy of the dialogue dates to the Old Babylonian period. Its author used rulings to divide its alternating boy/girl speeches. Early interpreters of the dialogue imagined that the man in the text was none other than King Hammurabi (see von Soden), but this reading is no longer accepted.

Texts and translations: M. HELD, "A Faithful Lover in an Old Babylonian Dialogue," *JCS* 15 (1961): 1–26; IDEM, "A Faithful Lover in an Old Babylonian Dialogue: Addenda and Corrigenda," *JCS* 16 (1962): 37–39. *Translation: BM²* 1.95–98. *Bibliography:* B. GRONEBERG, "'The Faithful Lover' Reconsidered: Toward Establishing a New Genre," in *Sex and Gender in the Ancient Near East* (2 vols.; ed. S. Parpola and R. M. Whiting; RAI 47; Helsinki: Neo-Assyrian Text Corpus Project, 2002), 1:165–83; W. VON SODEN, "Ein Zwiegespräch Ḫammurabis mit einer Frau," *ZA* 49 (1950): 151–94.

An Akkadian Love Song of Ištar and Dumuzi. This short Middle Babylonian text is our only Akkadian copy of a love poem between Dumuzi and Ištar, and it is also the only Akkadian text recovered so far that is listed in the large song catalogue discovered at Assur (*KAR* 158). According to the editor, this song does not appear to be a cultic text like the earlier Dumuzi/Inanna songs but rather an intimate conversation between a young man and a young woman. The present text has narrative-like qualities, as Ištar invites Dumuzi into her home—with the approval of her parents—and proceeds to speak intimately and provocatively to her lover.

Text and translation: BLACK, "Babylonian Ballads."

The Babylonian "Love Lyrics." There are several very fragmentary texts (see Lambert 1959; 1975) that were initially interpreted as love lyrics from a sacred rite during which the god Marduk copulated with the goddess Ištar of Babylon. This reading was based on a confluence of several features. Marduk exchanges very explicit love language with his "concubine" Ištar, and—as we might expect— the texts describe a mournful and angry response of Marduk's spouse, Zarpanitum. The discovery of an associated prescriptive ritual tablet confirmed that the lyrics were indeed used in a ritual context. All of these facts, however, can fit comfortably into the thesis of Edzard, which I tend to prefer. Edzard suggests that these texts should be associated with a jealousy ritual, designed to address in human life the same difficulties occasioned in Zarpanitum's experience by the sexual liaison between her husband and Ištar.

Texts and translations: W. G. LAMBERT, "Love Lyrics from Babylon," *JSS* 4 (1959): 1–15; IDEM, "The Problem of Love Lyrics," in *Unity and Diversity: Essays in the History, Literature, and Religion of the Ancient Near East* (ed. H. Goedicke and J. J. M. Roberts; Baltimore: Johns Hopkins University Press, 1975), 98–135. **Bibliography:** D. O. EDZARD, "Zur Ritualtafel der sog. 'Love Lyrics,'" in *Language, Literature, and History: Philological and Historical Studies Presented to Erica Reiner* (ed. F. Rochberg-Halton; New Haven: American Oriental Society, 1987), 57–69; G. LEICK, *Sex and Eroticism in Mesopotamian Literature* (New York: Routledge, 1994), 239–46.

Love Lyrics of Nabû and Tašmetu. This Neo-Assyrian tablet, and a few related texts that help us understand it, constitute our main evidence for sacred marriage rites during the first millennium. The love song contained on this tablet was recited during the sacred marriage rites of the god Nabû and his spouse, Tašmetu. To judge from one annual cultic calendar, this rite was observed annually on the second day of the month of Ajaru, when Nabû traveled to the temple of Eḫušaba to spend the night with his bride. The text is introduced with a brief prayer that praises both deities. The remaining balance of the tablet is an intimate dialogue between the parties, in which the couple express admiration for one another's physical attributes and speak in metaphor about the sexual intimacy they will enjoy. Unlike the Sumerian sacred marriage rites, this rite does not seem to have been a fertility ritual per se. Rather, it appears that the purpose of the rite was to protect and bless the king of Assyria. What better time to seek divine blessings than when the king provides the gods with lavish feasts and marital bliss? For a very similar text, see the Old Babylonian love lyrics of Nanay and Muat (above).

The love lyrics of Nabû and Tašmetu are similar to Song of Songs in a number of respects (see Nissinen). Both songs are poetic dialogues between male and female lovers, and both include frequent interjections by a chorus of onlookers. There are also many similar motifs in the two texts, such as detailed descriptions of the lovers' bodies, the use of garden imagery, and the woman's nocturnal yearning for her lover.

Texts and translations: J. J. A. VAN DIJK, "Textes divers du Musée Baghdad, II," *Sumer* 13 (1957): 26–27 (= TIM 9.54); A. LIVINGSTONE, *Court Poetry and Literary Miscellanea* (SAA 3; Helsinki: Helsinki University Press, 1989), 35–37. *Translations:* BM² 2.887–89; *COS* 1.128: 445–46. *Bibliography:* M. COHEN, *The Cultic Calendars of the Ancient Near East* (Bethesda, Md.: CDL Press, 1993), 311; E. MATSUSHIMA, "Le rituel hierogamique de Nabu," *ActSum* 9 (1987): 131–75; M. NISSINEN, "Love Lyrics of Nabû and Tasmetu: An Assyrian Song of Songs?" in *Und Mose schrieb dieses Lied auf—Studien zum Alten Testament und zum alten Orient: Festschrift für Oswald Loretz* (ed. M. Dietrich and I. Kottsieper; AOAT 250; Münster: Ugarit, 1998), 585–634; Y. SEFATI, *Love Songs in Sumerian Literature: Critical Edition of the Dumuzi-Inanna Songs* (Ramat Gan, Israel: Bar-Ilan University Press, 1998), 46–47.

4.2. Egyptian Love Poetry

All of our Egyptian love songs come from the Ramesside period (Nineteenth–Twentieth Dynasties, c. 1300–1150 B.C.E.), but it is possible that they were composed somewhat earlier. Inasmuch as these texts were used outside cultic contexts, they are perhaps closer to Song of Songs than the divine and royal love songs from Mesopotamia. The four most important exemplars are cited below, although several more fragmentary texts are extant (see Fox 1985, 77–81). Also included in this section are entries on the very unusual Turin Erotic Papyrus and on a text that is comparable to the Hymn to a Valiant Woman in Prov 31. For closely related Egyptian texts, see Fox 1985, 345–50.

Papyrus Harris 500. This Nineteenth Dynasty papyrus was discovered in a casket in the mortuary temple of Rameses II (the Ramesseum). In addition to the love songs, the verso of the papyrus includes copies of two tales, the Doomed Prince and the Capture of Joppa (see 8.1). As for the love poetry itself, its divisions are noted in the manuscript by pause marks as well as rubrics in red ink, which allow modern scholars to easily discern the text's structure. The fragmentary text falls into three groups, two short collections of independent love songs (Groups A and B) and a single three-stanza song (Group C). In Group A, the songs alternate between male and female speakers, but strictly speaking, the texts are not dialogues because the lovers do not respond to each other so much as they merely address each other. Group B, entitled Beginning of the Entertainment Song, contains only songs spoken by the female. The same goes for Group C, which is entitled the Flower Song: The Beginning of the Song of Entertainment. The tone of the texts is playful and quite erotic but not particularly explicit. Metaphor abounds in the texts, especially animal and plant imagery, although on one occasion the woman's vulva is depicted as "double-doors" with the "latch-bolt drawn back." In a manner reminiscent of Song of Songs, the lovers sometimes refer to each other as "brother" and "sister."

Text: E. A. W. BUDGE, *Facsimiles of Egyptian Hieratic Papyri in the British Museum, Second Series* (London: British Museum, 1923), pls. 41–46. **Translations:** *AEL* 2:189–92; *COS* 1.49: 126–27; FOSTER, *Hymns, Prayers, and Songs,* 164–66; FOWLER, *Love Lyrics of Ancient Egypt,* 3–30; FOX, *The Song of Songs and the Ancient Egyptian Love Songs,* 7–29; *LAE* 308–17. **Bibliography:** HERMANN, *Altägyptische Liebesdichtung,* 138–44; M. G. MASPERO, "Les Chants d'amour du Papyrus de Turin et du Papyrus Harris no. 500," *JA* 1 (1883): 5–47; WHITE, *A Study of the Language of Love in the Song of Songs and Ancient Egyptian Poetry.*

Papyrus Chester Beatty I. Discovered in a cache of papyri from Deir el-Medina, this Twentieth Dynasty papyrus contains a myth (Contending of Horus and Seth), two royal hymns, several business documents, and three love songs (Groups A, B, and C). The first love song bears the rubric "The Beginnings of the Sayings of the Great Entertainer," but for reasons we will see, Fox has dubbed it The Stroll. The seven-stanza poem bears a strong narrative flavor. In the alternating voices of boy and girl, we learn of their keen interest in one another and of the lovesickness that plagues them both. At the same time, as so often happens in matters of love, neither of the lovers suspects the degree of the other's interest, and resistance from their respective parents makes pursuit of the relationship even more difficult. In the poem's last three stanzas, we learn that the boy has been visited by the girl (stanza 5), that this happened as the girl strolled by his house and saw him inside (stanza 6), and that eight days later the boy misses her, is now quite sick with love, and can only be cured by a visit from his beloved (stanza 7). This poem is obviously a classic tale of adolescent love.

Group B is a much shorter poem, but its theme is similar to The Stroll. The girl expresses in three stanzas her longings for the boy, each introduced in the same way: "If only you would come to your sister swiftly." The girl's objective is expressed clearly in the concluding stanza: she wills that he might arrive at her "cave," an obvious circumlocution for her vagina.

The third set of poems, Group C, is introduced with this rubric: "The beginning of the sweet saying, which was found in a book container, and which the scribe Nakhtsobek from the necropolis wrote." Nakhtsobek's Song is arranged into seven stanzas, although the first two stanzas probably constitute a single poem. This first poem juxtaposes the topoi of festival, sacrifices, and sex in a manner similar to the depiction of prostitution in Prov 7:5–23; for this reason, Fox supposes that this Egyptian song also refers to the unbridled pleasures of prostitution. The speech sequence in the five remaining stanzas—stanzas 3–7—is boy, girl, girl, boy, boy. In the third stanza he extols her ability to capture his attention; in the fourth she notes that his indecision forced her to pursue him. The fifth stanza includes the sacrificial and sexual motifs found in the first two stanzas of Nakhtsobek's Song, but it is not at all clear that there is a relationship between this stanza and the first two. In any case, as the boy bends over during his cultic rites, it occasions an opportunity for the girl to observe her lover's phallus, which she describes as "longer than it is broad." The sixth and seventh stanzas present instances of a paraclausithyron ("serenade," see Copley), in which the rejected boy stands outside the girl's door and desperately pleas for her to let him in. This is an odd and surprising end to the sequence, particularly if Group C constitutes a single story. It is likely, however, that Group C is not a single story but rather a collection of disparate poems. The subtle and misleading impression that the collection is a narrative arises from two features. First, the alternating male and female voices create the false impression that there is a dialogue. And second, because the anthology juxtaposes different songs that reflect differing life circumstances, the collection produces a false sense of narrative movement in the reader.

Text: A. H. GARDINER, *The Library of A. Chester Beatty: The Chester Beatty Papyri, No. I.* (London: W. Walker, 1931), 27–38, pls. 16–17, 22–26, 29–30. *Translations: AEL* 2:181–89; *COS* 1.51: 128–29; FOSTER, *Hymns, Prayers, and Songs,* 162–64; FOWLER, *Love Lyrics of Ancient Egypt,* 57–78; FOX, *The Song of Songs and the Ancient Egyptian Love Songs,* 51–77; *LAE* 322–31. *Bibliography:* F. O. COPLEY, *Exclusus amator: A Study in Latin Love Poetry* (American Philological Monographs 17; Madison, Wisc.: American Philological Association, 1956); HERMANN, *Altägyptische Liebesdichtung,* 148–56; E. IVERSEN, "The Chester Beatty Papyrus, No. 1, Recto XVI, 9–XVII, 13," *JEA* 65 (1979): 78–88; WHITE, *A Study of the Language of Love in the Song of Songs and Ancient Egyptian Poetry.*

Cairo Love Songs. These songs from the Nineteenth and Twentieth Dynasties of Egypt were found inscribed on a vase at Deir el-Medina. Thirty-one fragments of the piece have been recovered to date, constituting most but not all of the still fragmentary piece. The text preserves two love songs (Groups A and B) in thirteen stanzas, but scholars surmise that the complete text would have included seven stanzas in each song, as we see in the seven-unit love poems of P.Chester Beatty 1. The poetry in Group A, entitled The Crossing by Fox, alternates between the male and the female speakers, but the speeches are soliloquies addressed to an audience rather than words for each other—hence, the text is not a dialogue. The text focuses on the stop-at-nothing, no-holds-barred commitment of the two lovers to each other. This is especially visible in one of the boy's speeches: "My sister's love is over there, on the other side [of the river]. The floodwaters are powerful in their season, and a crocodile waits on the sandbank. Yet I have gone down to the water. . . . I found the crocodile to be like a mouse, and the face of the waters like dry land to my feet. It is her love that makes me strong. . . . I see my heart's beloved standing right before my face!" Group B, entitled Seven Wishes, contains only the boy's speeches, which are cast as seven wishes that, if true, would put him in proximity with the body of the woman he fancies. For example: "If only I were her Nubian maid, her attendant in secret . . . she would grant me the hue of her whole body." As Fox correctly notes, the tones of Groups A and B are entirely different. The first poem describes the boy's tireless pursuit of the beloved who waits for him whereas the fantasizing boy in the second poem passively waits for circumstances that will likely never come to pass.

Text: G. POSENER, *Catalogue des ostraca hiératiques littéraires de Deir el Médineh* (DFIFAO 1, 18, 20, 25; Cairo: Imprimerie de l'Institut Français d'Archéologie Orientale, 1938–), 2:43–44, pls. 75–79a. *Translations: AEL* 2:193; *COS* 1.50: 127–28 (partial); FOWLER, *Love Lyrics of Ancient Egypt,* 31–48; FOX, *The Song of Songs and the Ancient Egyptian Love Songs,* 29–44; *LAE* 317–19. *Bibliography:* M. V. FOX, "The Cairo Love Songs," *JAOS* 100 (1980):

101–9; HERMANN, *Altägyptische Liebesdichtung*, 144–45; WHITE, *A Study of the Language of Love in the Song of Songs and Ancient Egyptian Poetry.*

The Turin Love Song. This song is preserved on a Twentieth Dynasty papyrus now found in the collection of the Egyptian Museum of Turin, Italy. Because the copyist wrote the first line of each unit in red, we know that the text is composed of three stanzas. The song plays on the theme of young lovers in hiding who needed to conceal their sexual intimacy behind the branches and foliage of plants and trees. Each stanza personifies a tree who comments on the couple's behavior beneath its branches. The first two trees, feeling neglected by the self-absorbed lovers, threaten to reveal their sins: "I won't be silent. . . . Then shall the misdeed be seen, and the beloved sister disciplined." The last tree provides the ideal hiding place, however, declaring, "The cloths are spread out beneath me, while the sister 'strolls about,' but my lips are sealed, so as not to tell I've seen their words." The motif of young people seeking forbidden love is common in the Egyptian love songs and is, of course, a perennial reality in human societies (cf. Song of Songs 8:1–2).

Text: E. SCAMMUZI, *Egyptian Art in the Egyptian Museum of Turin* (Turin: Fratelli Pozzo, 1964), pl. 89, nos. 28–30. *Translations:* FOWLER, *Love Lyrics of Ancient Egypt*, 49–56; FOX, *The Song of Songs and the Ancient Egyptian Love Songs*, 44–51; *LAE* 319–22. *Bibliography:* HERMANN, *Altägyptische Liebesdichtung*, 145–47; M. G. MASPERO, "Les chants d'amour du Papyrus de Turin et du Papyrus Harris no. 500," *JA* 1 (1883): 5–47; WHITE, *A Study of the Language of Love in the Song of Songs and Ancient Egyptian Poetry.*

The Turin Erotic Papyrus (Papyrus 55001). Found at Deir el Medina, this New Kingdom papyrus consists of a series of vignettes drawn on a papyrus scroll about 2.25 meters long and 20 cm high. The odd blend of scenes features animals engaged in human activities as well as a human couple engaged in erotic—some would say pornographic—sexual activities. Scholars normally interpret the animal scenes as a satire in which the beasts play the harp, wage war, and perform interspecies coitus (cat and goose). The erotic human images are ribald scenes that depict an unkempt man with an oversized phallus having sex in various and unusual positions with a younger, more attractive woman (Omlin could not bring himself to describe the scenes in German, so he resorted to Latin). Although we shall never be sure what the artist had in mind, his satirical depiction of animals behaving like humans probably implies that he viewed the sexual human behaviors that he depicted as suitable only for animals.

Text and translation: J. A. OMLIN, *Der Papyrus 55001 und seine satirisch-erotischen Zeichnungen und Inschriften* (Turin: Fratelli Pozzo, 1973). *Bibliography:* D. B. O'CONNOR, "Eros in Egypt," *Archaeology Odyssey* 4, no. 5 (September–October 2001): 43; WHITE, *A Study of the Language of Love in the Song of Songs and Ancient Egyptian Poetry.*

Petosiris's Song to Renpet-nefret. In this Ptolemaic tomb inscription, Petosiris lovingly extols the great qualities and virtues of his wife. It is comparable not only to the first stanza of The Stroll (P.Chester Beatty 1) but also to the Hymn to a Valiant Woman in Prov 31:10–31.

Text and translation: G. LEFEBVRE, *Le tombeau de Petosiris* (2 vols.; Cairo: Institut Français d'Archéologie Orientale, 1923–1924), 1:101; 2.34. *Bibliography:* FOX, *The Song of Songs and the Ancient Egyptian Love Songs,* 350; WHITE, *A Study of the Language of Love in the Song of Songs and Ancient Egyptian Poetry.*

4.3. Ugaritic Love Poetry

Rites of Divine Marriage (KTU 1.111). This bilingual Hurrian-Ugaritic text apparently prescribes rites for the sacred marriage between two little-known deities, the astral god Attaru-Šadi and the lunar goddess Ibbu. For a related text, see the following entry.

Text and translation: PARDEE, *Ritual and Cult at Ugarit,* 90–94. *Bibliography:* DEL OLMO LETE, *Canaanite Religion,* 84, 199–207.

A Ugaritic Marriage Song (KTU 1.24). The first part of this text is the story of the betrothal of Yariḫu, the West Semitic moon god, with Nikkal, a Mesopotamian moon goddess. A central theme of the tale is the negotiation between Yariḫu and Khirikhbi, the divine matchmaker. Khirikhbi initially rejects the generous marriage price offered by Yariḫu for Nikkal, suggesting that Yariḫu consider instead the goddess Padriya (daughter of Baal). Upon Yarhihu's insistence, however, the two are married. Nikkal is referred to as Nikkal-wa-Ibbu, apparently reflecting an attempt to identify her with Ibbu, the lunar goddess mentioned in the previous entry. The second part of the song mentions a human bride named PRBKHTH, evidence that this poem about divine marriage was used to celebrate human marriage.

Text and translation: PARKER, *Ugaritic Narrative Poetry,* 215–18. *Translation:* WYATT, *Religious Texts from Ugarit,* 336–41.

A Sacred Marriage Liturgy? (KTU 1.23). This text is unusual among the Ugaritic exemplars because it combines a mythical narrative poem with interspersed liturgical prescriptions. In highly erotic and explicit tones, the text narrates the sexual relationship of the god El with either one or two goddesses, that is, with Athirat-Rahmay or with Athirat and Rahmay (perhaps a hypostases of the sun goddess Šapšu). Some scholars have characterized the text as a rite of sacred marriage (de Moor), and some, as a famine-relief ritual (Pardee); still others connect it with royal marriage (Wyatt). For more on the mythological features of this text, see 10.4 ("A Ritual Theogony of the Gracious Gods").

Text and translation: PARKER, *Ugaritic Narrative Poetry,* 205–14. *Bibliography:* J. C. L. GIBSON, "The Ugaritic Literary Texts, I: The Mythological Texts," in *Handbook of Ugaritic*

Studies (ed. W. G. E. Watson and N. Wyatt; Leiden: Brill, 1999), 193–202; WYATT, *Religious Texts from Ugarit*, 324–35.

A Rite of Sacred Marriage? (KTU 1.132). This bilingual Hurrian-Ugaritic tablet lists a series of sacrifices taking place in a three-day rite that begins as the bed of the goddess Padriya (a daughter of Baal) is prepared with the "king's bed covers." It is generally presumed that the text has something to do with preparations for a rite of sacred marriage, but this is not certain.

Text and translation: PARDEE, *Ritual and Cult at Ugarit*, 96–99. ***Bibliography:*** DEL OLMO LETE, *Canaanite Religion*, 21, 24, 84, 207–12.

Concluding Observations

Near Eastern love songs were employed in a variety of contexts and served a corresponding variety of functions. In Mesopotamia, divine love lyrics were used to express the act of divine lovemaking and to facilitate the sexual liaison between the king and priestess during the annual rite of sacred marriage. In the latter case, the songs probably helped to sacralize a human sexual encounter that would otherwise have been unacceptable. These early Mesopotamian love poems, however, described more than the sex itself. The entire courtship of Dumuzi and Inanna, from inception to consummation—including all of the requisite frustrations and thrills—was laid out in these songs. It seems that in later periods Mesopotamia's kings no longer observed the rite of sacred marriage, but Mesopotamians continued to express the joys of divine sex in their love songs, such as in the love lyrics of Nabû and Tašmetu. These love poems were sometimes quite explicit in their depictions of physical anatomy and sexual intimacy, but in most cases metaphor partially concealed this. Especially prominent was the metaphor of "brother" and "sister," by which the lovers sometimes referred to each other.

Although the average Mesopotamian citizen was undoubtedly interested in love and sex, the Mesopotamian corpus of love poetry is somewhat thin regarding the concerns of the common man and woman. Nevertheless, we may safely assume that the cultic songs were often pressed into service for ordinary marriage ceremonies (note the Ugaritic marriage song *KTU 1.24*), and we should also note the few Mesopotamian exemplars that seem to reflect secular rather than cultic concerns (most notably Ki. 1063, the Persistent Woman, and the Akkadian Love Song of Ištar and Dumuzi). The same concern for common love appears in the Old Akkadian love charm, whose purpose was to secure sexual and relational fulfillment when none was present. The extent to which the love language of the poems penetrated everyday life is illustrated perhaps by Lu-dingira's semi-erotic description of his mother.

The Egyptian love songs offer more-realistic images of human love and sensuality than their Mesopotamian counterparts, and the rubrics in the texts explicitly identify them as works of "entertainment." From this we can surmise that the songs were recited and sung not only by the lover for the beloved but also in the royal courts, at weddings, at parties, and perhaps even in barrooms. As in the Mesopotamian exemplars, the Egyptian lovers address each other as "brother" and "sister," vividly describing each other's body through a wide range of floral and faunal metaphors. The situations presumed in the Egyptian songs are almost uniformly those encountered by young people, as their nascent desires for adolescent love and sex were proscribed by parents and by social mores. Nowhere is this more vividly expressed than in the Turin Love Song, where trees provide a hiding place for the pursuit of forbidden pleasure; similar frustrations of young love are articulated in The Stroll (see P.Chester Beatty 1) and in the Seven Wishes of the Cairo Songs (Group B). Of course, sexual frustration is not the only theme in the Egyptian songs. Images of relational and sexual fulfillment also appear in the texts. Undoubtedly, the most touching portrayal of love and commitment appears in The Crossing (Cairo Love Songs), which depicts a young man who will stop at nothing to reach the girl who eagerly awaits him. The realistic portrayals of eroticism and human intimacy in the Egyptian love songs provide our closest parallels to Hebrew love poetry. If there is an important difference between the Egyptian and the Israelite sources on this point, it would be that the Song of Songs' use of sexual metaphor is far bolder than that in its Egyptian counterparts (Fox 1985, 277).

Let us turn now to the Hebrew Song of Songs. The most difficult question that biblical scholars have faced in this work is the text's genre. It should be clear by now that some of the less popular readings of Song of Songs that interpret it as a sacred marriage text or as a love incantation of some sort are based on ritual exemplars from the Near Eastern evidence. If there are ritual dimensions in Song of Songs, however, these features are not so transparent as in the Near Eastern parallels. Consequently, for most biblical scholars, the song should not be viewed as a cultic text but rather as a work of secular love poetry akin to the Egyptian love songs. In this context, the primary generic choice faced by scholars is whether it is an anthology of disparate love poems or a more carefully structured work, perhaps a love story of some sort. Unfortunately, the Egyptian and Mesopotamian love songs do not provide comparative evidence to help us eliminate one of these possibilities. Some exemplars obviously reflect narrative progress (e.g., Dumuzi/Inanna songs; The Stroll; The Crossing) or some organizing structure (Seven Wishes in the Cairo Songs), but others exhibit strong anthological characteristics (e.g., the Manchester Tammuz; P.Harris 500; Nakhtsobek's Song). One implication of this observation is that neither the anthological nor the dramatic readings of Song of Songs should be given special preference in our readings; both are possible and sensible. On the other hand, where narrative movement is present in the Near Eastern texts, this movement has been fairly clear to modern scholars. It follows that the absence of obvious narrative momentum in Song of Songs might signal that an anthological reading should be preferred. If we assume, then, that the Song is an anthology of Hebrew love songs, we will find that this accentuates other unique features in the text.

In comparison with other Near Eastern love songs, it is perhaps the role of Solomon in the song that is most peculiar. This feature is sometimes linked to the king's role in the Mesopotamian sacred marriage songs, but there are problems with this comparison. Although the Mesopotamian sacred marriage featured either the gods or the living king, Song of Songs was composed several centuries after Solomon's lifetime, and its poems reflect no cultic or even religious overtones. For this reason, we should seek another explanation for Solomon's prominence in the text. In the absence of other plausible explanations, the most likely reason for the text's association with Solomon is that it was edited, like the other Solomonic texts (Proverbs, Qoheleth), to serve as a wisdom composition. My cautious suggestion is that the biblical Song of Songs is a wisdom text that took up and combined various love songs and then framed them to teach young Jewish women propriety in matters of love and sexuality. This reading of the song coheres nicely with its thrice-repeated refrain: "I adjure you, O daughters of Jerusalem . . . that you not stir up nor awaken love until it please" (Song 2:7; 3:5; 8:4; cf. 5:8). Because much of the book is focalized through the eyes of a woman, it is possible—but by no means certain—that its author was a female. The poems used by this author were already popular in the ancient context and included both royal and secular love songs. Perhaps some of these poems were influenced by, or originated in, the old tradition of the sacred marriage rite, but the signs of this ritual connection are no longer visible in the texts.

General Bibliography

S. ALLAM, "Quelques aspects du marriage dans l'Égypte ancienne," *JEA* 61 (1981): 116–35; B. ALSTER, "Marriage and Love in the Sumerian Love Songs," in *The Tablet and the Scroll: Near Eastern Studies in Honor of William W. Hallo* (ed. M. E. Cohen et al.; Bethesda, Md.: CDL Press, 1993), 15–27; J. A. BLACK, "Babylonian Ballads: A New Genre," in *Studies in Literature from the Ancient Near East: Dedicated to Samuel Noah Kramer* (ed. J. M. Sasson; AOS 65; New Haven: American Oriental Society, 1984), 25–34; A. M. BLACKMAN, "The Use of the Egyptian Word *ḥt* 'house' in the Sense of 'Stanza,'" *Or* 7 (1938): 64–67; J. BOTTÉRO, "Love and Sex in Babylon," in *Everyday Life in Ancient Mesopotamia* (Baltimore: Johns Hopkins University Press, 1992), 90–111; G. L. CARR, "The Love Poetry Genre in the Old Testament and the Ancient Near East: Another Look at Inspiration," *JETS* 25 (1982): 489–98; J. S. COOPER, "New Cuneiform Parallels to the Song of Songs," *JBL* 90 (1971): 157–62; IDEM, "Virginity in Ancient Mesopotamia," in *Sex and Gender in the Ancient Near East* (2 vols.; ed. S. Parpola and R. M. Whiting; RAI 47; Helsinki: Neo-Assyrian Text Corpus Project, 2002), 1:91–112; V. L. DAVIS, "Remarks on Michael V. Fox's 'The Cairo Love Songs,'" *JAOS* 100 (1980): 111–14; E. EBELING, *Ein Hymnenkatalog aus Assur* (Berliner Beiträge zur Keilschriftforschung 1.3; Berlin: Im Selbstverlage des Herausgebers, 1929); I. L. FINKEL, "A Fragmentary Catalogue of Lovesongs," *ActSum* 10 (1988), 17–18; J. L.

FOSTER, *Hymns, Prayers, and Songs: An Anthology of Ancient Egyptian Lyric Poetry* (SBLWAW 8; Atlanta: Scholars Press, 1995); B. H. FOWLER, *Love Lyrics of Ancient Egypt* (Chapel Hill: University of North Carolina Press, 1994); M. V. FOX, "The 'Entertainment Song' Genre in Egyptian Literature," *ScrHier* 28 (1982): 268–316; IDEM, "'Love' in the Love Songs," *JEA* 67 (1981): 181–82; IDEM, *The Song of Songs and the Ancient Egyptian Love Songs* (Madison: University of Wisconsin, 1985); A. HERMANN, *Altägyptische Liebesdichtung* (Wiesbaden: Harrassowitz, 1959); S. ISRAELIT-GROLL, "Ostracon Nash 12 and Chapter 5 of Song of Songs," in *Proceedings of the Tenth World Congress of Jewish Studies* (Jerusalem: World Union of Jewish Studies, 1990), 131–35; T. JACOBSEN, *The Harps That Once . . . Sumerian Poetry in Translation* (New Haven: Yale University Press, 1987); L. MANNICHE, "Some Aspects of Ancient Egyptian Sexual Life," *AcOr* 38 (1977): 11–23; T. J. MEEK, "Babylonian Parallels to the Song of Songs," *JBL* 43 (1924): 245–52; IDEM, "Canticles and the Tammuz Cult," *AJSL* 39 (1922–1923): 1–14; G. DEL OLMO LETE, *Canaanite Religion: According to the Liturgical Texts of Ugarit* (Bethesda, Md.: CDL Press, 1999); S. B. PARKER, ed., *Ugaritic Narrative Poetry* (SBLWAW 9; Atlanta: Scholars Press, 1997); D. PARDEE, *Ritual and Cult at Ugarit* (SBLWAW 10; Atlanta: Society of Biblical Literature, 2002); S. M. PAUL, "A Lover's Garden of Verse: Literal and Metaphorical Imagery in Ancient Near Eastern Love Poetry," in *Tehillah le-Moseh: Biblical and Judaic Studies in Honor of Moshe Greenberg* (ed. M. Cogan et al.; Winona Lake, Ind.: Eisenbrauns, 1997), 99–110; IDEM, "The 'Plural of Ecstasy' in Mesopotamian and Biblical Love Poetry," in *Solving Riddles and Untying Knots: Biblical, Epigraphic, and Semitic Studies in Honor of Jonas C. Greenfield* (ed. Z. Zevit, S. Gitin, and M. Sokoloff; Winona Lake, Ind.: Eisenbrauns, 1995), 585–97; J. M. SASSON, "A Further Cuneiform Parallel to the Song of Songs," *ZAW* 85 (1973): 359–60; IDEM, "Unlocking the Poetry of Love in the Song of Songs," *BR* 1 (1985): 10–19; S. SCHOTT, *Altägyptische Liebeslieder* (Zurich: Artemis, 1950); L. E. STAGER, "Key Passage," *ErIsr* 27 (2003): 240–45; W. G. E. WATSON, "Some Ancient Near Eastern Parallels to the Song of Songs," in *Words Remembered, Texts Renewed: Essays in Honour of John F. A. Sawyer* (ed. J. Davies, G. Harvey, and W. G. E. Watson; JSOTSup 195; Sheffield, England: Sheffield Academic Press, 1995), 253–71; J. G. WESTENHOLZ, "Love Lyrics from the Ancient Near East," *CANE* 4:2471–84; J. B. WHITE, *A Study of the Language of Love in the Song of Songs and Ancient Egyptian Poetry* (Missoula, Mont.: Scholars Press, 1975); J. T. WILLIS, "The Genre of Isaiah 5:1–7," *JBL* 96 (1977): 337–62; N. WYATT, *Religious Texts from Ugarit* (Sheffield, England: Sheffield Academic Press, 1998).

CHAPTER FIVE

Rituals and Incantations

Introduction

Although scholars have been interested in ritual for quite a while, ritual studies as a distinct scholastic enterprise appeared only in the 1970s. This interdisciplinary venture is presently engaged in a vibrant and ongoing debate about the nature, function, and origins of ritual behavior. We can better appreciate the contours of this debate by considering four preliminary questions: what is ritual, why does it exist, how should it be interpreted, and what nomenclature is used to describe it?

A standard scholarly answer to the first question is as follows (see Grimes). Ritual is *a symbolic religious act* that is (1) *repeated* (at regular intervals or in certain circumstances); (2) *sacred* (related to the divine); (3) *formalized* (following prescribed patterns); (4) *traditional* (usually believed to be ancient); and (5) *intentional* (as opposed to, e.g., unconscious gestures). Embedded in this definition is the belief that rituals create an ostensible intersection between this world and the divine realm, an intersection that we might describe as *sacred space* (the physical domain that is in contact with the divine) and *sacred time* (the period within which the divine connection is intact). Modern scholars, naturally, disagree about whether rituals point to an actual world beyond—a spiritual realm—or to a world existing only in our minds. This debate will not be tackled here. More important for our purpose is that scholars disagree about why this sacred link is important, which brings us to our second question: why does ritual exist?

On this question, ritual theorists tend to fall into one of four interpretive camps, namely, the traditional, the sociological, the psychological, and the myth-ritual approaches. Traditional theorists aver that our yearning for the sacred is basic to human identity, so that the sacred itself offers an adequate basis for ritual's existence (Eliade, R. Otto). In contrast, sociological theorists in the Durkheimian tradition believe that society provides the fundamental basis for human identity, so that rituals—like all human symbols—are coined by society to promote cultural order; it follows that social integration—not contact with the sacred per se—is the truer basis for ritual behavior. This view has been refined by theorists such as Geertz and Turner, for whom rituals serve this purpose by negating the effects of incoherence in our cultural systems. Psychological approaches, rooted especially in Freud's work, move in a very different direction (see Freud, Gay, Jensen). Freud argued that ritual sacrifice is a mythic drama that reenacts primordial events from human history. Primary among these events is our repressed memory of the "primal horde," wherein our apelike ancestors killed their father to gain access to his females. Every ritual sacrifice is a veiled rehearsal of this primal event from human evolution, an event that all humans harbor in our "collective unconsciousness." Although few theorists would buy this rather bizarre theory as a whole, some ritual scholars agree with Freud's conclusion that ritual is a symptom of unresolved neuroses. The psychological approach has been further developed in the work of R. Girard and W. Burkert, for whom ritual—especially sacrifice—provides a safe channel for the violent tendencies that developed during human evolution. For these scholars, social order is an important result of ritual, so their views combine the insights of Freud with those of the sociological school. Although this psychological approach suggests that primordial myths create ritual, the so-called myth-ritual school reverses this logic, averring that myths are composed in order to explain existing rituals (e.g., Gaster, Hooke). This conclusion follows from the evolutionary assumption that actions (including ritual actions) are logically prior to language. As we can see, when it comes to theory, the origins of ritual behavior are likely to remain obscure for some time. Nevertheless, it is likely that there is some truth in all four basic viewpoints regarding ritual: rituals link us to the sacred, bind society together, are symptoms of underlying fears and neuroses, and are often closely linked with myth.

How should rituals be interpreted? Our answer to this question should hinge in part on a theory of ritual origins, but there is, as we have seen, no consensus regarding this matter. Nevertheless, the mystery of ritual origins has not prevented theorists from reaching some consenses on the hermeneutics of ritual (see Gorman). Among the most important interpretive assumptions is that ritual study is based on the careful observation and description of the ritual's form (what is done), sequence (when it is done), and order (what is the relation between action and effect). A second assumption made by many theorists is that rituals exist as part of a larger ritual or cultural system, so that proper interpretation of ritual includes an effort to understand how it fits within, and contributes to, this system (e.g., Geertz, Turner). There are indeed new currents in ritual studies that question the validity of the "systems" approach to ritual, primarily because rituals, like habits, are often practiced without recourse to their meanings or, where meanings are given, the ritual participants often do not agree on these (see Bell, Staal, J. Z. Smith). Although this critique of the systems approach has certain merits, there can be little doubt that human beings tend to organize their ritual beliefs in a coherent way. Moreover, as we will see, the Near Eastern evidence suggests that ritual coherence was an important concern among the ancients.

What nomenclature is used to describe ritual? Scholars facilitate the description and comparison of rituals by employing a number of basic categories. Ritual behaviors are normally divided into two basic types, the confirmatory and the transformatory. These categories are not mutually exclusive, and a single ritual may fit comfortably into both in some way. *Confirmatory* rituals reinforce and preserve the boundaries that separate the sacred from the profane. A good example would be Israelite dietary law, the observance of which did not change one's ritual status so much as it preserved that status. In contrast, *transformatory* rites initiate changes in ritual status rather than preserve a status quo. One important type of transformatory rite is the *rite of passage,* which changes the ritual or social status of human beings (e.g., a wedding). According to the classic study of A. van Gennep, these rites feature a three-stage transition of persons from one status to another, including rites of "separation," "transition," and "incorporation." During this transition, the initiate traverses a "liminal phase" where the standard distinctions between the two statuses are blurred. Although most scholars agree that human beings address the ambiguity of social and ritual transition with this threefold ritual pattern, there is no agreement on why we feel the need to do so. Another important type of tranformatory ritual is the *elimination/ purgation rite,* which removes uncleanness by applying a ritual detergent (e.g., blood or water), by destroying it, or by transferring the pollution from sacred to profane space. Scholars have long pondered the origins of our inclination to perceive the presence of ritual pollution and to believe this pollution can be conveyed from one place to another, but no consensus has been reached. Nonetheless, I would suggest cautiously that the concept of communicable ritual impurity probably stems from everyday experiences with illness and contagion. Even in antiquity it was obvious that illnesses were contagious (see the Mari text, ARM 10.129 in Dossin), and it would have required only one short and logical step to conclude that sacred space needed protection from this contagion. The Mesopotamian evidence provides some support for this hypothesis, as we shall see.

Some transformational rituals effect change in a very direct way, serving as ready-made tools to provide blessings, curses, rain, fertility, and a host of other desired outcomes. We shall refer to these as *instrumental rituals,* but they are more commonly described as "magic," a term that presents certain problems. There is a long-standing debate about the definition of magic, mainly because scholars are attempting to employ as a technical word one that is in popular usage vague and imprecise (see Middleton; Morris; Ritner). Theological concerns further cloud the issue because the Judeo-Christian West has often contrasted theological "orthodoxy" with the evil "heterodoxy" of magic, a distinction that can scarcely be applied to the ancient Near East, where private rituals that we might describe as magic were performed by the same officials, and described with the same terminology, as public temple rituals (see Farber; Marett; Ritner). Roughly speaking, magical rituals can be classified as three functional types: productive, apotropaic/prophylactic, and malevolent magic. As the names imply, these types correspond to rituals that produce favorable outcomes (productive), those that remove or prevent unfavorable outcomes (apotropaic/prophylatic), and those that are intended to cause harmful outcomes (malevolent). Most of our Near Eastern ritual corpus fits into the first two of these three categories, but the distinctions are in practice difficult to maintain. For instance, many ancient rituals cured the sick (an apotropaic function) by causing harm to the demons causing the illness (a malevolent intention). In other words, our judgments about the nature of a ritual—for good or ill—are a function of our perspectives of what constitutes good and evil.

Because ritual is a religious behavior rather than a literary form, many kinds of ancient texts would fit comfortably into our discussion. Potential examples of ritual texts include sacrificial texts, medical texts, prayers, hymns, lamentations, omens, genealogies, and even a few narratives. For purposes of comparison, many of these exemplars are discussed elsewhere in this volume, so readers are encouraged to round out the present discussion of ancient ritual by consulting closely related chapters, especially the chapters on omens (ch. 6) and on hymns, prayers, and laments (ch. 3). In the present chapter our objective is to examine a range of Near Eastern texts that illustrate the most salient similarities and differences between the biblical and Near Eastern rituals. It is common and helpful to divide this ancient corpus into two text types: those describing the rituals (ritual descriptions) and those prescribing how they should be done (ritual prescriptions). Although this distinction is of some value and will be employed in the discussion that follows, it does not work so well in all cases.

One feature common to many of the ancient rites was the incantation, a verbal formula recited during the ritual procedure. Incantations appear as one of two basic types, spells and prayers. In magical spells (German, *Beschwörungen*), the recited words are deemed bearers of effective power and hence do not rely on the response of a deity. In contrast, prayer incantations (*Gebetsbeschwörungen*) are petitions to the deity, being effective only insofar as the uttered words move the divine will. For purposes of comparison, the magical incantations are treated in this chapter, and the prayer incantations are treated in 3.1.3.

5.1. Sacred Space: Cult Statues, Temple Construction, Temple Rites, and Topographic Texts

The ancients devoted a great deal of energy to creating and maintaining sacred space. At the center of sacred space stood the gods and goddesses, who existed as statues housed in private quarters of the temple's holy precinct (*cela*). The statues were generally made of wood overlaid with gold or silver and were adorned with jewelry and expensive attire. In Near Eastern theology, a chief function of humanity was to care for these gods, whose needs were not unlike the needs of their human caretakers. Consequently, the gods were regularly bathed and clothed, provided with food and drink, taken on trips by land and river, and even granted sexual liaisons with their divine spouses. The entries below focus on the construction of divine statues and on the sacred homes in which they lived.

The Mesopotamian* Mīs Pî *Ritual. The Mesopotamians fabricated new cult statues and restored older ones in a two-day rite of passage known as *Mīs Pî* ("mouth-washing") or *Pīt Pî* ("mouth-opening"). The two names reflect two distinct aspects of the ritual. Through *Mīs Pî* the statue was purified from the human contamination of those who created it, and through *Pīt Pî* the deity entered the statue, animating it so that praise hymns and food offerings could be received. If the statue fell into disrepair, the deity could abandon it, and if the cult image was lost or destroyed, it could not be restored unless the deity revealed a design for its restoration. This reflects the ancient belief that cult statues were divine designs rather than mere human creations. The *Mīs Pî* rites reinforced this belief by denying the human origins of the statue and strongly affirming its divine origins. During the ritual, the craftsmen who built the statue swore oaths, "I did not make [the statue]," while priestly incantations averred that the statue was "born in heaven," that is, constructed by the gods. For similar Egyptian rites, see the following entry. For a possible parallel in the biblical tradition, see the purification of Isaiah's lips in Isa ch. 6 (Hurowitz).

Text and translation: C. WALKER and M. B. DICK, *The Induction of the Cult Image in Ancient Mesopotamia: The Mesopotamian Mīs Pî Ritual* (SAALT 1; Helsinki: Helsinki University Press, 2001). *Bibliography:* A. BERLEJUNG, *Die Theologie der Bilder: Herstellung und Einweihung von Kultbildern in Mesopotamien und die alttestmentliche Bilderpolemik* (OBO 162; Freiburg, Switz.: Universitätsverlag, 1998); W. W. HALLO, "Cult Statue and Divine Image: A Preliminary Study," in *More Essays on the Comparative Method* (ed. Hallo, Moyer, and Perdue), 1–17; V. A. HUROWITZ, "Isaiah's Impure Lips and Their Purification in Light of Akkadian Sources," *HUCA* 60 (1989): 39–89; T. JACOBSEN, "The Graven Image," in *Ancient Israelite Religion: Essays in Honor of Frank Moore Cross* (ed. P. D. Miller Jr., P. D. Hanson, and S. D. McBride; Philadelphia: Fortress, 1987), 15–32; E. MATSUSHIMA, "Divine Statues in Ancient Mesopotamia: Their Fashioning and Clothing and Their Interaction with the Society," in *Official Cult and Popular Religion in the Ancient Near East* (ed. E. Matsushuma; Heidelberg: Universitätsverlag C. Winter, 1993), 209–19.

The Egyptian Mouth-Opening Ritual. This ritual, literally entitled the *Opening of the Mouth and Eyes,* was used in various permutations from the Old Kingdom down into the Roman period. Although it was commonly used in funerary contexts to revive the dead, one of its purposes—perhaps its original purpose—was to animate cult statues of gods and kings so that they could breathe, see, and receive food and drink. During the rite, special tools were applied to the mouth and eyes of the image. The most important tool was a ritual knife (the *psš-kf*), which appears to have been the same instrument used in Egypt to cut the umbilical cords of newborn babies. This suggests that the fashioning of the cult statue may have been understood as a kind of birth or rebirth (Roth), but not all would agree with this assessment (Lorton). Seven major copies of the rite are in our possession, dating from the New Kingdom down to the early Roman period. If the rite were observed using all of the elements in these texts, it would include seventy-five ritual episodes that fall into six basic sections of the rite: (1) preliminary rites (episodes 1–9); (2) rites of animation for the statue (episodes 10–22); (3) offerings addressing Upper Egypt (episodes 23–42); (4) offerings addressing Lower Egypt (episodes 43–46); (5) a funerary meal (episodes 47–71); and (6) concluding rites (episodes 72–75). The Opening of the Mouth portion of the rite would have included only the animation rites and the offerings (parts 1–4); the funerary offerings in part 5 were necessary only when the rite was being used to revive the dead. At any rate, it is clear that the focus of the rite was twofold: to animate the divine statue and to provide it with sustaining food and drink. For more on the funerary uses of this ritual, see below in 5.9.1.

Text and translation: E. OTTO, *Das ägyptische Mundöffnungsritual* (2 vols.; ÄgAbh 3; Wiesbaden: Harrassowitz, 1960). **Bibliography:** S. BJERKE, "Remarks on the Egyptian Ritual of 'Opening the Mouth' and Its Interpretation," *Numen* 12 (1965): 201–16; A. M. BLACKMAN, "The Rite of Opening the Mouth in Ancient Egypt and Mesopotamia," *JRitSt* 6 (1992): 13–42; GOYON, *Rituels funéraires de l'ancienne Égypte;* D. LORTON, "The Theology of Cult Statues in Ancient Egypt," in *Born in Heaven, Made on Earth* (ed. Dick), 123–210; A. M. ROTH, "Fingers, Stars, and the 'Opening of the Mouth': The Nature and Function of the ntrwy-Blades," *JEA* 79 (1993): 57–79; IDEM, "The PSŠ-KF and the 'Opening of the Mouth' Ceremony: A Ritual of Birth and Rebirth," *JEA* 78 (1992): 113–47.

Daily Temple Rites in Mesopotamia. Like their human counterparts, the gods had regular needs for food, drink, bathing, clothing, sex, and admiration. Ritual texts from the ancient Near East prescribed how these needs were met. Unfortunately, many of the prescriptive texts for daily sacrifices are fragmentary, so our reconstructions of the cultic ceremonies are necessarily partial and in some cases speculative. The primary source for the daily rite in Mesopotamia is a Seleucid-era copy of the daily rite for the gods of Uruk (AO 6451; see Linssen; Thureau-Dangin; *ANET* 338–39). The text is introduced by the words "Every day in the year," which mark it as a daily rite akin to the Hebrew *tāmîd* in Num 28:1–8. There follows a series of detailed prescriptions for the daily offerings, which included beverages, grains/bread, and meat offerings. Four meals are prescribed for each day, including large and small meals in both the morning and the evening. The prescriptions are presented in a list-like format, with rulings that separate each major section of the text. Interspersed with the offering lists are brief directions for those involved in the rites, including the priests, chefs, and the ritual slaughterers. The directions include ritual actions that must be done and liturgical compositions that should be recited. As we would expect at Uruk, Anu's provisions are listed first, followed by those of his spouse, Antu, and of the goddesses Ištar and Nanna. A few other deities are also mentioned. The author explicitly notes that his text does not cover all offerings for the daily rites of other deities dwelling at Uruk, nor does it address special cultic occasions. The colophon of the tablet mentions the name of the scribe who copied the text and in some detail enumerates how the text was copied from tablets that were at one time taken from Uruk by Nabopolossar of Babylon (sixth century B.C.E.). Additional insight into the daily Mesopotmian rites may be gleaned from another text, AO 6460, which covers the rites for days 16–17 of an unknown month at the Anu temple in Uruk (see Linssen; Thureau-Dangin).

As already noted, the general shape of the daily rite at Uruk parallels the daily *tāmîd* in the Hebrew Bible. Both offerings included unblemished animals, grains, and libations, and in both cases meals were provided in the morning and evening (two meals in Israel rather than four). One obvious difference between the Israelite and Mesopotamian rites is the scale of the offerings. The daily provision at Uruk—eighteen animals for the first meal alone—was much larger than that prescribed in the Hebrew Bible. But then again, there were many more deities to please in Uruk, and Uruk was a much larger city than even the largest towns of Israel and Judah.

Texts and translations: LINSSEN, *The Cults of Uruk and Babylon,* 172–83 (AO 6451), 245–51 (AO 6460); THUREAU-DANGIN, *Rituels accadiens,* 62–65, 74–86 (AO 6451), 68–69, 118–25 (AO 6460). *Translations: ANET* 338–39, 343–45; *TUAT* 1:55–57; 2:227–32. **Bibliography:** F. BLOME, *Die Opfermaterie in Babylonien und Israel* (Sacra scriptura antiquitatibus orientalibus illustrata 4; Rome: Pontificium Institutum Biblicum, 1934); M. HARAN, *Temples and Temple Service in Ancient Israel* (Winona Lake, Ind.: Eisenbrauns, 1985); W. G. LAMBERT, "Donations of Food and Drink to the Gods in Ancient Mesopotamia," in *Ritual and Sacrifice in the Ancient Near East* (ed. Quaegebeur), 191–201; LINSSEN, *The Cults of Uruk and Babylon,* 12–39; THUREAU-DANGIN, *Tablettes d'Uruk à l'usage des prêtres du temple d'Anu au temps des Séleucides,* no. 38; G. VAN DRIEL, *The Cult of Assur* (Assen: Van Gorcum, 1969).

Daily Temple Rites in Egypt. Surprisingly, all indicators suggest that the daily cults observed in ancient Egypt were of essentially the same form in every temple, large and small (Sauneron, 89). Our primary sources for reconstructing the daily rite include Ptolemaic-era depictions in the temples at Edfu and Dendera (see Derchain), depictions with accompanying hieroglyphic inscriptions from the mortuary temple of king Sety I at Abydos (1290–1279/8 B.C.E.), and several papyri from the Twenty-Second Dynasty (ca. 945–800 B.C.E.) that are presently in the Egyptian Museum of Berlin. The papyri include fragmentary copies of the cult for the goddess Mut (P.Berlin 3014 and 3053) and a very good manuscript of the daily rites for the god Amun-Re at Karnak (P.Berlin 3055). The ritual texts— let us consider P.Berlin 3055, for example—are essentially collections of incantation spells to be recited at certain points in the rite. Rubrics mark each ritual action (e.g., "Spell for seeing the god"), and each rubric is followed by the appropriate utterance (e.g., "Words to be said: My face is protected from the god and vice-versa. O gods, make way for me so that I might pass. It is the king who has sent me to see the god"). Several hymns and prayers are folded into these utterances, which perhaps illustrate how the cultic psalms of the Hebrew Bible would have been used.

We can reconstruct the daily rite by combining our evidence from the texts, depictions, and other sources. The rites began just before sunrise with the burning of incense before the *cela,* which was soon followed by a brief ceremony in which the *cela* was opened by breaking the clay seal and untying the cord that held its doors shut. Incantations accompanied the opening of the *cela,* and as its doors were opened, a powerful, full-voice choir sang the morning song: "Awake in peace, wake peacefully. . . . The gods rise early to honor your soul." The god's statue—normally of metal or wood and only 25 cm or so tall—was kept in a *naos,* a small granite or basalt structure with two wooden doors. Like the *cela* doors, the *naos* doors were sealed with clay and had to be ritually opened. When this was done, the high priest—here representing the pharaoh, as all priests did in such rites—took hold of the statue and "gave it his soul," reciting, as he did, this formula: "I adore your majesty with choice expressions and prayers that magnify your prestige, in your great names and in all the holy forms of manifestations in which you revealed yourself in the first moment [of the world]" (Sauneron, 81). At this phase in the rite, the priest observed various ritual prostrations, incense was offered, and hymns were sung. Next the deity was fed. A tray of cakes and bread was placed before it, and meat offerings were burned in the nearby altar room so that the god could consume its aroma. Through these rites the elaborate supplies of meat, bread, vegetables, and fruits in the adjoining altar room were symbolically passed to the god. Foodstuffs were also offered to other deities as well as to deceased kings and dignitaries whose statues were in the temple. Eventually the priests would eat the food after the gods had consumed its immaterial essence. Next the deity was offered a figurine of the goddess Maat—who personified justice, order, and harmony—and this was followed by various rituals of purification, most notably the anointing of the statue with oil. The deity was then washed, dressed, and purified as the rites drew to a close. The ceremonies ended with the replacement of the statue in the *naos,* the closing and sealing of the *naos* doors, and the ceremonial rite of Removing the Footprint, in which the priest departed the *cela* backwards while sweeping away all traces of his visit. Less elaborate rites—mostly cleansing rituals—were observed at midday, to be followed by a more elaborate evening ceremony akin to the morning service that we have just described. The day ended with the withdrawal of the priests and the closing of all doors and chambers in the temple.

Texts and translations: M. ALLIOT, *Le culte d'Horus à Edfou au temps des Ptolémées* (2 vols.; BdE 20; Cairo: Institut Français d'Archéologie Orientale, 1949–1954) (Edfu); A. ERMAN, ed., *Hieratische papyrus aus den königlichen Museen zu Berlin* (Leipzig: J. C. Hinrichs, 1901), pls. 1–37 (P.Berlin texts); A. MARIETTE, *Abydos* (2 vols.; Paris: A. Franck, 1869–1880), vol. 1 (Abydos); A. MORET, *Le rituel du culte divin journalier en Égypte* (Annales du Musée Guimet: Bibliothèque d'études 14; Paris: E. Leroux, 1902) (P.Berlin texts); J. OSING and G. ROSATI, *Papiri geroglifici e ieratici da Tebtynis* (2 vols.; Florence: Istituto Papirologico G. Vitelli, 1998) (daily rite for the god Sobek at Tebtunis). *Translations:* ANET 325–26; COS 1. 34:55–57; TUAT 2:391–405. *Bibliography:* J. ASSMANN, *The Search for God in Ancient Egypt* (Ithaca: Cornell University Press, 2001); A. R. DAVID, *Religious Ritual at Abydos (c. 1300 BC)* (Warminster, England: Aris and Phillips, 1973); P. DERCHAIN, "Du temple cosmique au temple ludique," in *Ritual and Sacrifice in the Ancient Near East* (ed. Quaegebeur), 93–97; IDEM, "Les scènes rituelles des temples d'époque gréco-romaine en Égypte et les règles du jeu 'Domino,'" in *Ritual and Sacrifice in the Ancient Near East* (ed. Quaegebeur), 99–105; D. LORTON, "The Theology of Cult Statues in Ancient Egypt," in *Born in Heaven, Made on Earth* (ed. Dick), 123–210; S. SAUNERON, *The Priests of Ancient Egypt* (Ithaca: Cornell University Press, 2000), 75–91; N. TACKE, "Das Opferritual des ägyptischen Neuen Reiches," in *Rituale in der Vorgeschichte, Antike, und Gegenwart: Studien zur vorderasiatischen, prähistorischen, und klassischen Archäologie, Ägyptologie, alten Geschichte, Theologie, und Religionswissenschaft* (ed. C. Metzner-Nebelsick et al.; Rahden, Germany: Marie Leidorf, 2004), 27–36.

Daily Rites in the Hittite Cult of Nerik. As the Hittites extended their empire to include various regions and cities, they also undertook efforts to assimilate the religious cults of conquered peoples into a more comprehensive Hittite religious system. A good example is provided by Hattušili III's effort to restore and reform the cult of the storm god at the city of Nerik. We have numerous texts that relate to this cult restoration project (see Haas), among them a brief but telling list of prescriptions for the daily rite at Nerik (KUB 31.113). The text is listed among the administrative fragments in *CTH* 275, but it is closely related to the Nerik cultic texts in *CTH* 671–78. The broken rubric of the tablet appears to identify the text as an "instruction" (literally, "covenant"), whose prescriptions regarded daily activities of the priests in the temple: "Constantly bring the water for the daily offering from gaurija-forest and the dunnariya-forest. . . . Always take that water for the cult of the god! And the daily bread that the king offers to god, you priests arrange it as follows: As soon as the priest and diviner go early into the temple, remove the old bread from the temple and put the new bread in place. When evening arrives, put a lamp in place and lock up the temple; a priest and the seer sleep at the [temple] gate." Following this overview of the daily rite, the text provides more detailed instructions regarding morning cultic activities and the placement and handling of the water and bread. The cultic activities described in this text are reminiscent of the Hebrew rites in Num 28 and of the priestly activities reflected in 1 Sam 3 (see Weinfeld).

Text and translation: HAAS, *Der Kult von Nerik*. **Bibliography:** M. WEINFELD, "Traces of Hittite Cult in Shiloh, Bethel, and in Jerusalem," in *Religionsgeschichtliche Beziehungen zwischen Kleinasien, Nordsyrien, und dem Alten Testament* (ed. Janowski, Koch, and Wilhelm), 455–72.

A Daily Rite from Ugarit (and Related Sacrificial Texts). The twin sites of Ras Shamra and Ras Ibn Hani—ancient Ugarit—have yielded an interesting corpus of almost one hundred ritual texts (see Pardee 2000). There is only one text from the site that may provide the daily rite of a temple in the city. It was the very first tablet recovered from Ugarit (RS 1.001 = *KTU* 1.39), distinguished from all others because it prescribes a one-day ceremony. The text prescribes a series of daytime and nighttime sacrifices to various deities. Although certain deities, such as Baal, appear in both the daytime and nighttime lists, there is a clear relationship between the times of day and the deities involved. Specifically, the nighttime sacrifices are directed toward the deities one would expect, such as chthonic deities, gods of fertility, and nocturnal gods such as Yariḫu (the moon god) and Šapši-Pagri (the sun as it passed through the underworld). Various types of offerings are listed, but modern scholars do not entirely understand the terminology. The offerings begin with an initial sequence of t^c-sacrifices for the god El, which were perhaps a type of atonement offering akin to the Hebrew ḥṭṭˀt ("sin/purification offering"). The remaining sacrifices were burnt offerings (perhaps like the He-brew *ʿlh*) as well as "peace offerings" (*šlm*), which were, like their Hebrew coun-terparts, communal sacrifices in which the gods and offerers shared a ritual meal from the meat of the sacrifice. Grain offerings were also included, but no liba-tions are mentioned. At the conclusion of the rites, the prescriptions direct the priests to "descend from the altars." There are obvious parallels between *KTU* 1.39 and the Hebrew *tāmîd* (see Num 28:1–8), which prescribed morning and evening sacrifices of meat, grain, and drink to Yahweh.

Apart from RS 1.001, there are no liturgies for daily temple rites from Ugarit. The remaining texts concern special liturgical days that were observed in the royal chapel of the king's palace and, to a lesser extent, in the major temples of the city, especially the temples of Baal and El. Some of these texts are liturgical schedules that cover several months of cultic activities, and others concern special festivals and cultic events. The ritual calendar of Ugarit was based on the lunar cycle, so the texts reflect a special interest in the beginning and middle of the month, that is, full moon and new moon. About three-quarters of the Ugaritic ritual texts mention the king, who played a significant role in the cultic life of Ugarit. The prominence of the king in the rituals is no surprise given that Ugaritic theology viewed the living king as a "son of god" and the deceased kings as gods (Wyatt, 560). A cadre of cultic personnel who were dependents of the king served in Ugarit's temples and chapels. The ritual texts specifically speak of "singers" (*šrm*), "holy ones" *qdšm*, and various exorcistic figures, and the administrative texts refer to "priests" (*khnm*) and the "chief of priests" (*rb khnm*). These last two titles are cognate to the corresponding Hebrew terms *khnm* ("priests") and *khn gdl* ("high priest"). Perhaps the most strik-ing difference between the Ugaritic and Israelite cultic literature is that the king has no prominent role in the priestly legislation of the Hebrew Bible. Most biblical scholars believe that this reflects only the postexilic context in which the Israelite Priestly Code was edited. It is likely that the king played a more prominent role in the temple cults of preexilic Israel and Judah.

It is interesting that the ritual prescriptions discovered at Ugarit seem to date mainly to the last few years of the kingdom (i.e., ca. 1200–1185). For this rea-son, it seems that the texts should not be regarded as representative of an ongoing *written* canonical tradition in the city. A more likely scenario is that we are deal-ing with ad hoc crib texts composed by priests to aide the performance of their ritual duties. If so, Ugarit's ritual tradition would have been perpetuated mainly as an oral tradition within the life of Ugarit's priestly guild. This conclusion could also be inferred from the laconic and cryptic nature of the instructions, which presume that the reader was already well versed in Ugarit's cultic lore.

Texts and translations: D. PARDEE, *Ritual and Cult at Ugarit*, 25–119; IDEM, *Les textes ritu-als* (2 vols.; Paris: Éditions Recherche sur les Civilisations, 2000). **Bibliography:** B. A. LEVINE, "The Descriptive Ritual Texts from Ugarit: Some Formal and Functional Features of the Genre," in *The Word of the Lord Shall Go Forth: Essays in Honor of David Noel Freed-man* (ed. C. L. Myers and M. O'Connor; Winona Lake, Ind.: Eisenbrauns, 1983), 467–75; IDEM, "Ugaritic Descriptive Rituals," *JCS* 17 (1963): 105–11; P. MERLO and P. XELLA, "The Ugaritic Cultic Texts, 1: The Rituals," in *Handbook of Ugaritic Studies* (ed. Watson and

Wyatt), 287–304; J.-M. DE TARRAGON, *Le culte à Ugarit* (CahRB 19; Paris: Gebalda, 1980);
N. WYATT, "The Religion of Ugarit: An Overview," in *Handbook of Ugaritic Studies* (ed.
Watson and Wyatt), 529–85.

Ugaritic God Lists. Although ancient god lists were sometimes products of theological reflection, most of our Ugaritic exemplars were sacrificial lists used in the
cult. A good example is *KTU* 1.118, which bears the "check marks" that priests
added as they completed each offering. The utility of this text for priests is illustrated by the fact that multiple copies have been found, including both Ugaritic
(*KTU* 1.47) and Akkadian exemplars (RS 20.024). The judgment that these god
lists were cultic texts rather than theological compositions is based primarily on
KTU 1.148, a liturgical tablet that bears the title "Sacrifice for the Gods of Mount
Zaphon" and also provides a list that parallels our three god lists exemplars. Sev-
eral features of the Ugaritic god lists are important for comparative purposes.
First, the texts refer to the gods collectively as the "gods of Zaphon," reflecting the
Ugaritic belief that all of the gods resided on the heavenly cosmic mountain (cf.
Mounts Zion, Sinai, and Seir in Israelite theology). Second, all of the lists place
the "god of the father" at the beginning, even before the great gods El, Dagan, and
Baal. This illustrates the relative prominence of the family deity in the theology of
Ugarit's royal household. Third, the god Baal appears in the lists seven times. This
was necessary because each of Baal's local manifestations—which were numerous—required a sacrifice. A similar religious phenomenon is visible in the
epigraphic evidence from Israel, which refers to "Yahweh of Samaria" and "Yahweh of Teman" (see 15.1).

Texts and translations: PARDEE, *Ritual and Cult at Ugarit,* 11–24, 44–49. *Translations:*
WYATT, *Religious Texts from Ugarit,* 360–62 (*KTU* 1.47, 1.118; RS 20.024), 427–29 (*KTU*
1.148). *Bibliography:* A. COOPER and M. H. POPE, "Divine Names and Epithets in the
Ugaritic Texts," in *Ras Shamra Parallels: The Texts from Ugarit and the Hebrew Bible* (ed.
L. R. Fisher; 3 vols.; AnOr 49–51; Rome: Pontificium Institutum Biblicum, 1972–1981),
3:333–469; J. C. DE MOOR, "The Semitic Pantheon of Ugarit," *UF* 2 (1970): 187–218; DEL
OLMO LETE, *Canaanite Religion,* 71–86; J. F. HEALEY, "The Akkadian 'Pantheon' List from
Ugarit," *SEL* 2 (1985): 115–23; IDEM, "The 'Pantheon' of Ugarit: Further Notes," *SEL* 5
(1988): 103–12.

Rural Sacrifices at Ugarit *(KTU 1.79; 1.80).* These two texts record sacrificial
ceremonies that were observed in nontemple contexts outside the city of Ugarit.
The offerings were apparently made on behalf of others by a fellow named Ṣitānu,
who was perhaps a rural priest empowered to slaughter animals outside temple
precincts. His acts of profane slaughter are distinguished from temple sacrifices
by using the term *ṭbḥ* ("to slaughter") instead of *dbḥ* ("to sacrifice"). Israelite tradition was also sensitive to the distinctions between cultic and profane slaughter.
Some strands of Israelite theology allowed for the profane slaughter of altar animals (Deut 12:15–16), and others did not (see Lev 17).

Texts and translations: PARDEE, *Ritual and Cult at Ugarit,* 119–22; C. VIROLLEAUD, *Textes
en cunéiformes alphabétiques des archives est, ouest, et centrales* (vol. 2 of *Le palais royal*

d'Ugarit; ed. C. F. A. Schaeffer; Mission de Ras Shamra 7; Paris: Imprimerie Nationale, 1955–), nos. 153, 154.

Mesopotamian Rituals for Divine Journeys. In the ancient world, transportation of the divine statue was an event accompanied by music, worship, incantations, and all manner of pomp and circumstance. Our three best-preserved exemplars include an old Sumerian ritual for transporting the goddess Nanna to Nippur and two Seleucid-era prescriptions regarding the god Anu. My comments will focus on the Seleucid exemplars. The first of the Seleucid texts, part of what was a ritual series, concerns the transport of Anu to the New Year festival at the Akitu house (on this structure, see 5.5). The text reflects the various stations through which the god passed, beginning with his departure from the chapel and passing through the ship dike of Anu, the ship dike of the Holy Quay, and the Royal Gate of the Akitu temple before finally arriving at the temple itself. The incantation priests (*mašmašu* [= *āšipu*]) figure prominently in the rites, offering numerous incantations along the way and at certain junctures joining other priests in the presentation of ŠUILLA prayers and blessings to the god. The blessings to be used in the rite are included in the tablet. The other Seleucid text concerns the Akitu (Akkadian *akītu*) procession itself, a trek in which Anu was joined by other gods and goddesses who were attending the festival. The singers, the lamentation priests, and the incantation priests played prominent roles in this public rite. For related texts from the Hebrew Bible, see 2 Sam 6 and 1 Chron 15–16, which describe ceremonies associated with the transport of the ark of the covenant.

Texts and translations: S. N. KRAMER, *Sumerian Literary Texts from Nippur in the Museum of the Ancient Orient at Istanbul* (AASOR 23; New Haven: Yale University Press, 1944), no. 39 (Nanna); LINSSEN, *The Cults of Uruk and Babylon*, 201–8 (Anu 2), 209–14 (Anu 1); F. THUREAU-DANGIN, "Le Procession du Nouvel an a Uruk," *RA* 20 (1923): 107–12 (Anu 1); IDEM, *Rituels accadiens*, 99–108 (Anu 2). *Translations:* ANET 342–43 (Anu 1); *TUAT* 2:175–89 (Nanna). *Bibliography:* A. FERRARA, *Nanna-Suen's Journey to Nippur* (Rome: Pontifical Biblical Institute, 1973).

Mesopotamian Temple Construction Narratives. Mesopotamian kings took great pride in temple construction/reconstruction and often narrated these deeds in their royal inscriptions. The three best Mesopotamian exemplars are the cylinders of Gudea (ca. 2100), the inscriptions of Samsuiluna (ca. 1750), and the inscriptions of Tiglath-pileser I (ca. 1100). These three texts seem to reflect the same basic narrative pattern: (1) the circumstances that prompted the divine decision to build; (2) preparations for the construction; (3) description and construction of the building; (4) dedication rituals for the temple; (5) promise or request for blessings upon the temple's builder. According to Hurowitz, this pattern appears in many Near Eastern construction narratives and constitutes a kind of literary topos that can be traced from the Sumerian period all the way down to Josephus. There can be little doubt that these similarities are linked at some level with the conventions of scribal literary tradition, but it is also likely that common cultural assumptions and ideologies explain some of the similarities. Biblical descriptions of temple construction appear in Exod 25–40, Ezek 40–48, 1 Kgs 5–8, and 2 Chron 2–7, and rituals for the temple's dedication appear in Exod 40 and Lev 9.

Texts and translations: D. FRAYNE, *Old Babylonian Period (2003–1595)* (RIME 4; Toronto: University of Toronto Press, 1990), 374–78 (Samsuiluna); A. K. GRAYSON, *Assyrian Rulers of the Early First Millennium BC* (2 vols.; RIMA 2–3; Toronto: University of Toronto Press, 1991–1996), 1:7–31 (Tiglath-pileser); E. J. WILSON, *The Cylinders of Gudea: Transliteration, Translation, and Index* (AOAT 244; Neukirchen-Vluyn: Neukirchener Verlag, 1996). *Translations:* ANET 268–69; COS 2.155: 417–33; T. JACOBSEN, *The Harps That Once . . . Sumerian Poetry in Translation* (New Haven: Yale University Press, 1987), 386–444. *Bibliography:* D. AVERBECK, "Sumer, the Bible, and Comparative Method: Historiography and Temple Building," in *Mesopotamia and the Bible: Comparative Explorations* (ed. M. W. Chavalas and K. L. Younger Jr.; Grand Rapids: Baker, 2002), 88–125; V. A. HUROWITZ, "The Priestly Account of Building the Tabernacle," *JAOS* 105 (1985): 21–30; IDEM, *I Have Built You an Exalted House: Temple Building in the Bible in Light of Mesopotamian and Northwest Semitic Writings* (JSOTSup 115; Sheffield, England: JSOT Press, 1992).

A Hittite Ritual for Building a Temple (CTH 413). As the text's rubric explicitly states, this rite was used "when they rebuild a temple that had been destroyed or a new house in a different place and they lay the foundations, they deposit under its foundations as follows . . ." The remainder of the text enumerates a series of offerings and rites that were observed as the temple's foundation was layed. The initial ritual apparently included a sympathetic magical act in which a piece of copper was ceremonially secured to the ground using four bronze pegs and an iron hammer. As this was done, an incantation was recited: "Just as this copper is secured, as moreoever it is firm, even so let this temple be secure. Let it be firm upon the dark earth." The text then continues with prescriptions for another incantation on behalf of the builder: "He who built this temple; let him likewise be firm before the gods." The bulk of the text prescribes a series of offerings—precious and semiprecious metals and stones—to be placed at various points in the temple's foundation, including especially at its center, at its four corners, and beneath its cult stand, hearth, and door. One of the incantations freed the new structure from human contamination by declaring, "This temple which we have built for thee, the god (he mentions the name of the god for whom they build it), it is not we who have really built it. All the gods have built it. The gods—those who are craftsmen—have built it. Telepinus has laid its foundations. The walls above them, Ea, the king of wisdom, has built them. Timber and stones, all the mountains have brought them, but the mortar the goddesses have brought." Readers should note the Mesopotamian influence on this text not only in the mention of Ea (Mesopotamian god of wisdom) but also in the motif whereby the craftsmen deny their role in building the temple, as we see in the above-mentioned Mesopotamian *Mīs Pî* ritual. For a related Hittite temple construction text, see *CTH* 415 (Tatishvili; Ünal).

Text: See list in *CTH* 413. *Translation:* ANET 356–57. *Bibliography:* A. M. DARGA, *Hitit mimarliği: Arkeolojik ve filolojik veriler* (Istanbul: Edebiyat Fakültesi Basımevi, 1985), 33–41;

HAAS, *Der Kult von Nerik*, 74; I. M. TATISHVILI, "Das neue hethitische Tempelbauritual (KBo XV 24)," *Arkeologiuri dzieban–Archaeological Researches* (1985): 133–46; A. ÜNAL, "'You Should Build for Eternity'—New Light on the Hittite Architects and Their Work," *JCS* 40 (1988): 97–106; M. WITZEL, *Hethitische Keilschrift-Urkunden in Transcription und Ueber- setzung* (Keilschriftliche Studien 4; Fulda, Germany: Verlag des Verfassers, 1924), 76–87.

A Hittite Ritual to Establish a New Temple (CTH 481). This six- or seven-day ritual was used to establish a new satellite temple for the "Goddess of the Night," an obscure deity in Kizzuwatna (southeastern Anatolia). According to one vari- ant, the rite's prescriptions were written by a "priest of the Deity of the Night," whereas another version attributes the text to "a Babylonian scribe and Ulippi, priest of the Deity of the Night." After introducing the rite's purpose and author, the text presents prescriptions for fashioning a new divine statue. These include an enumeration of the necessary construction materials and brief directions for the statue's fabrication. The remaining rites then have to do with transferring the divine presence from the original cult statue to the new one; this entailed rites at the old temple (days 1–5) and then at the new one (days 5 onward). An essential ritual on this occasion was a version of the ceremony, treated below (see *CTH* 483), by which the goddess was lured to her temple. This rite was performed at the old temple to insure her presence for a successful transfer, and it was subse- quently repeated at the new temple to facilitate her arrival there. Another impor- tant rite performed at both temples was a blood rite for cleansing the respective temples and statues. For additional Hittite rites that employed blood as a ritual detergent, see 5.4.

Text and translation: KRONASSER, *Die Umsiedelung der schwarzen Gottheit.* **Translation:** *COS* 1.70: 173–77. **Bibliography:** V. HAAS, "Ein hurritischer Blutritus und die Deponie- rung der Ritualrückstände nach hethitischen Quellen," in *Religionsgeschichtliche Bezie- hungen zwischen Kleinasien, Nordsyrien, und dem Alten Testament* (ed. Janowski, Koch, and Wilhelm), 67–85; H. A. HOFFNER, "Second Millennium Antecedents to the Hebrew ʾōb," *JBL* 86 (1967): 385–401; A. ÜNAL, "The Nature and Iconographical Traits of 'Goddess of Darkness,'" in *Aspects of Art and Iconography—Anatolia and Its Neighbors: Studies in Honor of Nimet Özgüç* (ed. M. J. Mellink, E. Porada, and T. Özgüç; Ankara: Türk Tarih Kurumu Basımevi, 1993), 639–44.

The Large Public Tent from Mari. The statues of gods and goddesses were nor- mally housed in their temples and so were protected from the elements. However, in some rituals and certainly during transportation from one place to another, the statues had overnight stays away from the temple precinct. Surely, in such cases the ancients did not fail to provide the statues with tents, and numerous texts confirm this assumption. Particularly striking is a text from Mari (M.6873) that describes the components of a huge tent and the number of men needed to transport it: "One large tent: 16 men; 10 framing[?] units: 20 men; 5 stands[?]: 5 men; 14 fence[?] units: 2 men; Total: 43 men pertaining to the large tent" (from Fleming). According to Fleming, other Mari texts confirm that this tent was used to house the gods when they attended sacrificial rituals.

Obviously this text is comparable, both conceptually and generically, to the portable shrine—the tabernacle—prescribed in Exod 25–40. Biblical scholars often suggest that the priestly tabernacle has little to do with real history but rather reflects a late, postexilic attempt to project the Jerusalem temple and its cult back into early Israelite history. Although I agree that the description of the priestly tabernacle in the Pentateuch is a late composition related theologically to the earlier Jerusalem temple, the Mari evidence makes it clear that there is nothing particularly late about the notion of large, portable tents for the temporary housing of the gods. The need for such structures existed in the ancient world long before Hebrew was a spoken tongue.

Text and translation: DURAND and GUICHARD, "Les rituels de Mari," 65–66. *Bibliography:* R. J. CLIFFORD, "The Tent of El and the Israelite Tent of Meeting," *CBQ* 33 (1971): 221–27; D. E. FLEMING, "Mari's Large Public Tent and the Priestly Tent Sanctuary," *VT* 50 (2000): 484–98; IDEM, "Recent Work on Mari," *RA* 93 (1999): 163–64.

Mesopotamian Temple Topographies. Mesopotamian scholars explored the accoutrements of their temples and cults in a genre that modern scholars call topography. Strictly speaking, this label is a misnomer arising from the fact that the best-known exemplar (TIN.TAR^{KI} = "Babylon") provides a topographical survey of the royal city of Babylon. In reality, however, most of the topographies are not geographical exercises so much as theological and cosmological explorations of the city's shrines. Temples are listed, along with their furnishings and features, and these are in turn provided with various theological interpretations. Some topographies provided detailed measurements of temples and their floor plans, such as the Neo-Assyrian text that carefully lays out the dimensions of Marduk's temple in Babylon (Esagil), providing north-south and east-west cross sections as well as the temple's overall dimensions and circumference (George, text 14). These metrics were important because the ancients believed that sacred dwellings were suitable for the gods only if their designs were divinely revealed. As Esarhaddon notes when he restored Esagil, "I laid its foundation platform directly on top of its ancient footings, according to its original plan: I did not fall short by one cubit, nor did I overshoot by half a cubit." The mundane details of architecture were theologically significant facts for the Mesopotamians, and this perhaps explains why the Hebrews were equally interested in the furniture and physical dimensions of their tabernacle (see Exod 25–40).

Text and translation: A. R. GEORGE, *Babylonian Topographical Texts* (OLA 40; Leuven: Peeters, 1992). *Bibliography:* A. R. GEORGE, *House Most High: The Temples of Ancient Mesopotamia* (Winona Lake, Ind.: Eisenbrauns, 1993).

Mesopotamian Rites for the Repair of the Temple and Its Kettledrum. As is the case with so many Mesopotamian temple rites, here again our primary exemplars are late copies from the Seleucid period. In this instance, however, there is surer evidence for what we suppose in other situations—that the late texts reflect much older traditions. The texts to be examined in this entry include a rite for repairing temples and a ritual for re-covering the bronze kettledrum in Anu's temple at Uruk. We have already noted in 3.1 that rites of this sort were conducted chiefly by lamentation priests (GALA/*kalû*) because preparations for temple construction usually began with demolition—an act that might anger the deity. By mourning for and with the gods, the lamentation priests believed that they could assuage this anger. Exorcistic priests (*āšipu/mašmašu*) also joined in the ceremonies, lending their expertise in acts of ritual purification.

The rite for repairing the temple is preserved in four similar texts (AO 6472; O 174; BE 13987; W 20030/2), the best of them a Seleucid text in the Louvre (AO 6472) and the oldest a Persian-era text from Babylon (BE 13987). The Babylonian copy confirms that the Seleucid tradition reflected in the other texts goes back at least a century or two. All four texts are introduced with the same rubric, "When the wall of the temple falls into ruin—for the purpose of demolishing and founding anew the temple in question . . ." The Louvre copy goes on to say, "you shall prepare three sacrificial stands for the god of the temple, the goddess of the temple, and the household god of the temple," indicating that the text was a multipurpose composition that could be used during the reconstruction of more than one temple. This introduction is followed by liturgical instructions that prescribe sacrifices for the temple's gods and for Ea, Marduk, and Šamaš, purification rituals using water and incense, and the recitation of a sequence of eight Sumerian laments. The rite ends with the rubric "The ritual of the *kalû* priest." A sequence of three *namburbû* rites follows, whose purpose was to avoid the outcomes predicted by unfavorable omens (on the *namburbûs*, see 5.8). All three *namburbû* rites include sacrifices, the recitation of laments, and rites of purification. The first is penitential and features the king's confession of sin. The second ends with a *kuppuru* ritual, such as was used during the Akitu festival (see 5.5). The third *namburbû* rite averts omens that portended the end of the king's reign.

None of the other three temple construction rites include *namburbû* rites, but their prescriptions for temple refurbishment are, in some respects, more detailed than in AO 6472. The three texts mention that diviners were consulted to confirm the suitability of reconstruction plans and to determine an "auspicious day" for the work to begin. Text O 174 further informs us that the appeasement rituals used at the outset of the construction continued even as the demolition and reconstruction were carried out. The same text also includes a catchline, showing that it was one tablet in a series of GALA rites. The unique feature in the third text, BE 13987, is that it prescribes the recitation of not only Sumerian compositions but also an Akkadian text, *Enūma Anu ibnû šamê*. The entire text of the piece is included on the ritual tablet.

Let us now consider the ritual for restoring the cover of the kettledrum. This rite is analogous in conception to the rites for refurbishing temples, since both include *kalû* laments during the repair of divine property. The drum repair rites were not observed, however, in the temple's holy precinct but in the *bīt mummi*, the temple workshop. Four versions of the kettledrum repair ceremony are extant and appear most recently in the work Linssen (cf. Thureau-Dangin; Mayer). Our most complete copy of the text, which is housed in the Louvre (AO

6479), is a Seleucid-period text from the Resh Temple in Uruk. Some of our other copies, however, are much older texts unearthed at Assur. Not only do these texts date to the Neo-Assyrian period; they are clearly copies of yet older Babylonian texts. So, at least in this instance, we have good evidence that our late Mesopotamian ritual texts are true to ancient tradition.

Let us consider the Louvre copy of the kettledrum ceremony in more detail. The text is prescriptive, offering a series of detailed liturgical directions marked off with rulings. The rite's purpose was to prepare the hide of a black bull for covering the kettledrum. After the bull was chosen—on the basis of careful inspection, since the bull needed to be unblemished—the animal was led into the workshop for the rite. At this point, the text instructs the priests to tie up the bull, conduct a series of lustration rites, and offer sacrifices to various deities. Most important among the rites was a series of procedures that paralleled the rites used in preparing divine statues. These included the *Mīs Pî* ("mouth-washing") rite and incantations that averred in the strongest terms that the gods had created the bull for this very purpose. The author of the Louvre text did not include the words of the incantations, but some of the lyrics appear in the older, Neo-Assyrian exemplars. After these preliminary rites, the bull was slaughtered, its parts were burned or buried, and another series of sacrifices and lustrations ensued. Although the drum was covered with bull skin at this point, it was not presented until the fifteenth day of the month, at which point still more sacrifices and lustrations were performed and another *Mīs Pî* rite was performed on the drum. The colophon concludes this portion of the series by warning that only "informed people" should observe these rituals or see the tablets that prescribe them. Only the end of the next tablet in the series is preserved; it provides a detailed list of the materials needed for the ritual and of the duties required of potters, woodworkers, and others.

The Hebrew Bible does not contain prescriptive rites for the refurbishment of the temple or its paraphernalia. The closest Israelite parallels to the Mesopotamian texts in this entry appear in the story of the restoration of the Jerusalem temple (Ezra 3:10–13; 6:13–18) and perhaps in the laconic priestly prescriptions for the dedication of the tabernacle in Exod 40:9–11. Although we could conclude from this that ancient Israel did not observe rituals akin to temple and kettledrum refurbishment rites, it is perhaps more sensible to presume, on the basis of the comparative material, that similar rites were used in the culture that gave us the Hebrew Bible.

Texts and translations: LINSSEN, *The Cults of Uruk and Babylon,* 252–82 (kettledrum texts), 283–305 (temple repair texts); W. R. MAYER, *Texte aus dem Res-Heiligtum in Uruk-Warka* (BagM 2; Berlin: Mann, 1980) (kettledrum texts); THUREAU-DANGIN, *Rituels accadiens,* 1–59 (kettledrum texts; temple repair texts). *Translations:* ANET 334–38 (kettledrum text), 339–42 (temple repair texts). *Bibliography:* W. HOROWITZ, "Antiochus I, Esagil, and a Celebration of the Ritual for Renovation of Temples," *RA* 85 (1991): 75–77; IDEM, "A Kettle-Drum Ritual during Iyar Seleucid Era 85," *NABU* 1991.080; LINSSEN, *The Cults of Uruk and Babylon,* 92–109; M. MALUL, "A Babylonian Ritual for Preparing a Skin for a Kettle Drum," *Tatzlil: A Forum for Music and Bibliography* 19 (1977): 96–102 (Hebrew).

A Hittite Ritual to Attract Missing Gods (CTH 483). Hittite tradition reflects a constant concern that gods in the region might abandon their temples and lend assistance to Hittite enemies. In this ritual, the diviner attempts to lure all possible missing gods back to Hatti by providing them with "trails" to sacrificial meals. Like many Hittite ritual texts, this one begins with the rite's title ("When the diviners attract the gods") and then follows with an enumeration of materials needed, the location of the rite, the ritual actions, and incantations/prayers. During the rite, the diviner uses trails of flour, honey, wine, oil, and other substances to lead the gods to a table decked in offerings. The first sequence of rites invites the "cedar gods" to return to Hatti. This is followed by a series of similar rites in which the gods are invited to return to their temples from the meadows, mountains, rivers, sea, springs, fire, heaven, and earth. Rites such as this one, which were designed to lure the gods into proximity with human beings, were commonly used by the Hittites. Scholars often refer to them as evocatio rites.

Text and translation: L. LUNTZ, *Un testa ittito di scongiuri* (Venice: Ferarri, 1937). *Translation:* ANET 351–53. *Bibliography:* V. HAAS and G. WILHELM, *Hurritische and luwische Riten aus Kizzuwatna* (AOAT 3; Neukirchen-Vluyn: Neukirchener, 1974), 7–33, 143–246 (for the text and translation of *CTH* 483, see pp. 182–210).

5.2. Temple Purgation Rituals

Maintenance of ritual purity in the temple *cela* was an ongoing concern in antiquity because ritual negligence could translate into divine anger on a grand scale. As we have seen, in most cases purification rites of some sort—using water, incense, anointing oil, and so forth—were observed on a daily basis. Several ancient cultures also addressed this issue in annual temple purgation rites that were observed at the New Year. Here our focus is on three such rites—one each from Mesopotamia, Hatti, and Ugarit—that are similar in purpose to Israel's annual purgation rite on the Day of Atonement. For comparative purposes, included is an Egyptian rite for protecting the temple scriptorium, where religious texts were written. Related texts are treated below in 5.3 and 5.4.

The Mesopotamian **Kuppuru.** The Mesopotamians often used rituals to transfer uncleanness from places where it was not wanted to objects or locations where the pollution could do no harm. One of the most common forms of this rite was the *kuppuru* ("to rub"), which entailed rubbing the object to be cleansed with substances that presumably absorbed the uncleanness. This material could then be removed, taking the uncleanness with it. Perhaps the best known of these rites was the *kuppuru* observed during the Akitu New Year festival (see 5.5). On day five of the festival (see *ANET* 331–34), a *kuppuru* ritual took place in the sanctuary of the god Nabû, who was visiting in Marduk's temple in Babylon. The ritual is not entirely understood, but it included the cleansing of demonic uncleanness from the sanctuary by slaughtering a ram and rubbing or wiping (*kuppuru*) the temple *cela* with its carcass. After this procedure, the ram's body was thrown into the river, and the exorcist priest who performed the ceremony left the city for open country, accompanied by the ram's slaughterer. Because of their uncleanness, both the exorcist priest and the ram's slaughterer could not return to Babylon until the Akitu was over. The purpose of this ritual is expressed explicitly in its incantation: "They purify the temple. . . . The god Marduk purifies the temple. . . . May the god Bel [i.e., Marduk] kill you, evil demon!"

In terms of form, content, and terminology, the Mesopotamian *kuppuru* is quite close to the Israelite *kippēr,* an atonement ritual that was also observed at the turn of the year (Lev 16). The similarities are too close to be explained by an amorphous pattern of cultural diffusion. It is more likely that the Israelite *kippēr* was intentionally fashioned to mimic the Mesopotamian *kuppuru.* This judgment is reinforced by the presence of the scapegoat ritual in Lev 16, which appears to be the older Israelite ritual to which the newer *kippēr* was attached. For more on the Akitu and the function of the *kuppuru* within it, see 5.5.

Texts and translations: LINSSEN, *The Cults of Uruk and Babylon,* 215–37; THUREAU-DANGIN, *Rituels accadiens,* 127–54. *Translation:* ANET 331–34. *Bibliography:* LINSSEN, *The Cults of Uruk and Babylon,* 148–51; WRIGHT, *The Disposal of Impurity,* 291–98.

A Ugaritic Purgation Ritual. This text (RS 1.002/*KTU* 1.40) is one of the few Ugaritic exemplars preserved in multiple copies, a clear indication of its importance. The text prescribes a series of rites that expiated sin, promoted upright behavior among the people, and fostered unity between the people of Ugarit and their gods. Because the ritual accentuated national unity, it is also comparable to the treaty/covenant texts in chapter 14, but here our concern is the text's purgation rite for sin. Like the Mesopotamian *kuppuru,* the Ugaritic rite entailed the sacrifice of a ram, but it differed from the *kuppuru* because it included a donkey sacrifice and because it expiated moral, ritual, and cultural uncleanness rather than demonic pollution. The sins of natives as well as foreigners living in Ugarit were at issue, and these sins were ritually confessed instead of denied. Unfortunately, the Ugaritic ritual is fragmentary, and we are not sure whether it was performed annually—which would make it more similar to the *kuppuru* and Hebrew Day of Atonement ritual—or at some other interval or on some other occasion. Because we have multiple copies of the text and at least two variant editions (cf. *KTU* 1.54; 1.84; 1.121; 1.122), most scholars believe that the ritual was observed at regular intervals, probably on an annual basis.

Text and translation: PARDEE, *Ritual and Cult at Ugarit,* 77–83. *Translation:* WYATT, *Religious Texts from Ugarit,* 342–47 (*KTU* 1.40). *Bibliography:* DEL OLMO LETE, *Canaanite Religion,* 144–60; N. WYATT, "The Religion of Ugarit: An Overview," in *Handbook of Ugaritic Studies* (ed. Watson and Wyatt), 529–85, here 564–66.

A Hittite Temple Purgation Ritual (CTH 480). This text, known also as the Ritual of Šamuḫa, prescribes a series of procedures for freeing the god and temple from ritual impurity. The impurities could be caused by careless speech or even by intentional curses aimed at the god or temple. The rites were essentially acts of sympathetic magic in which objects were ceremonially used to illustrate the desired effects of the rite. So, for instance, a soda plant was burned and turned into soap while an incantation was recited: "The god has cut down that thriving, abundant soda-plant like a harvester, and then reduced it to ashes. Like that soda-plant, let him also reduce to ashes and make into soap evil word, oath, curse, and uncleanness! So let it then no longer exist for my god. . . . Let god and sacrificer be free of that matter!" In another procedure, dangerous curses were loaded upon small model boats that were then sent through a ditch into the river. The associated incantation reads, "Just as the river has carried away the ship and no trace of it can be found any more—whoever has committed evil word, oath, curse, uncleanliness in the presence of the god—even so let the river carry them away." The ritual concluded with an offering of bread and cheese and with a scapegoat rite in which animals representing the king and queen carried away uncleanness. It is not clear whether these animals were sacrificed or whether they were released, as was the case in several Hittite scapegoat rites.

Text and translation: See *CTH* 480. *Translation: ANET* 346. *Bibliography:* J. FRIEDRICH, "Zum hethitischen Lexicon," *JCS* 1 (1947): 275–306, see pp. 298–99; A. GOETZE, "Contributions to Hittite Lexicography," *JCS* 1 (1947): 307–20, see pp. 315–16.

An Egyptian Ritual to Protect the House of Life (Papyrus Salt 825). This hieratic papyrus preserves an annual ritual to protect the "House of Life," the sacred scriptorium of Osiris's temple at Abydos. Although the text dates to the Persian or perhaps even Hellenistic period, scholars are fairly certain that it reflects much earlier Egyptian practices. The ritual describes an ideal House of Life, within which the god Osiris—here assimilated with the sun god Re—is protected by its four walls, representing the gods Isis, Nephthys, Horus, and Thoth, respectively. The ceiling of the structure was Nut ("heaven") and the floor was Geb ("earth"), thus forming a kind of microcosm. Vignettes drawn on the papyrus depict a schematic of this structure as well as drawings that picture Osiris's chief threat, Seth, bound back-to-back with an Asiatic (for this reason, Asiatics were not permitted to enter the sacred precinct; cf. Deut 23:1–7). The papyrus refers to sixteen books that were consulted during the rite and prescribes the fabrication of statues of both Osiris and his enemies. The Osiris statue was constructed using myrrh, pine resin, and incense. Each of these substances was ritually animated by giving it mythological origins: the myrrh grew from the tears of Horus, the pine resin from the tears of Geb, and the incense from the tears of Shu/Tefnut. The enemy statues were made from wax so that they could be ritually destroyed, either by incinerating them or by felling them with a flint knife and enclosing them in a ritual jar. Each Egyptian deity who attended the ritual was represented by an Egyptian official. A priest stood in for Shu, a ritual slaughterer for Horus, and a scribe for Thoth. The scribe's primary duty was to recite the divinely inspired ritual incantations: "The books . . . are the emanations of Re, wherewith to keep alive this god and to overthrow his enemies." The explicit purpose of the rite was to "overturn magical charms" and to "subjugate the entire universe," that is, to protect the purity of the scriptorium and hence of the ritual texts composed in it.

Text and translation: P. DERCHAIN, *Le Papyrus Salt 825 (B.M. 10051)* (Brussels: Palais des Académies, 1965). *Bibliography:* A. H. GARDINER, "The House of Life," *JEA* 24 (1938): 157–79; F.-R. HERBIN, "Les premieres pages du Papyrus Salt 825," *BIFAO* 88 (1988): 95–112; R. K. RITNER, *The Mechanics of Ancient Egyptian Magical Practice* (SAOC 54; Chicago: Oriental Institute of the University of Chicago, 1993).

5.3. "Scapegoat" Elimination Rituals

Near Eastern rituals commonly eliminated impurity by transferring it to objects or animals, but living animals were rarely used. Well-known exceptions to this rule appear in the Hittite texts and in a few other cases. These scapegoat disposal rites are comparable to the Hebrew atonement rituals found in Lev 14:49–57 (a ritual to cleanse a house with mildew) and Lev 16 (the Day of Atonement).

Hittite Scapegoat Rituals. The Hittites observed several rituals in which various evils—especially plagues—were transferred to substitutionary animals or persons in order to rid Hatti of the problems. A good example is Pulisa's Ritual to counteract a plague striking the Hittite army while on expedition. In such cases, the Hittites supposed that plagues were caused by angry deities from the attacked land. Their ritual response was to return a pair of captives (male and female) from the conquered land back to the offended foreign gods. The male prisoner was made a substitute for the Hittite king by dressing him in royal garb, and the female was apparently added to satisfy any offended goddesses. A bull and a ewe accompanied the human couple and were similarly adorned with royal symbols and images representing the plague. The significance of the imagery is explicitly laid out in the text: "Let this bull carry this plague back into the land of the enemy. Turn again in friendship to the king, to the princes, the lords, the army and to the land of Hatti." As in ancient Israel, Hittite scapegoat rites often identified the offerer/offerers with the animal by placing hands on the beast (Wright 1986). The major scapegoat texts from Hatti are the Pulisa Ritual (*CTH* 407), Ashella Ritual (*CTH* 394), Uhhamuwa Ritual (*CTH* 410), Ambazzi Ritual (*CTH* 391), Huwarlu Ritual (*CTH* 398), and Zarpiya Ritual (*CTH* 757). Note that the Hittites identified these rites by using the names of the specialists who supposedly concocted them (e.g., Pulisa's Ritual, Ashella's Ritual, etc.).

Texts and translations: (1) Pulisa's Ritual (*CTH* 407): text in KUB 15.1 and translations in *COS* 1.62: 161; WRIGHT, *The Disposal of Impurity,* 45–50; (2) Ashella Ritual (*CTH* 394): WRIGHT, *The Disposal of Impurity,* 50–51; (3) Uhhamuwa Ritual (*CTH* 410): *COS* 1.63: 162; *ANET* 347; (4) Ambazzi Ritual (*CTH* 391): *ANET* 348–49; (5) Huwarlu Ritual (*CTH* 398): H. KRONASSER, "Das hethitische Ritual KBo IV 2," *Die Sprache* 8 (1962): 89–107; (6) Zarpiya Ritual (*CTH* 757): *COS* 1.64: 162–63. *Bibliography:* B. JANOWSKI and G. WILHELM, "Der

Bock, der die Sünden hinausträgt: Zur Religionsgeschichte des Azazel-Ritus Lev 16,10.21f," in *Religionsgeschichtliche Beziehungen zwischen Kleinasien, Nordsyrien, und dem Alten Testament* (ed. Janowski, Koch, and Wilhelm), 109–70; H. M. KÜMMEL, *Ersatzrituale für den hethitischen König* (StBoT 3; Wiesbaden: Harrassowitz, 1967); B. SCHWARTZ, "The Hittite and Luwian Ritual of Zarpiya of Kezzuwatna," *JAOS* 58 (1938): 335–55; D. P. WRIGHT, *The Disposal of Impurity;* IDEM, "The Gesture of Hand Placement in the Hebrew Bible and Hittite Literature," *JAOS* 106 (1986): 433–46.

An Akkadian "Scapefish" Ritual. The transfer of ritual uncleanness to a substitute animal or object was widely practiced in Mesopotamia, but usually the animals were killed. A notable exception is what appears to be a "scapefish" *namburbû* rite, in which ritual pollution was transferred to a fish that was then released into the river. For more on the *namburbû*s and on related apotropaic rituals, see 5.8.

Text and translation: R. CAPLICE, "Namburbi Texts in the British Museum, V," *Or* 40 (1971): 133–83. *Bibliography:* WRIGHT, *The Disposal of Impurity.*

5.4. Blood as a Ritual Detergent

Ancient Near Eastern societies commonly used water and other substances to remove ritual pollution, but the use of blood as a ritual detergent was unusual. The Israelite propensity to use blood in this way makes the few comparative exemplars from the Near East especially important.

Hittite Blood Detergent Rituals. We have two cases in which blood was used in Hittite atonement rituals. Papanikri's Ritual (*CTH* 476) used the blood of sacrificed birds to purify a new birth stool, and Ulippi's Ritual (*CTH* 481) used sacrificial blood to remove uncleanness from new divine statues and from temple precincts. This second rite, treated above in 5.2, is particularly close to the biblical *kippēr* rite in Lev 16.

Texts and translations: KRONASSER, *Die Umsiedelung der schwarzen Gottheit;* F. SOMMER and H. EHELOF, *Das hethitische Ritual des Papanikri von Komana* (BoSt 10; Leipzig: Hinrichs, 1924). *Translation:* COS 1.70: 173–77 (Ulippi ritual). *Bibliography:* J. C. MOYER, "The Concept of Ritual Purity among the Hittites" (PhD diss, Brandeis University, 1969); WRIGHT, *The Disposal of Impurity.*

Blood Rites from Emar and Ugarit. Although blood rites certainly appear in texts from Emar (the *Zukru*) and Ugarit (various sacrifices), the tablets do not explicitly reveal the blood's significance in the rituals. The Hittite evidence, coupled with what we know from ancient Israel, provides contextual evidence that the rites from Emar and Ugarit probably used blood as a ritual detergent.

Texts, translations, and bibliography: See the above entries on Ugarit in 5.1 and 5.2 and the entry on the *Zukru* Festival of Emar in the following section (5.5).

5.5. Vernal and Autumnal Festivals

Public festivals were common and popular in the ancient Near East because they interrupted the monotony of daily rhythm and so provided social and psychological refreshment as the people ate, drank, danced, and soaked in the majesty of festive processions (see Renger). Shared experiences of this sort naturally reinforced social cohesion. Because ancient economies were agricultural, Near Eastern festivals were often observed around the vernal equinox and the autumnal equinox (i.e., planting and harvest). Near Eastern vernal and autumnal festivals are particularly important for comparative purposes because several Israelite feasts and rituals were observed during these periods (Passover and the Festival of Weeks in the spring; New Year, the Day of Atonement, and the Festival of Booths in autumn). Also of interest are the processions observed during many Near Eastern festivals, which are comparable to the processions described in texts such as 2 Sam 6 and 1 Chron 15–16.

The Mesopotamian Akitu Festival. The Mesopotamia Akitu was an annual festival whose essential rite was a procession of the gods to the "Akitu house," a special temple that was used on such occasions. The purpose was to honor some god or goddess with a festive gathering of other deities. Although the Akitu is often characterized as a New Year rite—and this it often was—the festival was actually observed at various times of the year, depending on the deity and city (see Thureau-Dangin, 88). For the god in question, the Akitu was the principle feast of the year. In certain instances, particularly in the case of the national deities (often Marduk or Assur), the god's Akitu was celebrated at the turn of the year and hence became a New Year rite. As in ancient Israel, the Mesopotamians maintained two calendars—civil and religious—and as a result, it turns out that first-millennium Babylon actually celebrated two Akitus, a primary one during Nisanu 1–12 (the first civil month) and another during Tashritu 1–12 (the seventh civil month, the first religious month). The two months obviously corresponded to the vernal equinox and the autumnal equinox, underscoring the solar and, by implication, agricultural dimensions of the rituals.

We are fortunate to have ritual prescriptions for several New Year Akitu rites. But regrettably, our primary texts are late (dating to the Seleucid period), and are also associated with two different deities. One text, preserved in duplicate, is part of a series relating to the Akitu of Marduk at Babylon and covers days two through five of the twelve-day affair (see Thureau-Dangin, 127–54; *ANET* 331–34). Another set of texts comes from a series of ritual prescriptions discovered at Uruk; they cover days seven through eleven of an Akitu rite for the god Anu (see Thureau-Dangin, 86–99; *TUAT* 2:23–27). The two texts also relate to different months in the calendar, since the first has to do with Marduk's Akitu in the month of Nisanu and the other with Anu's Akitu in the month of Tashritu. Nevertheless, there is no doubt that rites for the two months were essentially alike, for the scribe from Uruk sometimes reduced his workload by directing the priests to do their rite "as in the month of Nisanu." In sum, our image of the Akitu is the composite result of dovetailing disparate sources, but the image is essentially a valid one. Scholars are also quite certain the these late copies of the Akitu reflect much older ritual traditions.

As already mentioned, the New Year Akitu was a twelve-day affair observed at the year's beginning. During the Akitu, the gods decreed the "fates" for the coming year. Because these fates were decreed in the temple, ritual impurities could anger the gods and result in a year filled with pestilence, famine, and military defeat. The primary deities involved in the fates decree were Markuk, the chief god of Babylon, and his son Nabu, the patron god of scribal arts. Nabu's role was to inscribe the decrees, and Marduk's role was not only to decree the fates but also to dispel evil demonic presences that might derail them. According to the Mesopotamian tradition, Marduk had already defeated powerful demons in the great cosmic battle described in *Enuma Elish* (see 10.1.2). The priests replicated this victory by reciting the myth on day four of the Akitu. On the following day (day five) this triumph was ritually enacted by a *kuppuru* ritual (see 5.2), which removed from the temple any demonic pollution that might thwart the fate decrees. Following observation of the *kuppuru,* Marduk decreed the fates and Nabu "wrote" these down on the tablet of destinies. For comparative purposes, it is worth noting that the aforementioned rituals included a display offering with twelve loaves of bread (the significance of the number twelve is not so clear) as well as a "royal ordeal," in which the king averred his own innocence before Marduk: "I did not sin. . . . I was not neglectful of your godship. . . . I did not destroy Babylon," and so on. After this declaration of innocence, the priest slapped the king's face in what amounted to a kind of omen: "If, when he strikes the king's cheek, the tears flow, the god Bel is friendly; if no tears appear, the god Bel is angry: the enemy will rise up and bring about his [the king's] downfall."

Two additional features in the Akitu texts should be noted. First, the texts do not provide detailed prescriptions for the rites but depend instead on the priests' previous knowledge of the rites and incantations. This reminds us that most of the ancient priestly lore was perpetuated not in writing but rather through the oral traditions of the temple cult. Second, the colophons of the texts warn that only priestly scribes should read and copy their secret knowledge. It is difficult to say how carefully the priests followed this directive in any given historical period, but it appears that rites of the Akitu were widely known in the ancient world. The Persians adapted the rites for use in their temple at Persepolis (see Fenelly), and the Israelite Day of Atonement rite in Lev 16 also seems to mimic the Akitu. This is confirmed by the close verbal similarities between the Israelite and Mesopotamian rites (cf. *kippēr* and *kuppuru*), by the similar ritual actions in the ceremonies, and by the fact that both rites were observed as New Year temple purgation rites.

Texts and translations: LINSSEN, *The Cults of Uruk and Babylon,* 184–96 (Tashritu Akitu for Anu at Uruk), 197–200 (Nisanu Akitu for Anu at Uruk), 215–37 (Nisanu Akitu for Marduk at Babylon), 238–44 (Akitu for Ištar at Uruk); THUREAU-DANGIN, *Rituels accadiens,* 86–99 (Tashritu Akitu for Anu at Uruk), 99–108 (Nisanu Akitu for Anu at Uruk), 108–11 (Nisanu

Akitu for Anu at Uruk), 111–18 (Akitu for Ištar at Uruk), 127–54 (Nisanu Akitu for Marduk at Babylon). **Translations:** *ANET* 331–34 (Nisanu Akitu for Marduk at Babylon); *TUAT* 2:223–27 (Tashritu Akitu for Anu at Uruk). **Bibliography:** A. Y. AHMAD and A. K. GRAYSON, "Sennacherib in the Akitu House," *Iraq* 61 (1999): 187–89; J. A. BLACK, "The New Year Ceremonies in Ancient Babylon: 'Taking Bel by the Hand' and a Cultic Picnic," *Religion* 11 (1981): 39–59; A. FALKENSTEIN, "Akiti-Fest und akiti-Festhaus," in *Festschrift Johannes Friedrich zum 65. Geburtstag* (ed. R. von Kienle et al.; Heidelberg: C. Winter, 1959), 147–82; J. M. FENNELLY, "The Persepolis Ritual," *BA* 43 (1980): 135–62; A. K. GRAYSON, "Chronicles and the Akitu Festival," in *Actes de la XVIIe Rencontre assyriologique internationale* (ed. Finet), 160–70; J. KLEIN, "Akitu," *ABD* 1:38–40; W. G. LAMBERT, "The Conflict in the Akitu House," *Iraq* 25 (1963): 189–90; IDEM, "The Great Battle of the Mesopotamian Religious Year: The Conflict in the Akitu House," *Iraq* 25 (1963): 189–90; LINSSEN, *The Cults of Uruk and Babylon*, 61–91; S. A. PALLIS, *The Babylonian Akitu Festival* (Historisk-filologiske Meddelelser 12; Copenhagen: Høst & Søn, 1926); B. PONGRATZ-LEISTEN, *Ina Šulmi Irub: Die kulttopographische und ideologische Programmatik der akitu-Prozession in Babylonien und Assyrien im 1. Jahrtausend v. Chr.* (Baghdader Forschungen 16; Mainz am Rhein: P. von Zabern, 1994); W. VON SODEN, "Gibt es ein Zeugnis dafür, dass die Babylonier an die Wiederauferstehung Marduks geglaubt haben?" *ZA* 51 (1955): 130–66; F. THUREAU-DANGIN, *Tablettes d'Uruk à l'usage des prêtres du temple d'Anu au temps des Séleucides* (TCL 6; Paris: P. Geuthner, 1922); VAN DER TOORN, "The Babylonian New Year Festival"; WRIGHT, *The Disposal of Impurity*, 291–98.

The Mesopotamian Kislev Palm Festival. This Seleucid-era tablet contains prescriptions for several days of the palm festival at Esagil (Marduk's temple in Babylon), which was celebrated during the eighth month of Kislev (October/November). This timing coincided with the date harvest, dates being an important agricultural product in ancient Mesopotamia. The ceremonies of the palm festival included sacrifices, the singing of ŠUILLA prayers and BALAG laments (see 3.1.2), and the recital of the myth *Enuma Elish* before the god Marduk (see 10.1.2). At the point where the myth recalled the gift that Marduk received from his mother after his victory over Tiamat, a palm frond was presented as a gift to Marduk on a silver tray. This act was only one of many instances when palm fronds were either waved or offered to deities during the ritual. Portions of the rites focused on the underworld deity Zariqu (a form of Nergal), who, as a netherworld deity, was believed to be the nourisher of the roots of trees and plants. Although most of the ceremonies took place at Esagil, a few were observed at the nearby Akitu house (see previous entry). One of the most important participants in the ritual sequence was a slave who apparently rode upon a decorated bull, but the significance of this figure is not clear to modern scholars. On a comparative note, the practice of waving palm leaves during festivals is well attested in Israelite and Jewish tradition. Good examples include the seventh-month harvest festival of Sukkoth (Lev 23:39–43; Neh 8:13–18) and the eight-day Hanukkah festival (see 2 Macc 10:6–7), which was, like the Mesopotamian palm festival, a Kislev event.

Text and translation: G. ÇAĞIRGAN and W. G. LAMBERT, "The Late Babylonian Kislimu Ritual for Esagil," *JCS* 43–45 (1991–1993): 89–106. **Bibliography:** LINSSEN, *The Cults of Uruk and Babylon*, 118.

The Zukru *Festival of Emar.* Like many of our Emar texts, the *Zukru* festival texts come from the temple archive of the city's diviner, who was apparently a very important player in the ritual life of Emar. We possess two distinct versions of the *Zukru* festival prescriptions, corresponding to two different scales on which the festival was observed. The shorter but very fragmentary fourteenth-century edition (*Emar* 375) reflects an annual New Year rite held during the month of SAG.MU ("head of the year"). The rite began on the full moon (the fifteenth day) of the month with a procession of the god Dagan (and the city god dNIN-URTA) to an array of upright stones placed outside the city walls. These stones represented other deities, so that we have in essence an assembly that included the gods as well as the entire community of Emar. The stones were ritually anointed with oil and blood (cf. the use of blood in Israelite ritual), various sacrifices were offered, and the people of the town held a feast. Similar rites were observed on the seventh day of the festival, with the temple and the city of Emar underwriting all of these costs. The title "*Zukru*" is telling, for it reveals that the essential purpose of the rite was to swear an oath of allegiance to the gods (*nīš ilim zākaru*). In this respect the text should be compared with similar covenant texts in this chapter (see RS 1.002 in 5.2) and especially in chapter 14.

The longer version of the *Zukru,* from the thirteenth to the twelfth century (*Emar* 373), reflects a later development of the ritual. Our broken four-column tablet (two columns on each side) prescribed an elaborate rendition of the festival that was observed every seven years. Preparation for the ritual lasted one year, with the first rites being observed during the sixth year in the first and second months. Many offerings were given to the gods during this sixth-year rite, and many more during the actual observance of the *Zukru* in the following year (year seven). Because of the enormous costs involved in this seventh-year *Zukru,* the king of Emar played a prominent role in the provisions, although the town's citizens and temples participated as well. Our ritual text is organized into two parts, with one section listing the schedule of offerings and the other prescribing the ritual proper. Both divisions of the text are arranged chronologically, with major sections divided by double rulings and minor sections by single rulings. We do not know why this larger *Zukru* was observed only every seventh year, but its great expense for the city and king would have prohibited an annual festival of such magnitude.

Text and translation: D. E. FLEMING, *Time at Emar: The Cultic Calendar and the Rituals of the Diviner's Archive* (MC 11; Winona Lake, Ind.: Eisenbrauns, 2000), 48–140, 233–67. *Translation: COS* 1.123: 431–36. *Bibliography:* FLEMING, "The Emar Festivals: City Unity and Syrian Identity under Hittite Hegemony."

The Ugaritic Festival of First Wine. The autumnal festival of *Ra'šu-Yêni* ("first wine") has been reconstructed from two tablets unearthed at Ugarit (RS 1.003; 18.056 = *KTU* 1.41; 1.87). The text prescribes rites to be observed on days thirteen to twenty-one of the twelfth month as well as during the first month of the next year, suggesting that the event was not only a harvest festival but also a New

Year celebration. Our ritual text is essentially a distribution list for sacrifices made to about thirty gods during the event (including flesh offerings, unleavened bread, and other items), along with the barest outline of the ritual itself. Major sections of the text are separated with rulings. Most of the rites took place at the temple of the god El, with the king playing the most prominent role in the proceedings (as he did in most of the Ugaritic rites). The "New Moon" and days thirteen and fourteen of the month were particularly important in the ritual schedule. Near the rite's conclusion, the tablet refers to "dwellings" for the gods made of "cut branches" and placed upon the temple roof, a practice that is reminiscent of the Israelite Sukkoth (Booths) autumnal festival: "So the people went out and brought them, and made booths for themselves, each on the roofs of their houses, and in their courts and in the courts of the house of God, and in the square at the Water Gate and in the square at the Gate of Ephraim" (Neh 8:16).

Text and translation: PARDEE, *Ritual and Cult at Ugarit,* 56–65. *Translations:* COS 1.95: 299–301; WYATT, *Religious Texts from Ugarit,* 348–55 (*KTU* 1.41). *Bibliography:* B. A. LEVINE and J.-M. DE TARRAGON, "The King Proclaims the Day: Ugaritic Rites for the Vintage (*KTU* 1.41//1.87)," *RB* 100 (1993): 76–115; DEL OLMO LETE, *Canaanite Religion,* 106–28.

Hittite Festival Texts. The Hittites observed a dizzying number of festivals to honor the many gods of their empire. The official cultic calendar seems to have included about 165 festivals, many of them observed annually around the spring or fall of the year. One result of this practice is that the most numerous texts discovered at the Hittite capital of Boğazköy are the festival prescriptions. Festival prescriptions were essentially ritual manuals that provided step-by-step directions or outlines of all the rites pertaining to each festival. In the case of the well-documented KI.LAM festival, the textual evidence includes the following (see Singer): two forms of the ritual series (one enumerated by tablet number and the other by the festival days); a liturgical series featuring Hattic [not Hittite] songs and recitations; a ration series that enumerates food and beverage distributions to ritual participants; an outline series that provides an overview of the festival; and, finally, a library shelf list left behind by Hittite librarians.

It is difficult from our vantage point to determine which of the many festivals were deemed most important by the Hittites, but AN.TAH.ŠUM (thirty-eight days observed in the spring) and *Nuntariyašhaš* (twenty-one days observed in the fall) were among the most significant. Also important were the springtime Purulli festival, whose cult legend was the well-known Illuyanka myth (see 10.3), and the KI.LAM festival, a three day event that seems to be been observed in autumn. For a relatively complete list of the Hittite festival texts and fragments, see *CTH* 591–790.

Our documentation for the great fall festival (*Nuntariyašhaš*) is not so good, but texts from the spring AN.TAH.ŠUM festival are more plentiful (*CTH* 604–25). The festival takes its name from a plant that bloomed in spring, perhaps a kind of crocus. The festivities began with the king's trip from his winter home

to the city of Tahurpa. The remainder of the festival featured a somewhat rigorous itinerary as the king traveled to various temples and holy sites to observe the
appropriate ritual procedures. Most of the rites took place in the capital city of
Ḫattuša. The rites included not only sacrifices and feasts but also music, dancing,
athletic contests (footraces and horse races), funerary rituals (see day eleven),
"great assemblies" in the royal palace, and rites that featured cult objects, most
notably a "fleece" and the AN.TAḪ.ŠUM plant itself. Although many deities are
mentioned in the texts, the storm god of Hatti and the sun goddess of Arinna
were the most prominent. The climax of the festival was a ritual procession in
which the whole pantheon of the land of Hatti processed to a site known in Turkish as Yazilikaya, an open-air natural rock shrine, about three-quarters of a mile
northeast of Ḫattuša, where a fresh water spring once flowed. Reliefs on the stone
walls of Yazilikaya depict two processions—one of gods and the other of goddesses—advancing toward the center of the rear wall from each side. The Hittite
king is also depicted in the procession, bearing the cartouche of Tudhilays IV (ca.
1250–1220). Divine prossessions of this sort were common in Near Eastern festivals, as we have already noted in connection with the *Zukru* of Emar and the
Mesopotamian Akitu festival. For good overviews of the Hittite festivals, see
Bryce and also Popko 1995.

Texts and translations: E. BADALÌ and C. ZINKO, *Der 16. Tag des AN.TAH.ŠUM-Festes:
Text, Übersetzung, Glossar* (2d ed.; Scientia 20; Graz: Innsbrucker Gesellschaft zur Pflege
der Einzelwissenschaften und interdisziplinären Forschung, 1994); H. G. GÜTERBOCK,
"An Outline of the Hittite AN.TAḪ.ŠUM Festival," *JNES* 19 (1960): 80–89; IDEM, "The
North-Central Area of Hittite Anatolia," *JNES* 20 (1961): 85–97 (outline of Nuntari-
yašḫaš); G. MCMAHON, *The Hittite State Cult of the Tutelary Deities* (AS 25; Chicago: Ori-
ental Institute of the University of Chicago, 1991) (Festivals of protective deities);
I. SINGER, *The Hittite KI.LAM Festival* (2 vols.; StBoT 27–28; Wiesbaden: Harrassowitz,
1983–1984). *Translation: ANET* 358–61 (day sixteen of AN.TAḪ.ŠUM). *Bibliography:* G.
BECKMAN, "The Hittite Assembly," *JAOS* 102 (1982): 435–42; K. BITTEL et al., *Das hethi-
tische Felsheiligtum Yazilikaya* (Bogazöy-Hattusa 9; Berlin: Gebr. Mann 1975); T. BRYCE,
Life and Society in the Hittite World (Oxford: Oxford University Press, 2002), 187–210;
C. CARTER, "Athletic Contests in Hittite Religious Festivals," *JNES* 47 (1988): 185–87;
F. CORNELIUS, "Das hethitische ANTAḪŠUM (SAR)-Fest," in *Actes de la XVIIe Rencontre
assyriologique internationale* (ed. Finet), 171–74; H. FREYDANK, *Hethitische Rituale und
Festbeschreibungen* (KUB 55; Berlin: Akademie, 1985); H. G. GÜTERBOCK, "Some Aspects
of Hittite Festivals," in *Actes de la XVIIe Rencontre assyriologique internationale* (ed. Finet),
171–74; IDEM, "Yazilikaya: Apropos a New Interpretation," *JNES* 34 (1975): 273–77;
V. HAAS, "Betrachtungen zur Rekonstruktion des hethitischen Frühjahrsfestes (EZEN
purulliyaš)," *ZA* 78 (1988): 284–98; T. P. J. VAN DEN HOUT, "A Tale of Tiššaruli(ya): A
Dramatic Interlude in the Hittite KI.LAM Festival?" *JNES* 50 (1991): 193–202; J. G.
MACQUEEN, *The Hittites and Their Contemporaries in Asia Minor* (rev. and enl. ed.; London: Thames & Hudson, 1986), 123–32 (on Yazilikaya); H. OTTEN and C. RÜSTER, *Fest-
beschreibungen und Rituale* (KBo 30; Berlin: Gebr. Mann, 1984). M. POPKO, *Hethitische
Rituale und Festbeschreibungen* (KUB 58; Berlin: Akademie, 1988), 147–51; IDEM, *Religions
of Asia Minor* (Warsaw: Academic Publications Dialog, 1995); I. WEGNER and M. SALVINI,
Die hethitisch-hurritischen Ritualtafeln des (ḫ)isuwa-Festes (CHSTB 4; Rome: Multigrafica

Editrice, 1991); D. YOSHIDA, "Das AN.TAH.ŠUM-Fest im Tempel der Sonnengöttin," in *Cult and Ritual in the Ancient Near East* (ed. H. I. H. Prince Takahito Mikasa; BMECCJ 6; Wiesbaden: Otto Harrassowitz, 1992), 121–58; C. ZINKO, *Betrachtungen zum AN.TAH.ŠUM-Fest: Aspekte eines hethitischen Festrituals* (Scientia 8; Innsbruck: Scientia, 1987).

5.6. Priestly Ordination Texts

Ancient priests and priestesses were consecrated for their service to the gods through a series of ordination rituals. The entries below treat two different types of texts related to these rites as they were practiced in Mesopotamia. The first is a prescriptive text from Emar (fourteenth–twelfth century B.C.E.) that is particularly close to the ordination rites for Israelite priests in Exod 29 and Lev 8. The second text is of a different sort, including incantations that were used on the occasions when a new priest first entered service in the temple of Enlil and Ninlil at Nippur.

The Ordination of a High Priestess from Emar. Emar 369 is introduced by an appropriate incipit ("Tablet of rites for the NIN-DINGER of ᵈIM of Emar") and follows with prescriptions for a nine-day ordination ritual. The tablet is oriented around ritual time, with its major divisions marked by phrases such as "on the next day," "just before evening watch," "for seven days," and "on the seventh day." Horizontal rulings accompany these temporal cues and hence add visual dimensions to the text's structure. The rite of passage itself included the selection of the new high priestess by lot, her anointing with fine oil taken from the palace and temple, a communal meal, enthronement of the new priestess, seven days of festivities and rituals at the house of the priestess's father, and, finally, more sacrifices and the priestess's bridal procession from her father's house to the temple of ᵈIM, where she ascended the divine bed to become the god's spouse. We are not certain whether this act was symbolic only or whether, as elsewhere in Mesopotamia, she actually had sexual relations with the god's surrogate, that is, the king. The text concludes with a list of annual provisions for the priestess and with directions for distributions to the house of her father in the event of her death. So far as we can tell, the high priestess of the storm god was appointed to her position for life; this suggests that the ritual would have been observed only infrequently. For more on the closely related issue of sacred marriage, see the article by Klein as well as entries concerning Inanna/Dumuzi in 3.1.2 and 4.1. For the ritual of installation for another Emar priestess (*Emar* 370), see Fleming 1996.

Texts and translations: D. E. FLEMING, *The Installation of Baal's High Priestess at Emar: A Window on Ancient Syrian Religion* (HSS 42; Atlanta: Scholars Press, 1992); G. A. KLING-BEIL, *A Comparative Study of the Ritual of Ordination Found in Leviticus 8 and Emar 369* (Lewiston, N.Y.: Edwin Mellen, 1998). *Translation: COS* 1.122: 427–31. *Bibliography:* J. S. COOPER, "Sacred Marriage and Popular Cult in Early Mesopotamia," in *Official Cult and Popular Religion in the Ancient Near East* (ed. E. Matsushima; Heidelberg: Winter, 1993), 81–96; M. DIETRICH, "Das Einsetzungsritual der Entu von Emar (*Emar* VI/3, 369)," *UF* 21

(1989): 47–100; FLEMING, "The Emar Festivals: City Unity and Syrian Identity under Hittite Hegemony"; J. KLEIN, "Sacred Marriage," *ABD* 5:866–70; R. PATAI, "Hebrew Installation Rites," *HUCA* 20 (1947): 143–225; S. N. KRAMER, "The Dumuzi-Inanna Sacred Marriage Rite: Origin, Development, Character," in *Actes de la XVIIe Rencontre assyriologique internationale* (ed. Finet), 135–59.

The Ordination of a Priest of Enlil. This text has been pieced together from several broken Sumerian tablets. Preserved on them are portions of at least sixteen incantations that were used on the occasions when a new priest entered the temple of Enlil and Ninlil for the first time. Its author was, no doubt, a priest of Enlil at Nippur. The incantations are of varied length (from three to twenty-six lines) and are separated by rubrics and rulings. The first incantation is essentially a description of the actions required of the officiating priests. They were to lead the candidate into the washroom, inspect the candidate's physical condition, and then clean his body. The candidate could not enter the temple until he was "as pure as a golden statue, and the fear of god and humility are present in his body" (note the dual focus on both the exterior and interior qualities of the would-be priest). The significance of the incantations that follow is not entirely clear, but they accompanied rites in which soap and water were used to cleanse and shave the candidate. The god Marduk is frequently mentioned in the incantations as the one able to purify the initiate. Particular attention is given to protecting the candidate from an "an evil tongue," which was apparently understood to be harmful words from a demonic enemy (see IV.10–14). At a certain point near the end of the rite, it seems that the candidate could finally declare, "I am a priest of Enlil." The ritual probably dates no later than the end of the second millennium, but our copies are Neo-Assyrian and later.

Although they are not precise parallels, several texts in the Hebrew Bible feature a similar focus on the qualities necessary for an Israelite priest. These include not only Lev 21 and Num 8 but also certain Levitical psalms, such as Ps 15. Also relevant are the priestly ordination texts in Exod 29 and Lev 8.

Text and translation: R. BORGER, "Die Weihe eines Enlil Priesters," *BO* 30 (1973): 163–76, pls. 1–4. *Bibliography:* E. REINER, "Nabonidus and the Concern with the Past," in *Your Thwarts in Pieces, Your Mooring Rope Cut: Poetry from Babylonia and Assyria* (Michigan Studies in the Humanities 5; Ann Arbor: Horace H. Rackham School of Graduate Studies at the University of Michigan, 1985), 1–16 (the installation of Enanedu).

5.7. Other Priestly Instruction Texts

A Babylonian "Manual" of Sacrificial Procedure. This Old Babylonian text (UCLM 9–1910) provides detailed if laconic directions for carrying out the ritual slaughter of a sacrificial animal. The priest is directed to slaughter the sheep and drain its blood and then to follow a series of protocols for butchering the animal and for extispicy (see 6.1.1). Although the text is ostensibly a procedural manual, its bilingual form (Sumerian and Akkadian) suggests that it may have served instead as an exercise to introduce scribes to the technical vocabulary of sacrifice. The practice of draining the sacrificial animal's blood parallels the protocols observed in Israelite ritual (see Deut 12:16; 15:23; Lev 17).

Text and translation: D. A. FOXVOG, "A Manual of Sacrificial Procedure," in *DUMU-E2-DUB-BA-A: Studies in Honor of Åke W. Sjöberg* (ed. H. Behrens, D. T. Loding, and M. Roth; OPSNKF 11; Philadelphia: University Museum, 1989), 167–76.

The Hittite Priestly Instruction Manual. Although we do not possess extensive priestly protocol manuals from Egypt or Mesopotamia, the Hittites produced such a text (*CTH* 264). Our eight copies of this text date to the Empire period (ca. 1375–1180 B.C.E.), but the language of the text reflects older Hittite features. Like the Hittite law codes (see 13.3), the instructions feature both casuistic formulations and hortatory injunctions. Topics covered include regulations for ritual cleanliness (pigs and dogs are unclean; sexual intercourse makes one unclean), priestly grooming (hair and nails clipped), rites for priestly cleansing (especially bathing in water), rules for the consumption of sacrifices (priests can eat them), and regulations regarding who can enter the temple precinct (no women, children, or foreigners). Priests are commanded to attend all festivals and warned against misappropriating sacrifices and temple property. To transgress any of these commands constituted a "sin" against the god. Such infractions are generally dealt with severely, often eliciting a death sentence for the guilty party and for his family.

The instructions distinguish between various classes of priests—"high priests, lesser priests, and anointing priests"—and offer a further differentiation between priests and the nonpriestly guards who served outside the sacred precinct (although the guards could, under direction from the priests, assist inside). These arrangements parallel closely those in Hebrew priestly literature, where different classes of priests are recognized and where a rigid distinction is maintained between the priests and the nonpriestly Levites who provided security and service to the temple/tabernacle (see Milgrom; cf. 2 Kgs 25:18).

The closest Hebrew parallels to the Hittite priestly regulations are found in the Holiness Code of Leviticus (Lev 17–26). For other examples of the Hittite instructional genre, see 2.3.

Text and translation: E. H. STURTEVANT, *A Hittite Chrestomathy* (Philadelphia: Linguistic Society of America, University of Pennsylvania, 1935), 127–74. *Translations: ANET* 207–10; *COS* 1.83: 217–21. *Bibliography:* J. MILGROM, *Leviticus* (3 vols.; AB 3; Garden City: Doubleday, 1991–2001), 1:322–25, 352–56, 932–33; IDEM, "The Shared Custody of the Tabernacle and the Hittite Analogy," *JAOS* 90 (1970): 204–9; J. C. MOYER, "The Concept of Ritual Purity among the Hittites" (PhD diss., Brandeis University, 1969); IDEM, "Hittite and Israelite Cultic Practices: A Selected Comparison," in *More Essays on the Comparative Method* (ed. Hallo, Moyer, and Perdue), 19–38.

Punic Sacrificial Tariffs. The Phoenician populations that migrated to various coastland sites in the Mediterranean basin during the first millennium B.C.E. are referred to as the Punic peoples. Punic texts are important for students of the Hebrew Bible because like their Phoenician relatives, the Punic peoples shared many linguistic and cultural features with ancient Israel. Perhaps the most important of these comparative Punic texts are the sacrificial tariffs (i.e., payment lists), which date to between the fifth and third centuries B.C.E. Our most complete exemplar comes from the south of France (the Marseilles Tariff) and was inscribed on two blocks of stone. The inscription was originally displayed at the temple of the god Baal-Zaphon, where it provided priests and worshippers with easy access to its ritual prescriptions. The text is introduced by a brief prologue ("Tariff of payments set up by the men in charge of the payments . . .") and follows with a list of sacrifices classified according to the value of the animal to be offered, beginning with the most expensive item (i.e., oxen) and moving through smaller livestock to the less expensive items (birds and meal offerings). Distribution of the animal's flesh was prescribed to suit the type of sacrifice. In the event of a "complete whole offering" (*šlm kll*), the priest received only a monetary payment, but for the "whole offering" (*kll*), he received meat as well. Only in the case of the "communion offering" (*tsw't*) did both the priest and the offerer receive portions of the flesh. Wealthy worshippers were required to provide extra monetary payments, but the poor were permitted to keep portions of the sacrifice that were normally distributed to the priests. Near its conclusion, the inscription levies fines against priests and officers caught contravening its financial regulations, and it also refers to other written texts that provide additional payment schedules.

A fragmentary Punic inscription comparable to this one has been found at ancient Carthage. Both of these Punic tariffs are very similar in form and content to the sacrificial manual in Lev 1–7.

Texts and translations: G. A. COOKE, *A Text-book of North-Semitic Inscriptions* (Oxford: Clarendon, 1903), 112–24; *KAI* #69, #74. *Translations: ANET* 656–57; *COS* 1.98: 305–9 (Marseilles only). *Bibliography:* D. W. BAKER, "Leviticus 1–7 and the Punic Tariffs: A Form Critical Comparison," *ZAW* 99 (1987): 188–97; E. LIPINSKI, "Rites et sacrifices dans la tradition phénico-punique," in *Ritual and Sacrifice in the Ancient Near East* (ed. Quaegebeur), 257–81.

Ritual Calendars and Schedules. As a matter of convenience, ancient priests sometimes composed schedules for their cultic activities. These provided month-by-month and day-by-day lists of sacrifices, processions, rituals, and festivals that should be performed. There are too many exemplars to list them all, but several of the most important (from Mesopotamia, Emar, and Ugarit) are cited below in the bibliography. One of the Emar texts (*Emar* 446) attempts to integrate all of the city's rituals and festivals into a single schedule, but this arrangement would not have worked so well in a larger city such as Babylon, with its many rites and temples. The Near Eastern ritual calendars are comparable to those found in the Hebrew Pentateuch (Lev 23; Num 28–29; Deut 16).

Texts and translations: D. E. FLEMING, *Time at Emar: The Cultic Calendar and the Rituals from the Diviner's House* (MC 11; Winona Lake, Ind.: Eisenbrauns, 2000), 141–95, 268–93;

A. R. GEORGE, "Four Temple Rituals from Babylon," in *Wisdom, Gods, and Literature* (ed. George and Finkel), 259–99; S. LANGDON, "Calendars of Liturgies and Prayers," *AJSL* 42 (1926): 110–27; S. M. MAUL, "Die Frühjahrsfeierlichkeit in Aššur," in *Wisdom, Gods, and Literature* (ed. George and Finkel), 389–420; PARDEE, *Ritual and Cult at Ugarit*, 25–56. *Translation: COS* 1.124–25: 436–42. *Bibliography:* M. E. COHEN, *The Cultic Calendars of the Ancient Near East* (Bethesda, Md.: CDL Press, 1993); W. SALLBERGER, *Der kultische Kalender der Ur III-Zeit* (2 vols; Berlin: de Gruyter, 1993).

Mesopotamian Ritual Commentaries. Ancient priests and scholars sometimes turned their intellectual energies to the questions raised by their temple rituals. Some of their questions were matters of interpretation, and in this vein they produced a modest variety of texts in which various rites were given mystical and mythological explanations. For instance, one Neo-Assyrian commentator (VAT 9817, see Livingstone) explains that the cedar resin burned in a Ninurta ritual represented "the loose flesh of the evil gods." The commentator goes on to suggest that this ritual caused the demons to flee because they "smell the aroma and go into hiding." Similar comments are provided concerning a medical ritual: "The gypsum and bitumen that they smear on the door of the sick man: The gypsum is Ninurta. The bitumen is [the demon] Asakku. Ninurta pursues Asakku." In other words, the scholars attempted to explain the rituals in terms of their myths. Another purpose for the commentaries was to reconcile theological tensions and contradictions within the ritual tradition. For instance, one ancient scholar notes that the gods Anu and Enlil often failed to attend the Akitu festival as prescribed in the ritual. His proposed solution for this problem is that lesser gods attended the festival in their stead.

Although the ancient scholars who produced the ritual commentaries were intensely interested in the intellectual dimensions of their religious world, their thoughts and comments about ritual were not incorporated directly into the canonical ritual texts about which they wrote. For this reason, the absence of extensive ritual commentary in the priestly legislation of the Hebrew Bible should not be taken too quickly as evidence that the Israelite scribes were uninterested in the peculiarities of Israelite ritual.

Text and translation: A. LIVINGSTONE, *Mystical and Mythological Explanatory Works of Assyrian and Babylonian Scholars* (Oxford: Clarendon, 1986). *Bibliography:* VAN DER TOORN, "The Babylonian New Year Festival."

5.8. Other Apotropaic, Prophylactic, and Productive Rituals

Near Eastern cultures have left us with a large corpus of magical rites. Although some of these served productive purposes (e.g., to promote successful trade or to spark the interest of a potential lover), most were apotropaic/prophylactic attempts to remove or prevent troublesome outcomes ranging from illness, snake bite, domestic quarrels, infant mortality, and sexual impotence to the threats posed by ghosts, demons, witches, angry gods, and human enemies. In many cases, the problems addressed by rituals were of a medical nature. Good discussions of the medical dimensions of ancient Near Eastern ritual are provided in the monograph by Avalos.

5.8.1. Mesopotamian Apotropaic, Prophylactic, and Productive Rituals

The Mesopotamians traced the origins of illness and misfortune to a range of interrelated causes, including divine decrees, witchcraft, demonic influence, and even bad luck. These problems were addressed through a combination of treatments that we might divide into "medical" and "magical" categories. Medical treatments included setting bones, bandaging wounds, lancing boils, and pharmacology, and magical treatments included various rituals and incantations. These medical and ritual duties were carried out by two types of professionals, the *asû* ("physician") and the *āšipu* ("exorcist"), but there was no strict dividing line between their duties because our modern distinction between "medical" and "magical" did not hold for the ancients. Nevertheless, in rough outline, we may say that the *āšipu* was a ritual specialist and the *asû* a pharmacological specialist (see Scurlock). Here our interest is mainly in the incantations and rituals of *āšipūtu*, that body of tradition in which the *āšipu* was an expert. A good summary of the material included in *āšipūtu* is found in the *āšipu* instructional manual *KAR* 44 (see Zimmern; Bottéro, 65–112). According to Mesopotamian tradition, the lore of *āšipūtu* was authored by the wise god Enki/Ea (see the ancient catalogue published by Lambert), who in turn passed on this lore to his son Marduk. Consequently, Ea and Marduk appear prominently in the prescriptions for incantation rituals, although the god of justice, Šamaš, is also prominent in the texts.

Let us first consider the incantations and then turn to their associated rituals. Modern scholars distinguish two types of Mesopotamian incantations (Akkadian, *šiptu;* Sumerian, ÉN): the prayer incantation (German, *Gebetsbeschwörung*) and the magical incantation (*Beschwörung*). Both types were uttered in connection with ritual actions, but the petitionary element was not so strong in the magical incantations because they were understood not as prayers but as echoes of the divine word itself. One magical incantation put it this way: "This spell is not mine, but it is the spell of Ningirimma, Ea, and Asalluhi [i.e., Marduk]" (see *BM* 1.117). The entries that follow treat only the magical incantations. The prayer incantations are treated in 3.1.3. Because incantations were deemed effective on account of their antiquity, many were written and recited in the ancient Sumerian language. Some incantations included mythological introductions, which explained the origins of the problem to be addressed, or illustrated the solution that was needed. A good example is the Incantation against Toothache (see *ANET* 100–101). The text begins with the creation of the entire cosmos and works its way down to the creation of the worm, whose sucking at the dental patient's gums was deemed the cause of toothache (see *ANET* 100–101). After recitation of the myth, the tooth was ritually pulled: "Fix the pin and seize its foot [i.e., pull the tooth]. Because thou hast said this, May Ea smite thee, O worm, with the might of his hand!"

The ritual actions themselves were most often designed to address the problem of demonic oppression. Demons could gain influence in one's life if one's personal god withdrew protection on account of some moral or cultic lapse or perhaps because of influences from witchcraft. As we have seen, one obvious strategy for rectifying the problem was to seek assistance via prayer, but ritual actions were almost always practiced with such prayers. The three basic ritual strategies for removing demonic pollution were (1) removal by ritual detergent (e.g., the application of water or salve); (2) transfer and disposal (e.g., using an object, statue, or sacrificial animal); and (3) ritual destruction of the impurity (often by fire). Rituals and incantations were also used to counteract the effects of witchcraft.

In practice, the use of rituals and incantations was quite flexible. The selfsame incantation could appear on one-tablet prescriptions for use on a single occasion or in long and elaborate ritual collections such as *Maqlû, Šurpu, Mīs Pî,* and *Bīt Rimki.*

Sumerian Magical Incantations. The Sumerian incantations were magical spells rather than prayers. According to Falkenstein, these spells fall out into four basic types: (1) incantations that legitimized the incantation priest; (2) apotropaic/ prophylactic incantations that protected the laity from evil demons; (3) Ea/ Marduk incantations, in which demons and illness were removed by following the ritual directions that the god Ea gave to his son Marduk; and (4) incantations that consecrated objects to be used during exorcisms. Although we possess references to, and portions of, many such texts, our four primary collections of Sumerian incantations are UDUG.ḪUL.A.MEŠ (or *Utukkī Lemnūti,* against evil demons), SAG.GIG.GA.MEŠ (against headaches; cf. the SA.GIG medical diagnostic omens in the bibliography under "Other Omen Genres," 6.1.1), AZÁG.GIG.GA.MEŠ (or *Asakkī Marṣūti,* against fever sickness) and the ninth tablet of the *Šurpu* expiation series (see next entry). Our best copies of the texts date to the first millennium, but there is good evidence that these incantation collections were already taking shape during the Old Babylonian period and that their traditions date back to the Sumerian Ur-III period (so Falkenstein; Geller). In all cases but *Šurpu,* late copies of the Sumerian incantations also include Akkadian translations. Numerous nonserial Sumerian incantations have also been discovered. These include apotropaic spells (against snakes, scorpians, dogs, bad dreams, evil ghosts, evil eye, headache, demons, crying children, labor pains) and productive spells for purifying various objects (e.g., holy water, censers, perfumes, the royal throne, and even the army before battle) (see Alster; Van Dijk/Goetze/Hussey).

Texts and translations: B. ALSTER, "A Sumerian Incantation against Gall," *Or* 41 (1972): 349–58; O. R. GURNEY, "Babylonian Prophylactic Figures and Their Rituals," *AAA* 22 (1935): 31–96; J. B. NIES and C. E. KEISER, *Historical, Religious, and Economic Texts and Antiquities* (BIN 2; New Haven: Yale University Press, 1920), no. 22 (Neo-Babylonian copy of UDUG.ḪUL.A.MEŠ); E. REINER, *Šurpu: A Collection of Sumerian and Akkadian Incantations* (AfOB 11; Graz: Im Selbstverlage des Herausgebers, 1958); M. SIGRIST, "Une tablette d'incantations sumérienne," *ActSum* 2 (1980): 153–61; R. C. THOMPSON, *The Devils and*

Evil Spirits of Babylonia (2 vols.; London: Luzac, 1903–1904) (Neo-Assyrian editions of UDUG.ḪUL.A.MEŠ, SAG.GIG.GA.MEŠ, and AZÁG.GIG.GA.MEŠ); J. VAN DIJK, A. GOETZE, and M. I. HUSSEY, *Early Mesopotamian Incantations and Rituals* (YOS 11; New Haven: Yale University Press, 1985) (selections). *Translation: COS* 1.167: 539, 1.168: 539–40. *Bibliography:* G. CUNNINGHAM, "Summoning the Sacred in Sumerian Incantations," *SEL* 15 (1998): 41–48; A. FALKENSTEIN, *Die Haupttypen der sumerischen Beschwörung: Literarisch untersucht* (Leipzig: August Pries, 1931); M. J. GELLER, *Forerunners to Udug-Hul: Sumerian Exorcistic Incantations* (Freiburger altorientalische Studien 12; Stuttgart: F. Steiner, 1985); M. KREBERNIK, *Die Beschwörungen aus Fara und Ebla: Untersuchungen zur ältesten keilschriftlichen Beschwörungsliteratur* (Texte und Studien zur Orientalistik 2; Hildesheim, Germany: Olms, 1984); P. MICHALOWSKI, "The Early Mesopotamian Incantation Tradition."

The Mesopotamian Ritual Series Šurpu. This series was performed jointly by a priest and an incantation specialist, often as a medical therapy to alleviate physical suffering. As we have noted already, the inner logic of such rites traced medical difficulties back to gods or evil demons who tormented the patient. The response to this circumstance was a series of sympathetic rites in which objects were ceremonially burned after being declared carriers of the patient's sins and sufferings (hence the name Šurpu, literally, "burning"). The ritual prescriptions provided by Šurpu were not considered human concoctions; they were cast as Ea's instructions to his son Marduk, instructions that the ritual priests were in turn expected to imitate. Marduk's role in this regard reflects his status as the patron deity of exorcism, a role formerly played by his father, Ea, in the Sumerian tradition. Because the specific causes of illness were sometimes unknown, there was a gradual tendency for the series to grow as all possible causes of trouble were addressed. There was thus a correspoding tendency to use Šurpu in conjunction with other ritual series, such as *Ilī ul īdi* (literally, "My god, I do not know [what my sin is]").

Šurpu is preserved in several multitablet editions. Our most complete copies were written on nine tablets from Assurbanipal's library (seventh century B.C.E.), with the first tablet containing directions for magical operations (the "ritual tablet") and the remaining eight providing incantations, prayers, and other instructions for the exorcistic priests. Horizontal rulings between the various entries made it easier to read and consult the tablets. The text is mainly in Akkadian, with Sumerian ritual incantations featured in tablet nine. The dialect of the tablets points to its likely canonization well before our Neo-Assyrian copy, probably during the Kassite period (fifteenth–twelfth century B.C.E.), although the Sumerian incantations are probably much older. Šurpu's rituals probably existed independently or in small collections before they were finally collected into larger ritual compendiums—a pattern of growth that is visible in many Mesopotamian canonical texts.

Texts and translations: R. BORGER, "Šurpu II, III, IV, und VIII in 'Partitur,'" in *Wisdom, Gods, and Literature* (ed. George and Finkel), 15–90; E. REINER, *Šurpu: A Collection of Sumerian and Akkadian Incantations* (AfOB 11; Graz: Im Selbstverlage des Herausgebers, 1958). *Bibliography:* J. BOTTÉRO, *Mythes et rites de Babylone* (Paris: Champion, 1985), 163–219; M. J. GELLER, "The Shurpu Incantations and Lev 5:1–5," *JSS* 25 (1980): 181–92.

The Mesopotamian Ritual Series **Maqlû.** Whereas *Šurpu* often addressed problems of unknown origin, the ritual series *Maqlû* addressed a known problem: oppression from the spells of witchcraft. The standard form of *Maqlû* ("burning") contained a lengthy set of incantations and ritual prescriptions that were conveniently summarized on a ritual tablet, but we are relatively certain that the series originated as a much shorter sequence of ten incantations before it gradually reached its final form (Abusch 2002). Its rites included both direct and indirect treatments for the patient. Direct treatments included the patient's consumption of foodstuffs or the physical application of prepared substances to his or her body, whereas the all-important indirect method included the ritual burning, impaling, or drenching of the witch's effigy. Although we possess a large corpus of such texts that address the threat of witchcraft—not only *Maqlû* but also many other texts—so far as we can tell, not a single ritual prescription for carrying out witchcraft has been preserved. From this it is reasonable to conclude that the practice of witchcraft was more widespread in popular imagination than in reality. A new edition of *Maqlû* is now being prepared by Tz. Abusch.

Text and translation: G. MEIER, *Die assyrische Beschwörungssammlung Maqlû* (AfOB 2; Berlin: Im Selbstverlage des Herausgebers, 1937). *Bibliography:* TZ. ABUSCH, *Babylonian Witchcraft Literature* (BJS 132; Atlanta: Scholars Press, 1987); IDEM, *Mesopotamian Witchcraft: Toward a History and Understanding of Babylonian Witchcraft Beliefs and Literature* (AMD 5; Leiden: Brill, 2002); IDEM, "The Ritual Tablet and Rubrics of *Maqlû:* Toward the History of the Series," in *Ah, Assyria . . . Studies in Assyrian History and Ancient Near Eastern Historiography Presented to Hayim Tadmor* (ed. M. Cogan and I. Eph'al; ScrHier 33; Jerusalem: Magnes Press, 1991), 233–53; V. A. HUROWITZ, "Salted Incense—Exodus 30,35; Maqlu VI 111–113; IX 118–120," *Bib* 68 (1987): 178–94; M.-L. THOMSEN, "Witchcraft and Magic in Ancient Mesopotamia," in F. H. Cryer and M.-L. Thomsen, *Biblical and Pagan Societies* (London: Athlone, 2001), 3–95; IDEM, *Zauberdiagnose und schwarze Magie in Mesopotamien* (Copenhagen: Museum Tusculanum Press, 1987).

Prophylactic Omen Rituals: **Namburbû, Bīt Rimki, *and* Šar Pūḫi Rites.** Whenever omens portended evil, the Mesopotamians attempted to avoid the threat by performing prophylactic rites known as *namburbûs* (from the Sumerian NAM.BÚR.BI, meaning "undoing of it" [i.e., of portended evil]). These rites are preserved in noncanonical collections and in various omen texts, where they sometimes appear alongside the portents for which they are the prophalaxes (see ch. 6). The standard *namburbû* form included a title, prescriptions for the ritual, and an incantation prayer. According to Maul (1999), the *namburbû*'s objectives for the receiver of an evil omen were sixfold: (1) to placate the anger of the gods who sent the omen; (2) to effect a change in the gods' decision to render an evil fate; (3) to remove the impurities that come via the omen itself; (4) to remove ritual impurity from the person's house and possessions; (5) to return the person to a normal ritual state; and (6) to achieve a permanent state of protection against future evil omens. Although most of the *namburbûs* were small-scale rites, this was not always the case. The long ritual series *Bīt Rimki* ("house of the ritual bath," see Laessøe) was used to purify and protect the king from the evils portended by astronomical omens, especially eclipses, and the closely related *Šar Pūḫi* ("substitute king") included various rites as well as the temporary replacement of the threatened king by a substitute person. The substitute was killed after the threat to the king had dissipated (see Parpola). Although *namburbûs* were generally prophylactic procedures, they were sometimes used to combat existing problems, especially medical conditions.

Students of the Hebrew Bible will find the *namburbûs* particularly interesting when Israelite rituals also deal with the issues addressed by them. Such a comparison is possible concerning the problem of fungal infestations, which is treated both in the *namburbûs* and in Lev 14 (see Meier). In both cases, it was believed that the deity had sent the fungi (see Lev 14:33–34) and that, consequently, some type of response might be necessary. Priests were called in to offer a diagnosis, which was based mainly on the color of the fungus. If the color was unfavorable, the fungus was removed and purgation rites were performed in order to remove any ritual pollution.

Texts and translations: R. I. CAPLICE, "An Apotropaion against Fungus," *JNES* 33 (1974): 345–49; IDEM, "Namburbi Texts in the British Museum, I–V," *Or* 34 (1965): 105–31; 36 (1967): 1–38, 273–98; 39 (1970): 111–51; 40 (1971): 133–83; J. LAESSØE, *Studies on the Assyrian Ritual and Series Bît Rimki* (Copenhagen: Munksgaard, 1955); W. G. LAMBERT, "A Part of the Ritual for the Substitute King," *AfO* 18 (1957–1958): 109–12; 19 (1959–1960): 119. *Translations:* R. I. CAPLICE, *The Akkadian Namburbu Texts: An Introduction* (Sources from the Ancient Near East 1.1; Malibu, Calif.: Undena, 1974). *Bibliography:* P.-A. BEAULIEU, "Lion-Man: Uridimmu or urdimmu?" *NABU* 1990.121; J. BOTTÉRO, *Mesopotamia: Writing, Reasoning, and the Gods* (Chicago: University of Chicago Press, 1992), 138–55; A. R. W. GREEN, *The Role of Human Sacrifice in the Ancient Near East* (Missoula, Mont.: Scholars Press, 1975); R. LABAT, "Le sort des substituts royaux en Assyrie au temps des Sargonids," *RA* 40 (1945–1946): 123–43; S. M. MAUL, "How the Babylonians Protected Themselves against Calamities Announced by Omens," in *Mesopotamian Magic* (ed. Abusch and van der Toorn), 123–29; IDEM, *Zukunftsbewältigung: Eine Untersuchung altorientalischen Denkens anhand der babylonisch-assyrischen Löserituale (Namburbi)* (Baghdader Forschungen 18; Mainz: Philipp von Zabern, 1994); S. MEIER, "House Fungus: Mesopotamia and Israel (Lev 14:33–53)," *RB* 96 (1989): 184–92; S. PARPOLA, "Excursus: The Substitute King Ritual," in *Letters from Assyrian Scholars to the Kings Esarhaddon and Assurbanipal* (2 vols.; AOAT 5; Neukircken-Vluyn: Neukirckener Verlag, 1970–1983), 2:xxii–xxxii; J. H. WALTON, "The Imagery of the Substitute King Ritual in Isaiah's Fourth Servant Song," *JBL* 122 (2003): 734–43; WIGGERMANN, *Mesopotamian Protective Spirits*, 141–42.

The Series Bīt Mēseri *and Related Rites.* This entry covers a corpus of related rites that used prophylactic statues to protect homes and buildings from the threat of demonic presence. In some cases the rites addressed new construction, but in most instances the texts concern existing structures in need of protection because those living in them were sick. The major texts include the series *Bīt Mēseri*, which has been partially published by Borger and by Meier (see also Wiggermann, 105–18), and several similar texts published by Gurney and Wiggermann. Gurney's three texts (Gurney nos. 1–3) have been either reedited or collated as texts 1–3 in Wiggermann's monograph, which treats six texts in all. In sum, the texts to be considered include the series *Bīt Mēseri* (Borger; Meier; Gurney no. 3; Wiggermann no. 3) and a body of similar texts that were not a part of *Bīt Mēseri* (Gurney nos. 1–2; Wiggermann nos. 1–2, 4–6). All of these texts are prescriptive and reflect the same general tone and format. Their ritual directions are laconic, proceeding chronologically from the beginning of the rite to its end. The various sections of the rituals were marked off with rubrics and rulings, which made it easier for the *āšipu* to work through the rites. With this background in mind, let us consider the series *Bīt Mēseri* in more detail.

The objective of the series was to drive demons from the house of a sick person or to protect homes from demonic presences. Its apotropaic and prophylactic purposes are reflected in the title *Bīt Mēseri,* which means "enclosed house." According to an unpublished exorcistic catalogue (mentioned by Meier), the series originally contained four tablets, a ritual tablet followed by three tablets of ritual prescriptions. Unfortunately, we do not have the entire series, and there is debate about what tablets and fragments belong, or do not belong, to it. Scholars have managed to reconstruct tablet 2 of the series (Meier), and several parts of tablet 1 have also been published (see Borger; Wiggermann). Moreover, if Wiggermann is right, one of the rituals published by Gurney (no. 3) was performed during the rites of *Bīt Mēseri* and may originally have been a part of the series. In the absence of a complete text for *Bīt Mēseri,* the closely related texts published by Gurney and Wiggermann are important sources for reconstructions of the *Bīt Mēseri* rites.

The ritual method for protecting the home included the fabrication and animation of numerous prophylactic figures, which were eventually buried at strategic locations in and around the home. To judge from our nonseries texts and from what little is preserved of the series *Bīt Mēseri,* the protective figures included deities, *apkallu* sages (see 2.1), monsters, and perhaps zoomorphic figures, such as dogs. Our copies of *Bīt Mēseri* do not preserve the directions for fabricating the prophylactic images, but they suggest that the images were made from wood or were simply drawn on the walls of the house in question. The portion of the rite that covered the fabrication of the images can be filled out by consulting the nonseries texts mentioned above, but we should note that these texts prescribe a larger number of figures than *Bīt Mēseri* and that they also distinguish divine statues from nondivine figures by constructing the former from wood and the latter from clay.

So far as we can tell on the basis of the nonseries texts (Wiggerman nos. 1–2), the initial ritual actions of *Bīt Mēseri* would have unfolded as follows. The priest went out in the morning (i.e., as the sun god Šamaš appeared), taking his paraphernalia with him. These items included ritual tools as well as foodstuffs for offerings. When an appropriate tree was found, it was cleansed by a censer, torch, and holy water, and then offerings were made to the god Šamaš. Next, an incantation was recited over the tree, and it was cut down and immediately used to fashion an image. The texts provide very specific directions about the fabrication of the figures, but not so specific that one could follow them without previous knowledge of the rites. The process just enumerated, or something similar, was repeated numerous times until all of the prophylactic figures were ready. Before bringing the statues to the house of the sick patient, the figures were taken to the river and apparently left there overnight. The following morning (again, as the sun god Šamaš appeared), the figures underwent rites of consecration that were attended by the gods Ea, Šamaš, and Marduk. Ritual space for these gods was prepared by sweeping the ground, sprinkling it with holy water, setting up three empty chairs, and then making offerings before the chairs. At this point the prophylactic statues were consecrated by purifying them with water, censer, and torch. Only after these rites were completed could the figures be taken to the house and positioned in various places.

According to Wiggermann no. 1, after the figures were put in place, sacrifices were offered to several deities and to the three gods of the household, that is, to the god, goddess, and protective spirit (*lamassu*) of the house. A *kuppuru* elimination ritual was then performed on the structure (cf. the Akitu *kuppuru* in 5.2); in it various grains were rubbed on the home's surfaces and floor and then were swept up and thrown into the river, taking the home's demonic impurities with them. Final purification of the house included the use of a censer, a torch, and holy water in conjunction with the incantation "Evil go out." Because we have the second tablet of *Bīt Mēseri* and because we know that the first tablet was its ritual summary, it does not appear that the series *Bīt Mēseri* included ritual prescriptions for the foregoing procedures from Wiggerman no. 1. Such rituals would probably have been necessary, however, in *Bīt Mēseri*, so the ritual tablet would have directed in a summary fashion that they be done.

At this point, our copy of *Bīt Mēseri* picks up the rite. The *āšipu*-priest recited a series of Sumerian and/or Akkadian incantations before each group of figures, beginning with the god Marduk—who was represented only by an empty chair, as was the usual procedure with the great gods—and working his way down to include the prophylactic figures of the lower deities, *apkallū*, and monsters. We may judge from similar texts that the gods of the household (the family god and goddess as well as the house's protective *lamassu* spirit) were also addressed with sacrifices and incantations (see Wiggermann, 17), but they are not mentioned in *Bīt Mēseri*. Our copies of the series break off at this point, but we may surmise on the basis of Gurney no. 3 that this part of the ritual included Ea/Marduk incantations against evil demons (see Wiggermann, 113–14). Almost certainly, the prophylactic figures used in *Bīt Mēseri* were eventually buried at various points in and around the house, particularly in the bedroom and at the outer gate.

Several similarities between Israelite ritual and *Bīt Mēseri* should be noted. The temple-cleansing *kippēr* rite in Lev 16 is very close in form and rationale to the *kuppuru* that was used to purify the house in Wiggermann no. 1 and also perhaps in *Bīt Mēseri* itself. Another interesting comparative feature is that in the Mesopotamian rites the great gods were represented not as statues but by empty chairs. In certain respects, this is reminiscent of the Israelite idea that Yahweh's presence could be represented by the ark of the covenant.

Texts and translations: R. BORGER, "Die Beschwörungsserie *Bīt Mēseri* und die Himmelfahrt Henochs," *JNES* 33 (1974): 183–96; H. HUNGER and E. VON WEIHER, eds., *Spätbabylonische Texte aus Uruk* (3 vols.; Ausgrabungen der Deutschen Forschungsgemeinschaft in
Uruk-Waka 9, 10, 12; Berlin: Gebr. Mann, 1976–[1988]), vol. 2, nos. 8–11; G. MEIER, "Die
zweite Tafel der Serie Bīt Mēseri," *AfO* 14 (1941–1944): 139–52. *Bibliography:* E. A.
BRAUN-HOLZINGER, "Apotropaic Figures at Mesopotamian Temples in the Third and Second Millennia," in *Mesopotamian Magic* (ed. Abusch and van der Toorn), 149–72; A. R. W.
GREEN, "Neo-Assyrian Apotropaic Figures: Figurines, Rituals, and Monumental Art," *Iraq*
45 (1983): 87–96; O. R. GURNEY, "Babylonian Prophylactic Figures and Their Rituals,"
AAA 22 (1935): 31–96; E. REINER, "The Etiological Myth of the 'Seven Sages,'" *Or* 30
(1961): 1–11; WIGGERMANN, *Mesopotamian Protective Spirits.*

Other Mesopotamian Rituals and Incantations. If we set aside the important ritual collections described above, there remains a large corpus of Akkadian and
Sumerian incantation exemplars. These serial and nonserial exemplars appear in
medical texts (e.g., the ŠÀ.ZI.GA impotency rites), on individual tablets, and in
other ritual contexts. Most of the spells provided apotropaic protection from difficulties (bad dreams, crying children, scorpians, flies, labor pains, medical conditions, and a host of other problems), but a few were productive spells whose
effects were deemed positive by the ancients (e.g., love charms). These incantations bring us close to the experiences of the average Mesopotamian citizen (see
Ebeling).

Selected texts and translations: R. D. BIGGS, *ŠÀ.ZI.GA: Ancient Mesopotamian Potency In-
cantations* (TCS; Locust Valley, N.Y.: J. J. Augustin, 1957); S. A. L. BUTLER, *Mesopotamian
Conceptions of Dreams and Dream Rituals* (AOAT 258; Münster: Ugarit, 1998); J. VAN DIJK,
A. GOETZE, and M. I. HUSSEY, *Early Mesopotamian Incantations and Rituals* (YOS 11; New
Haven: Yale University Press, 1985); W. FARBER, *Beschwörungsrituale an Ishtar und Dumuzi*
(Akademie der Wissenschaften und der Literatur 30; Wiesbaden: Franz Steiner, 1977);
IDEM, *Schlaf, Kindchen, schlaf! Mesopotamische Baby-Beschwörungen und-Rituale* (MC 2;
Winona Lake, Ind.: Eisenbrauns, 1989); IDEM, "Zur älteren akkadischen Beschwörungs-
literature," *ZA* 71 (1981): 51–71; W. W. HALLO, "More Incantations and Rituals from the
Yale Babylonian Collection," in *Mesopotamian Magic* (ed. Abusch and van der Toorn),
275–89; F. KÖCHER, *Die babylonisch-assyrische Medizin in Texten und Untersuchungen* (6
vols.; Berlin: de Gruyter, 1963–); W. G. LAMBERT, "Fire Incantations," *AfO* 23 (1970):
39–45, pls. 1–11; D. SCHWEMER, *Akkadische Rituale aus Hattusa: Die Sammeltafel K Bo
XXXVI 29 und verwandte Fragmente* (TH 23; Heidelberg: C. Winter, 1998); R. C. THOMP-
SON, *Assyrian Medical Texts* (London: Oxford University Press, 1923); J. G. WESTENHOLZ,
"Help for Rejected Suitors: The Old Akkadian Love Incantation MAD V 8," *Or* 46 (1977):
198–219; R. WHITING, "An Old Babylonian Incantation from Tell Asmar," *ZA* 75 (1985):
179–87. *Translations:* BM^2 1.57–147, 2.824–83; COS 1.121: 426–27, 1.167: 539, 1.168:
539–40. *Bibliography:* R. D. BIGGS, "The Babylonian Sexual Potency Texts," in *Sex and
Gender in the Ancient Near East* (2 vols.; ed. S. Parpola and R. M. Whiting; RAI 47; Hel-
sinki: Neo-Assyrian Text Corpus Project, 2002), 1:71–78; E. A. BRAUN-HOLZINGER,
"Apotropaic Figures at Mesopotamian Temples in the Third and Second Millennia," in
Mesopotamian Magic (ed. Abusch and van der Toorn), 149–72; E. EBELING, *Aus dem
Tagewerk eines assyrischen Zauberpriesters* (Mitteilungen der altorientalischen Gesellschaft;
Leipzig: Harrassowitz, 1931); W. FARBER, "Lamaštu," *RlA* 6:439–46; IDEM, "*Mannam*

Lušpur ana Enkidu: Some New Thoughts about an Old Motif," *JNES* 49 (1990): 299–321;
M. J. GELLER, "Mesopotamian Love Magic: Discourse or Intercourse?" in *Sex and Gender
in the Ancient Near East* (2 vols.; ed. S. Parpola and R. M. Whiting; RAI 47; Helsinki: Neo-
Assyrian Text Corpus Project, 2002), 1:129–39; P. MICHALOWSKI, "The Early Mesopo-
tamian Incantation Tradition"; J. A. SCURLOCK, *Magical Means of Dealing with Ghosts in
Ancient Mesopotamia* (PhD diss., University of Chicago, 1988).

5.8.2. Egyptian Apotropaic, Prophylactic, and Productive Rituals

The Egyptian Execration Texts. From the burning of a witch's effigy to the substitute for a king, the patterns of ritual action often sympathetically represent its desired result. This sympathetic pattern is especially visible in the execration texts, an
Egyptian genre that has occasionally attracted the attention of biblical scholars.
From the Old Kingdom down through the Roman period, Egyptian priests ritually
cursed Egypt's enemies by shattering objects on which the names of its enemies
were inscribed. The textual evidence for execration rites includes both statues and
red pots that contain long lists of Egypt's enemies from the south (Nubia), east
(Mesopotamia, the Levant), west (Libya), and Egypt itself. Besides the inherent
value of these Egyptian lists as examples of sympathetic magic, biblical scholars
have been interested in the relationship between the Egyptian lists and the lists of
Israel's enemies in the prophetic books (Isa 13–27; Jer 45–51; Ezek 25–29; Amos
1–2). Some scholars have suggested that the prophetic lists were inspired by the
Egyptian execration texts and thus reflect a prophetic ritual that pronounced
curses upon Israel's enemies. The primary problem with this suggestion is that the
biblical books contain prophecies against foreign nations rather than simple lists,
and there is no evidence that these prophecies were ever attached to ritual ceremonies. Because this thesis has not enjoyed wide acceptance among biblical scholars,
the conceptual background of the Israelite prophecies against foreign nations remains an important question (for prophetic texts, see ch. 6).

Texts and translations: Y. KOENIG, "Les texts d'envoûtement de Mirgissa," *RdE* 41 (1990):
101–25; K. SETHE, *Die Ächtung feindlicher Fürsten, Völker, und Dinge auf altägyptischen
Tongefässcherben des Mittleren Reiches* (Berlin: Akademie der Wissenschaften, 1926). **Translations:** *ANET* 328–29; *COS* 1.32: 50–52. **Bibliography:** A. BENTZEN, "The Ritual Back-
ground of Amos I 2–ii 16," *OtSt* 8 (1950): 85–99; A. GOETZE, "Remarks on Some Names
Occurring in the Execration Texts," *BASOR* 151 (1958): 28–33; S. MORSCHAUSER, *Threat-
Formulae in Ancient Egypt: A Study of the History, Structure, and Use of Threats and Curses in
Ancient Egypt* (Baltimore: Halgo, 1991); S. PAUL, *Amos* (Hermeneia; Minneapolis: Fortress,
1991), 11–12; R. K. RITNER, *The Mechanics of Ancient Egyptian Magical Practice* (SAOC 54;
Chicago: Oriental Institute of the University of Chicago, 1993), 136–90; M. WEISS, "The Pat-
tern of the 'Execration Texts' in the Prophetic Literature," *IEJ* 19 (1969): 150–59.

Other Egyptian Apotropaic and Prophylactic Rites. Threats from angry deities,
demons, and ghosts were ever present in the Egyptian psyche, as were more
conventional difficulties presented by dangerous and venomous animals—especially snakes, scorpions, and crocodiles—and by illness in general. The Egyptian

effort to prevent and alleviate these problems usually took the form of magical rituals, most of them designed to address medical problems. The Egyptians often attributed medical troubles to digestive difficulties, in which the digestion of food was imagined a permutation of the more aggressive putrefaction that overtakes the body at death (Pinch). Egyptian medicine used rituals to halt the march of this putrefaction, thereby averting illness or death.

Apart from the funerary rites discussed in 5.9.1, the Egyptians were not prone to assemble canonical collections of apotropaic and prophylactic rituals. Consequently, our window into Egyptian ritual and medicine comes by way of a long list of different and, in some respects, idiosyncratic texts, most of them private collections of rites, incantations, and medical procedures preserved on papyri. Several common ritual motifs appear in this diverse corpus of ritual texts.

During the rituals, the ritual specialist often took on the persona and authority of a deity, usually Thoth or Isis. This slight of hand was achieved by claiming, "It is not me but the god X," a move that provided the ritual priest with the authority he needed to order troublesome demons and gods to take leave of the patient. At the same time, the suffering victim often took on the persona of the god Horus, a suitable metaphor given the miraculous healing of Horus in the Horus myths (see 10.2). The rituals themselves included a variety of ceremonial actions. Spitting and licking were commonly included, sometimes bearing positive imagery and other times representing ritual threats or pollution. Acts of swallowing were also needed, as patients ingested "medicinal" substances (dates, minerals, and similar prescriptions) as well as "magical" substances, such as holy water or water in which the ink of a written spell had been dissolved. Other common ritual actions included the binding, impaling, or destroying of one's enemies in effigy form, and also acts of execration, such as were described in the previous entry.

Most of the texts listed below come from the New Kingdom, although some of them, such as the Brooklyn Magical Papyrus (fourth–third century B.C.E.), date a good deal later. The most "scientific" exemplar in the bibliography is probably the famous Edwin Smith Surgical Papyrus (ca. 1550 B.C.E.), but even this text sometimes prescribes magical operations alongside its conventional medicine. Also interesting are the West Semitic magical incantations that appear in the London Medical Papyrus (see *COS* 1.101). This feature illustrates the tendency, visible in other Near Eastern rituals, to use foreign or esoteric languages in ritual incantations. Egyptian medical rituals were sometimes inscribed upon statue bases (see Klasens) or upon healing stelae called the Horus cippi (sing., Horus cippus, where *cippus* is Latin for "post"), which could be visited by the ill. The most famous of the Horus cippi texts is probably the Metternich Stela (see Scott). For good overviews of Egyptian magical rituals, see the studies of Pinch and Ritner.

Texts and translations: H. ALTENMÜLLER, "Der 'Socle Béhague' und ein Statuentorso in Wien," *OMRO* 46 (1965): 10–33; IDEM, "Ein Zaubermesser des Mittleren Reiches," *SAK* 13 (1986): 1–27; J. F. BORGHOUTS, *The Magical Texts of Papyrus Leiden I 348* (Leiden: Brill, 1971) (P.Leiden I 348); J. H. BREASTED, *The Edwin Smith Surgical Papyrus* (2 vols.; Chicago: Univeristy of Chicago Press, 1930) (P.Edwin Smith); A. ERMAN, *Zaubersprüche für Mutter und Kind* (Berlin: Verlag der Königlichen Akademie der Wissenschaften, 1901)

(P.Berlin 3027); H. GRAPOW, *Die medizinischen Texte in hieroglyphischer Umschreibung autographiert* (Berlin: Akademie, 1958) (P.Ebers); J. H. JOHNSON, "A Demotic Magical Text in Leiden," *Serapis* 3 (1975–1976): 9–15; IDEM, "Louvre E 3229: A Demotic Magical Text," *Enchoria* 7 (1977): 55–102; A. KLASENS, *A Magical Statue Base (Socle Béhague) in the Museum of Antiquities at Leiden* (Leiden: Brill, 1952); Y. KOENIG, *Le Papyrus Boulaq 6: Transcription, traduction, et commentaire* (BdE 87; Cairo: Institut Français d'Archéologie Orientale du Caire, 1981) (P.Boulaq 6); H. LANGE, *Der magische Papyrus Harris* (Copenhagen: A. F. Høst & Søn, 1927) (P.Harris 501); A. MASSART, *The Leiden Magical Papyrus I 343 + I 345* (Leiden: Brill, 1954) (P.Leiden I 343 + 345); C. SANDER-HANSEN, *Die Texte der Metternichstele* (Copenhagen: C. E. Sander-Hansen, 1956) (Metternich Stela); S. SAUNERON, *Le papyrus magique illustré de Brooklyn, Brooklyn Museum 47.218.156* (Brooklyn: Brooklyn Museum, 1970) (Brooklyn Magical Papyrus); N. SCOTT, "The Metternich Stele," *Bulletin of the Metropolitan Museum of Art* 9 (1950–1951): 201–17 (Metternich Stela); E. SUYS, "Le papyrus magique du Vatican," *Or* 3 (1934): 63–87 (Vatican Magical Papyrus); W. WRESZINSKI, *Der grosse medizinische Papyrus des Berliner Museum (Pap. Berlin 3038)* (Leipzig: J. C. Hinrichs, 1909) (P.Berlin 3038); IDEM, *Der Londoner medizinische Papyrus und der Papyrus Hearst* (Leipzig: J. C. Hinrichs, 1912) (London Medical Papyrus). **Translations:** *ANET* 12–14, 326, 328; J. F. BORGHOUTS, *Ancient Egyptian Magical Texts* (Nisaba 9; Leiden: Brill, 1978); M. CLAGETT, *Ancient Egyptian Science: A Source Book* (3 vols. in 4; Philadelphia: American Philosophical Society, 1989–1999), vol. 1, part 2, pp. 615–25; *COS* 1.101: 328–29. **Bibliography:** J. F. BORGHOUTS, "Akhu and Hekau: Two Basic Notions of Ancient Egyptian Magic and the Concept of Divine Creative Word," in *Magic in Egypt in the Time of the Pharaohs* (ed. Roccati and Siliotti), 29–46; IDEM, "The Edition of Magical Papyri in Turin: A Progress Report," in *Magic in Egypt in the Time of the Pharaohs* (ed. Roccati and Siliotti), 257–69; IDEM, "Magical Texts," in *Textes et langages* (vol. 3 of *Textes et langages de L'Égypte pharaonique: Cent cinquante années de recherches, 1822–1972;* Cairo: Institut Français d'Archéologie Orientale du Caire, 1974), 7–19; B. BRIER, *Ancient Egyptian Magic* (New York: Morrow, 1980); T. DZIERZYKARY-ROGALSKI, "The Magic Procedure of Breaking Bones in Ancient Egypt (Dakhleh Oasis)," *Africana-Bulletin* 30 (1981): 221–24; J. H. JOHNSON, "The Demotic Magical Spells of Leiden I 384," *OMRO* 56 (1975): 29–64; L. KÁKOSY, "Some Problems of the Magical Healing Statues," in *Magic in Egypt in the Time of the Pharaohs* (ed. Roccati and Siliotti), 171–86; IDEM, *Zauberei im alten Ägypten* (Budapest: Akadémiai Kiadó, 1989); J. R. OGDON, "Discussions in Ancient Egyptian Thought, 4: An Analysis of the 'Technical' Language in the Anti-snake Magical Spells of the Pyramid Texts (PT)," *DE* 13 (1989): 59–71; IDEM, "Studies in Ancient Egyptian Magical Thought, 1: The Hand and the Seal," *DE* 1 (1985): 27–34; PINCH, *Magic in Ancient Egypt;* J. PODEMANN SØRENSEN, "The Argument in Ancient Egyptian Magical Formulae," *AcOr* 45 (1984): 5–19; M. RAVEN, "Charms for Protection during the Epagomenal Days," in *Essays on Ancient Egypt in Honour of Herman te Velde* (Egyptological Memoirs 1; Groningen, Neth.: Styx, 1997), 275–91; IDEM, "Wax in Egyptian Magic and Symbolism," *OMRO* 64 (1983): 7–47; R. K. RITNER, *The Mechanics of Ancient Egyptian Magical Practice* (SAOC 54; Chicago: Oriental Institute of the University of Chicago, 1993).

5.8.3. Hittite Apotropaic, Prophylactic, and Productive Rituals

A Hittite Battle Ritual (CTH 422). The procedures prescribed in this text were observed before a military attack, "when they perform the ritual at the boundary of the enemy country." Sacrifices were offered to the gods and goddesses, including sheep for the god Zithariyas. As this sheep was offered, a long incantation was recited that depicted Zithariyas emploring the gods to assist the Hittites in their battle against the Kaškeans, tribal groups in the Black Sea region who often raided Hittite territory. In the event of battle against non-Kaškean enemies, we presume that the Kaškeans mentioned in the rite either represented these unnamed enemies or that the ritual officiant substituted a different enemy name at the place where the Kaškeans appear in the incantations. After the sacrifices and offerings were completed, the text prescribes that "they return to the army, and go to battle in this condition." From the Hittite point of view, this rite was an instance of productive magic that rendered the Hittite army ritually clean and ceremonially fit for battle. A similar concern for ritual purity during military campaigns is found in the book of Deuteronomy (Deut 23:9–14) and in the sectarian Jewish literature preserved among the Dead Sea Scrolls (see the War Scroll).

Text and translation: KUB 4.1; 31.146 (duplicates). *Translation:* ANET 354–55. *Bibliography:* E. VON SCHULER, *Die Kaškäer: Ein Beitrag zur Ethnographie des alten Kleinasien* (Berlin: de Gruyter, 1965), 168.

A Lustration Ritual for the Defeated Army (CTH 426). This text preserves prescriptions for a rite to be used when the Hittite armies were defeated in battle. Military failures were apparently attributed to the army's impurity, and the rite not only cleansed the troops but also prevented them from bringing ritual impurities back to the homeland. The Hittites designated the ritual as the "Behind the River" rite. It entailed the severing of a human being (probably a prisoner of war), a goat, a puppy, and a piglet, whose body parts were placed on both sides of a path that led to a hawthorn gate. The gate itself was flanked by fires on each side. The soldiers were directed to pass through the animal parts and gate before sprinkling themselves with clean water from the river. According to the text's conclusion, these procedures were to be repeated in the steppe before the army returned home.

The apotropaic features in this text are extreme in both their variety and their extent. It contains our only certain reference to human sacrifice in the Hittite rituals, and the animals sacrificed include a dog and swine, two creatures that were normally considered unclean. We can surmise that, in Hittite theology, the body parts somehow attracted and absorbed the impurities of the troops, but the inner logic of the rite escapes us. Perhaps the rationale was "like attracts like," that is, the unclean animals attracted the impurities. Also included in the rite were fire and water—both powerful cleansing agents—as well as a hawthorn gate. Gates of this sort were commonly used in Hittite rituals, apparently because dangerous impurities were thought to "catch" on their thorns as human beings passed through them. Turning to the Hebrew Bible, we find two covenant rites whose procedures are close to those in this Hittite rite. In Gen 15 the deity passed between the body parts of sacrificed animals, and the same sort of action was taken by Israelites as they covenanted with God in Jer 34:18–19. The functions of the Hittite and Hebrew rituals, however, were quite different.

Text and translation: H. M. KÜMMEL, *Ersatzrituale für den hethitischen König* (StBoT 3; Wiesbaden: Harrassowitz, 1967), 150–51. *Translation:* COS 1.61: 160–61. *Bibliography:* B. J. COLLINS, "The Puppy in Hittite Ritual," *JCS* 42 (1990): 211–26; S. EITREM, "A Purificatory Rite and Some Allied Rites of Passage," *Sources orientales* 25 (1947): 36–53; O. MASSON, "A propos d'un ritual hittite pour la lustration d'une armée: Le rite de purification par le passage entre les deux parties d'une victime," *RHR* 137 (1950): 5–25; J. C. MOYER, "Hittite and Israelite Cultic Practices: A Selected Comparison," in *More Essays on the Comparative Method* (ed. Hallo, Moyer, and Perdue), 19–38.

Other Hittite Apotropaic and Prophylactic Rituals. We have already noted several Hittite rituals of an apotropaic or prophylactic nature. The present entry treats remaining rites of this sort in summary fashion, a necessary concession given that hundreds of texts and fragments in the Hittite corpus fit this category. Roughly speaking, Hittite prescriptive rituals can be divided between state and private rituals. State rites usually involved the king and queen as either officiants or clients. Often the concern was to protect the king and queen from danger or illness or to preserve their ritual purity, which the Hittites guarded vigorously. One of these rites was a royal substitution rite analogous to the Mesopotamian *Šar Pūḫi*, but in Hatti it seems that the substitute—an enemy prisoner—was released and returned to his homeland rather than killed (see Kümmel; *ANET* 355–56; see entry on *Šar Pūḫi*). The Hittites also observed rites whose title ("mouth-washing") and function (purification) were similar to the Mesopotamian *Mīs Pî* rite (Haas 1984). The purpose of the rite was to purify the royal couple of Hatti, but its ritual operations were not so close to those used in Mesopotamian *Mīs Pî*. As for the private Hittite rites, these addressed a range of problems, ranging from childbirth, impotence, and family strife to witchcraft, defiled houses, and illnesses of various kinds.

Many of the Hittite rites were borrowed from nearby cultures and so reflect influences from other languages. This is particularly true of the rites that originated in Kizzuwatna (southeastern Anatolia) or Arzawa (western Anatolia), which bear influences from the languages of the respective regions (Hurrian in Kizzuwatna and Luwian in Arzawa). Hittite ritual prescriptions often bear the name of the specialist—sometimes male but often female—who designed the rite. For instance, the rite that addressed family quarrels bears the following rubric: "These are the words of Mastiggas, the woman from Kizzuwatna: If a father and son, or a husband and his wife, or a brother and sister quarrel, when I reconcile them, I treat them as follows." Such a rubric is characteristic of the Hittite rituals in that it identifies the rite's purpose and also the ritual's creator. In most texts, this rubric is followed by a list of the materials that were needed to perform the rite (food, ritual objects, sacrificial animals, etc.), which is in turn followed by a list-like enumeration of the ritual's actions and incantations. The ritual actions often included sympathetic magic, rites of contact, rites of substitution, and "attraction magic," which sought to harness divine power by drawing the gods to the people (cf. *CTH* 483 in 5.1). The specialists who performed the rite, whether a temple priest or one of the "old wise women," received payment from the foodstuffs included in the rite. Physicians sometimes assisted in the medical rites, but the ritual actions in prophylactic and apotropaic rites were almost always purely magical by our standards. For a list of the various rituals in ancient Hatti, see the ritual texts in *CTH* 390–500, 725–808.

Texts and translations: G. BECKMAN, *Hittite Birth Rituals* (StBoT 29; Wiesbaden: Harrassowitz, 1983); O. CARRUBA, *Das Beschwörungsritual für die Göttin Wišurijanza* (StBoT 2; Wiesbaden: Harrassowitz, 1966); A. GOETZE, *The Hittite Ritual of Tunnawi* (New Haven: American Oriental Society, 1938); V. HAAS, "Die hurritisch-hethitischen Rituale der Beschwörerin Allaiturah(h)i und ihr literarhistorischer Hintergrund," in *Hurriter und Hurritisch* (ed. V. Haas; Constance: Universitätsverlag Konstanz, 1988), 117–43; IDEM, "Ein hurritischer Blutritus und die Deponierung der Ritualrückstände nach hethitischen Quellen," in *Religionsgeschichtliche Beziehungen zwischen Kleinasien, Nordsyrien, und dem Alten Testament* (ed. Janowski, Koch, and Wilhelm), 67–85; IDEM, *Die Serien itkahi und itkalzi des AZU-Priesters, Rituale für Tasmisarri und Tatuhepa sowie weitere Texte mit Bezug auf Tasmisarri* (CHSTB 1; Rome: Multigrafica Editrice 1984); V. HAAS and I. WEGNER, *Die Rituale der Beschwörerinnen SAL.ŠU.GI* (CHSTB 5; Rome: Multigrafica Editrice, 1988); H. A. HOFFNER JR., "Paskuwatti's Ritual against Sexual Impotence (*CTH* 406)," *AuOr* 5 (1987): 271–87; M. HUTTER, *Behexung, Entsühnung, und Heilung: Das Ritual der Tunnawiya für ein Königspaar aus mittelhethitischer Zeit (KBo XXI 1–KUB IX 34–KBo XXI 6)* (OBO 82; Göttingen: Vandenhoeck & Ruprecht, 1988); L. JAKOB-ROST, *Das Ritual der Malli aus Arzawa gegen Behexung (KUB XXIV 9+)* (TH 2; Heidelberg: Carl Winter, 1972); H. KLENGEL, *Hethitische Gelübde und Traumtexte sowie Rituale und Festbeschreibungen* (Keilschrifturkunden aus Boghazköi 56; Berlin: Akademie, 1986); IDEM, *Hethitische Rituale und Festbeschreibungen* (Keilschrifturkunden aus Boghazköi 54; Berlin: Akademie, 1984); H. M. KÜMMEL, *Ersatzrituale für den hethitischen König* (StBoT 3; Wiesbaden: Harrassowitz, 1967); E. NEU, *Althethitische Ritualtexte im Umschrift* (StBoT 25; Wiesbaden: Harrassowitz, 1980); IDEM, *Ein althethitisches Gewitterritual* (StBoT 12; Wiesbaden: Harrassowitz, 1970); H. OTTEN, "Ein Ritual von Ašdu, der Hurriterin," in *Kaniššuwar: A Tribute to Hans G. Güterbock on His Seventy-Fifth Birthday, May 27, 1983* (ed. H. A. Hoffner Jr. and G. M. Beckman; AS 23; Chicago: Oriental Institute of the University of Chicago, 1986), 165–71; H. OTTEN and C. RÜSTER, *Luwische Texte und Huwassanna-Rituale* (KBo 29; Berlin: Gebr. Mann, 1983); H. OTTEN and V. SOUCEK, *Ein althethitisches Ritual für das Königspaar* (StBoT 8; Wiesbaden: Harrassowitz, 1969); M. POPKO, "Die hethitischen Ritualtexte: Probleme der Bearbeitung," in *Ägypten, Vorderasien, Turfan: Probleme der Edition und Bearbeitung altorientalischer Handschriften* (ed. H. Klengel and W. Sundermann; Berlin: Akademie, 1991), 82–84; IDEM, "Neue Fragmente der hurritischen SAL.ŠU.GI-Rituale," *AoF* 16 (1989): 84–88; J. PRINGLE, "Hittite Birth Rituals," in *Images of Women in Antiquity* (ed. A. Cameron and A. Kuhrt; Detroit: Wayne State University Press, 1983), 128–41; M. SALVINI and I. WEGNER, *Die Rituale des AZU-Priesters* (2 vols.; CHSTB 2; Rome: Multigrafica Editrice, 1986); D. SCHWEMER, *Akkadische Rituale aus Ḫattuša* (Heidelberg: Universitätsverlag C. Winter, 1998); G. SZABÓ, *Ein hethitisches Entsühnungsritual für das Königspaar Tuthaliia und Nikalmati* (TH 1; Heidelberg: Carl Winter, 1971); A. ÜNAL, *The Hittite Ritual of Ḫantitaššu from the City of Ḫurma against Troublesome Years* (Ankara: Turkish Historical Society Printing House, 1996); G. WILHELM, *Ein Ritual des AZU-Priesters* (CHSTB, Ergänzungsheft 1; Rome: Bonsignori Editore, 1995); D. YOSHIDA, "Ein hethitisches Ritual gegen Behexung (KUB XXIV 12) und der Gott Zilipuri/Zalipura," in *Essays on Ancient Anatolian and Syrian Studies in the 2nd and 1st Millennium B.C.* (ed. H. I. H. Prince Takahito Mikasa; BMECCJ 4; Wiesbaden:

Harrassowitz, 1991), 45–61. **Translations:** *ANET* 347–51, 55–58; *COS* 1.65: 164–65, 1.68: 168–71. **Bibliography:** B. J. COLLINS, "The Puppy in Hittite Ritual," *JCS* 42 (1990): 211–26; G. FRANTZ-SZABÓ, "Hittite Witchcraft, Magic, and Divination," *CANE* 3:2007–19; H. G. GÜTERBOCK, "An Initiation Rite for a Hittite Prince," in *American Oriental Society, Middle West Branch, Semi-centennial Volume: A Collection of Original Essays* (ed. D. Sinor; Asian Studies Research Institute, Oriental Series 3; Bloomington: Indiana University Press, 1969), 99–103; V. HAAS and G. WILHELM, *Hurritische and luwische Riten aus Kizzuwatna* (AOAT 3; Neukirchen-Vluyn: Neukirchener Verlag, 1974); A. ÜNAL, "Ritual Purity versus Physical Impurity in Hittite Anatolia: Public Health and Structures for Sanitation according to Cuneiform Texts and Archaeological Remains," in *Essays on Anatolian Archaeology* (ed. H. I. H. Prince Takahito Mikasa; BMECCJ 7; Wiesbaden: Otto Harrassowitz, 1993), 119–39; M. WEINFELD, "Traces of Hittite Cult in Shiloh, Bethel, and in Jerusalem," in *Religionsgeschichtliche Beziehungen zwischen Kleinasien, Nordsyrien, und dem Alten Testament* (ed. Janowski, Koch, and Wilhelm), 455–72; D. P. WRIGHT, "Analogy in Biblical and Hittite Ritual," in *Religionsgeschichtliche Beziehungen zwischen Kleinasien, Nordsyrien, und dem Alten Testament* (ed. Janowski, Koch, and Wilhelm), 473–508.

5.8.4. Ugaritic Apotropaic, Prophylactic, and Productive Rituals

Ugaritic Historiolae. Several Ugaritic ritual texts combine myth and rite in a genre that classical scholars refer to as historiola, a short mythological story that prefigures the desired results of magical action. For instance, one of the texts (*KTU* 1.114) narrates a drinking binge by the god El and his subsequent need to remedy his hangover. A line at the end of the myth introduces its ritual: "What is to be put on his [the drunken man's] forehead? Hairs of a dog. And he is to drink the head of the PQQ and its shoot mixed together with fresh olive oil." The ritual was obviously the treatment for a hangover. The myth was recited prior to the ritual in order to symbolically unleash the story's healing power. Other Ugaritic historiolae attempted to heal sick children (*KTU* 1.124) and to drive snakes from the land (*KTU* 1.100; 1.107). In one of these texts (*KTU* 1.124), Ditanu, the divine eponymous ancestor of the royal house of Ugarit, provided the ritual directions (see Brown). This feature should be compared to the similar roles played by the gods Enki/Ea and Marduk in the Mesopotamian incantation prescriptions.

As we shall see, historiolae were also common in the Egyptian funerary rites, where creation myths were recited because their creative power was believed to embody a desired ritual effect: resuscitation of the dead. For more on these Egyptian traditions, see the mortuary texts in 5.9.1 and the Egyptian myths in 10.2.

Text and translation: PARDEE, *Ritual and Cult at Ugarit*, 167–91. **Translations:** *COS* 1.94: 295–98; 1.97: 302–5; WYATT, *Religious Texts from Ugarit*, 378–87 (*KTU* 1.100), 391–95 (*KTU* 1.107), 404–13 (*KTU* 1.114), 423–25 (*KTU* 1.124). **Bibliography:** M. L. BROWN, "Was There a West Semitic Asklepios?" *UF* 30 (1998): 133–54; G. DEL OLMO LETE, *Canaanite Religion*, 359–73, 387–88; M. DIETRICH and O. LORETZ, "Die Bannung von Schlangengift (*KTU* 1.100 und *KTU* 1.107: 7b–13a, 19b–20), *UF* 12 (1980): 153–70; IDEM, "KTU 1.114: Ein 'Palimpsest.'" *UF* 25 (1993): 133–36; D. FRANKFURTER, "Narrating Power: The Theory and Practice of the Magical Historiola in Ritual Spells," in *Ancient Magic and Ritual Power* (ed. M. Meyer and P. Mirecki; Religions in the Greco-Roman World 129; Leiden: Brill, 1995), 457–76; B. A. LEVINE and J.-M. DE TARRAGON, "'Shapshu Cries Out in Heaven': Dealing with Snake-Bites at Ugarit (*KTU* 1.100, 1.107)," *RB* 95 (1988): 481–518; S. L. SANDERS, "A Historiography of Demons: Preterit-Thema, Para-myth, and Historiola in the Morphology of Genres," in *Proceedings of the XLV Rencontre assyriologique internationale: History and Historiography in the Cuneiform World* (ed. Tz. Abusch et al.; 2 vols.; Bethesda, Md.: CDL Press, 2001), 1:429–40; W. G. E. WATSON, "Comments on *KTU* 1.114: 29′–31′," *AO* 8 (1990): 265–67.

Other Ugaritic Incantations. For lack of use or owing to accidents of preservation, ritual incantations are poorly attested in the Ugaritic evidence. Our best prescriptive exemplars are poetic texts that address the threats posed by venomous snakes, scorpions, sorcerers, and the "evil eye" (see RS 92.2014; *KTU* 1.96). Other incantations address medical problems, such as male impotence (*KTU* 1.169 [= RIH 78/20]). The best preserved text is RS 92.2014, an incantation against snakes and scorpions. It includes words for warding off the creatures as well as an apotropaic incantation against would-be sorcerers who might instigate an attack from the animals. According to its colophon, this text was prepared for the benefit of a certain 'Urtēnu. Hence, this text is not a model copy but rather one destined for use in a specific ritual context.

Texts and translations: PARDEE, *Ritual and Cult at Ugarit,* 157–66; M. YON and D. ARNAUD, *Études ougaritiques* (Ras Shamra–Ougarit 14; Paris: Éditions Recherche sur les Civilisations, 2001), no. 52 [RS 92.2014]. ***Translations:*** *COS* 1.96: 301–2; 1.100: 327–28; WYATT, *Religious Texts from Ugarit,* 375–77 (*KTU* 1.96), 442–49 (*KTU* 1.169). ***Bibliography:*** Y. AVISHUR, "The Ghost-Expelling Incantation from Ugarit," *UF* 13 (1981): 13–25; A. CAQUOT, "Une nouvelle interprétation de la tablette ougaritique de Ras Ibn Hani 78/20," *Or* 53 (1984): 163–76; J. C. DE MOOR, "An Incantation against Evil Spirits (Ras Ibn Hani 78/20)," *UF* 12 (1980): 429–32; DEL OLMO LETE, *Canaanite Religion,* 373–86; D. E. FLEMING, "The Voice of the Incantation Priest (RIH 78/20)," *UF* 23 (1991): 141–54; E. LIPINSKI, "Ancient Types of Wisdom Literature in Biblical Narrative," in *Sepher Yiṣḥaq Arieh Seeligmann* (ed. Y. Zakovits and A. Rofé; Jerusalem: Rubenstein, 1983), 39–55; O. LORETZ and P. XELLA, "Beschwörungen und Krankenheilung in RIH 78/20," *Materiali lessicali ed epigrafici* 1 (1982): 37–46; W. G. E. WATSON, "Imagery in a Ugaritic Incantation," *UF* 24 (1992): 367–68.

5.9. Ritual and Death: Funerary Cults and Cults of the Dead

Whenever the trauma of human death occurs, rituals are observed to address the death itself (the funerary cult) and sometimes to serve the ongoing needs of the deceased (the cult of the dead). Both types of rites were observed in the ancient Near East, but ancient Egypt produced our largest corpus of mortuary texts. This was a natural outcome of the unique properties of Egyptian theology. Although other cultures in the Near East believed in the shadowy existence of the dead and even allowed in unique circumstances for the divinization of kings who joined the ranks of the gods, Egyptian theology took this a step further by allowing for a double passage that took one not only from life to death but also from death to a blessed immortality. This passage into immortality was accomplished through rituals, which were performed by the dead person on his or her own behalf and by the living on behalf of the deceased. For the most part, it seems that Israelite beliefs about the afterlife were quite different from those in Egypt, reflecting instead the theological notions prominent in other Near Eastern cultures. There is some evidence, however, particularly in the latest portions of the Hebrew Bible, that the idea of a dark and shadowy existence for the dead was gradually being replaced with concepts that were closer to the Egyptian viewpoint.

5.9.1. Egyptian Funerary Cults and Cults of the Dead

The Mummification Ritual. Prescriptions for this rite are preserved in two very late papyri, P.Boulaq 3 and P.Louvre 5.158. It is generally agreed that these attest to earlier ritual practices. The purpose of mummification was to preserve the body's elements so that they could be ritually reassembled for the afterlife. The primary methods for reanimating the body included the Opening of the Mouth rite (see below) and a series of funerary rituals that were performed by priests and by the deceased after burial (see Pyramid Texts, Coffin Texts, and Book of the Dead). The mythical prototype for this reanimation was the Osiris myth, in which the god Osiris was killed and dismembered by Seth, only to be reassembled later by his wife and sister, Isis (see 10.2). Mummification was already being practiced during the Predynastic period and the Old Kingdom, but the techniques of the embalmers were perfected during the New Kingdom. The rites were observed as late as the Roman and Byzantine periods.

The instructional manuals for the mummification rite are organized into chapters, each beginning with the words "And after doing that . . ." None of the manuscripts is complete. The text as we have it begins with the body already prepared by the removal of the viscera and by desiccation of the body and organs through a naturally occurring salt called natron. According to Herodotus, desiccation of the body required a total of about seventy days. At this stage, the head and body were anointed, the internal organs were placed in canopic jars, and then the body was wrapped in linen sheets and bandages. The embalmment priest— wearing the mask of Anubis, patron deity of embalming—recited various incantations at each stage in the process. One of these incantations clearly expresses the objectives of the rite: "So that you may unite with Osiris in the Great Shrine."

Text and translation: S. SAUNERON, *Rituel de l'embaumement: Pap. Boulaq III, Pap. Louvre 5.158* (Cairo: Imprimerie Nationale, 1952). *Translation: TUAT* 2:405–30 (P.Boulaq 3). *Bibliography:* S. D'AURIA, P. LACOVARA, and C. H. ROEHRIG, *Mummies and Magic: The Funerary Arts of Ancient Egypt* (Boston: Museum of Fine Arts, 1988); GOYON, *Rituels funéraires de l'ancienne Égypte;* J. E. HARRIS and E. WENTE, *An X-ray Atlas of the Royal Mummies* (Chicago: University of Chicago Press, 1980); F. JANOT, "Les instruments et la pratique des prêtres-embaumeurs," *BIFAO* 96 (1996): 245–63; J. F. QUACK, "Zwei

Handbücher der Mumifizierung im Balsamierungsritual des Apisstieres," *Enchoria* 22 (1995): 123–29; L. Troy, "Creating a God: The Mummification Ritual," *Bulletin of the Australian Centre for Egyptology* 4 (1993): 55–81; J. A. Wilson, "Funeral Services of the Egyptian Old Kingdom," *JNES* 3 (1944): 201–18.

The Egyptian Mouth-Opening Ritual for the Dead. Our demotic copies of this text are very late (first century C.E.) but probably attest to earlier developments. The texts preserve an abridged version of the Egyptian rite used to animate divine statues (see 5.1), adapted for the purpose of ritually reviving deceased Egyptians. Most of the ritual actions included in the earlier divine-statue rite (the fashioning of the statue, sacrifices, the use of the *psš-kf* implement, etc.) have been elimated, so that the late version of the ritual depends almost solely on the uttering of its incantations. Both the living and the dead employed the liturgy. The living recited it for their deceased relatives during the burial service, and the dead had copies of the text buried with them so that they might recite it during their trek to a blessed hereafter. The deity Osiris, with whom the deceased closely identified in the rites, figures more prominently in these demotic exemplars than in the earlier versions of the mouth-opening rites for divine statues.

Texts and translations: M. Smith, "An Abbreviated Version of the Book of Opening the Mouth for Breathing (Bodl. MS Egypt. c.9(P) + P.Louvre E 10605)," *Enchoria* 15 (1987): 61–91; 16 (1988): 55–76; idem, *The Liturgy of Opening the Mouth for Breathing* (Oxford: Griffith Institute, Ashmolean Museum, 1993). **Bibliography:** J. Assmann, "Death and Initiation in the Funerary Religion of Ancient Egypt," in *Religion and Philosophy in Ancient Egypt* (ed. W. K. Simpson; Yale Egyptology Series 3; New Haven: Yale University Press, 1989), 135–59; idem, "Egyptian Mortuary Liturgies," in *Studies in Egyptology Presented to Miriam Lichtheim* (ed. S. I. Groll; 2 vols.; Jerusalem: Magnes Press, 1990), 1:1–45; idem, *Tod und Jenseits im Alten Ägypten* (Munich: Beck, 2001); Goyon, *Rituels funéraires de l'ancienne Égypte;* J. A. Wilson, "Funeral Services of the Egyptian Old Kingdom," *JNES* 3 (1944): 201–18.

The Pyramid Texts, Coffin Texts, and Book of the Dead. In the Egyptian way of thinking, passage from death to a blessed afterlife depended on rituals that served three primary functions: to reanimate the body, to aver one's moral suitability for the afterlife, and to repel any impediments—demonic or divine—that might threaten the deceased's transition into the hereafter. Funerary rituals of this sort were performed not only by the living for the dead (as in mummification) but also as ritual duties undertaken by the deceased for themselves. For instance, while the living priest performed the "mouth opening" ritual before the mummy, the deceased could recite an appropriate incantation: "My mouth is opened by Ptah, My mouth's bonds are loosed by my city-god."

Beginning with the Old Kingdom, the Egyptians began to collect the incantations and rituals needed by the dead and to inscribe them on the passages and chambers of the royal pyramids (the Pyramid Texts, PT). This funerary tradition eventually developed into the Coffin Texts (CT) of the Middle Kingdom before culminating during the New Kingdom as the Book of the Dead (BD), a more democratic genre that was employed by a wider number of Egyptians. In preparation for their death, wealthy Egyptians commissioned scribes to prepare papyrus copies of the Book of the Dead with their name inserted at the appropriate junctures of its rituals.

The funerary tradition in PT, CT, and BD included numerous rites, hymns, and incantations that originated separately but were brought together early in Egyptian history. The development of this tradition included both textual and artistic dimensions. On the textual side, it is easy to discern changes in the number of spells included in the tradition as it passed from the Old Kingdom to the Late period. Although no single text included all of the spells, the PT drew from a corpus of about 750 spells, the CT from a total of about 1,200, and the later BD from a stock of about 200 spells. Scholars refer to these spells by their number (e.g., PT 150; CT 150; BD 150). The texts were continually revised, and various rubrics and titles were added as the tradition increasingly took on a more fixed order.

On the artistic side, vignettes depicting the rituals were gradually added in the papyrus copies of the BD. The vignettes and their associated rites and incantations took on a more-or-less canonical order by the Saite period (724–712 B.C.E.). To judge from our BD manuscripts, the most popular spell-vignette combination appears to have been the "Judgment of the Dead" (BD 125), which depicts the heart of a deceased man being weighed in the balance opposite the justice and order of *ma'at* (see 2.2). In the texts that accompany this scene, the deceased identifies himself with the god Osiris, utters secret names, and denies his sins in what amounts to a negative confession (although he also asks that the gods overlook his minor faults). It is clear from these late versions of the BD, and even in earlier ones, that the scribes were sometimes uncertain about the interpretation and significance of the archaic texts they were copying. This outcome was of little functional consequence, however, because the intended readers were the deceased, who could apparently manage the difficult archaic script better than the scribes.

The reader may wish to note that some of the rites and spells in the PT, the CT and the BD originated as funerary liturgies that were performed not by the dead but by priests on their behalf. These portions of the texts are visible in their interpersonal form, which addresses the deceased in the second person ("May you . . .") rather than in the first-person language of the deceased ("I am . . ."). For publication and discussion of these funerary liturgies, see Assmann 2002. Also noteworthy is a corpus of texts related to the PT, the CT, and the BD that modern scholars refer to as the Books of the Afterlife. These texts provided additional rites for the dead to use as well as topographies that could guide the deceased through the netherworld (Hornung 1997; see selections in Clagett).

We are, naturally, skeptical that deceased Egyptians could actually carry out these rites. The Egyptians, however, believed that they did, and they believed that the dead, once revived, could receive the food and drink offerings that were so necessary for a blessed hereafter. As happened so often with Egyptian funerary literature, such important rites were inevitably employed for the benefit of living Egyptians (Pinch).

Texts and translations: J. ASSMANN, *Altägyptische Totenliturgien* (Heidelberg: Universi-tätsverlag C. Winter, 2002–); E. A. W. BUDGE, *The Book of the Dead: The Papyrus Ani in the British Museum, The Egyptian Text with Interlinear Transliteration and Translation* (London: British Museum, 1895); R. O. FAULKNER, *The Ancient Egyptian Pyramid Texts* (2 vols; Oxford: Clarendon, 1969); IDEM, *The Ancient Egyptian Coffin Texts* (3 vols.; Warminster, England: Aris & Phillips, 1973–1978); É. NAVILLE, *Das aegyptische Todtenbuch der XVIII. bis XX. Dynastie aus verschiedenen Urkunden zusammengestelt und herausgegeben* (3 vols; Berlin: A. Asher, 1886). *Translations: ANET* 3–4, 7–8, 9–12, 32–36; ALLEN, *The Book of the Dead, or Going Forth by Day; COS* 1.2–8, 1.11–12, 1.17–21, 2.8–12; M. CLAGETT, *Ancient Egyptian Science: A Source Book* (3 vols. in 4; Philadelphia: American Philosophical Society, 1989–1999), vol. 1, part 2, pp. 407–546 (selections); R. O. FAULKNER, *The Ancient Egyptian Book of the Dead* (New York: Macmillan, 1985); E. HORNUNG, *Das Totenbuch der Ägypter: Eingeleitet, übersetzt, und erläutert* (Zürich: Artemis, 1979); *LAE* 245–77, 289–98 (partial). *Bibliography:* ALLEN, *The Book of the Dead, or Going Forth by Day;* J. ASSMANN, *Tod und Jenseits im alten Ägypten* (Munich: C. Beck, 2001); J. C. DARNELL, *The Enigmatic Netherworld Books of the Solar-Osirian Unity: Cryptographic Compositions in the Tombs of Tutankhamun, Ramesses VI, and Ramesses IX* (OBO 198; Freiburg, Switz.: Academic Press, 2004); E. HORNUNG, *The Ancient Egyptian Books of the Afterlife* (Ithaca: Cornell University Press, 1997); G. MILDE, "'Going Out into the Day': Ancient Egyptian Beliefs and Practices concerning Death," in *Hidden Features: Death and Immortality in Ancient Egypt, Anatolia, the Classical, Biblical, and Arabic-Islamic World* (ed. J. M. Bremer, T. P. J. van den Hout, and R. Peters; Amsterdam: University Press, 1994), 15–35; PINCH, *Magic in Ancient Egypt,* 22–23, 34–35; R. K. RITNER, *The Mechanics of Ancient Egyptian Ritual Practice* (SAOC 54; Chicago: University of Chicago Press, 1993); S. WIEBACH, *Phänomenologie der Bewegungs-abläufe im Jenseitskonzept der Unterweltbücher Amduat und Pfortenbuch und der litur-gischen "Sonnenlitanei"* (AAT 55; Wiesbaden: Harrassowitz, 2003).

5.9.2. Mesopotamian Funerary Cults and Cults of the Dead

The Mesopotamian Kispum. Apart from a few ritual texts, most of what we know about Mesopotamia's cult of the dead has been pieced together from various archaeological and archival sources, mainly letters and administrative records. Early sources attest that it was common practice to make offerings at the graves of ancestors in a ceremony known as the KISEGA/*kispum*, which included pouring water over the grave, food offerings, and prayers invoking the name of the dead (see Postgate; cf. Perlov). Inheritance documents from Nippur show that this ritual duty normally fell to the heir of the deceased, a custom that was related, no doubt, to the fact that the dead were often buried in the floor of the family home. Terracotta pipes designed to channel libations into graves have been found at the royal cemetery of Ur (third millenium B.C.E.; Postgate), demon-strating that the ancestor cult was alive and well at all levels of society during this early period.

Our primary textual evidence for the *kispum* comes from the Old Babylo-nian period, mainly from Akkadian texts unearthed at Mari. The most important text is M.12803 (see Birot; Durand and Guichard), a fragmentary ritual prescrip-tion associated with a visit to Mari from King Šamši-Adad, whose son Yasmah-

Addu ruled Mari before being ousted by Zimri-Lim (ca. 1775 B.C.E.). The text prescribes a *kispum* at the beginning of the month of Adar (i.e., at the new moon), to be observed in the city of Mari and its environs. The first sacrifices were to be offered to the god Šamaš, followed by *kispum* sacrifices in the "hall of thrones" before the statutes of Sargon and Naram-Sin (two kings who had ruled Akkad centuries earlier). These were followed by still other *kispum* sacrifices that were directed toward the deceased Amorite tribal ancestors of Šamši-Adad (for a related text, see the Genealogy of Hammurabi's Dynasty in 11.4). The reference to the "hall of thrones" in this text is not entirely understood. It may refer to the place where divine statues resided at the temple of Šamaš, or, perhaps more likely, it was the area where statues of royal ancestor figures were kept (note that the large ceremonial hall at Mari, room 65, has yielded a statue of Ištup-ilum, a king at Mari during the twenty-first century). Regardless, it is clear that Sargon and Naram-Sin were viewed here as divinized kings, and it is equally clear that these famous kings had no real connections with the dynasty of Šamši-Adad. The adoption of Sargon and Naram-Sin into Šamši-Adad's ancestral *kispum* originated from a desire to lend legitimacy and prestige to his ruling dynasty.

More about the *kispum* can be gleaned from archival sources at Mari. The city's administrators kept meticulous records of foodstuffs and supplies that moved in and out of the palace inventories. Among these are dated tallies of food disbursements for royal meals, food that was sometimes destined for the *kispum*. From this evidence, it becomes clear that the *kispum* was understood as a festival meal shared with the ghosts (*eṭemmū*) of the dynasty's ancestors at the full moon and the new moon (Malamat). It has been suggested that the term *kispum* derives from the verb *kasapu*, "to break," in the sense of breaking bread (see Durand and Guichard). Although much of our evidence is connected with the *kispum* as observed by royalty, other texts, most notably an Old Babylonian libation prayer (Wilcke), confirm that the *kispum* reflects beliefs and practices of private individuals (see Kraus; Kutscher and Wilcke). For a recent and very nice overview of the *kispum* at Mari, see Jacquet. Much later texts, such as the one published by Zimmern, show that the *kispum* was observed down into the first millennium.

Texts and translations: M. BIROT, "Fragment d'un rituel de mari relatif au *kispum*," in *Death in Mesopotamia* (ed. Alster), 139–50; DURAND and GUICHARD, "Les rituels de Mari," 63–71; D. A. FOXVOG, "Funerary Furnishings in an Early Sumerian Text from Adab," in *Death in Mesopotamia* (ed. Alster), 67–75; F. R. KRAUS, *Briefe aus dem British Museum (CT 43 und 44)* (AbB 1; Leiden: Brill, 1964), no. 106; R. KUTSCHER and C. WILCKE, "Eine Ziegel-Inschrift des Königs Takil-ilissu von Malgium," *ZA* 68 (1978): 95–128; B. PERLOV, "The Families of the Ensí's Urbau and Gudea and Their Funerary Cult," in *Death in Mesopotamia* (ed. Alster), 77–81; C. WILCKE, "Ein Gebet an den Mondgott von 3. IV. des Jahres Ammiditana 22," pp. 49–54 in "Nachlese zu A. Poebels, 'Babylonian Legal and Business Documents from the Time of the First Dynasty of Babylon Chiefly from Nippur' (*BE* 6/2)," *ZA* 73 (1983): 48–66; H. ZIMMERN, *Beiträge zur Kenntnis der babylonischen Religion* (Leipzig: Hinrichs, 1901), 164–67. **Bibliography:** A. ARCHI, "The Cult of the Ancestors and the Tutelary God at Ebla," in *Fucus: A Semitic/ Afrasian Gathering in Remembrance of Albert Ehrman* (ed. Y. L. Arbeitman; Philadelphia:

Benjamins, 1988), 103–12; J. BAUER, "Zum Totenkult im altsumerischen Lagasch," in *Vorträge* (ed. W. Voigt; 3 vols.; ZDMGSup 1; Wiesbaden: F. Steiner, 1969): 1:107–14; M. BAYLISS, "The Cult of the Dead in Assyria and Babylonia," *Iraq* 35 (1973): 115–25; J. BOTTÉRO, "Les inscriptions cunéiformes funéraires," in *La mort, les morts dans les sociétés anciennes* (ed. J.-P. Vernant; Paris: Maison des Sciences de l'Homme, 1982), 388–89; W. W. HALLO, "Disturbing the Dead," in *Minḥah le-Naḥum: Biblical and Other Studies Presented to Nahum M. Sarna in Honour of His 70th Birthday* (ed. M. Brettler and M. Fishbane; Sheffield, England: JSOT Press, 1993), 183–92; IDEM, "Royal Ancestor Worship in the Biblical World," in *"Shaʿarei Talmon": Studies in the Bible, Qumran, and the Ancient Near East Presented to Shemaryahu Talmon* (ed. M. Fishbane et al.; Winona Lake, Ind.: Eisenbrauns, 1992), 381–401; A. JACQUET, "Lugal-meš et malikum: Nouvel examen du kispum à Mari," in *Recueil d'études à la mémoire d'André Parrot* (ed. D. Charpin and J.-M. Durand; FM 6; Mémoires de N.A.B.U. 7: Paris: SEPOA, 2002), 51–69; A. MALAMAT, *Mari and the Early Israelite Experience* (Schweich Lectures of the British Academy 1984; Oxford: British Academy, 1989), 20–21, 24–25, 96–107; J. N. POSTGATE, *Early Mesopotamia: Society and Economy at the Dawn of History* (rev. ed.; London: Routledge, 1994), 99–101; SCHMIDT, *Israel's Beneficent Dead*, 27–46, 122–31; J. A. SCURLOCK, "Death and the Afterlife in Ancient Mesopotamian Thought," *CANE* 3:1883–93; Å. W. SJÖBERG, "Beiträge zum sumerischen Wörterbuch," in *Studies in honor of Benno Landsberger* (AS 16; Chicago: University of Chicago, 1965), 63–70; K. VAN DER TOORN, "Ilib and the 'God of the Father,'" *UF* 25 (1993): 379–87; IDEM, Gods and Ancestors in Emar and Nuzi," *ZA* 84 (1994): 38–59; A. TSUKIMOTO, *Untersuchungen zur Totenpflege (kispum) im alten Mesopotamien* (AOAT 216; Kevelaer, Germany: Butzon & Bercker, 1985).

5.9.3. Hittite Funerary Cults and Cults of the Dead

The Hittite Royal Funerary Ritual (CTH 450). Our knowledge of Hittite funerary beliefs and practices is limited mainly to the upper classes of Hittite society and, more specifically, to the royal couple, whose life was inextricably linked with the nation's health and identity. The death of the king or queen was immediately followed by a fourteen-day rite of passage entitled "When a great sin befalls Ḥattuša and the king or queen becomes a god" (see Otten), a title that reveals both the perceived causes of royal death and also the destiny of the deceased king or queen. Our copies of the ritual are from the fourteenth and thirteenth centuries, but the language reflects a composition no later than the Middle Hittite period (ca. 1500–1380) and perhaps as early as the Old Hittite period (ca. 1750–1500). The fragmentary and partial textual evidence relates mainly to days 1–2, 4, 7–9, and 12–13 of the ritual. The texts relate a complex and expensive ceremony that involved many people, the sacrifice of over one hundred animals, and large quantities of food and ritual objects. As was the case with many Hittite rites, this one was recorded on a series of tablets that originally included a ritual series, a liturgical series (with words and songs), a ration list, and a summary outline text.

In the initial phase of the rite, the body lay in state as sacrifices and offerings were made. The first of these sacrifices, an ox, was immediately identified with the king in an incantation: "As you have become, let this one become likewise, and let your soul descend in this ox." The king's soul was satisfied with these sacrifices and libations. Then his body was burned and his bones were recovered and wrapped in cloth by women. It is not entirely clear whether the cremation was done on the first or third day of the ceremony, but it was apparently completed early in the ritual series. The remains of the king were then placed on a chair, and the succeeding king and royal family ate a meal with the deceased (day 4). An effigy of the king was then manufactured, which represented his presence in the remainder of the rite. Numerous ritual activities followed, but the common denominator throughout is that the effigy regularly received offerings of food and drink. By the ritual's conclusion, the king's body had been interred in the mortuary chamber (day 6), and the effigy was either burned (the Hittite method for transferring bodies and objects to the afterworld) or placed in the temple for use in the ongoing royal ancestor cult. For a more detailed summary of the Hittite royal funerary rites, see Haas. For related comments concerning royal cults of the dead in Israel, see the entry on Ugaritic text *KTU* 1.161 in 5.9.4.

Texts and translations: A. KASSIAN, A. KOROLËV, and A. SIDEL'TSEV, *Hittite Funerary Ritual: Šalliš waštaiš* (AOAT 288; Münster: Ugarit, 2002); H. OTTEN, *Hethitische Totenrituale* (Berlin: Akademie, 1958); IDEM, "Eine Lieferungsliste zum Totenritual der hethitischen Könige," *WO* 2 (1954–1959): 477–79; IDEM, "Zu den hethitischen Totenritualen," *OLZ* 59 (1962): 229–33. *Bibliography:* T. R. BRYCE, *Life and Society in the Hittite World* (Oxford: Oxford University Press, 2002), 176–86; L. CHRISTMANN-FRANCK, "Le rituel des funérailles royales hittites," *RHA* 29 (1971): 61–111; V. HAAS, "Death and the Afterlife in Hittite Thought," *CANE* 3:2021–30; J. D. HAWKINS, "Late Hittite Funerary Monuments," in *Death in Mesopotamia* (ed. Alster), 213–25; T. P. J. VAN DEN HOUT, "Death as a Privilege: The Hittite Royal Funerary Ritual," in *Hidden Futures* (ed. Bremer, van den Hout, and Peters), 37–75; M. POPKO, *Hethitische Rituale und Festbeschreibungen* (KUB 58; Berlin: Akademie, 1988), 151–57.

5.9.4. Ugaritic Funerary Cults and Cults of the Dead

From king to commoner, it appears that the people of Ugarit provided ritual offerings of food and drink to their dead ancestors. Textual evidence reveals that the king and the nation honored Ugarit's deceased rulers with regular sacrifices, and archaeologists have discovered pipes from ground level that pass down into tomb vaults below (Lewis 1989, 172). For related texts from Ugarit, see the Ugaritic king lists in 11.3.

A Funeral Liturgy for the King of Ugarit (KTU 1.161). This is the only text from Ugarit that explicitly reflects a funerary context. Its liturgy marked the passing of Ugarit's king, Niqmaddu III, and the accession of its next and last king, Ammurapi III, and his queen mother, Tarriyelli (see Pardee). The rite's Ugaritic title is *spr dbḥ ẓlm*, which probably translates as "document of the sacrificial liturgy of the shades." So far as we can tell, the rite inducted Niqmaddu into the underworld, where he joined the ranks of his divinized royal ancestors. During the ceremony, the assembly of deceased kings (called by the dynastic name Ditanu) and others from the netherworld (the Rephaim, perhaps dead kings or deceased heroes) were invited to attend the sacrificial event. Apart from the deified kings, the most prominent deity in the rite was the sun goddess Šapšu. Her role was to usher Niqmaddu into the underworld as she passed through it during the night. The heart of the rite was a sequence of seven t^c-sacrifices that marked Niqmaddu's seven-step descent into the underworld. These were followed by a *šlm* sacrifice (cf. the biblical *šlm*, "peace offering") and by a prayer for the welfare of the new king, his queen mother, and the city of Ugarit. This text is unique among Ugaritic rituals because it is the only exemplar that is both a sacrificial liturgy and a poetic text. Its poetic character is best explained by the Ugaritic proclivity to speak of the gods in poetic language, as we see in the epic myths of Ugarit (see Pardee).

In ancient Israel, those who canonized the Hebrew Bible generally frowned upon funerary rites of this sort (Lev 19:17–18; Deut 14:1; 18:9–14; 26:14; 1 Sam 28:3–25; 2 Kgs 23:24; Jer 16:5–9). The biblical injunctions against necromancy (Exod 22:18; Lev 20:27; Deut 18:11) and against sacrifices for the deceased, however, presume that cultic rites for the dead were relatively common in ancient Israel (Schmidt; van Uchelen). Royal funerary rites were certainly observed upon the king's death, as were ongoing cults for deceased kings (see 2 Chron 6:13–14; 21:12–19; Ezek 43:7b–9; Gleis; Mailberger; Niehr; Schmidt). In this regard, readers should note the nineteen tumuli (man-made mounds) that lie to the east of Jerusalem. These sites may mark where ancient Judeans gathered to lament the deaths of their kings between the tenth and seventh centuries B.C.E. (see Barkay). For related comments, see the entry on Hittite royal funerary rites in 5.9.3.

Texts and translations: P. BORDREUIL, *Une bibliothèque au sud de la ville: Les textes de la 34e campagne (1973)* (Ras Shamra–Ougarit 7; Paris: Éditions Recherche sur les Civilisations, 1991), no. 90; PARDEE, *Ritual and Cult at Ugarit*, 85–88. ***Translations:*** COS 1.105: 357–58; WYATT, *Religious Texts from Ugarit*, 430–41 (*KTU* 1.161). ***Bibliography:*** G. BARKAY, "Mounds of Mystery: Where the Kings of Judah Were Lamented," *BAR* 29, no. 3 (2003): 32–39, 66, 68; P. BORDREUIL and D. PARDEE, "Le rituel funéraire ougaritique RS 34.126," *Syria* 59 (1982): 121–28; M. DIETRICH and O. LORETZ, "Neue Studien zu den Ritualtexten aus Ugarit (II): Nr. 6—epigraphische und inhaltliche Probleme in KTU 1.161," *UF* 15 (1983): 17–24; M. GLEIS, *Die Bamah* (BZAW 251; Berlin: de Gruyter, 1997), 218–21; E. LIPIŃSKI, "Ditanu," in *Studies in the Bible and the Ancient Near East Presented to Samuel E. Loewenstamm on His Seventieth Birthday* (ed. Y. Avishur and J. Blau; Jerusalem: Rubenstein, 1978), 91–110; LEWIS, *Cults of the Dead in Ancient Israel and Ugarit*, 5–46; P. MAILBERGER, "*pāgar, pægær,*" *TWAT*, 6:508–14; D. BODI, "Les expressions פגרי מלכיהם dans Ez 43,7b–9 et פגרי גלוליכם dans Lev 26,30 à la lumière des termes akkadiens *pagû(m)/ pagrā'u(m)* et *maliku(m)* des textes de Mari," in *Lectio difficilior probabilior?—l'exégèse comme expérience de décloisonnement: Mélanges offerts á Françoise Smyth-Florentin* (ed. T. Römer; Heidelberg: Wissenschaftlicher Theol. Seminar, 1991), 87–101; H. NIEHR, "The Changed Status of the Dead in Yehud," in *Yahwism after the Exile: Perspectives on Israelite Religion in the Persian Era* (ed. R. Albertz and B. Becking; Assen: Van Gorcum, 2003), 136–55; W. T. PITARD, "The Ugaritic Funerary Text RS 34.126," *BASOR* 232 (1978): 65–75; SCHMIDT, *Israel's Beneficent Dead*, 71–93, 100–122; D. TSUMURA, "The Interpretation of the Ugaritic Funerary Text KTU 1.161" in *Official Cult and Popular Religion in the Ancient*

Near East (Heidelberg: Universitätsverlag C. Winter, 1993), 40–55; IDEM, "Kings and Cults in Ancient Ugarit," in *Priests and Officials in the Ancient Near East* (Heidelberg: Universitätsverlag C. Winter, 1999), 215–38; N. VAN UCHELEN, "Death and the After-life in the Hebrew Bible of Ancient Israel," in *Hidden Futures* (ed. Bremer, van den Hout, and Peters), 77–90.

Memorial Inscriptions to Dagan (KTU 6.13, 6.14). Ugarit has yielded two stone stelae that record *pgr* sacrifices devoted to the god Dagan, one by the queen mother (Tarriyelli in *KTU* 6.13) and another by a local governor (Uzzinu in *KTU* 6.14). Interpretations of these texts are based largely on the somewhat earlier *pgr* sacrifices mentioned in the Mari sources (eighteenth century B.C.E.), in spite of the four centuries that separate Mari from Ugarit. At Mari, the rite's purpose was to share a ritual meal with the god and with living and deceased members of the royal line. If the same thing was going on at Ugarit—and we have no reason to doubt this—then these short texts provide good evidence for Ugarit's cult of the royal dead. From a comparative standpoint, the Ugaritic *pgr* stelae bring to mind the comments of Absalom in 2 Sam 18:18: "Now Absalom in his lifetime had taken and set up for himself a pillar that is in the King's Valley, for he said, 'I have no son to keep my name in remembrance'; he called the pillar by his own name. It is called Absalom's Monument to this day."

Text and translation: PARDEE, *Ritual and Cult at Ugarit*, 123–25. ***Bibliography:*** LEWIS, *Cults of the Dead in Ancient Israel and Ugarit*, 5–46, 53–79; SCHMIDT, *Israel's Beneficent Dead*, 49–53.

The marzeaḥ ***Texts from Ugarit.*** We possess eight texts from Ugarit that mention an institution known as the *marzeaḥ*. Four of these are Akkadian texts (RS 14.16; 15.70; 15.88; 18.01), and the remaining four were written in Ugaritic (*KTU* 1.21; 1.114; 3.9; 4.642). Although only one of these texts is a ritual text proper (*KTU* 1.114; see above, 5.8.4), some scholars believe that these texts reflect a funerary rite akin to the Mesopotamian *kispu*, in which the living shared a communal meal with their deceased relatives (see Pope). This conclusion is based mainly on three points: the royal funerary cult was prominent at Ugarit; one of the *marzeaḥ* texts reflects a ritual meal with the dead (RS 1.21); and Jer 16:5 mentions a "*marzeaḥ* house" in connection with Israelite funeral rites. From both Ugarit and Israel, however, there is good evidence that the *marzeaḥ* was not always associated with funerals. Most of the Ugaritic texts that mention the *marzeaḥ* are archival records of legal transactions in which one of the legal parties was a *marzeaḥ* association (all but *KTU* 1.21 and 1.114). Several such associations or societies existed, each in a different location or town and each with its own patron deity. The texts associate these *marzeaḥ* societies with vineyard ownership (*KTU* 4.642; RS 18.01) and with heavy drinking (*KTU* 1.114). A similar portrait appears in Amos 6:7, where the *marzeaḥ* (here *mirzaḥ*) is connected with drinking, eating, and festive living. Consequently, it does not appear that the *marzeaḥ* had any necessary connections with funerary rites. Rather, the *marzeaḥ* was a legal association of men who, among other things, drank and banqueted together. The connection of the term *marzeaḥ* with funerary rites was a consequence of the common denominator shared by the *marzeaḥ* meetings and funerals: both included the drinking of alcoholic beverages.

Texts and translations: *KTU* 1.21; 1.114; 3.9; 4.642; J. NOUGAYROL, *Textes accadiens et hourites des archives est, ouest, et centrales* (vol. 3 of *Le palais royal d'Ugarit;* ed. C. F. A. Schaeffer; Mission de Ras Shamra 6; Paris: Imprimerie Nationale, 1955–), 88, pl. 20 (RS 15.88); 130, pl. 17 (RS 15.70); IDEM, *Textes accadiens des archives sud* (vol. 4 of *Le palais royal d'Ugarit;* ed. C. F. A. Schaeffer; Mission de Ras Shamra 9; Paris: Imprimerie Nationale, 1955–), 230, pl. 77 (RS 18.01); PARDEE, *Ritual and Cult at Ugarit,* 167–70, 217–20 (*KTU* 1.114; 3.9); C. VIROLLEAUD, "Six textes de Ras Shamra provenant de la XIVe campagne (1950)," *Syria* 28 (1951): 163–79 (RS 14.16). **Translation:** WYATT, *Religious Texts from Ugarit,* 404–13 (*KTU* 1.114). **Bibliography:** D. B. BRYAN, "Texts Relating to the *marzeaḥ:* A Study of an Ancient Semitic Institution" (PhD diss., Johns Hopkins University, 1973); J. C. GREENFIELD, "The marzeaḥ as a Social Institution," in *Wirtschaft und Gesellschaft im alten Vorderasien* (ed. J. Harmatta and G. Komoróczy; Budapest: Akadémiai Kiadó, 1976), 451–55; T. J. LEWIS, *Cults of the Dead in Ancient Israel and Ugarit* (HSM 39; Cambridge: Harvard University Press, 1989), 80–94; J. L. MCLAUGHLIN, "The marzeah at Ugarit: A Textual and Contextual Study," *UF* 23 (1992): 265–81; D. PARDEE, "Marziḫu, kispu, and the Ugaritic Funerary Cult: A Minimalist View," in *Ugarit, Religion and Culture: Proceedings of the International Colloquium on Ugarit, Religion and Culture, Edinburgh, July 1994—Essays Presented in Honour of Professor John C. L. Gibson* (Münster: Ugarit, 1996), 273–87; M. H. POPE, "The Cult of the Dead at Ugarit," in *Ugarit in Retrospect* (ed. G. D. Young; Winona Lake, Ind.: Eisenbrauns, 1981); IDEM, "A Divine Banquet at Ugarit," in *The Use of the Old Testament in the New and Other Essays: Studies in Honor of W. F. Stinespring* (ed. J. M. Efird; Durham, N.C.: Duke University Press, 1972), 170–203; SCHMIDT, *Israel's Beneficent Dead,* 62–66.

A Royal Libation Ritual for the Gods and the Rephaim (**KTU 1.108**). This text invites a list of deities to attend a libation ritual provided by the king on their behalf. Although several deities are mentioned, the beginning and the end of the rite focus on Rapi'u, the eponymous leader of the underworld dead, collectively known as the Rephaim. The rite's purpose was to secure the Rephaim as envoys to the god Baal, from whom they would request a transfer of divine power to the king. It is possible, in light of the drinking motif, that this text is related in some way to the *marzeaḥ* institution (see previous entry), but almost as likely is that it has some relationship to Ugarit's *kispum*-like ancestral cult. The Rephaim mentioned in this and other Ugaritic texts are in some way related to the netherworld Rephaim that sometimes appear in the Hebrew Bible (Isa 14:9; 26:14–19; Ps 88:10 [MT 88:11]; Prov 2:18; 9:18; 21:16; Job 26:5; see Schmidt). In the Hebrew Bible, however, the term Rephaim was also a name given to the primeval inhabitants of Palestine (e.g., Deut 2:11, 20).

Text and translation: PARDEE, *Ritual and Cult at Ugarit,* 192–95. **Translation:** WYATT, *Religious Texts from Ugarit,* 395–98 (*KTU* 1.108). **Bibliography:** A. CAQUOT, "La tablette RS 24.252 et la question des Rephaïm ougaritiques," *Syria* 53 (1976): 295–304; DEL OLMO LETE, *Canaanite Religion,* 19, 184–92; M. DIETRICH and O. LORETZ, "Baal, RPU in *KTU* 1.108, 1.113 nach 1.17 VI 25–33," *UF* 12 (1980): 171–79; M. DIETRICH, O. LORETZ, and J. SANMARTÍN, " 'Der Neujahrs-psalm' RS 24.252 (= Ug. 5.S. 551–57, Nr. 2)," *UF* 7 (1975):

115–19; I. N. FORD, "The 'Living Rephaim' of Ugarit: Quick or Defunct?" *UF* 24 (1992): 73–101; B. A. LEVINE and J.-M. DE TARRAGON, "Dead Kings and Rephaim: The Patrons of the Ugaritic Dynasty," *JAOS* 104 (1984): 649–59; B. MARGULIS, "A Ugaritic Psalm (RS 24.252)," *JBL* 89 (1970): 292–304; S. B. PARKER, "The Feast of Rapi'u," *UF* 2 (1970): 243–49; SCHMIDT, *Israel's Beneficent Dead,* 267–73.

5.10. Other Texts

Circumcision in Egypt. Although Mesopotamians did not practice circumcision (note Ezek chs. 28, 31, 32), the Hebrew Bible and Near Eastern evidence reveal that the practice was widespread (cf. Jer 9:24–25). Two techniques were apparently used in the rite. In Egypt, a dorsal incision upon the foreskin liberated the glans penis, while in the West Semitic world the entire prepuce was removed (see Sasson). Bronze figurines from third-millennium Syria illustrate that the West Semitic practice was very old (Braidwood/Braidwood). The Egyptian word for "foreskin" is clearly a Semitic loanword, so it is possible that the Egyptians adapted the practice from their neighbors to the north. Nonetheless, the Egyptian practice is also old. Several Egyptian texts come into play here (see Jonckheere; Sasson). The two most important include the tomb inscription of Ankh-Mahor at Saqqarah and a stela found at Naga-ed-Der (both in *ANET*). In the first text, from the tomb of a physician, we find a picture of two young men undergoing circumcision (see Pritchard). One of them is being held fast by his fellow during the surgery. Its caption records the words of the officiating priest ("Hold on to him. Do not let him faint") as well as the response of his assistant ("I shall act to thy pleasure"). In the other picture, where the young man is not being restrained by anyone, we have the words of the circumcised youth ("Rub off what is there thoroughly") followed by the priest's response ("I shall make it heal"). In the second text from Naga-ed-Der, a young man records that he was circumcised along with 120 other youths. He claims that all of the surgeries turned out well.

Several comparative notes are in order. The Egyptian circumcision of 120 young men at one time is reminiscent of the mass circumcisions mentioned in Gen 17, Gen 34, and Josh 5. Also, one should note that Egyptian circumcision was apparently performed as rite of passage into manhood, and mainly on priests. This differs from the Hebrew rite, where the deed was performed on all males as infants (Lev 12:2–3).

Text and translation: F. JONCKHEERE, "La conception égyptienne du squelette," *Centaurus* 5 (1957): 323–38. ***Translations:*** ANET 326. ***Bibliography:*** R. J. BRAIDWOOD and L. S. BRAIDWOOD, *Excavations in the Plain of Antioch* (OIP 61; Chicago: University Press, 1960), 301, 240–46, pls. 56–64; R. G. HALL, "Circumcision," ABD 1:1025–31; J. B. PRITCHARD, ed., *The Ancient Near East in Pictures Relating to the Old Testament* (Princeton: University Press, 1954), 206; J. M. SASSON, "Circumcision in the Ancient Near East," *JBL* 85 (1966): 473–76; M. STRACMANS, "A propos d'un texte relative à la circoncision égyptienne," in *Mélanges Isidore Lévy* (Bruxelles: Secrétariat des Éditions de l'Institut, 1955), 631–39.

Mari Letter ARM 10.9/26.208. This fragmentary letter refers to a prophetic vision, in which the prophet witnessed an oath ceremony taking place in the heavenly council of the gods. Although the issue in question is not entirely clear, the ceremony itself can be made out rather easily. Before swearing their oath, the gods took dirt (or grease) from the city gate of Mari, dissolved it in water, and drank the concoction. There followed an oath in which the gods apparently promised not to harm the "brickwork" of a certain Mari official. The form and function of this divine oath are very similar to the Hebrew *Soṭah*, the ritual procedure prescribed for cases of a jealous husband (Num 5:11–31). An obvious difference between the two ceremonies regards the order of the rites, since in the Mari ceremony the drinking ritual preceded the oath while the order is reversed in Num 5.

Text and translation: G. DOSSIN, *La Correspondance feminine* (ARM 10; Paris: Librairie orientaliste P. Geuthner, 1967), no. 9; J.-M. DURAND, *Archives épistolaires de Mari I/1–2* (ARM 26; 2 vols.; Paris: Éditions Recherche sur les civilisations, 1988), no. 208. *Translations:* *ANET* 632; W. HEIMPEL, *Letters to the King of Mari: A New Translation, with Historical Introduction, Notes, and Commentary* (MC 12; Winona Lake, Ind.: Eisenbrauns, 2003), 258; M. NISSINEN, *Prophets and Prophecy in the Ancient Near East* (SBLWAW 12; Atlanta: Society of Biblical Literature, 2003), 42–43. *Bibliography:* J. M. SASSON, "An Apocalyptic Vision from Mari? Speculations on ARM X 9," *MARI* 1 (1982): 151–67; IDEM, "Mari Apocalypticism Revisited," in *Immigration and Emigration within the Ancient Near East: Festschrift E. Lipinski* (ed. K. van Lerberghe and A. Schoors; OLA 65; Leuven: Peeters, 1995), 285–98.

Letters from Neo-Assyrian Priests. Many letters have been recovered from the archives of the Sargonid kings, including a healthy correspondence between the priests and kings Esarhaddon and Assurbanipal. These sources give us an inside look into temple life and its relationship to the palace. We shall mention specifically only three of these letters. The first letter (SAA 3, no. 134) does not preserve its author's name, but it concerns a lamentation priest by the name of Pulu. With the emphatic words "They have changed the old rites," the author complains that Pulu constantly changed the ritual procedures and eliminated rites that should be performed in the temple. It seems that the author perceived Pulu's authority as the chief problem, since Pulu not only carried out these changes but also ordered silence on the matter (a directive that our author obviously did not follow). Perhaps we should take these criticisms of Pulu with a grain of salt, since the writer mentions that the temple fared far better when his father was a supervisor. The second letter (SAA 3, no. 169) also involves temple corruption, this time citing the theft of divine property by Nabû-epuš, priest of Ea. Here again, ulterior motives may be involved, since the author of the letter, Aššur-hamatu'a, comments that thefts were frequent and unreported in Ea's temple until he was stationed at his post. The third letter (SAA 3, no. 135) is somewhat cryptic, but it casts light on the ancient view of ritual. After enumerating a sequence of rituals scheduled for performance in the temple, the author avers, "This is not a ritual [*dullu*]; this is nothing. It is not ancient—your father introduced it." Although for this author a chief sign of ritual authenticity was the tradition's antiquity, this conceptual safeguard obviously could not insulate the rites from the whims of kings and priests.

The king's role in these three texts is particularly striking, as the priests constantly demured to his prerogatives in the actions that they took. This is not surprising given that the Assyrian king was viewed as the high priest—the *šangu*—of Assur. In addition to rituals, sacrifices, and temple corruption, the Neo-Assyrian priestly letters also address the following themes: the reconstruction of Babylon and its temples, the refurbishment of Assyrian temples, the cult of the royal image, divine processions and sacred marriage, prophecies, and deliveries of horses to Nabû's temple.

Text and translation: S. W. COLE and P. B. MACHINIST, *Letters from Priests to the Kings Esarhaddon and Assurbanipal* (SAA 3; Helsinki: Helsinki University Press, 1998).

Concluding Observations

The comments here on the comparative value of the Near Eastern rites and incantations for the study of Hebrew ritual will follow the contours of the priestly ritual literature in the Pentateuch. This material—nested especially in Exodus, Leviticus, and Numbers—can be represented in rough outline as follows:

Table 5.1

Exod 25–31, 35–40	Construction of the priestly tabernacle
Lev 1–7	Manual of sacrifices
Lev 8–9	Ordination and first service of the priests
Lev 11–15	Manual of impurities
Lev 16	Day of Atonement
Lev 17–26	Holiness Code (probably an early priestly composition)
Numbers	Various rites and priestly instructions

In their present form, these ritual and cultic materials are situated within a larger narrative context that begins with the creation and ends with Israel's conquest of the land. Scholars are reasonably certain that significant portions of this narrative story were composed by the same author(s) who assembled the priestly ritual material in Exodus to Numbers. For this reason, a thorough assessment of the priestly ritual materials will require that some consideration be given not only the rituals themselves but also to the closely related priestly narratives of the Hexateuch, which begin in Gen 1 and end, according to most scholars, with the allotment of tribal territories in Josh 13–21. Because of the staggering generic diversity in this priestly material, the relevant chapters of this volume include chapters 8 (Tales and Novellas), 9 (Epics and Legends), 10 (Myths), 11 (Genealogies and King Lists), 12 (Historiography), and 13 (Law Codes).

1. Construction of the Priestly Tabernacle (Exod 25–31, 35–40). The conceptual and generic features in the second half of Exodus fit nicely into the religious world of the ancient Near East. The large cultic tent from Mari shows that portable tent shrines like Israel's tabernacle were standard and necessary aspects of religious life, and the basic shape of the tabernacle, with its graduated sacred space leading to the *cela* of god, was standard fare in ancient religion. More specifically, the biblical tabernacle texts display a formal pattern common to Near Eastern temple construction narratives, in which the texts begin with divinely inspired prescriptions for the structure and follow with an account of its construction. The prescriptions are painstaking in detail and in this respect are comparable to the Babylonian topographical texts.

The accoutrements of the temple and cult in Exodus also find many parallels in ancient Near Eastern rites and cults. The ark of the covenant compares to the palanquins on which the ancient gods were carried, and the other features—priests, sacrifices, altars, incense, holy water, furniture, and so on—were standard elements in the cultic life of antiquity. In sum, the shape of the Israelite cult as depicted in the tabernacle construction narratives of Exodus is roughly the same as that found in other Near Eastern temple cults.

2. The Manual of Sacrifices (Lev 1–7). The form and content of this section of Leviticus is very close to the Punic ʾsacrificial tariffs and also, at least with respect to terminology, to the Ugaritic sacrificial system. Particularly noteworthy is that all three cults—Israelite, Punic, and Ugaritic—observed three primary types of sacrifices, namely, atonement offerings (e.g., sin offerings), offerings of religious devotion (e.g., burnt offerings), and communal meals with the deity (e.g., peace offerings). Because the Ugaritic and Punic sources reflect the West Semitic religious milieu of the second and first millennia, respectively, there is good reason to view this portion of Leviticus as the unique Israelite embodiment of broader generic patterns in Israel's ancient world. In this case, Leviticus contains prescriptive texts for both the offerers of the sacrifices (Lev 1:1–6:7) and for the priests who officiated during the rites (Lev 6:8–7:38). In these prescriptions, and also in the overall structure of the text, Lev 1–7 is very close to the Punic sacrificial tariffs. Because the Punic texts existed as a free-standing monumental text, it is very easy to presume—as many scholars do—that Lev 1–7 once existed as an independent manual of sacrificial prescriptions before it was folded into the book of Leviticus.

3. Priestly Ordinations (Lev 8–9). This portion of Leviticus provides a description of the Israelite ordination ritual for priests (Lev 8) and of the inaugural service over which they presided (Lev 9). The ceremonies correspond to the ordination prescriptions laid out in Exod 29, but they are also similar, in certain respects, to the Mesopotamian ordination rituals for the priest of

Enlil and for the high priestess of the city of Emar. Motifs common to the Mesopotamian and Israelite ordination rites include sacrifices, washing with water, anointing with oil, ritual meals, and ritual periods of seven days. Also noteworthy are parallels between the ordination of Enlil priests and certain emphases elsewhere in the Hebrew Bible, such as the importance of physical perfection in the priests (Lev 21:16–23) and the appropriate grooming of the priest's hair (cf. Lev 19:27; 44:20).

4. **Manual of Impurities (Lev 11–15).** This potion of Leviticus addresses three potential sources of ritual uncleanness: dietary uncleanness, discharges of bodily fluid, and contagious growths, whether on human skin or on some other surface (fungi). Let us consider each of the three in turn. (a) Dietary rules: Israelite conceptions of "clean" and "unclean" seem to have been very close to the views generally held in the ancient Near East. Clean species tended to include animals from the domestic flocks and herds that were commonly used as foodstuffs and for sacrifices, and unclean animals included species such as dogs and swine, which appear in Hittite texts as unclean animals. (b) Bodily fluids: Discharges of bodily fluids, whether from normal biological cycles or from illness, occasioned ritual uncleanness in the Near East. According to the Hittite Priestly Instructions, sexual activity rendered the priests ceremonially unclean, so that a ritual bath was necessary before the priests could resume their service in the temple. This is the same sort of law as appears in Lev 15:16–18. Although this Hebrew law was obviously intended for all Israelites rather than for priests only, its purpose was essentially the same: "Thus you shall keep the people of Israel separate from their uncleanness, so that they do not die in their uncleanness by defiling my tabernacle that is in their midst" (Lev 15:31). From a ritual standpoint, another particularly troubling circumstance for the ancients was the birth of a child. In most Near Eastern cultures, rituals were used to protect the mother and child, whose uncleanness made them vulnerable to demonic attacks. There is no evidence of this concern in Leviticus, but the book does prescribe a cleansing ritual on the occasion of childbirth in Lev 12. (c) Contagious growths: Perhaps the most pronounced similarity in this section of Leviticus is between the Israelite and Near Eastern responses to visible contagions. The Hebrews referred to growths of this sort as ṣāraʿt, whether they appeared as a kind of "leprosy" on the skin or as a fungus on leather, clothing, or mud-brick walls. In the case of skin infections, the Israelites, like their Near Eastern neighbors, responded by consulting their priests. The priests diagnosed the infections and, when necessary, treated them using medicinal and ritual means. In the case of fungal infestations on objects and structures, the Israelite response was closer still to Mesopotamian practice. As we have noted in our discussion of the Mesopotamian *namburbû* rites, both Israelite and Mesopotamian societies believed that the gods caused fungal growths and that priestly expertise was necessary to

treat the subsequent infestations. Priests diagnosed the situation on the basis of fungal color and then prescribed appropriate treatments, which normally entailed the removal of the fungus and the performing of elimination rites (see Lev 13:47–50, 14:33–57).

5. Day of Atonement (Lev 16). Israel's annual purgation of the temple included two somewhat different rites, a scapegoat ritual and a rite that cleansed the temple precinct by means of sacrifical blood. These two elements find their Near Eastern counterparts in two quite different contexts, the first in the Hittite scapegoat rites and the second in the Mesopotamian *kuppuru,* which was observed annually during the Akitu festival. What can we make of these similarities? The form, content, and New Year association of the Israelite *kippēr* is sufficiently close to the Mesopotamian *kuppuru* to suggest that the Israelite ritual was intentionally fashioned to mimic the Mesopotamian practice, perhaps to provide an Israelite alternative to Mesopotamian tradition. A theological adaptation of this sort would have been necessary during and after the exile as Jewish priests sought to inhibit the assimilation of their fellow Jews—and perhaps their fellow priests—to the dominant society of Mesopotamia. The Israelite version of the purgation rite differed, however, from its Mesopotamian couterpart on two key points. First, the Israelite ritual eliminated the uncleanness of human sin rather than uncleanness that stemmed from demonic presences. And second, whereas the Israelite high priest confessed the sins of Israel, the Mesopotamian king averred, "I have not sinned."

The correctness of this mimetic reading of Lev 16 is suggested by similar uses of mimesis in the Priestly writer, in which he mimicked Mesopotamian myths (Gen 1; see ch. 10) and Mesopotamian king lists (Gen 5; see ch. 11). It is unlikely, however, that the Priestly writer invented the Day of Atonement rite out of whole cloth. The scapegoat element of the rite probably represents an older native Israelite ritual, which provided the substrate for the more elaborate rite now prescribed in Lev 16. As we have seen, a scapegoat rite of this sort would have fit nicely into the Hittite-Levantine world of preexilic Israel.

6. The Holiness Code (Lev 17–26). This portion of Leviticus contains ritual prescriptions and various social and moral laws. For this reason, the Holiness Code is comparable at the same time to the Hittite Priestly Instructions and also to law codes in general (see ch. 13). Here we shall consider its ritual components. (a) Leviticus 17, 21, and 22 contains protocols for priestly service, including rules for priestly hygiene and purity as well as policies governing the consumption of sacred food from the temple. Priests are warned that they should keep these requirements "so that they may not incur guilt for it and die in it for having profaned it" (22:9). The Hittite Priestly Instructions included many rules of this sort, as well as similar warnings about the divine punishment that would result if the rules were contravened. (b) Leviticus 23 provides an abbreviated ritual calendar for the entire Israelite year, including the weekly Sabbaths and also Israel's spring and autumn festivals. Similar ritual calendars appear elsewhere in the Hebrew Bible (Num 28–29) and, as we have seen, in texts from Ugarit, Emar, Hatti, and Mesopotamia. (c) Leviticus 24:1–9 contains the prescriptions for Israel's perpetual presentation offering of twelve bread loaves. This practice is important on two scores. Not only does it represent the closest Israelite parallel to the Mesopotamian practice of presenting meals to the gods on trays; it also provides a very close parallel to the twelve-loaf offering presented to the diety during the Mesopotamian Akitu festival.

7. Ritual in Numbers. Priestly ritual prescriptions of diverse sorts are scattered about the book of Numbers. Here we shall consider only a few of these. (a) Numbers 5:11–31 prescribes a ritual ordeal in which a woman, accused of adultery, was made to swear an oath of innocence and then to drink a water-based concoction that contained dust from the temple floor. If guilty, the woman would respond to the drink with bitter suffering. A text from Mari (ARM 10.9) records a strikingly similar ritual in which the gods took an oath and then sealed it by drinking water in which dust from the city gate was dissolved. Another drink ordeal appears in the Hittite Priestly Instructions. (b) Numbers 15:32–36 contains a short tale illustrating the importance of the Israelite Sabbath law by briefly recounting the death sentence levied against a Sabbath breaker. This feature does not have a precise parallel in the texts examined in this chapter, but there is a similar element in the Hittite Instructions for Palace Personnel to Insure the King's Purity (see 2.3; see *ANET* 207): "At some time, I, the king, found a hair in the water pitcher in Sanahuitta. The king became angry and I expressed my anger to the water carriers: 'This is scandalous.' Then Arnilis said: 'Zuliyas was careless.' . . . Zuliyas . . . was found guilty . . . and he died." (c) Numbers 19 contains rites used to cleanse those who were made unclean through contact with a human corpse. Although the basic features of these rites suit the ritual patterns of Mesopotamia and the Levant, the text's emphasis on corpse contamination is unique. Perhaps the closest parallels appear in ancient Egypt, where death, as the ultimate form of putrefaction and uncleanness, required extensive rites to rid the deceased of impurities that might prevent a good transition into a blessed afterlife. (d) Numbers 28–29 contains the most detailed ritual calendar of the Hebrew Bible. It is basically a sacrificial schedule like that found at Emar and Ugarit; it covers the daily, Sabbath, and monthly rites, and the rites for the vernal and autumnal festivals. The daily rite of Israel, with its two meals of meat, drink, and grain, is quite comparable to the daily meals offered in the cults of Mesopotamia, Egypt, Hatti, and Ugarit. In all cases, it seems that the priests approached the gods with caution as they permeated the air with sweet-smelling incense and with songs. Perhaps the most important difference is that, unlike its neighbors, Israel did not present these meals to the deity in his *cela*. Entry into the *cela* was permited only once each year, on the Day of Atonement. This is, at least, how the priestly legislation describes it. The festival aspects of the Israelite calendar are also comparable to Near Eastern tradition. This counts not only for its general features, such as the vernal and autumnal festivals, but also in certain details. Perhaps the most striking comparative detail is Israel's use of booths during the great autumnal festival, a practice that is paralleled closely in Ugarit's autumnal wine festival. Another interesting parallel is the practice of waving palm leaves during festivals, as appears in the Mesopotamian Kislimu festival and in the seventh-month Israelite harvest festival of Sukkoth (Lev 23:39–43; Neh 8:13–18).

8. Orality and Writtenness in Ancient Ritual. Discussion of this subject will consider Mesopotamia, Ugarit, and then ancient Israel. The Mesopotamians produced a large corpus of prescriptive ritual texts that were consulted by priests and preserved over a long period of time in Mesopotamia's canonical tradition. Nevertheless, a thoughtful reading of these prescriptions reveals that they assumed a great deal of ritual competence in their readers. This indicates that, even in the comparatively literate context of the Mesopotamian cult, oral tradition played an important role in perpetuating ritual tradition. In Ugarit the role of orality seems to have been greater still. Not only are the Ugaritic ritual prescriptions cryptic; they also seem to be of a temporary nature. The texts are not the product of a lengthy canonical process so much as ad hoc crib texts, produced by the priests to assist them in their duties. If this is so, the Ugaritic texts are actually discrete glimpses into the otherwise oral world of Ugaritic ritual.

Regarding ancient Israel, modern scholars are divided on when to date the priestly ritual materials in the Pentateuch. A few scholars date them to the preexilic period, in part because of the similarities that we have noted between Israelite rituals and those from the second-millennium sources of Ugarit and Hatti. Most other scholars hold, to the contrary, that the priestly materials come mainly from the exilic and especially postexilic periods, not least because, as we have seen, the priestly materials reflect the indelible stamp of Mesopotamian influence (e.g., the Israelite *kippēr* and Mesopotamian *kuppuru*). Perhaps the comparative evidence suggests that we need not choose between these two options. A likely scenario is that Israel's ritual tradition was perpetuated orally before the Babylonian exile. As we might expect, this ritual corpus was, in most respects, similar to the rites observed at Ugarit, Hatti, and elsewhere in the Levant. The exile, however, had the effect of destroying the cultic context within which this oral tradition was transmitted. In such a circumstance, we can imagine that exiled Israelite priests attempted to preserve the tradition by submitting it to writing, and we can furthermore surmise that, during the course of the exilic and/or postexilic periods, the text was further systematized and at the same time shaped in conscious and unconscious ways by Jewish contacts with the Mesopotamian world.

9. The Divine Origins of Ritual. Although the Near Eastern ritual texts do not always state this explicitly, in many cases it appears that the rituals were understood as having divine origins. In the Egyptian ritual to protect the House of Life (see 5.2), the incanation books were understood to be the emanations of the god Re, and in the Mesopotamian incantations the instructions were commonly understood to have originated with the wise god Ea. Many other examples could be cited to illustrate this pattern. The Israelites also affirmed the divine origins of their priestly rituals, which in biblical literature are usually introduced with the formula "The Lord spoke to Moses," or "The Lord spoke to Moses and Aaron," or some permutation thereof.

Final Observations: It almost goes without saying that many of the rites and incantations discussed in this chapter have no parallels whatsoever in the Hebrew Bible. The monolatrous and monotheistic communities that produced and shaped the Hebrew canon, and Hebrew ritual with it, seem to have had their eye on distinguishing Israelite ritual practices from those in the Near East. This mono-Yahwist agenda had many consequences, but here we will mention only three important historical developments that began during the preexilic period and continued on into the postexilic period. First, Israel developed a unique aniconic tradition that forbade the fabrication of Yahwistic cult images. It is difficult to say with certainty when this development first appeared. Second, polytheistic ritual practices and ideologies were purged from the national temple cult, and attempts were made to centralize this monotheistic cult in Jerusalem. To the extent that this effort was successful, it had the effect of eliminating all sorts of rites and incantations that would previously have been associated with both Yahweh and with non-Yahwistic deities. Third, at the grassroots level, there were increasing efforts to eradicate the use of magical rituals in the popular religion of ancient Israelites. Consequently, while Near Eastern ritual texts describe flourishing death cults and all manner of magical rituals to address demons, ghosts, and various deities, one finds that corresponding rituals are not prominent in the formal cult of ancient Israel. Regarding these forbidden rituals, the biblical materials generally go no further than to polemicize against them: "No one shall be found among you who . . . practices divination, or is a soothsayer, or an augur, or a sorcerer, or one who casts spells, or who consults ghosts or spirits, or a wizard, or who seeks oracles from the dead" (Deut 18:10–11). Nevertheless, the polemic itself and the archaeological evidence (see Holladay; Schmidt; M. S. Smith; Torcznyer) suggest that many ancient Israelites practiced the very rituals and incantations that the biblical polemic demonized. Moreover, in later Judaism as exemplified by the Talmud, there appears to have been a greater comfort with some of these magical rites (Salvesen, 156).

General Bibliography

Tz. ABUSCH and K. VAN DER TOORN, eds., *Mesopotamian Magic: Textual, Historical, and Interpretative Perspectives* (AMD 1; Groningen, Neth.: Styx, 1999); T. G. ALLEN, *The Book of the Dead, or Going Forth by Day* (SAOC 37; Chicago: University of Chicago Press, 1974); B. ALSTER, ed., *Death in Mesopotamia: Papers Read at the XXVI Rencontre assyriologique internationale* (Mesopotamia 8; Copenhagen: Akademisk Forlag, 1980); J. ASSMANN, "Semiosis and Interpretation in Ancient Egyptian Ritual," in *Interpretation in Religion* (ed. S. Biderman and B.-A. Scharfstein; Leiden: Brill, 1992), 87–110; H. AVALOS, *Illness and Health Care in the Ancient Near East* (HSM 54; Atlanta: Scholars Press, 1995); R. D. BARNETT, "Bringing the God into the Temple," in *Temples and High Places in Biblical Times* (ed. A. Biran; Jerusalem: Nelson Glueck School of Biblical Archaeology of Hebrew Union College, 1981), 10–20; C. BELL, *Ritual: Perspectives and Dimensions* (Oxford: Oxford University Press, 1997); W. VAN BINSBERGEN and F. WIGGERMANN, "Magic in History: A Theoretical Perspective, and Its Application to Ancient Mesopotamia," in *Mesopotamian Magic: Textual, Historical, and Interpretative Perspectives* (ed. Tz. Abusch and K. van der Toorn; AMD 1; Groningen, Neth.: Styx, 1999), 3–34; J. BOTTÉRO, *Mythes et rites de Babylone* (Paris: Champion, 1985); J. M. BREMER, T. P. J. VAN DEN HOUT, and R. PETERS, eds., *Hidden Futures: Death and Immortality in Ancient Egypt, Anatolia, the Classical, Biblical, and Arabic-Islamic World* (Amsterdam: Amsterdam University Press, 1994); W. BURKERT, *Homo necans: The Anthropology of Greek Sacrificial Ritual and Myth* (Berkeley: University of California Press, 1983); D. M. CLEMENS, *Sources for Ugaritic Ritual and Sacrifice* (AOAT 284; Münster: Ugarit, 2001–), vol. 1; J. DANMANVILLE, "La libation en Mésopotamie," *RA* 49 (1955): 59–68; M. B. DICK, ed., *Born in Heaven, Made on Earth: The Making of the Cult Image in the Ancient Near East* (Winona Lake, Ind.: Eisenbrauns, 1999); G. DOSSIN, *Correspondance feminine* (ARM 10; Paris: P. Geuthner, 1978); J.-M. DURAND and M. GUICHARD, "Les rituels de Mari," in *Recueil d'études à la mémoire de Marie-Thérèse Barrelet* (ed. D. Charpin and J.-M. Durand; FM 3; Mémoires de N.A.B.U. 4; Paris: SEPOA, 1997), 19–78; E. DURKHEIM, *The Elementary Forms of Religions Life* (New York: Free Press, 1995); M. ELIADE, *The Sacred and the Profane: The Nature of Religion* (New York: Harcourt Brace, 1959); W. FARBER, "Witchcraft, Magic, and Divination in Ancient Mesopotamia," *CANE* 3:1895–1909; A. FINET, ed., *Actes de la XVIIe Rencontre assyriologique internationale* (PCBRHEAM 1; RAI 17; Ham-sur-Heure, Belgium: Comité Belge de Recherches en Mésopotamie, 1970); D. E. FLEMING, "The Emar Festivals: City Unity and Syrian Identity under Hittite Hegemony," in *Emar: The History, Religion, and Culture of a Syrian Town in the Late Bronze Age* (ed. M. W. Chavalas; Bethesda, Md.: CDL Press, 1996), 81–121; S. FREUD, *Totem und Tabu* (Leipzig: H. Heller, 1913); P. FRONZAROLI, "The Ritual Texts of Ebla," in *Literature and Literary Language at Ebla,* (ed. P. Fronzaroli; QS 18; Florence: Dipartimento di Linguistica, Università di Firenze, 1992), 165–85; T. H. GASTER, *Thespis: Ritual, Myth, and Drama in the Ancient Near East* (New York: Schuman, 1950); V. P. GAY, *Freud on Ritual: Reconstruction and Critique* (Missoula, Mont.: Scholars Press, 1979); C. GEERTZ, "Religion as a Cultural System," in *Reader in Comparative Religion* (ed. W. A. Lessa; New York: Harper & Row, 1979), 79–89; A. VAN GENNEP, *The Rites of Passage* (Chicago: University of Chicago Press, 1960); A. R. GEORGE and I. L. FINKEL, *Wisdom, Gods, and Literature: Studies in Assyriology in Honour of W. G. Lambert* (Winona Lake, Ind.: Eisenbrauns, 2000); R. GIRARD, *The Scapegoat* (Baltimore: Johns Hopkins University Press, 1986); IDEM, *Violence and the Sacred* (Baltimore: Johns Hopkins University Press, 1977); F. GORMAN, *The Ideology of Ritual: Space, Time, and Status in Priestly Theology* (JSOTSup 91; Sheffield, England: JSOT Press, 1990); J. C. GOYON, *Rituels funéraires de l'ancienne Égypte: Le rituel de l'embaumement, le rituel de l'ouverture de la bouche, les livres des respirations* (LAPO 4; Paris: Cerf, 1972); R. L. GRIMES, *Beginnings in Ritual Studies* (rev. ed.; Columbia: University of South Carolina Press, 1995); IDEM, *Research in Ritual Studies: A Programmatic Essay and Bibliography* (ATLA Bibliography Series; Metuchen, N.J.: Scarecrow, 1985); V. HAAS, *Der Kult von Nerik: Ein Beitrag zur hethitischen Religionsgeschichte* (Studia Pohl 4; Rome: Päpstliches Bibelinstitut, 1970); W. W. HALLO, J. C. MOYER, and L. G. PERDUE, eds., *More Essays on the Comparative Method* (Scripture in Context 2; Winona Lake, Ind.: Eisenbrauns, 1983); A. HAUSLEITER, "Totenrituale im Alten Vorderen Orient: Zum archäologischen Deutungspotential," in *Rituale in der Vorgeschichte, Antike, und Gegenwart: Studien zur vorderasiatischen, prähistorischen, und klassischen Archäologie, Ägyptologie, Alten Geschichte, Theologie, und Religionswissenschaft* (ed. C. Metzner-Nebelsick et al.; Rahden, Germany: Marie Leidorf, 2004), 17–26; J. S. HOLLADAY JR., "Religion in Israel and Judah under the Monarchy: An Explicitly Archaeological Approach," in *Ancient Israelite Religion: Essays in Honor of Frank Moore Cross* (ed. P. D. Miller Jr. et al.; Philadelphia: Fortress, 1987), 249–99; J. HOLM and J. BOWKER, eds., *Rites of Passage* (Themes in Religious Studies; New York: Pinter, 1994); S. H. HOOKE, *Myth and Ritual* (London: Oxford University Press, 1933); IDEM, *Myth, Ritual, and Kingship* (London: Oxford University Press, 1958); B. JANOWSKI, K. KOCH, and G. WILHELM, eds., *Religionsgeschichtliche Beziehungen zwischen Kleinasien, Nordsyrien, und dem Alten Testament* (OBO 129; Freiburg, Switz.: Universitätsverlag, 1993); A. E. JENSEN, *Myth and Cult among Primitive Peoples* (Chicago: University of Chicago Press, 1963); M. KREBERNIK, *Die Beschwörungen aus Fara und Ebla* (Texte und Studien zur Orientalistik 2; Zurick: Georg Olms, 1984); H. KRONASSER, *Die Umsiedelung der schwarzen Gottheit: Das hethitische Ritual KUB XXIX 4 (des Ulippi)* (SÖAW: Philosophisch-historische Klasse 241.3; Vienna: H. Böhlaus Nachf., Kommissionsverlag der Österreichischen Akademie der Wissenschaften in Wien, 1963); W. G. LAMBERT, "A Catalogue of Texts and Authors," *JCS* 16

(1962): 59–77; M. J. H. LINSSEN, *The Cults of Uruk and Babylon: The Temple Ritual Texts as Evidence for Hellenistic Cult Practices* (CM 25; Leiden: Brill, Styx, 2004); R. MARETT, "Magic (Introduction)," *ERE* 8:245–52; P. MICHALOWSKI, "The Early Mesopotamian Incantation Tradition," in *Literature and Literary Language at Ebla* (ed. P. Fronzaroli; QS 18; Florence: Dipartimento di Linguistica, Università di Firenze, 1992), 305–26; IDEM, "The Torch and Censer," in *The Tablet and the Scroll: Near Eastern Studies in Honor of William W. Hallo* (ed. M. E. Cohen, D. C. Snell, and D. B. Weisberg; Bethesda, Md.: CDL Press, 1993), 152–62; J. MIDDLE-TON et al., "Magic," *ER* 9:81–115; H. I. H. PRINCE TAKAHITO MIKASA, ed., *Cult and Ritual in the Ancient Near East* (BMECCJ 6; Wiesbaden: Otto Harrassowitz, 1992); B. MORRIS, *Anthropological Studies of Religion* (Cambridge: Cambridge University Press, 1987); G. DEL OLMO LETE, *Canaanite Religion: According to the Liturgical Texts of Ugarit* (Bethesda, Md.: CDL Press, 1999); R. OTTO, *The Idea of the Holy* (London: Oxford University Press, 1923); D. PARDEE, *Ritual and Cult at Ugarit* (SBLWAW 10; Atlanta: Scholars Press, 2002); G. PINCH, *Magic in Ancient Egypt* (Austin: University of Texas Press, 1994); J. QUAEGEBEUR, ed., *Ritual and Sacrifice in the Ancient Near East* (OLA 55; Leuven: Peeters, 1993), 319–32; J. RENGER, "Isinnam epēšum: Überlegungen zur Funktion des Festes in der Gesellschaft," in *Actes de la XVIIe Rencontre assyriologique internationale* (ed. A. Finet; PCBRHEAM 1; Ham-sur-Heure, Belgium: Comité Belge de Recherches en Mésopotamie, 1970), 75–80; R. K. RITNER, "Toward a Definition of Magic," in *The Mechanics of Ancient Egyptian Magical Practice* (SAOC 54; Chicago: University of Chicago Press, 1993), 1–28; A. ROCCATI and A. SILIOTTI, eds., *Magic in Egypt in the Time of the Pharaohs: International Study Conference, Milan, 29–31 October 1985* (Milan: Rassegna Internazionale di Cinematografia Archeologica: Arte e Natura Libri, 1987); A. SALVESEN, "The Legacy of Babylon and Nineveh in Aramaic Sources," in *The Legacy of Mesopotamia* (ed. S. Dalley et al.; Oxford: Oxford University Press, 1998), 139–61; B. B. SCHMIDT, *Israel's Beneficent Dead: Ancestor Cult and Necromancy in Ancient Israelite Religion and Tradition* (FAT 11; Tübingen: J. C. B. Mohr, 1994); J. SCURLOCK, "Physician, Exorcist, Conjurer, Magician: A Tale of Two Healing Professionals," in *Mesopotamian Magic: Textual, Historical, and Interpretative Perspectives* (ed. Tz. Abusch and K. van der Toorn; AMD 1; Groningen, Neth.: Styx, 1999), 69–79; J. Z. SMITH, *To Take Place: Toward Theory in Ritual* (Chicago: University of Chicago Press, 1987); M. S. SMITH, *The Early History of God: Yahweh and the Other Deities in Ancient Israel* (2d ed.; Grand Rapids: Eerdmans, 2002); J. A. SOGGIN, *Israel in the Biblical Period: Institutions, Festivals, Ceremonies, Rituals* (Edinburgh; New York: T & T Clark, 2001); K. L. SPARKS, "The Ark of the Covenant," in *Dictionary of the Old Testament Historical Books*, forthcoming; F. STAAL, "The Meaninglessness of Ritual," *Numen* 26 (1974): 2–22; F. THUREAU-DANGIN, *Rituels accadiens* (Paris: Leroux, 1921); IDEM, *Tablettes d'Uruk à l'usage des prêtres du temple d'Anu au temps des Séleucides* (TCL 6; Paris: P. Geuthner, 1922); K. VAN DER TOORN, "The Babylonian New Year Festival: New Insights from the Cuneiform Texts and Their Bearing on Old Testament Study," in *Congress Volume: Leuven, 1989* (ed. J. S. Emerton; VTSup 43; New York: Brill, 1991): 331–44; H. TORCZYNER, "A Hebrew Incantation against Night-

Demons from Biblical Times," *JNES* 6 (1947): 18–29; V. TURNER, *The Ritual Process: Structure and Anti-structure* (Chicago: Aldine, 1969); N. VELDHUIS, "The Poetry of Magic," in *Mesopotamian Magic: Textual, Historical, and Interpretative Perspectives* (ed. Tz. Abusch and K. van der Toorn; AMD 1; Groningen, Neth.: Styx, 1999), 35–48; C. WATANABE, "A Problem in the Libation Scene of Ashurbanipal," in *Cult and Ritual in the Ancient Near East* (ed. H. I. H. Prince Takahito Mikasa; Wiesbaden: Harrassowitz, 1992), 91–104; W. G. E. WATSON and N. WYATT, eds., *Handbook of Ugaritic Studies* (Leiden: Brill, 1999), 287–304; F. A. M. WIGGERMANN, *Mesopotamian Protective Spirits: The Ritual Texts* (CM 1; Groningen, Neth.: Styx, 1992); D. P. WRIGHT, *The Disposal of Impurity: Elimination Rites in the Bible and in Hittite and Mesopotamian Literature* (SBLDS 101; Atlanta: Scholars Press, 1987); E. M. ZEUSSE, "Ritual," in *The Encyclopedia of Religion* (ed. M. Eliade; 16 vols.; New York: Macmillan, 1987), 12:405–22; Z. ZEVIT, *The Religions of Ancient Israel: A Synthesis of Parallactic Approaches* (London; New York: Continuum, 2001); H. ZIMMERN, "Ein Leitfaden der Beschwörungskunst," *ZA* 30 (1915): 204–29.

CHAPTER SIX

Intermediary Texts: Omens and Prophecies

Introduction

Intermediation is a social phenomenon in which religious specialists serve as mediators between the spirit world and society. As a category, the phenomenon comprises Israelite prophecy and closely related genres from the Near East, not only the prophecies but also the omen literature. The primary difference between prophecies and omens rests in the mode of revelation. Omens communicate the divine will through signs that the diviner knows how to interpret, whereas the prophetic word passes to the intermediary more directly. The genres produced by the ancient prophets and diviners are often imagined to reflect prognostic exercises in telling the future—and this was often true—but a thoughtful examination of the evidence shows that prophets and diviners were also privy to the deity's perspective on the past and present. Although our corpus of Near Eastern prophecies is unfortunately small, the vast corpus of omen material left behind in Mesopotamia and elsewhere in the ancient Near East partially compensate for this dearth. For related texts, see chapter 7.

6.1. Mesopotamian Omens and Prophecies

In Mesopotamia the differences between divination and prophecy produced corresponding differences in the lifestyles and social contexts of ancient diviners and prophets. Diviners were well-educated scholars moving about the privileged classes of society whereas prophets and prophetesses were not scholars, were generally illiterate, and filled lower social niches than the priests and diviners. Generically speaking, diviners and prophets also produced very different kinds of texts, as we shall see.

6.1.1. Mesopotamian Omen Literature

As is the case in so many Mesopotamian genres, a large part of our omen corpus comes from Assurbanipal's library, so we must bear in mind that our picture of the omen literature is skewed toward the Neo-Assyrian phenomena. Nevertheless, scholars agree that Neo-Assyrian divination generally reflects both earlier and later practices in Mesopotamia. Mesopotamians believed that the gods spoke to them through signs of all sorts. Two types of omen are attested, *oblativa* and *impetrita*. In both cases strange and unusual events were viewed as signs from the gods, but the omen types differed on a crucial point. *Oblativa* were unsolicited signs that diviners passively awaited—for example, unusual historical events, strange animal behaviors, and unexpected meteorological or astronomical phenomena. In contrast, the signs observed in *impetrita* were actively solicited by diviners through physical manipulations—for example, the movement of oil poured upon water or the rising smoke of an incense brazier.

The two most important classes of omen literature were extispicy (omens based on the appearance of the *exta*, or entrails, of sacrificial animals) and astronomical observation (omens based on the movements of the sun, moon, planets, and stars). Like so many scholarly treatises from Mesopotamia, each omen was casuistic in form, containing a protasis followed by an apodosis: "If X is the observed phenomenon [protasis], Y is the predicted result [apodosis]." Omen series varied considerably in length; shorter collections included a few tablets with hundreds of entries, whereas longer collections, such as the astronomical omen series *Enūma Anu Enlil*, included several thousand entries on about seventy tablets. Each omen series developed over a long period of time, originating with observations of the ominous phenomena before scholars gradually systematized the texts to make them address theoretical circumstances. For instance, the protases in our astronomical omens include not only many *possible* empirical observations (such as a lunar eclipse on day fifteen) but also numerous astronomical *impossibilities* (such as a lunar eclipse on day twenty-one). This suggests that divination began as an empirical exercise before it developed in a more theoretical direction.

The gall bladder omens (a type of extispicy) conveniently illustrate the development of divination collections because we possess copies from the Old Babylonian, Middle Babylonian, Neo-Assyrian, and Seleucid eras (i.e., from the eighteenth to the second century). A comparison of these tablets (see Jeyes 2000) reveals that the materials underwent a high degree of organization between the Old Babylonian and Middle Babylonian periods, so that by the Middle Babylonian period the tradition was canonical and relatively stable. Nevertheless, some changes were made to the text in subsequent periods, reflecting a stronger tendency to add new omens than to remove old ones (seven added and two removed from a total of about eighty omens). There are also instances in which second apodoses were added, protases or apodoses were replaced, and obsolete words were eliminated. The overall evidence suggests that similar patterns of growth and development stand behind all of the major omen collections.

Who wrote the omen texts? According to one important tradition, it was the god Ea who wrote the great divination compendia for extispicy (*Barûtu*) and astronomical omens (*Enūma Anu Enlil*), but another popular view credited the primeval king Enmeduranki with these works, which were purportedly revealed to him by the gods Šamaš and Adad (Koch-Westenholz 1995, 74). Of course, we have good reason to question both of these traditions, but divine origin was central to any ancient view of omen literature. The human authors and editors of the texts were well aware of their own prominent role in composing and shaping the collections. How did they square this with the notion of divine authorship? Ancient scholars believed that the divination texts they produced were divinely inspired works (see 2.1). This phenomenon is comparable to the Mesopotamian claim that divine-cult statues were actually made by the gods themselves rather than by their ostensible human craftsmen (see 5.1). So it was surprisingly easy for Mesopotamians to harmonize the humanity of the scholar with his divinely inspired text.

Extispicy: **Barûtu** *and Related Texts.* Extispicy entailed the interpretation of the exta of sacrificial animals, but Mesopotamian diviners (*barû*) were particularly interested in the liver (hepatoscopy). By the Neo-Assyrian period, the lore of extispicy had emerged as a massive hundred-tablet diviner's manual known as *Barûtu*, a collection of ten "chapters" that concluded with a guide for interpreting the omens called *Multabiltu*. *Barûtu* was based on a still older omen compendium represented in *KAR* 423. Extispicy was generally practiced in support of the king and his administration. The king posed his questions to the gods, usually Adad or Šamaš, and the gods gave one of two responses through the omens: favorable or unfavorable. In other words, if the king's query was answered by the omen apodosis "the prince will be insulted by his servants," this did not mean that diviners expected the prince to be insulted; rather, the omen was simply unfavorable.

Two basic types of questions were asked of the gods. The first inquired whether anything dangerous would befall the king or country during a stated period of time. This period, called the *adunnu*, normally ranged from seven to about one hundred days. The second type was more specific and usually came from the king himself. During the Neo-Assyrian reign of Esarhaddon, from which many of these omen reports come, the standard form of the king's query was a clay tablet that included the king's question along with an appeal to the god for a favorable omen. The query tablet was given to the diviners, who usually added to it a list of *ezib* prayers designed to avert potential negative influences on the omens. When the query tablet was thus prepared, it was placed before Šamaš and the god was invited to "write" his verdict in the sacrificial animal's *exta*. As the ritual began, the behavior of the sacrificial sheep was carefully observed (because this too was omen-laden; see Ebeling; Leichty), and various *ikribu* prayers (see 3.1.2) were offered in which the diviner requested a good omen. After the sacrifice and the extispicy examination (which sometimes required second or third check-up extispicies for clarification), the observations were compared to the omen lists, tallied, and added to the tablet for return to the king. The results were presented as a list of features observed to be in the liver and *exta*, and if these features were "normal," the omen result was favorable. During the reign of Esarhaddon's son, Assurbanipal, these extispicy queries were cast in a new form, so that they became briefer, included fewer elements, and arranged these elements differently (see Starr 1990). Readers should note that, in addition to these royal queries, we also possess copies of private *tamitu* queries that date back to the Old Babylonian period (Lambert; Leichty 1990).

How often and to what extent was extispicy performed? The answer varies widely, depending in part on the historical venue. In Old Babylonian Mari it appears that between five hundred and six hundred extispicies were performed each month (Durand), whereas the more complex Neo-Assyrian extispicy rites yielded only two extispicies per day, one in the morning and the other in the evening (Cryer).

How were extispicy omens interpreted? As noted, the omen genres apparently originated with empirical observations, in the case of extispicy with observations of the liver. The significance of the liver's appearance was interpreted through loose associations, such as paronomasia (wordplay), contrasts, and especially analogy: "If the 'station' [a part of the liver] is long, the days of the prince will be long" (Starr 1985, 127). Conditions such as a split, a cut, a laceration, and atrophy were particularly unfavorable (but favorable for one's enemy). This empirical system eventually took a theoretical turn, which required that Mesopotamian scholars develop systematic rationales for interpreting the omens, rationales that modern scholars have been reasonably successful in identifying. One primary interpretive key in extispicy, as in other omen types, was the spatial opposition between left and right (Starr 1985; Guinan). The right side of the *exta* pertained to the inquirer and was positive, whereas the left side pertained to the enemy and was negative. For this reason, some divination prayers (*ikribu*) asked the gods to place favorable signs on the right sides of the organs and unfavorable signs on the left. Other oppositions of the right-left sort were also important, such as light versus dark, normal versus abnormal, firm versus infirm, and so forth. Unfortunately, there is as yet no complete modern edition of *Barûtu*.

Texts, translations, and discussions: R. D. BIGGS, "A Babylonian Extispicy Text Concerning Holes," *JNES* 33 (1974): 351–56; CRYER, *Divination in Ancient Israel and Its Near Eastern Environment,* 168–80; A. GOETZE, *Old Babylonian Omen Texts* (YOS 10; New Haven: Yale University Press, 1946); U. JEYES, *Old Babylonian Extispicy: Omen Texts in the British Museum* (Istanbul: Nederlands Historisch-Archaeologisch Instituut te Instanbul, 1989); U. KOCH-WESTENHOLZ, *Babylonian Liver Omens: The Chapters Manzāzu, Padānu, and Pān tākalti of the Babylonian Extispicy Series Mainly from Aššurbanipal's Library* (Copenhagen: Carsten Niebuhr Institute of Ancient Near Eastern Studies, University of Copenhagen, Museum Tusculanum Press, 2000); I. STARR, *Queries to the Sungod: Divination and Politics in Sargonid Assyria* (SAA 4; Helsinki: Helsinki University Press, 1990); IDEM, *The Rituals of the Diviner* (BMes 12; Malibu, Calif.: Undena, 1985). ***Bibliography:*** CRYER, *Divination in Ancient Israel and Its Near Eastern Environment;* J.-M. DURAND, "Introduction générale sur les Devins," in *Archives épistolaires de Mari,* vol. 1, part 1, pp. 3–68; E. EBELING, *Tod und Leben nach den Vorstellung der Babylonier* (Berlin: de Gruyter, 1931), 41–44; C. J. GADD, "Some Babylonian Divinatory Methods and Their Inter-relations," in *La divination* *en Mésopotamie ancienne et dans les régions voisines,* 21–43; A. K. GUINAN, "Left/Right Symbolism in Mesopotamian Divination," *SAA Bulletin* 10 (1996): 5–10; W. HEIMPEL, *Letters to the King of Mari: A New Translation, with Historical Introduction, Notes, and Commentary* (MC 12; Winona Lake, Ind.: Eisenbrauns, 2003), 173–248; V. A. HUROWITZ, "Eli's Adjuration of Samuel (1 Samuel III 17–18) in Light of A 'Diviner's Protocol' from Mari (AEM I/1, 1)," *VT* 44 (1994): 483–97; IDEM, "The Expression uqsamim beyadam (Num 22:7) in Light of Divinatory Practices from Mari," *HS* 33 (1992): 5–15; U. JEYES, "The Act of Extispicy in Ancient Mesopotamia: An Outline," *Assyriological Miscellanies* 1 (1980): 13–32; IDEM, "Assurbanipal's Bārûtu," in *Assyrien im Wandel der Zeiten: XXXIXe Rencontre assyriologique internationale* (ed. H. Waetzoldt and H. Hauptmann; Heidelberg: Heidelberger Orientverlag, 1997), 61–65; IDEM, "A Compendium of Gall-Bladder Omens Extant in Middle Babylonian, Nineveh, and Seleucid Versions," in *Wisdom, Gods, and Literature: Studies in Assyriology in Honour of W. G. Lambert* (ed. A. R. George and I. L. Finkel; Winona Lake, Ind.: Eisenbrauns, 2000), 345–73; IDEM, "Death and Divination in the Old Babylonian Period," in *Death in Mesopotamia* (ed. B. Alster; Mesopotamia 8; Copenhagen: Akademisk Forlag, 1980), 107–21; W. G. LAMBERT, "The *tamītu* Texts," in *La divination en Mésopotamie ancienne et dans les régions voisines,* 119–23; E. LEICHTY, "Ritual, 'Sacrifice,' and Divination in Mesopotamia," in *Ritual and Sacrifice in the Ancient Near East* (ed. J. Quaegebuer; Leuven: Peeters, 1993), 237–42; IDEM, "A *tamītu* from Nippur," in *Lingering over Words: Studies in Ancient Near Eastern Literature in Honor of William L. Moran* (Atlanta: Scholars Press, 1990), 301–4; T. RICHTER, "Untersuchungen zum Opferschauwesen, I: Überlegung zur Rekonstruktion der altbabylonischen *barûtum*-Serie," *Or* 62 (1993): 121–41; I. STARR, "Chapters 1 and 2 of the barûtu," *SAAB* 6 (1992): 45–53.

***Enūma Anu Enlil* and Related Texts (*Astronomical Omens*).** Like the extispicy omens, astrological omens are widely attested in the ancient world, appearing already in many early sites such as Hatti, Emar, Nuzi, Alalakh, Ugarit, and Elam as well as in Babylonia and Assyria proper. By the first millennium, astronomical omens became even more important and emerged as a rival of extispicy. From this period we possess copies of the very large astronomical omen compendium known as *Enūma Anu Enlil* as well as astronomical reports (Hunger) and an important catalogue of astronomical data called MUL.APIN (Hunger and Pingree), which includes star lists, celestial data, and a table for the use of water clocks to measure time. Most of the astronomical reports are Neo-Assyrian and come from the same period as the Neo-Assyrian extispicy reports (see above), but there are important differences between the two types of reports. Because astronomical omens were *oblativa* (scholars had to passively await the signs), it was inconvenient to use them for answering questions posed by the king. For this reason, the astronomical reports lack the query section that is so prominent in the extispicy reports. Because of the importance of celestial omens, ancient scholars devoted considerable energy to the task of predicting astronomical events, and this they did with ever increasing success. Sometime around the fifth century the astronomical predictions of Mesopotamian scholars became so accurate that the movements of the moon, sun, planets, and stars were no longer viewed as signs from the gods so much as patterns that directly determined life on earth. This development represented the first stages of the transition from astronomical omens to what would become astrology.

No complete publication of *Enūma Anu Enlil* has been completed (for partial publications, see below).

Texts and translations: E. REINER and D. PINGREE, *Babylonian Planetary Omens* (vols. 1, 2, Malibu, Calif.: Undena; vol. 3, Groningen, Neth.: Styx, 1975–) (partial); F. ROCHBERG-HALTON, *Aspects of Babylonian Celestial Divination: The Lunar Eclipse Tablets of Enūma Anu Enlil* (AfOB 22; Horn, Austria: Ferdinand Berger & Söhne, 1988) (partial); W. H. VAN SOLDT, *Solar Omens of Enuma Anu Enlil: Tablets 23(24)–29(30)* (Leiden: Nederlands Historisch-Archaeologish Instituut te Istanbul, 1995) (partial). ***Texts and translations of related texts:*** H. HUNGER, *Astrological Reports to Assyrian Kings* (SAA 9; Helsinki: Helsinki University Press, 1992); H. HUNGER and D. PINGREE, *MUL.APIN: An Astronomical Compendium in Cuneiform* (AfOB 89; Horn, Austria: Ferdinand Berger & Söhne, 1989). ***Bibliography:*** D. BROWN, *Mesopotamian Planetary Astronomy-Astrology* (CM 18; Groningen, Neth.: Styx, 2000); CRYER, *Divination in Ancient Israel and Its Near Eastern Environment,* 142–44; U. KOCH-WESTENHOLZ, *Mesopotamian Astrology: An Introduction to Babylonian and Assyrian Celestial Divination* (Copenhagen: Carsten Niebuhr Institute of Ancient Near Eastern Studies, Museum Tusculanum Press, University of Copenhagen, 1995); W. G. LAMBERT, "Babylonian Astrological Omens and Their Stars," *JAOS* 107 (1987): 93–96; E. REINER, "The Uses of Astrology," *JAOS* 105 (1985): 589–95; F. ROCHBERG-HALTON, "Benefic and Malefic Planets in Babylonian Astrology," in *A Scientific Humanist* (ed. Leichty, Ellis, and Gerardi), 23–38; N. M. SWERDLOW, *The Babylonian Theory of the Planets* (Princeton: Princeton University Press, 1998).

Šumma Ālu. Next to the extispicy and astronomical omens, the other major Mesopotamian omen corpus was known as *Šumma Ālu* ("If a city"), a long and amorphous collection of more than 120 tablets that interpreted many kinds of unusual events as omen-laden, including encounters with wild animals in the city, the growth of fungus, cries heard in the night, and types of lovemaking. These portents differed from those of extispicy and astronomy because most of them addressed private citizens rather than matters of the royal court. Hence, to the extent that the average Mesopotamians were concerned about omens, it would have been *Šumma Ālu*—not *Barûtu* or *Enūma Anu Enlil*—that interested them. Perhaps this explains why the largest collection of rituals designed to counter omen portents (*namburbûs) was compiled primarily to counter the portents of Šumma Ālu (numerous namburbûs were even included in the text of Šumma Ālu).*
 In at least one instance, there is evidence that the Israelites shared certain theological views that are expressed in *Šumma Ālu.* Just as in *Šumma Ālu* fungal growths were viewed as portents sent by the gods, so too in Israel it could be said that fungal infestations were sent by God (Lev 14:33–34). In both cultures, fungal infestations required a ritual response. For a comparison of the ritual responses in ancient Mesopotamia and ancient Israel, see the entry on *namburbûs* in 5.8.1.

Texts and translations: S. M. FREEDMAN, *If a City Is Set on a Height: The Akkadian Omen Series Šumma Ālu ina Mēlē Šakin,* (OPSNKF 17; Philadelphia: University Museum, 1998), vol. 1 (partial [tablets 1–21]); F. NÖTSCHER, "Die Omen-Serie Šumma Ālu ina Mêlê Šakin," *Orientalia Old Series* 31 (1928): 1–78; IDEM, "Haus-und Stadtomina der Serie Šumma Ālu ina Mêlê Šakin," *Orientalia Old Series* 39–42 (1929): 1–247; IDEM, "Haus-und

Stadtomina der Serie Šumma Ālu ina Mêlê Šakin," *Orientalia Old Series* 51–54 (1930): 1–243. **Bibliography:** CRYER, *Divination in Ancient Israel and Its Near Eastern Environment,* 161–67; A. K. GUINAN, "Erotomancy: Scripting the Erotic," in *Sex and Gender in the Ancient Near East* (2 vols.; ed. S. Parpola and R. M. Whiting; RAI 47; Helsinki: Neo-Assyrian Text Corpus Project, 2002), 1:185–201.

*Psephomancy (*LKA *137).* This divination procedure (sometimes called cleromancy) queried the gods by randomly selecting colored stones drawn from a sack or garment pocket. According to our primary text, a ritual prescription tablet (*LKA* 137), the diviner began the rite with an incantation inviting Šamaš to answer the question and then proceeded to draw images of Šamaš and other gods on the ground. This was an abbreviated way of achieving the divine presence that normally attended temple divination. At this point the diviner drew out one of two stones—a white stone (alabaster), which signaled a favorable answer, or a black stone (hematite), which signaled an unfavorable answer. For the portent to be valid, the procedure had to be repeated three times with the same result; mixed results indicated no answer from the gods. So far as we can see, psephomancy was a legitimate but second-rate form of divination that was used when standard forms of inquiry were not convenient or available. It is also the only Mesopotamian divination technique approved by Israel's priestly tradition (see *Urim* and *Thummim* in Exod 28:30; Lev 8:8; Num 27:21; 1 Sam 14:41).

Text, translation, and discussion: W. HOROWITZ and V. A. HUROWITZ, "Urim and Thummim in Light of a Psephomancy Ritual from Assur (*LKA* 137)," *JANES* 21 (1992): 95–115. *Translation: COS* 1.127: 444–45. **Bibliography:** B. T. ARNOLD, "Necromancy and Cleromancy in 1 and 2 Samuel," *CBQ* 66 (2004): 199–213; CRYER, *Divination in Ancient Israel and Its Near Eastern Environment,* 273–82; I. L. FINKEL, "In Black and White: Remarks on the Assur Psephomancy Ritual," *ZA* 85 (1995): 271–76; V. A. HUROWITZ, "True Light on the Urim and Thummim," *JQR* 88 (1998): 263–74; A. M. KITZ, "The Plural Form of ʾûrîm and thummîm," *JBL* 16 (1997): 401–10; C. VAN DAM, *The Urim and Thummim: An Old Testament Means of Revelation* (Winona Lake, Ind.: Eisenbrauns, 1993).

The Oneiromancy Series Ziqîqu *(Dream Omens).* In the ancient Near East there were essentially three types of dream speech from the gods: direct messages, interpreted symbolic messages, and uninterpreted symbolic dreams. In the first case the deity spoke unambiguously and directly to the dreamer, in the second case the deity provided a symbolic dream and its explanation, and in the third case the dream was given without an interpretation, prompting the need for a dream interpreter. In Mesopotamia, dream interpretations were done on the basis of the series Ziqîqu, which in our Neo-Assyrian editions includes not only omens but also three tablets (tablets I, X, and XI) of incantations and *namburbû* rituals (see 5.8.1) designed to avert any evils portended in the texts. Dream revelations were also quite common in the Hebrew Bible, but the Israelite interpreters did not consult omen compendia in their work (e.g., Gen 41; Dan 2).

Text and translation: A. L. OPPENHEIM, *The Interpretation of Dreams in the Ancient Near East: With a Translation of an Assyrian Dream Book* (TAPS, NS 46.3; Philadelphia: American Philosophical Society, 1956). *Bibliography:* M. BONECHI and J.-M. DURAND, "Oniro-mancie et magie à Mari à l'époch d'Ébla," in *Literature and Literary Language at Ebla* (ed. P. Fronzaroli; QS 18; Florence: Dipartimento di Linguistica, Università di Firenze, 1992), 151–61; J. BOTTÉRO, *Mesopotamia: Writing, Reasoning, and the Gods* (Chicago: University of Chicago Press, 1992), 105–24; S. A. L. BUTLER, *Mesopotamian Conceptions of Dreams and Dream Rituals* (AOAT 258; Münster: Ugarit, 1998); CRYER, *Divination in Ancient Israel and Its Near Eastern Environment,* 157–59; E. REINER, "Fortune-Telling in Mesopotamia," *JNES* 19 (1960): 23–35.

Hemerologies and Menologies. In Mesopotamian antiquity the hemerologies (from the Greek word for "calendar") were known as *uttuku* (from the Sumerian words meaning "good" and "day"). The texts contain entries that generally read, "In the month of Ayyaru, on the second day, favorable." Hemerologies were consulted in a variety of situations, including just before extispicy and in preparation for important undertakings, such as building projects or military campaigns. Closely related to the hemerologies were the menologies, such as *iqqur îpuš,* which were based on the month rather than the day (Labat 1965). Perhaps the best-known exemplar of the hemerological/menological genre is the Babylonian Almanac (Matoush; Labat 1941–1944).

Texts and translations: S. H. LANGDON, *Babylonian Menologies and the Semitic Calendars* (London: Oxford University Press, 1935); R. LABAT, "Un almanach babylonien (VR 48–49)," *RA* 38 (1941–1944): 13–40; IDEM, *Un calendrier babylonien des travaux des signes et des mois (series iqqur îpuš)* (Paris: H. Champion, 1965); IDEM, *Hémérologies et ménologies d'Assur* (Paris: Maisonneuve, 1939); I. MATOUSH, "L'almanach de Bakr-Awa," *Sumer* 17 (1961): 17–66. *Bibliography:* A. LIVINGSTONE, "The Case of the Hemerologies: Official Cult, Learned Formulation, and Popular Practice," in *Official Cult and Popular Religion in the Ancient Near East* (ed. E. Matsushima; Heidelberg: Universitätsverlag C. Winter, 1993), 97–113; A. SACHS, "Babylonian Horoscopes," *JCS* 6 (1952): 49–78.

Other Omen Genres. There was virtually nothing in the Mesopotamian experience through which the gods could not speak, as is vividly illustrated in the variety of omen types listed below. Note, however, that the medical series cited here, SA.GIG (also known as *Enūma ana bīt marṣi āšipu illaku*), is more of a diagnostic handbook than a compendium of medical omens (Labat; Heessel). For brief introductions to many of these omen types, see Cryer.

Texts, translations, and studies: **Aleuromancy (flour on water):** J. NOUGAYROL, "Aleuro-mancie babylonien," *Or* 32 (1963): 381–86 (omens of this type were incorporated into *Šumma Ālu*). **Cledonomancy (speech omens):** A. L. OPPENHEIM, "Sumerian: inim.gar, Akkadian: egirrû, Greek: kledon," *AfO* 17 (1954–1956): 49–55. **Lecanomancy (oil on water):** G. PETTINATO, *Die Ölwahrsagung bei den Babylonien* (2 vols.; Studi semitici 21–22; Rome: Istituto di Studi del Vicino Oriente, 1966); J. WALKER, "Funny Things Happen When Drops of Oil or Other Substances Are Placed on Water," *Scientific American* 249 (1983): 164–70. **Libanomancy (incense omens):** H. LUTZ, "An Old-Babylonian Divination Text," *University of California Publications in Semitic Philology* 9, no. 5 (1929): 367–77; G. PETTINATO, "Libanomanzia presso i Babilonesi," *RSO* 41 (1966): 303–27. **Physiognomy (omens based on human appearance and behavior):** B. BÖCK, *Die babylonisch-assyrische*

Morphoskopie (AfOB 27; Vienna: Institut für Orientalistik der Universität Wien, 2000); F. KÖCHER and A. L. OPPENHEIM, "The Old Babylonian Omen Text VAT 7525," *AfO* 18 (1957–1958): 62–80; F. R. KRAUS, *Die physiognomischen Omina der Babylonier* (MVAG 40.2; Leipzig: J. C. Hinrichs, 1935); IDEM, "Ein Sittenkanon in Omenform," *ZA* 43 (1936): 77–113; IDEM, *Texte zur babylonischen Physiognomatik* (Berlin: [n.p.], 1939); IDEM, "Weitere Texte zur babylonischen Physiognomatik," *Or* 16 (1947): 172–205. **Teratomancy (omens based on strange births):** J. BOTTÉRO, *Mythes et rites de Babylone* (Paris: Champion, 1985), 1–28; E. LEICHTY, *The Omen Series Šumma Izbu* (Locust Valley, N.Y.: J. J. Augustin, 1970). **Medical diagnostic omens:** I. L. FINKEL, "Adad-apla-iddina, Esagil-kīn-apli, and the Series SA.GIG," in *A Scientific Humanist* (ed. Leichty, Ellis, and Gerardi), 143–59; N. P. HEESSEL, *Babylonisch-assyrische Diagnostik* (AOAT 43; Münster: Ugarit, 2000) (new edition of SA.GIG tablets 15–33); J. V. KINNIER WILSON, "Two Medical Texts from Nimrud," *Iraq* 18 (1956): 130–46; 19 (1957): 40–49; IDEM, "The Nimrud Catalogue of Medical and Physiognomical Omina," *Iraq* 24 (1962): 52–62; R. LABAT, *Traité akkadien de diagnostics et pronostics médicaux* (2 vols.; Paris: Académie Internationale d'Histoire des Sciences, 1951) [dated publication of all forty tablets of SA.GIG]. ***Translation:*** COS 1.120: 421–26 (partial samples).

The Babylonian Diviner's Manual. The proliferation of omen types in Mesopotamia naturally raised an important question for ancient diviners: how do the various omens relate to each other? Mesopotamian scholars compiled all sorts of materials to facilitate their trade in divination, among them a treatise that addressed precisely this question. The Diviner's Manual is an index of tablets from two omen series, one entitled "If from the month of Arahsamna on" (fourteen tablets) and the other "If a star has a crest in front" (eleven tablets). This index helped diviners locate the appropriate materials for their work, but its author was particularly interested in explaining how to integrate the results of the terrestrial omens in the first text with the celestial omens in the second. The author concluded that a portent was valid only when it was simultaneously confirmed by terrestrial, astronomical, and hemerological data. Since we posses no other copies of the Diviner's Manual, we do not know how widely this rationale was adopted.

Text and translation: A. L. OPPENHEIM, "A Babylonian Diviner's Manual," *JNES* 33 (1974): 197–220.

6.1.2. Mesopotamian Prophecies

Apart from the Hebrew Bible, prophecies from the Near East are few and far between. Our primary sources from Mesopotamia include the Old Babylonian prophecies from Mari and Ešnunna and the Neo-Assyrian prophecies from the Sargonid dynasty. Miscellaneous cuneiform texts, recently published in a collection by Nissinen, provide additional contextual background for our understanding of these prophecies (see Nissinen 2003, 179–99).

The Old Babylonian Mari Prophecies. We possess more than fifty letters in which prophetic oracles or visions were reported to Zimri-Lim, the king of Mari (eighteenth century B.C.E.). The oracles reflect two primary concerns: the king's welfare (encouragement, warnings of danger, advice for success) and, to a lesser extent, the king's neglect of the gods and their cults. Because the prophets worked in temples and viewed the king as an important benefactor of the cult, these themes are not surprising. The Mari corpus includes prophecies from at least ten deities (but mostly from the West Semitic deities, Dagan, Annunitum, and Adad). Generically speaking, the texts reflect the epistolary form in which they were transmitted, but it appears that the original oracles were stylistically elevated and included proverbs, lyrical forms, poetic repetition, and various kinds of imagery. Although the prophets may have been decent poets, they were apparently illiterate. Consequently, scribes recorded all of the Mari oracles, at the behest of either the prophet himself or, more usually, at the behest of royal and temple functionaries who suspected that the king would be interested in the oracle's content.

The prophets mentioned in the Mari letters are both male and female, and the terms used to describe them include *muḫḫû*, *āpilū*, and *assinnū*, among others. It appears that all three types of prophet were of the temple entourage, but they played somewhat different roles. The *muḫḫû* were ecstatic prophets, as suggested by the derivation of their title from the verb *maḫû*, "to rave, go mad, go into a frenzy." It was such a prophet who publicly skinned and ate a raw lamb, dramatically illustrating his claim that an epidemic would strike Mari's livestock unless Zimri-Lim restored property stolen from Dagan's temple and exiled the guilty party (see Nissinen, 38–39). Although this oracle was delivered in a public forum, we are relatively sure that prophets did not receive the oracle in public. To judge from the present evidence, *muḫḫû* prophets normally received their oracles in the temple, where a fit of ecstasy was immediately followed by the delivery of an oracle in which the deity seized the prophet and spoke through his mouth. Important exceptions to this rule were the dream oracles that prophets received while they were sleeping, but even in these cases the prophet dreamt that he was receiving the oracle in the temple. Similarly ecstatic were the *assinnū* prophets, cult singers who were perhaps castrated males serving in the temple of the goddess Annunitum (i.e., Ištar). The *āpilū* were prophetic interpreters of omen signs, an interpretive role implied by their title (derived from *apālu*, "to answer"). We surmise that after the omens were taken, the *āpilū* stepped forward in order to supplement or further interpret the results of divination. Because omen interpretations were essentially either favorable or unfavorable, this practice added propositional content to the divine message. The close association of the *āpilū* with the respected institution of divination suggests that they enjoyed a higher status than the *muḫḫû*. The *āpilū* tended to be men (sixteen men to one woman) whereas the lower-class *muḫḫû* were more evenly divided (about twenty men to eight women). In spite of these status distinctions, it appears that all of the prophetic types were essentially peripheral figures in the Mari political establishment (although their roles in the respective cults were perhaps more central).

How did the prophetic oracles reach King Zimri-Lim? Ancient kings could not rule or protect their kingdoms without timely information, and for this reason they ordered their functionaries to report anything of interest to the court. Temple prophets, aware of this, usually passed oracular messages to the king through his

royal deputies, directly or by letter. Within Mari proper, the messages were often
entrusted to the most influential women in Zimri-Lim's life (especially his wife
Šiptu), but messages from the provinces and abroad were given to male deputies.
Eventually a written report of the oracle reached the king. Once the oracle arrived
in the royal court, its message was not immediately accepted but was instead submitted to Mari's diviners for further verification. This ritual method of verification,
called *piqittum*, required a lock of the prophet's hair or a fringe of his garment, but
its purpose is not entirely clear. Some scholars believe that this divination ritual was
designed to authenticate the prophet or his oracle, but others believe that it was to
determine a proper response to the oracle. How carefully was the prophet's message
guarded during its transmission? In the one instance where we possess several versions of a message passing to Zimri-Lim (ARM 26.197; 26.199; 26.202), it is clear
that the envoy's ideological concerns reshaped the oracle almost as soon as it left
the prophet's mouth (see Sasson 1994).

Texts and translations: J.-M. DURAND, "Les textes prophétiques," in *Archives épistolaires
de Mari,* vol. 1, part 1, pp. 377–452; NISSINEN, *Prophets and Prophecy in the Ancient Near
East,* 13–91. **Translations:** W. HEIMPEL, *Letters to the King of Mari: A New Translation, with
Historical Introduction, Notes, and Commentary* (MC 12; Winona Lake, Ind.: Eisenbrauns,
2003), 249–70, 325, 422; J. J. M. ROBERTS, "The Mari Prophetic Texts in Transliteration and
English Translation," in *The Bible and the Ancient Near East: Collected Essays* (Winona
Lake, Ind.: Eisenbrauns, 2002), 157–253; ANET 623–25, 629–32 (partial). **Bibliography:**
M. ANBAR, "Mari and the Origin of Prophecy," in *kinattutu ša dârâti: Raphael Kutscher
Memorial Volume* (ed. A.F. Rainey; Tel Aviv: Tel Aviv University, 1993), 1–5; D. CHARPIN,
"Le contexte historique et géographique des prophéties dans les textes retrouvés à Mari,"
Bulletin of the Canadian Society for Mesopotamian Studies 23 (1992): 28–32; J. F. CRAGHAN,
"The ARM X 'Prophetic' Texts: Their Media, Style, and Structure," *JANES* 6 (1974): 39–57;
IDEM, "Mari and Its Prophets: The Contributions of Mari to the Understanding of Biblical
Prophecy," *BTB* 5 (1975): 32–55; F. ELLERMEIER, *Prophetie in Mari und Israel* (Herzberg am
Harz, Germany: Erwin Jungfer, 1968); ELLIS, "Observations on Mesopotamian Oracles
and Prophetic Texts"; R. P. GORDON, "From Mari to Moses: Prophecy at Mari and in An-
cient Israel," in *Of Prophets' Visions and the Wisdom of Sages* (ed. H. A. McKay and D. J. A.
Clines; Sheffield, England: Sheffield Academic Press, 1993), 63–79; J. H. HAYES, "Prophe-
tism at Mari and Old Testament Parallels," *AThR* 49 (1967): 397–409; H. B. HUFFMON, "A
Company of Prophets: Mari, Assyria, Israel," in *Prophecy in Its Ancient Near Eastern Context* (ed. Nissinen), 47–70; IDEM, "The Expansion of Prophecy in the Mari Archives: New
Texts, New Readings, New Information, in *Prophecy and Prophets: The Diversity of Con-
temporary Issues in Scholarship* (ed. Y. Gitay; SemeiaSt; Atlanta: Scholars Press, 1997), 7–22;
A. MALAMAT, "The Forerunner of Biblical Prophecy: The Mari Documents," in *Ancient Is-
raelite Religion: Essays in Honor of Frank Moore Cross* (ed. P. D. Miller Jr., P. D. Hanson, and
S. D. McBride; Philadelphia: Fortress, 1987), 33–57; IDEM, "A Mari Prophecy and Nathan's
Dynastic Oracle," in *Prophecy* (ed. J. A. Emerton; Berlin: de Gruyter, 1980), 68–82; IDEM,
"A New Prophetic Message from Aleppo and Its Biblical Counterparts," in *Understanding
Poets and Prophets* (ed. A. G. Auld; Sheffield, England: Sheffield Academic Press, 1993),
236–41; IDEM, "Prophetic Revelations in the New Documents from Mari and the Bible," in
Volume du congrès: Genève, 1965 (VTSup 15; Leiden: Brill, 1966), 207–27; W. L. MORAN,
"New Evidence from Mari on the History of Prophecy," *Bib* 50 (1969): 15–56; E. NOORT,
Untersuchungen zum Götterbescheid in Mari (AOAT 202; Neukircken-Vluyn: Neukirch-

ener Verlag, 1977); S. B. PARKER, "Official Attitudes toward Prophecy at Mar and in Israel," *VT* 43 (1993): 50–68; B. PONGRATZ-LEISTEN, *Herrschaftswissen in Mesopotamien: Formen der Kommunikation zwischen Gott und König im 2. und 1. Jahrtausend v. Chr.* (SAAS 10; Helsinki: Helsinki University Press, 1999); J. M. SASSON, "Mari Dreams," *JAOS* 103 (1983): 283–93; IDEM, "The Posting of Letters with Divine Messages," in *Recueil d'études à la mémoire de Maurice Birot* (ed. D. Charpin and J.-M. Durand; FM 2; Mémoires de N.A.B.U. 3; Paris: SEPOA, 1994), 299–316; A. SCHART, "Combining Prophetic Oracles in Mari Letters and Jeremiah 36," *JANES* 23 (1995): 75–93; A. SCHMITT, *Prophetischer Gottesbescheid in Mari und Israel: Eine Strukturuntersuchung* (Stuttgart: Kohlhammer, 1982); K. VAN DER TOORN, "From the Oral to the Written: The Case of Old Babylonian Prophecy," in *Writings and Speech in Israelite and Ancient Near Eastern Prophecy* (ed. Ben Zvi and Floyd), 219–34; IDEM, "Mesopotamian Prophecy between Immanence and Transcendence: A Comparison of Old Babylonian and Neo-Assyrian Prophecy," in *Prophecy in Its Ancient Near Eastern Context* (ed. Nissinen), 71–87; WILSON, *Prophecy and Society in Ancient Israel*, 109–10.

The Old Babylonian Ešnunna Prophecies. Two eighteenth-century tablets from Ešnunna record oracles from the goddess Kititum (i.e., Ištar) to King Ibalpiel II (ca. 1779–1765). The reports are cast in the form of letters from the goddess. The better preserved of the two texts promises divine support for the faithful king, including Kititum's vow to establish a "protective spirit" for the king. No prophetic figures are mentioned in the texts, but the tablets are undoubtedly scribal records of actual prophetic utterances.

Texts and translations: M. DEJ. ELLIS, "The Goddess Kititum Speaks to King Ibalpiel: Oracle Texts from Ischali," *MARI* 5 (1987): 235–66; NISSINEN, *Prophets and Prophecy in the Ancient Near East*, 93–95. *Bibliography:* ELLIS, "Observations on Mesopotamian Oracles and Prophetic Texts"; HUFFMON, "Ancient Near Eastern Prophecy," *ABD* 5:477–82; W. L. MORAN, "An Ancient Prophetic Oracle," in *Biblische Theologie und gesellschaftlicher Wandel: Für Norbert Lohfink* (ed. G. Braulik et al.; Freiburg im Breisgau: Herder, 1993), 252–59.

The Neo-Assyrian Prophecies. When we turn from Mari and Ešnunna to the Neo-Assyrian prophecies, we leap over an entire millennium of history into a new historical era. The ruling Sargonid dynasty controlled vast stretches of the Near East, from Elam in the East to Egypt in the West. As with any large kingdom, the pressures on its stability were considerable from both within and without, and propaganda was an important element in the effort to stem the tide of entropy. The Assyrian prophecies of the seventh century B.C.E. represented one facet of the complex ideological network that reinforced Sargonid authority. The Assyrian prophecies comprise a small but telling corpus of seven oracle reports and four collections of prophetic oracles. Because the reports are the more basic of the two genres, being the sources from which the collections were composed, let us consider them first. Neo-Assyrian prophetesses and prophets were cultic personnel supported by the temple, in most cases by a temple of Ištar (in Arbela) or by a temple of Ištar's other manifestations (e.g., Mullissu in Assyria). Most of the intermediaries were females in the goddess cult, but male prophets, often castrates, were also devoted to the Ištar cult. Although our oracles date only to the seventh century, it is known that prophets and prophetesses served in the Ištar cult at least as early as the second millennium and perhaps earlier (Parpola). By the Neo-Assyrian period their native titles were *raggimu/raggimtu* ("shouter"), apparently ecstatics like the earlier *muḫḫû* from Mari. Because of the close relationship between the king and the Ištar cult, however, the Assyrian prophetesses were more centrally located than the peripheral prophets of Mari. For this reason extispicy was rarely used to confirm Neo-Assyrian prophecies. The messages of the oracles were almost exclusively words of encouragement for the royal family, in which Ištar said, "Fear not," and cited her past support of the dynasty as a basis for confidence in the present and future. Granted, Ištar's prophetesses sometimes demanded faith, praise, and cultic support for their goddess as well, and they were even critical of the king and his behavior at times. Nevertheless, other texts show that prophets were sternly warned against speaking "any evil, improper, ugly word which is neither seemly nor good to Assurbanipal, the great crown prince designate, son of Esarhaddon" (Parpola). Failure to support the regime was the hallmark of "false prophecy" in Assyria (Nissinen 1996).

Assyrian prophetesses delivered their oracles in a variety of cultic and noncultic contexts, so, contrary to the pattern in Mari, oracles did not have to be delivered in the temple of the god or goddess in question. The rhetorical power and persuasiveness of the oracles were accentuated by various rhythmic and poetic patterns, as was the case with the earlier Mari prophecies. When oracles were delivered, the royal deputies had them committed to writing and passed them on to the king. These copies were composed on tablets with a horizontal orientation, which were used for temporary reports that would later be discarded. More important oracles were then transferred onto larger archival tablets for preservation in the state archive. These new copies were recast in the *ṭuppu* format, which employs the vertical columns used in archival texts (see Parpola, liii). When editors transferred the oracles to an archival format, they sometimes combined them into larger collections.

We possess four such collections from the Neo-Assyrian period, but one of these (the fourth collection) is fragmentary. The first collection contains at least ten oracles of encouragement addressed to King Esarhaddon by different prophets. Preservation and rereading of these oracles reminded the king of Ištar's continuing faithfulness during difficult periods in his reign. The thematic rationale behind the collection differs somewhat from the biblical collections, where authorship was often—but not always—the basis of the collection. The second collection also contains oracles of encouragement and dates to a period when Esarhaddon was facing threats from disloyal elements in his kingdom. Once again the collection includes oracles from several prophets. The third collection, the Covenant of Assur, includes oracles that were delivered in connection with a covenant ritual performed during Esarhaddon's coronation (681 B.C.E.), in which the god Assur promised to protect and preserve the king's dynasty. These oracles warned Assyrians to "listen" to Esarhaddon (collection 3, line 2), motivating them to do so with vivid descriptions of the punishments received by recent rebels and traitors. Copies of these oracles were then deposited before the divine images housed in the Assur temple. This covenant collection was probably the earliest of the three collections from Esarhaddon's reign, but all three were compiled and composed by the same scribe. Hence, it was a single scribal redactor, not the prophets themselves, who determined the content of the collections and their ultimate arrangement. The Neo-Assyrian evidence provides a suggestive glimpse into a prophetic process that began with oral speech and ended with written oracle collections stored in an archive. This process is, naturally, interesting to students of the Hebrew Bible because the biblical prophetic books are ostensibly products of a similar process. In the case of the Neo-Assyrian prophecies, however, the time frame between their oral delivery and their compilation into collections was very short, in stark contrast to the centuries of transmission that followed the composition of the canonical prophetic texts in the Bible. For this reason, if the Neo-Assyrian evidence illuminates our study of Israelite prophecy, it does so primarily in the initial stages of the process that created the Hebrew prophetic books (Nissinen, "Spoken"). For closely related texts, see the Neo-Assyrian oracle letters in the following entry.

Texts and translations: NISSINEN, *Prophets and Prophecy in the Ancient Near East,* 97–177; S. PARPOLA, *Assyrian Prophecies* (SAA 9; Helsinki: Helsinki University Press, 1997). *Translation:* ANET 449–51, 605–6. *Bibliography:* ELLIS, "Observations on Mesopotamian Oracles and Prophetic Texts"; F. M. FALES and G. B. LANFRANCHI, "The Impact of Oracular Material on the Political Utterances and Political Action in the Royal Inscriptions of the Sargonid Dynasty," in *Oracles et prophéties dans l'antiquité* (ed. J.-G. Heintz; Paris: De Boccard, 1997), 99–114; H. B. HUFFMON, "A Company of Prophets: Mari, Assyria, Israel," in *Prophecy in Its Ancient Near Eastern Context* (ed. Nissinen), 47–70; M. NISSINEN, "City as Lofty as Heaven: Arbela and Other Cities in Neo-Assyrian Prophecy," in *"Every City Shall Be Forsaken": Urbanism and Prophecy in Ancient Israel and the Near East* (ed. L. L. Grabbe and R. D. Haak; JSOTSup 330; Sheffield Academic Press, 2001), 174–209; IDEM, "Falsche Prophetie in neuassyrischer und deuteronomisticher Darstellung," in *Das Deuteronomium und seine Querbeziehungen* (ed. T. Veijola; Helsinki: Finnische Exegetische Gesellschaft, 1996), 172–95; IDEM, *References to Prophecy in Neo-Assyrian Sources* (SAAS 7; Helsinki: Helsinki University Press, 1998); IDEM, "The Socioreligious Role of the Neo-Assyrian Prophets," in *Prophecy in Its Ancient Near Eastern Context* (ed. Nissinen), 89–114; IDEM, "Spoken, Written, Quoted, and Invented: Orality and Writtenness in Ancient Near Eastern Prophecy," in *Writings and Speech in Israelite and Ancient Near Eastern Prophecy* (ed. Ben Zvi and Floyd), 235–71; B. PONGRATZ-LEISTEN, *Herrschaftswissen in Mesopotamien: Formen der Kommunikation zwischen Gott und König im 2. und 1. Jahrtausend v. Chr.* (SAAS 10; Helsinki: Helsinki University Press, 1999); M. WEIPPERT, "Assyrische Prophetien der Zeit Asarhaddons und Assurbanipals," in *Assyrian Royal Inscriptions: New Horizons in Literary, Ideological, and Historical Analysis* (ed. F. M. Fales; Rome: Istituto per l'Oriente, Centro per le Antichità e la Storia dell'Arte del Vicino Oriente, 1981), 71–115; WILSON, *Prophecy and Society in Ancient Israel,* 111–19.

Neo-Assyrian Letters from the Gods. Among our Sargonid-era tablets are several fragmentary texts that purport to be letters sent from the gods to Neo-Assyrian kings. The letters are clearly literary texts rather than standard letters, not only because they come from the gods but also because the texts were carefully formatted using rulings. The texts are divine responses to letters sent from the kings. For instance, in one exemplar, the god Aššur responds to Assurbanipal's favorable report on the war with Šamaš-šum-ukin, his "rebel" brother ruling in Babylon. Aššur insists that Assurbanipal's victories over his brother were the result of divine favor, which the god had lavished upon Assurbanipal because of Šamaš-šum-ukin's "evil deeds" and sins. Assurbanipal's attack on Babylon was apparently unpopular in some circles, and there is plenty of evidence that he undertook an extensive propaganda campaign to secure his support after the battle. Priestly diviners of the royal court likely composed this text as a part of that campaign. The king would have accepted this letter and our other exemplars as messages of encouragement during tough times.

Readers should note a closely related literary dialogue between Assurbanipal and the god Nabu (see 3.1.2) and an additional text from the Middle Babylonian period that may be a letter from the goddess Belit-balati to an individual named Nusku-taqishu-bullit (see Grayson). For letters written *to* the gods, see 3.1.2.

Text and translation: A. LIVINGSTONE, *Court Poetry and Literary Miscellanea* (SAA 3; Helsinki: Helsinki University Press, 1989), 107–15. *Bibliography:* A. K. GRAYSON, "Literary Letters from Deities and Diviners: More Fragments," in *Studies in Literature from the Ancient Near East: Dedicated to Samuel Noah Kramer* (ed. J. M. Sasson; AOS 65; New Haven: American Oriental Society, 1984), 143–48; B. PONGRATZ-LEISTEN, *Herrschaftswissen in Mesopotamien: Formen der Kommunikation zwischen Gott und König im 2. und 1. Jahrtausend v.Chr.* (SAAS 10; Helsinki: Helsinki University Press, 1999), 210–65.

6.2. Egyptian Prophecies and Omens

The paucity of Egyptian omen literature makes Egypt a notable exception in the ancient world. Extispicy seems never to have been practiced there, and astronomical omens appeared only late in Egyptian history through influence from Mesopotamia. The primary indigenous forms of Egyptian intermediation included oneiromancy (dream omens) and priestly oracles.

Egyptian Dream Omens. Oneiromancy appears in Egyptian texts from as early as the Nineteenth Dynasty (ca. 1300–1100) and as late as the second century B.C.E. (see Gardiner and Volten, respectively). The omens they contain are comparable to the Mesopotamian dream omens, so it is possible—perhaps likely—that they were inspired by practices in Mesopotamia.

Texts and translations: A. H. GARDINER, *Hieratic Papyri in the British Museum, Third Series: Chester Beatty Gift* (2 vols.; London: British Museum, 1935), 1:9–23; A. VOLTEN, *Demotische Traumdeutung (Pap. Carlsberg XIII und XIV Verso)* (Copenhagen: Munksgaard, 1942). *Translations:* ANET 495; COS 1.33: 52–54. *Bibliography:* A. L. OPPENHEIM, *The Interpretation of Dreams in the Ancient Near East: With a Translation of an Assyrian Dream Book* (TAPS, NS 46.3; Philadelphia: American Philosophical Society, 1956), 243–45.

Egyptian Oracles. From the New Kingdom onward—and probably in earlier periods as well—one could submit verbal or written questions to the god as his statue was transported by bark during festivals. The god was concealed within a portable shrine on such occasions, so petitions were answered "yes" or "no" through the bark's movements. Because the bark was carried by laymen, we can imagine that its movements were somehow directed by the priests who conducted the divine procession. Oral petitions to the god were answered by the statue's movement toward or away from the petitioner, whereas the written queries were presented to the god in the form of two short texts, which often took the form of "So and so is right" and "So and so is wrong." The two texts were laid before the god, and the god indicated his choice by walking toward one of them (although in the later period the statue apparently answered the question in words, thanks to a speaking tube used by a priest concealed in the statue). Because the oracles often had legal implications, the results of the petitions were frequently written down and preserved in the archives for later reference. As a result, our textual evidence for the oracles includes two text types: very short oracle queries (see Cerný 1935, 1942, 1972) and longer texts that record query results (e.g., P.Brooklyn 47.218.3; see Parker). There are also numerous texts and depictions that refer to the oracles and hence fill out our picture of this religious institution.

The gods for whom we have evidence of the practice—either oracles or references to oracles—include Amun, Mut, Khons, and Mont (all of Thebes) as well as Isis (Abydos), Ptah (Memphis), and Setekh (Dakhleh). The vast majority of our oracle queries, however, have been found at Deir el-Medinah, where the divinized Pharaoh Amenhotep I was often consulted for oracles (see Kruchten 2000; Ryholt). It is likely that the principle god of each town was sometimes approached when difficult and important decisions needed to be made, especially thorny judicial cases (see Jin; Cerný 1962). In another common custom, parents asked the god whether their young child would live—not a surprising practice given infant mortality in the ancient world. In a few cases, Egyptian kings claim to have been selected by oracles given to them or to others, but it is likely that these royal inscriptions were works of propaganda rather than history (see *ANET* 446–48).

Texts and translations: A. M. BLACKMAN, "Oracles in Ancient Egypt," *JEA* 11 (1925): 249–55; 12 (1926): 176–85; J. CERNÝ, "Nouvelle série des questions adressées aux oracles," *BIFAO* 41 (1942): 13–24; IDEM, "Questions adressées aux oracles," *BIFAO* 35 (1935): 41–58; IDEM, "Le tirage au sort," *BIFAO* 40 (1941): 135–41; IDEM, "Troisième série des questions adressées aux oracles," *BIFAO* 72 (1972): 49–69; J.-M. KRUCHTEN, *Le grand texte oraculaire de Djehoutymose, intendant du domaine d'Amon sous le pontificat de Pinedjem II* (Monographies Reine Élisabeth 5; Brussels, 1986); IDEM, "Un Oracle d' 'Amenhotep du Village' sous Ramsès III: Ostracon Gardiner 103," in *Deir el-Medina in the Third Millennium AD: A Tribute to Jac. J. Janssen* (ed. R. J. Demarée and A. Egberts; Egyptologische Uitgaven 14; Leiden: Nederlands Instituut voor het Nabije Oosten, 2000), 209–16; PARKER, ed., *A Saite Oracle Papyrus from Thebes in the Brooklyn Museum [P. Brooklyn 47.218.3];* K. RYHOLT, "Two New Kingdom Oracle Petitions, O. BMFA 72.659, 72.666," *REg* 48 (1997): 279–82. *Translation:* G. ROEDER, *Ägyptische Mythologie* (3 vols.; Düsseldorf: Artemis & Winkler, 1998), 3:191–272 (partial). *Bibliography:* J. CERNÝ, "Egyptian Oracles," in

A Saite Oracle Papyrus from Thebes in the Brooklyn Museum [P. Brooklyn 47.218.3] (Providence: Brown University Press, 1962, 35–48); IDEM, "Une expression désignant la réponse négative d'un oracle," *BIFAO* 30 (1931): 491–96; V. DOMINIQUE and H. GENEVIÈVE, "Les Questions oracularies d'Égypte: Histoire de la recherche, nouveautés, et perspectives," in *Egyptian Religion—the Last Thousand Years: Studies Dedicated to the Memory of Jan Quaegebeur* (ed. W. Clarysse, A. Schoors, and H. Willems; 2 vols.; OLA 84–85; Leuven: Petters, 1998), 2:1055–71; S. HERRMANN, "Prophetie in Israel und Ägypten: Recht und Grenze eines Vergleiches," in *Congress Volume: Bonn, 1962* (VTSup 9; Leiden: Brill, 1963), 47–65; S. JIN, "Ein Gottesurteil im pBoulaq X: Ein Fall von 'Balance of Power' bei dem Gottesorakel?" *JESHO* 44 (2001): 95–102; J. LECLANT, "Éléments pour une étude de la divination dans l'Égypte pharaonique," in *La divination* (ed. A. Caquot and M. Leibovici; 2 vols.; Presses Universitaires de France, 1968), 1:1–23; S. SAUNERON, *The Priests of Ancient Egypt* (new ed.; Ithaca: Cornell University Press, 2000), 96–103; WILSON, *Prophecy and Society in Ancient Israel*, 124–28, 217–23.

Egyptian Hemerologies. Like the Mesopotamians, the Egyptians composed calendars that labeled the days of the year as either lucky or unlucky. The nature of a given day was tied to the mythological traditions, where events in the heavens on a given date—for good or ill—were believed to affect events on earth as well, portending evil or good for people born on particular days. Charms and other magical operations could apparently alleviate such fates to some extent. In other respects, the calendars were used to plan activities in the present and future, with important undertakings being scheduled to coincide with auspicious dates in the calendar. The most complete exemplars are the Cairo Calendar (see Bakir 1966) and P.Sallier IV (Chabas; Budge), but several others are known (see Bakir 1948).

Texts and translations: A. EL-MOHSEN BAKIR, "The Cairo Calendar of Lucky and Unlucky Days (Journal d'Entrée, 86637)," *ASAE* 48 (1948): 425–31; IDEM, *The Cairo Calendar No. 86637* (Cairo: Government Press, 1966); E. A. W. BUDGE, *Egyptian Hieratic Papyri in the British Museum, Second Series* (London: British Museum, 1923), pls. 88–111 (P.Sallier IV); F. CHABAS, *Le calendrier des jours fastes et néfastes de l'année égyptienne (Papyrus Sallier, IV)* (Paris: [s.d.], 1890) (P.Sallier IV); C. LEITZ, *Tagewählerei: das Buch ḥȝt nḥḥ pḥ.wy ḏt und verwandte Texte* (2 vols.; ÄgAbh 55; Wiesbaden: Harrassowitz, 1994) (Cairo Calendar). ***Bibliography:*** T. A. BACS, "Prolegomena to the Study of Calendars of Lucky and Unlucky Days," in *Magic in Egypt in the Time of the Pharaohs* (ed. A. Roccati and A. Siliotti; Verona: Rassegna Internazionale di Cinematografia Archeologica Arte e Natura Libri, 1987), 245–56; A. EL-MOHSEN BAKIR, "The Cairo Calendar of Lucky and Unlucky Days (Journal d'Entrée, 86637)," *ASAE* 48 (1948): 425–31; W. R. DAWSON, "Some Observations on the Egyptian Calendars of Lucky and Unlucky Days," *JEA* 12 (1926): 260–64.

6.3. West Semitic and Hittite Intermediation

Many omen texts have also been unearthed at Ugarit, Hatti, and elsewhere in the ancient Near East, but these exemplars are generally dependent upon the Mesopotamian omen tradition. Regarding prophecy, our sources are much poorer, being limited primarily to the Deir 'Alla Inscription (see below) and to several references to West Semitic prophecy in the Egyptian story of Wenamun (see 8.1), the Amman Citadel Inscription (see 15.2), the Aramaic Zakkur Inscription (see 15.2), and the Hebrew Lachish Letters (see 15.1).

Hittite Omens and Oracles. The most common type of native Hittite divination appears to have been the "KIN-oracle" (Kammenhuber), a form of psephomancy (lot-casting) performed by an elder female cult functionary. Another preferred omen type was ornithomancy, based on the observation of bird flight and behavior (see Archi). Most of the other omen types represented in the Hittite corpus reflect strong Mesopotamian influences. One of the more interesting of these is *KUB* 5.7 (= *ANET* 497–98), which records a series of extispicy queries by which the diviners attempted to determine why the gods were angry at Hatti. Several offenses against the gods were discovered, but unfortunately the text breaks off before the diviners arrive at a final answer (if, indeed, they ever did). One of the problems uncovered by the diviners was that the temple precinct had been defiled by invalids and mutilated people who had entered its doors. As a result, the text prescribed that the Hittite old woman (a cult functionary) would "perform a rite for the god in the manner to which she is accustomed." The notion that physically impaired people could defile the sacred precinct should be compared to 2 Sam 5:6–8, Lev 21:16–23, and Deut 23:1.

Texts and translations: See list in *CTH* 531–82; O. R. GURNEY, "A Hittite Divination Text," in D. J. WISEMAN, *The Alalakh Tablets* (OPBIAA 2; London: British Institute of Archaeology at Ankara, 1953), 116–18; *KUB* 5.7. ***Translations:*** *ANET* 497–98 [*KUB* 5.7]; *COS* 1.78–79: 204–11. ***Bibliography:*** A. ARCHI, "L'ornitomanzia ittita," *Studi micenei ed egeoanatolici* 16 (1975): 62–77; S. R. BIN-NUN, "Some Remarks on Hittite Oracles, Dreams, and Omina," *Or* 48 (1979): 118–27; A. KAMMENHUBER, *Orakelpraxis, Träume, und Vorzeichenschau bei den Hethitern* (TH 7; Heidelberg: C. Winter, 1976); E. LAROCHE, "Éléments d'haruspicine hittite," *RHA* 54 (1952): 19–48; IDEM, "Lécanomancie hittite," *RA* 52 (1958): 150–62; K. K. RIEMSCHNEIDER, *Babylonische Geburtsomina in hethitischer Übersetzung* (StBoT 9; Wiesbaden: Harrassowitz, 1970); M. SCHOUL, "Die Terminologie des hethitischen SU-Orakels," *AoF* 21 (1994): 73–124; WILSON, *Prophecy and Society in Ancient Israel*, 223–27.

Ugaritic Omens. Although we have no direct evidence of prophetic intermediation at Ugarit, omen procedures were apparently used there, including extispicy, astrology, teratomancy, and oneiromancy. Our evidence for these practices includes liver and lung models (extispicy), astrological reports (astrology), and several divination compendia for teratomancy, oneiromancy, and lunar omens. All of these omen procedures were widely used elsewhere in the Near East. Ugarit seems to have adopted these omen forms from Mesopotamia.

Text and translation: D. PARDEE, *Ritual and Cult at Ugarit* (SBLWAW 10; Atlanta: Scholars Press, 2002), 127–48. ***Translations:*** *COS* 1.90–93: 287–94. ***Bibliography:*** DEL OLMO LETE, *Canaanite Religion*, 345–59.

Royal Necromancy at Ugarit. The deceased kings of Ugarit were divinized, and they participated with the living royal family in an ongoing funerary cult (see

5.9.4). One aspect of this cult was apparently necromancy, in which the deceased kings delivered oracles to those still alive. Little is known about this practice, although ritual texts sometimes refer to it or imply that it was done. The one text that seems to describe necromancy directly is RS 1.124 (Pardee, 170–72), in which Ditanu, the eponymous ancestor of Ugarit's royal dynasty, was consulted on behalf of a royal child who was ill. Ditanu provided a ritual remedy for the problem, but we do not know how this remedy was communicated to the sitting king. Mesopotamian medical rituals similar to this were often placed in the mouths of gods—especially Ea and Marduk—so it is possible that RS 1.124 was a type of ritual prescription rather than a true oracle. According to del Olmo Lete, other texts relevant to Ugaritic necromancy might include *KTU* 1.41, 1.87, 1.104, 1.106, and 1.112 (see Pardee). The obvious comparative text from the Hebrew Bible is Saul's consultation with Samuel through the sorceress of Endor (1 Sam 28:3–25).

Text and translation: D. PARDEE, *Ritual and Cult at Ugarit* (SBLWAW 10; Atlanta: Scholars Press, 2002), 170–72. ***Bibliography:*** DEL OLMO LETE, *Canaanite Religion*, 212–53, 306–16, 346–47.

The Deir ʿAlla Inscription. This poetic story, entitled the "Book of Balaam Son of Beor" and dating to the eighth century B.C.E., was discovered at Deir ʿAlla in Transjordan (near the Jabbok River in ancient Ammon). Although the text is essentially a tale and so would fit nicely in chapter 8 below, for comparative purposes it is included here. The tale was written in red and black ink on the plaster wall of a building that was not a temple (cf. the writing on plastered stone in Deut 27:1–8). The inscription's language stands between Aramaic and the Canaanite dialects of Palestine. Although the broken state of the text precludes certainty, scholars have managed to piece together two sequences of text (combinations I and II). In the opening sequence, the god El reveals to Balaam a vision of doom, which Balaam relates to his people on the following day. Here we learn that the gods are plotting to force Shagar, a goddess of light and fertility, to seal up the heavens and thereby to prevent life-giving light and rain from reaching the people. What follows is obscure, but it appears that Balaam thwarts this plan by offering a series of oracles and magical rituals. The second sequence is too fragmentary to summarize, but clearly the two sequences are related to the biblical story of Balaam son of Peor in Num 22–24. If the historical Balaam lived during the ninth century B.C.E., as Margalit supposes, then this would establish a terminus a quo for the biblical tradition. In certain respects, the Deir ʿAlla stories are comparable to the prophetic biographies found in the Hebrew prophetic books (e.g., Jeremiah).

Texts and translations: J. A. HACKETT, *The Balaam Text from Deir ʿAlla* (HSM 31; Chico, Calif.: Scholars Press, 1984); J. HOFTIJZER and G. VAN DER KOOIJ, *Aramaic Texts from Deir ʿAlla* (Leiden: Brill, 1976); *KAI* #312; B. A. LEVINE, "The Deir ʿAlla Plaster Inscriptions," *JAOS* 101 (1981): 195–205. ***Translation:*** COS 2.27: 140–45. ***Bibliography:*** W. E. AUF-RECHT, "A Bibliography of the Deir ʿAlla Plaster Texts," *Newsletter for Targumic and Cognate Studies* Supplement 2 (1985): 1–7; M. L. BARRÉ, "The Portrait of Balaam in Numbers

22–24," *Int* 51 (1997): 254–66; G. COATS, "Balaam: Sinner or Saint?" *BR* 18 (1973): 21–29;
J. HOFTIJZER and G. VAN DER KOOIJ, eds., *The Balaam Text from Deir ʿAlla Re-evaluated*
(New York: Brill, 1991); B. MARGALIT, "Ninth-Century Israelite Prophecy in the Light of
Contemporary NWSemitic Epigraphs," in *Und Mose schrieb dieses Lied auf—Studien zum
Alten Testament und zum alten Orient: Festschrift für Oswald Loretz* (ed. M. Dietrich and
I. Kottsieper; AOAT 250; Münster: Ugarit, 1998), 515–32; M. S. MOORE, *The Balaam Tra-
ditions: Their Character and Development* (SBLDS 113; Atlanta: Scholars Press, 1990); C.-L.
SEOW, "West Semitic Sources," in Nissinen, *Prophets and Prophecy in the Ancient Near East*,
201–18; J. VAN SETERS, "From Faithful Prophet to Villain: Observations on the Tradition
History of the Balaam Story," in *A Biblical Itinerary—in Search of Method, Form, and Content: Essays in Honor of George W. Coats* (ed. E. E. Carpenter; JSOTSup 240; Sheffield, England: Sheffield Academic Press, 1997), 126–32.

Concluding Observations

Six key issues are presently matters of debate or discussion in the study of
Hebrew intermediation. Although the comments offered here will give attention
to all of the comparative Near Eastern data, the Mesopotamian materials constitute the bulk of the Near Eastern evidence and so figure prominently in the
conclusions.

1. **Poetry and Prophecy.** Some biblical scholars have argued that the Israelite
prophets were essentially religious poets. This equation is perhaps too
simple, but it is true that many of the Bible's prophetic oracles are poetic.
Poetry was also a feature in the Near Eastern prophecies, although the poetic nature of the Mari texts is more pronounced than in the Neo-Assyrian
exemplars. In the oral culture of ancient Mesopotamia, the poetic qualities
of the oracles would have enhanced the receptivity of the listening audience. The same can be said of the biblical prophecies.

2. **Orality, Writing, and Prophecy.** Mesopotamian prophecies were delivered
orally and then preserved in writing. During this process the prophecies
underwent at least three stages of editorial shaping. As we see in the
Mari texts, the oracle reports were strongly influenced by the ideological
perspectives and concerns of those who wrote them. Consequently, the rhetorical shaping of the oracles was an immediate and unavoidable phenomenon. A second level of editorial influence is visible in the Neo-Assyrian
evidence, as the state apparatus decided to preserve some oracles in an archival form for later consultation. In this case, it was the choice to preserve
the oracle in a certain way that gave it a kind of nascent canonical status.
The third stage of editorial shaping appeared in the Neo-Assyrian practice
of creating small oracle collections, which joined together disparate oracles
on the basis of theme and content. What do these observations tell us about
the Hebrew prophetic books? First, an obvious point is that the biblical

prophecies probably do not give us a verbatim record of ancient Israelite prophetic oracles. If we can judge from the Mesopotamian oracles, this conclusion would seem to hold even if the oracles were recorded and preserved sometime close to their delivery. Second, and perhaps more important, the rhetorical and ideological shaping of the Near Eastern oracles became progressively more profound as the text passed from one context to the next. Given the complexity of Israel's prophetic literature, the long period during which it was transmitted, and the many different ideological hands through which it passed, we should expect that each prophetic book is the end product of a lively editorial and theological process.

3. Prophecy, the State, and the Transmission of Hebrew Prophecies. Nearly all of our Near Eastern prophetic sources were recorded by and preserved for a state apparatus. It is likely that the royal courts in ancient Israel also preserved records of prophetic oracles. The short book of Nahum, which contains a collection of oracles against Assyria, is very similar to the Neo-Assyrian oracle collections and may have come to us by way of Judean archival records. On this point, however, there are certain complications with comparing the Israelite and Near Eastern exemplars. With the exception of a few instances from Mari, the ancient states tended to preserve only prophetic oracles that supported the state apparatus. Indeed, Neo-Assyrian law specifically forbade prophecies that openly criticized the state. By comparison, the Hebrew prophets frequently disparaged the governments of Israel and Judah. Jeremiah offered many extensive criticisms of the state, even predicting the state's downfall. This evidence invites us to consider another context in which the prophetic words of Jeremiah could have been perpetuated. The book of Jeremiah makes the specific claim that a circle of prophetic supporters—including especially the scribe Baruch—wrote down and preserved the prophet's sayings. Although this claim can never be proved, the authors and editors of Jeremiah would not have gained anything by inventing the idea (see 15.1). Nevertheless, it is clear that our Hebrew prophetic corpus was preserved and transmitted through some combination of state and non-state contexts.

4. Prophetic Biographies and Tales. One feature that clearly distinguishes the biblical prophetic books from their much shorter and less complex Near Eastern counterparts is the presence of biographical narratives about the Hebrew prophets. The comparative evidence does preserve the prophetic tale about Balaam and his oracles, so it is not impossible to imagine that similar tales about the Israelite prophets were composed and preserved along with the oracles. The fact that the Hebrew prophets were often peripheral figures who stood up against the status quo would likely have spawned heroic stories about them, such as we have concerning Elisha and Elijah. It is difficult, however, to imagine how these biographical and legendary details were written, collected, and preserved apart from the state apparatus. This difficulty is in principle not much different than the problem of how the oracles themselves came to appear in the prophetic books.

5. Canonicity and Intermediation. The Near Eastern prophecies were composed soon after the delivery of the oracles that they record and so were not the product of a long canonical process. For this reason, although the prophecies might shed some light on the initial stages of the creation of the Israelite prophetic books, they tell us very little about the subsequent development of the books. Fortunately, the Near East provides us with reasonably good comparative exemplars for the study of Israel's canonical prophecies: the omen compendia. The omen compendia are canonical texts that reflect a long and arduous process of composition and editing. Though the omens were not prophecies, their authority in matters of intermediation caused the ancients to preserve them and also to add to them. The resulting editorial process was painstaking and systematic. It seems likely that the long and multifarious character of the Hebrew prophetic books—especially books such as Isaiah and Jeremiah—can be attributed to such a canonical process.

6. Divination in Ancient Israel. Although the biblical sources may leave us with the impression that divination was neither acceptable nor widely practiced in ancient Israel, scholars are fairly certain that this is a misperception. The old story of Elisha in 2 Kgs 13:14–20 shows the prophet engaged in omens by arrow, and the ongoing rhetoric against divination, such as appears in Deut 18:9–22 and 2 Kgs 17:17, can only be an indication that divination was widely practiced. Moreover, there is at least one kind of divination that the Hebrew canon endorsed: psephomancy. Unfortunately, we know very little about this priestly use of the Urim and Thummim (see Exod 28:30; Lev 8:8; Num 27:21) apart from what may be gleaned from the Mesopotamian evidence. Most scholars date the priestly endorsement of the Urim and Thummim to the postexilic period, when Jews were under strong and continuous influences from Mesopotamia. This step could have been an act of resistance against the influences of Mesopotamian divination. By adopting and endorsing psephomancy, the Israelite priests not only embraced the simplest form of divination but also rejected forms of divination that viewed the created world—especially the stars, planets, sun, and moon—as divinely ordered expressions of the divine will. This theological posture would have been in keeping with the monotheistic conceptions of the Priestly writer's account of creation (Gen 1). At the same time, postbiblical Judaism apparently became increasingly more comfortable with certain forms of Mesopotamian divination. Passages in the Babylonian Talmud provide ritual prescriptions for lecanomancy (oil omens), in which the gods Ea, Sin, Šamaš, and Marduk are demythologized as the sea and three luminaries (see Salvesen, 155–56).

General Bibliography

R. C. BAILEY, "Prophetic Use of Omen Motifs: A Preliminary Study," in *The Biblical Canon in Comparative Perspective* (ed. K. L. Younger Jr., W. W. Hallo, and B. F. Batto; Scripture in Context 4; Lewiston, N.Y.: Mellen, 1991), 195–215; H. M. BARSTAD, "No Prophets? Recent Developments in Biblical Prophetic Research and Ancient Near Eastern Prophecy," *JSOT* 57 (1993): 39–60; E. BEN ZVI and M. H. FLOYD, eds., *Writings and Speech in Israelite and Ancient Near Eastern Prophecy* (Atlanta: Scholars Press, 2000); R. BERCHMAN, ed., *Mediators of the Divine: Horizons of Prophecy, Divination, Dreams, and Theurgy in Mediterranean Antiquity* (Atlanta, Ga.: Scholars Press, 1998); F. CRYER, *Divination in Ancient Israel and Its Near Eastern Environment: A Socio-historical Investigation* (JSOTSup 142; Sheffield, England: JSOT Press, 1994); *La divination en Mésopotamie ancienne et dans les Régions voisines: 14e Rencontre assyriologique internationale* (Paris: Presses Universitaires de France, 1966); J.-M. DURAND, *Archives épistolaires de Mari* (ARM 26; Paris: Éditions Recherche sur les Civilisations, 1988–); M. DEJ. ELLIS, "Observations on Mesopotamian Oracles and Prophetic Texts: Literary and Historiographic Considerations," *JCS* 41 (1989): 127–86; A. JEFFERS, *Magic and Divination in Ancient Palestine and Syria* (Studies in the History and Culture of the Ancient Near East 8; Leiden: Brill, 1996); A. M. KITZ, "Prophecy as Divination," *CBQ* 65 (2003): 22–42; U. KOCH-WESTENHOLZ, *Mesopotamian Astrology: An Introduction to Babylonian and Assyrian Celestial Divination* (Copenhagen: Carsten Niebuhr Institute of Ancient Near Eastern Studies, Museum Tusculanum Press, University of Copenhagen, 1995); M. KÖCKERT and M. NISSINEN, eds., *Propheten in Mari, Assyrien, und Israel* (FRLANT; Göttingen: Vandenhoeck & Ruprecht, 2003); W. G. LAMBERT, "The Qualifications of Babylonian Diviners," in *Tikip santakki mala bašmu: Eine Festschrift für Rykle Borger* (ed. S. M. Paul; CM 10; Groningen, Neth.: Styx, 1998), 141–55; E. LEICHTY, "The Origins of Scholarship," in *Die Rolle der Astronomie in den Kulteren Mesopotamiens* (ed. H. D. Galter; Grazer morgenländische Studien 3; Graz: Druck & Verlagsgesellschaft, 1993), 20–29; E. LEICHTY, M. DEJ. ELLIS, and P. GERARDI, eds., *A Scientific Humanist: Studies in Memory of Abraham Sachs* (OPSNKF 9; Philadelphia: University Museum, 1988); A. R. MILLARD, "La prophetie et l'Écriture—Israel, Aram, Assyrie," *RHR* 2002, no. 2 (1985): 125–45; W. L. MORAN, "An Ancient Prophetic Oracle," in *Biblische Theologie und gesellschaftlicher Wandel* (ed. G. Braulik, W. Gross, and S. McEvenue; Freiburg in Breisgau: Herder, 1993), 252–59; M. NISSINEN, ed., *Prophecy in Its Ancient Near Eastern Context: Mesopotamian, Biblical, and Arabian Perspectives* (SemeiaSt 13; Atlanta: SBL, 2000); IDEM, *Prophets and Prophecy in the Ancient Near East* (SBLWAW 12; Atlanta: Scholars Press, 2003); G. DEL OLMO LETE, *Canaanite Religion: According to the Liturgical Texts of Ugarit* (Bethesda, Md.: CDL Press, 1999); A. L. OPPENHEIM, "Divination and Celestial Observation in the Last Assyrian Empire," *Centaurus* 14 (1969): 97–135; R. A. PARKER, ed., *A Saite Oracle Papyrus from Thebes in the Brooklyn Museum [P. Brooklyn 47.218.3]* (Providence: Brown University Press, 1962); F. ROCHBERG-

HALTON, "Empiricism in Babylonian Omen Texts and the Classification of Mesopotamian Divination as Science," *JAOS* 119 (1999): 559–69; H. W. F. SAGGS, *The Encounter with the Divine in Mesopotamia and Israel* (London: Athlone Press, 1978); A. SALVESEN, "The Legacy of Babylon and Nineveh in Aramaic Sources," in *The Legacy of Mesopotamia* (ed. S. Dalley et al.; Oxford: Oxford University Press, 1998), 139–61; M. WEINFELD, "Ancient Near Eastern Patterns in Prophetic Literature," *VT* 27 (1977): 178–95; R. R. WILSON, *Prophecy and Society in Ancient Israel* (Philadelphia: Fortress, 1980); H. WOHL, "The Problem of the *maḫḫû*," *JANES* 3 (1970–1971): 113–18.

CHAPTER SEVEN

Apocalyptic and Related Texts

Introduction

Because the visions in the book of Daniel represent the only full-scale apocalypses in the Hebrew Bible, our interpretation of these visionary genres depends profoundly on insights gained from comparative material. Generally speaking, this comparative material satisfies in varying degrees the definition of apocalypse adopted by scholars from the Society of Biblical Literature Genres Project:

> An apocalypse is a genre of revelatory literature with a narrative framework, in which a revelation is mediated by an otherworldly being to a human recipient, disclosing a transcendent reality which is both temporal, in so far as it envisages eschatological salvation, and spatial insofar as it involves another, supernatural world. (*Semeia* 14 [1979]: 9)

> [The genre normally serves] to interpret the present, earthly circumstances in light of the supernatural world and of the future, and to influence both the understanding and the behavior of the audience by means of divine authority. (*Semeia* 36 [1986]: 7)

Central to this definition is that true apocalypses narrate the event of revelation and that the revelation presents salvation in its eschatological dimensions. Deliverance does not arrive from within human history but only through a divine intervention that brings history to a decisive end. Moreover, this divine cosmological reality has both temporal and spatial aspects. These two aspects correspond to two distinct but closely related types of apocalypses: the *historical apocalypse* and the *otherworldly journey*. The historical apocalypse forecasts the *temporal* march of human history as it leads up to the eschaton. By comparison, the otherworldly journey is *spatial* because it narrates the prophet's visionary experience in the heavens or in the underworld. The close connection between these two types of apocalypse is illustrated by the presence of both in a single Jewish text (*1 Enoch,* see Evans). Few Near Eastern texts will pass for apocalypses so defined, but several reflect traits that are prominent in Daniel and in later Jewish apocalypses.

The discussion below presumes the standard scholastic dogma that the visionary materials in Daniel are pseudoprophetic and that they were composed in response to the Hellenistic oppression experienced by Jews during the second century B.C.E. Although a few religiously conservative scholars continue to date the book using the ostensible sixth-century setting of its visions, the comparative data adduced in this chapter lend further support to the later date assumed by most scholars.

For related texts, see *OTP,* vol. 2.

7.1. Mesopotamian Pseudoprophecies

In the eyes of many scholars, the Babylonian prose prophecies are the earliest recognizable predecessors to the Jewish apocalypses. These prophecies are perhaps better described as pseudoprophecies because their "predictions" were made after the predicted events had occurred. The usual pattern was to establish the text's credibility using *vaticinia ex eventu* ("prophecies after the event") and then to follow this with either a prediction or an attempt to legitimize an institution. Apart from fragmentary texts, there are five important exemplars known to scholars from clay tablets. According to Grayson and Lambert, two of these include first-person autobiographical prophecies (the prophetic speeches of Marduk and Šulgi), and the others appear to be third-person prophecies (Text A, the Dynastic Prophecy, and the Uruk Prophecy). T. Longman has recently pointed out, however, that the broken introductions of both the Uruk and the Dynastic prophecies also appear to be autobiographical and that Text A is so similar to these texts that it, too, may share this feature. Longman's inferences are necessarily speculative given the broken state of the texts, but they are also reasonable, for it is difficult to imagine that these writers would have cast their pseudoprophecies as anonymous compositions. Although our discussion will presume Grayson's distinction between first-and third-person prophecies, this distinction should be regarded as provisional and tentative. A somewhat different text, Kummaya's Dream Vision, is also included in this discussion, primarily because it shares features with apocalypses and because it has recently been compared to the biblical book of Daniel.

The Marduk Prophetic Speech. This pseudonymous address was ostensibly spoken by the god himself, making it comparable not only to apocalypses but also to the pseudoautobiographies discussed in 9.1.2. Although our copy of the text comes from Assurbanipal's Neo-Assyrian library, the speech was likely composed during the twelfth century, when Nebuchadnezzar I (ca. 1125–1104 B.C.E.) elevated the god Marduk to the chief position in the Mesopotamian pantheon (Lambert). The speech supports this cultic innovation by asserting through

vaticinia ex eventu that Marduk had "predicted" his rise to prominence beforehand. In this respect, the Marduk text differs from the other Babylonian prophecies because it ends with an *ex eventu* prophecy rather than a genuine prediction
(contra Roberts). Our seventh-century copy of the Marduk speech ends with a
catch line that joins it to another Babylonian prophecy, the prophetic speech of
King Šulgi (see the following text). This suggests that the ancients, no less than
modern scholars, recognized the similarities between the two exemplars.

Texts and translations: R. BORGER, "Gott Marduk und Gott-König Šulgi als Propheten,"
BO 28 (1971): 3–24; GRAYSON and LAMBERT, "Akkadian Prophecies" (see Text D). *Translations: COS* 1.149: 480–81; T. LONGMAN, *Fictional Akkadian Autobiography*, 233–35. *Bibliography:* W. G. LAMBERT, "The Reign of Nebuchadnezzar I: A Turning Point in the
History of Ancient Mesopotamia," in *The Seed of Wisdom* (ed. W. S. McCullough; Toronto:
University of Toronto Press, 1964), 3–13; T. LONGMAN, *Fictional Akkadian Autobiography*,
132–42; J. J. M. ROBERTS, "Nebuchadnezzar I's Elamite Crisis in Theological Perspective,"
in *Essays on the Ancient Near East in Memory of J. J. Finkelstein* (ed. M. deJ. Ellis; Hamden,
Conn.: Archon Books, 1977), 183–87.

The Šulgi Prophetic Speech. This pseudonymous piece of propaganda purports
to be a revelation given to the renowned King Šulgi (ca. 2094–2047 B.C.E.), in
which the king "predicts" the history of Babylon down to the twelfth century
B.C.E. It is relatively easy, however, to correlate these prophecies with actual history down to the twelfth-century Kassite period; this suggests that the prophecies
are of the ex eventu type. These ex eventu prophecies are followed by a prediction
of Babylon's restoration (emancipation from the Kassites?), but the text's broken
condition makes it difficult to identify the author's ultimate agenda. The most
obvious divergence of the Šulgi and Marduk speeches from genuine apocalypses
is the complete absence of eschatology in both texts.

Texts and translations: R. BORGER, "Gott Marduk und Gott-König Šulgi als Propheten,"
BO 28 (1971): 3–24; GRAYSON and LAMBERT, "Akkadian Prophecies" (see Text C). *Translation:* LONGMAN, *Fictional Akkadian Autobiography*, 236–37. *Bibliography:* LONGMAN, *Fictional Akkadian Autobiography*, 146–49.

Text A. This exemplar is one of four texts (A, B, C, and D) studied by Grayson and
Lambert; C and D have turned out to be portions of the Šulgi and Marduk texts
(see above) whereas B is of a different sort altogether (see Biggs; *ANET* 451–52,
606–7). Unlike the Marduk and Šulgi prophecies, Text A appears to be framed in
the third person rather than as an autobiography. Our copy dates to 614 B.C.E., but
the date of composition is uncertain, mainly because the tablets are fragmentary.
Text A's author "predicts" a series of good and bad kings, introducing each with
an anonymous phrase, "A prince will arise and rule for N years." Each reign, save
one, is carefully separated from the others with rulings. The detailed descriptions
of the reigns and the very specific chronological data they provide suggest that
the prophecies are not genuine but of the *ex eventu* type. Although the text's poor
condition makes it difficult to discern its author's aims, the detailed chronologi-

cal information in Text A distinguishes it from the four other Babylonian prophecies. The author apparently derived this chronology from other sources, probably
from astrological diaries (Biggs). This distinctive feature casts some doubt upon
Longman's conjecture (see the introduction to this section) that Text A was composed as a fictional autobiography, since his conjecture was based on the assumption that Text A is in most respects like the other Akkadian prophecies.

Text and translation: GRAYSON and LAMBERT, "Akkadian Prophecies." *Translation:*
LONGMAN, *Fictional Akkadian Autobiography,* 240–42. *Bibliography:* R. D. BIGGS, "Baby-
lonian Prophecies, Astrology, and a New Source for 'Prophecy Text B,'" in *Language, Liter-
ature, and History: Philological and Historical Studies Presented to Erica Reiner* (AOS 67;
New Haven: American Oriental Society, 1987), 1–14; *ANET* 606–7; LONGMAN, *Fictional
Akkadian Autobiography,* 152–63.

The Uruk Prophecy. This prophecy is cast as a third-person narrative and stands
chronologically between the other two third-person prophecies, Text A and the
Dynastic Prophecy. Like Text A, the Uruk text presents the "future" as a sequence
of good and bad kings whom it introduces anonymously in this fashion: "A king
will arise, and he will [or will not] grant justice to the land." The last two kings in
the sequence, the tenth and eleventh kings, provide the key to the text's interpretation (following Hunger and Kaufman; Beaulieu; alternative views in Goldstein;
Lambert). It predicts that the tenth king would renovate Uruk's temples and return the statue of Uruk's protective goddess from Babylon; this description fits
Nebuchadnezzar II (604–562 B.C.E.) so well that its must be an ex eventu prediction of his reign. The eleventh king would then arise in Uruk (presumably
Nebuchadnezzar's son, Evil-Merodach, 561–560 B.C.E.), whose dynasty would
forever rule the world and "exercise dominion like the gods." This second prediction was obviously a genuine attempt at prophecy, since no such eschatological
kingdom appeared in Uruk. For this reason, we can safely presume that the text
was written after Nebuchadnezzar's reign during the reign of his son, Evil-
Merodach. The Uruk Prophecy was therefore composed during the Late Babylonian period when a priest in Uruk took up his stylus to support a dynasty favorably disposed to his city. In addition to the text's eschatological tone and use of
vaticinia ex eventu, in at least one other respect it is reminiscent of apocalypses.
The Uruk Prophecy, like Text A, schematizes history as a series of discrete political periods, in this case as a series of good and bad kings. Schematic presentations
of political history are also common in later Jewish apocalypses, such as the book
of Daniel.

Text and translation: H. HUNGER and S. KAUFMAN, "A New Akkadian Prophecy Text,"
JAOS 95 (1975): 371–75. *Translation:* LONGMAN, *Fictional Akkadian Autobiography,*
237–38. *Bibliography:* P.-A. BEAULIEU, "The Historical Background of the Uruk Prophecy,"
in *The Tablet and the Scroll: Near Eastern Studies in Honor of William W. Hallo* (ed. M. E.
Cohen et al.; Bethesda, Md.: CDL Press, 1993), 41–52; J. GOLDSTEIN, "The Historical Set-
ting of the Uruk Prophecy," *JNES* 47 (1988): 43–46; W. G. LAMBERT, *The Background of
Jewish Apocalyptic* (London: Athlone Press, University of London, 1978), 10–12; LONG-
MAN, *Fictional Akkadian Autobiography,* 146–49.

The Dynastic Prophecy. This text is later than the Uruk Prophecy and dates to the Hellenistic period. It predicts with remarkable accuracy the rise and fall of various dynasties and empires, including Assyria, Babylon, Persia, and Macedonia; this suggests that here we are dealing with *ex eventu* prophecy. Although the text breaks off just after the Macedonian Empire, we can deduce how it probably ended. The text characterizes the ruling dynasties in an alternating pattern of good and evil. The next dynasty apparently would have been the "evil" Seleucids, implying that a genuine prophecy of the Seleucid downfall followed. If this reconstruction is accurate, then the Dynastic Prophecy—like the Jewish book of Daniel—presented a message of hope that the Hellenistic Seleucids would be destroyed and replaced by a favorable native Babylonian dynasty. Book 3 of the Sibylline Oracles (see 7.3) seems to confirm that anti-Seleucid sentiments were common in Babylon at the time.

Text and translation: GRAYSON, *Babylonian Historical-Literary Texts,* 2–37. ***Translations:*** *COS* 1.150: 481–82; LONGMAN, *Fictional Akkadian Autobiography,* 239–42. ***Bibliography:*** LONGMAN, *Fictional Akkadian Autobiography,* 149–52.

Kummaya's Dream Vision of the Netherworld. In this text, Prince Kummaya relates the story of his descent into the underworld court, where he was greeted by a cadre of terrible hybrid gods—part human, part animal—and was ushered into court to face the enthroned god, Nergal. The god considers a permanent imprisonment for Kummaya because of his cultic impiety, but Kummaya is released when Nergal's counselor suggests that the prince has learned his lesson and would be more valuable as the god's supplicant among the living. Kummaya is transparently a pseudonym for the Neo-Assyrian king Assurbanipal, and the example of pious behavior shown to him is that of his anti-Babylonian grandfather, Sennacherib. From this, scholars have surmised that the text was composed by Assyrian scribes in their struggle against a pro-Babylonian movement that had been initiated by Assurbanipal's father, Esarhaddon. For this purpose, they concocted a vision of the divine punishment that awaited Assurbanipal if he did not return to the pro-Assyrian policies of his grandfather (for a closely related text, see the Sin of Sargon in 9.1.3). In employing a fictional tale to make a point with the royalty, the author(s) of the Dream Vision of the underworld followed a strategy similar to that employed by the Israelite prophet Nathan when he addressed problems in the life of King David through a fictional story (see 2 Sam 12).

    Kummaya's Dream Vision has been known for some time, but only recently has H. Kvanvig asserted that its composite underworld beasts played a significant role in the development of apocalyptic themes, such as the hybrid beasts in Dan 7 (see Kvanvig 1981; 1988). Whether this text provided the inspiration for Daniel's dream vision (Dan 7), as Kvanvig claims, is debatable. Nevertheless, it is possible that Kummaya's vision, or traditions like it, provided early inspiration for the genre of the otherworldly journey, which would later appear in Ezekiel during the Babylonian exile and more prominently in the postexilic Jewish apocalypses.

Texts and translations: A. LIVINGSTONE, *Court Poetry and Literary Miscellanea* (SAA 3; Helsinki: Helsinki University Press, 1989), 68–76; W. VON SODEN, "Die Unterweltsvision eines assyrischen Kronprinzen," *ZA* 9 (1936): 1–31. *Translation: ANET* 109–10. *Bibliography:* H. KVANVIG, "An Akkadian Vision as Background for Daniel 7," *ST* 35 (1981): 85–89; IDEM, *Roots of Apocalypticism: The Mesopotamian Background of the Enoch Figure and of the Son of Man* (WMANT 61; Neukirchen-Vluyn: Neukirchener Verlag, 1988), 355–441.

7.2. Egyptian Apocalypses

Although ancient Egypt produced no full-blown apocalypses, several comparative exemplars are of particular importance for the study of apocalyptic. One of these texts is the very old Prophecy of Neferti, and the others are much later texts dating to the Persian, Greek, and Roman periods.

The Prophecy of Neferti. This text was composed during the Middle Kingdom and includes two parts, a prose narrative and a poetic prophecy. According to the narrative, Pharaoh Snofru of the Old Kingdom invited sage Neferti to entertain the king in his royal court. Because the king preferred a word about the future rather than a story about the past, Neferti offered up a prophecy: he predicted that Egypt would fall into disarray until a "king from the south" named Ameny would arise and restore Egypt's fortunes. Because Ameny is the short form of Amenemhet I, a Middle Kingdom pharaoh, and because the text was composed in good Middle Egyptian, this clearly was not a genuine oracle but rather an *ex eventu* attempt to legitimize Pharaoh Amenemhet I (1991–1962 B.C.E.) by showing that his reign had been predicted many centuries earlier during the reign of Pharaoh Snofru (ca. 2575–2551 B.C.E.). Hence, like the Babylonian Marduk Prophecy, the Prophecy of Neferti used *ex eventu* predictions to legitimize an existing institution. In order to present Amenemhet as a savior figure, the text's author painted Egypt as a nation in tragic disarray. As we see elsewhere, the theme of national distress was a favorite motif in the Middle Kingdom literature (see the Admonitions of Ipuwer in 2.2.2). Our primary copy of the Prophecy of Neferti is the recto of Papyrus 1116B in the Ermitage Museum, Leningrad, but several partial and fragmentary texts on writing tablets and ostraca have also been discovered.

Text and translation: W. HELCK, *Die Prophezeiung des Nfr.tj: Kleine ägyptische Texte* (Wiesbaden: Harrassowitz, 1970). *Translations: AEL* 1:139–45; *ANET* 444–46; *COS* 1.45: 106–10; *LAE* 214–20; R. B. PARKINSON, *The Tale of Sinuhe and Other Ancient Egyptian Poems: 1940–1640 BC* (Oxford: Clarendon, 1997), 131–43. *Bibliography:* H. GOEDICKE, *The Protocol of Neferyt* (Baltimore: Johns Hopkins University Press, 1977); G. POSENER, *Littérature et politique dans l'Égypte de la XIIe dynastie* (Bibliothèque de l'École des hautes études 307; Paris: Champion, 1956), 21–60, 145–57.

The Demotic Chronicle. The designation "chronicle" is strictly speaking a misnomer created by E. Revillout's initial publication of this papyrus, but even he soon recognized that the text was more prophetic than historical. A better name for the chronicle would be the Demotic Oracle Commentary, for it purports to be a commentary on an older collection of prophetic oracles. The commentary interpreted the prophecies so that predictions leading up to the reign of Pharaoh Teos (365–60 B.C.E.) had already been fulfilled and predictions of events after Teos lay in the future. Hence, the author wanted readers to believe that his commentary was composed during the reign of Teos, when Egypt was confronted by a threat from Persia.

The commentary describes the oracles as a series of tablets, but because portions of the text are missing, only tablets 7–13 and part of tablet 6 are treated in the commentary. Each section of the commentary begins with a reference to the oracle tablet to be discussed and follows with a sequence of quotes from it. Each quotation is then provided with an interpretative gloss. One of these glosses predicts the return of Persian rule after Egypt's brief independence from Persia during the Twenty-Eighth to Thirtieth Dynasties (404–343 B.C.E.). Several features in the text, however, cast doubt on the authenticity of this "prediction."

The commentary reflects knowledge not only of events during the Persian period but also of events during the Greek era. Moreover, the commentary and the oracle it supposedly elucidates were composed in the same language and style. From these facts we can surmise that the commentary—and the oracle it interprets—are the creations of a single author who used *ex eventu* prophecy to establish the credibility of his authentic predictions. What were his authentic predictions, and what purpose did they serve? The writer predicted that "a man of Herakleopolis" would restore Egyptian independence and that during his reign the high priest of the god Harsaphes (in Herakleopolis) would "rejoice after the Greeks" (i.e., after the Ptolemies). Various stages of this new king's rebellion against the Greeks were also predicted, but we have no evidence that these corresponded to any actual events on the ground. For this reason, the usual reading of the Demotic Chronicle is that it was composed by, or on behalf of, the priesthood of Harsaphes in Herakleopolis. The likely objective was to spawn a rebellion against Greece by which both Egypt and the Harsaphes priesthood could profit. This objective was closely related to a secondary purpose of the chronicle, namely, its attempt to provide standards for legitimate Egyptian kingship. In a manner reminiscent of the biblical books of Kings, the Demotic Chronicle presents the kings of the Twenty-Eighth to Thirtieth Dynasties as a series of good and bad kings whose behavior dictated their fates. For instance, it is said of Pharaoh Hakoris, "He was overthrown because he abandoned the law and did not have concern for his brothers" (DC IV, 9–10). By way of contrast, the predicted savior king from Herakleopolis would "not abandon the law" (DC III, 16). In this way, the text not only sought to restore native Egyptian rule but also to dictate the patterns that this restored dynasty ought to follow.

Text and translation: W. SPIEGELBERG, *Die sogenannte demotische Chronik des Pap. 215 der Bibliothèque nationale zu Paris* (Demotische Studien 7; Leipzig: Hinrichs, 1914). ***Transla-***

tion: H. FELBER, "Die demotische Chronik," in *Apokalyptik und Ägypten* (ed. Blasius and Schipper), 65–111. *Bibliography:* J. BERGMAN, "Introductory Remarks on Apocalypticism," in *Apocalypticism in the Mediterranean World and the Near East* (ed. D. Hellholm), 51–60; J. G. GRIFFITHS, "Apocalyptic in the Hellenistic Era," in *Apocalypticism in the Mediterranean World and the Near East* (ed. D. Hellholm), 273–93; J. H. JOHNSON, "The Demotic Chronicle as an Historical Source," *Enchoria* 4 (1974): 1–17; IDEM, "The Demotic Chronicle as a Statement of a Theory of Kingship," *JSSEA* 13 (1983): 61–72; C. C. MCCOWN, "Hebrew and Egyptian Apocalyptic Literature," *HTR* 18 (1925): 357–411.

Other Egyptian Texts. Several other Egyptian texts figure prominently in discussions of apocalyptic literature. The Oracle of the Potter (a copy from ca. second–fourth century C.E.), the Prophecy of the Lamb (ca. third century B.C.E.), and the fragmentary text known as Nectanebo's Dream (ca. second century B.C.E.) are, like the Demotic Chronicle, *ex eventu* political prophecies. The Oracle of the Potter and Nectanebo's Dream predict national deliverance from the Greeks, and the Prophecy of the Lamb foretells national relief from an anonymous assailant. The other relevant text, the Admonitions of Ipuwer, is discussed in 2.2.2. Readers may also wish to note a fragmentary pseudoprophetic text recently treated by Quack.

Texts and translations: L. KOENEN, "The Dream of Nektanebos," *BASP* 22 (1985): 171–94 (Nectanebo's Dream); L. KOENEN and R. MERKELBACH, "Prophezeiungen des 'Töpfers,'" *ZPE* 3 (1968): 137–209 (Oracle of the Potter); K.-T. ZAUZICH, "Das Lamm des Bokchoris," in *Festschrift zum 100–jährigen Bestehen der Papyrussammlung der Österreichischen National-bibliothek: Papyrus Erzherzog Rainer (P. Rainer Cent.)* (Vienna: In Kommission bei Verlag Brüder Hollinek, 1983), 165–74 (Prophecy of the Lamb). *Translations:* H. GRESSMANN, *Altorientalische Texte zum Alten Testament* (Berlin: de Gruyter, 1926), 48–50; *LAE* 445–49 (Prophecy of the Lamb); MCCOWN, "Hebrew and Egyptian Apocalyptic Literature," 392–99 (partial). *Bibliography:* L. KOENEN, "Die Apologie des Töpfers an König Ameno-phis, oder das Töpferorakel," in *Apokalyptik und Ägypten* (ed. Blasius and Schipper), 139–87; B. E. PERRY, "The Egyptian Legend of Nectanebus," *TAPA* 97 (1966): 327–33; J. F. QUACK, "Ein neuer prophetischer Text aus Tebtynis (Papyrus Carlsberg 399 + Papyrus PSI INV. D. 17 + Papyrus Tebtuis Tait 13 VS.)," in *Apokalyptik und Ägypten* (ed. Blasius and Schipper), 253–74; K. RYHOLT, "Nectanebo's Dream or the Prophecy of Petesis," in *Apokalyptik und Ägypten* (ed. Blasius and Schipper), 221–41; H. J. THISSEN, "Das Lamm des Bokchoris," in *Apokalyptik und Ägypten* (ed. Blasius and Schipper), 113–38.

7.3. Persian and Greek Apocalypses

From the Babylonian exile onward, Jewish tradition subsisted within an increasingly complicated matrix of ideas that included inspiration not only from Mesopotamia and Egypt but also from regions farther east (Persia) and west (Greece). Our purpose here is to explore these last two sources of tradition.

Persian Pahlavi Texts and Zand-i Vohuman Yasn. Until recently, scholars assumed that the rather sudden emergence of eschatology in Second Temple Judaism was a result of Persian influence. Persian apocalypses were thought to be earlier than the

Judaic sources, and they included many of the features found in Jewish apocalyptic, such as religious dualism, angels, demons, millennialism, judgment, afterlife, and the periodization of history. This assumption, however, has been questioned in recent years, mainly because the most important Persian apocalypses turn out to be very late Pahlavi texts that date to the ninth century C.E. The most discussed of the Pahlavi texts is the *Zand-i Vohuman Yasn* (or *Bahman Yasht*), in which the deity (Ahura Mazda) grants the prophet Zoroaster a vision of the future. The vision takes the form of a tree with four branches of gold, silver, copper, and iron, respectively. Each metal represents a kingdom, with the final, iron kingdom marking the end of one millennium, which would be followed by another millennium and by a series of eschatological events. Chapter 3 of the *Zand* expands this vision by placing seven branches on the tree, but the final kingdom is the same in both visions. Although these features are obviously similar to the historical schematics of the Akkadian and Egyptian apocalypses, the allegory of four metals is particularly close to the book of Daniel (see Dan 2). It is not clear how much of this Persian material can be traced back to the pre-Christian era, but there is substantial evidence that the basic shape of Persian apocalyptic existed by 600 B.C.E., several centuries before Daniel and the other Jewish apocalyptic works were written (Hartman). This makes it more likely that the conceptual and generic features of Jewish apocalyptic were influenced by Persian ideas.

Text: B. T. ANKLESARIA, *Zand-i Vohuman Yasn* (Bombay: Camay Oriental Institute, 1967). *Translation:* C. G. CERETI, *The Zand I Wahman Yasn: A Zoroastrian Apocalypse* (Rome Oriental Series 75; Rome: Istituto Italiano per il Medio ed Estremo Oriente, 1995). *Bibliography:* COLLINS, *The Apocalyptic Imagination,* 29–33; S. S. HARTMAN, "Datierung der jungavestischen Apokalyptik," in *Apocalypticism in the Mediterranean World and the Near East* (ed. D. Hellholm), 61–75; A. HULTGÅRD, "Forms and Origins of Iranian Apocalypticism," in *Apocalypticism in the Mediterranean World and the Near East* (ed. D. Hellholm), 387–411.

Hesiod's Works and Days. The Greek traditions were rich in motifs and themes found in Jewish apocalyptic, and some of these Hellenistic traditions are undeniably old. Hesiod's Works and Days (ca. 700 B.C.E.), for instance, allegorically presents human history as a sequence of four races: gold, silver, bronze, and iron (although a heroic race of demigods appears between the bronze and iron dispensations). The fourth race, of iron, represents the common humanity of Hesiod's day, a race that never rests from labor and sorrow and that is ever degenerating into bitterness and evil. As a result of this moral deterioration, it is predicted that Zeus would eventually intervene and destroy mortal humanity. This eschatological viewpoint and its allegorical mode of presentation are similar to the book of Daniel, providing good evidence that Greek authors in the seventh century B.C.E. were already using generic conventions that would later become important in Jewish historical apocalypses.

Texts and translations: H. G. EVELYN-WHITE, *Hesiod: The Homeric Hymns and Homerica* (LCL; Cambridge: Harvard University Press, 1982), 2–65; R. HAMILTON, E. RAINIS, and

R. RUTTENBERG, *Hesiod's Works and Days* (Bryn Mawr, Penn.: Thomas Library, Bryn Mawr College, 1988). **Bibliography:** J. S. CLAY, *Hesiod's Cosmos* (Cambridge: Cambridge University Press, 2003); W. J. VERDENIUS, *A Commentary on Hesiod: Works and Days, vv. 1–382* (Leiden: Brill, 1985); M. L. WEST, *Hesiod, Works and Days* (Oxford: Clarendon, 1978).

The Sibylline Oracles. Although many other Greek texts are worthy of discussion, the Sibylline Oracles brings us chronologically closer to the Jewish apocalypses. These oracles, attributed to old women (Sibyls) who uttered ecstatic prophecies, were widely attested in the Hellenistic world. The title "Sibyl" has never been adequately explained; perhaps it was once the name of a famous prophetess. Because many early Sibyls were Asiatic, it is commonly presumed that the Sibylline institution originated in Asia and then spread to Greece from the East, but this is a matter of dispute. Later Jewish and Christian authors adopted the Sibyl as a spokesperson for their causes, pseudepigraphically placing in her mouth predictions that aided their political and religious agendas. Because the pagan Sibylline Oracles have been preserved only in fragments, the twelve Jewish and Christian texts provide our primary access to the pagan Sibylline tradition (see Evans). Fortunately, one of the Jewish oracles, book 4, originated as a pagan oracle. Once stripped of its Jewish modifications, the text provides us with an example of the older Hellenistic Sibyls. Book 4 originally served a political agenda, legitimizing Alexander the Great's Macedonian Empire by "predicting" that it would be the fourth kingdom to follow after Assyria, Media, and Persia. This *ex eventu* strategy is very similar that used in Marduk's prophetic speech and in the Prophecy of Neferti, and the oracle's fourfold periodization of history into Assyrian, Median, Persian, and Greek segments is reminiscent of many Hellenistic-era texts, including the Akkadian Dynastic Prophecy and the book of Daniel. Because of intertextual similarities such as these, it is commonly presumed that Sibylline motifs, themes, and ideas contributed to the emergence of similar Near Eastern genres (and vice versa), and this partially explains why Jewish apocalyptic first appeared during the Hellenistic period. As we have noted, book 4 of the Sibylline Oracles was later expanded by Jewish writers, who added the Roman Empire to the prophecy (Rome was not integrated into the book's original four-kingdom scheme) and displaced the text's original historical climax in the time of Alexander with an eschatological climax during the Roman period.

Text and translation: OTP 1:317–472 (translations with publication information). *Bibliography:* H. W. ATTRIDGE, "Greek and Latin Apocalypses," *Semeia* 14 (1979): 159–86; COLLINS, *The Apocalyptic Imagination,* 116–33; H. W. Parke, *Sibyls and Sibylline Prophecy in Classical Antiquity* (London: Routledge, 1988).

Concluding Observations

In looking prospectively at the book of Daniel, there are four key features in our comparative texts that should be highlighted. First, many of the texts were cast as the autobiographical speeches of gods or famous kings (e.g., Marduk and Šulgi). Obviously, this practice enhanced the text's authority, for in one fell swoop the prophecy became the ancient utterance of a deity or hero.

A second feature of the texts is that in many cases the authors lent clout to their real predictions by presenting history as a sequence of discrete periods, each of which culminated in an "accurate" *ex eventu* prophecy. These *ex eventu* predictions are discernible to us because, on the one hand, they are too detailed and accurate to be genuine prophecies and, on the other hand, they contrast sharply with the real predictions that failed. Dating the prophecy texts is therefore a relatively straightforward enterprise: one only needs to recognize when the predictions go awry. When appraised from our modern purview, pseudoprophecies may seem inauthentic and even morally tendentious, but this needn't have been the case for the ancients. *Ex eventu* prophecy was a standard generic convention in Babylonian scribal circles, and we can perhaps surmise what made this convention legitimate. Mesopotamian scholars viewed history as a recurring cycle of events, and they also believed that historical patterns from the past could yield accurate predictions of the future (see 6.1.1). It is quite feasible to conclude that Babylonian scholars expressed this belief by illustrating through *ex eventu* "prophecies" that the rules governing history—past, present, and future—were immutable. There is no doubt, of course, that this pseudoprophetic device would have duped some readers, but it is perhaps more helpful to view the practice as a pious ruse rather than as a mendacious attempt to mislead.

A third feature of the texts regards their ideological aim. For instance, the Marduk speech did not conclude with a real prediction but rather with yet another *ex eventu* prophecy. Its author did not aspire to give a prognosis; he hoped to promote the ideology of Marduk's prominence. The propaganda of Kummaya's Dream Vision and the Egyptian Demotic Chronicler were equally transparent. Although it is true that the other Akkadian prophecies offered genuine predictions, it would be rather artificial to separate these prognoses from the ideological concerns of their writers. It cannot be doubted, for instance, that the author of the Uruk Prophecy hoped that his prophecy of Uruk's restoration would come true. In all cases, then, the texts that we have examined were composed for their ideological value as much as for their predictive value because the writers certainly knew—implicitly if not explicitly—that their prophecies might stimulate the very courses of action that they predicted.

Fourth, and finally, we should note the social context of these works. In at least one case, the text was composed in support of changes made by those with political clout (the Marduk Prophecy), but in most other cases, the authors appear to represent relatively marginalized communities. This lends some support to the assertion, made by some scholars, that apocalyptic literature is normally produced by oppressed communities.

The two non-Jewish texts that stand closest to Daniel generically and contextually are the Babylonian Dynastic Prophecy and the Egyptian Demotic Chronicle. All three texts present history as a cycle of rising and falling kingdoms, use esoteric or symbolic language, practice *vaticinia ex eventu,* and follow their pseudoprophecies with genuine prophecies. Moreover, all three texts respond to Hellenistic oppression (Seleucid or Ptolemaic) by predicting deliverance through a native ruler. The major distinction between the three texts is that whereas the Egyptian and Babylonian authors imagined a solution from within the normal confines of history, this was not the case for the eschatologically minded author(s) of Daniel. If Daniel and these other texts were indeed responses to Hellenistic oppression, then the importance of their prophecies rested not in their predictive value so much as in the encouragement they offered to suffering people.

General Bibliography

J. BERGMAN, "Introductory Remarks on Apocalypticism," in *Apocalypticism in the Mediterranean World and the Near East* (ed. D. Hellholm), 51–60; A. BLASIUS and B. U. SCHIPPER, eds., *Apokalyptik und Ägypten: Eine kritische Analyse der relevanten Texte aus dem griechisch-römischen Ägypten* (OLA 107; Sterling, Va.: Peeters, 2002); J. J. COLLINS, *The Apocalyptic Imagination: An Introduction to Jewish Apocalyptic Literature* (2d ed.; Grand Rapids: Eerdmans, 1998); J. EGGLER, *Influences and Traditions Underlying the Vision of Daniel 7:2–14* (OBO 177; Freiburg, Switz.: University Press, 2000); C. A. EVANS, *Ancient Texts for New Testament Studies* ([rev. ed. of *A Guide to Nonbiblical Texts for New Testament Interpretation;* Peabody, Mass.: Hendrickson Publishers, 1992] Peabody, Mass.: Hendrickson Publishers, forthcoming); A. K. GRAYSON, *Babylonian Historical-Literary Texts* (TSTS 3; Toronto: University of Toronto Press, 1975); A. K. GRAYSON and W. G. LAMBERT, "Akkadian Prophecies," *JCS* 18 (1964): 7–30; J. G. GRIFFITHS, "Apocalyptic in the Hellenistic Era," in *Apocalypticism in the Mediterranean World and the Near East* (ed. D. Hellholm), 273–93; G. F. HASEL, "The Four World Empires of Daniel 2 against Its Near Eastern Environment," *JSOT* 12 (1979): 17–30; D. HELLHOLM, ed., *Apocalypticism in the Mediterranean World and the Near East* (2d ed.; Tübingen: J. C. B. Mohr, 1988); T. LONGMAN III, *Fictional Akkadian Autobiography: A Generic and Comparative Study* (Winona Lake, Ind.: Eisenbrauns, 1991); C. C. MCCOWN, "Hebrew and Egyptian Apocalyptic Literature," *HTR* 18 (1925): 357–411; M. NISSINEN, "Neither Prophecies nor Apocalypses: The Akkadian Literary Predictive Texts," in *Knowing the End from the Beginning: The Prophetic, the Apocalyptic and Their Relationships* (ed. L. L. Grabbe and R. D. Haak; JSPSup; London; New York: Continuum, 2004), 134–48; D. S. RUSSELL, *The Method and Message of Jewish Apocalyptic* (Philadelphia: Westminster, 1964); J. M. SASSON, "An Apocalyptic Vision from Mari? Speculations on ARM X:9," *MARI* 1 (1982): 151–67; M. SMITH, "On the History of ΑΠΟΚΑΛΥΤΩ and ΑΠΟΚΑΛΥΨΙΣ," in *Apocalypticism in the Mediterranean World and the Near East* (ed. D. Hellholm), 9–20.

CHAPTER EIGHT

Tales and Novellas

Introduction

Every society produces short stories that are creative works of fiction. Scholars commonly refer to these short narratives as *tales*, but as a category this comprises a broad spectrum of exemplars ranging from simple folktales to highbrow literature. Consequently, it is helpful to distinguish the more elaborate and refined tales as *novellas*, creative literature in the highest order. In comparison with other tales, novellas are emplotted more intricately, reflect more varied staging and casting, and develop their characters in more detail. Simple tales are, by comparison, shorter, more episodic, less complex, and may bear the marks of oral composition. So, although tales and novellas share a common status as short, fictional narratives, the novella is a particular type of tale. Another type of tale is the so-called fairy tale (German, *Märchen*), whose chief features include fabulous make-believe plots and characters that lie outside the bounds of the writer's physical and metaphysical reality. Since the time of Gunkel and Frazer, scholars have sometimes discussed this genre in connection with the Hebrew Bible, but it is not at all clear that much material in the Hebrew Bible or the Near East fits the fairytale category. The task of isolating Hebrew fairy tales in the biblical corpus is particularly difficult because it is not easy to distinguish Israelite notions of the miraculous from Israelite notions of fancy.

Many texts that are conventionally labeled myth or legend would undoubtedly fit the category of tales or novellas, but for purposes of classification this chapter excludes mythic genres (stories about gods), legendary genres (stories about cultural heroes and institutional origins), and epic genres (long narrative poems). Because nearly all of our Mesopotamian, Hittite, and Ugaritic narratives fit these excluded types, the entries in this chapter focus especially on Egypt, which is undoubtedly our richest source of Near Eastern tales and novellas. It should be stressed, however, that this chapter leaves out some of the most important comparative exemplars for understanding Hebrew narrative, namely, the apocryphal Jewish tales about Tobit, Judith, Susanna, and Daniel. For more on these important Jewish exemplars, see Evans.

8.1. Egyptian Tales and Novellas

Although the Egyptian Old Kingdom produced many prayers, rituals, instructional texts, and autobiographies, it is generally admitted that the literary quality of these texts is not comparable to the literature of Egypt's classical age, the Middle Kingdom. Many of our best Egyptian tales and novellas come from this period, so here we shall begin with the Middle Kingdom Tale of King Cheops's Court and then proceed chronologically through the Egyptian sources. It is reasonable to inquire about what made Middle Kingdom Egypt such a rich source of tales and novellas. The explanation cannot be simple, but the development can be attributed partially to emergence of a class of wealthy Twelfth Dynasty intellectuals who sponsored literary activities that were no longer constrained by the concerns of the royal court and its propaganda (Parkinson). Texts that playfully belittled royal functionaries, such as the Tale of the Eloquent Peasant, attest to these developments.

One genre that will not be discussed in detail is the so-called *Königsnovelle*, supposedly a kind of historical novel that the Egyptians wrote about the lives of their kings (see A. Hermann; S. Herrmann; Loprieno). Although this label creates the impression that the genre was of a discrete and recognizable type, the exemplars cited by Hermann include many variations, not only annals and mortuary biographies but also royal inscriptions of every type—including even fictional texts such as the Bentresh Stela (see 9.3). Consequently, the texts that have sometimes been labeled as *Königsnovellen* appear in various parts of this volume. For a discussion and critique of the relative usefulness of the generic category *Königsnovella*, see Van Seters.

The Tale of King Cheops's Court (Papyrus Westcar). This story was set in the Fourth Dynasty of the Old Kingdom but was composed about seven centuries later, during the Middle Kingdom (ca. 2040–1650 B.C.E.). It is a cycle of tales within a tale, through which we can glimpse both the Egyptian tale genre as well as its most important contextual home, the royal court. As the story goes, Pharaoh sought relief from palace boredom by summoning his princes to entertain him with wonderful stories. Among these stories was the tale of a "wax crocodile" that, like the serpent staff of Moses (Exod 4:3–4), could be transformed from a wax model to a full-fledged reptile and back again. After this and several other tales were told, Prince Hordedef stepped forward with the complaint that in these tales "truth cannot be told from falsehood," and he promised to usher into the king's presence a real flesh-and-blood wonder-worker. At the king's bidding he introduced one, and this miracle worker performed several impressive marvels. The magician rounded out his presentation with a prophetic prediction that the sun god would impregnate a mortal with three sons, one of whom would supplant the sitting king's Old Kingdom dynasty. Several important features of the Egyptian tales are reflected in this text.

The story presents the royal court as fertile ground for the composition and recitation of entertaining tales. The creative and fanciful tone of the tale fits this entertaining purpose, and although in this case the tale is obviously a literary composition, its short, episodic, and colloquial character reflects influences from oral-tale types (Parkinson). As is often the case in folktales, the tale's protagonist wonder-worker, Djedi, was a commoner rather than a god or prince. Common folk often figure prominently in such tales, in part because folk tales often originate among common people and in part because the unexpected rise and success of a commoner is an entertaining theme. Nevertheless, like most court tales, this one looked beyond the commoner and attempted to flatter its Middle Kingdom royal audience. It accomplished this through a playful *ex eventu* prophecy, which "predicted" the fall of an Old Kingdom dynasty as well as the rise of a Middle Kingdom dynasty to replace it. The theme and poetic nature of the text suggest that Egyptian bards recited it to entertain the palace and upper-crust society.

Text and translation: A. M. BLACKMAN, *The Story of King Kheops and the Magicians: Transcribed from Papyrus Westcar (Berlin Papyrus 3033)* (Reading, England: J.V. Books, 1988). *Translations:* AEL 1:215–22; LAE 13–24; R. B. PARKINSON, *The Tale of Sinuhe and Other Ancient Egyptian Poems* (Oxford: Clarendon, 1997), 102–27. *Bibliography:* C. J. EYRE, "Fate, Crocodiles, and Judgment of the Dead: Some Mythological Allusions in Egyptian Literature," SAK 4 (1976): 103–14; IDEM, "Yet Again the Wax Crocodile: P. Westcar 3, 12ff.," JEA 78 (1992): 280–81; E. S. MELTZER, "The Art of the Storyteller in Papyrus Westcar: An Egyptian Mark Twain?" in *Essays in Egyptology in Honor of Hans Goedicke* (ed. B. M. Bryan and D. Lorton; San Antonio, Tex.: Van Siclen, 1994), 169–75.

The Tale of Sinuhe. This poetic tale was the best and most popular of the ancient Egyptian novellas. After its composition during the Middle Kingdom, the tale was read and copied by scribes for almost eight centuries. Sinuhe was a royal official who served in the courts of Pharoah Amenemhat I. When Amenemhat I died, Sinuhe feared the new regime of Senwosret I and fled for his life to Syria-Palestine. There Sinuhe achieved greatness and became the ruler of the whole region, after which he was invited by the new Egyptian king to return home for a suitable burial in his homeland. Not only does this tale intend to say that Egyptians in foreign lands always rise to the top; it also wants us to see that, even after reaching this pinnacle, the only option left for the hero is a return to his Egyptian homeland. The Tale of Sinuhe is therefore a literary statement about the qualitative difference between life in Egypt and life in a foreign land and, more specifically, about the differences between Egyptians and foreigners (Baines; Sparks).

The tale is a textbook case of generic extension and generic assimilation, but this cannot be fully appreciated apart from another Egyptian genre: the autobiography. Autobiographies developed during the Old Kingdom as commemorative tomb inscriptions that addressed the gods and passersby with a flattering self-portrait of the entombed (see 12.2.1 for exemplars). The purpose of this genre was twofold: to preserve the deceased's reputation and to secure offerings for his life in the hereafter. Early exemplars were inscribed on the tomb itself, but in later periods the autobiographies were written on small stelae that could be placed closer to Abydos, holy city of the god Osiris (god of the dead). A comparison of Sinuhe with these funerary autobiographies reveals that the writer of Sinuhe borrowed his framework (introduction and conclusion) from the funerary autobiographies but extended this form in numerous ways. Sinuhe is a literary composition written on papyrus rather than an inscription on stone, and the story's purpose was not to secure an afterlife so much as to extol Egyptian values. The author inserted his fictional narrative into an autobiographical framework and then folded into it many other generic elements, such as eulogies, royal decrees, letters, prayers, and ritual lyrics.

From the moment it was discovered and for some time afterward, many scholars presumed that Sinuhe was a factual and historical autobiography. This was mainly because the story is similar to the authentic autobiographies and because the tale reflects an authentic historical setting, the transition from King Amenemhat I to Senwosret I. As early as 1916, however, Gardiner pointed out that the text reflected little accurate knowledge of either the culture or the geography of Syria-Palestine. This observation eventually led scholars to appreciate more fully the literary character of the work. As a creative and fictional narrative, Sinuhe was not an autobiographical apology but rather an entertaining attempt to promote Egyptian society by extolling its virtues. As one can see, fiction and history look very much alike, particularly when the fiction is intentionally set into an autobiographical literary context and when its fictional plot subsists on actual events in history.

Biblical scholars have been aware for some time that Sinuhe and the biblical Joseph story share the same basic exile-restoration plot, in which the unfortunate protagonist enters a foreign land under duress and, through wisdom and cunning, becomes its ruler. For this reason, it is commonly presumed that the Joseph story's author was either directly or indirectly influenced by the Sinuhe tale, a conclusion that is reinforced by the Egyptian setting and coloring of the Joseph story (King; Meinhold).

Text and translation: R. KOCH, *Die Erzählung des Sinuhe* (BAeg 17; Brussels: Fondation Égyptologique Reine Élisabeth, 1990). ***Translations:*** *AEL* 1:222–35; *ANET* 18–23; *COS* 1.38: 77–82; *LAE* 54–66; PARKINSON, *The Tale of Sinuhe and Other Ancient Egyptian Poems,* 21–53. ***Bibliography:*** S. ALLAM, "Sinuhe's Foreign Wife (Reconsidered)," *DE* 4 (1986): 15–16; M. BARTA, *Sinuhe, the Bible, and the Patriarchs* (Prague: Czech Institute of Egyptology, 2003); J. BAINES, "Contextualizing Egyptian Representations of Society and Ethnicity," in *The Study of the Ancient Near East in the Twenty-First Century: The William Foxwell Albright Centennial Conference* (ed. J. S. Cooper and G. M. Schwartz; Winona Lake, Ind.: Eisenbrauns, 1996) 339–84; J. W. B. BARNES, "Sinuhe's Message to the King: A Reply to a Recent Article," *JEA* 53 (1967): 6–14; A. M. BLACKMAN, "Some Notes on the Story of Sinuhe and Other Egyptian Texts," *JEA* 22 (1936): 35–44; E. BLUMENTHAL, "Zu Sinuhes Zweikampf mit dem Starken von Retjenu," in *Fontes atque pontes: Eine Festgabe für Hellmut Brunner* (ed. M. Görg; AAT 5; Wiesbaden: Harrassowitz, 1983), 42–46;

P. DERCHAIN, "La réception de Sinouhé à la cour de Sésostris Ier," *RdE* 22 (1970): 79–83; J. L. FOSTER, "Cleaning Up *Sinuhe*," *JSSEA* 12 (1982): 81–85; A. H. GARDINER, *Notes on the Story of Sinuhe* (Paris: Champion, 1916); H. GOEDICKE, "The Route of Sinuhe's Flight,"*JEA* 43 (1957): 77–85; IDEM, "Sinuhe's Reply to the King's Letter," *JEA* 51 (1965): 29–47; J. KAHL, "Es ist von Anfang bis zum Ende so gekommen, wie es in der Schrift gefunden worden war: Zur Überlieferung der Erzählung des Sinuhe," in *Und Mose schrieb dieses Lied auf—Studien zum Alten Testament und zum alten Orient: Festschrift für Oswald Loretz* (ed. M. Dietrich and I. Kottsieper; AOAT 250; Münster: Ugarit, 1998), 383–400; J. R. KING, "The Joseph Story and Divine Politics: A Comparative Study of a Biographic Formula from the Ancient Near East," *JBL* 106 (1987): 577–94; IDEM, "Sinuhe's Duel," *JARCE* 21 (1984): 197–201; G. LANCZKOWSKI, "Die Geschichte vom Riesen Goliath und der Kampf Sinuhes mit dem Starken von Retenu," *MDAIK* 16 (1958): 214–18; A. LOPRIENO, *Topos und Mimesis zum Ausländer in der ägyptischen Literatur* (ÄgAbh 48; Wiesbaden: Harrassowitz, 1988), 41–59; A. MEINHOLD, "Die Geschichte des Sinuhe und die altestamentlich Diasporanovelle," *Wissenschaftliche Zeitschrift für Ernst-Moritz-Ardnt Universität* 20 (1971): 277–81; K. L. SPARKS, *Ethnicity and Identity in Ancient Israel* (Winona Lake, Ind.: Eisenbrauns, 1998), 77–85.

The Tale of the Eloquent Peasant. This Middle Kingdom tale appears in four different manuscripts, two of them Middle Kingdom papyri that also include copies of the Tale of Sinuhe. The plot unfolds as follows. While on a trip to purchase provisions for his hungry wife and children, a poor man named Khunanup is robbed by a gentry-class man named Nemtinakht. The peasant—here depicted as a kind of noble savage—quickly approaches the region's chief magistrate and sought justice through a series of nine beautiful and articulate pleas for help. After the peasant's first petition, the magistrate covertly arranges to have food provided to his family, but he does not tell Khunanup. Paradoxically, the peasant's pleas are so eloquent that the magistrate feigns ignoring them in order to churn up yet more eloquent petitions. When, after nine "failed" petitions, the peasant finally despairs of living, the magistrate reports to Khunanup that all of his petitions have been dutifully recorded on a new scroll and will be read before the king. In this way the story playfully accounts for its own composition and illustrates the usual way of accessing ancient stories: as listeners, not readers. In the end, Khunanup's case is heard and all matters are set aright by the king. Although the tale was obviously entertaining, it also defended the value of rhetoric and offered a playful critique of civic justice. The text is often viewed as a wisdom composition.

Text and translation: R. B. PARKINSON, *The Tale of the Eloquent Peasant* (Oxford: Oxford University Press, 1991). ***Translations:*** AEL 1:169–84; ANET 407–10; COS 1.43: 98–104; *LAE* 25–44; PARKINSON, *The Tale of Sinuhe and Other Ancient Egyptian Poems,* 54–88. ***Bibliography:*** R. B. PARKINSON, "The Date of the 'Tale of the Eloquent Peasant,'" *RdE* 42 (1991): 171–81; IDEM, "Literary Form and the *Tale of the Eloquent Peasant*," *JEA* 78 (1992): 163–78; E. PERRY, "A Critical Study of the Eloquent Peasant," (PhD diss., Johns Hopkins University, 1986); N. SHUPAK, "A New Source for the Study of the Judiciary and Law of Ancient Egypt: 'The Tale of the Eloquent Peasant,'" *JNES* 51 (1992): 1–18; W. K. SIMPSON, "The Political Background of the Eloquent Peasant," *GM* 120 (1990): 95–99.

The Story of Wenamun. Although Egyptian literature reached its creative heights during the Middle Kingdom, the New Kingdom also produced several interesting pieces, including the story of Wenamun, its greatest literary achievement. The story, introduced by a standard Egyptian date formula, takes the form of an administrative travel report from a certain Wenamun, an official from the temple of Amon. The date given in the text corresponds to the actual date of its composition (ca. 1100 B.C.E.), when Egyptian strength and vitality were rapidly disintegrating. Wenamun explains how he faced numerous obstacles in his effort to procure lumber from the Phoenicians at Byblos, primarily because the Phoenicians were aware of Egypt's social and economic decline. Although this might suggest that the story of Wenamun is a real travel report, its narrative style, the subtlety of its language, its sarcastic tone, and the careful development of its dialogues betray the text's true character. It offers a self-critical parody of Egyptian society. The argument against the authenticity of Wenamun's travel report is simple: such artistic and literary beauty never appears in the Egyptian report genre. So, in Wenamun as in the Tale of Sinuhe, we have a fictional text that was intentionally framed with a historical genre (a report). According to Eyre, precisely by blurring the border between history and fiction, these works became effective commentaries on Egyptian society. The historical circumstances presumed in Wenamun, however, are so close to the difficult realities of late New Kingdom life that it can be fruitfully compared to modern historical novels, which also situate fictional events in otherwise historical contexts.

Text and translation: GARDINER, *Late-Egyptian Stories,* 61–76. *Translations: AEL* 2:224–30; *ANET* 25–29; *COS* 1.41: 89–93; *LAE* 116–24. *Bibliography:* C. J. EYRE, "Is Egyptian Historical Literature 'Historical' or 'Literary?'" in *Ancient Egyptian Literature* (ed. Loprieno), 415–33; A. H. GARDINER, *Egypt of the Pharaohs* (Oxford: Oxford University Press, 1961), 306–13; C. F. NIMS, "Second Tenses in Wenamun," *JEA* 54 (1968): 161–64.

The Tale of the Shipwrecked Sailor. This New Kingdom story was written in the style of a simple folktale but has a complex structure that places "a tale within a tale within a tale." As a dejected ship captain prepares to face the king at the end of an unsuccessful journey, one of his deckhands explains through a tale how he once faced the same trouble. Within the deckhand's tale is yet another tale, in which the deckhand is in turn encouraged by a giant serpent. While the fable-like character of the tale obviously reflects its fictional genre, so does another more subtle indicator. In his dialogue with the reptile, the deckhand reflects no fear or surprise, either at his initial meeting with the great serpent or in the subsequent conversation. This is a hallmark of fictional literature: the characters in the story do not behave or respond as normal human beings should. Although this feature and the story's fairy-tale and fable motifs imply a make-believe world, the tale does not fail to convey a wise message: as each one is encouraged in times of trouble (e.g., the deckhand by the serpent), let him encourage his neighbor (as the deckhand does to the ship's captain).

Text and translation: A. M. BLACKMAN, *Middle Egyptian Stories* (BAeg 2; Brussels: Fondation Égyptologique Reine Élisabeth, 1932), 41–48. *Translations:* AEL 1:211–15; COS 1.39: 83–85; LAE 45–53; PARKINSON, *The Tale of Sinuhe and Other Ancient Egyptian Poems,* 89–101. *Bibliography:* J. BAINES, "Interpreting the Story of the Shipwrecked Sailor," *JEA* 76 (1990): 55–72; E. BRUNNER-TRAUT, *Altägyptische Märchen* (2d ed.; Dusseldorf: Diederichs, 1965), 5–10; B. BRYAN, "The Hero of the 'Shipwrecked Sailor,'" *Serapis* 5 (1980): 3–13; G. BURKARD, *Überlegungen zur Form der ägyptischen Literatur: Die Geschichte des Schiffbrüchigen als literarisches Kunstwerk* (AAT 22; Wiesbaden: Harrassowitz, 1993); P. DER MANUELIAN, "Interpreting 'The Shipwrecked Sailor,'" in *Gegengabe: Festschrift für Emma Brunner-Traut* (ed. I. Gamer-Wallert and W. Helck; Tübingen: Attempto, 1992), 223–33; J. L. FOSTER, "The Shipwrecked Sailor: Prose or Verse?" *SAK* 15 (1988): 69–109; A. LOPRIENO, "The Sign of Literature in the Shipwrecked Sailor," in *Religion und Philosophie im alten Ägypten: Festgabe für Philippe Derchain zu seinem 65. Geburtstag am 24. Juli 1991* (ed. U. Verhoeven and E. Graefe; OLA 39; Leuven: Peeters, 1991), 209–18; G. A. RENDSBURG, "Literary Devices in the Story of the Shipwrecked Sailor," *JAOS* 120 (2000): 13–23; A. SPALINGER, "An Alarming Parallel to the End of the Shipwrecked Sailor," *GM* 73 (1984): 91–95.

The Tale of Two Brothers. This tale describes how a wayward wife took interest in, and made advances toward, her younger brother-in-law living in the same household. Because the younger brother rejects these advances, the wife feigns that he has sexually assaulted her, forcing him to flee. After a sequence of bizarre episodes, the younger brother, Bata, becomes the king and judges the wife of his older brother, Anubis. The two brothers are eventually reconciled, and upon Bata's death, Anubis succeeds him on the throne. The author hints at the fictional character of his work by introducing fable-like elements (a talking cow) and, more important, by bestowing divine names upon his human characters (Anubis and Bata). These divine protagonists are an obvious reflection of the Egyptian view that the human pharaoh was also a god. Although the purpose of this tale it is not entirely clear, it is often believed to address disturbances in the royal household, especially as they relate to royal succession. Specifically, Wettengel has suggested that the text relates to a crisis at the end of the Nineteenth dynasty, just before the coronation of Seti II as crown prince, when it was necessary to explicate the descent of Ramesside kingship from a dynastic deity (here Bata). The parallels between this tale and the story of Joseph in Potiphar's house (Gen 39) are transparent.

Text and translation: GARDINER, *Late-Egyptian Stories,* 9–29. *Translations:* AEL 2:203–11; ANET 23–25; COS 1.40: 85–89; LAE 80–90. *Bibliography:* S. T. HOLLIS, *The Ancient Egyptian "Tale of Two Brothers"* (Norman: University of Oklahoma Press, 1990); V. VIKENTIEV, "Nâr-Ba-Thai," *JEA* 17 (1931): 67–80; W. WETTENGEL, *Die Erzählung von den beiden Brüdern: Der Papyrus d'Orbiney und die Königsideologie der Ramessiden* (OBO 195; Freiburg, Switz.: Universitätsverlag, 2003).

The Victory of Truth over Falsehood. Although the beginning of this story from papyrus Chester Beatty II is not preserved, we can surmise that the tale began as follows. Falsehood has taken his brother Truth before the divine court, falsely al-

leging that Truth had stolen his wondrous dagger. As we pick up the story, Falsehood is describing this great dagger to the Ennead (the great gods of Egypt) and
then requests that the court blind Truth and make him Falsehood's servant. The
Ennead does so. However, once this request is granted, Falsehood cannot bear to
live in proximity with the more virtuous qualities of Truth. In response, Falsehood directs his servants to feed Truth to a lion. This plan is eventually foiled, allowing Truth to bear the son who would avenge him in the divine court. This his
son accomplishes, when he justly accuses Falsehood of having stolen a great ox.
At the story's conclusion, the Ennead orders that Falsehood be blinded and made
the servant of Truth's household. The moral of this tale is clear enough. Our copy
dates to the 19th dynasty of the Egyptian New Kingdom.

Text: GARDINER, *Late-Egyptian Stories,* 30–36. *Translations:* AEL 2.211–14; *LAE* 104–7. *Bibliography:* L. COULON, "Le rhétorique et ses fictions: Pouvoirs et duplicité du discours à
travers la literature égyptienne du Moyen et du Nouvel Empire, *BIFAO* 99 (1999): 103–32;
J. G. GRIFFITHS, "Wahrheit und Lüge," *LÄ* 4:1140–42; L. H. LESKO, "Three Late Egyptian Stories Reconsidered," in *Egyptological Studies in Honor of Richard A. Parker* (Hanover, N.H.:
Published for Brown University Press by University Press of New England, 1986), 98–103.

The Tale of the Doomed Prince. This little tale appears in Hieratic Egyptian on
the verso of Papyrus Harris 500, along with another story known as The Capture
of Joppa (see next entry). Here we read of a childless king, whose prayers for
progeny were finally answered with a son. Unfortunately, the son was fated by the
gods to die by crocodile, snake, or dog. The remainder of the tale relates how the
prince's family and then wife attempted to protect him from these three dangers.
Regrettably the papyrus breaks off before the story's conclusion, but the tone of
what remains suggests a happy ending in which all three fates were averted. For
this reason, the traditional title "Doomed Prince" is probably misleading. Animals routinely speak in the story, providing sure evidence of the tale's fairy-tale
and fable-like character.

Text: E. A. W. BUDGE, *Facsimiles of Egyptian Hieratic Papyri in the British Museum, Second
Series* (London: British Museum, 1923), pls. 48–52. *Translations:* AEL 2:200–3; *LAE*
75–79. *Bibliography:* M. PIEPER, "Das Märchen von Wahrheit und Lüge und seine
Stellung unter den ägyptischen Märchen," *ZÄS* 70 (1934): 42–97; G. POSENER, "On the
Tale of the Doomed Prince," *JEA* 39 (1953): 107; W. SPIEGELBERG, "die Schluīzeilen der
Erzählung vom verwunschenen Prinzen, *ZÄS* 64 (1929): 86–87.

The Capture of Joppa. On the verso of Papyrus Harris 500 is this fictional tale, inspired by the Asiatic military campaigns of Thutmose III (15th c. B.C.E.). The
story's chief protagonist was one of Thutmose's generals named Djehuty (i.e.,
Thuti; Thoth). Although Djehuty lived during the Middle Kingdom, the present
text was written in Late Egyptian and dates to the New Kingdom. From this we
may surmise that the text is a legendary elaboration on the general's life. Still, the
officer's fame is no fiction. We have recovered numerous texts, as well as an inscribed gold bowl given to Djehuty by Thutmose, that confirm his renown. The

story's beginning is not preserved. What we have describes a ruse, in which Djehuty feigned a change of allegiance from Egypt to Joppa (on the Mediterranean coast of southern Palestine) and then captured the city by sending it "giftbaskets" filled with Egyptian soldiers. It is possible that this story inspired the similar motif found in the stories of the Trojan Horse and Ali Baba.

Text: E. A. W. BUDGE, *Facsimiles of Egyptian Hieratic Papyri in the British Museum, Second Series* (London: British Museum, 1923), pl. 47. **Translations:** *ANET* 22–3; A. ERMAN, *The Literature of Ancient Egypt* (London: Methuen, 1927), 167–69; *LAE* 72–74. **Bibliography:** H. GOEDICKE, "The Capture of Joppa," *Chronique d'Egypte* 43 (1968): 219–33.

Other Egyptian Tales and Novellas. Although the remaining tales and fables from ancient Egypt are numerous, many are also fragmentary. The more important exemplars are translated in major anthologies (see *AEL, ANET,* and *LAE*), and a number of fragmentary texts are discussed in an article by Parkinson.

Texts, translations, and studies: *AEL* 3:151–59; *ANET* 22–23; *LAE* 112–15, 450–52, 492–96; R. B. PARKINSON, "Teachings, Discourses, and Tales from the Middle Kingdom," in *Middle Kingdom Studies* (ed. S. Quirke; New Malden, England: SIA, 1991), 91–122.

8.2. Mesopotamian Tales and Novellas

Although Egyptian literature is a rich source of tales and novellas, numerous Mesopotamian stories are known as well, some written in Sumerian and others in Akkadian. A few texts cited elsewhere in this volume would also fit here nicely (e.g., the Sin of Sargon in 9.1.3), just as some of the texts cited here could be included in other chapters. The discussion begins with our oldest Sumerian exemplars and then moves chronologically forward.

Sumerian Tales of the King's Courtroom. Among the Sumerian tales preserved in our Old Babylonian sources are several entertaining stories about the king's wise judgments in the royal courts, of which the Tale of the Three Ox Drivers is an early example. The tale begins, "There were once three friends, citizens of Adab, who fell into a dispute with each other and went to seek justice. . . . One man had an ox, one a cow, and one a wagon." As the three traveled along to fetch water, the cow conceived by the ox and birthed a calf, which subsequently ate the load in the wagon. To whom, asked the three, did the calf belong? The king took council with the *sekrum,* a "cloister woman," and then presented a judgment that satisfied "each man's heart." The text is broken and we do not know what this judgment was, but it was obviously a wise and imaginative verdict that solved an apparently irresolvable conundrum. The Tale of the Old Man and the Young Girl is a second exemplar from this genre. Although the beginning of the story is missing, it is clear that an impotent old man appeared before the king's court with a young lady. After taking council with the cloister woman, the king pronounced his ruling: the old man could enter her house and become her husband, an arrangement

that the young lady happily—and paradoxically—accepted. The royal protagonists of these Sumerian courtroom tales were always anonymous, so we should
not imagine the stories to be works of royal propaganda unless one envisions
them as general apologies on behalf of the monarchy. It is in fact far more likely
that these tales were parodies of royalty, as is suggested by the source of the king's
wisdom, a cloister woman, and by the nature of the cases, which were absurd.
This would explain the burlesque and entertaining character of the tales, in which
Lipinski suggests the pens of wisdom scribes were playfully turned on the
monarchy.

An obvious biblical parallel to these Sumerian texts is the story of Solomon's wise verdict in 1 Kgs 3:16–28, in which the shrewd and cunning king was
able to solve what appeared to be an irresolvable case. Scholars have often noted
that the biblical story itself provides only anonymous actors, "the king" and the
two prostitutes, and this suggests that the story may have originated as an entertaining anonymous tale before it was secondarily applied to Solomon by the
author of 1 Kings (Lipinski).

Text and translation: H. DE GENOUILLAC, *Textes religieux sumériens du Louvre* (TCL 16;
Paris: P. Geuthner, 1930), nos. 80 and 83. *Bibliography:* B. R. FOSTER, "Humor and Cu-
neiform Literature," *JANES* 6 (1974): 69–85; GRESSMANN, "Das salomonische Urteil";
E. LIPINSKI, "The King's Arbitration in Ancient Near Eastern Folk-Tale," in *Keilschriftliche
Literaturen: Ausgewählte Vorträge der XXXII. Rencontre assyriologique internationale* (ed.
K. Hecker and W. Sommerfeld; BBVO 6; Berlin: Dietrich Reimer, 1986), 137–42; M. A.
ZIPOR, "The Cannibal Women and Their Judgment before the Helpless King (2 Kings
6:24ff)," *AbrN* 35 (1998): 84–94.

The Fowler and His Wife. This Sumerian tale is preserved in Old Babylonian copies of Sumerian Proverb Collection 24 (see 2.1.1). The ostensible plot concerns a
drunken bird-catcher and his wife's criticisms of his failure as a hunter, but it
seems likely that we have here a double entendre. The text is almost certainly a
critique of the husband's sexual achievement.

Text and translation: B. ALSTER, "Paradoxical Proverbs and Satire in Sumerian Literature," *JCS* 27 (1975): 201–30. *Bibliography:* B. ALSTER, "Proverb Collection XXIV,"
Assyriological Miscellanies 1 (1980): 33–50; IDEM, "Two Sumerian Short Tales Reconsidered," *ZA* 82 (1992): 186–201; P. MICHALOWSKI, "On 'The Fowler and His Wife,'" *RA* 75
(1981): 170.

The Slave and the Scoundrel. According to this tale, Hala-Bau was a manumitted
slave who had some wealth but also a bad disposition that caused everyone to reject her. She was somehow taken and locked up by a certain Nanna-ildumu, who,
with his daughter, proceeded to live like a king for six months and fifteen days,
that is, until they exhausted Hala-Bau's fortune. The tale seems to end with Hala-
Bau and Nanna-ildumu roaming the streets in poverty. Roth identifies the tale as
a "comic morality tale," suggesting that it should be associated with the Sumerian

wisdom tradition. Our copies of the story come from an Old Babylonian tablet discovered at Nippur.

Text and translation: M. T. ROTH, "The Slave and the Scoundrel," *JAOS* 103 (1983): 275–82. *Bibliography:* B. ALSTER, "Two Sumerian Short Tales Reconsidered," *ZA* 82 (1992): 186–201.

The Poor Man from Nippur. This five-episode Akkadian tale proves that it is a blunder to conclude, as some have, that "the man of Mesopotamia was a stranger to laughter" (Contenu). Sick, poor, and destitute, Gimil-Ninurta was a desperate pauper in the city of Nippur. He purposed to go out into the city and trade some of his clothes to buy a sheep, but this failing, he ended up with a goat, which, according to social custom, he could eat only with friends and relations. Having none of these, the poor fellow decided to invite the mayor of Nippur to dinner. Gimil-Ninurta fully expected the mayor to accept the offer and to volunteer beer and other accoutrements for the feast. When the mayor rejected Gimil-Ninurta's offer and had him driven from the royal house, Gimil-Ninurta vowed a threefold vengeance upon the mayor. The mayor, amused by the vow, laughed the rest of the day. The remainder of the story explains how Gimil-Ninurta, through three different ruses, managed to give the mayor sound thrashings. After the third beating, the text says that the mayor "entered the city more dead than alive."

This poetic tale was copied by an apprentice scribe in the *bīt mummi,* a school-and-workshop attached to a temple in Sultantepe. The tablet, dated to 701 B.C.E., was found with other texts in the private library of a scholar-scribe named Qurdi-Nergal, for whom the colophon explicitly says the text was prepared. Later variations of the tale appear in manuscripts of the *Arabian Nights.* Whatever other purposes the text may have served, one of its primary functions was obviously entertainment.

Texts and translations: O. R. GURNEY, "The Tale of the Poor Man of Nippur," *AnSt* 6 (1956): 145–64; O. R. GURNEY and J. J. FINKELSTEIN, *The Sultantepe Tablets* (2 vols.; OPBIAA 3, 7; London: British Institute of Archaeology at Ankara, 1957–1964), nos. 38–39. *Bibliography:* G. CONTENAU, *Everyday Life in Babylon and Assyria* (London: E. Arnold, 1954), 302; J. S. COOPER, "Structure, Humor, and Satire in the Poor Man of Nippur," *JCS* 27 (1975): 163–74.

The Aramaic Story of Ahiqar. Although our oldest copies go back to the fifth century B.C.E., it is generally assumed that the story of Ahiqar is somewhat older, perhaps as old as the seventh century (Lindenberger, Aramaic Proverbs, 1983). The primary text was discovered in the community archive of a Jewish military colony at Elephantine. The tale shows no signs of Jewish influence or authorship (VanderKam), but Jews of the period had likely already adopted Ahiqar as one of their own, as is reflected in the apocryphal book of Tobit (Tob 1:21–22). A collection of wisdom sayings (see 2.3) follows the story in the manuscript, and this has prompted some scholars to suggest that these two components—story and wisdom—originated separately. This conclusion is reasonable given that the wisdom sayings reflect a somewhat older Aramaic dialect, although it should be noted that traditional materials such as proverbs are more likely to preserve older linguistic features. As for the story itself, our Aramaic copy is fragmentary and must be filled out with later versions in demotic, Greek, Syriac, Arabic, and a number of other languages. In many cases these later versions provide more elaborate renditions of the tale.

According to the tale, Ahiqar was the wisest of Assyria's counselors during the reigns of Sennacherib and Esarhaddon. When he became aged and lacked a son, the sage adopted his nephew Nadin as both son and scholarly apprentice. When Nadin finally succeeded Ahiqar, he quickly turned on his father by framing him in a series of forged letters. Esarhaddon subsequently sentenced Ahiqar to death and commissioned an officer, Nabushumishkun, to carry out the penalty. Fortunately, Ahiqar had previously spared Nabushumishkun's life, and Nabushumishkun responded in kind by feigning Ahiquar's death and concealing the sage from Esarhaddon. The Aramaic text breaks off at this point, but later versions suggest the following conclusion: When news of wise Ahiqar's death reached Egypt, Pharaoh quickly challenged Assyria to a duel of wits, in which Assyria had to "build a castle in the air" or "pay three years of revenue." When Nadin could not solve this puzzle, Esarhaddon bemoaned the loss of Ahiqar's wisdom. To Esarhaddon's delight, at this opportune moment Nabushumishkun reproduced Ahiqar, who handled the Egyptian challenge and returned home with the booty from Egypt. Ahiqar was then rewarded with a position overseeing the king's household. The tale concludes with Ahiqar beating the underhanded Nadin to death.

Does the story of Ahiqar give us history or a good tale? Substantial evidence has been adduced to show that figures by the names Nabushumishkun and Nadin indeed served in Esarhaddon's courts. Moreover, it appears that each filled a historical role that was reminiscent of the tale: Nabushumishkun was a high-ranking army officer, and a certain Nadin was accused of subversive activities (Lindenberger, "Ahiqar," 1985). The figure of Ahiqar presents problems, however. There is a very late Seleucid-era text (second century B.C.E.) that mentions him as the chief court scholar of Esarhaddon (Van Dijk), but this reference could easily be based on the story of Ahiqar itself. For this reason, the story's genre should be ascertained mainly on the basis of its content. Our first observation is that the tale's plot is inherently improbable, reflecting a theme common in Mesopotamian tradition, that of "the disgrace and rehabilitation of a minister" (Krappe). The tale also reflects a fourfold pattern that appears in many Near Eastern folktales (Niditch/Doron): (1) a person of lower status is called before a person of higher status to answer a difficult question or problem; (2) the person of high status poses the problem that no one else can solve; (3) the person of lower status solves the problem; (4) the person of lower status is rewarded with gifts, authority, and status. These stock plots are in turn joined to the theme of the ungrateful nephew, which was also a common Mesopotamian motif (Reiner). When the possible historicity of the tale's characters is viewed alongside these folklorish elements, many scholars inevitably view the story as a piece of historical fiction. Nevertheless, many other scholars would be willing to concede that the story was inspired by the life of a scholar named Ahiqar and perhaps reflects real events in his life (Dalley; Greenfield).

What was the purpose of this composition? Reversal of fortune is an entertaining theme that runs through the story, suggesting that the author wished to amuse his readers. If the tale's first readers served as scholars in the royal courts, as seems likely, then the tale would also have encouraged courtiers who faced the threat or reality of rejection by their royal superiors. This tale would have given the courtiers new confidence because it averred, in a strong dose of retributive dogma, that the guilty would ultimately be punished and the innocent vindicated. The story's relationship to the collection of wisdom maxims that follow it is perhaps germane to its composition. The Aramaic language of the proverbs is older than that in the story itself, suggesting that the story may have been composed to enhance the value of the sayings by attributing them to the famous Ahiqar (Lindenberger, "Ahiqar," 1985). It is impossible to determine whether the tale originated as an addition to the proverbs or, as seems more likely, as a separate composition that was later added to them.

Text and translation: J. M. LINDENBERGER, *The Aramaic Proverbs of Ahiqar* (Baltimore: Johns Hopkins University Press, 1983). *Translations: ANET* 427–30; J. M. LINDENBERGER, "Ahiqar: A New Translation and Introduction," *OTP* 2:479–507. *Bibliography:* F. C. CONYBEARE, J. R. HARRIS, and A. S. LEWIS, *The Story of Aḥikar* (Cambridge: Cambridge University Press, 1913); S. DALLEY, "Assyrian Court Narratives in Aramaic and Egyptian: Historical Fiction," in *Proceedings of the XLV Rencontre assyriologique internationale: History and Historiography in the Cuneiform World* (ed. Tz. Abusch et al.; 2 vols.; Bethesda, Md.: CDL Press, 2001), 149–61; J. C. GREENFIELD, "The Wisdom of Ahiqar," in *Wisdom in Ancient Israel: Essays in Honour of J. A. Emerton* (Cambridge: Cambridge University Press, 1995), 43–52; A. H. KRAPPE, "Is the Story of Aḥikar the Wise of Indian Origin?" *JAOS* 61 (1941): 280–84; A. R. MILLARD, "Judith, Tobit, Ahiqar, and History," in *New Heaven and New Earth: Prophecy and the Millennium: Essays in Honour of Anthony Gelston* (ed. P. J. Harland and C. T. R. Hayward; Leiden: Brill, 1999), 195–203; S. NIDITCH and R. DORON, "The Success of the Wise Courtier: A Formal Approach," *JBL* 96 (1977): 179–93; E. REINER, "The Etiological Myth of the 'Seven Sages,'" *Or* 30 (1961): 1–11; J. C. VANDERKAM, "Ahikar/Ahiqar," *ABD* 1:113–15; IDEM, "Ahiqar, Book of," *ABD* 1:119–20; J. VAN DIJK, "Die Inschriftenfunde," in *XVIII. Vorläufiger Bericht über die von dem Deutschen Archäologischen Institut und der Deutschen Orient-Gesellschaft aus Mitteln der Deutschen Forschungsgemeinschaft unternommenen Ausgrabungen in Uruk-Warka: Winter 1959/60* (ed. H. J. Lenzen; Berlin: Gebr. Mann, 1962), 39–62.

8.3. Hittite Tales

Appu and His Two Sons. Here we meet Appu, a wealthy and successful man who was nonetheless childless. He offered sacrifices to the sun god (here, Šamaš, Mesopotamian god of justice), who subsequently took the form of a young man and appeared to Appu. After their conversation, the sun god arranged for the man to receive two sons, whom Appu named Wrong and Right. The two sons eventually inherited their father's estate and sought to divide it up, but the tale makes it clear that Wrong did this unfairly, taking the best ox for himself and giving his brother a bad cow. The sun god thwarted this injustice by making Right's bad cow become good, and in the text's broken conclusion we find the gods making a series of just verdicts on behalf of Right. The basic message of the text is expressed in the proem of *CTH* 360, which affirms that divine retribution will always vindicate the righteous person and frustrate the plans of the evil person.

Text and translation: J. SIEGELOVÁ, *Appu-Märchen und Hedammu-Mythus* (StBoT 14; Wiesbaden: Harrassowitz, 1971). *Translation:* HOFFNER, *Hittite Myths,* 63–65. *Bibliography:* FRIEDRICH, "Churritische Märchen und Sagen in hethitischer Sprache."

The Sun God, the Cow, and the Fisherman. This very broken text (*CTH* 363) is reminiscent of the tale in the previous entry about Appu and his sons. It recounts two episodes in which the sun god comes down and provides children to a childless parent. In the first instance it is a cow that receives calves, apparently because the sun god copulated with the cow. (This explains the birth of a calf with two legs.) In the second instance the sun god causes a fisherman to find a child in the mountains. The fisherman, recognizing this as a blessing from the sun god, takes the child home and requests that his wife "lie down on the bed, and wail . . . so that the whole city will hear and say: The fisherman's wife has borne a child." The tablet's colophon indicates that there is more to come in the story, but we do not have copies of the next tablet. Some scholars believe that this tale is part of the Appu tale.

Text and translation: FRIEDRICH, "Churritische Märchen und Sagen in hethitischer Sprache." *Translation:* HOFFNER, *Hittite Myths,* 65–67. *Bibliography:* H. A. HOFFNER, "The Hurrian Story of the Sungod, the Cow, and the Fisherman," in *Studies on the Civilization and Culture of Nuzi and the Hurrians in Honor of E. R. Lacheman* (ed. M. Morrison and D. I. Owen; Winona Lake, Ind.: Eisenbrauns, 1981), 189–94.

Kessi the Hunter and His Beautiful Wife. According to this tale (*CTH* 361), Kessi became so enamored with his beautiful wife that he no longer hunted in the mountains and no longer offered sacrifices to the gods. When his mother complained that Kessi no longer hunted and brought her game to eat, Kessi took to the mountains to hunt. Unfortunately, the gods, angered by Kessi's impiety, would not allow him to find any game. Kessi remained in the mountains for three months, too embarrassed to return to his city empty-handed. Our broken copy of the text concludes with Kessi receiving a series of dreams, which his mother is about to interpret. Fragmentary tablets of a Hurrian version of Kessi have been found also, but these have not yet been published.

Text and translation: FRIEDRICH, "Churritische Märchen und Sagen in hethitischer Sprache." *Translation:* HOFFNER, *Hittite Myths,* 67–68.

Concluding Observations

Although the texts examined in this chapter served a variety of functions, we can infer that entertainment was a common motivation for their writers and readers. Even the more serious texts, such as the story of Ahiqar, the Tale of Sinuhe, and Wenamun, reflect entertaining themes; on the other hand, the latter three texts were more than entertainment. Ahiqar was composed to teach an ideology of retributive wisdom; Sinuhe, to extol the propaganda of Middle Egyptian virtues; and Wenamun, to critique an Egypt in decline. So, although Near Eastern tales and novellas were commonly entertaining, it is equally clear that in many cases more than laughter was at stake.

If tales and novellas are superficially similar to histories and sometimes reflect historical realities, on what basis do scholars judge them to be works of fiction? One important trait of fiction is the presence of fanciful and marvelous events in the narrative. Wax crocodiles, story-telling serpents, and talking cows are the motifs of fable and make-believe, and it is perfectly sensible and reasonable on one level to infer from these motifs that a text is fictional. On the other hand, this assumption reflects a strain of modern bias that was not prevalent among the ancients, for whom the miraculous sometimes constituted a real possibility. Although fanciful and marvelous themes are potential signs of fiction, this equation is not as straightforward as we might imagine.

Another trait that commonly appears in fiction is historical improbability, of which there are two varieties, internal and external. In the first instance, the story itself seems quite improbable. It is not very likely, for instance, that the poor man from Nippur could so easily deceive the city's mayor on three different occasions, nor is it sensible to imagine a Sumerian king who regularly gets legal advice from a cloister woman. Even when a tale's characters seem to be historical figures, as in Ahiqar, the plot's improbabilities cause scholars to doubt its historicity. Although these instances of internal evidence mark a work as fiction, external evidence can also play this role. Sometimes the events described in a narrative do not stand up to historical verification. For instance, even though we know a good amount about the reign of the Assyrian king Esarhaddon, there is no evidence that a fellow named Ahiqar was granted the prominence that the tale ascribes to him. Sometimes the relevant external evidence is of a linguistic sort. Although the Tale of King Cheops's Court is set in the Fourth Dynasty (ca. 2600–2450 B.C.E.), its Egyptian dialect turns out to be from the Middle Kingdom (ca. 2040–1650 B.C.E.). In this way, the text's "prophetic predictions" turn out to be playful and fictional etiologies written after the fact. As we can see, external evidence often figures prominently in our effort to distinguish fact from fiction.

Paradoxically, another important trait of fiction is that it sometimes assumes the superficial form of a historical genre but deviates from this in other important respects. The Tale of Sinuhe was framed as an autobiography and Wenamun's story as a travel report, but in both cases the literary quality and artistic character of the text betrays its fictive character. Narrative strategies such as these, which blur the distinction between fiction and history, are particularly effective because of the realism they lend to the story and its message. One common strategy for promoting this verisimilitude (the appearance of being true or real) is to set the story within a well-known historical period or to adopt well-known figures of the past as key or supporting characters. It was precisely this practice that made the tales of Sinuhe, Wenamun, and Ahiqar so popular and rhetorically effective.

Another reason for judging a text to be fictional is generic analogy: when a narrative's motifs and themes appear in other texts that we have already appraised as fictional, it stands to reason that we might suspect our story is also of the fictional type. The primary difficulty with this assumption is that "fictional" motifs often originate in historical realities and historical accounts are always emplotted using narrative strategies similar to those used in fictional works. For this reason, the criterion of generic analogy should be wielded with some care, although it must remain a valid and important tool in our effort to make generic distinctions successfully.

In the Hebrew Bible, some of the biblical texts that scholars have often identified as fictional tales or novellas include the Joseph story, Ruth, Jonah, Esther, and the tales in the first half of the book of Daniel. The comparative evidence adduced above seems to bear out these judgments. In some of these cases, the external evidence suggests the biblical tales should be so adjudged. There is, for instance, no evidence for a Hebrew vizier in Egypt named Joseph, or for a Hebrew queen named Esther in Persia, or for a Jewish Daniel so high in the Babylonian administration, or for the religious reform of Assyria and its king, as Jonah might suggest. Other evidence reinforces these conclusions. In the case of the Joseph story, its plot line is very similar to the Egyptian Tale of Sinuhe and draws upon two other Egyptian traditions, the Tale of Two Brothers (cf. Gen 39) and the motif of seven years of plenty or famine (cf. Gen 41; the Famine Stela in 9.3). The Joseph story in turn influenced later Jewish tales, such as Esther, Daniel and Tobit, in which faithful Jews, living in the royal courts of a foreign king, were tested with a choice between their Judaism and death. Their decision to stand firm in the face of this threat resulted in their improbable rise to power and prominence.

Because these works were fictional, their characters strike thoughtful readers as artificial. For instance, Persian kings were not so easily entrapped by their own decrees as Daniel and Esther suggest (Dan 6; Esth 8–9), and there is little chance that a Babylonian king would plan to execute all of his wise men (Dan 2:12) or that a Persian king would decree that Jews could fight and kill thousands of Persian soldiers (Esth 8–9). The characters in the book of Ruth are also fictional, for they bear names that symbolically reflect their roles in the story. Ruth means "companion," Orpah "disloyal," and Boaz "strength," and Naomi, who finally settles happily in Israel, sports a name that roughly translates as "peaceful" (see Sasson; Soggin). Only in fiction do names correspond so nicely with narrative roles. In the book of Esther, its chief protagonist and antagonist, Mordecai of Kish and Haman the Agagite, correspond precisely to earlier literary prototypes from 1 Sam 15, Saul the son of Kish and King Agag. Strictly speaking, the death of

Agag and his family in 1 Samuel precludes the historicity of the story. Daniel the Jew was also a fictional character, whose origins can be traced back to Danel (cf. Ezek 14:14; 28:3), a hero in the literary traditions of second-millennium Ugarit (see the entry on Aqhat in 9.2). Such a development should occasion no surprise, given that the Jews often adopted foreign figures as their own (e.g., Noah, Ahiqar, and Enoch).

This brief overview includes only the longest and most prominent fictional tales in the Hebrew Bible. Many shorter exemplars are nested in the narratives of the Pentateuch and the Deuteronomistic History. Notable examples include the tale of Solomon's wise verdict (1 Kgs 3; cf. "Sumerian Tales of the King's Courtroom"; Zipor; Gressman), the story of the man of God from Judah (1 Kgs 13; see Dozeman), and the three wife-sister tales in Genesis (Gen 12, 20, 26; see Niditch 1987). Fiction also plays an important role in Israel's epic and legendary traditions (see ch. 9).

Some religious communities are naturally uncomfortable with the suggestion that portions of their Scripture may be fictional. Although this is not the place to debate the theological issues, it is perhaps helpful to recall these words: "We may say that history by opening us to the different, opens us to the possible, while fiction, by opening us to the unreal, opens us to the essential" (Ricoeur, 177). Neither fiction nor history necessarily has the upper hand when it comes to expressing religious truth, and this is nowhere more vividly illustrated than in the Near Eastern tradition itself. Among the most interesting peculiarities of Near Eastern literature is a general dearth of discourse genres—that is, texts that formally and directly treat subjects in theoretical terms. The primary ancient substitute for our modern theoretical discourse was narrative, and this suggests that many ancient narratives were creative expressions of theology and ideology rather than reports of actual events. It is worthwhile to note, however, on the basis of the comparative evidence, that Hebrew tales and novellas were not necessarily works of theology in every case or in every respect. The tales were certainly entertaining as well, and entertainment counts in any culture—ancient Israel being no exception.

General Bibliography

A. AARNE, *Verzeichnis der Märchentypen* (Helsinki: Suomalainen Tiedeakalemian Toimituksia, 1910); A. AARNE and S. THOMPSON, *The Types of the Folktale: A Classification and Bibliography* (2d ed. rev.; Folklore Fellows Communications 75, no. 184; Helsinki: Suomalainen Tiedeakatemia, Academia Scientiarum Fennica, 1964); D. ALEXANDER, "Jonah and Genre," *TynBul* 36 (1985): 35–59; R. ALTER, *The Art of Biblical Narrative* (New York: Basic Books, 1981); M. BAL, *Narratology: Introduction to the Theory of Narrative* (Toronto: University of Toronto Press, 1985); W. R. BASCOM, "Four Functions of Folklore," in *The Study of Folklore* (ed. Dundes), 279–98; D. BEN-AMOS, *Folklore Genres* (Austin: University of Texas

Press, 1976); S. B. BERG, *The Book of Esther: Motifs, Themes, and Structure* (SBLDS 44; Missoula, Mont.: Scholars Press, 1979); A. BERLIN, *Poetics and Interpretation of Biblical Narrative* (Sheffield, England: Almond, 1983); D. E. BYNUM, "The Generic Nature of Oral Epic Poetry," in *Folklore Genres* (ed. Ben-Amos), 35–58; G. W. COATS, ed., *Saga, Legend, Tale, Novella, Fable: Narrative Forms in the Old Testament* (JSOTSup 35; Sheffield, England: JSOT Press, 1985); J. J. COLLINS, "The Court-Tales in Daniel and the Development of Apocalyptic," *JBL* 94 (1975): 218–34; P. W. COXON, "The 'List' Genre and Narrative Style in the Court Tales of Daniel," *JSOT* 35 (1986): 95–121; L. DÉGH and A. VÁZSONYI, "Legend and Belief," in *Folklore Genres* (ed. Ben-Amos, 1976), 94–123; T. B. DOZEMAN, "The Way of the Man of God from Judah: True and False Prophecy in the Pre-deuteronomic Legend of 1 Kings 13," *CBQ* 44 (1982): 379–93; A. DUNDES, ed., *The Study of Folklore* (Englewood Cliffs, N. J.: Prentice-Hall, 1965); C. A. EVANS, *Ancient Texts for New Testament Studies* ([rev. ed. of *A Guide to Nonbiblical Texts for New Testament Interpretation;* Peabody, Mass.: Hendrickson Publishers, 1992] Peabody, Mass.: Hendrickson Publishers, forthcoming); J. G. FRAZER, *Folktale in the Old Testament* (New York: Macmillan, 1923); J. FRIEDRICH, "Churritische Märchen und Sagen in hethitischer Sprache," *ZA* 49 (1950): 213–54; A. H. GARDINER, *Late-Egyptian Stories* (BAeg 1; Brussels: Fondation Égyptologique Reine Élisabeth, 1932); G. GENETTE, *Narrative Discourse: An Essay in Method* (Ithaca: Cornell University Press, 1980); IDEM, *Narrative Discourse Revisited* (Ithaca: Cornell University Press, 1988); H. GRESSMANN, "Das salomonische Urteil," *Deutsche Rundschau* 130 (1907): 212–28; H. GUNKEL, *The Folktale in the Old Testament* (trans. M. D. Rutter; Sheffield, England: Almond, 1987); A. HER-MANN, *Die ägyptische Königsnovelle* (New York: J. J. Augustin, 1938); S. HERR-MANN, "Die Königsnovelle in Ägypten und Israel," *Wissenschaftliche Zeitschrift der Karl-Marx Universität Leipzig* 3, no. 1 (1953–1954): 51–62; H. A. HOFFNER, *Hittite Myths* (SBLWAW 2; Atlanta: Scholars Press, 1990); W. L. HUMPHREYS, "A Life-Style for Diaspora: A Study of the Tales of Esther and Daniel," *JBL* 92 (1973): 211–23; D. IRVIN, *Mytharion: The Comparison of Tales from the Old Testament and the Ancient Near East* (AOAT 32; Neukirchen-Vluyn: Neukirchener Verlag, 1978); J. R. KING, "The Joseph Story and Divine Politics: A Comparative Study of a Bio-graphic Formula from the Ancient Near East," *JBL* 106 (1987): 577–94. P. G. KIRKPATRICK, *The Old Testament and Folklore Study* (JSOTSup 62; Sheffield, Eng-land: Sheffield Academic Press, 1988); A. J. LEVINE, "Tobit: Teaching Jews How to Live in the Diaspora," *BRev* 8 (1992): 42–51; A. LOPRIENO, ed., *Ancient Egyptian Literature: History and Forms* (PA 10; New York: Brill, 1996); IDEM, "The 'King's Novel,'" in *Ancient Egyptian Literature,* 277–95; A. MEINHOLD, "Die Gattung der Josephsgeschichte und des Esterbuches: Diasporanovelle," *ZAW* 87 (1975): 306–24; 88 (1976): 72–93; P. J. MILNE, *Vladimir Propp and the Study of Structure in Hebrew Biblical Narrative* (Bible and Literature Series 13; Sheffield, England: Sheffield Academic Press, 1988); S. NIDITCH, *Folklore and the Hebrew Bible* (Min-neapolis: Fortress, 1993); IDEM, *Oral World and Written Word* (Louisville: West-minster John Knox, 1996); IDEM, *Underdogs and Tricksters: A Prelude to Biblical Folklore* (San Francisco: Harper & Row, 1987); S. NIDITCH and R. DORON, "The

Success of the Wise Courtier: A Formal Approach," *JBL* 96 (1977): 179–93;
A. OLRIK, "Epic Laws of Folk Narrative," in *The Study of Folklore* (ed. Dundes),
129–41; IDEM, *Principles for Oral Narrative Research* (Folklore Studies in Transla-
tion; Bloomington: Indiana University Press, 1992); V. PROPP, *Morphology of the
Folktale* (2d ed.; Austin: University of Texas Press, 1968); IDEM, *Theory and His-
tory of Folklore* (Minneapolis: University of Minnesota Press, 1984); P. RICOEUR,
"The Narrative Function," *Semeia* 13 (1978): 177–202; W. RÖLLIG, "Volksliteratur
in mesopotamischer Überlieferung," in *Keilschriftliche Literaturen: Ausgewählte
Vorträge der XXXII. Rencontre assyriologique internationale* (ed. K. Hecker and W.
Sommerfeld; BBVO 6; Berlin: Dietrich Reimer, 1986), 81–87; L. A. ROSENTHAL,
"Die Josephsgeschichte mit den Buchem Ester und Daniel verglichen," *ZAW*
15 (1895): 278–84; J. M. SASSON, *Ruth: A New Translation with a Philological
Commentary and a Formalist-Folklorist Interpretation* (2d ed.; Sheffield, England:
Sheffield Academic Press, 1989); W. K. SIMPSON, "Belles Lettres and Propaganda,"
in *Ancient Egyptian Literature* (ed. Loprieno), 435–43; J. L. SKA, *Our Fathers Have
Told Us: Introduction to the Analysis of Hebrew Narratives* (SubBi 13; Rome:
Editrice Pontificio Istituto Biblico, 1990); J. A. SOGGIN, *Introduction to the Old
Testament* (3d ed.; Louisville: Westminster John Knox, 1989); M. STERNBERG, *The
Poetics of Biblical Narrative* (Bloomington: University of Indiana Press, 1985); S.
THOMPSON, *The Folktale* (New York: Holt, Rinehart, and Winston, 1946); IDEM,
The Motif-Index of Folk-Literature (2d ed.; 6 vols.; Bloomington: Indiana Univer-
sity Press, 1955–1958); IDEM, "The Star Husband Tale," in *The Study of Folklore*
(ed. Dundes), 415–59; F. L. UTLEY, "Oral Genres as Bridge to Written Literature,"
in *Folklore Genres* (ed. Ben-Amos), 3–15; J. VAN SETERS, *In Search of History* (New
Haven: Yale University Press, 1983); H. M. WAHL, "Das Motiv des 'Aufstiegs' in
der Hofgeschichte: Am Beispiel von Joseph, Esther, und Daniel," *ZAW* 112 (2000):
59–74; M. A. ZIPOR, "The Cannibal Women and Their Judgment before the Helpless King (2 Kings 6:24ff)," *AbrN* 35 (1998): 84–94.

CHAPTER NINE

Epics and Legends

Introduction

Although the terms *epic* and *legend* usually imply somewhat different things, in due course we shall see why, in the context of ancient Near Eastern studies, the genres can be conveniently treated together. The term *epic* is patently easier to define: it is an analytical genre spawned from the study of prominent Greek texts from which it took its name. In Greek antiquity, *epic* (Gr. *epos*) referred to the unique metrical pattern followed in many poems, most notably in the Homeric poems, the *Iliad* and the *Odyssey* (Hardie). In our era the term is applied to texts that are similar to these old Greek works in form and content; that is, epics are essentially texts that narrate the acts of gods and cultural heroes in extended poetry. The genre can be conveniently subdivided into *epic myths,* which treat primarily the deeds of the gods, and *epic legends,* whose primary focus is on the deeds of great men. Because myths will be treated in the following chapter, in this chapter our emphasis will be on the legendary epics. The category of legendary epic obviously assumes some definition of legend, which provides a segue to our discussion of that genre.

In Near Eastern studies *legend* is commonly used in two different ways, and both senses of the term are so standard and conventional that neither can be ignored (Hals). In the first instance, legends are narratives that treat the lives of great heroes or the origins of important social or religious institutions. The genre therefore serves as society's link to its ancient roots. In the second instance, scholars often use *legend* to describe nonhistorical traditions that the ancients popularly regarded as historical (Dégh and Vázsonyi). The key issue in this second case is the difference between the supposed mode of composition, which was fictional, and the mode of reception, which imagined the story to be true. Modal contrasts of this sort are to be expected because old and venerable stories are likely to be viewed as historical even when they are not, especially when the stories treat matters of cultural importance. This chapter takes the first and broader route, which defines legend as *a traditional story that treats cultural heroes and institutions.*

From a modern viewpoint, this definition leaves room for both historical and nonhistorical narratives, and from the ancient viewpoint, it can include stories that the ancients may or may not have believed. This flexibility is important because our study of these ancient traditions frequently trips on precisely these two questions: were these traditions composed referentially or fictionally, and did the ancient audience believe—or not believe—these stories?

Epic and legend are inseparably linked in Near Eastern studies because the most popular Near Eastern epics also narrated the exploits (*res gestae*) of legendary heroes from the remote past. There are many examples of these texts, some more or less complete and others quite fragmentary. Although the sheer number of exemplars dictates that our survey must be selective, it is not difficult to highlight the best-known legendary epics as well as a few less familiar texts. Among the most important texts are the Gilgamesh traditions, the traditions about the kings of Akkade (Sargon and Naram-Sin), and the two famous Ugaritic epics, Kirta and Aqhat. Among the lesser-known texts are the epic tales of Enmerkar and Lugalbanda (both closely related to Gilgamesh), the story of Idrimi, the Tale of Sarbanapal and Sarmuge, and the Egyptian Setne tales. One may infer from this list that our focus will be on the heroic legends rather than on legends of institutional origin, but the two types cannot be easily disentangled. Most of the heroic legends are about kings, and there was no institution so important and influential in the ancient world as kingship.

One of the most debated issues among Near Eastern epic scholars has been the question of orality. Were the epics composed orally and subsequently committed to writing, or were they literary compositions in the first place? The studies of M. Parry and A. Lord have played an important role in this debate. With the apparent support of modern comparative material from Yugoslavian oral epics, these scholars have argued that illiterate Greek poets composed the Homeric epics in a formulaic language that fundamentally differed from literary poetry. The chief function of these epics was to glorify Greek culture by anchoring the present in the traditions of the past, a functional end that was achieved by expressing the traditional content in a traditional form, namely, in highly formulaic epic poetry. Consequently, according to Parry and Lord, the presence of traditional formulas in a piece of epic poetry points to its oral origins.

Numerous studies have followed the Parry-Lord paradigm by attempting to isolate the traditional oral formulas behind the Near Eastern literary epics (e.g., Hecker). But in recent years, this project has been criticized from two directions. Classical scholars have raised serious questions about the validity of the Parry-Lord model, and Near Eastern scholars have raised questions about the comparative value of the Homeric compositions vis-à-vis the Near Eastern epics (see Russo). In this milieu of uncertainty, many epic scholars confess agnosticism on the question of oral composition. But there is at the same time an emerging consensus that some epics were composed for oral performance before an audience, as is reflected in this excerpt from tablet one of the Gilgamesh Epic:

Of him who found out all things, I shall tell the land, Of him who experienced everything, I shall teach the whole. . . . Look for the copper tablet-box, Undo its bronze lock, Open the door to its secret, Lift out the lapis-lazuli tablet and read it, The story of that man, Gilgamesh, who went through all kinds of sufferings. He was superior to other kings, a warrior lord of great stature.

The poem's reciter introduces the text in the first person and follows up with an invitation to "read" (i.e., listen to) the story. Similar patterns are visible in other Near Eastern heroic-epic texts. Because of the oral-aural character of the texts, it will always be difficult to determine whether their oral characteristics stem directly from their oral composition or from the literary effort to compose the texts for oral performance.

9.1. Mesopotamian Epics and Legends

9.1.1. Epic Tales of Enmerkar, Lugalbanda, and Gilgamesh

The Epic Tales of Enmerkar and Lugalbanda. Although our Enmerkar and Lugalbanda texts come mainly from the Old Babylonian period, fragmentary evidence suggests that cycles of Sumerian poems about these characters began to circulate in Mesopotamia during the Ur III period (ca. 2100–2000). Some of the traditions concerned Enmerkar alone, while others were in some way related to both Enmerkar and Lugalbanda. We begin with the poetic Sumerian tale known as Enmerkar and the Lord of Aratta, which pitted Enmerkar, priest-king of Uruk and son of the god Šamaš, against his royal counterpart in Aratta, a city lying to the east of Mesopotamia in the Iranian mountains. Both kings were considered spouses to the goddess Inanna and copulated with her during an annual rite of sacred marriage—a rite that secured the blessing of the goddess upon their respective cities. Because Enmerkar wished to control Aratta because it was a source of stone and precious metals, he used his superior relationship with Inanna to coax the goddess into abandoning Aratta, thus removing its rainfall and fertility. When the goddess complied and Enmerkar subsequently demanded Aratta's surrender, the king of Aratta challenged Enmerkar to a dual of wits. Eventually Ishkur, brother of Inanna, brought rainfall to Aratta and so squelched Enmerkar's plans. Although the text is somewhat fragmentary near its end, it appears that a compromise ended the standoff: a female sage suggested that the two cities barter to meet their respective needs for goods and materials. Folded into the tale are two linguistic etiologies, one that made Enmerkar the inventor of written language and letters, and another that credited the wise god Enki for the origins of human languages, which he apparently created by confusing languages in a manner akin to that described in Gen 11 (see Jacobsen 1992; Kramer 1968; Swiggers).

We are not sure why Enmerkar and the Lord of Aratta was written, but Jacobsen suggests that it was recited—like other Sumerian epics—to entertain

those in the royal courts of Uruk. Such a purpose would have been especially fitting when envoys from the east were present. Although this explanation might
suit the text's concluding compromise, a similar tale that plays on the same motifs (Enmerkar and En-suhkešdanna) ends with Enmerkar besting the king of
Aratta. The common motifs in the two tales include the following: (1) a contest
between Enmerkar and the king of Aratta; (2) a focus on the affections of Inanna;
(3) the role of envoys in communication between the parties; and (4) the wise
elder woman.

     Lugalbanda's connection with the Enmerkar traditions appears to rest in
Lugalbanda's original identity as the god of Kullab, a small town that merged with
Uruk. The epic tradition remembers the god Lugalbanda as an early king of Uruk
and as a high officer in Enmerkar's army. Three texts tell us his tale. In the oldest
and shortest of these, we learn that Lugalbanda married the cow goddess Ninsuna
in the eastern mountains and brought her back to Uruk. The two longer tales (let
us call them Lugalbanda I and II) were composed by different authors and appear
never to have been joined as a single text, although the second text presupposes
the first (Kramer 1952; Jacobsen, *Harps;* contra Wilcke). Lugalbanda I—known
also as Lugalbanda in the Mountain Cave, Lugalbanda and Hurrumkura, and
Lugalbanda in the Wilderness—begins with the creation of heaven and earth, the
giving of the city of Uruk to Enmerkar, and then Enmerkar's military campaign
against Aratta. It is on this campaign that our protagonist, Lugalbanda, becomes
injured and is subsequently left behind by the army in a mountain cave. The
focus of the text then turns to Lugalbanda's piety, as he entreats various gods for
help. He next leaves his cave, builds a fire, and traps several animals. Divine approval to consume the animals is then given in a dream, and the gods join
Lugalbanda in the repast (i.e., a sacrifice). Because the text begins with creation, it
is likely that this text deals with the origins of eating animal flesh and also of fire
making. The rationale here is like that in the Hebrew Priestly literature (Hallo
1979; Milgrom), where ritual sacrifice rendered the consumption of meat acceptable. Lugalbanda II (variously known as the Lugalbanda Epic, Lugalbanda and
the Thunderbird, Lugalbanda and Anzu, Lugalbanda and Enmerkar, and the Return of Lugalbanda) picks up with the protagonist's departure from the cave and
his trek to overtake the advancing army of Uruk. Fortunately he meets the enormous and usually dangerous Anzu bird, who reveals to him the path taken by the
army and bestows upon Lugalbanda anything he asks. Lugalbanda requests speed
and endurance, and these gifts are granted. Sometime later, Uruk's siege against
Aratta begins to fail, and king Enmerkar decides to send a messenger to inquire of
the goddess Inanna at Uruk. Lugalbanda volunteers, and with the help of the
bird's gifts—speed and endurance—he quickly consults with Inanna and brings
back her directions for Enmerkar. The text breaks off at this point in the story, but
we may suppose that Enmerkar carried out Inanna's plan and succeeded in conquering Aratta. Kramer (1952) notes that the story was tailored to accentuate the
role of political messengers and may have been composed to flatter envoys
visiting in the royal courts of Ur (note his similar comments about Enmerkar and
the Lord of Aratta).

Enmerkar—Texts and translations: A. BERLIN, *Enmerkar and Ensuhkešdanna: A Sumerian Narrative Poem* (Occasional Publications of the Babylonian Fund 2; Philadelphia: University Museum, 1979); S. N. KRAMER, *Enmerkar and the Lord of Aratta: A Sumerian Epic Tale of Iraq and Iran* (Philadelphia: University Museum, University of Pennsylvania, 1952); VANSTIPHOUT, *Epics of Sumerian Kings,* 1–96. *Translations: COS* 1.170: 547–50 (partial); JACOBSEN, *The Harps That Once,* 275–319. *Bibliography:* B. ALSTER, "An Aspect of 'Enmerkar and the Lord of Aratta,'" *RA* 67 (1973): 101–10; J. S. COOPER, "The Incipit of Enmerkar and Ensuhkesdana," *NABU* 1997/118: 1.1; T. JACOBSEN, "The Spell of Nudimmud," in *'Sha'arei Talmon': Studies Presented to Shemaryahu Talmon* (ed. M. Fishbane and E. Tov; Winona Lake, Ind.: Eisenbrauns, 1992), 403–16; J. KLEIN, "The Origin and Development of Languages on Earth: The Sumerian versus the Biblical View," in *Tehillah le-Moshe: Biblical and Judaic Studies in Honor of Moshe Greenberg* (Winona Lake, Ind.: Eisenbrauns, 1997), 77–92 (Hebrew); S. N. KRAMER, "The Babel of Tongues: A Sumerian Version," *JAOS* 88 (1968): 108–11; P. SWIGGERS, "Babel and the Confusion of Tongues," in *Mythos im Alten Testament und seiner Umwelt: Festschrift für Hans-Peter Müller zum 65. Geburtstag* (ed. A. Lange et al.; BZAW 278; Berlin: de Gruyter, 1999), 182–95; H. L. J. VANSTIPHOUT, "Enmerkar's Invention of Writing Revisited," in *DUMU-E²-DUB-BA-A* (ed. Behrens, Loding, and Roth), 515–24; IDEM, "The Matter of Aratta: An Overview," *OLP* 26 (1995): 5–20; IDEM, "Problems in the 'Matter of Aratta,'" *Iraq* 45 (1983): 35–42; IDEM, "Repetition and Structure in the Aratta Cycle," in *Mesopotamian Epic Literature: Oral or Aural?* (ed. M. E. Vogelzang and H. L. J. Vanstiphout; Lewiston, N.Y.: Edwin Mellen, 1992), 247–64.

Lugalbanda—Texts and translations: W. W. HALLO, "Lugalbanda Excavated," in *Studies in Literature from the Ancient Near East* (ed. Sasson), 165–80 (outline and portions of Lugalbanda I); VANSTIPHOUT, *Epics of Sumerian Kings,* 1–21, 97–165; C. WILCKE, *Das Lugalbandaepos* (Wiesbaden: Harrassowitz, 1969) (Lugalbanda II and portions of Lugalbanda I). *Translation:* JACOBSEN, *The Harps That Once,* 320–44. *Bibliography:* B. ALSTER, "Lugalbanda and Ninsuna," *JCS* 41 (1986): 69–86; IDEM, "Lugalbanda and the Early Epic Tradition in Mesopotamia," in *Lingering over Words* (ed. Abusch, Huehnergard, and Steinkeller), 59–72; J. A. BLACK, *Reading Sumerian Poetry* (London: Athlone, 1998) (Lugalbanda and the Thunderbird); R. S. FALKOWITZ, "Notes on 'Lugalbanda and Enmerkar,'" in *Studies in Literature from the Ancient Near East* (ed. Sasson), 103–14; W. W. HALLO, "Leviticus and Ancient Near Eastern Literature," in *The Torah: A Modern Commentary III—Leviticus* (ed. B. J. Bamberger; New York: Union of American Hebrew Congregations, 1979), xxiii–xxxi; J. MILGROM, "A Prolegomenon to Leviticus 17:11," *JBL* 90 (1971): 149–56.

The Gilgamesh Epic. The stories of Gilgamesh were the most popular in ancient Mesopotamia and are, arguably, next to the flood stories, the Mesopotamian texts most familiar to modern readers. Although the final canonical form of the epic included twelve carefully structured tablets, it is now clear that the traditio-historical process that created the epic was quite complex. Gilgamesh was a king in ancient Uruk sometime between 2800 and 2500 B.C.E. At some point—we are not certain when, but no later than 2150 B.C.E.—Sumerian poets began to express the king's fame in heroic tales of his exploits. Similar stories were also circulated about Lugalbanda (Gilgamesh's father?) and Enmerkar (Gilgamesh's grandfather?). We might suppose that a rather long interval passed before the heroic legends arose, but we know from Mari texts that similar poetic legends were being composed about its king during his own lifetime (see 9.1.3, Epic of Zimri-Lim). Consequently, it is difficult to determine precisely when the Gilgamesh traditions first appeared. At any rate, by 2150 the kings of the Third Dynasty of Ur were particularly taken with Gilgamesh and claimed him as their ancestor. This prompted their court poets to compose and recite these tales at royal banquets. From this early period, modern scholars know at least five Sumerian compositions that treated the life of Gilgamesh.

Sumerian tradition paints Gilgamesh as a Promethean figure, the progeny of both a mortal (sometimes Lugalbanda) and a goddess (Ninsum). Some of the stories stressed his wisdom (Gilgamesh and Agga) whereas others accentuated his vigor and physical prowess, along with the strength of his sidekick, Enkidu (Gilgamesh and Huwawa [also known as Gilgamesh and the Land of the Living], Gilgamesh and the Bull of Heaven). The theme of death and afterlife were features in two other texts (Gilgamesh, Enkidu, and the Netherworld [also known as Gilgamesh and the Halub Tree]; the Death of Gilgamesh). With the exception of Gilgamesh and Agga, all of these stories were eventually rolled into the epic version of Gilgamesh's life. Although other Sumerian stories were also incorporated into the epic version (Descent of Inanna into the Netherworld; the flood story), during the Sumerian period these had no direct relationship to Gilgamesh. As Jacobsen has noted, the early Gilgamesh tales fall into two distinct groups. In one, Gilgamesh was a death-defying hero who sought fame and an immortal reputation through feats of strength and wisdom. In the other, Gilgamesh grimly faced the death he feared but could not evade. It was this second theme that ultimately shaped the epic version of Gilgamesh's life.

The first known attempt to thematically integrate these poetic stories into a single epic is a fragmentary Akkadian text from the Old Babylonian period (contra Bing, who argues for an older Sumerian version). The detail of how this was done is not entirely clear. But the thematic concerns of this epic version were certainly derived from some of the Sumerian stories that addressed the deaths of Enkidu and Gilgamesh and Gilgamesh's confrontation with mortality (Wolff). This mortality theme was then systematically applied to the various traditions, causing the author or authors to take many liberties with the older stories. For instance, in the Akkadian epic, the story of Gilgamesh and Huwawa was transformed from a Sumerian tale in which Gilgamesh sought fame by felling the famous trees of Cedar Mountain into a quest to kill Huwawa and achieve immortality (Tigay 1985).

Although the Old Babylonian epic represented an obvious step forward in the development of the Gilgamesh traditions, the standard epic tradition, dating from about 1250 B.C.E. and current in the first millennium, introduced other changes (according to the version found at Nineveh, the compiler of the standard version was Sin-leqe-unnini, a scholar and incantation priest from the Kassite period). The most significant modification introduced in the standard version was the addition of a prologue and an epilogue, which framed the epic so that the heroic value of Gilgamesh's deeds became less important than the wisdom he acquired through his experiences. Other important changes included the incorporation of the flood story (tablet 11) and, somewhat later, the addition of traditions paralleling the Sumerian story of Gilgamesh, Enkidu, and the Netherworld (tablet 12). Although it has not been proved that tablet 12 is a later addition to the standard version, two features make this likely: (1) Enkidu, the friend of Gilgamesh who died in tablet 7, is suddenly alive again, and (2) the style of the text is a literal rendering from the Sumerian version rather than a creative adaptation, such as appears elsewhere in the Akkadian epic. According to Vulpe, this addition was made because the poem ended too abruptly and required a narrative outlet for grasping the simple humanity of Gilgamesh and, by implication, of the reader. Our latest copy of Gilgamesh is a fragmentary text from Seleucid-era Uruk, but the episode covered in this fragment does not appear in the standard version.

The heroic deeds of Gilgamesh inspired and entertained many Near Eastern kings—and not a few commoners. This spawned an active tradition about his deeds, a tradition that developed from various independent stories into full-length epic accounts of Gilgamesh's life. These epics carried the tradition a step further by reflecting on the significance of the hero's pursuit of fame and immortality. Although Gilgamesh and his story achieved long-lasting fame, his search for immortality ended in disappointment.

There is good evidence that the pessimism of Gilgamesh influenced the biblical author of Qoheleth. Parallels between these two texts are at points very close and include not only content but also the order of presentation (see Day; Tigay 1993). Qoheleth 9:5–6 follows closely Šiduri's speech to Gilgamesh in tablet 10 (see OB X.111.6–14), and other parallels include the imagery of a threefold cord that cannot be broken (cf. Eccles 4:12; Gilgamesh and Huwawa, lines 106–10, Epic Version, 5.2.20–25), the comparison of human toil with "the wind" (cf. Eccles 1:14; YBC 2178), and the introspective tone of the two works. Some biblical scholars believe that the Gilgamesh story also influenced portions of the Jacob story in Genesis. Middle Babylonian fragments discovered at Tell Harmal describe a nighttime dream in which Gilgamesh struggled with a wild bull that unexpectedly turned out to be his patron god, Šamaš (see Hendel, 106–7; Cavigneaux/Al-Rawi 2000). Jacob's all-night struggle with God at Peniel in Gen 32:22–32 is a very similar tradition.

Texts and translations: A. CAVIGNEAUX and F. N. H. AL-RAWI, "La fin de Gilgamesh, Enkidu, et les Enfres d'après les manuscrits d'Ur et de Meturan (Textes de Tell Haddad VIII)," *Iraq* 62 (2000): 1–19; IDEM, *Gilgamesh et la mort: Textes de Tell Haddad VI, avec un appendice sur les textes funéraires sumériens* (CM 19; Groningen, Neth.: Styx, 2000); IDEM, "Gilgamesh et Taureau de Ciel (cul-mè-kam) (Textes de Tell Haddad IV)," *RA* 87 (1993): 97–129, pls. I–III; D. O. EDZARD, "Gilgamesh und Huwawa: Zwei Versionen der sumerischen Zedernwaldepisode nebst einer Edition von Version 'B,'" *Sitzungberichte der Bayerischen Akademie der Wissenschaften. Philosophisch-historische Klasse* 1993.4: 1–61; IDEM, "Gilgamesh und Huwawa A," *ZA* 80 (1990): 165–203; 81 (1991): 165–233; A. R. GEORGE, *The Babylonian Gilgamesh Epic: Introduction, Critical Edition, and Cuneiform Texts* (2 vols.; Oxford: Oxford University Press, 2003); A. GOETZE and S. LEVY, "Fragment of the

Gilgamesh Epic from Megiddo," *Atiqot* 2 (1959): 121–28; V. A. HUROWITZ, "Splitting the Sacred Mountain: Zechariah 14,4 and Gilgamesh V ii 4–5," *UF* 31 (1999), 241–45; D. KATZ, *Gilgamesh and Akka* (Groningen, Neth.: Styx, 1993); T. ORNAN, "Picture and Legend: The Case of Humbaba and the Bull of Heaven," *ErIsr* 27 (2003): 18–32 [Hebrew]; S. N. KRAMER, "The Death of Gilgamesh," *BASOR* 94 (1944): 2–12; S. PARPOLA, *The Standard Babylonian Epic of Gilgamesh: Cuneiform Text, Transliteration, Glossary, Indices, and Sign List* (SAA Cuneiform Texts 1; Helsinki: Neo-Assyrian Text Corpus Project, 1997); W. H. P. RÖMER, *Das sumerische Kurzepos "Gilgamesh and Akka"* (AOAT 290; Neukirchen-Vluyn: Neukirchener Verlag, 1980); R. C. THOMPSON, *The Epic of Gilgamesh* (London: Luzac, 1928). **Translations:** *ANET* 44–52, 72–99, 503–7; *COS* 1.132: 458–60; 1.171: 550–52 (partial); DALLEY, *Myths From Mesopotamia*, 50–135; B. R. FOSTER, D. FRAYNE, and G. BECKMAN, *The Epic of Gilgamesh: A New Translation, Analogues, Criticism* (New York: Norton, 2001) (includes translations of Akkadian, Sumerian, and Hittite exemplars); M. KOVACS, *The Epic of Gilgamesh* (Stanford, Calif.: Stanford University Press, 1985). **Bibliography:** J. D. BING, "On the Sumerian Epic of Gilgamesh," *JANES* 7 (1975): 1–11; J. BLENKINSOPP, "Gilgamesh and Adam: Wisdom through Experience in *Gilgamesh* and in the Biblical Story of the Man, the Woman, and the Snake," in *Treasures Old & New: Essays in the Theology of the Pentateuch* (Grand Rapids: Eerdmans, 2004), 85–101; M. CIVIL, "Reading Gilgamesh," *AuOr* 17–18 (1999–2000): 179–89; J. DAY, "Foreign Semitic Influence on the Wisdom of Israel and Its Appropriation in the Book of Proverbs," in *Wisdom in Ancient Israel: Essays in Honour of J. A. Emerton* (ed. J. Day et al.; Cambridge: Cambridge University Press, 1995), 55–70; N. FORSYTH, "Huwawa and His Trees: A Narrative and Cultural Analysis," *ActSum* 3 (1981), 13–29; S. GREENGUS, *Old Babylonian Tablets from Ishchali and Vicinity* (UNHAII 44; Leiden: Nederlands Historisch-Archaeologisch Instituut, 1979); A. HEIDEL, *The Gilgamesh Epic and Old Testament Parallels* (2d ed.; Chicago: University of Chicago Press, 1949); R. S. HENDEL, *The Epic of the Patriarch* (HSM 42; Atlanta: Scholars Press, 1987); T. JACOBSEN, "The Gilgamesh Epic: Romantic and Tragic Vision," in *Lingering over Words* (ed. Abusch, Huehnergard, and Steinkeller), 231–49; J. KLEIN, "The 'Bane' of Humanity: A Lifespan of One Hundred Twenty Years," *ActSum* 12 (1990), 57–70; S. N. KRAMER, "Gilgameš and Agga," *AJA* 53 (1949): 1–18; W. G. LAMBERT, "The Theology of Death," in *Death in Mesopotamia: Papers Read at the XXVIe Rencontre assyriologique internationale* (ed. B. Alster; Mesopotamia 8; Copenhagen: Akademisk Forlag, 1980), 53–66; A. MILLARD, "Gilgamesh X: A New Fragment," *Iraq* 26 (1964): 99–105; W. L. MORAN, "The Epic of Gilgamesh: A Document of Ancient Humanism," *Bulletin of the Canadian Society for Mesopotamian Studies* 22 (1991): 15–22; IDEM, "The Gilgamesh Epic: A Masterpiece from Ancient Mesopotamia," *CANE* 4:2327–36; IDEM, "Rilke and the Gilgamesh Epic," *JCS* 32 (1980): 208–10; W. VON SODEN, "Untersuchungen zur Babylonischen Metrik I," *ZA* 71 (1981): 161–204; W. E. STAPLES, "Epic Motifs in Amos," *JNES* 25 (1966): 106–12; J. TIGAY, *The Evolution of the Gilgamesh Epic* (Philadelphia: University of Pennsylvania Press, 1982); IDEM, "The Evolution of the Pentateuchal Narratives in the Light of the Evolution of the Gilgamesh Epic," in *Empirical Models for Biblical Criticism* (ed. J. Tigay; Philadelphia: University of Pennsylvania Press, 1985), 21–52; IDEM, "On Evaluating Claims of Literary Borrowing," in *The Tablet and the Scroll: Near Eastern Studies in Honor of William W. Hallo* (ed. M. E. Cohen, D. C. Snell, and D. B. Weisberg; Bethesda, Md.: CDL Press, 1993), 250–55; N. VULPE, "Irony and the Unity of the Gilgamesh Epic," *JNES* 53 (1994): 275–83; H. N. WOLFF, "Gilgamesh, Enkidu, and the Heroic Life," *JAOS* 89 (1969): 392–98.

9.1.2. The Legends of Sargon, Naram-Sin, and the Other Sargonid Kings

Here again our texts are concerned with heroic kings whose achievements gave them lasting reputations: the first and third from Sargon of Akkade's dynasty (ca. 2310–2273 B.C.E.), that is, Sargon himself and Naram-Sin (ca. 2246–2190 B.C.E.). Many scholars believe, however, that the texts in fact deal with traditions about all five of the dynasty's kings that were subsequently associated with the two most prominent rulers. Poetic accounts of the royal exploits of these kings were widespread, covering a period from the third to the first millennium and appearing in Akkadian and even in a few Hittite translations. Copies have been found in Mesopotamia, Egypt, and Hatti. This distribution attests to the international popularity of the stories and of their namesakes, who were worshipped as divine by later kings. Fortunately, Westenholz has published a catalogue of the texts; for the sake of convenience, we will use her numerical system, which designates the texts as 1 through 22 (but note that not all of these texts are epics).

The epics of Sargon and Naram-Sin can be classified broadly into two categories, the legendary accounts of their deeds and the fictional autobiographies. (The generic debate surrounding these texts is complex. See Kraus, Lewis, Longman, Reiner and Westenholz.) The autobiographical texts are sometimes called *narû* (stela) texts because their style and arrangement mimicked the autobiographical royal inscriptions and because they explicitly claimed in some instances to have been written upon a stela (for the royal inscriptions, see chs. 12 and 15). Our copies of these texts are on tablets, not stelae, however, and scholars now agree that the works were never royal inscriptions but were instead pseudonymous texts published long after the two kings ruled. The rationale for this practice is clear enough: the ancients gave new concepts and ideas authority by attributing them to heroes from the past. This they accomplished, so it seems, by publishing "stelae" in the names of their ancient and more famous predecessors. A chief trait of the Mesopotamian fictional autobiographies was their three-part structure, which included a first-person introduction (e.g., I, Sargon . . .), a first-person narrative, and a concluding epilogue. Four subgenres can be differentiated within this class of texts on the basis of the epilogues: texts that end with (1) blessings and/or curses, (2) a didactic lesson, (3) a donation to the temple, or (4) a prophecy (Longman). Here we will discuss exemplars that suit the first three categories, leaving the prophetic autobiographies for chapter 7 (see 7.1).

Also included in this section is an entry on the Curse of Akkad, a Sumerian text that blamed the fall of the Sargonid dynasty on the careless impiety of King Naram-Sin. In some respects this text defies generic labels, but it fits the epic/legend category as well as any other.

The Sargon Birth Legend. This title is something of a misnomer, based as it is on the story of Sargon's birth, which takes up only the text's first ten lines. The title stuck, however, for reasons that will be obvious. According to the tale, Sargon was born to an EN-priestess who was apparently prohibited from bearing children.

She successfully concealed his birth and then abandoned him in a watertight bas-
ket at the river's edge. Aqqi, a water-drawing agriculturalist, found and raised
Sargon. As an adult, Sargon took up the family trade, but he soon drew the attention of the goddess Ištar, who interceded to make him the king of Akkade. The
text then follows with a list of Sargon's greatest accomplishments and concludes
by pronouncing a blessing upon future kings, that they too might enjoy a long
reign and success. A natural question arises: to what end would such a text have
been written? Although composed in the poetic style of earlier epics, the Akkadian dialects of the Birth Legend exemplars are Neo-Assyrian and Neo-Babylonian.
These dialects were in use over a millennium after Sargon of Akkad lived. The
Birth Legend is therefore now generally regarded as a composition of the Neo-
Assyrian king Sargon II (709–705 B.C.E.), who composed the text in honor of his
namesake and, in doing so, placed a blessing for himself in the elder Sargon's
mouth (Lewis). Thus, the text was probably composed to extol the virtues of
Sargon II and to legitimate his reign.

Scholars commonly believe that the similarities between this story and the
birth of Moses in Exodus are best explained by the biblical author's use of
the Sargon tradition. The artificial attachment of the concealment theme to the
Moses tradition is suggested by the sudden and unexplained disappearance of
the infant-killing motif after Moses was found at the river's edge. Rabbinic tradition attempted to account for this strange feature: "Moses was cast into the Nile
to make the [Egyptian] astrologers think that Israel's savior had already been
thrown into the Nile, so that from that day on they would call off the search for
him. Indeed from that day on, the decree was annulled, for they divined that Israel's savior had already been attacked by water" (see Greenberg). Although the
rabbinic solution might strike us as artificial, the rabbis recognized the problem.
The infant-killing motif and the resulting concealment do not cohere with the
Moses story so nicely as they do in the case of the Sargon Birth Legend. This suggests that the Hebrew writer took up the motif from the Sargon legend, where it
fit very satisfactorily, and applied it to Moses in order to portray Israel's lawgiver
as a similar hero. Why was this done? It has been suggested that the biblical presentations of Moses were reshaped from time to time in order to counter political
and theological challenges from Assyria, Babylon, and Persia (Otto). In the case
of the exposure motif, this may reflect an attempt to contrast the heroic Moses
with the enslaving presence of the Neo-Assyrian king Sargon II (721–705 B.C.E.).
We may, then, conclude that not only the social dynamics in ancient Israel but
also the external political forces faced by ancient Israel have shaped the Moses
tradition.

Text and translation: WESTENHOLZ, *Legends of the Kings of Akkade,* no. 2. *Translations:*
ANET 119; *COS* 1.133: 461. *Bibliography:* B. S. CHILDS, "The Birth of Moses," *JBL* 84
(1965): 109–22; IDEM., *Exodus* (OTL; Philadelphia: Fortress, 1974), 8–9; M. GREENBERG,
Understanding Exodus (New York: Behrman, 1969), 39–41; W. W. HALLO, *The Book of the
People* (BJS 225; Atlanta: Scholars Press, 1991); B. LEWIS, *The Sargon Legend: A Study of the
Akkadian Text and the Tale of the Hero Who Was Exposed at Birth* (ASOR Dissertation Se-
ries 4; Cambridge, Mass.: ASOR, 1980); LONGMAN, *Fictional Akkadian Autobiography,*

53–60, 215–16; E. Otto, "Mose und das Gesetz: Die Mosefigur als Gegenentwurf politi-
scher Theologie zur neuassyrischen Königsideologie im 7. Jh. v. Chr," in *Mose: Ägypten
und das Alte Testament* (ed. E. Otto; SBS 189; Stuttgart: BKW, 2000), 43–83; D. B.
Redford, "The Literary Motif of the Exposed Child," *Numen* 14 (1967): 209–28.

The Sumerian Sargon Legend. This fragmentary composition relates the rise of
Sargon of Akkad to power, focusing especially on how he eventually supplanted
kings Urzababa of Kish and Lugalzagesi of Uruk. Our copies of the text are not
very good, but the general outline of the story can be made out. Sargon was serving as the cupbearer in the courts of Urzababa. At that time, the gods Anu and
Enlil decreed that the rule of Urzababa would come to an end and that Sargon
was their new favorite. The gods revealed their plan to Sargon in a dream, which
predicted a painful and horrible death for Urzababa. As soon as Urzababa learned
of the dream, he made a series of attempts on Sargon's life. In one of these plots,
Urzababa dispatched Sargon as a messenger to Lugalzagesi of Uruk, with Sargon
apparently bearing a tablet whose words would lead to his own death. In order to
make this possible, it appears that Urzababa invented the clay envelope to conceal
the tablet's content from Sargon (so Alster; contra Cooper). At any rate, this and
other plots against Sargon's life failed. Although the text breaks off before the
story ends, we may safely presume that the tale ended happily for Sargon and un-
happily for Urzababa and Lugalzagesi.

Ancient sources confirm that the personalities involved in the story are essentially historical, including even the detail that Sargon served in the court of
Urzababa (Cooper/Heimpel). The patrimony of Sargon in this text may also be
true to life, since it identifies Sargon's father as La'ibum and so contradicts the
Sargon Birth Legend, where Sargon does not know his father. In spite of these historical details, scholars surmise that the story itself is largely fictional and served
one of two purposes, depending on when it was written. (1) Because the text's dialect appears to be from the late OB period, it is possible that it was written long
after Sargon lived. If this is the case, then the story was composed as didactic lesson, to teach readers that our destinies are determined by the gods and should not
be resisted. As Cooper and Heimpel note, this text would then be one of a series of
exemplars that provided ideological/theological reflections on the downfalls of
major Mesopotamian hegemonies prior to the OB period: Uruk and Kish (the present text), Akkad (Curse of Akkad), and the Ur III Dynasty (Ur Laments). (2) The
other possibility is that this text actually goes back to the Ur III period itself. In
this case, the text would have been composed to secure the legitimacy of the new
Ur dynasty. Essentially, the claim would have been as follows: Just as the gods have
previous granted authority to Urzababa, Lugalzagesi, and Sargon, so too they
have now granted authority to the family of Ur-Nammu of Ur (see Cooper).

The most obvious parallels between the Sumerian Sargon Legends and the
Hebrew Bible would include the Story of David's Rise to Power (1 Sam 16–2 Sam
6), Joseph's dream interpretations in the house of Pharoah (Gen 37), and the
story of Uriah the Hittite, in which the protagonist naively bore a letter that
sealed his own death (2 Sam 11).

Text and translation: J. S. COOPER and W. HEIMPEL, "The Sumerian Sargon Legend," *JAOS* 103 (1983): 67–82. *Bibliography:* V. AFANASJEVA, "Des Sumerische Sargon-Epos: Versuch einer Interpretation," *AoF* 14 (1987): 237–46; B. ALSTER, "A Note on the Uriah Letter in Sumerian Sargon Legend," *ZA* 77 (1987): 169–73; J. S. COOPER, "Paradigm and Propaganda: The Dynasty of Akkade in the 21st Century," in *Akkad, The First World Empire: Structure, Ideology, Traditions* (ed. M. Liverani; Padova: Sargon, 1993), 11–23; WESTENHOLZ, *Legends of the Kings of Akkade,* 4, 51.

The Cruciform Monument of Maništušu. This autobiographical text was inscribed on a twelve-sided cross and purports to be an inscription of Maništušu, son of Sargon the Great. After a brief narrative that recounts the king's victories over rebel vassals, the text concludes with a very long list of booty that was captured and then donated to the god Šamaš. Grammatical and morphological features in the inscription reveal that it is a forgery, probably composed by priests of Ebabbar (the temple of Šamaš) in order to inspire more donations for their shrine. The text may date to as early as the Old Babylonian period or, more likely, as late as the Neo-Babylonian period.

Text and translation: E. SOLLBERGER, "The Cruciform Monument," *Jahrbericht "Ex oriente lux"* 20 (1968): 50–70. *Translations:* G. A. BARTON, *The Royal Inscriptions of Sumer and Akkad* (New Haven: Yale University Press, 1929), 130–35; LONGMAN, *Fictional Akkadian Autobiography,* 79–83, 218–21. *Bibliography:* I. J. GELB, "The Date of the Cruciform Monument of Maništušu," *JNES* 8 (1949): 346–48; L. W. KING, "The Cruciform Monument of Maništušu," *RA* 9 (1912): 91–105; J. D. PRINCE, "An Akkadian Cruciform Monument,"*AJSL* 29 (1912–1913): 95–110.

The Cuthean Legend of Naram-Sin. Naram-Sin's best-known fictional autobiography is the so-called Cuthean Legend or, as Westenholz has named it, Naram-Sin and the Enemy Hordes (Westenholz §§20–22). The name Cuthean Legend stems from the text's claim that it was written upon a stela that was placed in the *cela* of the god Nergel in Cutha. The widespread popularity of the epic explains why it exists in several different recensions. These differ substantially in length, from about 600 lines of poetry in the Old Babylonian version to about 180 lines in the first-millennium Standard Babylonian text. The incipit (lines 1–3) is a fictional trope that is characteristic of the so-called *narû* literary genre: "Open the tablet-box and read out the stela, which I, Naram-Sin, son of Sargon, have inscribed and left for future days." As the narrative unfolds, we discover what the author hoped to say to future kings.

    Our story begins with Naram-Sin's confrontation with a horde of divinely created barbarians with "partridge bodies" and "raven faces." When this horde threatened his kingdom, Naram-Sin followed standard Mesopotamian procedure by seeking guidance through omens. Although the omens were negative, Naram-Sin proceeded with his campaign, which failed miserably. The distraught Naram-Sin was then approached by the wise god Ea, who counseled that a New Year festival accompanied by prayer and sacrifice was in order. Naram-Sin followed this advice and then took new omens, which portended success for his attack. Although the

ensuing battle went well indeed, Naram-Sin stopped short of destroying the bar-
barians because the goddess Ištar commanded him to do so. Here the text concludes with these words (lines 149–166):

> You, whoever you are, be it governor or prince or anyone else, whom the gods will
> call to perform kingship, I made a tablet-box for you and inscribed a stela for you.
> In Kutha, in the Emeslam, in the cella of Nergal, I left (it) for you. Read this stele!
> Hearken unto the words of this stele! Be not bewildered! Be not confused! Be not
> afraid! Do not tremble! Let your foundations be firm! You, within the embrace of
> your wife, do your work! . . . Strengthen your walls! Fill your moat with water! Your
> chests, your grain, your money, your goods, your possessions, bring into your
> stronghold! Tie up your weapons and put (them) in the corners! Guard your cour-
> age! Take heed of your own person! Let him [the enemy] roam through your land!
> Go not out to him! . . . You who have read my inscription and thus have gotten
> yourself out (of trouble), you who have blessed me, may a future (ruler) bless you!

Although the didactic purpose of this conclusion is clear enough, there are
two common ways of understanding its message. Some scholars argue that the
work advocates religious piety by encouraging kings to heed the messages of divinely given omens (Grayson); others hold to a political reading, in which the author criticizes imperialism and seeks to promote an agenda of pacifism and
domestic duty (Longman; Westenholz). Although I prefer the latter reading, in
either scenario the text clearly highlights the threats that arise when royal hubris
is given free reign. By depositing his pseudepigraphic composition in the temple,
the author of the Cuthean Legend added the voice of Naram-Sin to his ideological agenda (because the conclusion of the Old Babylonian version is not preserved, we do not know whether this ideology was reflected in the original version
of the epic or only in the Neo-Babylonian version).

One scholar has suggested that the Neo-Babylonian version of the Cuthean
Legend may have influenced Ezekiel's prophecies about Gog in Ezek 38–39
(Astour), but this view has not been widely adopted.

Text and translation: WESTENHOLZ, *Legends of the Kings of Akkade,* nos. 20–22. *Translation:* LONGMAN, *Fictional Akkadian Autobiography,* 103–17, 228–31. *Bibliography:* M. C.
ASTOUR, "Ezekiel's Prophecy of Gog and the Cuthean Legend of Naram-Sin," *JBL* 95
(1976): 567–79; A. K. GRAYSON, "Assyrian and Babylonia," *Or* 49 (1980): 140–94; LONG-
MAN, *Fictional Akkadian Autobiography,* 103–17, 228–31.

The Great Revolt against Naram-Sin. When we turn to the Great Revolt against
Naram-Sin (see Westenholz §§15–19) and compare it with the Cuthean Legend,
an interesting generic pattern emerges. Although both tales are autobiographical
in form and content, the tradition of the Great Revolt is not entirely fictional but
can be traced back to events described in Naram-Sin's royal inscriptions (see
Tinney). So, although Naram-Sin narrates the revolt as a confrontation with superhuman adversaries (as in the Cuthean Legend), there is little doubt that the revolt tradition goes back to real events. The fact that our text dates to the third
millennium and cannot be too far removed from those events illustrates how

quickly history becomes the fodder for legendary elaboration. The various recensions of the Great Revolt attest to the perceived value of its didactic message. According to the story, Naram-Sin's vassals swore an oath of fidelity to Naram-Sin but later revolted. Their revolt was ill fated because Naram-Sin had the help of the gods and so utterly defeated the vassals in battle. The didactic point is clear even to modern readers: no one ought to break a solemnly sworn treaty oath unless he wishes to face the wrath of the king and his gods. Centuries later the Neo-Assyrian kings drew upon this popular motif in their political propaganda (Livingstone).

Text and translation: WESTENHOLZ, *Legends of the Kings of Akkade,* nos. 3–9, 12–13, 15–19. *Bibliography:* D. CHARPIN, "La version mariote de l' 'Insurrection générale contre Narâm-Sîn,'" in *Recueil d'études à la mémoire de Marie-Thérèse Barrelet* (ed. D. Charpin and J.-M. Durand; FM 3; Mémoires de N.A.B.U. 4; Paris: SEPOA, 1997), 9–17; LIVINGSTONE, *Court Poetry and Literary Miscellanea,* 64–66; T. POTTS, "Reading the Sargonic 'Historical-Literary' Tradition: Thoughts on *The Great Revolt against Naram-Sin,*" in *Proceedings of the XLV Rencontre assyriologique internationale* (ed. Abusch et al.), 1:391–408; S. TINNEY, "A New Look at Naram-Sin and the 'Great Rebellion,'" *JCS* 47 (1995): 1–14.

The Historical Epics of Sargon and Naram-Sin. There are heroic legends of Sargon and Naram-Sin that appear to be more historically grounded than the didactic pieces examined above. The most important exemplars are Sargon the Conquering Hero (Westenholz §6), Sargon in Foreign Lands (§7), Sargon, King of Battle (§9), Naram-Sin and the Lord of Apišal (§12), and Erra and Naram-Sin (§13). Each of these texts can be traced back to events in the respective king's life. Like the Gilgamesh legends before them, these traditions were cast as third-person narratives rather than as autobiographies, and they extolled the king's wisdom and military valor. The military prowess of Sargon is expressed most vividly in the frequently used epithet *šar tamḫāri* ("king of battle"), which he shared with the gods Nergal and Ninurta. The conflicts faced by the kings are never just human, for behind each conflict are the divine participants, so that Sargon and Naram-Sin often stand alongside one god (e.g., Nergal, Erra) in the fight against enemies backed by another god (usually Enlil). The king's dependence on the gods was therefore a prominent theme in the heroic legends of Sargon and Naram-Sin.

Text and translation: WESTENHOLZ, *Legends of the Kings of Akkade,* nos. 3–9, 12–13. *Bibliography:* H. G. GÜTERBOCK, "Ein neues Bruchstück der Sargon-Erzählung 'König der Schlact,'" *MDOG* 101 (1969): 14–26; W. G. LAMBERT, "Naram-Sin of Ešnunna or Akkad?" *JAOS* 106 (1986): 793–95; IDEM, "A New Fragment of the King of Battle," *AfO* 20 (1963): 161–62; IDEM, "Studies in Nergal," *BO* 30 (1973): 357–73; J. NOUGAYROL, "Un chef d'oeuvre inédit de la literature babylonienne," *RA* 45 (1951): 169–83.

The Curse of Akkad. This third-person poetic narrative, written several centuries after the fall of the Sargonid dynasty of Akkad, explains why the city was destroyed and, equally important, why it was never rebuilt. The history of the city is recounted in terms of the divine will of Enlil and the gods. Enlil initially established the house of Sargon and made Akkad a prosperous city, blessed to overflowing by its chief goddess, Inanna. But during the reign of Sargon's son Naram-Sin (historically, he was Sargon's grandson), Enlil rebuffed Naram-Sin's proposal to refurbish Enlil's temple (Ekur) at Nippur. This rebuff was taken as an ominous sign: Inanna abandoned Akkad, the gods withdrew the city's claim to kingship, and Naram-Sin experienced visions of Akkad's destruction. The king responded with seven years of penitence, but when Enlil did not answer, Naram-Sin moved arrogantly against Nippur and destroyed and plundered Enlil's temple. As a result, Enlil sent the barbarian Gutians to destroy Akkad (ca. 2100 B.C.E.), and the gods declared a great curse upon the city so that it would never be rebuilt. The finality of this curse is expressed in the concluding words, "Akkad was destroyed." The legendary character of the text is revealed when it is read alongside genuine history. Although the Curse of Akkad associates the fall of Akkad with the reign of Naram-Sin, Naram-Sin's dynasty did not end in disaster during his lifetime but instead lasted for three more generations. It is indeed true that Naram-Sin razed the temple of Enlil in preparation for its refurbishment, which was completed by his son Sharkalisharri, but he did not destroy, plunder, and abandon the temple site as this text would have us remember it.

The text was composed during the Sumerian renaissance of the Ur III dynasty and provided a theological explanation for the transition from Akkad in the north to Ur in the south. Its author clearly succeeded in this aim, but his more subtle motivations for composing the text are not clear. Was it written out of sympathy for Inanna's loss of Akkad (as might be suggested by the text's rubric, "Praise Song [*Zami*] for Inanna"), or did the text serve a propagandistic function by attributing Ur's prominence—and Akkad's destruction—to divine election? Such questions are part of an ongoing discussion among Assyriologists and Sumerologists. But scholars now generally reject (see Cooper) the thesis that the text was vehemently *anti*-Akkadian (see Wilcke).

An important theological feature in the Curse of Akkad is its lamentation over Ekur, a cultic act whose purpose was to appease the heart of Enlil in the wake of his temple's destruction and desecration. This theme and the more general theme of divine anger provided much of the literary inspiration for the later Sumerian city laments, discussed in 3.1.2.

Text and translation: J. S. COOPER, *The Curse of Agade* (Baltimore: Johns Hopkins University Press, 1983). *Translation:* JACOBSEN, *The Harps That Once*, 359–74. *Bibliography:* J. COOPER, "Literature and History: The Historical and Political Referents of Sumerian Literary Texts," in *Proceedings of the XLV Rencontre assyriologique internationale* (ed. Abusch et al.), 131–47; D. O. EDZARD, "Das 'Wort im Ekur' oder die Peripetie in 'Fluch über Akkade,'" in *DUMU-E²-DUB-BA-A* (ed. Behrens, Loding, and Roth), 99–105; A. FALKENSTEIN, "Fluch über Akkade," *ZA* 57 (1965): 43–124; C. WILCKE, "Politische Opposition nach sumerischen Quellen—der Konflikt zwischen Königtum und Ratsversammlung: Literaturewerke als politische Tendenzschriften," in *La voix de l'opposition en Mésopotamie* (ed. A. Finet; Brussels: Institut des Hautes Études de Belgique, 1974), 37–65.

9.1.3. Other Epics and Legends from Mesopotamia

The Etana Legend. According to Mesopotamian tradition, Etana was a heroic king of the First Dynasty of Kish who ruled in the period immediately following the great flood. The Sumerian King List remembers him this way: "Etana, a shepherd, the one who ascended to heaven." This reference alludes to our legend, which begins as a fable. An eagle and a serpent lived happily together in a tree until the eagle consumed one of the serpent's offspring. When the serpent appealed to Šamaš, god of justice, the god instructed him to hide in a dead animal carcass and to strike the eagle when he came to consume the carrion. The serpent did so and clipped the bird's wings, plucked him, and cast him into a pit. At this point Etana enters the story. He was childless and in need of the heavenly "plant of birth." When he appealed to Šamaš, the deity instructed him to rescue the eagle, who would in turn fly Etana into the heavens. All of this came to pass, and Etana's trip to heaven was going well until, high in the sky, he feared for his life and released his grip on the bird in order to return to the earth. Unfortunately, our texts break off at this point. Some scholars believe that the legend ends with Etana's fall and hence is a warning against human arrogance, but Mesopotamian tradition remembers Etana as one who ascended into heaven, and it identifies his son and heir as Balikh. For this reason, it is probably better to assume that he eventually reached his goal (Haul).

The Etana Legend survives in Old Babylonian, Middle Assyrian, and Standard Babylonian versions, but the tradition itself goes back to the third millennium because cylinder seals from the Old Akkadian period (ca. 2400–2250 B.C.E.) depict Etana on the back of an eagle (see Collon; Steinkeller). The late version of the tale omits some episodes that are crucial for understanding the story. From a comparative standpoint, the story of Etana's ascent into heaven is sometimes compared to Enoch's heavenly ascent in Gen 5:22–24.

Texts and translations: J. V. KINNIER WILSON, *The Legend of Etana* (Warminster, England: Aris & Phillips, 1985); J. R. NOVOTNY, *The Standard Babylonian Etana Epic: Cuneiform Text, Transliteration, Score, Glossary, Indices, and Sign List* (SAA Cuneiform Text 2; Helsinki: Neo-Assyrian Text Corpus Project, 2001). *Translations:* ANET 114–18, 517; COS 1.131: 453–57; DALLEY, *Myths from Mesopotamia,* 189–202. *Bibliography:* D. COLLON, *Catalogue of Western Asiatic Seals in the British Museum: Cylinder Seals* (London: British Museum, 1962–), vol. 2, nos. 151–52; M. HAUL, *Das Etana-Epos: Ein Mythos von der Himmelfahrt des Königs von Kiš* (Göttinger Arbeitshefte zur altorientalischen Literatur 1; Göttingen: Seminar für Keilschriftforschung, 2000); W. HOROWITZ, "Two Notes on Etana's Flight to Heaven," *Or* 59 (1990): 511–17; G. SELZ, "Die Etana-Erzählung: Ursprung und Tradition eines der ältesten epischen Texte in semitischer Sprache," *ActSum* 20 (1998): 135–79; P. STEINKELLER, "Early Semitic Literature and Third Millennium Seals with Mythological Motifs," in *Literature and Literary Language at Ebla* (ed. P. Fronzaroli; QS 18; Florence: Dipartimento di Linguistica, Università di Firenze, 1992), 243–75.

The Epic of Zimri-Lim. This interesting text has not yet been published, but one finds scattered references to it in discussions of Mari literature (M. Guichard announced plans to publish an edition of the text in 1995 [see *NABU* 1995, p. 105], but his edition has not yet appeared). The epic was composed during the first six years of Zimri-Lim's reign (1779–1757 B.C.E.) and honored the Mari king as a warrior and as the beloved of the gods, his soldiers, and his people (Durand). Although we might suppose that rather long intervals must pass before heroic legends of this sort arise, this text provides good evidence that poetic legends were being composed about King Zimri-Lim even during his own lifetime.

Table 9.1

Epic of Zimri-Lim: List of Published Lines

line 3	*MARI* 4 (1985): 328, n. 159.
lines 17–23	*MARI* 4 (1985): 325, n. 137.
lines 18–23	ARM 26/1, 428.
lines 25–28	*MARI* 4 (1985): 328.
lines 74–76	FM 1, p. 119, n. 3.
lines 97–98	*AfO* 36–37 (1989–90): 106.
lines 112–114	*MARI* 4 (1985): 332, n. 189.
lines 112–123	FM 1, p. 122, n. 9.
lines 137–142	ARM 26/1, 393.
lines 141–142	*MARI* 5 (1987): 661.
line 145	ARM 26/1, 57, n. 280.
lines 145–148	ARM 26/1, 393.
lines 164–167	ARM 26/1, 475.
lines 165–166	*MARI* 4 (1985): 325, n. 140.

References provided by J. M. Sasson

Bibliography: D. CHARPIN and J.-M. DURAND, "La prise du pouvoir par Zimri-Lim," *MARI* 4 (1985): 293–343; J.-M. DURAND, *Archives épistolaires de Mari I/1* (ARM 26.1; Paris: Éditions Recherche sur les civilisations, 1988); IDEM, "De la Joie à l'Orage," *Mari* 5 (1987): 661; IDEM, "Précurseurs syriens aux Protocoles néo-assyriens," in *Marchands, diplomates, et empereurs: Études sur la civilisation mésopotamienne offertes à Paul Garelli* (ed. D. Charpin and F. Joannès; Paris: Éditions Recherche sur les Civilisations, 1991), 13–71 (see p. 46); M. FLEURY and J.-M. DURAND, *Recueil d'études en l'honneur de Michel Fleury* (FM 1; Paris: Société pour l'étude du Proche-Orient Ancien, 1991); M. NISSINEN, *Prophets and Prophecy in the Ancient Near East* (SBLWAW 12; Atlanta: Society of Biblical Literature, 2003), 90.

The Statue Inscription of King Idrimi. Another important heroic vita is the autobiographical statue of Idrimi, king of Alalakh (ca. 1500 B.C.E.). Its place in this discussion hinges in part on the artifact's date, which has a bearing on whether its genre is better characterized as history or legend. The statue sports an Akkadian account of Idrimi's life that is vaguely chronological and narrates his exploits after being exiled from his home in Aleppo, including his rise to kingship in Alalakh and his accomplishments after seizing the throne of Alalakh. The damaged statue was found in the twelfth-century destruction level of a temple, where someone carefully collected the pieces of the statue and buried them in the

temple floor. This was probably done because the text promised a blessing to anyone who preserved the statue and a curse for anyone who damaged it. Idrimi's
story is actually a pseudoautobiography, for it mentions both the length of his
reign and the succession of his son after his death (although neither Adadniniari
nor Niqmepa is mentioned by name). Moreover, although many scholars have
dated the text to the period immediately following Idrimi's death, there is some
evidence that it may have been composed about three hundred years later (ca.
1200). This later date reflects the archaeological level in which the statue was
found, and it also suits the style of the sculpture and the period in which the
scribe mentioned in the text, Šarruwa, probably would have lived (see Sasson).

The highly folkloristic motifs in Idrimi's story reinforce the fictional character of the text (Lemche; Liverani). Idrimi, the youngest of his brothers, fled the
trappings of civilized life to seek adventure in the desert. After enduring a seven-
year exile from his homeland, he assembled around himself a band of warriors,
received favorable omens from the gods, and made his move to regain Alalakh.
His first strategic move was to enact a treaty with the powerful king Sutarna, who
granted Idrimi kingship in Alalakh. Idrimi then undertook successful expeditions
against the Hittites—a seemingly impossible feat at this point in history—and
completed various administrative and building programs in his city. The folkloristic tropes and historical improbabilities of the story have caused most scholars to view it as a mixture of historical fact and fictive imagination. Whether one
dates the text to the fifteenth or the twelfth century, its primary purpose was the
same: to extol and support the royal dynasty of Alalakh by appealing to the heroic
deeds of its ancient founder, Idrimi. When viewed in its Near Eastern generic
context, the story of Idrimi seems to lie somewhere on the historical continuum
between the more fanciful epics of Sargon and the propagandistic Assyrian Annals (see 12.1.1). Biblical scholars have sometimes compared this story of Idrimi
to the political propaganda in the biblical stories about David's and Solomon's
rise to power in 1–2 Samuel (see Lemche).

Texts and translations: E. L. GREENSTEIN and D. MARCUS, "The Akkadian Inscription of
Idrimi," *JANES* 8 (1976): 59–96; S. SMITH, *The Statue of Idri-mi* (OPBIAA 1; London: Brit-
ish Institute of Archaeology in Ankara, 1949). *Translations: ANET* 657–58; *COS* 1.148:
479–80. *Bibliography:* M. DIETRICH and O. LORETZ, "Die Inschrift der Statue des Königs
Idrimi von Alalaḫ," *UF* 13 (1981): 201–68; A. KEMPINSKI and N. NA'AMAN, "The Idrimi
Inscription Reconsidered," in *Excavations and Studies: Essays in Honor of Shemuel Yeiven*
(ed. Y. Aharoni; Tel Aviv: Carta, 1973), 211–20 (Hebrew); N. P. LEMCHE, *Prelude to Israel's
Past: Background and Beginnings of Israelite History and Identity* (trans. E. F. Maniscalco;
Peabody, Mass.: Hendrickson, 1998), 157; M. LIVERANI, "Memorandum on the Approach
to Historiographic Texts," *Or* 42 (1973): 178–94; LONGMAN, *Fictional Akkadian Autobiography*, 60–66; 216–18; G. H. OLLER, "The Inscription of Idrimi: A Pseudo-autobiography?"
in *DUMU-E²-DUB-BA-A* (ed. Behrens, Loding, and Roth), 411–17; J. M. SASSON, "On
Idrimi and Šarruwa the Scribe," in *Studies on the Civilization and Culture of Nuzi and the
Hurrians in Honor of Ernest R. Lacheman on His Seventy-fifth Birthday* (ed. M. A. Morrison
and D. I. Owen; Winona Lake, Ind.: Eisenbrauns, 1981), 309–24; J. VAN SETERS, *In Search
of History* (New Haven: Yale University Press, 1983), 188–91.

The Autobiography of Kurigalzu. As in the Cruciform Monument of Maništušu (see above), here we seem to have a pseudonymous composition designed to promote donations to a temple. The text, ostensibly the royal inscription of a Kassite king named Kurigalzu (ca. end of the fifteenth century B.C.E.), is preserved on two late tablets. In it Kurigalzu claims to have granted a large tract of land for the support of the cult of the goddess Ištar. The text pronounces a curse on anyone who contravenes this arrangement. Most scholars suspect that the text was composed in the later period by devotees—probably priests—of Ištar in order to secure resources for their work.

Text and translation: A. UNGNAD, "Schenkungsurkunde des Kurigalzu mar Kadašman-Ḫarbe," *AfK* 1 (1923): 19–23. *Translation: BM²* 1.279–80. *Translation and study:* LONGMAN, *Fictional Akkadian Autobiography,* 88–91, 224–25.

The Agum-kakrime Inscription. This tale recounts how the Kassite king Agum recovered the stolen statues of Marduk and his consort from the "Haneans" (probably a reference to the Hittites) and then, after returning them to Babylon, lavished upon them many gifts. Our copies of the text date to the Neo-Assyrian period at a time several centuries removed from the Kassite period. For this reason, although it remains possible that the tablets are copies of a genuine inscription (see *BM²* 1.274–78), most scholars presume that this text, like the Cruciform Monument of Maništušu and the Autobiography of Kurigalzu (see above), is a pseudonymous composition designed to encourage donations to a temple, in this case to Marduk's temple.

Text and translation: P. JENSEN, "Inschrift Agum-Kakrimi's d. i. Agum's des Jungeren," in *Sammlung von assyrischen und babylonischen Texten* (ed. E. Schrader; vol. 3 of *Keilinschriftliche Bibliothek;* Berlin: Reuther, 1892), 134–52. *Translation: BM²* 1.274–78. *Translation and study:* LONGMAN, *Fictional Akkadian Autobiography,* 83–88, 221–24.

The Tukulti-Ninurta Epic. This text was composed after the Assyrian king Tukulti-Ninurta I (1243–1207 B.C.E.) defeated king Kaštilaš of Babylon and sacked his city in 1235. Although the text is fragmentarily preserved in our Middle and Neo-Assyrian sources, scholars are reasonably sure that its basic shape can be reconstructed. The plot, which falls into three parts, centers on the conflict between the respective kings. Part one introduces the two kings as protagonist and antagonist, asserting that Tukulti-Ninurta is a pious and peace-loving man whereas Kaštilaš of Babylon is so evil that the gods of Babylon elected to abandon their temples. Part two provides an account of the hostilities, which erupt when Kaštilaš breaks his solemn treaty with Assyria and attacks his neighbor to the north. This endeavor is doomed from the start because divine favor is on the side of Tukulti-Ninurta. Kaštilaš offers a soliloquy on his impending defeat even as Tukulti-Ninurta utters accusing speeches against him. Eventually Babylon is defeated, and the spoil is seized and returned to Assyria, where it is dedicated to the temples of the Assyrian gods. Part three of the text celebrates the victory with praises lavished upon the gods and especially upon Tukulti-Ninurta, who is proclaimed the new and legitimate king of Babylon. Underlying the entire work is the theme of treaty fidelity, in which Kaštilaš is repeatedly berated for breaking the treaty with Assyria whereas Tukulti-Ninurta is praised for keeping it. The epic was clearly a piece of political propaganda, composed to justify Assyria's prosecution of its war against Babylon.

Generically speaking, the poetic, thematic, and historical dimensions of the text make it comparable to the historical epics of Sargon and Naram-Sin. Biblical scholars have sometimes compared the text to Ezekiel because both texts contain the motif of the divine abandonment of cities and temples (Babylon and Jerusalem, respectively; cf. Ezek 10–11; Block).

Text and translation: P. B. MACHINIST, *The Epic of Tukulti-Ninurta I: A Study in Middle Assyrian Literature* (PhD diss., Yale University, 1978). *Translation: BM²* 1.211–30. *Bibliography:* D. I. BLOCK, "Divine Abandonment: Ezekiel's Adaptation of an Ancient Near Eastern Motif," in *Perspectives on Ezekiel: Theology and Anthropology* (ed. M. S. Odell and J. T. Strong; SBLSymS 9; Atlanta: Scholars Press, 2000), 15–42; IDEM, *The Gods of the Nations: Studies in Ancient Near Eastern National Theology* (2d ed.; Grand Rapids: Baker, 2000), 121–23; D. DAMROSCH, *The Narrative Covenant: Transformations of Genre in the Growth of Biblical Literature* (San Francisco: Harper & Row, 1987), 71–75; P. B. MACHINIST, "Literature as Politics: The Tukulti-Ninurta Epic and the Bible," *CBQ* 38 (1976): 455–82.

The Neo-Assyrian Royal Epics. These texts extoll the heroic accomplishments of Neo-Assyria's kings. Although their content is similar to the propagandistic Neo-Assyrian Annals and other royal inscriptions, the poetic genre of the epics distinguishes them from those prose compositions. The best-preserved exemplar is an epic of Shalmaneser III, but it is quite fragmentary, as are the epics concerning Sargon II and Assurbanipal.

Texts, translations, and studies: W. G. LAMBERT, "The Sultantepe Tablets, VIII: Shalmaneser in Ararat," *AnSt* 11 (1961): 143–58; LIVINGSTONE, *Court Poetry and Literary Miscellanea,* 45–53. *Bibliography:* R. BORGER and W. SCHRAM, *Einleitung in die assyrischen Königsinschriften* (Leiden: Brill, 1961–), 2:81.

The Sin of Sargon. According to this Neo-Assyrian tale, Sennacherib of Assyria discovers through divination that his own father, Sargon II (721–705), had sinned against the gods by neglecting the cults of Babylon. Sennacherib responds quickly to this revelation by assuming a new posture of worship and respect toward Babylon and its chief god, Marduk. As the text concludes, Sennacherib encourages his son to continue this pro-Babylonian policy, warning Esarhaddon to persevere through the resistance from Assyrian scholars and to "reconcile the gods of Babylonia with your [Assyrian] gods!" Although modern scholars at first read this text as a historical report, it turns out that Sennacherib cannot be its historical protagonist because he was infamous for one great sin: the destruction of Babylon. Assyria's turn toward Babylon should instead be associated with Sennacherib's son Esarhaddon, who worked hard to atone for his father's sins by rebuilding Babylon and restoring its temples. It follows that the Sin of Sargon was a

fictional work of propaganda sponsored by Esarhaddon, whose goal was to promote a renewal of the Babylonian cults in the face of resistance from Assyria's
scribal elite. For their own part, the pro-Assyrian party eventually responded to
the Sin of Sargon with a fictional composition of their own: Kummaya's Dream
Vision (see 7.1).

Text and translation: LIVINGSTONE, *Court Poetry and Literary Miscellanea,* 77–79. *Bibli-
ography: ARAB* 2:242–44; LONGMAN, *Fictional Akkadian Autobiography,* 117–18, 231–33;
G. ROUX, *Ancient Iraq* (2d ed.; New York: Penguin, 1980), 300; H. TADMOR, B. LANDS-
BERGER, and S. PARPOLA, "The Sin of Sargon and Sennacherib's Last Will," *SAAB* 3
(1989): 3–51; C. WALKER and M. B. DICK, *The Induction of the Cult Image in Ancient
Mesopotamia: The Mesopotamian mīs pî Ritual* (SAALT 1; Helsinki: Helsinki University
Press, 2001), 24–27.

The Tale of Sarbanapal and Sarmuge. Although this unusual papyrus, P.Amherst
63, comes from Upper Egypt (fourth–third century B.C.E.), it is directly relevant to
the study of Mesopotamian tradition. The text, written in Aramaic with an Egyptian demotic script, contains a New Year liturgy for Aramaic-speaking exiles in the
region, but it also includes—for reasons that are not entirely clear—a tale about
two competitors for the royal throne, Sarbanapal and Sarmuge. The tale is introduced by a lament over the ruins of Nineveh (Neo-Assyria's capital), a clue that has
helped scholars recognize that Sarbanapal and Sarmuge are none other than
Assurbanipal and Šamaš-šum-ukin, Esarhaddon's rival sons, who contended with
each other for their father's throne. Some historical background is in order.

Before Esarhaddon died, he divided his realm between his two sons, placing
Assurbanipal on the throne in Assyria and Šamaš-šum-ukin on the throne in Babylon. Although the division was ostensibly between equals, Assurbanipal covertly assumed control of Babylon, and when Esarhaddon died, he forced Šamaš-šum-ukin
to take an oath of loyalty and exacted new taxes from the Babylonians. This resulted in a Babylonian plot to rebel that Assurbanipal at first attempted to foil
through various political maneuvers. When these failed, he ordered a full-scale
siege of Babylon. The city eventually fell to Assyria, and Šamaš-šum-ukin perished
in the conflagration. Assurbanipal then carried many of the survivors back to Assyria as spoil, and he mutilated and flayed the bodies of Babylon's leaders.

Although this historical review might suggest that Assurbanipal was a villain of sorts, our papyrus tells a different story. According to the legend, it was
Sarbarnapal, not his father, who had appointed Sarmuge to the Babylonian
throne, and the duty given to Sarmuge was not so much to rule Babylon as to ensure that tribute was sent back to Assyria. When the ungrateful and devious
Sarmuge rebelled against Assyria, Sarbarnapal's response was measured and patient, and when war became necessary, he requested that Sarmuge be captured
alive. The papyrus tells us that when Sarmuge nonetheless died in the carnage
of Babylon's fall, Sarbarnapal lamented the passing of his dead brother and,
upon advice from his generals, published this "true" account of the events that
transpired. From this we can deduce that the account goes back to Assurbanipal
himself, who had it composed to bolster his claim to the Babylonian throne.

Propagandistic messages of this sort were disseminated through letters and by word of mouth (see Moran; Crown; Hurowitz). In this case, the original tale was historical insofar as it purported to be an account of actual events, but it was fictional insofar as its composition included not only an ideological shaping of the story but also outright fabrications of fact. That the tale became the stuff of popular legend is confirmed by its fascinating history, during which it began as a semihistorical piece of propaganda in the seventh century B.C.E. and reached Egypt as a third-century Aramaic folktale wrapped in a ritual. The tradition appears in various guises in later Greek and Roman literature, as well as in modern works like Byron's tragedy "Sardanapalus" and Delacroix's famous painting "The Death of Sardanapalus" (Frahm). As we can see, the traditions generated by propaganda can be quite resilient.

For more on P.Amherst 63, see the appropriate entry in 3.2.

Texts and translations: R. C. STEINER and C. F. NIMS, "Ashurbanipal and Shamash-shum-ukin: A Tale of Two Brothers from the Aramaic Text in Demotic Script," *RB* 92 (1985): 60–81; IDEM, "You Can't Offer Your Sacrifice and Eat It Too: A Polemical Poem from the Aramaic Text in Demotic Script," *JNES* 43 (1984): 89–114. *Translation: COS* 1.99: 309–27. *Bibliography:* A. D. CROWN, "Tidings and Instructions: How News Travelled in the Ancient Near East," *JESHO* 17 (1974): 244–71; E. FRAHM, "Images of Ashurbanipal in Later Tradition," *ErIsr* 27 (2003): 37–48; V. A. HUROWITZ, "Spanning the Generations: Aspects of Oral and Written Transmission in the Bible and Ancient Mesopotamia," in *Freedom and Responsibility: Exploring the Challenges of Jewish Continuity* (ed. R. M. Geffen and M. B. Edelman; Hoboken: KTAV, 1998), 11–30; I. KOTTSIEPER, "Die literarische Aufnahme assyrischer Begegenheiten in frühen aramäischen Texten," in *La circulation des biens, des personnes, et des idées dans le Proche-Orient ancien: Actes de la XXXVIIIe Rencontre assyriologique internationale* (ed. D. Charpin and F. Joannès; Paris: Éditions Recherche sur les Civilisations, 1992), 283–89; W. L. MORAN, "Assurbanipal's Message to the Babylonians (*ABL* 301), with an Excursus on Figurative *Biltu*," in *Ah, Assyria . . . Studies in Assyrian History and Ancient Near Eastern Historiography Presented to Hayim Tadmor* (ed. M. Cogan and I. Eph'al.; ScrHier 33; Jerusalem: Magnes Press, 1991), 320–31; R. C. STEINER, "The Aramaic Text in Demotic Script: The Liturgy of a New Year's Festival Imported from Bethel to Syene by Exiles from Rash," *JAOS* 111 (1991): 362–63; IDEM, "Papyrus Amherst 63: A New Source for the Language, Literature, Religion, and History of the Arameans," in *Studia aramaica: New Sources and Approaches* (ed. M. J. Geller et al.; JSSSup 4; Oxford: Oxford University Press, 1995), 199–207; R. C. STEINER and A. M. MOSHAVI, "A Selective Glossary of Northwest Semitic Texts in Egyptian Script," *DNWSI* 1249–66.

The Adad-guppi Inscription. Although cast as an autobiography of the mother of the Neo-Babylonian king Nabonius, this text was apparently composed after her death by priests of Sin in order to inspire devotion to their temple in Harran. The basic theme of the story is that Adad-guppi prospered because she was a devotee of Sin, the basic point being that the reader should follow her example. Nabonidus (555–539 B.C.E.), the self-proclaimed savior of the cult of Sin at Harran, likely sponsored the text.

Text and translation: C. J. GADD, "The Harran Inscriptions of Nabonidus," *AnSt* 8 (1958): 35–92. *Translations: ANET* 560–62; *COS* 1.147: 477–78; LONGMAN, *Fictional Akkadian*

Autobiography, 97–103, 225–28. **Bibliography:** M. B. DICK, "The 'History of David's Rise to Power' and the Neo-Babylonian Succession Apologies," in *David and Zion: Biblical Studies in Honor of J. J. M. Roberts* (ed. B. F. Batto and K. L. Roberts; Winona Lake, Ind.: Eisenbrauns, 2004), 3–19; B. LANDSBERGER, "Die Basaltstele Nabonids von Eski-Harran," *Halil-Edhem Hâtira Kitabi* 1 (1947): 116–52; J. LEWY, "The Late Assyro-Babylonian Cult of the Moon and Its Culmination at the Time of Nabonidus," *HUCA* 19 (1946): 405–89.

9.2. The Ugaritic Epics

It is extremely unusual for ancient texts to divulge their sponsors and authors, but in the case of the Ugaritic tales Aqhat and Kirta, we have both. Our tablets come from the library of Attanu-Purlianni, the high priest of Baal in the city's main temple. The priest dictated these and other texts to a scribe, Ilimilku of Shubbani, whose meticulousness and precision are still visible in the hardened clay. The dictation and copying of the text was sponsored by King Niqmaddu II of Ugarit, who reigned ca. 1375–1345 B.C.E. We do not know how far back the traditions in these epics go, but as S. Parker has noted, at Ugarit we are not dealing with long and open-ended literary histories, such as we face in the case of many ancient texts. Both of these poems were composed with beautiful parallelism and, according to some scholars, with a rhythmic meter as well. There is another set of narratives, known as the Rephaim Texts, that may be related to the Aqhat tradition in some way, but the exemplars are quite fragmentary and little understood. Some copies of these Rephaim Texts were apparently written by the same Ilimilku who composed Aqhat and Kirta, and others not. In terms of genre, it is not at all clear whether the Rephaim Texts are best understood as myth, epic, or some other genre.

The Kirta Epic. The prologue introduces us to Kirta, king of Khubur (not of Ugarit!), a Job-like figure who was bereft of family through divorce, pestilence, war, and other disasters and so faced an apparent end to his dynasty. But Kirta's sorrow caught the attention of the god El, who approached Kirta in a dream and explained in detail how the king could acquire a new wife and, through her, a royal heir. Kirta followed these directions exactly, performing sacrifices and then organizing a military excursion to seize the daughter of King Pabil of Udum (Edom?). Midway through his seven-day journey to Udum, he took his only diversion from El's directions: he vowed to bring rich gifts to the goddess Asherah if she granted success on his adventure. Kirta succeeded in his campaign and was quickly blessed by El with many children. But as we might expect, he neglected to keep this vow to Asherah. In the second episode, which is again reminiscent of Job, Kirta was struck down by a severe illness—the result of his broken vow. The king's illness eventually spawned a serious famine in his kingdom, which prompted El to intercede. El challenged the divine council to heal Kirta, but this failing, he fashioned a creature that restored the king's health. The third and final episode follows, in which Yassub, Kirta's heir, proposed to depose his father

because Kirta's illness had prevented him from protecting widows and the oppressed in the royal courts (note, however, that Kirta was already cured of this illness in the previous story). Kirta subsequently cursed his son, but with this the
text unfortunately ends in midsentence. The text is therefore partial, and apparently we are missing episodes before and after what is preserved. Nevertheless,
what we do possess allows us to imagine the nature of the whole.

The episodes in Kirta address three perennial threats to kingship: lack of
dynastic progeny, illness, and the threat of deposition (Knoppers). The central
themes binding these episodes together are the survival of the dynasty in the face
of these threats, and the key role that the deity, El, plays in its survival. As Parker
has noted, it is nevertheless transparent that the three episodes were originally independent and were combined into a single text. Kirta's vow to Asherah was awk-
wardly added to the first episode in order to connect it with the second, and the
king's healing in the second episode is in obvious tension with his continuing illness in the third. The connections between the three stories are clearly artificial.
Although Kirta's tradition history is much shorter and less complex that that of
the Gilgamesh Epic, the two texts reflects a similar pattern of composition, in
which separate stories have been combined to create a larger epic whole. There is,
however, at least one very important difference. Although Gilgamesh was a historical figure, there is no evidence for the existence of Kirta, nor does the epic endeavor to situate him in a concrete historical context. The same can be said of the
protagonist in the other great Ugaritic legend, Aqhat.

Text and translation: PARKER, *Ugaritic Narrative Poetry,* 9–48. *Translations:* ANET
142–49; COOGAN, *Stories from Ancient Canaan,* 52–74; COS 1.102: 333–43. *Bibliography:*
G. N. KNOPPERS, "Dissonance and Disaster in the Legend of Kirta," *JAOS* 114 (1994):
572–82; B. MARGALIT, "The Legend of Keret," in *Handbook of Ugaritic Studies* (ed. Watson
and Wyatt), 203–33; D. J. O'CONNOR, "The Keret Legend and the Prologue-Epilogue of
Job," *ITQ* 55 (1989): 1–6; IDEM, "The Keret Legend and the Prologue-Epilogue of Job—a
Postscript," *ITQ* 55 (1989): 240–42.

The Legend of Aqhat. This text is fragmentary and its plot is only partially
known. Like the Kirta story, Aqhat introduces us to a childless man, Danel, who
was a pious and respected elder (or king) known for his just verdicts at the city
gate. Desperate to acquire an heir, he offered sacrifices in the temple of Baal while
imploring the god to help. After seven days of sacrifices, Baal took Danel's request
to El—the god who handled such things (cf. Kirta)—and El in turn blessed Danel
with a son, who was named Aqhat. The craftsman god Kothar was quite taken
with Danel's son and presented Aqhat with a beautiful bow, which quickly attracted the attention of the goddess Anat. When Aqhat rebuffed Anat's bids to
acquire the bow—including an offer of eternal life—the goddess took her complaints to El. Anat was soon authorized to take whatever action she wished, and
the goddess quickly enlisted YTPN (a deity?) to help her kill Aqhat. Aqhat was
swiftly murdered, but the bow was destroyed in the process. The immediate effects of Aqhat's death were agricultural problems similar to those created by
Kirta's illness in the first epic. The agricultural blight was eventually squelched

when Danel and Paghit (Aqhat's sister) performed appropriate rituals, but the text breaks off abruptly at this point, just as Paghit is embarking on a quest to avenge her brother's murder.

Although our knowledge of Aqhat is even more fragmentary than that of Kirta, it is fairly easy to see that Aqhat's episodes are more integrated than those in its sister text. The net effect is that Aqhat seems more like an epic novella and less like a collection of separate epic legends. The Kirta and Aqhat stories, however, obviously share many similar motifs, including the theme of childlessness, the role of El in providing children, and the agricultural blight that is associated with illness and death. But this brings us no closer to an answer for the question of why Aqhat was composed. One part of the answer hinges on whether Aqhat was an elder/chieftain (Margalit) or a king (Koch), but we will not explore this here.

Although some scholars believe that the origins of Aqhat should be traced back to a much earlier myth (Xella), there is an increasing consensus that Aqhat is a single creative literary work without much prehistory (del Olmo Lete; Parker). On the purpose of this work, scholars have often pointed out that Aqhat is especially concerned with social roles and family piety. This has prompted some scholars to view the text as a wisdom composition. Other scholars have suggested that its concern for family tradition reflects instead a conflict between its author's kinship-based identity and Ugarit's political institutions. Margalit in particular has argued that the goddess Anat's violence toward Aqhat reflects the oppressive nature of Ugarit's Rephaite warrior class against traditional society and values. Parker wisely suggests that it is probably impossible to grasp the text's primary significance in our present state of knowledge; nevertheless, it remains true that the universal values reflected in Aqhat made it a very satisfying story. As noted, Aqhat, like Kirta, is apparently a fictional legend treating a fictional character. The priestly scribe responsible for copying the text may well have known Aqhat to be fictive, but this would not have prevented others from reading it as history.

Two similarities between Aqhat and the Hebrew Bible are striking. First, Aqhat and Kirta share with the Hebrew patriarchal narratives the motif of acquiring heirs in the face of barrenness, and in both traditions it is the chief god El who can miraculously overcome the threat of human infertility. The significance of this parallel is heightened if one imagines, as some scholars do, that the patriarchal narratives are based on older epic sources. Second, many scholars are convinced that Ezekiel's allusions to Danel in Ezek 4:14, 14:20, 28:3 are related to the Danel mentioned in the Aqhat story. Several lines of evidence suggest that this inference is correct. Ezekiel's references to Danel mention him in the company of Noah and Job. Because these two figures can be legitimately identified as non-Israelites, Danel was probably a foreign hero. This likelihood is reinforced by Ezekiel's oracle against the king of Tyre (Ezek 28), which presupposes that the Phoenicians were familiar with Danel (Ezek 28:3). Although at first sight it may seem artificial to assume a connection between second-millennium Ugarit and first-millennium Phoenicia, we should recall that Ugarit was a cultural ancestor of Phoenicia and that there is substantial evidence the Ugaritic epic tradition was preserved in Phoenicia at least until the Hellenistic period (Attridge and Oden).

It is therefore very likely that the Hebrew Daniel represents a Jewish adaptation of the much older, Ugaritic Danel. In a nutshell, this suggests that the Jewish Daniel began his career as a Ugaritic hero before he was subsequently adopted by Diaspora Jews as a mantic sage (the Aramaic tales of Dan 1–6) and then later as an apocalyptic prophet (the Hebrew apocalypses of Dan 7–12). Judaism is known to have adopted other foreign characters as its own, most notably Ahiqar (see chs. 2 and 8 above).

Texts and translations: B. MARGALIT, *The Ugaritic Poem of AQHT* (BZAW 182; New York: de Gruyter, 1989); PARKER, *Ugaritic Narrative Poetry,* 49–80. *Translations: ANET* 149–55; COOGAN, *Stories from Ancient Canaan,* 27–47; *COS* 1.103: 343–56. *Bibliography:* H. W. ATTRIDGE and R. A. ODEN JR., *Philo of Biblos: The Phoenician History* (CBQMS 9; Washington: Catholic Biblical Association, 1981); J. DAY, "The Daniel of Ugarit and Ezekiel and the Hero of the Book of Daniel," *VT* 30 (1980): 174–84; K. KOCH, "Die Sohnesverheissung an den ugaritischen Daniel," *ZA* 24 (1967): 211–21; G. DEL OLMO LETE, *Mitos y leyendas de Canaan según la tradición de Ugarit* (Fuentes de la ciencia biblica 1; Madrid: Cristianidad, 1981); S. B. PARKER, *The Pre-biblical Narrative Tradition* (SBLRBS 24; Atlanta: Scholars Press, 1989); N. WYATT, "The Story of Aqhat" (*KTU* 1.17–19), in *Handbook of Ugaritic Studies* (ed. Watson and Wyatt), 234–58; P. XELLA, "Una 'rilettura' del poema di Aqhat," in *Problemi del mito nel Vicino Oriente antico* (Supplemento agli Annali dell'Istituto Orientale di Napoli 7; Naples: Istituto Orientale di Napoli, 1976), 61–91.

The Ugaritic Rpum Texts. The so-called *Rpum* texts (or Rephaim Texts) are preserved in three tablet fragments, *KTU* 1.20 (= RS 3.348), 1.21 (= RS 2.019), and 1.22 (= RS 2.024). All three texts are narratives, but scholars are not certain whether the fragments are parts of the same story or of several different but similar texts. About all that can be said of the story is that the Rephaim are invited to attend a weeklong banquet held at a threshing floor (a common cultic site in the ancient world), but the purpose of this banquet is not entirely understood. The most common scholarly interpretation is that the Rephaim were the ghosts of deceased kings or nobility who traveled by chariot to attend an assembly of gods, dead kings, and living kings in Ugarit's funerary or mortuary cult. Other common readings interpret the Rephaim as deities, as the dead in general, as a class of living chariot warriors associated with the king, or as some combination of the above. For more on the Rephaim, see the Ugaritic funerary and ritual texts treated in 5.9.4.

Text and translation: PARKER, *Ugaritic Narrative Poetry,* 196–205. *Bibliography:* W. T. PITARD, "The *Rpum* Texts," in *Handbook of Ugaritic Studies* (ed. Watson and Wyatt), 259–69.

9.3. Legends from Egypt and Hatti

The Bentresh Stela. This text was inscribed on a black sandstone stela that includes a relief of Ramses II offering incense to the god Khons. Below the relief is the tale a demon-possessed princess (Bentresh) whom Khons healed when Ramses II transported the god's statue to the princess in Bakhtan. The stela was placed in the temple of Khons, where it obviously served the shrine as a fictional piece of propaganda. Although the stela dates to the fourth–third century B.C.E., its author made the text look ancient by inscribing it in Middle Egyptian hieroglyphs and by presenting it as an ancient royal inscription of Ramses II (1304–1237 B.C.E.). Similar fictional inscriptions are treated in the next entry and in several entries in chapter 9 ("Epics and Legends").

Texts and translations: K. A. KITCHEN, *Ramesside Inscriptions, Historical and Biographical* (Oxford: Blackwell, 1975–), 2:284–87. *Translations: AEL* 4:90–94; *ANET* 29–31; *COS* 1.54: 134–36; *LAE* 361–67. *Bibliography:* G. LEFEBVRE, "Encore la stèle de Bakhtan," *Chronique d'Égypte* 19 (1944): 214–18; G. POSENER, "A propos de la stèle de Bentresh," *BIFAO* 34 (1934): 75–81.

The Famine Stela. Like the Bentresh Stela, this late text was falsely presented as an old royal inscription. The stela sports a relief of King Djoser (ca. 2650 B.C.E.) making offerings to the gods of the Nile's cataract region—especially to Khnum— and follows with a text that purports to be a royal decree, in which the Pharaoh recounts his dream vision that Khnum would provide relief from a severe seven-year famine. As an act of gratitude, Djoser decrees that all revenue from Elephantine to Takompso should be given to the Khnum temple. Although the text dates to the second century B.C.E., a few scholars consider it to be a late copy of an old and authentic royal decree. Scholars more often assess this text as a fictional attempt by priests to secure tax revenues for their temple. Like the author of the Bentresh Stela, this author proffered his fiction by composing the text in Middle Egyptian and by presenting it as the royal inscription of a long-dead Pharaoh. The similarity of the tale to the famine story of Genesis is quite striking, not only because of its Egyptian setting and seven-year famine but also because of the motifs of taxation (Gen 41:33–49; 47:13–26), dream omens (41:1–32), and preservation of priestly land (47:22).

Texts and translations: P. BARGUET, *La stèle de la famine à Séhel* (Cairo: Institut Français d'Archéologie Orientale, 1953). *Translations: AEL* 3:94–103; *ANET* 31–32; *COS* 1.53: 130–34; *LAE* 386–92. *Bibliography:* H. BRUNNER, "Die Hungersnotstele," in *Kindlers Literatur Lexikon* (Zürich: Kindler, 1967), 111; M. LICHTHEIM, "The Naucratis Stela Once Again," in *Studies in Honor of George R. Hughes* (SAOC 39; Chicago: Oriental Institute of the University of Chicago, 1977), 142–44.

The Egyptian Stories of Setne Khamwas. Khamwas was the fourth son of Ramses II (thirteenth century B.C.E.) and served as the high priest of Ptah at Memphis, where he became famous as a builder and restorer of sacred monuments. Popular memory eventually shaped this fame into the legendary scholar and magician who appears in the demotic tales of the Ptolemaic period (ca. third century B.C.E.). Two separate papyri exist, yielding three different episodes. The episodes are not closely linked together, suggesting that we have a cycle of popular tales rather than a thematically unified story about Setne Khamwas. In this, the tales of Khamwas follow a pattern visible in the other legendary traditions of the Near East.

The first papyrus (Setne I) explains how Setne Khamwas is tempted by a deceased magician named Naneferkaptah to steal from his grave a book written by the god Thoth (patron deity of learning and magic). Although Naneferkaptah has paid for the book with his own life and with the life of his family, the lure of the magical book is strong: it promises to give Setne the power to understand animal languages, to wield power over nature, and to resurrect the dead. Setne indeed succeeds in his venture to recover the book, but in the end two skilled magicians induce him to return it to the grave. The tale was entertaining but also taught the essential Egyptian belief that magical secrets belong to the gods.

Although the second papyrus is often called Setne II, the hero of its two tales (tales A and B) is Setne's son Si-Osire rather than Setne himself. In tale A, Si-Osire's birth is revealed beforehand to Setne in a dream vision, which suitably portends a son who turns out to be a wonder-working child with unusual wisdom and strength. Using this wisdom, Si-Osire guides his father into the netherworld, where Setne sees that the righteous are blessed and that sinners are forever tormented. Greek concepts of the afterlife have obviously influenced the story. Si-Osire's wisdom is also the theme of the second tale (tale B). Here a Nubian chieftain arrives in the court of the pharaoh with a sealed letter. When the chieftain challenges the king to provide a wise Egyptian who can read the letter without opening its envelope, the king naturally turns to his greatest scholar, Setne. But Setne too becomes deeply troubled by the Nubian challenge. When the situation looks hopeless even to sage Setne, Si-Osire steps forward and volunteers to read the letter. After doing so, Si-Osire reveals that he is really Horus-son-of-Paneshe, sent as Setne's son by the god Osiris in order to save Egypt's reputation in this battle of wits with the Nubians. Si-Osire then vanishes without a trace, and Setne makes offerings to Horus-son-of-Paneshe for the remainder of his life.

Although the two tales in this papyrus were obviously entertaining, both were apparently motivated by more-constructive religious concerns. The authors co-opted Setne and his family as protagonists in order to teach a certain theology about the afterlife (tale A) and to promote the cult of Horus-son-of-Paneshe. The second papyrus clearly combines two originally separate tales about Si-Osire; this reflects the same literary phenomenon that we have seen in other legends: the tales originate separately and are later combined.

Text and translation: F. L. GRIFFITH, *Stories of the High Priests of Memphis: The Sethon of Herodotus and the Demotic Tales of Khamuas* (2 vols.; Oxford: Clarendon, 1990). *Translations: AEL* 3:125–51; *LAE* 453–91. *Bibliography:* P. A. PICCIONE, "The Gaming Episode in the Tale of Setne Khamwas as Religious Metaphor," in *For His Ka: Essays Offered in Memory of Klaus Baer* (ed. D. Silverman; SAOC 55; Chicago: Oriental Institute of the University of Chicago, 1994), 197–204; I. RUTHERFORD, "Kalasiris and Setne Khamwas: Greek Novels and Egyptian Novels," *ZPE* 117 (1997): 203–9.

Kanesh and Zalpa: A Tale of Two Cities. In this Hittite tale (*CTH* 7.1), the queen of Kanesh in Hatti begot thirty sons in a single year and because she was reluctant to raise them, she placed them in baskets and sent them down the river toward the Black Sea. There the gods found the boys and raised them in the land of Zalpa.

Meanwhile the queen again begot thirty children, this time thirty girls. On a trip to Kanesh, the boys heard the story of the thirty missing sons and recognized the queen as their lost mother. When the boys approached the queen, she did not recognize them and wanted to give her daughters to them as wives. The story ends with the brothers debating the appropriateness of such a course of action. The text breaks off at this point, and it is difficult to perceive the author's objective or purpose for the story. It is very interesting that later, as the tablet again becomes legible, we find that the story has progressed from legendary prehistory to the historical period of the kings Labarna, Hattušili I, and Muršili I. From this we may surmise that the tale provided an introduction to an account of political and social relations between the Hittite state and the city of Zalpa on the Black Sea.

Text and translation: H. OTTEN, *Eine althethitische Erzählung um die Stadt Zalpa* (StBoT 17; Wiesbaden: Harrassowitz, 1973). *Translations:* COS 1.71: 181–82; H. A. HOFFNER, *Hittite Myths* (SBLWAW 2; Atlanta: Scholars Press, 1990), 62–63. *Bibliography:* H. G. GÜTERBOCK, "Die historische Tradition und ihre literarische Gestaltung bei Babyloniern und Hethitern bis 1200," ZA 44 (1938): 45–149 (101–5, Zalpa Text); IDEM, "Hittite Historiography: A Survey," in *History, Historiography, and Interpretation: Studies in Biblical and Cuneiform Literatures* (ed. H. Tadmor and M. Weinfeld; Jerusalem: Magnes Press, 1983), 21–35 (27–28, Zalpa Text); H. A. HOFFNER, "Histories and Historians of the Ancient Near East: The Hittites," Or 49 (1980): 283–332 (289–91, Zalpa Text); A. KAMMENHUBER, "Die hethitische Geschichtsschreibung," *Saeculum* 9 (1958): 136–55; G. F. DEL MONTE and J. TISCHLER, *Die Orts-und Gewässernamen der hethitsichen Texte* (Wiesbaden: Ludwig Reichert, 1978), 490–92.

Concluding Observations

Two types of legendary epic appear among the Near Eastern exemplars we have examined. One type treated fictional characters, such as Lugalbanda, Kirta, and Aqhat, and the other narrated the deeds of historical figures, such as Gilgamesh, Sargon, Tukulti-Ninurta and Assurbanipal. Apart from historical information from outside the narratives themselves, it would be difficult in some cases to determine the historical status of the protagonists in these texts. Here we shall consider in summary fashion the differences between these two types of legendary epic, as well as some of the generic features in the epical and legendary genres.

1. **Fictional Protagonists.** These texts were entertaining compositions but not bereft of ideology and theology. Lugalbanda integrated the old Kullub god into the Uruk tradition by converting him into an early king of Uruk, and the legends of Kirta and Aqhat conveyed Ugarit's dynastic theology, El's divine power to grant progeny, and perhaps, in the case of Aqhat, a critique of Ugaritic society. These texts remind us that entertainment and ideology were not mutually-exclusive aims in ancient literature, nor did serious ideological or theological narratives demand historical protagonists. The

role of sources in the compositions varied. Although Aqhat appears to have been a literary composition without much prehistory, both Lugalbanda and Kirta originated as cycles of disparate tales that were eventually combined by scribes.

2. **Historical Protagonists.** The texts that treated historical figures can be subdivided into two types, those whose plots were essentially fictional and those that were tied, more or less, to known historical events (historical epics). Some of the fictional epics were pseudoautobiographies, which co-opted the voice of an ancient and well-known figure in support of some ideology or agenda. The Cuthean Legend made Naram-Sin an advocate of pacifism and domestic duty rather than military conquest, and Sargon II (721–705 B.C.E.) had his Birth Legend composed to legitimize his rule by exploiting the reputation of the much earlier Sargon of Akkad (2334–2279 B.C.E.). Similarly, Setne as depicted in Egyptian lore was far removed from the historical protagonist. Although Egyptian history teaches us that Setne was a high priest of Ptah and restorer of sacred monuments during the thirteenth century B.C.E., the demotic tales that date ten or more centuries later remembered him as a colorful scholar and magician who begot a wonder-working son. Unlike the Cuthean Legend and the Sargon Birth Legend, the Setne tales were entertaining products of popular tradition rather than serious ideological compositions, but all three exemplars teach us the same point: the historical status of a narrative's protagonist tells us little about the narrative's historicity. The same can be said for several priestly compositions, in which the priests created legendary traditions in order to secure legitimacy or support for their cults and temples. The usual strategy was to place support for the cult in the mouth of a famous king from the past. This propagandistic strategy appears in Egyptian texts, such as the Famine and Bentresh Stelas, as well as in Akkadian texts, such as the Cruciform Monument of Maništušu, the Autobiography of Kurigalzu, and the Agum-kakrime Inscription.

As we have just noted, the plots of the historical epics were more closely tied to genuine history, but here, too, political and ideological agendas shaped the texts. The Great Revolt against Naram-Sin narrated the king's victories over would-be rebels in order to dissuade vassals from breaking their oaths of allegiance, and the other Sargonid epics, such as the King of Battle, elaborated and magnified the feats of the kings in support of their dynastic legitimacy. The Tukulti-Ninurta Epic was similarly historical and propagandistic. The Curse of Akkad, too, was closely tied to historical events, most notably to the fall of Akkad and the Rise of Ur III, but its author proffered two fictions: one made Naram-Sin the last king of Akkad, and the other made him the cause of the city's fall and abandonment. This simple etiology was apparently based on theological speculation that interpreted Naram-Sin's pious refurbishment of Enlil's temple as an impious desecration of Ekur. It is no longer possible to distill what belonged to the author and what belonged to the traditions he inherited, but the legendary shaping of the Naram-Sin tradition is clear enough in this exemplar.

3. **Epic and Legend as Tradition.** The traditional nature of legend is especially illustrated by two very different exemplars, the Gilgamesh Epic and the Tale of Sarbanapal and Sarmuge. The Gilgamesh tradition began as a series of entertaining oral and written tales that were eventually combined to form still longer compositions. These materials reflect the natural inclination to fictively embellish the lives of cultural heroes and thereby exaggerate their accomplishments. The early epic version was profoundly shaped by its editor, who took the diverse traditions about the long-dead king and used them to explore the philosophical and theological dimensions of human mortality. A still later editor, responsible for the so-called standard edition, added the flood story and transformed the epic into a wisdom composition by adding a prologue and an epilogue. In sum, the creation of the standard epic in 1250 B.C.E. was the last major step in a millennium-long oral and literary odyssey, and even after this, other editors made subtle changes to the text. So, if the Gilgamesh Epic is our example, then the creation of epic literature could involve a long and lively process in the scribal tradition.

Stranger still is the progression of tradition that created our Tale about Sarbanapal and Sarmuge. The story began as a piece of royal propaganda for the Neo-Assyrian king Assurbanipal and turned up several centuries later in an Aramaic ritual text from Egypt. Nevertheless, in comparison with the other exemplars examined above, the tale preserves Assurbanipal's original propaganda with remarkable fidelity. The likely explanation for this is that the tale was orally preserved by migrants who valued the story for its nostalgia and antiquity but for whom its propaganda served no vital purpose. If such was the case, there would have been no occasion for altering the tradition. The Tale of Sarbanapal and Sarmuge illustrates a scenario in which legendary traditions can faithfully preserve historical memory for a long period of time.

In connection with epic and tradition, we should not fail to highlight the still unpublished Epic of Zimri-lim. From what we know of it, the ancient scribes were flattering their king even as he lived by presenting him in heroic colors. So, while it was often true that heroic elaborations on the lives of historical persons took place many years after such persons lived, it was not always true. Consequently, we cannot merely suppose that all of the miraculous and heroic elements in the ancient epics were the result of a lengthy and complex process in the oral and/or literary tradition.

4. Legend, Epic, and the Hebrew Bible. The Hebrew Bible does not contain epic texts, nor, for the most part, does it include texts that as a whole could be characterized as legend. Nevertheless, epic and legend appear to have been prominent among the sources used by Israelite historians. Regarding epic sources, the Hebrew Bible may allude to such sources when it refers to the "Book of Jashar" (Josh 10:13; 2 Sam 1:18) and to "the Book of the Wars of the LORD" (Num 21:14), and scholars have long suspected that remnants of the Hebrew epic tradition are preserved in poems such as the Blessing of Jacob (Gen 49), the Song of Miriam (Exod 15), the Oracles of Balaam (Num 24), the Blessing of Moses (Deut 33), the Song of Deborah (Judg 5), and the lament over Saul and Jonathan (2 Sam 1). Although this evidence is circumstantial and inconclusive, the theory that Hebrew historians had access to epic sources is not entirely reckless so long as the theory is treated as a possibility or probability rather than as a fact (see Albright; Cassuto; Conroy; Cross; Damrosch; Hendel; Mowinckel; Parker). There can be no doubt that poetic narrative sources existed in ancient Israel; that these were substantial epic works in the Homeric sense is only an educated guess.

As for legend, most scholars believe that old legendary sources played an important role in the composition of ancient Hebrew histories. These legends recounted the origins of Israel's national and religious institutions and spoke of its cultural heroes, especially Israel's ethnic forefathers (Abraham, Isaac, Jacob, Joseph), religious and military leaders (Moses, Joshua, Samuel, and the judges), prophetic personalities (Elijah, Elisha), and royalty (Saul, David, and Solomon). The historical value of Israel's legendary traditions is a matter of intense debate, partly because of an academic interest in Israelite history but also because of theological concerns. Comparative materials from the Near East cast some light on this issue. First, although the legendary sources sometimes preserved accurate memories of the past, these memories were colored in greater or lesser degrees by the ideological hands through which the traditions passed. Only when the tradents had little or no interest in a tradition's content—for example, the Tale of Sarbanapal and Sarmuge—was it preserved without significant alteration. Second, the historical value of the legendary traditions varied considerably from one exemplar to another. Although the Tukulti-Ninurta Epic preserved useful historical content from the king's reign, in other texts not only the narrative but even the chief characters of the story were fictive. It follows that the historical value of legendary sources must be carefully weighed on a case-by-case basis. Third, the Near Eastern exemplars reflect an obvious tendency in the ancients to elaborate and embellish the lives of their cultural heroes and the stories of their national institutions. On this basis, it is reasonable to anticipate that the Bible's legendary traditions were similarly shaped by the Israelite imagination and by political and theological elaboration.

All of this said, it is clear enough from the Near Eastern evidence that many legends were designed to look much older than they were. This was particularly true of fictional priestly legends like the Famine and Bentresh Stelas, the Cruciform Monument of Maništušu, the Autobiography of Kurigalzu, and the Agum-kakrime Inscription. Similarly, modern scholars suspect that many of the Bible's stories concerning priestly or cultic legitimacy were composed late in Israel's history but were written or edited to make them appear very old, in many cases creating the impression that the story went back to the earliest days of Israelite history. Possible examples might include the story of Melchizedek in Gen 14 (legitimizing the Jerusalem priesthood?), Abraham's sacrifice of Isaac (the origins of vicarious animal sacrifice), Jacob's dream at Bethel in Gen 28 (an origin legend of Bethel sanctuary), the story of the Golden Calf in Exod 32 (legitimizing Levites but critiquing the Aaronid priesthood), the conflict between Moses and Miriam/Aaron in Num 12 (against Aaronid ethnic prejudices?), the rebellion of Korah, Dathan, and Abiram in Num 16 (supporting Aaronid legitimacy against Korahite claims), and the story of David's Evil Census in 2 Sam 24 (legitimizing the temple site in Jerusalem). Other stories may have been invented to teach the Israelites piety, as could have been the case in the story of Nadab and Abihu (Lev 10) and the story of the sabbath-breaker in Num 15:32–36.

General Bibliography

Tz. ABUSCH et al., eds., *Proceedings of the XLV Rencontre assyriologique internationale: History and Historiography in the Cuneiform World* (2 vols.; Bethesda, Md.: CDL Press, 2001); Tz. ABUSCH, J. HUEHNERGARD, and P. STEINKELLER, eds., *Lingering over Words: Studies in Ancient Near Eastern Literature in Honor of William L. Moran* (Atlanta: Scholars Press, 1990); W. F. ALBRIGHT, *Yahweh and the Gods of Canaan* (London: University of London, 1968); H. BEHRENS, D. T. LODING, and M. ROTH, eds., *DUMU-E²-DUB-BA-A: Studies in Honor of Åke W. Sjöberg* (OPSNKF 11; Philadelphia: University Museum, 1989); D. BEN-AMOS, ed., *Folklore Genres* (Austin: University of Texas Press, 1976); D. E. BYNUM, "The Generic Nature of Oral Epic Poetry," in *Folklore Genres* (ed. Ben-Amos), 35–58; U. CASSUTO, "The Beginning of Historiography among the Israelites," *Biblical and Oriental Studies* 1 (1973): 7–16; IDEM, "The Israelite Epic," *Biblical and Oriental Studies* 2 (1975): 69–109; C. CONROY, "Hebrew Epic: Historical Notes and Critical Reflections," *Bib* 61 (1980): 1–30; M. D. COOGAN, *Stories from Ancient Canaan* (Louisville: Westminster, 1978); F. M. CROSS JR., *Canaanite Myth and Hebrew Epic: Essays in the History of the Religion of Israel* (Cambridge: Harvard, 1973); S. DALLEY, *Myths from Mesopotamia* (Oxford: Oxford University Press, 1989); D. DAMROSCH, *The Narrative Covenant: Transformations of Genre in the Growth of Biblical Tradition* (San Francisco: Harper & Row, 1987); L. DÉGH and A. VÁZSONYI,

"Legend and Belief," in *Folklore Genres* (ed. Ben-Amos), 93–123; R. M. HALS, "Legend," in *Saga, Legend, Tale, Novella, Epic: Narrative Forms in Old Testament Literature* (ed. G. W. Coats; Sheffield, England: JSOT Press, 1985), 45–55; P. R. HARDIE, "Epic," *OCD* 530; K. HECKER, *Untersuchungen zur akkadischen Epik* (AOAT Sonderreihe; Neukirchen-Vluyn: Neukirchener Verlag, 1974); R. S. HENDEL, *The Epic of the Patriarch* (HSM 42; Atlanta: Scholars Press, 1987); T. JACOBSEN, *The Harps That Once . . . Sumerian Poetry in Translation* (New Haven: Yale University Press, 1987); F. R. KRAUS, "Der Brief des Gilgameš," *AnSt* 30 (1980): 109–21; A. LIVINGSTONE, *Court Poetry and Literary Miscellanea* (SAA 3; Helsinki: Helsinki University Press, 1989); T. LONGMAN III, *Fictional Akkadian Autobiography: A Generic and Comparative Study* (Winona Lake, Ind.: Eisenbrauns, 1991); A. B. LORD, *The Singer of Tales* (Harvard Studies in Comparative Literature 24; Cambridge: Harvard University Press, 1960); S. MOWINCKEL, "Hat es ein israelitisches Nationalepos gegeben?" *ZAW* 53 (1935): 130–53; S. B. PARKER, *The Prebiblical Narrative Tradition* (SBLRBS 24; Atlanta: Scholars Press, 1989); IDEM, *Ugaritic Narrative Poetry* (SBLWAW 9; Atlanta: Scholars Press, 1997); M. PARRY, "Studies in the Epic Technique of Oral Verse-Making, I: Homer and the Homeric Style," *HSCP* 41 (1930): 73–147; IDEM, "Studies in the Epic Technique of Oral Verse-Making, II: The Homeric Language as the Language of Oral Poetry," *HSCP* 43 (1932): 1–50; E. REINER, "Die akkadische Literatur," *Altorientalische Literaturen* (ed. W. Röllig; Neues Handbuch der Literaturwissenschaft; Wiesbaden: Harrassowitz, 1978), 150–210; J. A. RUSSO, "Oral Theory: Its Development in Homeric Studies and Applicability to Other Literatures," in M. E. Vogelzang and H. L. J. Vanstiphout, eds., *Mesopotamian Epic Literature: Oral or Aural?* (Lewiston, N.Y.: Edwin Mellen, 1992), 7–21; J. M. SASSON, ed., *Studies in Literature from the Ancient Near East: Dedicated to Samuel Noah Kramer* (AOS 65; New Haven: American Oriental Society, 1984); S. SPIEGAL, "Noah, Danel, and Job: Touching on Canaanite Relics in the Legends of the Jews," in *Louis Ginzberg Jubilee Volume* (New York: American Academy for Jewish Research, 1945), 305–55; H. L. J. VANSTIPHOUT, *Epics of Sumerian Kings: The Matter of Aratta* (SBLWAW 20; Atlanta: Society of Biblical Literature, 2003); W. G. E. WATSON and N. WYATT, eds., *Handbook of Ugaritic Studies* (Leiden: Brill, 1999); J. G. WESTENHOLZ, *Legends of the Kings of Akkade* (Winona Lake, Ind.: Eisenbrauns, 1997).

CHAPTER TEN

Myth

Introduction

In the Near Eastern creation myth *Enuma Elish,* the Babylonian god Marduk created the heavens and earth by splitting the dragon goddess Tiamat into two halves. According to one modern scholar, "no one but a lunatic under the influence of hashish could ever arrive at the theory" (Cornford, 111). Although other scholars might not express this so derisively, it remains the case that many ancient and modern students of myth have asked this question: why do human beings compose and believe such fanciful stories? This question gets to the heart of a theoretical problem: the problem of mythic composition.

Modern scholarship has proffered numerous theories about the origins of myth, some of them quite speculative. According to the psychoanalyst S. Freud, myths reflect the distorted vestiges of unconscious national wish fantasies. Hence, for Freud, myths were to nations what dreams were to individuals. In a similarly negative vein, Lévy-Bruhl and E. B. Tylor viewed myth as the product of primitive and prescientific modes of thought, a step on the evolutionary ladder that leads to modern humanity. C. Lévi-Strauss, the structural anthropologist, has offered a different and more positive solution. He argues that human beings seek to construct rational, all-embracing systems that help us interpret our experiences. Where these systems are inadequate, myths provide the "logical model" capable of overcoming any remaining contradictions. Another common approach to myth is that of the so-called myth-ritual school, which argues that myths originate as the stories that explain ritual practices, which in turn foster social cohesion (Harrelson). This theory, which appears to have developed from the work of J. G. Frazer, assumes that ritual practices are more basic human behaviors than myth composition, so that the latter is necessarily the result of the former. Although it must be true that some myths were composed to explain ritual practices, this theory is proved wrong by the fact that some myths seem to have no ritual connections at all. Essentially, the result of this debate is that scholars have not reached a consensus about the origins of myth, nor are they likely to do so. This theoretical issue is tied closely to a second problem that is perhaps more fundamental for our purposes: the problem of definition.

Although no one seems to doubt that a story such as *Enuma Elish* is a myth, scholars have vigorously debated which texts pass, or do not pass, as myths (see Bolle; Kirk). Two common definitions of the genre have emerged from this dispute (see M. S. Day). The more general of these definitions sees myth as a story about gods or supernatural beings. The primary analytical criterion in this definition is therefore the *content* of the tradition. A second and more restrictive approach applies a *functional* criterion. For these theorists, myths are sacred histories that either explain the human condition or validate social institutions (Eliade). Although it is certainly true that many so-called myths do precisely this, several factors dictate that the first definition probably serves our purposes best. First, scholars habitually label stories about gods as myths, even when these stories play no vital social or religious role. It seems futile to swim against this tide unless there are compelling reasons to do so. Second, as we shall see, there are a bewildering variety of functions served by "god stories," so that the second definition, which views myths as sacred stories, is simply too restrictive. It is more profitable to regard the sacred myths as one type within the broader discussion of stories about gods and demigods. Third, a consensus is emerging that there is "no single type of myth . . . and unitary theories of mythical function are largely a waste of time" (Kirk). In light of the practical realities and theoretical ambiguities, the broad definition adopted here is useful because it comprises all of the ancient texts that are commonly discussed as myths. In other words, so long as the jury is out on the nature and function of biblical and Near Eastern myths, the broadest possible definition of myth is warranted.

10.1. Mesopotamian Myths

Generally speaking, the Sumerian and Akkadian myths from Mesopotamia were works of epic poetry, a genre introduced in the previous chapter. In the case of the Sumerian myths, the texts reflect a variety of topics, including especially the themes of creation, flood, and fertility. Although these were potentially serious theological themes, several of the myths were composed for entertainment if Jacobsen is correct. The two Sumerian creation traditions were associated with the cities of Nippur and Eridu, respectively. The Nippur tradition featured the cosmic motif of marriage between "heaven and earth," whereas the Eridu tradition centered on the chthonic motif of Enki's life-giving, subterranean waters (Clifford). Later Akkadian myths generally picked up where the Sumerian texts left off, so that, regarding myths, "no neat distinction can be drawn between Sumerian and Akkadian texts" (Clifford; Lambert, 1992). In general, the Akkadian texts provided new versions of the old myths or adopted and reworked the Sumerian mythic motifs to create new compositions. Because of the various historical theological processes, the names of the gods and goddesses used in the ancient myths are confusing and inconsistent for modern readers (see, e.g., Lambert 1975). For a helpful list of the deities, along with explanations for their names, temples, and functions, see S. Dalley, *Myths from Mesopotamia,* 317–31.

Readers should note that the myths regarding the amorous relationship between the gods Dumuzi and Inanna are treated in chapter 4 above (see 4.1).

10.1.1. Sumerian Myths

The Song of the Pickaxe. Our copies date from the Old Babylonian period, but the tradition itself likely goes back to the Sumerian early Dynastic period (ca. 2500). The song displays the marks of the Nippur creation tradition, in which creation was spawned by the marriage of heaven and earth. An (heaven) and Ki (earth) were united as one until the birth of Enlil, their first child, who became the space between them and so formed the room for creation to take place. Enlil then planted the center of the world in Duranki, the home of his temple in Nippur. He accomplished this by using a pickax, which is the primary subject of the myth. Humanity appeared when Enlil used this tool to produce people, who sprouted like plants from the soil of KALAM (= Sumer). In a mixed metaphor that is not entirely understood by scholars, the text also has humanity created with the use of a brick mold. After these creative acts, Enlil entrusted his pickax technology to human beings so that they might provide sacrifices to the gods through their agricultural efforts.

Text and translation: D. O. EDZARD, "U 7804 // UET VI/1 26: 'Gedicht von der Hacke,'" in *Wisdom, Gods, and Literature: Studies in Assyriology in Honour of W. G. Lambert* (ed. A. R. George and I. L. Finkel; Winona Lake, Ind.: Eisenbrauns, 2000), 131–35. *Translation:* COS 1.157: 511–13. *Bibliography:* CLIFFORD, *Creation Accounts in the Ancient Near East and in the Bible,* 30–32; G. FARBER, "'Das Lied von der Hacke,' ein literarischer Spass?" in *Landwirtschaft im Alten Orient: Ausgewählte Vorträge der XLI. Rencontre Assyriologique International* (ed. H. Klengel and J. Renger; BBVO 18; Berlin: Dietrich Reimer, 1999), 369–73; S. N. KRAMER, *From the Poetry of Sumer: Creation, Glorification, Adoration* (Berkeley: University of California Press, 1979), 25–26.

Enki and Ninhursag. Whereas the Nippur tradition featured the creative power of Enlil, the Eridu tradition featured Enki, god of wisdom, as the creator and the god of sweet waters for agriculture. Two texts, the story of Enki and Ninhursag and the so-called Eridu Genesis (see below), suitably represent this tradition.

The story of Enki and Ninhursag is actually two myths that have been loosely linked. The setting for the tale, Dilmun, was borrowed from the first of these myths. Although early translators of the text identified Dilmun as a paradise like the Eden of Genesis, it is now more common to view it as a virginal and inchoate place, lacking life, fresh water, and human culture (see Alster, Batto). In this context, Enki impregnated Ninsikila, a local goddess of Dilmun, and produced the city, which still lacked water. Upon Ninsikila's request, Enki promised, and then provided the city with, both fresh water and a harbor quay. As a result,

Dilmun became a mecca for trade. The plot then transitions to the second myth, where the Dilmun goddess Ninsikila is equated with Nintur/Ninhursag, the mother goddess.

In this second story, Enki incestuously fathered a series of goddesses. The sequence began when he had relations with the chthonic deity Nintur (= Ninhursag), who birthed his daughter (Ninmu). Enki then had relations with Ninmu, who birthed his granddaughter (Ninkurra). When Ninkurra birthed Enki's great-granddaughter, Uttu, however, things became more complicated. Ninhursag counseled Uttu to reject Enki's sexual advances until he offered her a gift of apples, cucumbers, and grapes. Enki accomplished this by providing the waters for human agriculture, which, of course, resulted in apple, cucumber, and grape offerings that he could offer to Uttu. Thereafter Uttu slept with him, but instead of bearing yet another divine offspring, this time Ninhursag used Enki's semen to create eight plants. Enki then ate these plants in order that he might "know" them and set their destiny, but this angered Ninhursag, who vowed to withdraw from Enki and the divine council until Enki was dead. In her absence Enki soon grew both sad and weak, so that the Annunaki—the great gods—sought help from a fox who could lure Ninhursag back to them. The fox quickly accomplished this, and upon her return Ninhursag healed Enki's eight injuries by birthing eight new deities—one for each plant that Enki had eaten. The last of these deities was Ensak, lord of Dilmun. So the story begins with the creation of Dilmun and ends with the birth of its patron deity.

This myth viewed Enki's sexual activity as agriculturally productive, so that his relationship with Ninhursag caused "his phallus to water the dikes." Enki's pursuit of sexuality through the giving of gifts also had this productive effect because the gifts were acquired from human agriculture, requiring that he water the land appropriately. On the other hand, when no sexual partners were accessible to Enki and when the mother goddess Ninhursag withdrew her life-giving powers, Enki's weakness led to drought and agricultural blight. The text therefore supposes a divine explanation for variations in the supply of water, and it also provides an etiology for the presence of good aquifers in ancient Dilmun (Larsen). An implicit but more important theme of the text is the emergence of Dilmun's economic prosperity. According to Jacobsen, this suggests that the myth's author combined pleasure and politics to entertain Dilmunite traders visiting in the Sumerian port of Ur.

Texts and translations: P. ATTINGER, "Enki et Ninhursaga," *ZA* 74 (1984): 1–52; S. N. KRAMER, *Enki and Ninhursag: A Sumerian "Paradise" Myth* (ASOR Supplementary Studies 1; New Haven: American Schools of Oriental Research, 1945). *Translations: ANET* 37–41; JACOBSEN, *The Harps That Once,* 181–83. *Bibliography:* B. ALSTER, "Dilmun, Bahrain, and the Alleged Paradise in Sumerian Myth and Literature," in *Dilmun* (ed. Potts), 39–74; B. F. BATTO, "Paradise Reexamined," in *The Biblical Canon in Comparative Perspective* (ed. K. L. Younger Jr., W. W. Hallo, and B. F. Batto; Scripture in Context 4; Lewiston, N.Y.: Mellen, 1992), 33–66; CLIFFORD, *Creation Accounts in the Ancient Near East and in the Bible,* 35–38; T. JACOBSEN, "The Eridu Genesis," *JBL* 100 (1981): 513–29; KRAMER and MAIER, *Myths of*

Enki, the Crafty God, 22–30; C. E. LARSEN, "The Early Environment and Hydrology of Ancient Bahrain," in *Dilmun* (ed. Potts), 3–22.

Enki and Ninmaḫ. Compositionally speaking, this creation story should be compared with the previous myth of Enki and Ninhursag (= Ninmaḫ), which also combined two originally separate stories (Jacobsen). In the first episode, the minor gods complained that their physical labors on behalf of the gods were too great to bear. Wise Enki then proposed a solution—the creation of humanity—which he asked his mother Nammu to implement. With the goddess Ninmaḫ serving as her midwife, Nammu used the moist clay of Apsu to produce human beings "without the sperm of a male," so that humans resulted from the joining of Enki's rational wisdom (represented by the waters of Apsu) with Nammu's physical properties as the womb goddess. At this point the second story begins, and we find ourselves at a feast in celebration of humanity's creation. As inebriation took hold of the divine celebrants, Ninmaḫ challenged Enki and asserted her prerogative as midwife to determine what would become of her human creation, for good or ill. Enki in turn claimed that he could mitigate any ill she created. In response, Ninmaḫ used the moist clay of Apsu to create a series of human misfits, each with a physical defect. But Enki found a station in life for each of the handicapped souls. Having endured the challenge, Enki then produced a creature from clay and asked Ninmaḫ to produce a woman to birth it. But the creature, Umul, was born prematurely, so that Ninmaḫ was unable to care for it. For reasons that are not entirely clear, Ninmaḫ's defeat threatened her chief city: "My city is destroyed, my house wrecked, my children taken captive, I am a fugitive driven out of Ekur, I myself, even, have not escaped out of your hands!" Enki responded with the encouragement that only Ninmaḫ could provide what Umul needed: full gestation in the womb (Kilmer). The text then concludes with a reminder that life requires both Enki and Ninmaḫ but that Enki bested Ninmaḫ in the contest. Hence, the two myths combined in this exemplar each illustrate that both male and female are necessary for human procreation. They also provide mythical etiologies for the existence of handicapped human beings and, presumably, for premature births.

Text and translation: BENITO, "'Enki and Ninmah' and 'Enki and the World Order.'" *Translations: COS* 1.159: 516–18; JACOBSEN, *The Harps That Once,* 151–66. *Bibliography:* CLIFFORD, *Creation Accounts in the Ancient Near East and in the Bible,* 39–46; A. D. KILMER, "Speculations on Umul, the First Baby," in *Kramer Anniversary Volume: Cuneiform Studies in Honor of Samuel Noah Kramer* (ed. B. L. Eichler; AOAT 25; Kevelaer, Germany: Butzon & Bercker, 1976), 265–70; KRAMER and MAIER, *Myths of Enki, the Crafty God,* 31–37; J. SAUREN, "Nammu and Enki," in *The Tablet and the Scroll: Near Eastern Studies in Honor of William W. Hallo* (ed. M. E. Cohen, D. C. Snell, and D. B. Weisberg; Bethesda, Md.: CDL Press, 1993), 198–208.

Enki and the World Order. In this myth Enki is praised for his success in establishing the order of creation. He assigned the gods to their respective temples and duties, created sweet waters and fertile soil, established the nations and their boundaries, and bestowed upon humanity all implements of life and culture. At one point Enki decreed the destinies of several cities and nations, pronouncing blessings upon Mesopotamia's cities and curses upon their traditional enemies. This motif is similar to the blessings and curses pronounced by certain biblical figures, such as Jacob (Gen 49) and Moses (Deut 33). Concluding the myth is a complaint from the goddess Inanna, who apparently felt shortchanged in Enki's division of divine labor. Enki responds with praise for the goddess, but the text peters out at that point. It is likely that the emphasis on Inanna at the text's conclusion reflects a theological effort to explain her prominence among the gods (Kramer and Maier).

Text and translation: BENITO, " 'Enki and Ninmah' and 'Enki and the World Order.' " *Bibliography:* CLIFFORD, *Creation Accounts in the Ancient Near East and in the Bible,* 34–35; KRAMER and MAIER, *Myths of Enki, the Crafty God,* 38–56 (with translation and commentary).

Enki and Inanna: The Theft of the Arts of Civilization. This broken text recounts an effort by the goddess Inanna (i.e., Venus) to pilfer the cultural norms (the ME) from Enki's abode at Eridu and return them to her native city of Uruk. She succeeded in this endeavor (Kramer and Maier), but at least one scholar speculates that Enki punished Inanna by making her descend and return from the underworld in an eternal cycle (see Alster). Human beings were similarly punished by a cycle of propagation and death; they could enjoy the benefits of the ME, but no individual could enjoy them forever. Regardless of how one interprets the exemplar, especially valuable for students of wisdom literature and Mesopotamian civilization is the text's enumeration of ninety-four ME that represented the fundamental powers, duties, norms, and standards that made civilized life possible. For more on the ME, see 2.1.

Text and translation: G. FARBER-FLÜGGE, *Der Mythos Inanna und Enki unter besondere Berücksichtigung der Liste der me* (Studia Pohl 10; Rome: Biblical Institute Press, 1973). *Translation:* COS 1.161: 522–26. *Bibliography:* B. ALSTER, "On the Interpretation of the Sumerian Myth 'Inanna and Enki,'" ZA 64 (1974): 20–34; KRAMER and MAIER, *Myths of Enki, the Crafty God,* 57–68 (with translation and commentary).

The Eridu Genesis. The so-called Eridu Genesis is a fragmentary but fascinating text whose structure is similar to that of Gen 1–11. The oldest exemplar is from ca. 1600 B.C.E. Though it is missing the first two-thirds of a six-column tablet, the essential outline of the plot can be tentatively reconstructed from versions of the same tradition. Extant portions of the text begin with Nintur's pity for the nomadic existence of human beings. This she remedied by establishing civilization, founding cities, and providing kingship. Eridu was named as the first city and was given to Enki, followed by the creation of several other cities that were in turn bestowed upon their patron deities. Later versions of the text show that this section probably included a list of antediluvian rulers as well. Following a break in the text, we meet a saddened Nintur, mourning because the great gods had decreed a flood to destroy her human creation. But Enki interceded by warning Ziusudra (cf. Utnapishtim, Atrahasis), the Sumerian flood hero, who constructed a boat and was saved from the flood. In the end, Ziusudra was rewarded with eternal life in Dilmun. Thus there were three main themes in the Eridu Genesis: (1) the creation of civilization, (2) the flood, and (3) the flood hero (see Civil).

Texts and translations: T. JACOBSEN, "The Eridu Genesis," *JBL* 100 (1981): 513–29; A. POEBEL, *Historical and Grammatical Texts* (PBS 5; Philadelphia: University Museum, 1914). *Translations: COS* 1.158: 513–15; JACOBSEN, *Harps That Once,* 145–50. *Bibliography:* M. CIVIL, "The Sumerian Flood Story," in W. G. LAMBERT and A. R. MILLARD, *Atrahasis: The Babylonian Story of the Flood* (Oxford: Clarendon, 1969; repr., Winona Lake, Ind.: Eisenbrauns, 1999), 138–45; P. D. MILLER, "Eridu, Dunnu, and Babel: A Study in Comparative Mythology," *HAR* 9 (1985): 227–51.

The Assur Bilingual Creation Story (KAR 4). This eleventh-century bilingual myth is from the library of Tiglath-pileser I. Although it could be an Akkadian translation of an older Sumerian composition, the Sumerian seems very late, and some of the text's motifs appear only in Akkadian myths (especially the use of divine blood to create human beings). It is perhaps better to view the text as a bilingual composition from its inception. The myth begins with the first acts of creation after heaven and earth had been separated and after the gods had established their plan (GIŠ.ḪUR) for the cosmos. At this point the gods created the Tigris, the Euphrates, and an irrigation system, and then they slew two rebel deities and used their blood to create human beings to do the work of the gods. The first human couple, named Ullegarra and Annegarra, were planted in Nippur and were commanded to "multiply" and see to the prosperity of the land, cattle, sheep, animals, fishes, and birds. The myth includes features that parallel motifs in the creation story of Gen 1 (the themes of proliferation, human dominion, and prosperity/blessing) and especially in the creation story of Gen 2 (the first human couple, symbolic names for the couple, rivers in their primeval home, and the task of cultivation).

Text and translation: G. PETTINATO, *Das altorientalische Menschenbild und die sumerischen und akkadischen Schöpfungsmythen* (Heidelberg: Winter, 1971), 74–81. *Translations and discussions: BM*[3], 491–93; J. BOTTÉRO and S. N. KRAMER, *Lorsque les dieux faisaient l'homme: Mythologie mésopotamienne* (Paris: Gallimard, 1989), 77–79; CLIFFORD, *Creation Accounts in the Ancient Near East and in the Bible,* 49–51.

The Bilingual Creation of the World by Marduk. Although preserved on a Late Babylonian tablet from Sippar, it is likely that this bilingual myth goes back to an earlier Sumerian composition in which Enki rather than Marduk played the chief role. As the text begins, the primeval cosmos included only the sea and a water pipe, which presumably connected the upper world to the sweet waters of Apsu below. Although the text is broken, it appears that Marduk's creative acts were as follows: (1) the creation of his "Eridu," i.e., Babylon and Marduk's temple, Esagil [note that Eridu was the sacred city of Enki]; (2) the creation of dry land, which was formed by placing soil upon a raft floated in the sea; (3) the creation of human beings, animals, and geographical features; (4) establishment of the boundaries between dry land and the sea by Enki and Marduk jointly; and (5) the formation of bricks, brick molds, cities (Nippur; Uruk), and temples (Ekur; Eanna). This text obviously has many affinities with other Mesopotamian creation myths as well as with the biblical traditions in Genesis, but its idiosyncrasies are visible as well. Perhaps its most notable feature is that the creation of some cities and of Marduk's temple takes place before the formation of dry land.

Text: CT 13, plates 35–38. *Translations: BM³,* 491–93; J. BOTTÉRO, *Mythes et rites de Babylone* (Paris: Champion, 1985), 302–12. *Bibliography:* HEIDEL, *The Babylonian Genesis,* 68–71; HOROWITZ, *Mesopotamian Cosmic Geography,* 129–32.

The Ninurta Myth, Lugal-E. This epic myth, known by its incipit, Lugal-E, combines three originally separate myths about Ninurta, the god of spring thunderstorms and floods. The first episode recounts his victory over Azag, an opponent in the mountains; the second, the irrigation engineering by which he guided mountain waters into the Tigris River basin each year; and the third, how Ninurta determined the destinies of different types of stone by passing judgment on them. All three tales appear to have been etiological, the first two accounting for Ninurta's power to control mountain waters and the third explaining the properties and typical uses of different kinds of stone.

Text and translation: J. VAN DIJK, *LUGAL UD ME-LÁM-bi NIR-GÁL: Le récit épique et didactique des travaux de Ninurta, du déluge, et de la nouvelle création* (2 vols.; Leiden: Brill, 1983). *Translation:* JACOBSEN, *The Harps That Once,* 233–72. *Bibliography:* J. A. BLACK, "Some structural features of Sumerian narrative poetry," in *Mesopotamian Epic Literature: Oral or Aural?* (ed. M. E. Vogelzang and H. L. J. Vanstiphout; Lewiston, N.Y.: Edwin Mellen, 1992), 71–101; M. J. GELLER, "Notes on Lugale," *BASOR* 8 (1985): 215–22.

The Marriage of Amurru. This fragmentary Sumerian text (CBS 14061) was discovered in the temple library at Nippur and dates from about 2000 B.C.E. Modern scholars normally relate the text to the appearance of new Amorite populations in Mesopotamia around the end of the third millennium B.C.E. (see Mendenhall). The central theme of the myth seems to be the desire of the god Amurru (dMARTU) to find a wife in order to secure better offerings, presumably because offering portions corresponded to the number of members in each family. Kupper has shown that the protagonist deity, Amurru, was an entirely new god invented as a part of the Mesopotamian's effort to integrate the rise of the Amorites into their theology. In introducing Amurru to the Mesopotamian pantheon, the Sumerians did not fail to satirize the new Amorite arrivals, whom they characterized as uncivilized nomads who ate raw meat, did not bury their dead, and did not live in houses.

Texts and translations: E. CHIERA, *Sumerian Epics and Myths* (OIP 15, Cuneiform Series 3; Chicago: University of Chicago Press, 1934), 67–68; IDEM, *Sumerian Religious Texts* (Crozer Theological Seminary Babylonian Publications 1; Upland, Penn.: n.p., 1924),

14–23. *Bibliography:* S. N. KRAMER, *Sumerian Mythology* (New York: Harper & Brothers, 1961), 98–101; J.-R. KUPPER, *L'iconographie du dieu Amurru* (Brussels: n.p., 1961); G. E. MENDENHALL, "Amorites," *ABD* 1:199–202; J. N. POSTGATE, *Early Mesopotamia: Society and Economy at the Dawn of History* (London: Routledge, 1992), 84, 271.

Dumuzi and Inanna Myths. Sumerian traditions about the relationship between Dumuzi and Inanna were mythologically important, particularly because of their theme of the dying and rising deity, whose disposition was believed to reflect the undulating tides of the annual agricultural cycle. Although these texts would fit here nicely, for the sake of convenience the Dumuzi/Inanna myths are handled in our discussion of love poetry (see 4.1).

10.1.2. Akkadian Myths

Atrahasis. The story of Atrahasis has often been called the Mesopotamian flood story, but this epic tale was thematically more complex. The plot initially unfolds as a conflict between the lower gods (the Igigi) and the more powerful gods, led by Enlil (the Anunnaki). Weary from the task of digging irrigation canals, these weaker deities picketed Enlil's residence and demanded release from their menial tasks. In response, Enlil determined to create human beings as an alternative labor force to "carry the toil of the gods." Using the design of the wise god Enki, the birth goddess (Nintu) fashioned humanity by mixing clay with the blood of a slain god, one of the rebel deities. This use of divine blood had two unanticipated effects: humans were both immortal and rebellious. Consequently, after twelve hundred years of growth, humanity had developed into a noisy and clamoring presence that disturbed Enlil's sleep. Although Enlil sought to reduce this human population through plague, drought, and famine, Enki, who sought to preserve his creation, each time thwarted these genocidal strategies. In a final act of desperation, Enlil and the other gods purposed to destroy humanity in a great flood.

Although the gods nearly succeeded in this endeavor, the ever wise Enki intervened by covertly instructing one of his devotees, Atrahasis ("extra wise"), to build a boat. Atrahasis did so, taking both his family and all species of animals on board. Meanwhile, as the great storm began and intensified, the gods and goddesses had to reckon with the unanticipated problem that their source of food and drink—the sacrifices—had perished with humanity. As a result, when the flood ended and the pious Atrahasis offered his sacrifices, the deities were drawn to his offerings "like flies." Only Enlil appears to have been disturbed by the survival of Atrahasis, but even he was finally won over by Enki. The text concludes with Enlil's request that Enki and Nintu take steps to control the population growth of humanity. This was accomplished by establishing certain classes of people who would not bear children (priestesses), by allowing demons to rob human mothers of their offspring, and by decreeing human death for the first time. Atrahasis was therefore an etiological tale that explained both the origins of humanity and its mortality, and it did so by combining the creation and flood traditions into a single narrative framework. In its basic structure and even in some of its details, Atrahasis is very close to what we have in the primeval history of Gen 1–11, especially regarding the flood tradition (Gen 6–9). For this reason, many scholars believe that the Genesis author was familiar with Atrahasis or with a similar text.

Our oldest copies of Atrahasis, from the Old Babylonian period, are nearly identical to our first-millennium Neo-Assyrian copies. For texts and translations, see Lambert and Millard.

Text and translation: W. G. LAMBERT and A. R. MILLARD, *Atra-Hasis: The Babylonian Story of the Flood* (Oxford: Clarendon, 1969; repr., Winona Lake, Ind: Eisenbrauns, 1999). *Translations: ANET* 104–6, 512–14; *COS* 1.130: 450–52; DALLEY, *Myths from Mesopotamia,* 1–38. *Bibliography:* D. M. CARR, *Reading the Fractures of Genesis: Historical and Literary Approaches* (Louisville: Westminster John Knox, 1996), 241–46; W. M. CLARK, "The Flood and the Structure of the Prepatriarchal History," *ZAW* 83 (1971): 184–211; I. M. KIKIWADA and A. QUINN, *Before Abraham Was: A Provocative Challenge to the Documentary Hypothesis* (Nashville: Abingdon, 1985); A. R. MILLARD, "A New Babylonian 'Genesis' Story," *TynBul* 18 (1967): 3–18; W. L. MORAN, "The Creation of Man in Atrahasis I 192–248," *BASOR* 200 (1970): 48–56; IDEM, "Some Consideration of Form and Interpretation in Atrahasis," in *Language, Literature, and History: Philological and Historical Studies Presented to Erica Reiner* (ed. Francesca Rochberg-Halton; AOS 67; New Haven: American Oriental Society, 1987), 245–56; R. A. ODEN JR., "Divine Aspirations in Atrahasis and in Genesis 1–11," *ZAW* 93 (1981): 197–216; VON SODEN, "Konflicte und ihre Bewältigung in babylonischen Schöpfungs-und Fluterzählungen."

The Myth of Anzu. The popular modern title is something of a misnomer because the myth's two versions, Old Babylonian and Standard Babylonian, were not composed to honor Anzu so much as the gods Ningirsu (OB) and Ninurta (SB). The tale's plot pivoted on the "tablet of destinies," which gave its possessor the authority to "decree the fates" for both the gods and human beings. The tablet was stolen from the great god Enlil by his trusted doorkeeper, Anzu, prompting an all-out effort by the gods to recover it. The heroic response eventually came from Enlil's son, Ningirsu, who defeated Anzu, recovered the tablet of destinies, and was subsequently praised by the gods with a list of honorific epithets. In the Standard Babylonian version, the chief protagonist Ningirsu (patron god of Girsu) was replaced by Ninurta, whose cult center was at Kalḫu. As we shall see, the Anzu Myth inspired many features in the later but better-known creation myth *Enuma Elish.*

Texts and translations: A. ANNUS, *The Standard Babylonian Epic of Anzu* (SAA Cuneiform Texts; Helsinki: Helsinki University Press, 2001); W. W. HALLO and W. MORAN, "The First Tablet of the SB Recension of the Anzu Myth," *JCS* 31 (1979): 65–115; B. HRUŠKA, *Der Mythenadler Anzu in der Literatur und Vorstellung des alten Mesopotamien* (Budapest: n.p., 1975); H. W. F. SAGGS, "Additions to Anzu," *AfO* 33 (1986): 1–29; M. E. VOGELZANG, *Bin Šar Dadmē: Edition and Analysis of the Akkadian Anzu Poem* (Groningen, Neth.: Styx, 1988). *Translations: ANET* 111–13; DALLEY, *Myths from Mesopotamia,* 203–27.

Enuma Elish. This seven-tablet epic myth was known in antiquity by its incipit ("When on high . . ."), which was composed to mimic the title of Atrahasis,

Inūma ilu awīlum ("when the gods like men"). This and other evidence suggests that *Enuma Elish* was deliberately fashioned to supplant the older Atrahasis story (Batto). The epic began with a theogony, when the mingling waters of the oldest primordial beings, Apsu (waters of earth) and Tiamat (waters of the sea), produced the first generation of gods and goddesses [Note that Apsu and Tiamat do not appear to be deities]. Soon after their birth, however, this noisy generation of young deities annoyed father Apsu, who then moved—against the wishes of his wife, Tiamat—to destroy them. This plan was thwarted when Ea (= Enki), the god of wisdom, recited a magic spell and killed Apsu. Ea then built his abode upon the waters of Apsu, which served as the explanation for Ea's status as the god of fresh water and "king of Apsu." Here, in this holy temple, Ea and his spouse Damkina conceived Marduk, the patron deity of Babylon and key protagonist of our story.

Meanwhile Ea's murder of Apsu naturally enraged his consort, Tiamat. She was a formidable opponent surrounded by a host of demons, including Kingu, a powerful demon god whom Tiamat had adopted as her new consort and to whom she had entrusted the "tablet of destinies," which gave its possessor the authority to "decree the fates" for both the gods and human beings. When Ea and all other deities recoiled from this hoard of demon gods, Marduk agreed to battle Tiamat in exchange for the authority to decree the fates. When the gods agreed to these terms, Marduk waged his war against the forces of chaos. He let loose a wind into Tiamat's mouth, shot an arrow into her distended belly, and extinguished her life. When her supporting cast dispersed in response, Marduk seized Kingu and the tablet of destinies.

With his victory secured, Marduk turned his attention to creation. He split the body of Tiamat into two parts, "like a fish for drying," and fashioned the heavens from one half and the earth from the other. After placing the sun, moon, and twelve constellations in the heavens, Marduk concluded his creative work by providing the blueprint for human beings, whose service would alleviate the toil of the gods. The wise god Ea then fashioned human beings according to Marduk's plan, using the blood of the rebel demon-god Kingu as the life force to animate humanity. In honor of this feat, the gods constructed the city of Babylon and Marduk's temple-home, Esagil. The epic concludes with the gods proclaiming Marduk's glory by pronouncing his fifty names. Although the tablet of destinies was ultimately returned to the high god Anu, the epilogue nonetheless says that Marduk was "the Enlil of the gods . . . the utterance of his mouth no god shall change." The praise here lauded upon Marduk reflects the transition of this Mesopotamian tradition from a creation myth to a national myth with Babylon as its focus. Obviously, praise for Babylon's chief god did not play well in rival Assyria, where versions of *Enuma Elish* featured Assur in the place of Marduk (Lambert, 1997).

Enuma Elish shares several important motifs with the Anzu Myth, including the tablet of destinies, the conflict between the good and evil gods, and the pronouncement of special names upon the victor. The author of *Enuma Elish*, or someone who influenced him, apparently took up themes used to honor Ninurta in the Anzu Myth and transferred them to Marduk (Lambert, 1986). Although some scholars associate this exaltation of Marduk with Nebuchadnezzar I's restoration of the god's statue to Babylon (from Elam in the twelfth century B.C.E.), Dalley suggests that the text was quite a bit older. At any rate, although *Enuma Elish* was composed as a piece of theological propaganda, it later became an important part of the annual Akitu festival (see 5.5), during which the myth was recited because it was believed that narrating Marduk's victory over demons would repel demons from the temple during the festival. We have already highlighted a similar use of myth in the rituals of ancient Egypt (see above). Many scholars believe that *Enuma Elish* influenced the author of the biblical creation story in Gen 1 (Batto), in which Yahweh moved over the watery *tehom* (cf. Tiamat, the primeval sea), separated the waters above from the waters below (cf. the splitting of Tiamat by Marduk), and then created the heavenly bodies and human life (the sequence as in *Enuma Elish*).

Texts and translations: L. W. KING, *The Seven Tablets of Creation, or The Babylonian and Assyrian Legends Concerning the Creation of the World and of Mankind* (2 vols.; London: Luzac, 1902); R. LABAT, *Le poème babylonien de la création* (Paris: Adrien-Maissonneuve, 1935); W. G. LAMBERT and P. WALCOT, "A New Babylonian Theogony and Hesiod," *Kadmos* 4 (1965): 64–72. *Translations: ANET* 60–72, 501–3; *COS* 1.111: 390–402; DALLEY, *Myths from Mesopotamia,* 228–77. *Bibliography:* B. F. BATTO, "Creation Theology in Genesis," in *Creation in the Biblical Traditions* (ed. Clifford and Collins), 16–38; HEIDEL, *The Babylonian Genesis;* T. JACOBSEN, "The Battle between Marduk and Tiamat," *JAOS* 88 (1968): 104–8; W. G. LAMBERT, "The Assyrian Recension of Enuma Eliš," in *Assyrien im Wandel der Zeiten: XXXIXe Rencontre assyriologique internationale* (ed. H. Waetzoldt and H. Hauptmann; Heidelberg: Heidelberger Orientverlag, 1997), 77–79; IDEM, "Kosmogonie," *RlA* 6:218–22; IDEM, "Ninurta Mythology in the Babylonian Epic of Creation," in *Keilschriftliche Literaturen: Ausgewählte Vorträge der XXXII. Rencontre assyriologique internationale* (RAI 32; ed. K. Hecker and W. Sommerfeld; BBVO 6; Berlin: Dietrich Reimer, 1986), 55–60; TSUMURA, *The Earth and the Waters in Genesis 1 and 2;* VON SODEN, "Konflikte und ihre Bewältigung in babylonischen Schöpfungs-und Fluterzählungen."

The Flood Tradition in the Gilgamesh Epic. An alternative to the Atrahasis creation story thus appears in *Enuma Elish.* In addition, an alternative to the Atrahasis flood story appears in the eleventh tablet of the Gilgamesh Epic (see 9.1.1). As pointed out in the previous chapter, the epic describes Gilgamesh as a man deeply troubled by his own mortality, especially after the death of his companion Enkidu. It was this problem that led Gilgamesh to visit the flood hero, Utnapishtim (cf. Atrahasis or Ziusudra), the only human being who had not experienced death. When Gilgamesh asked Utnapishtim how he had acquired immortality, Utnapishtim's answer was the flood story.

Utnapishtim explained to Gilgamesh that when the gods purposed the great flood, Ea had secretly warned him to build a ship and escape its effects. He completed the ark, whose dimensions were those of a great cube, in only seven days. Utnapishtim then loaded the boat with provisions, his family, and animals. The deluge that followed frightened even the gods. After seven days of torrential

rain and storm, the ship came to a rest atop Mount Nisir. Utnapishtim then released a series of birds—two doves followed by a swallow—in order to seek out
dry land. The last bird succeeded, and they disembarked. His first action was to
offer a sacrifice to the gods, which delighted them because they hungered from
the lack of sacrifices—an unanticipated consequence of the flood. Enlil, however,
was none too pleased by this outcome and indicted Ea for being disloyal to the
gods. Even so, Ea was able to calm Enlil so that immortality could be conferred
upon Utnapishtim and his wife. Although the story is fascinating, its implications
for Gilgamesh were straightforward: there was no way to duplicate Utnapishtim's
unique experience in order to acquire immortality. As consolation, Utnapishtim
told Gilgamesh of a plant in the depths of Apsu that had the power to restore
youth and preserve life. Although Gilgamesh followed this advice and successfully retrieved the plant, a serpent subsequently purloined it. This is clearly an etiology for the serpentine habit of shedding and renewing skin: "As [the snake]
took it away, it shed its scaly skin." Gilgamesh's quest for immortality had
obviously ended in failure and disappointment.

The biblical materials in Genesis dovetail with this episode in Gilgamesh at
two key points. Most obvious is the connection with the flood story in Gen 6–9,
which in almost every respect is quite close to the Mesopotamian version (see
Heidel). The other motif concerns the plant of life and its theft by a serpent,
which reminds us of the biblical episode in which the serpent robbed Adam and
Eve of their access to the tree of life (Gen 3). This might imply that the biblical
tree of life should be understood as bestowing immortality not through a single
eating of its fruit but rather through the continuing renewal its fruit offered.

Texts and translations: See "The Gilgamesh Epic" in 9.1.1. ***Bibliography:*** J. AZZOPARDI,
"The Flood in Genesis and the Epic of Gilgamesh," *MelT* 32 (1981): 1–5; E. FISHER,
"Gilgamesh and Genesis: The Flood Story in Context." *CBQ* 32 (1970): 392–402; A. HEI-
DEL, *The Gilgamesh Epic and Old Testament Parallels* (Chicago: University of Chicago
Press, 1949); S. W. HOLLOWAY, "What Ship Goes There: The Flood Narrative in the
Gilgamesh Epic and Genesis Reconsidered in Light of Ancient Near Eastern Temple Ideol-
ogy," *ZAW* 103 (1991): 328–55; I. RAPAPORT, *Tablet XI of the Gilgamesh Epic and the Biblical
Flood Story: A Refutation of the Generally Held View That Genesis Chapters 6–9 Is Based
upon a Babylonian Prototype* (Tel Aviv: Tel Aviv University Press, 1981); G. J. WENHAM,
"The Coherence of the Flood Narrative," *VT* 28 (1978): 336–48.

The Story of Adapa. Lost immortality is also a central theme in the mythical tale
of the great pre-flood *apkallu* sage, Adapa (see 2.1; for an ancient *apkallu* list, see
the Sumerian King List in 11.1). Adapa's story began with an act of hubris in
which he cursed the south wind and so angered the great god Anu. Adapa was
quickly ushered into the divine court for trial, but Anu pitied Adapa because his
wisdom and hubris were not his own doing; rather, the god Ea had disclosed to
Adapa "what pertains to heaven and earth." For this reason, in lieu of punishment, Anu offered to Adapa the "water" and "food" of [immortal] life, an offer
that Adapa refused because he was warned to forego it by his patron deity, Ea.
When Adapa naively obeyed Ea's instructions, Anu responded, "Come, Adapa,

why didn't you eat? Why didn't you drink? Didn't you want to be immortal? . . . Take him and send him back to his earth." So, in the final analysis, Ea disclosed to Adapa the wisdom of heaven and earth, but he also deceived Adapa in the matter of immortality, perhaps because he did not wish to lose the service of this wise devotee. The theme of human mortality was obviously an important one in Mesopotamian literature, for it appears in narrative traditions as early as the Sumerian Gilgamesh stories and continues down into the later traditions of the Gilgamesh Epic, Atrahasis, and Adapa; mortality was also an important theme in Mesopotamia's wisdom tradition.

Our best copy of Adapa was discovered in the fourteenth-century B.C.E. Amarna archive, where Egyptian scribes apparently used it to study Akkadian and as a source of cultural insight. One peculiarity of this exemplar is that the scribes attempted to mark off the text's poetic meter with a series of red dots—obvious evidence of their literary interests. Both earlier and later fragments of Adapa survive. Neo-Assyrian copies show that the text was known down into the first millennium, and a Sumerian copy from the Old Babylonian period suggests both the antiquity and the original language of the text. Both the Sumerian and the Neo-Assyrian copies contain conclusions that mark them as ritual incantations, and the Sumerian copy, which has been announced but not published (see Cavigneaux and al-Rawi), is also peculiar because it formed part of a larger narrative that described the time just after the deluge, with the ensuing feeding of the gods and the organization of humankind.

Adapa is an important comparative exemplar for students of the Hebrew Bible. Not only might Adapa's name be understood, like Adam's, to mean "human being" (Sumerian A.DA.AB, Akkadian *a-mi-lu*, "man"; see Batto); the two tales also share the following themes: (1) portrayal of the protagonists as primeval humans; (2) the problem of humans with divine knowledge; (3) the revelation of divine knowledge by a crafty god/creature (i.e., the serpent and Ea); (4) the problem of hubris; (5) a missed opportunity for immortality; (6) the deception of human beings; and (7) the consumption of food as a metaphor for knowledge/immortality. The wide geographical and chronological distribution of Adapa suggests that Hebrew writers would have had ample opportunity to become familiar with this Mesopotamian text.

Texts and translations: S. IZRE'EL, *Adapa and the South Wind: Language Has the Power of Life and Death* (MC 11; Winona Lake, Ind.: Eisenbrauns, 2001); J. KNUDTZON, *Die El-Amarna Tafeln* (2 vols.; Vorderasiastische Bibliothek 2; Leipzig: Hinrichs, 1906–1915), 1:964–68 (Amarna copy). *Translations:* ANET 101–3; COS 1.129: 449; S. DALLEY, *Myths from Mesopotamia,* 181–88. *Bibliography:* N. E. ANDREASEN, "Adam and Adapa: Two Anthropological Characters," *AUSS* 19 (1981): 179–81; B. F. BATTO, *Slaying the Dragon: Mythmaking in the Biblical Tradition* (Louisville: Westminster John Knox, 1992); J. D. BING, "Adapa and Humanity: Mortal or Evil?" *JANES* 18 (1986): 1–2; IDEM, "Adapa and Immortality," *UF* 16 (1984): 53–56; G. BUCCELLATI, "Adapa, Genesis, and the Notion of Faith," *UF* 5 (1973): 61–66; E. BURROWS, "A Note on Adapa," *Or* 30 (1928): 24; A. CAVIGNEAUX and F. AL-RAWI, "New Literary Texts from Tell Haddad (Ancient Meturan): A First Survey," *Iraq* 55 (1993): 232–48; W. W. HALLO, "Adapa Reconsidered: Life and Death in Contextual

Perspective," *Scriptura* 87 (2004): 267–77; IZRE'EL, *The Amarna Scholarly Tablets;* T. JACOB-SEN, "The Investiture and Anointing of Adapa in Heaven," *AJSL* 46 (1930): 201–3; D. MANFRIED, "Wurde Adapa um das ewige Leben betrogen? Der Amarna-Text 356 und sein Beitrag zur Traditionsgeschichte babylonischer Mythen in Ägypten," *Mitteilungen für Anthropologie und Religionsgeschichte* 6 (1991): 119–32; P. MICHALOWSKI, "Adapa and the Ritual Process," *Rocznik orientalistyczny* 41, no. 2 (1980): 77–82; H.-P. MÜLLER, "Erkenntis und Verfehlung: Prototypen und Antitypen zu Gen 2–3 in der altorientalischen Literatur," in *Glaube und Toleranz: Das theologische Erbe der Aufklärung* (ed. T. Rendtorff; Gütersloh: Gütersloher Verlagshaus Gerd Mohn, 1982), 191–210; IDEM, "Mythos als Gattung archaischen Erzählens und die Geschichte von Adapa," *AfO* 29–30 (1983–1984): 75–89; W. H. SHEA, "Adam in Ancient Mesopotamian Traditions," *AUSS* 15 (1977): 27–41.

Nergal and Ereškigal. According to this myth, Ereškigal, goddess of the underworld, beguiled the war god Nergal into taking up residence with her in the land of the dead. Nergal went to the underworld to meet the legendary queen, who charmed him into sharing her bed and so sealed his doom. Because of Nergal's copulation with Ereshkigal, the gods refused his return to the heavens. Thus the two wedded and became the joint overseers of the underworld. Our copies of the myth include a fourteenth-century exemplar from the Amarna archive (EA 357) as well as later copies from Sultantepe (seventh century B.C.E.; see Gurney) and Uruk (Seleucid period; see Hunger/von Weiher). The two later copies are substantially longer and more complex than the Amarna exemplar, so most scholars suspect that the Amarna version, though older, represents an abbreviated edition of the myth. Nevertheless, even with the three texts together, the story is incompletely preserved, and it is difficult to determine its theological significance for the ancients.

Texts and translations: O. R. GURNEY, "The Sultantepe Tablets, VII: The Myth of Nergal and Ereškigal," *AnSt* 10 (1960): 105–31 (Sultantepe version); H. HUNGER and E. VON WEIHER, eds., *Spätbabylonische Texte aus Uruk* (3 vols.; Ausgrabungen der Deutschen Forschungsgemeinschaft in Uruk-Waka 9, 10, 12; Berlin: Gebr. Mann, 1976–[1988]), 1:17–19 (Uruk version); IZRE'EL, *The Amarna Scholarly Tablets,* 51–61, 132–39 (Amarna version). ***Translations:*** *ANET* 103–4, 507–12; *COS* 1.109–10: 384–90; DALLEY, *Myths from Mesopotamia,* 163–81. ***Bibliography:*** M. HUTTER, *Altorientalische Vorstellungen von der Unterwelt: Literar-und religionsgeschichtliche Überlegungen zu "Nergal und Ereškigal"* (OBO 63; Freiburg, Switz.: Universitätsverlag, 1985); E. REINER, *Your Thwarts in Pieces, Your Mooring Rope Cut: Poetry from Babylonia and Assyria* (Ann Arbor: University of Michigan Press, 1985), 50–60.

The Erra Myth. Although our discussion of the Akkadian myths has been preoccupied with thematic concerns, at least one text provides a profound glimpse into the modal processes that produced these mythic compositions. The Erra Myth is a five-tablet myth composed to explain the twin disasters that befell Babylon sometime between 1100 and 750 B.C.E.: civil war within Babylon and the overrunning of its outlying client cities by nomadic invaders. The text explains how the chief god of Babylon, Marduk, was lured away from his city by a ruse when Erra (i.e., Nergal, plague god of the underworld) suggested that Marduk's temple was in need of repair. In Marduk's absence, Erra's influence spawned social upheaval and military disintegration in the Babylonian ranks, but upon Marduk's return, Erra confessed his error and promised to bless Babylon anew. Incidentally, it is interesting that in Marduk's speech the god credits himself with having sent the great flood.

The story is introduced with the formula of an oral epic, "I sing of the son of the king [Erra]," and follows with an extended dialogue rather than a full-blown narrative. For this reason, the "myth" label is a loose one. What is most important from a compositional perspective, however, is that the text's author, a Babylonian priest, provides very specific details about the mode of the myth's composition: "The one who put together the composition about him [i.e., Erra] was Kati-ilani-Marduk son of Dabibi. (Some god) revealed it to him in the middle of the night, and when he recited it upon waking, he did not leave anything out, nor add a single word." From this evidence we can deduce that one of two modes of composition were at work in the Erra Myth. We can first imagine that the priest's theological and mythological reflections upon Babylon's troubles induced the dream, which he interpreted as divine revelation. This is a very sensible reading of the situation, and we can with little doubt imagine that similar processes gave rise to many of the ancient myths. On the other hand, there is another less elegant modal possibility, perhaps best illustrated by the words of Socrates in Plato, *Republic* 3.21: "How, then," Socrates asks, "might we contrive one of those opportune falsehoods of which we were just now speaking, so as by one noble lie to persuade if possible the rulers themselves, but failing that the rest of the city?" (Shorey, 1:301). Two lines of evidence suggest that this second option may be the correct one. First, the author of the Erra Myth seems to have incorporated anachronisms that deliberately made the epic appear older than it was; and second, the reference to a "man of Akkad" who would restore Babylon appears to have been a pseudoprophecy, composed not centuries before but rather near the time of this new ruler (usually thought to be either Nabu-nasir, ca. 740 B.C.E., or Merodach-Baladan II, ca. 700 B.C.E.). In sum, although this myth might have come to the priest in a dream, it is more likely that Kabti-ilani-Marduk's myth was a "noble lie," crafted to encourage both the king and his people by painting Babylon's future in bright and promising colors. In any case, it is transparent that the Erra Myth was the product of a priest's mythological contemplation of world events.

As a theological explanation for the fall of Babylon, the Erra Myth is comparable to the Deuteronomistic History of the Hebrew Bible, which sought to provide a theological explanation for the Fall of Jerusalem and the subsequent deportation of Jews to Mesopotamia.

Text and translation: L. CAGNI, *The Poem of Erra* (SANE 1.3; Malibu, Calif.: Undena, 1977). *Translations: COS* 1.113: 404–16; DALLEY, *Myths from Mesopotamia,* 282–312. **Bibliography:** D. DAMROSCH, *The Narrative Covenant: Transformations of Genre in the Growth of Biblical Literature* (San Francisco: Harper & Row, 1987), 75–85; P. B. MACHINIST, "Rest and Violence in the Poem of Erra," in *Studies in Literature from the Ancient Near East: Dedicated to Samuel Noah Kramer* (ed. J. M. Sasson; AOS 65; New Haven: American Oriental Society, 1984), 221–26; P. SHOREY, ed., *Plato: The Republic* (LCL; Cambridge: Harvard University, 1930–35).

The Ordeal of Marduk. In his war to exterminate Babylon, the Neo-Assyrian king Sennacherib commissioned his scribes to produce a myth whose focal point was a divine legal proceeding in which the Babylonian god Marduk was found guilty. We do not possess copies of the myth itself, but five somewhat different versions of a Neo-Assyrian commentary on the myth have come to light (Livingstone, 1986). It is possible, perhaps even likely, that the text was composed when Sennacherib destroyed Babylon in 689 B.C.E. and deported Marduk's statue to Assyria (von Soden). A central purpose of the myth would have been to reconfigure theologically the annual Akitu festival so that Assur's theological prominence supplanted that of Marduk.

Texts, translations, and studies: A. LIVINGSTONE, *Court Poetry and Literary Miscellanea* (SAA 3; Helsinki: Helsinki University Press, 1989), xxix–xxx, 82–91; IDEM, *Mystical and Mythological Explanatory Works of Assyrian and Babylonian Scholars* (Oxford: Clarendon, 1986), 205–53; W. VON SODEN, "Gibt es ein Zeugnis dafür, dass die Babylonier an die Wiederauferstehung Marduks geglaubt haben?" *ZA* 51 (1955): 130–66.

A Myth of the King's Creation. This fragmentary text from the Vorderasiatisiches Museum of Berlin was composed in a Neo-Babylonian script and reflects motifs that are found in Atrahasis and *Enuma Elish.* Human beings were created to ease the labor of the gods, and then the king was created to rule humanity. The king's creation was prompted by Ea, who directed the birth goddess Belet-ili to form the king with attractive features and to endow him with the crown and with divine weapons. The text concludes by pronouncing curses upon anyone who rebelled against the king. This conclusion is very similar to Assurbanipal's coronation prayer (see "Akkadian Coronation Prayers" in 3.1.2) and suggests that our text may have been used in a similar ritual ceremony. Three similar texts in the Hebrew Bible include the description of the king of Tyre in Ezek 28:12–19, the creation of humanity in Gen 2, and the creation of the Israelite king in Ps 2:5.

Text and translation: W. R. MAYER, "Ein Mythos von der Erschaffung des Menschen und des Königs," *Or* 56 (1987): 55–68. *Translations: BM³,* 495–97; *COS* 1.146: 467–77. *Bibliography:* H.-P. MÜLLER, "Eine neue babylonische Menschenschöpfungserzählung im Licht keilschriftlicher und biblischer Parallelen: Zur Wirklichkeitsauffassung im Mythos," *Or* 58 (1989): 61–85; J. H. TIGAY, "Divine Creation of the King in Psalms 2:6," *ErIsr* 27 (2003): 246–51; J. VAN SETERS, "The Creation of Man and the Creation of the King," *ZAW* 101 (1989): 333–42.

Mesopotamian Cosmic Geographies. Biblical scholars are understandably interested in Mesopotamian cosmologies because these may help us to understand better the Israelite cosmologies in Genesis and in other biblical texts. The Mesopotamian creation myths and legends are important sources in this inquiry (e.g., *Enuma Elish,* Atrahasis, Etana Legend), but other cosmological and geographical texts should be considered. The most important exemplars are found in Horowitz's standard discussion, and here a few exemplars are highlighted: (1) Two Akkadian texts depict the universe as a structure composed of several heavenly and earthly levels. According to *KAR* 307, the universe includes three levels of heaven (upper, middle, and lower) and three terrestrial levels (upper, middle, and lower). Inhabiting these levels are Anu and the three hundred Igigi gods (upper heaven); Bel (i.e., Marduk) and other Igigi (middle heaven); the stars (lower heaven); humanity (upper earth); Ea (middle earth); and the six hundred Anunnaki gods, whom Marduk locked in the underworld because of their rebellion (lower earth). A shorter description of the heavens provided by AO 8196 matches *KAR* 307, but there is evidence for an earlier Sumerian conception of "seven heavens and seven earths" (Horowitz, 208–20). The Akkadian copies of these texts date to the first millennium, but it is likely that the texts go back to the Kassite period. (2) Various incantations, prayers, hymns, astronomical texts, and theological commentaries reflect Mesopotamian beliefs about the cosmos. Particularly interesting for students of the Hebrew Bible are texts that reveal the Mesopotamian belief that the heavens were composed of water (cf. Gen 1; Ps 104:3; 148:4). This is explicitly stated in *Enuma Elish* IV. 137–46 and is fleshed out in the ancient cosmological commentaries (e.g., series I.NAM.GIŠ.ḪUR.AN.KI.A; see Livingstone), which interpret the Akkadian word for "heavens" (*šamê*) as *ša mê* ("[made] of water"). As in Hebrew cosmology (Gen 7:11), rainfall was generally understood to come from heavenly ducts that allowed these waters to fall (see the prayer to An for Rim-Sîn in Charpin [= U 7745, originally published as UET 6: 102]). (3) An important geographical text is the Babylonian *mappa mundi* ("map of the world"), preserved on a late Akkadian tablet from Nippur (BM 92687). The exemplar provides a map with labeled features, noting not only sites within Mesopotamia but also features on the extreme horizon of terrestrial geography. For example, an arrow pointing north on the map is labeled the "Great Wall—6 leagues in between where the sun is not seen," probably reflecting the fact that the sun never appears in the northern sky from Mesopotamian latitudes. (4) Another important geographical text, the Sargon Geography, describes the Neo-Assyrian Empire of Sargon II by noting the relative positions of lands and peoples. The sizes of the most important geographical regions are listed in terms of their circumference (e.g., "90 leagues is the circumference of Elam"). Our copies date to the Neo-Assyrian and Late Babylonian periods (see VAT 8006 and BM 64382+82955), and are now published in the new edition of W. Horowitz (see Horowitz 67–95), which contains many other relevant cosmological and geographical texts as well as a synthetic discussion.

Texts and translations: D. CHARPIN, *Le clergé d'Ur au siècle d'Hammurabi* (Hautes études orientales 22; Genève: Librairie Droz, 1986), 275–78 (prayer for Rim-Sin); W. HOROWITZ, *Mesopotamian Cosmic Geography;* A. LIVINGSTONE, *Mystical and Mythological Explanatory Works of Assyrian and Babylonian Scholars* (Oxford: Clarendon, 1986), text 32:6 (I.NAM. GIŠ.ḪUR.AN.KI.A). **Bibliography:** C. BLACKER and M. LOEWE, eds., *Ancient Cosmologies* (London: Allen & Unwin, 1975); B. HALPERN, "The Assyrian Astronomy of Genesis 1 and the Birth of Milesian Philosophy," *ErIsr* 27 (2003): 74–83; J. KOCH, *Neue Untersuchungen zur Topographie des babylonischen Fixsternhimmels* (Wiesbaden: Harrassowitz, 1989); D. MEIJER, ed., *Natural Phenomena: Their Meaning, Depiction, and Description in the Ancient Near East* (New York: Royal Netherlands Academy of Arts and Sciences, 1992).

10.2. Egyptian Myths

Full-length myths are comparatively rare in our collection of Egyptian texts, perhaps because myths were transmitted orally in the corpus of secret priestly lore (van Dijk). Barring a few papyri devoted to myths, most of our Egyptian exemplars are preserved in the funerary literature, namely, in the Pyramid Texts (PT), the Coffin Texts (CT), the Book of the Dead (BD), and related literature (for more on the funerary literature, see 3.2 and 5.9.1). Our task here is to cull from these sources a range of mythic episodes that are of comparative value for students of the Hebrew Bible, focusing especially on the Egyptian creation traditions but including other valuable samples as well. As is the case in so many ancient cultures, the Egyptian creation stories dealt with both the origins of the gods (theogony) and the origins of the cosmos (cosmogony). For related expressions of Egyptian creation theology, see the Egyptian hymnic literature (especially the hymn to Amon in P.Leiden I 350).

Atum Creation Stories (PT 600, CT 335, BD Spell 17). The funerary literature preserves two well-known Atum creation stories, one from the Heliopolis tradition and the other from Hermopolis. Both texts presume that a primeval mound, the first dry land, emerged from the preexistent primeval waters of Nun. In the Heliopolis tradition (PT 600), the sun god Atum stood upon this primeval hill and sneezed into existence the second-generation gods, Shu (god of air) and Tefnut (goddess of moisture), and then continued with other acts of creation (in a variation, Shu and Tefnut were created by Atum's masturbation [see PT 527]). The primordial mound where these creative acts took place was the future site of the sanctuary of Heliopolis, in this way reflecting the uniqueness and legitimacy of its sacred shrine. The myth goes on to invite Egypt's great gods to join Atum in protecting the king's pyramid and thereby to restore and preserve the king's life in the hereafter. Apparently, the rising pyramid symbolized the primeval hillock and could, by the creative power of Atum and his myth, become a place for the king's new life to emerge after his death.

Our access to the Hermopolis creation tradition comes via the Middle Kingdom Coffin Texts (text 335) and the New Kingdom Book of the Dead (spell 17). Although the New Kingdom editions reflect substantial glosses, the essentials of the spell are the same in all of the texts. This time Atum—here equated with the sun god Re—brought himself into being out of the primeval waters (Nun) and began the creation from his station upon the primeval mound of earth. Instead of creating Shu and Tefnut by sneezing or masturbation, as in the Heliopolis tradition, in this text he created the Ennead (the great gods of Egypt) by naming the parts of his body. All of this took place "before the liftings of Shu," which we know from Coffin text 76 referred to Shu's creation of space for further creation by pushing Geb (the earth god) away from Nut (the goddess of the sky). As in the first Atum myth, the use of a creation myth in ritual reveals the story's power to re-create life for those who were deceased, but this text differs from the Heliopolis tradition because it claims that the primeval mound of creation was not in Heliopolis but at the sacred precinct in the Hermopolis temple. Other Egyptian cult centers, such as Memphis and Thebes, also asserted their primacy with myths of this sort.

Two comparisons with the biblical tradition spring to mind. First, the Egyptian creation stories depict the first land rising from the primeval waters and the creation of a life-sustaining order through the separation of earth and sky. These themes are surely reminiscent of the creation story in Gen 1, and although most scholars see a direct relationship between Gen 1 and the Mesopotamian traditions, connections with Egyptian tradition cannot be ruled out (see also the Egyptian iconographic evidence in O. Keel). The second comparison regards the tendency to associate temple sites with important events in the past. Just as the Egyptians linked their temple sites to creation, so too did the Israelite traditions associate the Jerusalem temple with Abraham's sacrifice of Isaac (cf. Gen 22; 2 Chron 3:1) and with David's sacrifice to avert the destruction of Jerusalem after his evil census (2 Sam 24).

Texts and translations: E. A. W. BUDGE, *The Book of the Dead* (London: British Museum, 1895); R. O. FAULKNER, *The Ancient Egyptian Pyramid Texts* (2 vols; Oxford: Clarendon, 1969); IDEM, *The Ancient Egyptian Coffin Texts;* E. NAVILLE, *Das Aegyptische Todtenbuch der XVIII. bis XX. Dynastie* (Berlin: A. Asher, 1886). *Translations: ANET* 3 (PT 600); *ANET* 3–4 (BD spell 17); *COS* 1.3: 7 (PT 527); 1.4: 7–8 (PT 600); 1.10: 15–17 (CT 335; BD spell 17). *Bibliography:* ALLEN, *Genesis in Egypt,* 13–18, 30–35.

The Memphite Theology. This creation account rivaled the Atum traditions (see previous entry) by attributing creation to the god Ptah of Memphis. The text is also known as the Shabaka Stone because the Nubian king Shabaka (716–702 B.C.E.) claims to have "found" an ancient copy of the text and to have recopied it anew. Although some scholars believe that the tradition goes back about two thousand years earlier than Shabaka, others believe that Shabaka's discovery of the text was an eighth-century fiction designed to legitimize Ptah's prominence by claiming that the text was very old. In any case, in contrast to the Atum creation stories, here the primeval waters and primeval hillock do not precede Ptah's appearance because he is amalgamated as a single deity with both Tatenen (the god of the primeval hillock) and Nun (as Ptah-Nun, the primeval waters). Ptah's first creative acts included the creation of the god Atum and the other eight members of the Ennead. This was accomplished when Ptah expressed his thoughts in verbal commands, a logos creation theology that is reminiscent of Genesis: "God said . . . and it was so." The myth's composers were aware of their theological innovation: "Whereas the Ennead of Atum came into being by his semen and his fingers, the Ennead (of Ptah), however, is the teeth and lips in this mouth, which pronounced the name of everything." According to the Memphite Theology, one result of this creative process was that Ptah was in "every body and in every mouth of all gods, all men, [all] cattle, all creeping things, and (everything) that lives." Although some theogonic details appear in the text, cosmological aspects of creation are treated briefly, and the details about humanity's origins are conspicuously absent. For related texts, see *COS* 1.12–14.

Text and translation: S. SHARPE, *Egyptian Inscriptions from the British Museum and Other Sources* (2 vols.; London: Moxon, 1837–1841), vol. 1, pls. 36–38. *Translations:* AEL 1:51–57; *ANET* 4–6; *COS* 1.15: 21–23. *Bibliography:* ALLEN, *Genesis in Egypt*, 42–47; J. H. BREASTED, "The Philosophy of a Memphite Priest," *ZÄS* 39 (1902): 39–54; A. ERMAN, *Ein Denkmal memphitischer Theologie* (Berlin: Pruessischen Akademie der Wissenschaften, 1910); K. KOCH, "Wort und Einheit des Schöpfergottes in Memphis und Jerusalem," *ZTK* 62 (1965): 251–93; WESTERMANN, *Genesis* 1:38–40.

The Egyptian Book of Nut. Although this text perhaps dates to the Middle Kingdom, our copies appear in two New Kingdom inscriptions (of Seti I and Rameses IV) and with commentary in two demotic papyri from the second century B.C.E. (P.Carlsberg I and II). The myth is perhaps our clearest expression of Egyptian cosmology, in which the goddess Nut forms a canopy-like vault above the earth (the god Geb) while the god of the atmosphere (Shu) separates the two. Below the earth lies the Duat, the underworld abode through which the sun passes each night. Surrounding this structure in every direction is water, visible above as the sky and below in the fresh waters of the Nile. In Seti's copy from Abydos and in the demotic version, the disappearance and reappearance of the stars are attributed to Nut's "swallowing" of the stars and Shu's decree that they be born again each time. An inscribed picture of this cosmology accompanies the text. The comparative value of this exemplar concerns mainly Hebrew cosmological texts, such as Ps 19 and especially Gen 1, where a "firmament" above the atmosphere (the heavens) separates the "waters above" from the "waters below." Although the similarities between Hebrew and Egyptian cosmology are obvious, it is unlikely that Egyptian theology directly influenced the biblical authors; more likely is that Gen 1 and the Book of Nut reflect cosmological views that were common in the ancient world. At any rate, we should notice that the closest Egyptian parallel to Gen 1 is, in certain respects, a scientific text. Our modern distinction between myth and science did not hold in antiquity.

Texts and translations: H. FRANKFORT, *The Cenotaph of Seti I at Abydos I* (2 vols.; London: Egypt Exploration Society, 1933); R. A. PARKER, *The Early Decans* (vol. 1 of *Egyptian Astronomical Texts;* Providence: Brown University Press, 1960) (all four texts). *Translation:* *COS* 1.1: 5–6. *Bibliography:* ALLEN, *Genesis in Egypt*, 1–9; J. D. CURRID, "An Examination of the Egyptian Background of the Genesis Cosmogony," *BZ* 35 (1991): 18–40; HORNUNG, *The Ancient Egyptian Books of the Afterlife*, 112–16; O. KEEL, *The Symbolism of the Biblical World: Ancient Near Eastern Iconography and the Book of Psalms* (Winona Lake, Ind.: Eisenbrauns, 1997), 26–47.

The Book of Knowing the Creations of Re and of Overthrowing Apophis. The Egyptians believed that an underworld demon named Apophis each evening threatened the daily circuit of the sun god Re. They addressed this threat in a series of rituals known collectively as the Beginning of the Book of Overthrowing Apophis, and here our eyes land on a portion of the papyrus known as the Book

of Knowing the Creations of Re and of Overthrowing Apophis, a myth that includes the creation of humanity. This myth, whose words were to be recited verbatim, runs as follows. Re existed in the primeval waters of Nun and there
planned his creation. The first deities, Shu and Tefnut, were created through acts
of masturbation and spitting. These two gods in turn created other deities who
assisted in the creative process. Humanity was created from the tears of Re himself, who cried when he lost his "Eye" (a powerful divine force). This last etiology
was based on a pun between the Egyptian words for "tears" (*remy*) and "humanity" (*remet*). As the directions in the ritual explain, the ritual repulsed not only
the enemies of Re but also the enemies of the pharaoh. The daily appearance of
the sun therefore confirmed not only the ritual's success in the divine realm but
also its efficacy on behalf of the king. As in the other funerary creation stories
mentioned above, ritual recitation of this narrative was believed to put into mo-
tion creative powers of renewal on behalf of the dead. For background and bibliography on related texts, see Hornung.

Text and translation: R. O. FAULKNER, *The Papyrus Bremner-Rhind (British Museum No.
10188)* (BAeg 3; Brussels: Fondation Égyptologique Reine Élisabeth, 1933). *Translations:*
ANET 6–7; COS 1.9: 14–15. *Bibliography:* HORNUNG, *The Ancient Egyptian Books of the
Afterlife*, 26–117.

The Destruction of Humankind. Although the Egyptians had no flood story, they
possessed a myth in which the human beings narrowly averted complete destruction. Here again, the tale is found in Egyptian funerary literature, in this case in a
longer text known as the Book of the Cow of Heaven. In this tale, the sun god Re
discovered a human plot against him and so moved to destroy civilization. His violent "Eye" assumed the form of his daughter Hathor, who brutally began to destroy humanity. The job progressed well until the human suffering moved Re to
compassion, prompting him to end the mayhem before it was too late. He accomplished this by pouring a mix of red beer upon the land. When Hathor mistook
this for blood, she drank the brew and became so inebriated that she did not see
her human victims. The remainder of the text describes how a weary Re withdrew
to the sky and commissioned the other gods to govern the cosmos; various etiologies for names and customs follow, most notably an etiology for the custom of alcohol consumption at the Feast of Hathor. Although the text perhaps originated
as an etiological composition, our copies were put to a different use. All five come
from the Book of the Cow of Heaven, which appears on the tomb walls of several
New Kingdom pharaohs. Perhaps it was believed that this myth of humanity's
preservation could also ritually revive the lives of deceased kings.

Text and translation: E. HORNUNG, *Der ägyptische Mythos von der Himmelskuh: Eine
Ätiologie des Unvollkommenen* (2d ed.; OBO 46; Freiburg, Switz.: Universitätsverlag, 1991).
Translations: AEL 2:197–99; ANET 10–11; COS 1.24: 36–37; LAE 289–98. *Bibliography:*
E. BRUNNER-TRAUT, *Altägyptische Märchen* (2d ed.; Düsseldorf: Diederichs, 1965), 69–72;
HORNUNG, *The Ancient Egyptian Books of the Afterlife*, 148–51.

The Contending of Horus and Seth. Papyrus Chester Beatty I (Egyptian Late period) preserves a strange tale about the conflict between Horus and Seth, but the story cannot be understood apart from a foray into other aspects of Egyptian tradition. According to Egyptian tradition, the god Seth killed and dismembered his brother Osiris and scattered the body in fourteen parts about Egypt. Isis, the wife of Osiris, was able to recover these parts excepting the penis, because it had been consumed by a Nile fish. Nevertheless, Isis fashioned a substitute member and became impregnated, finally giving birth to Osiris's son, Horus. Our myth answered the question "Who would take the place of the departed Osiris?"

According to the Contending of Horus and Seth, most of the gods in the divine council preferred Horus as the successor of Osiris, which did not please the sun god, here represented as Pre-Harakhti. The debate among the gods was relentless and nearly fruitless, but as the council began to lean in favor of Horus, Seth threatened the gods with his heavy mace. In response to the impasse, Pre-Harakhti advised that Horus and Seth be sent to a deserted island in order to fight it out. He instructed the ferryman, Nemty, to prevent any intrusions on the fight, especially from Horus's mother, Isis. Isis deceived Nemty, however, and taking the form of an attractive woman, she seduced Seth and used this relationship to tell him a tale of woe. In a story reminiscent of Nathan's parable to David (2 Sam 12), Isis explained to Seth that her deceased husband was a cattleman whose son's inheritance a stranger had illegitimately claimed. When Seth judged this interloper, Isis revealed herself and identified Seth as the culprit. Seth immediately grew angry because this somehow thwarted his plans. The gods then punished Nemty for allowing the intrusion of Isis.

Several conflicts ensued, most notably when Seth had his way with Horus by sticking his erect penis between Horus's thighs and ejaculating. Horus grabbed the semen with his hand and went to Isis, who, now horrified, cut off his hand and threw it into the water. She then covertly placed some of Horus's semen on the lettuce of Seth, which in turn made Seth pregnant. When Seth laid claim to kingship because he had had his manly way with Horus, Isis called forth the semen of both Seth and Horus; Seth's semen came out of the water (where Isis had thrown it) whereas the semen of Horus was in Seth, thus implying that it was Horus—not Seth—who had treated Seth like a woman. The gods eventually determined that Horus was the legitimate heir of Osiris.

At least one prominent Egyptologist has suggested that the story's primary purpose was entertainment (Simpson), but its theological themes were very significant. Pharaoh himself was the embodiment of Horus as well as the reincarnation and living son of the deceased pharaoh, Osiris. For this reason, Van Dijk has suggested that the pharaoh's legitimacy as Egypt's ruler rested on the Osiris-Horus genealogy and so upon the myths that expressed it. For related texts, see the following entry.

Text and translation: A. H. GARDINER, *Late-Egyptian Stories* (BAeg 1; Brussels: Fondation Égyptologique Reine Élisabeth, 1932), 37–60. *Translations: AEL* 2:214–23; *LAE* 91–103. *Bibliography:* W. K. SIMPSON, *The Literature of Ancient Egypt* (New Haven: Yale University

Press, 1972), 108–26; J. Van Dijk, "Myth and Mythmaking in Ancient Egypt," *CANE* 3:1705.

Horus Myths from Edfu. Inscribed on the walls of the temple of Horus at Edfu (Upper Egypt) is a series of five late Egyptian texts that share the theme of Horus's victory over Seth (see previous entry). In the first text, the Legend of the Winged Disk, Horus, here appearing as Horus of Beḥdet, acted on behalf of his father, Re. Horus took on the form of a winged disk and entered the heavens to destroy the evil enemies of Re, most notably Seth. Although Horus succeeded in dismembering Re's enemies, the pieces fell to the earth and became crocodiles and hippopotamuses in the Nile. The remainder of the tale recounts Horus's pursuit of these enemies as he uses a harpoon and other weapons to progressively eliminate them from various regions of Upper and Lower Egypt. The text as a whole provides an etiology for Horus's prominence in Egyptian theology while on a more modest scale the myth provides many etiologies for place-names, rituals, and various religious institutions and festivals. Aside from Horus and Seth, the most prominent deities in the text are Re, who repeatedly requests that Horus defeat his enemies, and Thoth, who provides magical spells to protect Horus and pronounces various place-names in honor of Horus's victories.

The second text is a version of the myth described in the previous entry (Contending of Horus and Seth), in which Horus appeared as the son of Osiris and Isis rather than as Horus of Beḥdet. Although these two images, of Horus the son of Osiris and Horus of Beḥdet, tended to become merged into a single deity, there were occasions when they were treated as separate manifestations of Horus (see below). The third text appears to provide the script for a sacred drama in which the victories of Horus over Seth were ritually acted out in the temple. At its conclusion, the myth provides two versions of Seth's dismemberment and of the distribution of his body parts among the various gods and cities. Texts four and five provide two more accounts of Horus's victory over Seth, with Seth appearing in these tales as a red hippopotamus and a red donkey, respectively. In this final sequence, we find Isis asking Horus of Beḥdet to assist her youthful son Horus, thus reflecting the flexibility in which the various manifestations of Horus were used in the tradition.

For students of the Hebrew Bible, among the most important comparative observations is how the Edfu inscriptions combine seemingly contradictory mythical narratives into a single five-part inscription. These myths were valued not for their supposed narrative coherence but for their utility in honoring Horus and in expressing his divine attributes. Similarly, we can surmise that the two quite different creation stories juxtaposed in Gen 1 and 2 probably occasioned less annoyance among ancient Israelites than they sometimes do among modern commentators.

Text and translation: E. Chassinat, *Le temple d'Edfou* (Cairo: Institut Français d'Archéologie Orientale du Caire, 1931). **Translations:** A. M. Blackman and H. W. Fairman, "The Myth of Horus at Edfu—II," *JEA* 28 (1942): 32–38; *JEA* 29 (1943): 2–36; *JEA* 30 (1944): 5–22; H. W. Fairman, "The Myth of Horus at Edfu—I," *JEA* 21 (1935): 26–36;

D. KURTH, *Treffpunkt der Götter: Inschriften aus dem Tempel des Horus von Edfu eingeleitet, übersetzt, und erläutert* (Zurich: Artemis, 1994).

Cultic Abomination of the Pig (CT 157). This mythical incantation also provided etiologies to explain (1) why Buto in Lower Egypt belonged to the god Horus; (2) why there was a luminary contrast between the sun and moon; and (3) why Egyptian followers of Horus observed a prohibition against eating pork. The myth accomplished this by playing on the traditional enmity between Seth and Horus, in which Seth took the form of a black pig and struck a blow to Horus's eye (the moon). The pig thereby became an abomination to Horus, and the god Re in turn gave Buto to Horus as compensation for his eye injury. This short myth may well have originated as a playful and entertaining etiology for dietary rules, but its presence in a Coffin Text ritual (and later, in the Book of the Dead) suggests that some Egyptian readers took it seriously. The companion text, *CT* 158, adds that this incantation should "not be said while eating pork." The obvious comparative value of this text is its similarity to the dietary rules of Deut 14 and Lev 11.

Text and translation: FAULKNER, *The Ancient Egyptian Coffin Texts.* **Translations:** ANET 10; *COS* 1.19: 30–31. **Bibliography:** W. L. DARBY, P. GHALIOUNGUI, and L. GRIVETTI, *Food: The Gift of Osiris* (London: Academic Press, 1977), 171–209; R. L. MILLER, "Hogs and Hygiene," *JEA* 76 (1990): 125–40.

Papyrus Jumilhac. This hieratic papyrus contains a collection of mythical and religious lore from the nineteenth nome of Ptolemaic-era Egypt. Its focus was on the god Anubis, who was the patron deity of embalming and, during the period in question, the chief deity of Egypt's nineteenth nome. In addition to numerous minor myths, two traditions emerge as important in the text. The first is a version of the Tale of Two Brothers (see 8.1), which in its original rendition narrated a story of estrangement between the gods Anubis and Bata and the eventual restoration of their relationship. In this late version of the story, however, Bata is equated with the god Seth and becomes the enemy of Anubis. The second tradition contains the theme of Osiris's dismemberment by Seth and Anubis's subsequent role in collecting and reanimating the body of Osiris (see entries on the Horus myths in this chapter). The text also contains various lists, including lists of gods and their ranks, of geographical and topographical features with their mythological significance, of sacred hills, trees, lakes, and serpents, and of religious and cultural behaviors that were forbidden in the nome. The text is replete with etiologies that provided explanations for place-names and for various cultural and religious practices. Later scribes added brief notes to the text, which appear as demotic glosses in the margins of the papyrus.

Text and translation: J. VANDIER, *Le papyrus Jumilhac* (Paris: Centre National de la Recherche Scientifique, 1962). **Bibliography:** S. T. HOLLIS, *The Ancient Egyptian "Tale of Two Brothers"* (Norman: University of Oklahoma Press, 1990), 47–48, 171–76 (includes partial translations); K.-T. ZAUZICH, "Zu einigen demotischen Glossen im Papyrus Jumilhac," *Enchoria* 4 (1974): 159–61.

10.3. Hittite Myths

The Hittite myths were of two primary types, those that were originally Hattian and those that were Hurrian. The central *topos* of the Hattian myths was the motif of the vanishing deity, in which the disappearance of a god—usually the storm god or his son—caused the rains to cease and the fertility of land and livestock to wane. These myths were apparently used in rituals either to lure back the missing god or perhaps to preempt his or her departure. Although our copies of the texts generally date to the New Kingdom (1380–1200 B.C.E.), scholars are fairly certain that the Hattian myths date back to the Old Kingdom (1750–1500 B.C.E.). The Hurrian myths, on the other hand, centered on a conflict between the gods Kumarbi and Tessub, who competed to secure their respective claims to kingship over the gods. Tessub, the great storm god of Hatti, was the ultimate victor in this contest.

Several related ritual texts that are known to scholars are not treated here either because they are too fragmentary or because their mythic elements are abbreviated in comparison with their ritual components (see Hoffner, texts 8, 10, 12, 13).

The Illuyanka Myth. A single tablet preserves two versions of this myth (*CTH* 321), which was recited or sung during the little-understood springtime Purulli festival (see 5.5). The scribe who produced our copy, Pihaziti, identified the text as a composition of "Kella, the GUDU-priest." The myth attributed poor spring seasons to weakness in the storm god, who was fragile after his defeat by a powerful serpent named Illuyanka. To correct this problem, the storm god called for a festival, to be attended by his daughter Inara and by a mortal man named Hupasiya, whom she had bribed with sex to assist her. Inara invited the serpent to the feast, and when he became drunk, Hupasiya tied him up. After this victory for the storm god, the text breaks off with Hupasiya weeping to be permitted to return to his home. In the second version, the serpent took the "heart and eyes" of the storm god. In response, the storm god sired a son who then married the serpent's daughter and worked in the house of the serpent for her hand. Eventually the son demanded as his bride-price the heart and eyes of his father, which the son received and then dutifully returned to his father. When the rejuvenated storm god approached to destroy the serpent, the storm god's son responded, "Include me with them; have no pity on me." In this way the son died with the serpent. The text ends with a series of somewhat obscure ritual instructions.

Text and translation: G. BECKMAN, "The Anatolian Myth of Illuyanka," *JANES* 14 (1982): 11–25. *Translations: ANET* 125–26; *COS* 1.56: 150–51; HOFFNER, *Hittite Myths*, 10–14. *Bibliography:* HAAS, *Hethitische Berggötter und hurritische Steindämonen;* IDEM, "Betrachtungen zur Rekonstruktion des hethitischen Frühjahrsfestes (EZEN purulliyas)," *ZA* 78 (1988): 284–98; "Jason's Raub des goldenen Vliesses im Lichte hethitischer Quellen," *UF* 7 (1975): 227–33.

The Telipinu Myths and Related Texts. Telipinu was a storm god as well as the son of Hatti's great storm god. The three versions of his myth (*CTH* 324) recount his disappearance, the resulting loss of fertility in Hatti, and the all-out search to find him and return him to his ailing land. In each case the search fails until a tiny bee, sent out by the mother goddess Hannahanna, discovers Telipinu and returns him to his father. A series of rituals designed to appease Telipinu's anger follows, including the burning of brushwood that sympathetically represented the removal of Telipinu's wrath and frustration. Several similar storm god myths are also known.

Text and translation: LAROCHE, *Textes mythologiques hittites*, 29–50. ***Translations:*** ANET 126–28; COS 1.57: 151–53, 1.69: 172–72; HOFFNER, *Hittite Myths*, 14–20 (Telipinu myths), 20–25 (other exemplars). ***Bibliography:*** G. KELLERMAN, "The Telepinu Myth Reconsidered," in *Kaniššuwar: A Tribute to Hans G. Güterbock on His Seventy-Fifth Birthday, May 27, 1983* (ed. H. A. Hoffner Jr. and G. Beckman; Chicago: Oriental Institute of the University of Chicago, 1986), 115–24; IDEM, "La déesse Hannahanna: Son image et sa place dans la mythes anatoliens," *Hethitica* 7 (1987): 109–48; H. OTTEN, *Die Überlieferung des Telipinu-Mythus* (Leipzig: Voerderasiatisch-Aegyptische Gesellschaft, 1942).

The Disappearance of the Sun God. Here again (*CTH* 323) at issue is the disappearance of a god, but in this case the result is not a loss of infertility (as in the Telipinu myths) but rather the extreme cold caused by the disappearance of the sun god. Although the text's conclusion is somewhat fragmentary, the mother goddess, Hannahanna, apparently lures the sun god back with promises that sacrifices would result. According to the text's colophon, its ancient title was the Invocation of the Sun God and Telipinu.

Text and translation: LAROCHE, *Textes mythologiques hittites*, 21–28. ***Translation:*** HOFFNER, *Hittite Myths*, 26–28. ***Bibliography:*** BERNABÉ, *Textos literarios hetitas*, 61–64; B. DE-VRIES, *The Style of Hittite Epic and Mythology* (Ann Arbor: University Microfilms, 1967).

The Kumarbi Cycle. This Hurrian mythic cycle includes five tales that feature a conflict between the gods Kumarbi and Tessub over divine kingship. The first tale, the Song of Kumarbi, depicts an alternating series of god-kings from each family line and their respective efforts to secure kingship over the gods. Kumarbi, a netherworld deity, eventually loses this quest to Tessub, who is a celestial deity. The four remaining tales—the Song of the God LAMA, the Song of Silver, the Song of Hedammu, and the Song of Ullikummi—appear to recount the stories of Kumarbi's sons, a series of gods and monsters begotten in his effort to drive Tessub from the throne. Although a group of netherworld deities sides with Kumarbi and a group of celestial deities assists Tessub, the key divine figure in the cycle is the Mesopotamian god of wisdom, Ea. Although Ea initially sides with Kumarbi in the conflict, during the course of the cycle one can discern a gradual shift in his allegiance from Kumarbi to Tessub. From this we can discern that the text's primary purpose was to explain how Tessub became the supreme storm god of Hatti. Especially interesting to students of religious tradition is the way that

Greek authors later took up and developed the first of the compositions, the Song of Kumarbi (see Güterbock; Walcott).

Texts and translations: H. G. GÜTERBOCK, "The Hittite Version of the Hurrian Kumarbi Myths: Oriental Forerunners to Hesiod," *AJA* 52 (1948): 123–34; IDEM, *The Song of Ullikummi: Revised Text of the Hittite Version of a Hurrian Myth* (New Haven: American Schools of Oriental Research, 1952) (Song of Ullikummi = *CTH* 345); H. A. HOFFNER, "The Song of Silver," in *Documentum Asiae Minoris antiquae: Festschrift für Heinrich Otten zum 75. Geburtstag* (ed. E. Neu and C. Rüster; Weisbaden: Harrassowitz, 1988), 143–66; LAROCHE, *Textes mythologiques hittites,* 145–52 (Song of the God LAMA = *CTH* 343), 169–76 (Song of Hedammu = *CTH* 348), 153–61 (Song of Kumarbi = *CTH* 344), 177–82 (Song of Silver = *CTH* 364). *Translation:* HOFFNER, *Hittite Myths,* 38–61. *Bibliography:* BERNABÉ, *Textos literarios hetitas;* W. BURKERT, "Von Ullikummi zum Kaukasus—die Felsgeburt des Unholds: Zur Kontinuität einer mündlichen Erzählung," *Würzburger Jahrbücher für die Altertumswissenschaft* 5 (1979): 253–61; G. GIORGADZE, "On the Word for 'Silver' with Reference to Hittite Cuneiform Text," *AoF* 15 (1988): 69–75; HAAS, *Hethitische Berggötter und hurritische Steindämonen;* G. KOMORÓCZY, " 'The Separation of Sky and Earth': The Cycle of Kumarbi and the Myths of Cosmogony in Mesopotamia," *Acta antiqua* 21 (1973): 21–45; P. WALCOTT, *Hesiod and the Near East* (Cardiff: University of Wales Press, 1966).

Elkunirša and Ašertu: An Ugaritic Myth in Hatti. This text (*CTH* 342) has been partially reconstructed from the fragments of two or three different copies. The myth apparently relates the story of a conflict between Baal and Ašertu, but for our purposes the most salient point is that the Hittites were reading and translating Ugaritic mythical texts. The translator misunderstood the phrase "El, Creator of the Earth," and rendered it as Elkunirša.

Texts and translations: LAROCHE, *Textes mythologiques hittites,* 139–44; H. OTTEN, "Ein kanaanäischer Mythus aus Boğazköy," *MIOF* 1 (1953): 125–50. *Translations:* ANET 519; *COS* 1.55: 149; HOFFNER, *Hittite Myths,* 69–70. *Bibliography:* H. A. HOFFNER JR., "The Elkunirša Myth Reconsidered," *RHA* 23 (1965): 5–16.

10.4. Ugaritic Myths

In Ugaritic tradition, creation was attributed to the god El and his consort Athirat (= Asherah), who carried the epithets *bny bnwt* ("the creator of creatures") and *qnyt 'ilm* ("creator of the gods"), respectively (see Pope). The Hebrew Bible and inscriptional evidence similarly indicates that Yahweh/Elohim was the creator god and that at least some Israelites viewed Asherah as his consort (see 15.1). Although El and Athirat were prominent in Ugaritic theology as the parents of the gods and creators of the cosmos, tales about them are generally wanting. There were, however, numerous Ugaritic myths that featured the storm god Baal as the protagonist. These are frequently referred to as the Baal Cycle. Several shorter mythic texts, many of them fragmentary, are also preserved in the Ugaritic corpus. Many of these are best described as "historiolae," myths recited because their stories were paradigms to induce a ritual effect. Entries on these exemplars are found in our discussion of the ritual texts (see 5.8.4).

Myths of the Baal Cycle. As the title implies, the Baal Cycle reflects a collection of episodic stories that are loosely connected with each other. The frailty of these connections has raised many questions about how the six fragmentary tablets (*KTU* 1.1–6) relate to each other. Although various options have been suggested, most scholars agree that *KTU* 1.3–6 represents a single narrative. That *KTU* 1.1 and 1.2 originally preceded *KTU* 1.3–6 is less certain. Whatever the case, the tablets available to us relate at least three episodes from the life of the god Baal: his struggle with Yamm (the sea god) in *KTU* 1.1–2, the construction of his palace in 1.3–4, and his struggle with Mot (god of death) in 1.5–6. The central theme of the composition appears to be a contest, carried out under the supervision of the great god El, for the divine kingship over gods and men.

Baal's conflict with Yamm echoes the pattern of conflict in Marduk's struggle with the waters of Tiamat in *Enuma Elish,* and it has indeed been argued that the Babylonian myth depended on the Ugaritic (Jacobsen). Yamm's messengers, appearing as flames of fire (cf. Ps 104:4), announced that Yamm would become king of the pantheon and demanded that the god Baal be turned over to him as his slave. After El, the chief god, acquiesced to these demands, Baal resisted with weapons he had received from the craftsman deity, Kothar. Baal then defeated and drank Yamm (the sea). The text breaks off at this point, but many scholars believe that a creation account similar to that in *Enuma Elish* followed. At any rate, when the text is again legible, we find Baal seeking to assume his role as king of the pantheon and requesting El's permission to build a palace. In response to the appeals of the goddesses Asherah and Anat, El reluctantly permitted such a palace on Mount Zaphon (about twenty-five miles north of Ugarit), which he commissioned Kothar to build.

After another break in the text, we again find Baal in conflict with a rival god, this time with Mot (Death), who defeated and swallowed Baal. As in the Ugaritic epics (See 9.2), fertility withered in the wake of the protagonist's death. The gods El and Anat therefore mourned Baal's passing, and Anat took Baal's body and buried it on Mount Zaphon. After an ill-fated attempt to restore fertility by replacing Baal with Athtar, god of the stars, Anat angrily pursued Mot and killed him. El immediately had a dream that the fertility of the earth had returned, which foreshadowed the emergence of Baal from death. Although Baal reappeared and resumed his role at the head of the pantheon, after seven years Mot also reappeared, and there ensued a great battle between them. Although the battle ended in a draw, Shapshu (the divine messenger) convinced Mot to accept his role as god of the underworld or face overthrow by El.

These curious myths can be interpreted in a variety of ways (see Smith). One common approach views the stories as etiologies. Baal's victory over Mot and the ensuing truce between them not only assured humanity of Baal's life-giving rain but also preserved the ever present threat of death through Mot (Parker). At the same time, the pattern of Baal's death and resurrection mirrored and thus accounted for the seasonal cycle of life and death (Day; Mettinger). Those who accept this seasonal-myth interpretation often suggest that the text was recited during annual fertility rituals (de Moor). Other scholars have stressed the political nature of the myths over their etiological features (Smith). Baal was the patron deity of the Ugaritic king, and King Niqmaddu II (1375–1345 B.C.E.) of Ugarit apparently sponsored our copies of the Baal myth. It is easy to imagine how Baal's victory in the face of so many serious threats might have played an apologetic role for the king and provided an encouraging message for the royal family.

Texts and translations: KTU 1.1–6; PARKER, *Ugaritic Narrative Poetry,* 81–180; M. S. SMITH, *The Ugaritic Baal Cycle* (VTSup 55; Leiden: Brill, 1994–) (vol. 1 includes plates of the tablets as well as an introduction and a commentary on tablets 1–2). *Translations:* ANET 129–42; COS 1.86: 241–74. **Bibliography:** J. DAY, "Baal," ABD 1:545–49; GIBSON, "The Ugaritic Literary Texts, I"; J. H. GRONBAEK, "Baal's Battle with Yam—a Canaanite Creation Fight," JSOT 33 (1985): 27–44; T. JACOBSEN, "The Battle between Marduk and Tiamat," JAOS 88 (1968): 104–8; T. N. D. METTINGER, "The Elusive Essence: YHWH, El, and Baal and the Distinctiveness of Israelite Faith," in *Die hebräische Bible und ihre zweifache Nachgeschichte: Festschrift für Rolf Rendtorff zum 65. Geburtstag* (ed. E. Blum et al.; Neukirchen-Vluyn: Neukirchener Verlag, 1990), 393–417; J. C. DE MOOR, *The Seasonal Pattern in the Ugaritic Myths of Baʿlu* (AOAT 16; Neukirchen-Vluyn: Neukirchener Verlag, 1971); M. H. POPE, *El in the Ugaritic Texts* (VTSupp 2; Leiden: Brill, 1955); N. H. WALLS JR., *The Goddess Anat in the Ugaritic Texts* (SBLDS 135; Atlanta: Scholars Press, 1992), 5–6, 68; P. L. WATSON, "The Death of 'Death' in the Ugaritic Texts," JAOS 92 (1972): 60–64.

*A Ritual Theogony of the Gracious Gods (***KTU 1.23***).* This liturgical tablet preserves a sexually explicit narrative poem, but the poem's interpretation is fraught with difficulties. Clearly, El plays the male role in the story, but the female role is filled by a single goddess bearing a compound name, Athirat-Rahmay, or by two goddesses named Athirat and Rahmay, respectively. The sexual relationship between El and the goddess(es) results in the birth of new deities, but here again there is confusion about how many gods are birthed. Some scholars believe that two individual deities are born, Šahar and Šalim ("dawn" and "dusk"), as well as a group of deities collectively called the "gracious gods." Other scholars simplify matters by identifying Šahar and Šalim as the gracious gods. At any rate, upon their creation, these gracious gods immediately began to consume the birds of the air and fish of the sea. El put a stop to their destructive behavior by sending the gods and their mothers into the desert to hunt for food. During their seven-year desert trek, the gods met a "watchman of the sown land," who provided them with food and drink. Perhaps this theogonic myth was composed to explain the origins of the several gods and to explicate the divine need for sacrifices from humanity. As for the liturgical side of the text, it is still not clear how the text was employed ritually. For more on the ritual dimensions of this text, see 4.3.

Certainly, the closest Near Eastern parallel to El's begetting of "dawn" and "dusk" as the first created gods is the biblical creation story in Gen 1, where the motif of "morning" and "evening" plays an important role.

Text and translation: PARKER, *Ugaritic Narrative Poetry*, 205–14. *Translation:* COS 1.87: 274–83. *Bibliography:* GIBSON, "The Ugaritic Literary Texts, I"; N. WYATT, "Les mythes des Dioscures et l'idéologie royale dans les littératures d'Ougarit et d'Israël," *RB* 103 (1996): 481–516; IDEM, *Religious Texts from Ugarit* (Sheffield, England: Sheffield Academic Press, 1998), 324–35.

Concluding Observations

1. **Authors and the Composition of Myth.** Near Eastern myths were nearly always anonymous compositions, the important exceptions being the Egyptian funerary myths, supposedly penned by the gods, and a few exemplars from Mesopotamia and Hatti. Attribution of the Egyptian myths to the gods was a matter of long-standing tradition, but there is no easy way for modern readers to deduce whether the earliest traditions were viewed as divine or whether divine authorship was postulated after the texts were written. The latter option is more probable, since the texts themselves made no explicit claims to divine authorship. More direct are the claims of Kati-ilani-Marduk, the Babylonian priest who wrote the Erra Myth. He maintained that the gods revealed his myth in a dream, but again we have no way of knowing whether we should attribute this claim to an authentic religious experience or to a kind of pious deception. At any rate, the exemplar is clear evidence for a nexus between myth, the priesthood, and divine revelation. The priestly role in mythic composition is similarly illustrated by the Hittite Illuyanka Myth, which was explicitly attributed to "Kella, the GUDU-priest." Regardless of who composed the myths, whether priest or scholar or someone else, it is clear that Near Eastern myths were composed in response to the needs and condition of the author's community. The Ordeal of Marduk (Neo-Assyrian) mythically illustrated Assyria's climb to prominence, and the Erra Myth was written to explain troubles in Babylon. Although the scribes who wrote these two texts did so with great confidence in their theology, we can also surmise that, in some cases, myths were composed as speculative fictions rather than as confident expressions of theology. Nothing would prevent later readers from embracing such speculative compositions as sources of theological or historical truth.

2. **The Functions of Myth.** Ancient myths served many different purposes, in most cases more than one. Some myths provided the foundations for cultural beliefs and institutions whereas others were less serious compositions. The exemplars surveyed in this chapter attest to the following major functional categories:

   a. Myth and Ritual. Scholars have long recognized myth's close association with ritual, and this relationship is clearly born out in the evidence surveyed here. Myths were associated with rituals in two important ways. Some of the ritual myths were historiola, narratives that symbolically embodied the ritual's desired effects (e.g., Egyptian creation myths; *Enuma Elish*). Others narrated the conditions that made the rituals necessary (the Hittite myths, as well as exemplars treated in 5.8.1).

b. Myth as Theology. Theological verities were expressed through myths, verities that were often closely associated with historical realities. Myths explained the relative prominence of deities (e.g., Ninurta in *Lugal-E;* Marduk in *Enuma Elish*), the divinity of kings (e.g., Pharaoh in the Horus myths), the significance of city temples (e.g., Egyptian creation texts from Heliopolis, Hermopolis, and Memphis), the sacking of cities (the Erra Myth), the emergence of new political entities (Assyria and its god Assur in the Ordeal of Marduk), and the ever present threat of death (Mot in the Baal Cycle). It is difficult from our modern vantage to distinguish between theological compositions that the authors wholeheartedly believed and those that were products of theological speculation, but in either case, later readers took the compositions as serious expression of truth.

c. Myth as Propaganda. The theological intentions of the myths obviously did not preclude their propagandistic purposes. The Memphite Theology, for instance, was not only a theological explanation for the city's prominence but also a polemical document that took the side of the god Ptah against Atum. Similarly polemical were the Ordeal of Marduk and Assyrian versions of *Enuma Elish,* which were composed to nourish Assyria's national identity by exalting its god Assur. What is interesting about these polemical exemplars is how close their content and form was to the myths with which they competed. This suggests, not surprisingly, that polemical myths were most effective when they adhered closely to accepted mythical patterns.

d. Myth as Etiology. As we have seen, practically every ancient myth had its etiological dimensions. Myths explained the origins and structure of the cosmos (creation myths; the Book of Nut), the seasonal patterns of the year (Dumuzi/Inanna myths; Hittite myths), the ritual uncleanness of certain meats (Abomination of the Pig), and even the properties of various types of stone (*Lugal-E*). On a larger scale, myths provided the very foundations of society's beliefs and institutions.

e. Myth as Praise. Because myths recounted the great deeds of the gods, they were also suitable expressions of praise and admiration for the deity. This is why stories of Horus's victories over Seth were inscribed at his temple at Edfu, Egypt.

f. Myth as Entertainment. Although it is natural for readers influenced by the western monotheistic tradition to imagine that every text with a god or gods must be a serious and religiously important text, it is clear that several exemplars examined in this chapter were composed as pleasure myths. This was particularly true of the Sumerian myths used to entertain visitors in the royal courts, but even serious myths could have their entertainment quotient.

g. Myth and History. Mesopotamian scribes sometimes attempted to provide longer and more coherent accounts of early history than were offered in the conventional myths. The most obvious examples are the Eridu Genesis and Atrahasis, which were produced by integrating various myths and motifs into linear narratives. This suggests, of course, that our modern distinction between myths and history would not hold so easily in the minds of the ancient scribes. Often, they viewed their myths as history.

h. Myth and Science. Modern scholars commonly distinguish ancient myths from ancient scientific texts, but several exemplars that we have examined demonstrate that this distinction would not have resonated with the ancients. The Mesopotamian cosmic geographies were scholarly scientific texts, whose portraits of the cosmos were derived from, or were quite close to, the cosmologies in myths like *Enuma Elish.* Similarly, some copies of the Egyptian Book of Nut included scholarly commentaries on the cosmological implications of the text. To be sure, these ancient texts often expressed cosmological ideas in mythological language, and sometimes even in mythological pictures (see Keel), but this does not contradict the conceptual point: for the ancients, their cosmological myths also reflected their scientific ideas about the cosmos.

3. **Collections of Myth.** Ancient scribes sometimes assembled collections of myths associated with particular deities; the Horus myths at Edfu and the Anubis myths in P.Jumilhac are good examples. In other cases, confluences of myth appear to have been more accidental, as myths associated with the same deity were gradually combined. This pattern is particularly visible in the Sumerian myths of Enki and Ninmaḫ and Enki and Ninhursag, each a combination of two older mythic episodes now joined into a single composition.

4. **Myth and Theological Consistency.** In one respect, it is not a surprise that Near Eastern myths sometimes offer us contradictory portraits of divine realities. Such outcomes were an inevitable consequence of political and ideological conflicts fought out on theological turf. More surprising, however,

are the instances where myths about the same god, and used by the same community, offered "contradictory" accounts of heavenly events. A case in point is the temple of Horus at Edfu, where five myths that offer quite different accounts of Horus's victory over Seth are inscribed side by side. The coherence of these myths rested not in their rigid historical coherence but rather, more narrowly, in their value as expressions of Horus's power and divine attributes. Although it would be a mistake to divorce all ancient myths from the category of sacred history—for the ancients often believed in the history of their myths—it is clear that, in some cases, myths were neither histories nor allegories but rather expressions of key theological ideas and themes. This observation applies also to mythical traditions elsewhere in the Near East, where myths were not so much histories as serious works of philosophical and theological speculation that sought in the acts and deeds of the gods an explanation for the circumstances of human life and experience.

5. The Recycling of Mythic Motifs. Although mythic composition certainly required some degree of innovation, these innovations were rarely clothed in novelty but rather were steeped in older plots, motifs, and themes (Lambert, in *CANE*). Good examples of such themes are the primeval hillock of the Egyptian creation myths, humanity's service to the gods in Mesopotamian myth, the disappearing deity in Hittite mythology, and, for a more specific example, the cluster of motifs from Ninurta mythology used by the author of *Enuma Elish* to honor Marduk. Duplications of this sort are not unexpected, given that new myths generally involved modifications of accepted belief rather than radical reformulations of religious heritage. As a general rule, the traditional societies of antiquity would not have embraced excessive theological novelty.

6. Editorial Aspects of Myth. Ancient myths were frequently revised for a variety of reasons. Scribes replaced Marduk with Assur in Assyrian versions of *Enuma Elish,* and late versions of the Anzu Myth substituted Ninurta for Ningirsu. As these examples show, revisions were often prompted by variations in the prominence of cult centers and their gods, variations that were closely related to political and historical realities. Changes in a myth's function also elicited editorial work. For example, although both early and late versions of Adapa attest to its function as a ritual text, the abbreviated copy from Amarna, Egypt, excludes the ritual elements in favor of the text's philosophical value.

7. Myth as an International Genre. The presence of Mesopotamian myths at Ugarit, Hatti, and Egypt demonstrates that ancient myths were sometimes known beyond the bounds of their host culture. Although in some cases these texts were used merely to teach foreign languages, in others scribes were apparently interested in the myths themselves (e.g., Adapa). There are also instances in which the transfer of myth from one society to another entailed some adaptation of the myth to its new context. It is fairly clear, for instance, that the Ugaritic and Babylonian conflict myths reflect renditions of the same basic plot; less clear in this case is the direction of influence, which probably moved from the Levant to Mesopotamia.

8. **Hebrew Myth in Comparative Perspective.** The Hebrew materials that fall within the purview of our discussion include mainly the narratives in Gen 1–11 and the poetic texts that allude to mythic episodes.

The traditions in Genesis that are most naturally viewed as myth include the creation traditions, the flood, and the tower of Babel. An assessment of these stories is complicated by the fact that our present text in Gen 1–11 is a conflation of two different compositions, one composed by the Yahwistic author (J) of the Pentateuch, who referred to the deity as Yahweh, and the other by the Priestly writer (P), who in Genesis referred to the deity as Elohim and whose contributions to the Pentateuch reflect priestly and cultic concerns (see chs. 5 and 12 of this study). Thus the primeval history presents us with two creation stories (Gen 1 [P]; Gen 2–3 [J]), two genealogies between creation and the flood (Gen 4 [J]; Gen 5 [P]), two beginnings for the flood story (7:1–4 [J]; 7:11–13 [P]), two conclusions for the flood (8:20–22 [J]; 9:1–17 [P]), and then two concluding genealogies (Gen 10 [J]; Gen 11 [P]). Duplications of this sort should occasion no surprise in light of the Near Eastern evidence, which presents us with many native variations of the basic myths about creation, the flood, and cosmic conflict. Also unsurprising is that the final editor of the Pentateuch was comfortable juxtaposing these two different accounts, since we have seen that Near Eastern scribes often combined "contradictory" myths and traditions into single compositions (e.g., the Horus myths from Edfu).

The overall shape of J's primeval history (creation-genealogy-flood-genealogy) closely parallels the literary pattern in the Eridu Genesis and Atrahasis. This is likely not a coincidence but rather one effect of the Genesis author's familiarity with Mesopotamian tradition. This is suggested by the many other details in J that find parallels in Mesopotamia, such as the creation of Adam from clay, the divine animation of his body, the work allotted to humanity (tilling the ground; see Hutter), the name of Adam (cf. Adapa), the deception of a human couple by one wise and crafty (cf. Adapa), and the role of a serpent in robbing us of the plant of life (see 9.1.1). Even the confusion of languages at Babel, which has no parallel in either Atrahasis or the Eridu Genesis, is a motif found in Mesopotamian tradition (see the Enmerkar Epic in ch. 9, above). In comparison with the Near Eastern texts, the uniqueness of J's myths is most visible in the way that he demythologized ancient tradition by removing the presence of all gods excepting

Yahweh and also in the unique way that the various mythic motifs were combined to present the Yahwist's unique view of the creation, the fall, and humanity.

As for P, here again its overall structure parallels closely the Mesopotamian texts, and its details are also based on Mesopotamian models. The creation story of P, with its emphasis on the primeval sea (*tehom*) and the subsequent separation of heavens and earth, is very close to Marduk's creation in *Enuma Elish*, in which he defeated Tiamat and split her body to form the structures of heaven and earth, placing the waters in the heavens, just as in Genesis. We have already seen that P's primeval genealogy in Gen 5 was designed to mimic the Sumerian King List tradition (see the introduction and ch. 11's conclusion below), and P's flood story shows clear signs of demythologizing a Mesopotamian source. This is most evident in the case of Ištar's colorful necklace, which, according to the Mesopotamian flood tradition, she wore to remind her never again to send a flood. P makes the necklace into a rainbow, but the rainbow continues to serve the same function as the necklace, namely, to remind the Israelite deity not to destroy the earth with a flood. The presence of these motifs in P should not distract us from the reality that the Priestly writer had his eyes not only on Mesopotamian myths but also on the Hebrew myths that preceded him in J.

Influences of Near Eastern myth on Israelite theology are also discernible in the biblical allusions to mythical episodes. Among the most important examples is the myth of cosmic conflict, in which the deity must fight and defeat evil or demonic enemies. This motif is central in *Enuma Elish* and in Baal's victory over Yamm. Although the Hebrew Bible does not preserve an Israelite version of the myth itself, F. M. Cross has argued that the Song of the Sea in Exod 15 preserves a demythologized rendition of the myth, in which Yahweh destroys the army of Pharaoh. Whether Cross is correct is a matter of debate, but there can be no doubt that the theme of Yahweh's cosmic conflict with the sea and sea monsters—usually known as Leviathan or Rahab—appears often in Hebrew poetic texts, such as Ps 74:13–14: "You divided the sea by your might; you broke the heads of the dragons in the waters. You crushed the heads of Leviathan, you gave him as food for the creatures of the wilderness." Many similar examples could be cited (Gen 6:1–4; Job 4:18; 15:15; 28:5; Ps 82; Isa 14:12–14; 24:21–23; 27:1; Ezek 28:11–28; for discussions, see J. Day; Page). The significance of this conflict myth in Israelite tradition is illustrated by its juxtaposition with the all-important Exodus tradition in Isa 51:9–10: "Awake, awake, put on strength, O arm of the LORD! Awake, as in days of old, the generations of long ago! Was it not you who cut Rahab in pieces, who pierced the dragon? Was it not you who dried up the sea, the waters of the great deep; who made the depths of the sea a way for the redeemed to cross over?" Another kind of mythic allusion appears in descriptions of Yahweh and in the divine epithets referring to him. For instance, the Israelites sometimes depicted Yahweh as "riding on a . . . cloud" (Isa 19:1; cf. Ps 18:9–10), which is comparable to Ugaritic descriptions of Baal after he defeated Yamm: "Hail, Baal the Conqueror! Hail, Rider on the Clouds! For Prince Sea is our captive, Judge River is our captive." (See Ohler for many similar epithets.)

None of the biblical epithets and allusions, or any of the Israelite narratives, reflect the theme of theogony (the origins of God). In this, Israelite theology was somewhat different from its Near Eastern counterparts. Although this unique trait is certainly a result of Israelite monotheism, the content of the Bible's mythic allusions suggests that we should avoid two extreme and false conclusions: imagining that Israelites were in all periods and instances intensely monotheistic, and underestimating the strong heno- and monotheistic influences in its literature.

General Bibliography

J. P. ALLEN, *Genesis in Egypt: The Philosophy of Ancient Egyptian Creation Accounts* (San Antonio, Tex.: Van Siclen, 1988); S. AUSBAND, *Myth and Meaning, Myth and Order* (Macon, Ga.: Mercer University Press, 1983); J. BAINES, "Myth and Literature," in *Ancient Egyptian Literature: History and Forms* (ed. A. Loprieno; PA 10; New York: Brill, 1996), 361–77; C. A. BENITO, "'Enki and Ninmah' and 'Enki and the World Order'" (PhD diss., University of Pennsylvania, 1969); A. BERNABÉ, *Textos literarios hetitas* (Madrid: Alianza Editorial, 1987); C. BLACKER and M. LOEWE, *Ancient Cosmogonies* (London: Allen & Unwinn, 1975); K. W. BOLLE, "Myth," *ER* 10:261–73; R. J. CLIFFORD, *The Cosmic Mountain in Canaan and the Old Testament* (Cambridge: Harvard University Press, 1972); IDEM, *Creation Accounts in the Ancient Near East and in the Bible* (CBQMS 26; Washington: Catholic Biblical Association, 1994); R. J. CLIFFORD and J. J. COLLINS, eds., *Creation in the Biblical Traditions* (CBQMS 24; Washington: Catholic Biblical Association, 1992); F. M. CORNFORD, *The Unwritten Philosophy and Other Essays* (Cambridge: Cambridge University Press, 1950), 111; F. M. CROSS JR., "The Song of the Sea and Canaanite Myth," in *Canaanite Myth and Hebrew Epic* (Cambridge: Harvard University Press, 1973), 112–44; S. DALLEY, *Myths from Mesopotamia* (Oxford: Oxford University Press, 1989); D. DAMROSCH, *The Narrative Covenant: Transformations of Genre in the Growth of Biblical Literature* (San Francisco: Harper & Row, 1987); J. DAY, *God's Conflict with the Dragon and the Sea* (Cambridge: Cambridge University Press, 1985); M. S. DAY, *The Many Meanings of Myth* (Lanham, Md.: University Press of America, 1984); M. DIETRICH, "Vom mythischen Urbild zu Realbild," in *Mythos im Alten Testament und seiner Umwelt: Festschrift für Hans-Peter Müller zum 65. Geburtstag* (ed. A. Lange et al.; BZAW 278; Berlin: de Gruyter, 1999), 17–28; W. G. DOTY, *Mythography: The Study of Myths and Rituals* (Tuscaloosa: University of Alabama Press, 1986); A. DUNDES, *The Flood Myth*

(Berkeley: University of California Press, 1988); IDEM, *Sacred Narrative: Readings in the Theory of Myth* (Berkeley: University of California Press, 1984); M. ELIADE, *Myth and Reality* (New York: Harper, 1963); R. O. FAULKNER, *The Ancient Egyptian Coffin Texts* (3 vols.; Warminster, England: Aris & Phillips, 1973–1978); J. G. FRAZER, *The Golden Bough* (12 vols.; London: Macmillan, 1917–1920); S. FREUD, "The Relation of the Poet to Day-Dreaming," in *Collected Papers* (5 vols.; New York: International Psycho-analytical Press, 1924–1950), 4:182; J. C. L. GIBSON, "The Ugaritic Literary Texts, I: The Mythological Texts," in *Handbook of Ugaritic Studies* (ed. W. G. E. Watson and N. Wyatt; Leiden: Brill, 1999), 193–202; V. HAAS, *Hethitische Berggötter und hurritische Steindämonen: Riten, Kulte, und Mythen* (Mainz: Philipp von Zabern, 1982); W. HARRELSON, "Myth and Ritual School," *ER*, 10:282–85; G. F. HASEL, "The Polemic Nature of Genesis Cosmology," *EvQ* 46 (1974): 81–102; IDEM, "The Significance of the Cosmology in Genesis 1 in Relation to Ancient Near Eastern Parallels," *AUSS* 10 (1972): 1–20; A. HEIDEL, *The Babylonian Genesis: The Story of Creation* (2d ed.; Chicago: University of Chicago Press, 1951); H. A. HOFFNER JR., *Hittite Myths* (SBLWAW 2; Atlanta: Scholars Press, 1990); E. HORNUNG, *The Ancient Egyptian Books of the Afterlife* (Ithaca: Cornell University Press, 1999); W. HOROWITZ, *Mesopotamian Cosmic Geography* (MC 8; Winona Lake, Ind.: Eisenbrauns, 1998); V. A. HUROWITZ, "Mesopotamian Myth in Biblical Metamorphosis," *Sevivot* 34 (1995): 52–62 [Hebrew]; M. HUTTER, "Adam als Gärtner und König (Gen 2,8.15)," *BZ* 30 (1986): 258–62; S. IZRE'EL, *The Amarna Scholarly Tablets* (CM 9; Groningen, Neth.: Styx, 1997); T. JACOBSEN, *The Harps That Once . . . Sumerian Poetry in Translation* (New Haven: Yale University Press, 1987); IDEM, *The Treasures of Darkness: A History of Mesopotamian Religion* (New Haven: Yale University Press, 1976); O. KEEL, *The Symbolism of the Biblical World: Ancient Near Eastern Iconography and the Book of Psalms* (Winona Lake, Ind.: Eisenbrauns, 1997); A. D. KILMER, "The Mesopotamian Counterpart of the Biblical *Nepilim*," in *Perspectives on Language and Text: Essays and Poems in Honor of Francis I. Andersen's Sixtieth Birthday* (ed. E. W. Conrad and E. G. Newing; Winona Lake, Ind.: Eisenbrauns, 1987), 39–43; G. S. KIRK, *Myth: Its Meaning and Function in Ancient and Other Cultures* (Berkeley: University of California Press, 1970); S. N. KRAMER and J. MAIER, *Myths of Enki, the Crafty God* (New York: Oxford University Press, 1989); W. G. LAMBERT, "The Historical Development of the Mesopotamian Pantheon: A Study in Sophisticated Polytheism," in *Unity and Diversity: Essays in the History, Literature, and Religion of the Ancient Near East* (ed. H. Goedicke and J. J. M. Roberts; Baltimore: Johns Hopkins University Press, 1975), 191–200; IDEM, "Myth and Mythmaking in Sumer and Akkad," *CANE* 3:1825–35; IDEM, "A New Look at the Babylonian Background of Genesis," *JTS* 16 (1965): 287–300; IDEM, "The Relationship of Sumerian and Babylonian Myth as Seen in Accounts of Creation," in *La circulation des biens, des personnes, et des idées dans le Proche-Orient ancien: Actes de la XXXVIIIe Rencontre assyriologique internationale* (ed. D. Charpin and F. Joannès; Paris: Éditions Recherche sur les Civilisations, 1992), 129–35; B. LANG, "Non-Semitic Deluge Stores and the Book of Genesis: A Bibliographical and Critical Survey," *Anthropos* 80 (1985): 605–15; E. LANGE et al., eds., *Mythos im Alten Testa-*

ment und seiner Umwelt: Festschrift für Hans-Peter Müller zum 65. Geburtstag
(BZAW 278; Berlin: de Gruyter, 1999); E. LAROCHE, Textes mythologiques hittites
en transcription (Paris: Klincksieck, 1969); L. LÉVY-BRUHL, How Natives Think
(London: Allen & Unwin, 1928); C. LÉVI-STRAUSS, Myth and Meaning (New
York: Schocken, 1978); IDEM, Structural Anthropology (2 vols.; Harmondsworth,
England: Penguin, 1963–1973); C. H. LONG, The Myths of Creation (Chico, Calif.:
Scholars Press, 1963); P. D. MILLER JR., "Eridu, Dunnu, and Babel: A Study in
Comparative Mythology," HAR 9 (1985): 227–51; W. L. MORAN, "A Mesopo-
tamian Myth and Its Biblical Transformation," in W. L. Moran, The Most Magic
Word: Essays on Babylonian and Biblical Literature (ed. R. S. Hendel; CBQMS
35; Washington: Catholic Biblical Association, 2002), 59–74; J. O'BRIEN and
W. MAJOR, In the Beginning: Creation Myths from Ancient Mesopotamia, Israel,
and Greece (Chico, Calif.: Scholars Press, 1982); A. OHLER, Mythologische Ele-
mente im alten Testament (Düsseldorf: Patmos, 1969); J. OSWALT, "The Myth of
the Dragon and Old Testament Faith," EvQ 49 (1977): 163–72; H. R. PAGE, The
Myth of Cosmic Rebellion: A Study of Its Reflexes in Ugaritic and Biblical Literature
(Leiden: Brill, 1996); S. B. PARKER, ed., Ugaritic Narrative Poetry (SBLWAW 9; Atlanta: Scholars Press, 1997); D. T. POTTS, ed., Dilmun: New Studies in the Archaeology and Early History of Bahrain (Berlin: Dietrich Reimer, 1983); D. B. REDFORD,
The Ancient Gods Speak: A Guide to Egyptian Religion (Oxford: Oxford University
Press, 2002); P. RICOEUR, "Myth and History," ER 10:273–82; S. SCHOTT, Mythe
und Mythenbildung im alten Ägypten (Leipzig: Hinrichs, 1945); M. S. SMITH,
"Mythology and Myth-Making in Ugaritic and Israelite Literatures," in Ugarit and
the Bible: Proceedings of the International Symposium on Ugarit and the Bible,
Manchester, September 1992 (ed. G. J. Brooke et al.; Münster: Ugarit, 1994),
293–341; W. VON SODEN, "Konflicte und ihre Bewältigung in babylonischen
Schöpfungs-und Fluterzählungen," MDOG 111 (1979): 1–34; K. L. SPARKS, "The
Problem of Myth in Ancient Historiography," in Rethinking the Foundations—
Historiography in the Ancient World and in the Bible: Essays in Honor of John Van
Seters (Berlin: de Gruyter, 2000), 269–80; D. T. TSUMURA, The Earth and the
Waters in Genesis 1 and 2 (JSOTSup 83; Sheffield: Sheffield Academic Press,
1989); E. B. TYLOR, Primitive Culture (London: Murray, 1913); J. VAN DIJK, "Myth
and Mythmaking in Ancient Egypt," CANE 3:1696– 1709; P. VEYNE, Did the
Greeks Believe Their Myths? An Essay on the Constitutive Imagination (Chicago:
University of Chicago Press, 1988); C. WESTERMANN, Genesis: A Commentary
(3 vols.; Minneapolis: Augsburg, 1984–1986), vol. 1; R. WHITING, ed., Mythology
and Mythologies: Methodological Approaches to Intercultural Influences (Melammu
2; Helsinki: Helsinki University Press, 2001); R. H. WILKINSON, The Complete
Gods and Goddesses of Ancient Egypt (London: Thames & Hudson, 2003); N. WYATT,
"The Expression bekor mawet in Job xviii 13 and Its Mythological Background,"
VT 40 (1990): 207–16; IDEM, Myths of Power: A Study of Royal Myth and Ideology
in Ugaritic and Biblical Tradition (Munster: Ugarit, 1996).

CHAPTER ELEVEN

Genealogies, King Lists, and Related Texts

Introduction

Whether out of curiosity or a desire for pedigree, human beings are interested in their ancestral heritage. In most cultures this heritage is expressed in genealogies, the written or oral compositions that depict ancestral relationships. The biblical writers were no exception to this rule, and one can trace an interest in genealogies from the earliest biblical writers through the Christian and Judaic literature into modern times. What becomes clear from these genealogies is that human beings attach a great deal of significance to the ancestral links that connect them with other people. This applies not only to ethnic and family ties but also to political and social institutions (e.g., priesthood and kingship) whose authority structures tend to follow the contours of ancestry. For this reason, many cultures preserve lists of political rulers—"king lists"—that connect contemporary generations of rulers with their ancient counterparts. Both genealogies and king lists were prominent genres in the ancient Near Eastern world.

It is appropriate to join together our discussions of the genealogies and king lists because the two genres overlap considerably in form and function. Generally speaking, both fit within a larger generic category that J. Goody has called the list genre, and for obvious reasons the dynastic king lists tend to follow genealogical lines. Moreover, we shall find that the king lists cannot be fully appreciated apart from the special insight we gain from the genealogies and that certain features in the biblical genealogies cannot be fully explained apart from the king lists.

11.1. Mesopotamian King Lists and Related Texts

King lists provided a chronological roll of former rulers, often noting the length of each monarch's reign as well as dynastic transitions, which were marked by horizontal lines, summary notations, or both. Some texts also noted gaps in the sequence. Because royal traditions tend to be dynastic and hereditary in character, all or part of each king list was also genealogical. The king lists were closely related to several other Near Eastern list genres. Ancient scribes were required to manage many date-sensitive archival materials, especially business and legal documents. In order to date these properly, they compiled various types of chronological lists, including not only king lists but also Babylonian date-year lists (e.g., *ANET* 269–71) and Assyrian eponym lists, which named each year after an Assyrian high official. The dating and preservation of records contributed to social and political stability, but the lists also provided chronological information for the king lists and chronicles composed by Mesopotamian scholars.

The Eblaite King Lists. These two lists are our oldest Mesopotamian exemplars, dating from near the destruction of the city of Ebla (Tell Mardikh) about 2400 B.C.E. The first text (Archi 1986) is an offering list that includes ten deceased but deified kings and six gods, each of whom received an offering of sheep. This text was probably used in the royal mortuary cult and is comparable to the Genealogy of Hammurabi's Dynasty, to be discussed below. The second text provides a bare list of seventy-two names, which was probably a scribal exercise tablet (Archi 2001). The early portions of the text move in reverse chronology beginning with the most recent king, but later on, the list is ordered according to the first cuneiform sign in the names (i.e., "alphabetically"). Reverse ordering of lists can be a natural consequence of following oral tradition, since it is the order we usually follow when our memory is unaided by written sources (Archi 2001).

Text and translation: A. ARCHI, "Die ersten zehn Könige von Ebla," *ZA* 76 (1986): 213–17. ***Bibliography:*** A. ARCHI, "The King-Lists from Ebla," in *Proceedings of the XLV Rencontre assyriologique internationale: History and Historiography in the Cuneiform World* (ed. Tz. Abusch et al.; 2 vols.; Bethesda, Md.: CDL Press, 2001), 1:1–13; G. PETTINATO, *Old Canaanite Cuneiform Texts of the Third Millennium* (Monographs on the Ancient Near East 1.7; Malibu, Calif.: Undena, 1979).

The Sumerian King List and Related Lists. The Sumerian King List (SKL) originated about 2000 B.C.E. Several different editions of the text survive, revealing a complicated literary history that probably goes back to a single original composition. In its most complete form, the text includes a list of antediluvian kings, followed by a reference to the flood itself, followed by a list of postdiluvian kings. The latest copy goes down to Damiq-ilišu (ca. 1816–1794 B.C.E.), the last king of Isin. The SKL notes the length of each king's reign, but the reign lengths are often exceptionally long, particularly in the case of the pre-flood kings (e.g., Alalgar reigned 36,000 years!). However, this pre-flood portion of the list was apparently not a part of the original composition because it does not appear in some manuscripts and because the kings mentioned in it are sometimes duplicated in the post-flood list (e.g., both Dumuzi and Enmenunna).

According to Jacobsen, the SKL was composed from two types of sources: date lists and legendary epics. Date lists provided the structural and chronological backbone of the text, and the epics are reflected in brief anecdotes associated with certain kings. So, for instance, when the SKL describes king Etana as "a shepherd, the one who ascended to heaven," it undoubtedly refers to his ascension in the Etana Legend (see 9.3.1). The chronological data in the SKL are sometimes peculiar, particularly in those early sections of the list that covered primeval periods for which the author could not have had date lists. In these cases, the lengths of reign are absurdly long and seem to have been derived using astronomical figures (for the antediluvian chronology) and operations from sexagesimal mathematics (for the postdiluvian chronology; see Young 1988, "Mathematical").

When and why was the SKL first composed? It presents kingship as a single succession of divinely appointed leaders that originated at the beginning of time. It is therefore reasonable to presume that the SKL was composed to legitimize a specific king by painting him as the one and only authentic king. Jacobsen believes that this king was Utu-hegel, king of Uruk, and that the list was composed to legitimize his reign after he liberated Sumer from Gutian domination about 2100 B.C.E. To be sure, the list also seems to legitimize the Isin dynasty at points (ca. 2017–1794 B.C.E.), but most scholars view this as a later adaptation of the older Utu-hegel list (e.g., Hallo 1963), a notable exception being Michalowski, who believes that the SKL was composed during the Isin period. Regardless, whether written for Utu-hegel or for the kings of Isin, the list spawned a literary tradition that lasted through Mesopotamian history (see the Dynastic Chronicle [12.1.1]) down into the Hellenistic period (the Seleucid King List in Akkadian [see Van Dijk]; Berossus's history in Greek [see 12.1.1]). The fact that the kinglists outlasted their original function in the Uruk and Isin periods suggests that scribes preserved them mainly out of antiquarian and historical interest. However, a comparison of the exemplars from the earliest to the latest copies reveals that the order and number of the kings varied somewhat from text to text. This fluidity was probably the result of various efforts to make the lists suit the necessities of political propaganda.

Some later exemplars in the SKL tradition, such as the Seleucid King List (Van Dijk, 43–52), were expanded to include not only the Mesopotamian kings but also their royal counselors. The counselors who lived before the flood were very wise superhuman figures known as the *apkallū*, and those who lived after the flood were called the *ummānū*. The *ummānū* were wise like the *apkallū* but entirely human (for more on the *apkallū* and *ummānū*, see 2.1). Although there is much variation in these late lists, the seventh of the pre-flood kings and counselors is often unique in some way. King Enmeduranki is the most common figure in this position; he was famous in Mesopotamia as the first human recipient of omen and astrological lore (Lambert). Tradition has it that he was taken to the heavenly assembly to receive this lore, and in another text—from the incantation series *Bīt Mēseri* (see 5.8.1)—we learn that his *apkallu* counselor, Utuabzu, also "ascended into heaven" (see Borger; Reiner).

The biblical genealogy that begins in Gen 5 and ends in Gen 11 is obviously similar to SKL tradition. Both exemplars are linear in form, both begin with creation, both are interrupted by the flood, and both include very long life spans prior to the flood. In Genesis, as in the Mesopotamian lists, the seventh figure (in this case Enoch) was unique because he ascended into heaven (see VanderKam). Moreover, the chronology in Gen 5 and 11 was apparently derived, like the chronology of its Mesopotamian counterparts, from Babylonian mathematical and astronomical data (Etz; Labuschagne; Young 1988 ["Application"]; 1990). Most scholars attribute these biblical materials to the exilic and/or postexilic Priestly source, which would explain why the biblical author was so familiar with Mesopotamian tradition. This Priestly author likely sought to enhance Jewish identity by composing a history that mimicked the traditions of his more powerful and influential Mesopotamian neighbors.

Texts and translations: R. BORGER, "Die Beschwörungsserie *Bīt Mēseri* und die Himmelfahrt Henochs," *JNES* 33 (1974): 183–96 (Neo-Assyrian ritual text with list of *apkallu*); GLASSNER, 117–27; T. JACOBSEN, *The Sumerian King List* (AS 11; Chicago: University of Chicago Press, 1939) (critical edition of the SKL); S. LANGDON, *Historical Inscriptions: Containing Principally the Chronological Prism, W-B. 444* (Oxford Editions of Cuneiform Texts 2; Weld-Blundell Collection 2; Oxford: Oxford University Press, 1923), 1–26, pls. I–VI (best manuscript of the SKL); VAN DIJK, "Die Inschriftenfunde" (Seleucid-era the Uruk King List with royal advisors). ***Translation:*** *ANET* 265–67 (SKL), 566–67 (SKL). ***Bibliography:*** EDZARD, "Königslisten und Chroniken, A"; D. V. ETZ, "The Numbers of Genesis V 3–31: A Suggested Conversion and Its Implications," *VT* 43 (1993): 171–89; B. GOODNICK, "Parallel Lists of Prediluvian Patriarchs," *Dor le Dor* 13 (1984): 47–51; GRAYSON, "Königslisten und Chroniken, B"; W. W. HALLO, *The Ancient Near Eastern Background of Some Modern Western Institutions* (Leiden: Brill, 1996), 1–15; IDEM, "Beginning and End of the Sumerian King List in the Nippur Recension," *JCS* 17 (1963): 52–57; T. C. HARTMAN, "Some Thoughts on the Sumerian King List and Genesis 5 and 11b," *JBL* 91 (1972): 25–32; G. F. HASEL, "The Genealogies of Gen 5 and 11 and Their Alleged Babylonian Background," *AUSS* 16 (1978): 361–74; J. KLEIN, "A New Nippur Duplicate of the Sumerian Kinglist in the Brockmon Collection, University of Haifa," in *Velles paraules: Ancient Near Eastern Studies in Honor of Miguel Civil* (ed. P. Michalowski et al.; AuOr 9; Barcelona: Editorial AUSA, 1991), 123–29; F. R. KRAUS, "Zur Liste der älteren Könige von Babylonien," *ZA* 50 (1952): 29–60; C. J. LABUSCHAGNE, "The Life Spans of the Patriarchs," in *New Avenues in the Study of the Old Testament: A Collection of Old Testament Studies* (ed. A. S. van der Woude; OTS 25; New York: Brill, 1989), 121–27; W. G. LAMBERT, "Enmeduranki and Related Matters," *JCS* 21 (1967): 126–38; P. MICHALOWSKI, "History as Charter: Some Observations on the Sumerian King List," in *Studies in Literature from the Ancient Near East: Dedicated to Samuel Noah Kramer* (ed. J. M. Sasson; AOS 65; New Haven: American Oriental Society, 1984), 237–48; E. REINER, "The Etiological Myth of the 'Seven Sages,'" *Or* 30 (1961): 1–11; M. B. ROWTON, "The Date of the Sumerian King List," *JNES* 19 (1960): 158–62; E. SOLLBERGER, "New Lists of the Kings of Ur and Isin," *JCS* 8 (1954): 135–36; J. C. VANDERKAM, *Enoch: A Man for All Generations* (Columbia: University of South Carolina Press, 1995), 6–14; VAN SETERS, *In Search of History*, 70–72; G. P. VERBRUGGHE and J. M. WICKERSHAM, *Berossos and Manetho, Introduced and Translated: Native Traditions in Ancient Mesopotamia and Egypt* (Ann Arbor: University of Michigan Press, 2001), 13–91; C. VINCENTE, "The Tell Leilan Recension of the Sumerian King List," *ZA* 85 (1995): 234–70; J. WALTON, "The Antediluvian Section of the Sumerian King List and Genesis 5," *BA* 44 (1981): 207–8; C. WILCKE, "Genealogical and Geographical Thought in the Sumerian King List," in *DUMU-E2–DUB-BA-A: Studies in Honor of Åke*

Sjöberg (ed. H. Behrens, D. T. Loding, and M. Roth; OPSNKF 11; Philadelphia: University Museum, 1989), 557–71; D. W. YOUNG, "The Influence of Babylonian Algebra on Longevity among the Antediluvians," *ZAW* 102 (1990): 321–35; IDEM, "A Mathematical Approach to Certain Dynastic Spans in the Sumerian King List," *JNES* 47 (1988): 123–29; IDEM, "On the Application of Numbers from Babylonian Mathematics to Biblical Life Spans and Epochs," *ZAW* 100 (1988): 332–61.

The Lagaš King List. According to its original publisher, E. Sollberger, BM 23103, also known as the Lagaš King List (LKL), is closely related to the SKL. Like the SKL, the LKL includes a reference to the flood, the provision of kingship by the gods afterward, and a list of postdiluvian kings. But by comparison, the LKL is peculiar for two reasons. Although modern scholars know the names of the rulers of Lagaš during this period, most of the kings in the list are entirely unknown apart from it. Moreover, the list attributes extremely long reigns to the kings, not only the ancient ones, as in the SKL, but also more recent ones. According to Sollberger, this suggests that the LKL parodies the SKL because the Sumerian list had failed to include the rulers of Lagaš. The new text legitimized Lagašite claims to the throne by tracing kingship through Lagaš rather than through Kish, Uruk, and Ur as in the SKL. This is a reasonable appraisal, which demonstrates that similar texts can be composed through quite different modes of composition. It is a classical example of generic extension, in which the king list genre was extended to create a new type of text: the parody king list. If Gen 5 and 11 were composed to mimic the SKL tradition, as suggested above, then Genesis was not the first text to do so.

Texts and translations: GLASSNER, 144–49; E. SOLLBERGER, "The Rulers of Lagaš," *JCS* 21 (1967): 279–91. *Bibliography:* EDZARD, "Königslisten und Chroniken, A."

The Assyrian Eponym Lists and Chronicles. From early in the second millennium onwards, Assyrian documents were dated with the formula "day X, month Y, *līmu* PN," where *līmu* meant "eponym" and PN was the name of the government official after whom the year was named. This dating system depended on preserving a long, continuous list of date formulas, and it is to this effort that we owe the Assyrian eponym canons. The eponym manuscripts were compiled in two forms, called Canon A (eponym lists) and Canon B (eponym chronicles). Manuscripts in Canon A contain bare lists of the eponyms whereas those in Canon B include brief historical entries. Our oldest list of Assyrian eponyms dates to about 1200 B.C.E., but this list is fragmentary and cannot be connected to the continuous list that modern scholars have reconstructed for the period between 910 to 649 B.C.E. Ancient Assyrian scholars certainly used the eponym lists to construct their kings lists (see the next entry), and the eponym chronicles—which included historical information—were apparently consulted by the authors of the Babylonian Chronicles (see Weissert).

Although the use of eponyms is normally associated with Assyrian culture, readers should note the five fragmentary copies of an Old Babylonian eponym chronicle recovered from Mari (see Glassner).

Texts and translations: GLASSNER, 160–76; A. UNGNAD, "Datenlisten," *RlA* 2:131–94; IDEM, "Eponym," *RlA* 2:412–57. *Translations: ANET* 274 (partial); *COS* 1.136: 465–66 (partial). *Bibliography:* M. BIROT, "Les chroniques 'assyriennes' de Mari," *MARI* 4 (1985): 219–42; I. L. FINKEL and J. E. READE, "Assyrian Eponyms, 873–649 BC," *Or* 67 (1998): 248–54; IDEM, "Lots of Eponyms," *Iraq* 57 (1995): 167–72; J. J. FINKELSTEIN, "Mesopotamia," *JNES* 21 (1962): 73–92; A. R. MILLARD, "Assyrian Royal Names in Biblical Hebrew," *JSS* 21 (1976): 1–14; IDEM, *The Eponyms of the Assyrian Empire, 910–612 BC* (SAAS 2; Helsinki: Helsinki University Press, 1994); VAN SETERS, *In Search of History*, 69–70; E. WEISSERT, "Interrelated Chronographic Patterns in the Assyrian Eponym Chronicle and the 'Babylonian Chronicle': A Comparative View," in *La circulation des biens, des personnes, et des idées dans le Proche-Orient ancient: Actes de la XXVIIIe Rencontre assyriologique internationale* (ed. D. Charpin and F. Joannès; Paris: Éditions Recherche sur les Civilisations, 1992), 273–82.

The Assyrian King Lists. The Assyrian king lists (AKL) exist in three formal varieties (A, B, and C), each with its peculiar features and functions (Röllig). The earliest manuscript of AKL-A dates to the tenth century B.C.E., and the most recent copies date to the late eighth century B.C.E. The text includes four sections: (1) a list of seventeen names followed with the final notation "seventeen kings who lived in tents"; (2) a genealogy of ten kings that moves chronologically backward and ends with the notation "ten kings who are ancestors"; (3) a list of six kings whose "eponyms are missing"; and (4) a long list of kings that moves chronologically forward and includes brief, scattered narrative anecdotes. Yamada has worked out the explanation for this structure and its idiosyncrasies and for the general composition history of the text.

According to standard readings of AKL-A, the text was composed to legitimize the rule of Šamši-Adad I, an Amorite usurper who seized the Assyrian throne ca. 1813 B.C.E. (contra Van Seters; Yuhong). Three major sources were used in the composition, including a list of Amorite "tent dwellers" (section one), a list of leading forefathers from Šamši-Adad's family (section two), and a list of Assur's kings from the collapse of the Ur III empire until the reign of Šamši-Adad (sections three and four). The first section, of tent-dwelling kings, includes many of the names found in the ancestral cult's Genealogy of Hammurabi's Dynasty (see below), so it is believed that a similar source was consulted here. The similarities stem from the common Amorite background shared by Hammurabi and Šamši-Adad. The second section of the AKL apparently originated as a list of leaders from Šamši-Adad's family. Its separate origin is confirmed by its genealogical form, whose chronological sequence is the reverse of the rest of AKL-A (cf. the second Ebla list, above). The third and fourth sections were apparently composed from king lists and an eponym chronicle of some sort, as is suggested by the text's confession that some "eponyms were missing" and by the fact that numerous dates in these sections were cited as eponyms. Certain fictions were necessary to make the scheme work (e.g., Puzur-Ashur II was *not* the son of Naram-Sin, as AKL-A says; see Van Seters). After a lengthy dormancy in the tradition, a second edition of AKL-A was composed to legitimize the reign of Bēlu-bāni (ca.1600 B.C.E.). This conclusion can be reached by comparing AKL-A with other sources available from the period. The third edition of AKL-A followed, appearing in the Middle Assyrian period when Tukulti-Ninurta I (1243–1207) greatly expanded Assyrian influence and power. From this period on, the text was periodically updated with reliable contemporary data. It no longer functioned to legitimate a particular king or dynasty so much as it became an expression of Assyrian pride. In the later periods the text served two other purposes. In its amulet form, it served as a ritual blessing for the royal family, and in its standard tablet form it became an important source of chronographic and historical information. This historical interest prompted scribes to add to the text anecdotal comments that served no purpose in the chronological scheme but reflected instead a natural tendency for the chronographers to expand their lists by adding historical notes. The chronographic form of the document naturally precluded excesses in that direction.

The Assyrian chronographic tradition is more clearly expressed in the generic innovation of AKL-B (Weidner). This tradition, sometimes referred to as the Synchronistic Chronicle, is arranged in parallel columns that correlate the reigns of Assyrian kings with their Babylon contemporaries. As they did with AKL-A, ancient scholars consulted these texts in their chronographic and historical research. The third variety of Assyrian king list, AKL-C, is a bare list of Assyrian kings without genealogical references or lengths of reign. Its purpose is unclear, but it obviously did not serve a chronographic function.

Texts and translations: I. J. GELB, "Two Assyrian King Lists," *JNES* 13 (1954): 209–30; GLASSNER, 136–45; E. NASSOUHI, "Grand liste des rois d'Assyrie," *AfO* 4 (1927): 1–11; A. POEBEL, "The Assyrian King List from Khorsabad," *JNES* 1 (1942): 247–306, 460–92; IDEM, "The Assyrian King List from Khorsabad—Concluded," *JNES* 2 (1943): 56–90; E. F. WEIDNER, "Die grosse Königsliste aus Assur," *AfO* 3 (1926): 66–71. *Translations:* ANET 272–74 (AKL-B), 564–66 (AKL-A); *COS* 1.135: 463–65 (AKL-A). *Bibliography:* J. A. BRINKMAN, "Comments on the Nassouhi Kinglist and the Assyrian Kinglist Tradition," *Or* 42 (1973): 306–19; GRAYSON, "Königslisten und Chroniken, B," 101–25; F. R. KRAUS, "Könige, die in Zelten wohnten," *Mededelingen der Koninklijke Nederlandse Akademie van Wetenschappen* 28 (1965): 123–43; B. LANDSBERGER, "Assyrische Königsliste und 'Dunkel Zeitalter,'" *JCS* 8 (1954): 31–133; A. MALAMAT, *Mari and the Early Israelite Experience* (Schweich Lectures of the British Academy 1984; Oxford: Oxford University Press, 1989), 98–101; RÖLLIG, "Zur Typologie und Entstehung der babylonischen und assyrischen Königslisten"; SPARKS, *Ethnicity and Identity in Ancient Israel,* 44–51; J. VAN SETERS, *In Search of History,* 72–76; Sh. YAMADA, "The Editorial History of the Assyrian King List," *ZAW* 84 (1994): 11–37; IDEM, "Notes on the Genealogical Data of the Assyrian King List," *ErIsr* 27 (2003): 265–275; W. YUHONG, "Did the Assyrian King List Attempt to Prove the Legitimacy of Šamši-Adad?" *Journal of Ancient Civilizations* 5 (1990): 25–37.

The Ur-Isin King List. This list, which we know from two copies, covers both the Third Dynasty of Ur (Ur-Nammu to Ibbi-Sin, 2112–2004 B.C.E.) and the First Dynasty of Isin (Išbi-Irra to Damiq-ilišu, 2017–1794). The text ends with the fourth year of Damiq-ilišu and so was composed about 1813–1812 B.C.E. Its purpose was probably chronographic, as is the case with a number of texts already discussed.

Text and translation: E. SOLLBERGER, "New Lists of the Kings of Ur and Isin," *JCS* 8 (1954): 135–36. *Bibliography:* GRAYSON, "Königslisten und Chroniken, B," 90–96.

The Larsa King List. This list, composed about 1738 B.C.E., provides a simple register of Larsa's fourteen dynastic kings from Naplanum to Rim-Sin I, followed by Hammurabi, conqueror of Larsa, and his son, Samsu-iluna. The complete list thus includes sixteen names along with the length of their reigns in Larsa. The document was composed from date lists and served primarily to legitimize Hammurabi's rule in Larsa.

Text and translation: GRAYSON, "Königslisten und Chroniken, B," 89. *Bibliography:* GRAYSON, "Königslisten und Chroniken, B," 89; E. GRICE, *Chronology of the Larsa Dynasty* (YOS 4.1; New Haven: Yale University Press, 1919), 1–43.

The Babylonian King Lists. Röllig has identified three varieties of Babylonian king lists (BKL): A, B, and C. These three texts are generically similar, so it is sufficient to examine only the larger text, BKL-A. Although the date and provenance of BKL-A are uncertain, the list covers the period from the First Dynasty of Babylon (ca. 1894–1595 B.C.E.) until the founding of the Neo-Babylonian Chaldean dynasty at the end of the seventh century B.C.E. It is arranged according to dynastic succession, and each section of the text includes a dynastic list of kings along with the lengths of their reigns, followed by a summary statement such as "132 (years) 6 months, 11 kings, dynasty of Isin," followed by a horizontal line. The accuracy of the text suggests that it stands at the end of a long tradition of similar chronographic texts. In this respect, its functional character is like the late—but not early—uses of AKL-A.

Texts, translations, and studies: ANET 271 (BKL-B), 272 (BKL-A); GRAYSON, "Königslisten und Chroniken, B," 96–97, 100 (BKL-A,-B, and-C); RÖLLIG, "Zur Typologie und Entstehung der babylonischen und assyrischen Königslisten."

Seleucid-Era King Lists. We possess two somewhat different king lists from the Seleucid period. The first is a fragmentary text from Uruk, which provides a list of kings that begins with the Babylonians, passes through the Persian period, and ends with the Greek king Seleuces II. The length of each king's reign is included (e.g., "7 Years: Alexander"). The other text, the so-called Seleucid King List, begins with Alexander the Great and works its way through the Hellenistic period. The entries in the text take this form: "Year 32: Antiochus, son of Seleucus, became king. He ruled for 20 years. Year 51, month Ajaru, 16th day: Antiochus, the great king, died. Year 52: Antiochus (II), son of Antiochus (I), became king. He ruled for 15 years." The author of the list often notes when the king's death involved unusual circumstances, such as "Seleucus . . . was killed in the West" or "Antiochus the king was put to death upon the command of his father." In this respect, the list sometimes takes on the character of a kind of chronicle.

Texts and translations: A. J. SACHS and D. J. WISEMAN, "A Babylonian King List of the Hellenistic Period," *Iraq* 16 (1954): 202–11 (Seleucid King List); VAN DIJK, "Die

Inschriftenfunde" (Uruk King List). **Bibliography:** R. BORGER, "Der Aufstieg des Neu-babylonischen Reiches," *JCS* 19 (1965): 59–78; GRAYSON, "Königslisten und Chroniken, B," 97–100; J. SCHAUMBERGER, "Die neue Seleukidenliste BM 35603 und die makkabäische Chronologie," *Bib* 36 (1955): 423–35.

11.2. Egyptian King List

There is only one text from pharaonic times that attempts to provide a chronological list of Egyptian kings along with the lengths of their reigns: the Turin Canon. In addition, several groupings of royal names and/or royal images have been found in the mortuary temples of ancient Egypt.

Mortuary Royal Assemblies. How one defines "king list" determines whether these three lists lie within the scope of this discussion, but excepting the Karnak list, the exemplars clearly enumerate the Egyptian kings in chronological order, albeit incompletely and without chronological information. The lists, inscribed in mortuary temples, registered the names of deceased kings who were to be honored during ancestral banquets. In this respect, the texts are similar to the Ebla and Ugaritic king lists and also to the Genealogy of Hammurabi's Dynasty. The Egyptian lists are selective and exclude especially the "heretic" Amarna kings, among others. The major exemplars come from Karnak (Thutmose III, Eighteenth Dynasty), Abydos (Seti I, Nineteenth Dynasty), and Saqqara (tomb of the "overseer of works," reign of Ramses II, Nineteenth Dynasty).

Texts and translations: A. CAULFEILD and T. ST. GEORGE, *The Temple of the Kings at Abydos I* (London: Quaritch, 1902) (Abydos); E. MEYER, *Aegyptische Chronologie* (Berlin: G. Reimer, 1904) (Abydos; Saqqara); K. SETHE and W. HELCK, *Urkunden der 18. Dynastie* (5 vols.; Urk 4; Leipzig: Hinrichs, 1906–1909 [vols. 1–4, Sethe]; Berlin: Akademie, 1958 [vol. 5, Helck]), 2:607–610 (Karnak). **Translations:** COS 1.37A–C: 68–71. **Bibliography:** J. MÁLEK, "Special Features of the Saqqara King-List," *JSSEA* 12 (1982): 21–28; REDFORD, *Pharaonic King-Lists, Annals, and Day-Books;* D. WILDUNG, "Aufbau und Zweckbestim-mung der Königliste von Karnak," *GM* 9 (1974): 41–48.

The Turin Canon and Its Tradition. Our copy is papyrus no. 1874 of the Egyptian Museum of Turin. It was composed during the New Kingdom reign of Ramsees II (1290–1224 B.C.E.) but includes more than three hundred earlier kings. It traces Egyptian kingship from a mythological period, in which the gods ruled, until the reign of the Hyksos kings (1640–1532 B.C.E.), then there is a break in the text. The mythological and legendary character of the list's early portions is similar to the SKL, the difference being that the Turin Canon's list is composed exclusively of deities in the first two sections. These deities are followed by a list of "heroes" and then by the dynasty of Menes, traditional founder of Egypt's First Dynasty. The Turin Canon includes sixteen sections, with groupings based on the location of the royal residence, on genealogical continuity, or on periods of foreign rule. Each section is prefaced by a heading and ends with a summation such as this: "Total of kings of the Residence [Itj-towy], 8; making 213 years, 1 month, 17 days." The first word of each heading and closing summary is written in red ink, a feature that made it easier to consult the text for chronological and historical purposes. These summary statements are reminiscent of those used in AKL-A and of *toledoth* statements found in the pentateuchal genealogies (Gen 2:4; 5:1; 6:9; 10:1; 11:10; 11:27; 25:19; Num 3:1). Like some of the Mesopotamian exemplars, the Turin Canon (TC) also includes scattered historical anecdotes.

The author of the TC had access to accurate sources from the Eleventh Dynasty onward, and the more curious names in the list are best explained as misreadings of an earlier hieratic source. The TC's list of early kings is not very accurate, as a comparison with the older and more dependable Palermo Stone shows (see 12.2.1). The TC's author was obviously hard pressed to find sources for the early periods of Egyptian history, and as in many king lists, he resorted to the inclusion of deities, heroes, and legendary figures in his rendition of kingship's early history. The text therefore adheres to a pattern that appears in the Sumerian list as well: it began with the most reliable and available sources—other lists—and then filled in the gaps with a combination of traditional sources and scholarly speculations. The stability of the tradition established by the TC is illustrated by its close similarity to the much later list provided in Manetho's third-century B.C.E. history of Egypt (Redford). The TC was carefully structured so that it could be easily consulted for chronological purposes, but its brief narrative anecdotes attest to antiquarian concerns as well. So we see that both Mesopotamian and Egyptian scribes found it difficult to confine their interests to mere chronography (cf. SKL and AKL-A).

Texts: A. H. GARDINER, *The Royal Canon of Turin* (Oxford: Griffith Institute, 1959); W. G. WADDELL, *Manetho* (LCL; Cambridge: Harvard University Press, 1980). *Translation:* COS 1.37D: 71–3 (partial). *Bibliography:* J. MÁLEK, "The Original Version of the Royal Canon of Turin," *JEA* 68 (1982): 93–106; P. F. O'MARA, *The Chronology of the Palermo and Turin Canons* (La Canada, Calif.: Paulette, 1979); REDFORD, *Pharaonic King-Lists, Annals, and Day-Books*, esp. 1–18, 203–332; G. P. VERBRUGGHE and J. M. WICKERSHAM, *Berossos and Manetho, Introduced and Translated: Native Traditions in Ancient Mesopotamia and Egypt* (Ann Arbor: University of Michigan Press, 2001), 95–215.

11.3. Ugaritic King Lists

The Ugaritic King Lists. Our exemplars of the Ugaritic king lists include one fragmentary Ugaritic text (RS 24.257 = *KTU* 1.113) and four Akkadian texts, of which three are complete (RS 94.2518). The first text, known for some time, has come into clearer focus only with the discovery of syllabic Akkadian exemplars. The lists are texts from a ritual associated with the shades of Ugarit's deceased kings, here understood as divine beings (e.g., "the god who is Niqmepa"). Many scholars view the texts as part of an ongoing royal mortuary cult akin to the Mesopotamian *kispum* (see 5.9.2; del Olmo Lete), although it is still possible that such rites were used only occasionally, when recently deceased kings joined the company of their ancestors (as in *KTU* 1.161; see 5.9.4). In this second case, ongoing provisions for deceased kings would have been provided through the regular sacrificial cult rather than through a special mortuary cult. The names in the Ugaritic and Akkadian lists are not easily reconcilable. Two somewhat different schemes have been worked out to explain their differences (cf. Pardee; Arnaud), but it seems, in the end, that the two texts do not offer us identical lists of Ugarit's kings.

Texts and translations: D. ARNAUD, "Prolégomènes à la rédaction d'une histoire d'Ougarit II: Les bordereaux de rois divinisés," *Studi micenei ed egeo-anatolici* 41 (1998): 153–73 (RS 94.2518); D. PARDEE, *Ritual and Cult at Ugarit* (SBLWAW 10; Atlanta: Society of Biblical Literature, 2002), 195–210. *Translation: COS* 1.104: 356–7 (*KTU* 1.113). *Bibliography:* T. J. LEWIS, *Cults of the Dead in Ancient Israel and Ugarit* (HSM 39; Atlanta: Scholars Press, 1989), 47–52; G. DEL OLMO LETE, *Canaanite Religion: According to the Liturgical Texts of Ugarit* (Bethesda, Md.: CDL Press, 1999); B. B. SCHMIDT, *Israel's Beneficent Dead: Ancestor Cult and Necromancy in Ancient Israelite Religion and Tradition* (FAT 11; Tübingen: J. C. B. Mohr, 1994).

11.4. Near Eastern and Greek Genealogies

Genealogies are oral or written texts that represent the ancestral relationships between people. The two basic forms of genealogy are *linear* (it includes only one person from each generation, thus producing a serial list) and *segmented* (it includes more than one person from each generation, thus producing various branches, like a family tree). These two basic forms correspond generally to different kinds of genealogical functions, as we will see. Two corresponding genealogical features are depth and breadth. *Depth* corresponds to how many generations are included in a genealogy whereas *breadth* refers to how many individuals are included in each generation. Thus the biblical genealogy that includes Noah and his three sons has a depth of two generations and a maximum breadth of three individuals. Although the breadth and depth of a genealogy could theoretically grow indefinitely, research demonstrates that there is a strong tendency for genealogies to simplify over time by eliminating individual names and even genealogical segments that are no longer useful, especially older components of the genealogies. Omissions such as these can be deliberate, but more often they are an accidental result of "structural amnesia," a propensity to forget unimportant elements in the genealogy (Barnes). To summarize, although genealogies naturally tend to add new elements over time, for a variety of reasons they also tend to become more streamlined and simplified.

Recent studies of biblical and Near Eastern genealogies are beholden to modern anthropology, which has the advantage of observing how oral genealogies work in living cultures. Let us consider just one example. The Humr people of Sudan trace their lineage back to a fictional ancestor named Humr, who fathered sons and grandsons who in name and number corresponded to the Humr tribes (Cunnison). Eponymous ancestors such as these are common in oral gene-alogies and provide a reasonable, if speculative, explanation for the origins of tribes and peoples. Two other important features also emerge from the Humr sources. First, political and domestic genealogies sampled from the same time period do not match because they reflect two different sets of relational contin-gencies, and second, a comparison of Humr political genealogies from 1905 and 1955 reveals that the genealogies changed to reflect new political realities. We thus learn from the Humr samples that genealogical content can be fluid because it varies with function and because it sometimes adjusts to reflect changing circumstances.

Genealogy of the Hammurabi Dynasty. This genealogy was composed for the great-great-grandson of Hammurabi, Ammiṣaduqa. With this text, Ammiṣaduqa invited his deceased ancestors, including Hammurabi, to attend a ritual *kispum* meal in their honor (see Malamat). This was probably an attempt to secure the favor of these potentially restless ancestral spirits. The genealogy can be divided into four sections. Section one (lines 1–19) includes a list of what modern schol-ars describe as "tribal eponyms," "geographical toponyms," and "early kings," but for the ancients these nineteen names represented consecutive rulers. Sections two and three (lines 20–38) provide a nine-generation genealogy of the Babylo-nian dynastic kings and a list of those overlooked in the first two sections, partic-ularly tribal entities associated with the dynasty and fallen soldiers who had perished on the dynasty's behalf. A statement at the end identifies the genre of the text: "come ye, eat this, drink this, (and) bless Ammiṣaduqa the son of Ammiditana, the king of Babylon." This text has often been compared to the ge-nealogies in Gen 10 because it includes eponymous ancestors (e.g., the fictional king Heana) who are the ostensible forefathers of tribal groups (e.g., the tribal Haneans). Genesis 10 similarly presents the Assyrians as the children of a man named Assur, the Canaanites as the children of a man named Canaan, and so on. A closer parallel to Gen 10 is found, however, in the Pseudo-Hesiodic Catalogue of Women (see below).

Text and translation: J. J. FINKELSTEIN, "The Genealogy of the Hammurapi Dynasty," *JCS* 20 (1966): 95–118. *Translation: COS* 1.134: 462–63. *Bibliography:* M. CHAVALAS, "Genea-logical History as 'Charter,'" in *Faith, Tradition, and History: Old Testament Historiography in Its Near Eastern Context* (ed. A. R. Millard et al.; Winona Lake, Ind.: Eisenbrauns, 1994), 103–28; W. G. LAMBERT, "Another Look at Hammurapi's Ancestors," *JCS* 22 (1968): 1–2; A. MALAMAT, *Mari and the Early Israelite Experience* (Oxford: Oxford University Press, 1989), 96–107; RÖLLIG, "Zur Typologie und Entstehung der babylonischen und assyr-ischen Königslisten."

Egyptian Priestly Genealogies. Our sources from the Egyptian Late period in-clude a number of linear priestly genealogies that vary in depth from ten or more to about sixty generations. The length and linear form of these genealogies is a consequence of their function, which was to legitimize the authority of priestly families by linking them to the priesthood of hoary antiquity. Long priestly genealogies first appeared during the first millennium, when royal power at Thebes was ebbing and the priestly families of Thebes moved to secure their sacred office and advance their political aspirations (Wilson). The fact that earlier lists are not preserved suggests that these new genealogies were based at least in part on pious fictions rather than legitimate sources. When the genealogies were shortened through telescoping—and they often were—the connection with antiquity was preserved by excising the middle rather than the beginning of the list. Although most of the Egyptian priestly genealogies were linear in form and legitimizing in function, a recently republished segmented genealogy from the Cairo Museum (JE 38224) has yielded a seventh-century priestly genealogy that includes both male and female elements (Leahy/Leahy). Like a similar list from Copenhagen (AeIN 1040), the Cairo exemplar includes pictures of the deceased male ancestors but represents females only as names in the text. These genealogies apparently enumerated forefathers who would receive offerings during ancestral cultic activities. The most important comparative exemplars from the Hebrew Bible are the postexilic priestly genealogies in 1 Chron 5:27–41 (Eng. 6:1–15); 6:35–38 (Eng. 6:50–53); 9:11–13; Ezra 7:1–5; and Neh 11:10–14; 12:10–11 (see Johnson). A comparison of these biblical genealogies reveals a pattern of telescoping (cf. 1 Chron 5:27–41; Ezra 7:1–5) and fluidity (cf. 1 Chron 5:27–41; 9:10–11) like that which appears in the Egyptian texts. Also, it is perhaps not a coincidence that the Hebrew priestly genealogies appeared, like their Egyptian counterparts, in conjunction with the historical demise of a strong native monarchy.

Texts and translations: L. BORCHARDT, *Die Mittel zur zeitlichen Festlegung von Punkten der ägyptischen Geschichte* (Cairo: Selbstverlag, 1935), 96–112 (Memphite genealogy); L. M. LEAHY and A. LEAHY, "The Genealogy of a Priestly Family from Heliopolis," *JEA* 72 (1986): 133–47. *Bibliography:* M. D. JOHNSON, *The Purpose of the Biblical Genealogies* (Cambridge: Cambridge University Press, 1969), 37–44; H. KEES, *Das Priestertum im ägyptischen Staat vom neuen Reich bis zur Spätzeit* (Leiden: Brill, 1953); K. A. KITCHEN, "Some Egyptian Background to the Old Testament," *TynBul* 5 (1960): 14–18; J. QUAEGE-BEUR, "Contribution à la prosopographie des prêtres memphites à l'époque ptolémaïque," *AncSoc* 3 (1972): 77–109; IDEM, "The Genealogy of the Memphite High Priest Family in the Hellenistic Period," in *Studies on Ptolemaic Memphis* (ed. D. J. Crawford, J. Quaegebeur, and W. Clarysse; Studia hellenistica 24; Leuven: n.p., 1980), 43–81; REDFORD, *Pharaonic King-Lists, Annals, and Day-Books,* 62–64.

The Pseudo-Hesiodic Catalogue of Women. Greek genealogies provide some of the closest comparative exemplars for the biblical genealogies, particularly for the segmented genealogies in Gen 10 and elsewhere. An excellent and early example is the sixth-century B.C.E. Catalogue of Women, a work of antiquarian historiography that was in antiquity attributed to Hesiod but is now viewed as Pseudo-Hesiodic. The text accounts for the origins of the Hellenic tribes by postulating a common eponymous forefather named Hellen, who begot sons and grandsons whose names reflect the various Greek ethnic groups (Doros [Dorians], Aiolos [Aeolians], Ion [Ionians], Akhaios [Achaeans], etc.). A comparison of this genealogy with later genealogies, such as those of Euripides (fifth century B.C.E.), re-veals that these ethnic genealogical traditions were rather fluid (Hall, 40–51). The Catalogue accounts for the origins of foreign nations in a similar way, citing eponymous ancestors and drawing genealogical relationships between them in a manner akin to that used by the author of Gen 10 (although the Catalogue does not appear to construct a genealogy that leads back to one individual, as Gen 10 does). Genealogies in the Catalogue often reflect numerical aesthetics, preferring the chief characters to have progeny that number two, three, ten, twelve, fifty, and so forth. This is comparable to Israel's tribal lists, which reflect a preference for ten or twelve tribes (see Sparks 2003; cf. Judg 5; Gen 49; Deut 33; Ezek 48). In spite of the striking similarities enumerated here, Hess has cautioned that there are also important differences between the Catalogue and the Hebrew genealo-gies (Hess). For more on the historiographical aspects of the Catalogue of Women, see 12.6.

Text and translation: H. G. EVELYN-WHITE, *Hesiod: The Homeric Hymns and Homerica* (LCL; Cambridge: Harvard University Press, 1982), 2–65. *Bibliography:* J. HALL, *Ethnic Identity in Greek Antiquity* (Cambridge: Cambridge University Press, 1997); R. S. HESS, "The Genealogies of Genesis 1–11 and Comparative Literature," *Bib* 70 (1989): 241–54; G. N. KNOPPERS, "Greek Historiography and the Chronicler's History: A Reexamination," *JBL* 122 (2003): 627–50; SPARKS, *Ethnicity and Identity in Ancient Israel*, 51–75, 298; IDEM, "Genesis 49 and the Tribal List Tradition in Ancient Israel," *ZAW* 115 (2003): 327–47; R. THOMAS, *Oral Tradition and Written Record in Classical Athens* (Cambridge: Cambridge University Press, 1989); J. VAN SETERS, "The Primeval Histories of Greece and Israel Com-pared," *ZAW* 100 (1988): 1–22; P. VEYNE, *Did the Greeks Believe in Their Myths? An Essay on the Constitutive Imagination* (Chicago: University of Chicago Press, 1988); M. L. WEST, *The Hesiodic Catalogue of Women: Its Nature, Structure, and Origins* (Oxford: Oxford University Press, 1985).

Concluding Observations

The Near Eastern materials discussed in this chapter include lists of kings and royal functionaries, priestly genealogies, and, in a few cases, dynastic genealo-gies used in ancestral cults. The bulk of the materials served chronographic, his-torical, or legitimizing functions. In some cases, the lists began as works of propaganda but were later copied and studied for their historical value (SKL; AKL-A). In at least one instance, it appears that a king list was deliberately in-vented to mimic and parody another list (LKL). Five key tendencies can be identi-fied in these lists. First, their authors used whatever sources were convenient and available. Although date lists, eponym lists, and other king lists were the sources of choice, in their absence the authors resorted to all sorts of traditions that we might view as legendary or traditional, particularly in the portions of the lists that dealt with hoary antiquity (see SKL; AKL-A; Turin Canon). Second, the compilers of the lists were frequently inclined to add brief narrative anecdotes from nonlist sources. Although the functions of the texts generally prevented excesses in this direction, this natural tendency to expand the lists into narratives attests to the antiquarian and historical interests of the scribes. Third, when the lists were composed for purposes of legitimation, the scribes often took liberties with their source materials in the effort to compose lists that accomplished their aims. Fourth, when the king lists and genealogies outlived their original functions as propaganda, they were sometimes preserved as objects of historical and anti-quarian interest (SKL; AKL-A). And finally, in the case of some king lists (AKL-A) and ancestral genealogies (the Genealogy of Hammurabi's Dynasty), there is evidence that the authors—or the sources that they consulted—used eponyms to account for the origins of various cultures and peoples.

In comparison with the Mesopotamian traditions, the Greek genealogies in the Catalogue of Women were quite different because they reflect a greater prefer-ence for sociocultural and etiological functions and display a more pronounced tendency toward invention and fluidity. This is in part because fluidity was a nec-essary feature in the sociocultural genealogies of Greece (which changed to re-flect shifting social realities), but it is also a straightforward result of the freedoms enjoyed by Greek genealogists, who, unlike their Mesopotamian counterparts, were unhindered by the narrow constraints of royal sponsorship. The Greek au-thors were free to explore all matter of ethnography, history, and tradition. In doing so, they invented connections between originally separate genealogies, pos-tulated eponymous ancestors to explain their own origins and the origins of other nations and peoples, and liberally reformulated and combined these gene-alogies to suit their ideological interests and historiographical pursuits.

What are the implications of these data for the biblical genealogies and king lists? Each of the major genealogical types in the Hebrew Bible—segmented gene-alogies, linear genealogies, and priestly genealogies—is similar to one or more texts in the Near Eastern material. The segmented genealogies of Genesis (e.g., Gen 10) and the biblical tribal lists (e.g., Gen 49; Deut 33; Judg 5) find their closest parallels in the Greek traditions, AKL-A, and the Genealogy of Hammurabi's Dynasty. Most striking in these sources is the common use of eponymous ancestors to explain the origins of various peoples and nations (Gen 10; Catalogue of Women) and a simi-lar use of genealogies and eponyms to account for the origins of tribal groups (Gen 49; AKL-A; Genealogy of Hammurabi's Dynasty). By postulating that the forefa-thers of similar tribal groups were the children of a common forefather, the an-cients were able to explain simultaneously both cultural dissimilarity (different tribal identities) and cultural similarity (common language and cultural patterns). Genealogical invention is visible in many other instances as well. A good example is the genealogy of Samuel in 1 Chron 6:1–13 [Eng. 6:16–28]. The original genealogy in 1 Sam 1:1 presented Samuel as an Ephraimite, but this created certain problems for the Chronicler because of Samuel's prominent role in temple and sacrificial ac-tivities. The Chronicler's genealogy therefore tied Samuel into a Levitical genealogy and so legitimized his participation in cultic affairs.

The linear genealogies of Gen 5 and 11 have a very close relationship to the Mesopotamian king lists as represented in the SKL tradition. Important points of contact between the Hebrew and the Mesopotamian texts include their basic form

(list–flood–list), the long life spans of pre-flood figures, and the use of astronomical and/or mathematical information to create the chronological schemes. The
similarities are in fact so close that we may safely assume that the biblical authors
deliberately mimicked the SKL tradition, a practice for which we find precedent in
the LKL. Also noteworthy is that the author of the genealogy in Gen 5 appears to
have taken his list of patriarchs from the earlier list now found in Gen 4 (see Wilson, 158–66). In this, his use of sources parallels the Mesopotamian practice of
consulting earlier king lists in order to produce new ones.

The linear priestly genealogies of the Hebrew Bible, which appear in
1 Chron 5:27–41 (Eng. 6:1–15); 6:35–38 (Eng. 6:50–53); 9:11–13; Ezra 7:1–5; and
Neh 11:10–14; 12:10–11 are comparable to the Egyptian priestly genealogies,
sharing with them not only their priestly content but also a common form (linear), function (legitimizing), historical context (demise of kingship and rise
of the priesthood), and compositional strategy (use of invention; see Johnson).
The priestly genealogies reflect the same pattern of telescoping (cf. 1 Chron
5:27–41; Ezra 7:1–5) and fluidity (cf. 1 Chron 5:27–41; 9:10–11) that appears in
their Egyptian counterparts.

Finally, a few comments on the king lists in the Hebrew Bible. Insofar as we
can reconstruct them, the Hebrew king lists include features that are comparable to
those in the Near Eastern lists. A straightforward example is the Edomite King List
in Gen 36:31–39 (cf. 1 Chron 1:43–50; see Bartlett), but scholars have been able to
isolate several other lists that are now partially concealed by their present literary
context. For instance, biblical scholars are fairly certain that the book of Judges
was composed by combining various stories about the "major judges" (Gideon,
Deborah, etc.) with a chronological list of "minor judges" about whom no stories
appear (Tola, Jair, etc.; see discussion in de Vaux). The primary evidence for this is
that the chronological data for the minor judges includes precise numbers (3, 23,
22, 18, 6, etc.) whereas round numbers are used in the chronology of the major
judges (20, 40, 80 years). Another set of "concealed" king lists is reflected in
1–2 Kings, which seem to have been composed using two different king lists, one
from the north and one from the south (Bin-Nun). The best evidence for this is
that the regnal formulas used in 1–2 Kings vary inflexibly with the two kingdoms.
The northern formulas are, "PN2 (the son of PN1) reigned over Israel in (Tirzah/
Samaria) n years," and, "PN reigned over Israel n years in (Tirzah/Samaria),"
whereas the southern formula is, "And he reigned n years in Jerusalem."

General Bibliography

W. E. Aufrecht, "Genealogy and History in Ancient Israel," in *Ascribe to the Lord:
Biblical and Other Studies in Memory of Peter C. Craigie* (ed. L. Eslinger and
G. Taylor; JSOTSup 67; Sheffield, England: Sheffield Academic Press, 1988),
206–35; J. A. Barnes "The Collection of Genealogies," *Rhodes-Livingstone Journal*
5 (1947): 48–55; J. R. Bartlett, "The Edomite King-List of Genesis XXXVI.

31–39 and Chronicles I. 43–50," *VT* 16 (1965): 301–14; S. R. BIN-NUN, "Formulas from the Royal Records of Israel and Judah," *VT* 18 (1968): 414–32; L. BOHAN-NAN, "A Genealogical Charter," *Africa* 22 (1952): 301–15; P. BOHANNAN, "The Migration and Expansion of the Tiv," *Africa* 24 (1954): 2–16; I. CUNNISON, *Baggara Arabs: Power and the Lineage in the Sudanese Nomad Tribe* (Oxford: Clarendon, 1966); D. O. EDZARD, "Königslisten und Chroniken, A: Sumerisch," *RlA* 6:77–86; J.-J. GLASSNER, *Mesopotamian Chronicles* (SBLWAW 19; Atlanta: Society of Biblical Literature, 2004); J. GOODY, *The Domestication of the Savage Mind* (Cambridge: Cambridge University Press, 1977); A. K. GRAYSON, "Königslisten und Chroniken, B: Akkadisch," *RlA* 6:86–135; W. HOROWITZ, "The Isles of the Nations: Genesis X and Babylonian Geography," in *Studies in the Pentateuch* (ed. J. A. Emerton; VTSup 41; Leiden: Brill, 1990), 35–43; M. D. JOHNSON, *The Purpose of the Biblical Genealogies* (Cambridge: Cambridge University Press, 1969); G. N. KNOPPERS, "The Relationship of the Priestly Genealogies to the History of the High Priesthood in Jerusalem," in *Judah and the Judeans in the Neo-Babylonian Period* (ed. O. Lipschits and J. Blenkinsopp; Winona Lake, Ind.: Eisenbrauns, 2003), 109–33; A. MALAMAT, "King Lists of the Old Babylonian Period and Biblical Genealogies," *JAOS* 88 (1968): 163–73; IDEM, "Tribal Societies: Biblical Genealogies and African Lineage Systems," *Archives européennes de sociologie* 14 (1973): 126–36; I. MAYER, "From Kinship to Common Descent: Four-Generation Genealogies among the Gusii," *Africa* 35 (1965): 366–84; N. NA'AMAN, "Sources and Redaction in the Chronicler's Genealogies of Asher and Ephraim," *JSOT* 49 (1991): 99–111; T. J. PREWITT, "Kinship Structures and the Genesis Genealogies," *JNES* 40 (1981): 87–98; D. B. REDFORD, *Pharaonic King-Lists, Annals, and Day-Books: A Contribution to the Study of the Egyptian Sense of History* (SSEA Publication 4; Mississauga, Ont.: Benben, 1986); W. RÖLLIG, "Zur Typologie und Entstehung der babylonischen und assyrischen Königslisten," *AOAT* 1 (1969): 265–77; S. SCHIMMEL, *The Mystery of Numbers* (Oxford: Oxford University Press, 1993); K. L. SPARKS, *Ethnicity and Identity in Ancient Israel: Prolegomena to the Study of Ethnic Sentiments and Their Expression in the Hebrew Bible* (Winona Lake, Ind.: Eisenbrauns, 1998); IDEM, "Genesis 49 and the Tribal List Tradition in Ancient Israel," *ZAW* 115 (2003): 327–47; Y. B. TSIRKIN, "Japheth's Progeny and the Phoenicians," in *Phoenicia and the Bible* (ed. E. Lipinski; OLA 44; Studia Phoenicia 11; Leuven: Peeters, 1991), 117–34; J. VAN DIJK, "Die Inschriftenfunde," in *XVIII. vorläufiger Bericht über die von dem Deutschen Archäologischen Insitut und der Deutschen Orient-Gesellschaft aus Mitteln der Deutschen Forschungsgemeinschaft unternommenen Ausgrabungen in Uruk-Warka* (Berlin: Gebr. Mann, 1962), 39–62; J. VAN SETERS, *In Search of History: Historiography in the Ancient World and the Origins of Biblical History* (New Haven: Yale University Press, 1983); J. C. VANDERKAM, "Jewish High Priests of the Persian Period: Is the List Complete?" in *Priesthood and Cult in Ancient Israel* (ed. G. A. Anderson and S. M. Olyan; JSOTSup 125; Sheffield, England: Sheffield Academic Press, 1991), 67–91; R. DE VAUX, *Histoire ancienne d'Israël: La période des juges* (Paris: J. Gabalda, 1973), 14–17; R. R. WILSON, *Genealogy and History in the Biblical World* (YNER 7; New Haven: Yale University Press, 1977).

CHAPTER TWELVE

Historiography and Royal Inscriptions

Introduction

Historiography is commonly defined as a "written account of the past based on source inquiry," but modern scholars differ markedly on how this definition should be employed. Some scholars take their cue from the Greek historian Herodotus. For Herodotus, history writing was based not only on "inquiry" (*histōria*) but especially on *critical* inquiry, which involved a cautious and measured skepticism toward historical sources. When historiography is defined in this way, the category naturally excludes ancient works that seem somewhat gullible and uncritical in perspective, especially many of the historical texts from the ancient Near East. Other scholars hold that less critical works can also include an effort to inquire about the past by consulting sources. It appears to me that both of these theoretical postures are potentially helpful. On the one hand, there are striking differences between the critical inquiries of Greek historians—which generally eschewed miracles and the supernatural—and the histories written by Israelite authors and by other Near Eastern scholars. On the other hand, one can hardly ignore the obvious generic similarities between the source-based narratives of the ancient Near East and the works of the Greek historians. Given that both approaches have their taxonomical benefits, which is best for our purposes?

An implicit, if not explicit, issue in the study of ancient Israelite historiography is how it compares to modern history writing. Modern historians normally sift through their sources to determine which are most beneficial, mainly because their objective is to present an account of the past that is as accurate as possible. Some biblical scholars believe that the Israelite authors who composed the narratives in the Hebrew Bible carried out their work along these same lines; other scholars assert that nothing could be further from the truth. So long as these questions are in play, it seems wise to adopt a broad definition of historiography that includes both critical and uncritical narratives of the past. One scholar has recently attempted to do this by defining historiography as "a narrative that presents a past" (Brettler). Such a definition is clearly a step in the right direction, but it is perhaps too broad because it includes not only modern and ancient histories but also narratives that might be based mainly or even exclusively on the human imagination, such as epics, legends, myths, and novellas.

My own solution to this taxonomic problem employs the commonly used terms *historiography* and *history writing*. In my nomenclature, *historiography* refers to any text that presents the past on the basis of its author's source inquiry, and the term *history writing* is a still narrower category that includes historiographies that define the significance of past events through an extended, selective, and chronologically sensitive narrative. Each of these categories needs to be unpacked. The broad category of historiography is necessary in this discussion because numerous ancient works present accounts of the past but without using a narrative form. Such texts are certainly different from the narrative histories in the Hebrew Bible, but they are important for helping us understand the kinds of sources that were available to ancient historians, how the ancient writers used these sources, how they construed the past, and how nonnarrative historical genres may have contributed to the development of narrative histories. The narrower term *history writing* is necessary because it describes the instances in which historiography is presented in narrative or story form. In such cases, the historian's presentation must assume some rationale of historical causation and employ some criteria for evaluating the significance of the narrated events. This ideological perspective or bias is often identified by the use of the German word *Tendenz*. Although an author's *Tendenz* may reflect a unique perspective, there can be little doubt that history writers—both ancient and modern—hope to persuade readers to share their viewpoint.

It is theoretically useful at this point to distinguish between *proximate* and *nonproximate* histories. The first type of history is composed by writers who have ready access to good sources for their narratives, perhaps even eyewitness accounts. In contrast, the writers of nonproximate histories face more serious source limitations, as they are separated from the events they narrate by comparatively wide temporal, geographical, or cultural rifts. In such cases, the sources are often poor and difficult for the historian to assess properly. It is the nature of things that histories of the distant past are usually compositions of the nonproximate sort.

The present chapter considers two kinds of texts. It treats mostly texts that fit more or less comfortably into the categories of historiography and history writing as defined above. Because the focus of these texts was often on the king himself, many of them could be characterized not only as royal inscriptions but also as biographies or autobiographies. The balance of the chapter deals with texts of another kind, which may not be historiographic but will be of interest to students of Hebrew history and historiography. Good examples are the ration dockets of King Jehoiachin. These are archival texts that preserve a record of food distributions made to Judah's king while he lived in Babylon during the exile (see 12.1.2).

12.1. Mesopotamian Historiography

12.1.1. Mesopotamian Chronicles and Annals

Scholars of Near Eastern historiography refer most frequently to two Mesopotamian genres, the chronicles and the annals, which are distinguished especially by their form and manner of composition. The chronicles were essentially
chronologically ordered lists of events composed on the basis of information
gathered by consulting sources about the past, often the distant past. Insofar as
these texts tended to be lists rather than full-blown narratives, they also test the
limits of our definition of history writing. In contrast, the annals were literary
narratives composed on a regular basis to describe the king's deeds during each
year of his reign (hence "annal"). This was generally achieved by combining records from recent years with older information that was gleaned from earlier
copies of the annals.

All of the Mesopotamian exemplars treated in this chapter were composed
in Akkadian, excepting the Sumerian Tummal Chronicle and the Greek history of
Berossus. For a discussion on the general absence of historiography written in
Sumerian, see Kramer.

The Tummal "Chronicle." This unique Sumerian text relates a brief history of
Ninlil's Tummal sanctuary in Nippur. The founding of the goddess's sanctuary is
described, as well as a series of five occasions on which the holy site fell into ruin.
At the text's conclusion, it appears that the sanctuary had been restored: "Ninlil
went (several times) to the Tummal." Stylistically, the composition is similar to
the Sumerian King List (Glassner), but the text is so short that it barely passes as a
"chronicle." Ten OB copies of the text are extant, all of them from Ur and Nippur.

Texts and translations: GLASSNER, 156–59; E. SOLLBERGER, "The Tummal Inscriptions," *JCS*
16 (1962): 40–47. *Bibliography:* KRAMER, "Sumerian Historiography"; J. OELSNER, "Aus den
sumerischen literarischen Texten der Hilprecht-Sammlung Jena: Der Text der Tummal-
Chronik," in *Literatur, Politik und Recht in Mesopotamien: Festschrift für Claus Wilcke* (ed.
W. Sallaberger, K. Volk, and A. Zgoll; Wiesbaden: Harrassowitz, 2003), 209–24.

The Weidner Chronicle. This is the oldest known Akkadian chronicle. Although
our three copies date to the Neo-Assyrian period and later, it is fairly clear that
the piece was composed late in the second millennium near the end of the Kassite
period or during the early Isin II period (ca. 1150 B.C.E.). The chronicle's primary
interest was the provision of fish for Marduk's temple between 2500 and 2000
B.C.E. The author attempted to show that kings who neglected the cult of the god
Marduk always met an unhappy end. Although he seems to have consulted omen
materials at certain points and also some other sources, the primary source for
the narrative was the author's imagination, for it is highly anachronistic to suggest that Marduk's temple was of such importance so many years before Babylon
rose to historical prominence. Consequently, scholars normally presume that the

chronicle was a tendentious composition whose content was derived mainly from the author's imagination. Though this may be true, the religious anachronism and selective character of the history can also be explained by the author's *Tendenz*, which could not fathom a time when Marduk's temple was unimportant or a monarch who succeeded while neglecting it. The schematic historical pattern that followed from this *Tendenz* is comparable to the Hebrew history in Joshua–2 Kings (which judged Israel's history according to the Deuteronomic law) and even more so to the Hebrew Chronicler, who believed that history unfolded according to the inflexible forces of immediate retribution.

Texts and translations: GLASSNER, 263–69; GRAYSON, *Assyrian and Babylonian Chronicles,* 43–45, 145–51, 278–79. *Translation: COS* 1.138: 468–70. *Bibliography:* B. T. ARNOLD, "The Weidner Chronicle and the Idea of History in Israel and Mesopotamia," in *Faith, Tradition, and History* (ed. Millard et al.), 129–48; GRAYSON, "Königslisten und Chroniken, B," 88; VAN SETERS, *In Search of History,* 88.

The Assyrian Chronicles. Our four fragments of the Assyrian Chronicles come from Middle Assyrian period, in at least one case probably from the library of Tiglath-pileser I (1114–1076 B.C.E.). The chronicles concern the kings Enlil-Narari, Arik-din-ili, Ashur-resah-ishi I, and Tiglath-pileser I. Unfortunately, the texts are too fragmentary to characterize in detail, but they display some of the same characteristics found in the later Babylonian Chronicles, such as their chronological format, the use of rulings to separate each year, their third-person narrative focalization, and the list-like literary style of the compositions. Several differences, however, should be noted. Although we surmise that these fragmentary texts originally included dates and also covered more than one king in a series, the texts themselves cannot confirm this. As it is, we have separate fragments concerning four different kings. Another and perhaps more important difference between the Assyrian and Babylonian texts might be in the area of propaganda. Whereas the Babylonian Chronicles are devoid of explicit propaganda, the Assyrian texts seem to provide propagandistic details about the king's accomplishments—such as how much booty he captured—and they also refer to the king's "military prowess."

Texts and translations: GLASSNER, 184–91; GRAYSON, *Assyrian and Babylonian Chronicles,* 184–89, 288–89. *Bibliography:* R. BORGER, *Einleitung in die assyrischen Königsinschriften,* v. 1 (Leiden: Brill, 1961), 31, 105; N. NA'AMAN, "Assyrian Chronicle Fragment 4 and the Location of Idu," *RA* 88 (1994): 33–35; H. TADMOR, "The Campaigns of Sargon II of Assur," *JCS* 12 (1958): 22–40, 77–100; VAN SETERS, *In Search of History,* 82–83; E. F. WEIDNER, "Die Bibliothek Tiglatpilesers I," *AfO* 16 (1952–53): 197–215, esp. 208.

The Assyrian Annals. The most significant Assyrian contributions to the Mesopotamian historiographic tradition were the annals. The Assyrian Annals belong to an older and broader category of texts called royal inscriptions. These inscriptions varied in length from simple labels on foundation stones to longer narratives of commemoration. The texts were invariably propagandistic and glorified the king and his many accomplishments. Some of the exemplars were public documents prominently inscribed in palaces and temples, and others were buried in foundation deposits of the king's construction projects. There are also a few clay tablet versions that were used for drafts, archival copies, and student exercises (Levine). The similarities between the royal inscriptions and the annals show that the annals represent a generic innovation that developed from the propagandistic inscription genre.

The first annals appeared during the reign of Adad-narari I (1306–1274 B.C.E.), and the genre continued in use until the reign of Assurbanipal (668–627 B.C.E.). The texts were cast as autobiographies in which the king offered a year-by-year narrative of his activities, highlighting especially his divine election, military campaigns, building projects, and deeds in support of the religious cult. Scribes sometimes accentuated the king's accomplishments by increasing to astronomical proportion the size of his army, the size of enemy armies he had defeated, or the booty that he seized. This may have been done by multiplying known figures by 10 (so, for instance, when the text suggests that the king defeated an army of 75,000, it was perhaps only 7,500; see De Odorico 1995; cf. the large census figures in Num chs. 1–2, 26). Depictions of the king were invariably flattering, so that failures or setbacks were rarely mentioned. Exceptions to this rule appear mainly in the royal apologies. A good example is Esarhaddon's Apology, which appears in one section of his historical prism from Nineveh (Prism A; n.b., as the name partly implies, prisms were multi-sided clay objects prepared to receive cuneiform writing). This composition addresses two themes. First, it explains how Esarhaddon became the crown prince when he was not the oldest son of Sennacherib. This deviation from the pattern of primogeniture, said Esarhaddon, was a decision of his father that had been fully confirmed through divination. Thus the Apology asserts that Esarhaddon's legitimacy rested in both royal and divine election. The other point made by Esarhaddon was to assert in the strongest possible terms that he played no role in the coup attempt that led to the murder of his father, Sennacherib. Esarhaddon blamed his bellicose brothers for the patricide, who fought vainly for a throne that neither their father nor the gods would give them. Although we might expect that this apology was published when Esarhaddon rose to power, it appears instead to have been composed when Esarhaddon chose his younger son, Assurbanipal, as his successor. It is very easy to see that the story of Esarhaddon's own rise to power—which did not follow the pattern of primogeniture—would have provided ideological support for this choice. Twenty copies of Prism A have been found so far, reflecting the importance of this propaganda for Esarhaddon's regime. The apologetic history of Esarhaddon has been compared to the stories of David and Solomon in Samuel-Kings, where the Davidic regime defended itself against charges that it had brutally killed the house of Saul (see Sparks).

The physical locations in which the annals were found illustrate well their propagandistic function. Many of the texts were inscribed on large statues and on the walls and floors of temples and palaces, where courtiers and scholars could read them and be persuaded thereby to lend their allegiance and support to the regime. The impressive physical dimensions of the texts certainly added to their persuasive power (see Russell). The common people in antiquity were illiterate, and at any rate, they did not have access to these texts. The usual way to disseminate propaganda to the masses was public readings, by which the regime's message passed into the matrix of everyday conversation (for more on this oral dimension of royal propaganda, see the Tale of Sarbanapal and Sarmuge in 9.1.3). Our other major source of Assyrian Annals was the foundation deposit, for texts and other items were buried in the foundations of the king's construction projects. Likely readers for these texts would have been the gods and also future kings, who would discover the texts during temple refurbishment projects. Thus the target of Assyrian royal propaganda was not only the people of the Assyrian Empire but also those in the heavens and those in the future.

The literary process that gave rise to the annals can be illustrated by comparing three editions of Shalmaneser III's annals (858–825 B.C.E.). One of the earliest editions, the Monolith Inscription, was inscribed upon a large stela found at Kurkh in 1861. It was composed in 853–852 B.C.E. and covered the first six years of the monarch's reign. So far as we can tell, this composition was based mainly on temporary notes that were discarded after use. A second edition of the annals, composed on two monumental bull figures found at Kalḫu, covers the period down to the eighteenth year of the king. Its account of the king's first six years is virtually identical to that of the earlier Monolith Inscription; this suggests that at regular intervals, perhaps on an annual basis, new editions of the annals were composed by culling information from previous editions and adding to this a narrative of the more recent periods. A third edition of Shalmaneser's annals, probably the final edition, was composed in 828–827 B.C.E. It narrates the king's activities down to his thirty-first year. A comparison of this text with the earlier Monolith Inscription reveals a propensity for later annalists to summarize content from the earlier editions. Whereas seventeen lines were devoted to Shalmaneser's accession year in the earlier editions, in this later version the account is just four lines, which were slavishly copied from the first four lines of the older editions. Copying from these older editions did not require the scribes to consult the inscriptions themselves because they had convenient access to archival copies of the texts (see the annalistic tablet discovered at Aššur in Grayson, 2:32–41). It has been suggested that the primary sources used by the annalists were temporary notes that were discarded after the compositions were completed (Van Seters). Although this was surely so, later editions of the annals sometimes reflect expansion and modifications of earlier editions. In such cases, it appears that the scribes consulted archival sources of some kind (Cogan).

Although the annals pass for historiography, upon closer examination it is clear that they do not pass for history writing on two key points. First, they are lacking as narrative plots. This is primarily because the annals were composed as a series of short annual entries rather than as complete literary narratives of the past. Although this creates the impression of a long, nonproximate history, the annals are instead a collection of brief, proximate histories. Second, the annals reflect a limited use of source materials. Events of past years were simply recopied or abbreviated from earlier annals, and recent events were culled mainly from a narrow scope of temporary records. Propagandistic concerns generally precluded the annalists from inquiring seriously about the events of the past. Consequently, the annalists projected monarchic perspectives into history more than they sought to discover it.

The Assyrian Annals are significant sources for the study of ancient Israelite history and historiography. Regarding history, they include many references to Israelite and Judean kings and also provide an important window into the political and military circumstances of Palestine during the eighth and seventh centuries B.C.E. Regarding historiography, the texts illustrate the unique role that narrative history plays in disseminating political propaganda. Careful attention to this pattern can help us recognize more easily the propagandistic properties in Israelite historiography and to compensate for this in our assessments of Israelite history. The standard translation of the Assyrian Annals is still Luckenbill's *Ancient Records of Assyria and Babylon*. But Luckenbill's work has been superseded in part by the Royal Inscriptions of Mesopotamia series of the University of Toronto Press, although the latter project is no longer being funded and unfortunately seems to have ended without covering the period after 745 B.C.E. As the bibliography shows, however, there are several very good editions of the post-745 B.C.E. texts.

Texts and translations: R. BORGER, *Beiträge zum Inschriftenwerk Assurbanipals* (Wiesbaden: Harrassowitz, 1996); IDEM, *Die Inschriften Asarhaddons, Königs von Assyrien* (AfOB 9; Graz: Im Selbstverlage des Herausgebers, 1956); E. FRAHM, *Einleitung in die Sanherib-Inschriften* (AfOB 16; Vienna: Institut für Orientalistik der Universität Wien, 1997); A. FUCHS, *Die Annalen des Jahres 711 v. Chr. nach Pismenfragmentum aus Ninive und Assur* (SAA Studies 8; Helsinki: Helsinki University Press, 1998); IDEM, *Die Inschriften Sargons II. aus Khorsabad* (Göttingen: Cuvillier, 1994); A. K. GRAYSON, *Assyrian Rulers of the Early First Millennium BC* (2 vols.; RIMA 2–3; Toronto: University of Toronto Press, 1991–1996); H. TADMOR, *The Inscriptions of Tiglath-pileser III, King of Assyria: Critical Edition, with Introductions, Translations, and Commentary* (Jerusalem: Israel Academy of Sciences and Humanities, 1994). ***Translations:*** ANET 274–301; COS 2.113–119: 261–306 (Annals and other inscriptions); D. D. LUCKENBILL, *Ancient Records of Assyria and Babylon* (2 vols.; Chicago: University of Chicago Press, 1926–1927). ***Bibliography:*** R. BORGER and W. SCHRAM, *Einleitung in die assyrischen Königsinschriften* (Leiden: Brill, 1961–), vol. 1; M. COGAN, "A Plaidoyer on Behalf of the Royal Scribes," in *Ah, Assyria* (ed. Cogan and Eph'al), 121–28; M. DE ODORICO, "Compositional and Editorial Processes of Annalistic and Summary Texts of Tiglath-pileser I," SAAB 8 (1994): 67–112; IDEM, *The Use of Numbers and Quantifications in the Assyrian Royal Inscriptions* (SAAS 3; Helsinki: University of Helsinki, 1995); F. M. FALES, ed., *Assyrian Royal Inscriptions: New Horizons in Literary, Ideological, and Historical Analysis* (Orientis antiqui collectio 17; Rome: Istituto per l'Oriente, 1981); F. M. FALES, "Assyrian Royal Inscriptions: Newer Horizons," SAAB 13 (1999–2001): 115–44; IDEM, "Narrative and Ideological Variations in the Account of Sargon's Eighth Campaign," in *Ah, Assyria* (ed. Cogan and Eph'al), 129–47; P. GARELLI, "La propagande royale assyrienne," *Akkadica* 27 (1981): 16–29; T. ISHIDA, "The Succession Narrative and Esarhaddon's Apology: A Comparison," in *Ah, Assyria* (ed. Cogan and Eph'al), 166–73; M. T. LARSEN, *Power and Propaganda: A Symposium on Ancient Empires*

(Mesopotamia 7; Copenhagen: Akademisk Forlag, 1979); L. D. LEVINE, "Preliminary Remarks on the Historical Inscriptions of Sennacherib," in *History, Historiography, and Interpretation* (ed. Tadmor and Weinfeld), 58–75; A. R. MILLARD, "Large Numbers in the Assyrian Royal Inscriptions," in *Ah, Assyria* (ed. Cogan and Eph'al), 213–22; B. ODED, " 'The Command of the God' as a Reason for Going to War in the Assyrian Royal Inscriptions," in *Ah, Assyria* (ed. Cogan and Eph'al), 223–30; J. RENGER, "Neuassyrische Königsinschriften als Genre Keilschriftliteratur: Zum Stil und zur Kompositionstechnik der Inschriften Sargons II. von Assyrien," in *Keilschriftlich Literaturen: Ausgewählte Vorträge der XXXII. Rencontre assyriologique internationale* (ed. K. Hecker and W. Sommerfeld; Berlin: Reimer, 1986), 109–28; J. M. RUSSELL, *The Writing on the Wall: Studies in the Architectural Context of Late Assyrian Palace Inscriptions* (MC 9; Winona Lake, Ind.: Eisenbrauns, 1999); K. L. SPARKS, "Propaganda (Apology of David)"; H. TADMOR, "Autobiographical Apology in the Royal Assyrian Literature," in *History, Historiography, and Interpretation* (ed. Tadmor and Weinfeld), 36–57; IDEM, "Observations on Assyrian Historiography," in *Essays on the Ancient Near East in Memory of Jacob Joel Finkelstein* (ed. Ellis), 209–13; VAN SETERS, *In Search of History,* 60–68; N. K. WEEKS, "Causality in the Assyrian Royal Inscriptions," *OLP* 14 (1983): 115–27; E. WEISSERT, "Creating a Political Climate: Literary Allusions to Enuma Eliš in Sennacherib's Account of the Battle of Halule," in *Assyrien im Wandel der Zeiten: XXXIXe Rencontre assyriologique internationale* (ed. H. Waetzoldt and H. Hauptmann; Heidelberg: Heidelberger Orientverlag, 1997), 191–202.

The Synchronistic History. Regarding the chronicle genre, the best-known Assyrian chronicle is the Synchronistic History (not to be confused with the synchronistic king list in *ANET* 272–74; see 11.1). This text outlines Assyro-Babylonian relations from the first half of the fifteenth century B.C.E. down to the reign of Adad-nerari III (810–783 B.C.E.). Its author viewed military engagements between the two countries as resulting from Babylonian border violations of the boundary between the two nations. Each skirmish led to a Babylonian defeat, presumably because the gods invoked in the agreements—particularly the Assyrian god Assur—had intervened on behalf of the Assyrians. The text appears to have been composed immediately after the reign of Adad-nerari III, when Assyria was weak and particularly vulnerable to Babylonian attack. The author refers only to Assyrian victories over Babylon, an ideological *Tendenz* that he preserved on at least two occasions by fictively imagining defeats as victories (Grayson, 52). The particular boundary line assumed in the work was also imaginary. Although the author makes the disingenuous claim that the chronicle was engraved upon an official stela, it would be incorrect to characterize the piece as pure fiction. The author studiously avoided mentioning Assyrian kings who had no dealings with Babylon, and this can only mean that he gave at least some attention to the sources that he consulted, which appear to have been royal inscriptions. He probably consulted other chronicles as well. According to Grayson, the purpose of the text was to encourage Assyrians in their struggle against Babylonian incursions. It would also perhaps have served a useful deterrent role in the hands of Babylonian readers.

The Synchronistic History is structured in panels that deal with the reign of each king, the entries separated by rulings, as was the norm in Mesopotamian chronicles. Because the kings treated in the text were from both Assyria and Babylon, the author had to negotiate through the chronologies of the two nations. His effort was comparable in certain respects to the synchronistic strategy employed by the Deuteronomistic Historian in his accounts of the northern and southern kingdoms in 1 and 2 Kings. For sources, the content of the Synchronistic History suggests that its author consulted the royal inscriptions of Assyrian kings as well as other chronicles.

Texts and translations: GLASSNER, 176–83; GRAYSON, *Assyrian and Babylonian Chronicles,* 51–56, 157–69. *Bibliography:* GRAYSON, "Königslisten und Chroniken, B," 88; H. TAD-MOR, "Observations on Assyrian Historiography," in *Essays on the Ancient Near East in Memory of Jacob Joel Finkelstein* (ed. Ellis), 209–13; VAN SETERS, *In Search of History,* 83–84, 86–87, 295–96.

The Babylonian Chronicle Series. The most noteworthy Babylonian contribution to the historiographic genre is the Babylonian Chronicle Series. The series comprises a number of texts, connected to each other by catchlines, that cover the reign of Nabu-naṣir (747–734 B.C.E.) down to the reign of Seleucus II (245–226 B.C.E.), in other words, from the advent of the Neo-Babylonian dynasty down to the Seleucid period. Although the first documents in the series were composed close to Nabu-naṣir's reign, our extant copies date from a somewhat later period—in the case of the series's first chronicle, from the reign of Darius I of Persia (521–486 B.C.E.). If all of the texts were in our possession, we would have a continuous narrative of Babylonian history from the middle of the eighth century down to the middle of the third century B.C.E. Only thirteen texts are available, however, and these leave us with substantial breaks in the sources. In outlook, phraseology, and structure, the genre has its own perspective that distinguishes it markedly from the annalistic tradition of the Assyrians. The chronicles are selective and do not provide a record of each year; rather, on average, they record about one year in three (Brinkman). They are arranged in segments, each demarcated by dividing lines and a regnal date formula, such as "The Nth year of PN." The end of each reign is also marked with a formula of sorts: "For N years PN1 ruled in Babylon. PN2 ascended the throne in Babylon." The authors consulted written source material while compiling the chronicles, as is confirmed by the confession that source materials were not always available: "The battle which Nabu-nasir waged against Borsippa is not written" (no. 1, line 8).

The chronicles are concerned with a number of different topics, especially with kingship and the process of royal succession. The compilers were also interested in occasions when gods (in statue form) failed to attend religious festivals, when gods were abducted from their temples, when military activities took place, and when coup attempts either threatened or altered an orderly monarchic succession. The accounts are narrated in the third person and are dispassionate from a political point of view, interested not only in Babylonian kingship but also in the politics of neighboring states that affected Babylon. Both the victories and the military defeats of Babylon are included. Thus these texts seem to reflect a genuine intellectual interest in the history of Babylon itself.

Because the chronicles did not serve the propagandistic functions of the Assyrian Annals, they also lacked bombastic and superlative descriptions of the king as well as the Assyrian penchant for self-aggrandizing descriptions of monarchic building projects, military feats, and booty lists. J. A. Brinkman has offered a reasonable explanation for the ideological differences between the Assyrian Annals and the Babylonian Chronicles. Whereas the annals were composed under the sponsorship of the Assyrian kings as part of the state's official propagandistic effort, the chronicles reflect private (or at least nonofficial) scribal activities freed from the influence of the Babylonian court. This difference in context and *Tendenz* gave rise to two distinct genres and interests, one in promoting the Assyrian state (the Annals), the other in discovering the history of Babylon (the chronicles).

What kinds of sources were consulted to compose the Babylonian Chronicle Series? Some time ago, D. J. Wiseman suggested that the chronicles were based on some kind of "running account" of the events going on in Babylon. He suggested that such a source could be found in the astronomical diaries that provide a dated record of day-to-day events in each month (see Sachs/Hunger; Rochberg-Halton; Pinches/Strassmaier). The diaries include observations of an astronomical and meteorological nature along with statements about market prices, the height of the river, and matters of historical interest. Two additional lines of evidence have been cited in support of Wiseman's conclusion. First, the Babylonian Chronicle Series begins with the reign of Nabu-naṣir, and a serious effort to compile astronomical diaries began precisely at this point (although some efforts along these lines may have begun as early as the tenth century B.C.E.). Second, Grayson has noted that there are certain correspondences between the chronicles and the diaries in content and phraseology. In recent years, however, the theory that the chroniclers consulted astronomical diaries has been questioned on two fronts. Brinkman has argued that there are striking differences between the diaries and the chronicles in the one instance where they cover the same historical events (see Brinkman). At the same time, Weissert has satisfactorily demonstrated that, in at least one case, the Babylonian chroniclers consulted Assyrian sources, namely, the Assyrian Eponym Chronicle (see 11.1). Although the observations of Brinkman and Weissert should curb our enthusiasm for the astronomical-diary theory, it is still necessary to hypothesize that the Babylonian chroniclers had access to some sort of running account of the history that they narrated (so Grayson). At any rate, all of these sources aside, the date lists, eponym lists, and king list traditions provided the essential chronological backbone of the chronicles (see ch. 11).

Perhaps the best way to characterize the Babylonian Chronicles is as only one of many genres produced by Mesopotamian "list science." The Babylonian scholars were inquisitive souls, with a penchant for compiling lists of nearly everything that they found useful or interesting. It was only a matter of time before history seized their research interests, and the result was a genre whose aims were truly historiographic. Like the Assyrian Annals, however, the chronicles test the limits of my definition of true history writing. From a literary point of view, they are better characterized as lists with brief notations than as historical narratives. Moreover, although the dispassionate and even-handed perspective of the chronicles makes them wonderful sources for modern history, the ancient authors did not explicitly present the significance of past events for their readers. Indeed, there may well be some kind of implied *Tendenz* in the compositions; still, the most obvious purpose of the chroniclers was to produce a catalogue of events in their nation's past. I. Finkel and B. van der Spek are preparing a new edition of the Babylonian Chronicles, which will appear as *Babylonian Chronicles of the Hellenistic Period*.

Texts and translations: GLASSNER, 193–206, 214–57; GRAYSON, *Assyrian and Babylonian Chronicles*, 8–28, 69–124. *Translations:* ANET 301–7 (partial); COS 1.137: 467–68 (partial). *Bibliography:* J. A. BRINKMAN, "The Babylonian Chronicle Revisited," in *Lingering over Words: Studies in Ancient Near Eastern Literature in Honor of William L. Moran* (ed. Tz. Abusch et al.; Atlanta: Scholars Press, 1990), 73–104; GRAYSON, "Chronicles and the Akitu Festival"; IDEM, "Königslisten und Chroniken, B," 86–87; W. W. HALLO, "Dating the Mesopotamian Past: The Concept of Eras from Sargon to Nabonassar," *Bulletin of the Society for Mesopotamian Studies* 6 (1983): 7–18; IDEM, "The Nabonassar Era and Other Epochs in Mesopotamian Chronology and Chronography," in *A Scientific Humanist: Studies in Memory of Abraham Sachs* (ed. E. Leichty, M. deJ. Ellis, and P. Gerardi; OPSNKF 9; Philadelphia: University Museum, 1988), 175–90; T. G. PINCHES and J. N. STRASSMAIER, *Late Babylonian Astronomical and Related Texts* (ed. A. J. Sachs; Brown University Studies 18; Providence: Brown University Press, 1955), xii–xxi, 46–149; F. ROCHBERG-HALTON, "The Babylonian Astronomical Diaries," *JAOS* 111 (1991): 323–32; A. SACHS, "A Classification of the Babylonian Astronomical Tablets of the Seleucid Period," *JCS* 2 (1949): 271–90; A. SACHS and H. HUNGER, *Astronomical Diaries and Related Texts from Babylonia* (5 vols.; Vienna: Verlag der Österreichischen Akademie der Wissenschaften, 1988–2001); E. WEISSERT, "Interrelated Chronographic Patterns in the Assyrian Eponym Chronicle and the 'Babylonian Chronicle': A Comparative View," in *La circulation des biens, des personnes, et des idées dans le Proche-Orient ancien: Actes de la XXXVIIIe Rencontre assyriologique internationale* (ed. D. Charpin and F. Joannès; Paris: Éditions Recherche sur les Civilisations, 1992), 273–82; D. J. WISEMAN, *Chronicles of the Chaldaean Kings (626–556 B.C.) in the British Museum* (London: Trustees of the British Museum, 1956).

Supplements to the Babylonian Chronicle Series. According to Van Seters, three of the Babylonian Chronicles—Chronicle P, the Chronicle of Early Kings, and the Eclectic Chronicle—appear to reflect attempts to stretch the history provided in the Babylonian Chronicle Series back into earlier times. This theory naturally presupposes that these texts originated after the series (i.e., after the middle of the eighth century B.C.E.). Like the chronicle series itself, these three texts reflect a detached historical tone and display the same format, in which kings and events are treated in a series of entries divided by rulings.

The Chronicle of Early Kings is preserved on two late Babylonian tablets, which cover the period from Sargon of Akkad (ca. 2334–2279 B.C.E.) down to Agum III (ca. 1450 B.C.E.). The author's major sources of information were the Weidner Chronicle (see above) and the omen texts (see 6.1.1), as may be discerned from the fact that all of the chronicle's information about Sargon and Naram-Sin appears in the same order and format as in the protases of omen compendia (Grayson, 46).

As for Chronicle P, it is named after its first editor, T. G. Pinches. Only about one-third of Chronicle P's tablet is preserved. Each section of the chronicle treats the reign of a Babylonian king during the Kassite period. The entries are of unequal length and are marked off with rulings. We do not know the provenance of the text, but its language is Standard Babylonian. Grayson suggests that the text was probably written between the twelfth and eighth centuries B.C.E., but the fragmentary state of the text prevents us from surmising its author's purpose. A date earlier than the eighth century necessarily precludes Van Seters's theory that Chronicle P was composed as a supplement to the Babylonian Chronicle Series.

The Eclectic Chronicle seems to be a late composition, written in Standard Babylonian on a small tablet apparently for private use. The chronicle selectively narrates events relating to Babylon from the eleventh century B.C.E. down to the reign of Shalmeneser V (the eighth century B.C.E.), but the tablet is broken and in its original form likely covered a period running from the twelfth to the seventh century. Numerous kings who might have been included are omitted from the sequence. The author's two major criteria for including a king were apparently the king's influence on Babylon and the relative importance of his reign. These criteria explain the omission of several Babylonian kings and the inclusion of several Assyrian kings who controlled Babylon.

A fourth text, recently published by Walker, seems to fill in historical gaps between Chronicle P and the Eclectic Chronicle. It is a private document derived from sources that were very similar to—or perhaps identical with—those used by the authors of Chronicle P and the Eclectic Chronicle. It also shares with those texts the same format and the same interest in political history. This new text has been named Chronicle 25, signaling that it is an addition to the corpus of twenty-four chronicles published in Grayson's basic collection.

One obvious difference between these four texts and the Babylonian Chronicle Series regards the sources that the respective authors used. Whereas the Babylonian chronicler seems to have had access to some kind of running account of the history he narrated, the authors of the Chronicle of Early Kings, Chronicle P, the Eclectic Chronicle, and Chronicle 25 did not have this advantage for the earlier periods that they covered. Consequently, they were forced to use a wider variety of source types, including omen texts, historical epics, legendary materials, and older chronicles, such as the Weidner Chronicle. This evidence attests to a natural pattern in historiography, whereby authors must resort to a variety of generic source materials in their effort to narrate the events of remote antiquity.

Texts and translations: GLASSNER, 268–88; GRAYSON, *Assyrian and Babylonian Chronicles,* 45–49, 152–56 (Chronicle of Early Kings); 56–59, 170–77 (Chronicle P); 63–65, 180–83 (Eclectic Chronicle); W. G. LAMBERT, "Samsu-iluna in Later Tradition," in *De la Babylonie à la Syrie, en passant par Mari: Mélanges offerts à Monsieur J.-R. Kupper à l'occasion de son 70e anniversaire* (ed. Ö. Tünca; Liège: Université de Liège, 1990), 27–34; C. B. F. WALKER, "Babylonian Chronicle 25: A Chronicle of the Kassite and Isin II Dynasties," in *Zikir Šumim: Assyriological Studies Presented to F. R. Kraus on the Occasion of His Seventieth Birthday* (ed. G. Van Driel et al; Leiden: Brill, 1982), 398–417. **Bibliography:** GRAYSON, "Königslisten und Chroniken," 88–89; VAN SETERS, *In Search of History,* 86–88.

The Sins of Nabû-šuma-iškun. This text depicts the eighth-century reign of Nabû-šuma-iškun of Babylon as a series of increasingly unwise and impious acts against the state and the gods. He stopped going out to war, forced priests to break laws, sold Babylonians into slavery, profaned temples and seized their goods, brought foreign deities into Babylon, and ignored oaths that were solemnly sworn before the gods. Obviously, competitors for power found it expeditious to compose and preserve this scathing review of the king's life. Our copy of the text comes from the late Babylonian period.

Texts and translations: GLASSNER, 300–313; E. VON WEIHER, *Spätbabylonische Texte aus Uruk, v. 3* (Berlin: Mann, 1988), no. 58. *Bibliography:* S. W. COLE, "The Crimes and Sacrileges of Nabû-šuma-iškun," *ZA* 84 (1994): 220–52.

The Esarhaddon Chronicle. Preserved on a single broken tablet, this text chronicles the Neo-Assyrian reign of Esarhaddon (681–669 B.C.E.). A comparison of the text with parallel sections of the Babylonian Chronicle Series suggests that one of the author's aims was to present Esarhaddon in the best light possible, since he studiously omitted references to Esarhaddon's failures and setbacks, such as the sack of Sippar by the Elamites (year six of Esarhaddon). It is therefore noteworthy that the evidence points to a Babylonian rather than an Assyrian author. History tells us that the Babylonians officially recognized Esarhaddon as their king, and this Babylonian author apparently agreed with that sentiment.

Texts, translations, and discussions: GLASSNER, 206–10; GRAYSON, *Assyrian and Babylonian Chronicles,* 30–32, 125–28; IDEM, "Königslisten und Chroniken," 87.

The Šamaš-šum-ukin Chronicle. This text, preserved on a tablet for private use, contains an account of the reigns of four kings—including Šamaš-šum-ukin—which was eclectically derived from other sources. The text is divided into two sections; the first section falls chronologically after the second. Each panel treats two kings, but we do not know what the author's interest was.

Texts, translations, and discussions: GLASSNER, 210–13; GRAYSON, *Assyrian and Babylonian Chronicles,* 32–34, 128–30; IDEM, "Königslisten und Chroniken," 87.

The Dynastic Chronicle. This eighth-century Neo-Assyrian document was composed in Akkadian and Sumerian. Like many of the chronicles, this one is more nearly a king list than a narrative account of the past. The text covers Babylonian history from the time before the flood down to the eighth century B.C.E., but there are many lacunae in the tablet, and the complete text may have included many more kings. The author arranged his text according to a dynastic pattern, citing the kings in each dynasty and then providing a summary statement (e.g., "Three kings of the dynasty of the Sealand ruled for twenty-three years") before moving on to the next dynasty. The same pattern appears in the SKL (see 11.1), which in some form probably inspired this author. The order of the antediluvian dynasties in the chronicle, however, differs from the SKL, and the author of our chronicle also penned several chronological discrepancies. One unusual feature of the Dynastic Chronicle is its peculiar interest in the place where kings were buried. Perhaps its author believed that this indicated something about the king's legitimacy.

Texts, translations, and discussions: GLASSNER, 126–35; GRAYSON, *Assyrian and Babylonian Chronicles,* 40–44, 139–44. *Bibliography:* I. L. FINKEL, "Bilingual Chronicle Fragments," *JCS* 32 (1980): 65–80; GRAYSON, "Königslisten und Chroniken," 87–88; VAN SETERS, *In Search of History,* 71–72.

The Chronicle of Market Prices. Little is preserved of this fragmentary tablet, but what remains allows us to recognize it as a selective record of market prices from the time of Hammurabi (eighteenth century B.C.E.) down to at least the eighth century B.C.E. A likely source of the author's information was the astronomical diaries, since these also contained entries regarding market prices. We do not know why the text was composed, but the author may have considered market prices to be a significant indicator of the king's legitimacy.

Texts, translations, and discussions: GLASSNER, 294–97; GRAYSON, *Assyrian and Babylonian Chronicles,* 60–62, 178–79. *Bibliography:* GRAYSON, "Königslisten und Chroniken," 88–89; VAN SETERS, *In Search of History,* 90.

Religious Chronicles: The Akitu Chronicle and the Religious Chronicle. Two Babylonian texts chronicle religiously significant events rather than political history. The first, the Akitu Chronicle, is a private document of unknown date and provenance. It catalogued all interruptions of the Akitu (New Year) festival during the period between Sennacherib's sack of Babylon in 689 B.C.E. and the accession of Nabopolassar in 626 B.C.E. Grayson suggests that the text was composed "out of sheer interest in the subject matter" (Grayson, *Assyrian and Babylonian Chronicles*), but its author certainly viewed interruptions of the Akitu festival as religiously significant, perhaps because he was interested in correlating these interruptions with historical events known from other sources. This text shows how easily the chronicle genre could be extended to address other issues besides royal succession.

The so-called Religious Chronicle is similar to the Akitu Chronicle in that it concerns interruptions of the festival, but its author was even more interested in "bizarre events," particularly the appearance of wild animals within the city. It is likely that the author's interest in the bizarre stemmed from the Mesopotamian propensity to see unusual events as omen-laden in some way. His chronicle covers a period of about a hundred years at the end of the eleventh and beginning of the tenth centuries B.C.E. It is reasonable to suppose that the text was composed after the latest period that it covers, namely, during the tenth century. The fact that our Neo-Babylonian copies date several centuries later reflects the strong tendency of Babylonian scholars to preserve the chronographic sources that they inherited.

Texts and translations: GLASSNER, 212–15, 296–301; GRAYSON, *Assyrian and Babylonian Chronicles,* 35–36, 131–32 (Akitu Chronicle); 36–39, 133–38 (Religious Chronicle).

Bibliography: GRAYSON, "Chronicles and the Akitu Festival"; IDEM, "Königslisten und Chroniken," 87.

The Juridical Chronicle. This fragmentary text from Seleucid-era Babylon appears to be a chronicle of judicial proceedings, dealing with instances of theft of temple property. In each case, the defendants were eventually found guilty and were either punished or executed. It is possible that the text was composed to dissuade temple personnel from pilfering divine property. If so, it is interesting to note that several defendants who were initially pronounced innocent were subsequently re-tried after one of them quickly died in prison. Upon further interrogation, the accomplices were also found guilty and were burned to death. This element in the text was perhaps a way of introducing the threat of divine justice alongside the threat of human justice in matters of the temple treasury.

Texts, translations, and discussions: GLASSNER, 156–59; F. JOANNÈS, "Une chronique judiciaire d'époque hellénistique," in *Assyrologica et Semitica: Festschrift für Joachim Oelsner anlässlich seines 65. Geburtstages am 18. Februar 1997* (ed. J. Marzahn and H. Neumann; AOAT 252; Münster: Ugarit-Verlag, 2000), 193–211.

Berossus's History of Babylonia. Berossus was a Babylonian priest serving at Esagil, the great temple of the god Marduk. He composed his history of Babylon in Greek at the beginning of the third century B.C.E. No copies of the history itself survive, but modern scholars have been able to reconstruct portions of the work from fragments quoted by other Greek writers. So far as we can tell, the history was composed of three books, beginning with creation and ending with the time of Berossus. The basic shape of the work was (1) creation, (2) astrological/astronomical wisdom, (3) a pre-flood king list, (4) the flood, and (5) a post-flood history down to the third century B.C.E. The sources that Berossus used to write his history were similar to those we know from other Mesopotamian traditions. His creation myth comes from *Enuma Elish,* his pre-flood king list is similar to our late copies of the Sumerian King List tradition, his flood story parallels the other Mesopotamian flood stories, and his post-flood history contains limited information of the type found in the Babylonian Chronicle Series. Particularly interesting is Berossus's description of the *apkallū,* the monsterlike beings—half fish and half man—who lived before the flood and revealed to humanity all that was necessary for settled and civilized life (see 2.1). These beings appear in other Mesopotamian texts, including the late Seleucid-era version of the SKL (see 11.1). According to Berossus, the wisdom given by these monsters survived the deluge because the Mesopotamian flood hero buried tablets containing their wisdom at Sippar, where they were recovered after the flood.

Although Berossus composed his work rather late in Mesopotamian history, it is as important for the study of Hebrew historiography as any of the earlier historiographic texts. Not only is the fundamental structure of Berossus's history paralleled in Genesis; it is increasingly clear to modern scholars that the two basic components of Genesis—the histories of the Yahwist and the Priestly writers (see the conclusion of ch. 10)—were composed not long before the time of Berossus, probably during the sixth–fifth centuries B.C.E. Also intriguing from a comparative point of view is that Berossus attempted to present his native history in a form that mimicked the literature of his Greek overlords. It seems likely that the earlier Hebrew histories, written during the Babylonian and Persian periods, were also mimetic works, composed to present the traditions of Israel in a form that paralleled Mesopotamian tradition.

Text and translation: JACOBY, *Die Fragmente der griechischen Historiker,* 3:364–97. *Translations:* S. BURSTEIN, *The Babyloniaca of Berossus* (SANE 1.5; Malibu, Calif.: Undena, 1978); VERBRUGGHE and WICKERSHAM, *Berossos and Manetho, Introduced and Translated,* 1–91. *Bibliography:* R. DREWS, "The Babylonian Chronicles and Berossus," *Iraq* 37 (1975): 39–55; B. KOMOROCZY, "Berosos and the Mesopotamian Literature," *AcAntHung* 21 (1973): 125–52; A. KUHRT, "Berossus' *Babyloniaka* and Seleucid Rule in Babylonia," in *Hellenism in the East* (ed. A. Kuhrt and S. Sherwin-White; London: Duckworth, 1987), 53–56; W. G. LAMBERT, "Berossus and Babylonian Eschatology," *Iraq* 38 (1976): 170–73; P. SCHNABEL, *Berossos und die babylonisch-hellenistische Literatur* (Leipzig: Teubner, 1923).

12.1.2. Other Mesopotamian Texts and Sources

A Neo-Sumerian "Amphictyony." During the Neo-Sumerian period (twenty-first century B.C.E.), the various provinces in southern Mesopotamia took turns in supplying sacrifices for the temples at the religious capital in Nippur. This practice may be deduced from a calendar text that outlines the sequence of provincial contributions by month (see Hallo) and also from archival texts that record the contributions themselves (see Sigrist). Some scholars have described this arrangement as an amphictyony on the basis of an analogy with Greek culture. *Amphiktyonia* is the name that the Greeks gave to their sacral leagues, in which various Greek tribes were united in their commitment to, and defense of, a central religious shrine (e.g., the Delphic League). This analogy is important because of a further analogy for which biblical scholars have argued, namely, that early Israel, as depicted in Joshua and Judges (esp. Judg 5), was a sort of amphictyony that joined the twelve tribes in a common commitment to Yahweh's shrine and to each other (Noth). This hypothesis concerning early Israel has fallen into disfavor in recent years (de Geus), but there may yet be some comparative value in the theory (Sparks).

Texts and translations: W. W. HALLO, "A Sumerian Amphictyony," *JCS* 14 (1960): 88–114; M. SIGRIST, *Neo-Sumerian Account Texts in the Horn Archaeological Museum* (Andrews University Cuneiform Texts 1; Berrien Springs, Mich.: Andrews University Press, 1984), text 209. *Translation:* COS 3.144: 315–16. *Bibliography:* U. VON ARX, *Fragen im Horizont der Amphiktyoniehypthese von Martin Noth* (vol. 1 of *Studien zur Geschichte des alttestamentlichen Zwölfersymbolismus;* Europaische Hochschulschriften, Reihe 23, Theologie 397; New York: Lang, 1990); F. CAUER, "Amphiktyonie," PW 1:1904–35; H. E. CHAMBERS, "Ancient Amphictyonies, Sic et Non," in *More Essays on the Comparative Method* (ed. W. W. Hallo, J. C. Moyer, and L. Perdue; Scripture in Context 2; Winona Lake, Ind.: Eisenbrauns, 1983), 39–59; C. H. J. DE GEUS, *The Tribes of Israel: An Investigation into Some of the Presuppositions of Martin Noth's Amphictyony Hypothesis* (SSN 18; Assen, Neth.: Van

Gorcum, 1976); G. FOHRER, "Altes Testament: 'Amphiktyonie' und 'Bund'?" *TLZ* 91 (1966): 801–16, 893–904; N. P. LEMCHE, "The Greek Amphictyony: Could It Be a Prototype for the Israelite Society in the Period of the Judges?" *JSOT* 4 (1977): 48–59; M. NOTH, *Das System der zwölf Stämme Israels* (BWANT 52; Stuttgart: Kohlhammer, 1930); J. PENROSE-HARLAND, "The Calaurian Amphictyony," *AJA* 29 (1925): 160–71; SPARKS, *Ethnicity and Identity in Ancient Israel*, 109–21.

Mesopotamian Travel Itineraries. Scholars have unearthed itineraries that outline the trips taken by ancient travelers. The best-known exemplar is an Old Babylonian itinerary known as the Road to Emar, which is preserved in three copies (UIOM 2134; UIOM 2370; YBC 4499). The copies cover the same trip, but they are not identical and appear to enumerate the same journey in different ways. Essentially, the texts are lists of the overnight stations visited during the trip. Each station is described in this way: "day X, place Y," where "Y" refers to an overnight station along the route and "X" refers to the number of days at the site. In most cases "X" is a single day. Where more than one day is given, the author often includes a brief account of some incident that took place at the site. We may surmise that these accounts were given as explanations for delays in the trip. The purpose of the texts is not transparent. Although the copies obviously recorded real trips motivated by trade or military concerns, it is not clear whether we have canonical texts that were used as guides for travel or whether we have administrative records of some sort. Among other things, these eighteenth-century itineraries allow us to deduce that traveling soldiers or merchants covered a distance of about 12.5 to 18.5 miles per day. Other data from the Near East, however, suggest that armies could cover significantly longer distances in a single day when necessary and that couriers traveling alone or in small groups could cover still more ground (see Crown). The advent of horseback riding during the ninth to eighth centuries B.C.E., of course, improved these speeds. Mesopotamian itineraries also appear in the ninth-century Assyrian Annals of Tukulti-Ninurta II and Assurnaṣirpal II. Both exemplars begin with a dated rubric followed by a list of stations in the following form: "I departed from city A, in city B I spent the night" (see Davies 1974). For more on the Assyrian Annals, see 12.1.1.

The parade example of a Hebrew itinerary is Num 33:1–49, although texts in Num 21:10–20 and Deut 10:5–7 work as well. The entries in Num 33 take the form "They departed from place A, in place B they spent the night." This finds its closest parallel in the itineraries of the Assyrian Annals.

Text and translation: W. W. HALLO, "The Road to Emar," *JCS* 18 (1964): 57–88. *Bibliography:* G. COATS, "The Wilderness Itinerary," *CBQ* 34 (1972): 132–52; A. D. CROWN, "Tidings and Instructions: How News Travelled in the Ancient Near East," *JESHO* 17 (1974): 244–71; G. I. DAVIES, "The Wilderness Itineraries: A Comparative Study," *TynBul* 25 (1974) 46–81; IDEM, "The Wilderness Itineraries and the Composition of the Pentateuch," *VT* 33 (1983): 1–13; P. GARELLI, "La notion de route dans les texts," *RA* 52 (1958): 117–27.

Mesopotamian and Syrian Census Lists. Census lists are common in the archival materials unearthed from the ancient Near East. The lists were essentially registration documents that enumerated those who were responsible for taxes or for military service (although, note the religious motivations behind the census at Chagar Bazar; see Talon). Important exemplars include texts from ancient Alalakh, Nineveh, and Khafajeh. From Alalakh we have numerous lists of names that are associated with certain towns or groups of towns. Where the texts served a military function, this is sometimes visible in the fact that they enumerate those who were "warriors" or owned chariots. The Neo-Assyrian texts from Nineveh reflect a full-scale census of the region around Harran. Although the basic content of these tablets is comparable to the Alalakh census texts, the detail of the Neo-Assyrian records is sometimes quite striking, as this example shows: "Il-šimki, gardener; 1 son, of 3 spans' height; 1 woman; 1 daughter, weaned: a total of 4 people. 7,000 stalks of vine. Total, in the town of Aku'anu near the city of Haran." It is obvious that a chief purpose of this Assyrian census was taxation. As for Khafajeh, this site has yielded several muster lists, which recorded the names of soldiers who had been called up for military duty. A total of 17 texts are included in this find.

Several census lists were also discovered at Ugarit (see *KTU/CTU*), and census surveys are mentioned in the Mari texts (Kupper) and also in Egypt, where Pharaohs carried out regular surveys of their population (Mendenhall; Griffith). The closest parallels from ancient Israel would be the two Hebrew census inscriptions from Tell 'Ira and from the Ophel in Jerusalem (see 15.1). For related texts in Hebrew Bible, see Numbers (chs. 1–4, 26), Ezra (chs. 2, 8), and Nehemiah (chs. 7, 11–12).

Texts and translations: F. M. FALES and J. N. POSTGATE, *Imperial Administrative Records* (2 vols.; SAA 7, 11; Helsinki: University Press, 1992–1995), 2.xxx-xxxiv, 122–45; S. GREEN-GUS, *Old Babylonian Tablets from Ischali and Vicinity* (Istanbul: Nederlands Historisch-Archaeologisch Instituut, 1979), 45, 71–74, pls. ci–cix; *KTU*, 2.39, 4.80, 4.102, 4.128, 4.340, 6.25; F. L. GRIFFITH, *The Petrie Papyri: Hieratic Papyri from Kahun and Gurob* (London: B. Quaritch, 1898), vol 1., 19–25, pls. ix–xi; D. J. WISEMAN, *The Alalakh Tablets* (London: British Institute of Archaeology at Ankara, 1953), 64–78. **Translation:** *COS* 3.125–26: 276–17 (Alalakh). **Bibliography:** G. E. MENDENHALL, "The Census Lists of Numbers 1 and 26," *JBL* 77 (1958): 52–66; J.-R. KUPPER, "Le recensement dans les texts de Mari," in *Studia Mariana* (ed. A. Parrot; Leiden: Brill, 1950), 99–110; E. A. SPEISER, "The Alalakh Tablets," *JAOS* 74 (1954): 18–25; P. TALON, *Old Babylonian Texts from Chagar Bazar* (*Akkadica Suppl.* 10; Brussels: FAGD/ASGD, 1997), 14–17.

Jehoiachin's Ration Dockets. These are archival records that enlighten us about the fate of Judah's King Jehoiachin after he was exiled to Babylon. The texts record disbursements of oil and other supplies for foreigners who were under the care of Babylon's royal household. One of the texts (Bab 28122) mentions "eight men from Judah," and another (Bab 28186) refers to "Jehoiachin, King of Judah," and his five sons. Other nationalities mentioned in the archive include people from Ashkelon, Tyre, Byblos, Arvad, Egypt, Media, Persia, Lydia, and Greece. The texts attest not only to the reality of the Babylonian exile itself but also, and more specifically, to the general accuracy of the report at the end of 2 Kgs 25 that the king of Babylon provided for Jehoiachin (2 Kgs 25:27–30). For related texts, see the following entry.

Text and translation: E. F. WEIDNER, "Johachin, König von Jud, in babylonischen Keilschrifttexten," in *Mélanges syriens offerts à monsieur René Dussaud, secrétaire perpétuel de l'Académie des inscriptions et belles-lettres* (2 vols.; Bibliothèque archéologique et historique 30; Paris: Geuthner, 1939), 2:923–35. ***Translation:*** *ANET* 308.

Jews in Mesopotamian Archival Texts (and the Al Yaḥudu Inscriptions). In addition to the ration dockets mentioned in the previous entry and the Murašû family archive from Nippur (see ch. 1), several other Mesopotamian archival texts witness to the presence of exiled Jewish populations in Mesopotamia. Numerous Hebrew names appear in the texts, often bearing some form of the theophoric element YHWH. One group of texts, from Šēḫ Ḥamad in eastern Syria, attests to Jews living in the region early in the reign of Nebuchadnezzar of Babylon (ca. 604–601 B.C.E.; see Postgate; Fales). Because this was before the Babylonian deportations, we may surmise that these Jews were exiled there during earlier deportations of the Neo-Assyrian era. Deportations associated with the Babylonian exile are reflected in a later group of archival records from the early days of Persian-era Babylon (see Joannès/Lemaire). These texts list a group of Jews living in a place called *al Yaḥudu* (URU *ia-a-ḫu-du*), "city of Judah." This is the same name given to Jerusalem by the Babylonians in the Babylonian Chronicles (see 12.1.1), so we may surmise that Jews living in Mesopotamia named their new settlement after the homeland capital. Biblical scholars commonly believe that a large portion of the Hebrew Bible was written or edited by Jewish scribes living in the eastern Diaspora. Perhaps this "city of Judah," or some place like it, provided the intellectual center for their scribal activities. Only one published text mentions *al Yaḥudu*, but I am told that Kathleen Abraham (Bar-Ilan University) will soon publish similar exemplars from the private collection of Sh. Moussaïff.

Texts and translations: F. JOANNÈS and A. LEMAIRE, "Trois tablettes cunéiformes à onomastique oust-sémitique," *Transeuphratène* 17 (1999): 17–34; J. N. POSTGATE, "The Four 'Neo-Assyrian' Tablets from Šēḫ Ḥamad," *SAAB* 7 (1993): 109–24. ***Bibliography:*** F. M. FALES, "West Semitic Names in the Šēḫ Ḥamad Texts," *SAAB* 7 (1993): 139–50; D. VANDERHOOFT, "Babylonian Strategies of Imperial Control in the West," in *Judah and the Judeans in the Neo-Babylonian Period* (ed. O. Lipschits and J. Blenkinsopp; Winona Lake, Ind.: Eisenbrauns, 2003), 235–62; K. L. YOUNGER JR., "Yahweh at Ashkelon and Calaḫ? Yahwistic Names in Neo-Assyrian," *VT* 52 (2002): 207–18.

The Verse Account of Nabonidus. Nabonidus, a usurper of the Babylonian throne, was the last king of the Neo-Babylonian Empire. He was most remembered in antiquity as the king who shunned Babylon and withdrew to the city of Harran, where he devoted himself to the lunar god Sin, whose temple he lavishly restored (see the Babylonian Chronicles, above). The royal inscriptions of

Nabonidus describe these actions—for which he claimed divine sanction from both Sin and from Babylon's god Marduk—but the inscriptions also refer to the strong resistance Nabonidus faced from citizens, officials, and priests in Babylon and in other major cult centers in the empire, such as Borsippa, Nippur, Ur, Uruk, and Larsa (see *ANET* 562–63; Smith, 44–45).

The author of the present text capitalized on these facts. His objective was to present the last ruler of Babylon in the most unfavorable way possible, and this he accomplished by depicting Nabonidus as an arrogant, unjust king who had impiously neglected the chief cults of Babylon. The text was written in Akkadian verse and hence was designed for public readings, through which its propaganda could be disseminated more widely (although a more suitable language for reaching the general populace would have been Aramaic). The composition clearly served as propaganda for the incoming Persian regime of Cyrus, but the author is believed to have been a native Babylonian priest from the temple of Marduk, who viewed Cyrus as a restorer of the home cult and seized one last opportunity to exact revenge on Nabonidus, the king who had snubbed his god.

The historical figure of Nabonidus stands behind the story about Nebuchadnezzar's madness in Dan 4. This conclusion is based on several facts that cohere nicely. First, the description of Nebuchadnezzar's madness in Daniel suits the life and reputation of Nabonidus better than Nebuchadnezzar. Second, an Aramaic text found among the Dead Sea Scrolls—the *Prayer of Nabonidus* (4QPrNab[ar])—reveals that Jews were familiar with the traditions about Nabonidus's madness (see Jongeling/Labuschagne/van der Woude; *COS* 1.89)). Third, the author of Daniel incorrectly identified Belshazzar as the son of Nebuchadnezzar rather than of Nabonidus; this suggests that the popular traditions about Nabonidus were somehow shifted to the more famous Nebuchadnezzar.

Text and translation: S. SMITH, *Babylonian Historical Texts Relating to the Capture and Downfall of Babylon* (London: Methuen, 1924), 27–97. *Translations:* ANET 312–14, 562–63 (related royal inscription of Nabonidus); B. JONGELING, C. J. LABUSCHAGNE, and A. S. VAN DER WOUDE, *Aramaic Texts from Qumran* (Leiden Brill, 1976–), vol. 1 (*Prayer of Nabonidus*). *Bibliography:* P.-A. BEAULIEU, *The Reign of Nabonidus, King of Babylon, 556–539 B.C.* (New Haven: Yale University Press, 1989); S. COHEN and V. A. HUROWITZ, "חקות העמים הבל הוא (Jer 10:3) in Light of Akkadian *parṣu* and *zaqīqu* Referring to Cult Statues," *JQR* 89 (1999): 277–90; P. W. COXON, "Another Look at Nebuchadnessar's Madness," in *The Book of Daniel in the Light of New Findings* (ed. A. S. van der Woude; Leuven: Leuven University Press/Peeters, 1993), 211–22; H. SCHAUDIG, *Die Inschriften Nabonids von Babylon und Kyros' des Grossen, samt den in ihrem Umfeld entstandenen Tendenzschriften: Textausgabe und Grammatik* (AOAT 256; Münster: Ugarit, 2001).

Ethnic Massacre Decrees. The biblical story of Esther includes an event—historically improbable it would seem—in which Persia announced its plans to massacre its Jewish population eleven months before the pogrom would take place (Esth 3:5–15). Even more implausible is the book's claim that the Jews responded by slaughtering over 75,000 Persians (Esther 9:1–17). As unlikely as these events strike us on historical grounds, there is evidence from Persian and

Syrian contexts that in some cases ancient kings announced ethnic massacres well in advance and that these slaughters could result in great loss of life. Herodotus tells us that the Persians conducted large-scale massacres of Scythians and Magi (Herodotus, 1.106, 3.79), and Cicero describes the extermination of 80,000 Romans by Mithridates VI of Pontus (in Asia Minor) in 88 B.C.E. (see Pro Lege Manilia, 3.7; Bickerman). The killing was to be done everywhere at the same time, on the thirtieth day after the royal order was given. However, a one-month lead-time is not so long as eleven months given in the book of Esther, and the orders of Mithridates to his satraps and cities were sealed, unlike the public decree given in Esther.

Texts and translations: A. D. GODLEY, trans., *Herodotus* (4 vols.; LCL; Cambridge: Harvard, 1920–25); H. G. HODGE, trans., *Cicero: Pro lege Manilia, Pro Caecina, Pro Cluentio, Pro Rabirio Perduellionis* (LCL; Cambridge: Harvard University Press, 1979); L. ROBERT, *Inscriptions Séleucides de Phrygie et d'Iran* (Hellenica 7; Limoges: A. Bontemps, 1949), 22. *Bibliography:* E. BICKERMAN, *Four Strange Books in the Bible: Jonah, Daniel, Koheleth, Esther* (New York: Schocken, 1967), 190; D. J. A. CLINES, *Ezra, Nehemiah, Esther* (NCBC; Grand Rapids: Eerdmans, 1984), 257; R. GORDIS, "Religion, Wisdom and History in the Book of Esther—A New Solution to an Ancient Crux," *JBL* 100 (1981): 359–388, esp. 383.

12.2. Egyptian Historiography

Ancient Egyptian documents reflect an intense interest in the past and an ongoing inclination to preserve records of the past for posterity. The relevant sources include annalistic records and compositions, royal annals, and funerary biographies. One genre not addressed here in detail is the much discussed *Königsnovelle,* supposedly a kind of historical novel that the Egyptians wrote about the lives of their kings (see 8.1). The natural appeal of the *Königsnovelle* is that it may shed light on the development of royal histories in Israel, particularly those of David and Solomon, but it seems that better parallels can be found in the royal apologies from Mesopotamia, Hatti, and Persia, treated in the present chapter.

12.2.1. Egyptian Chronicles, Annals, and Biographies

The Gnwt and Daybooks. The *gnwt* (sing., *gnt*—tentatively pronounced "genut") were annalistic records that appeared early in Egyptian history. The texts were written on papyrus and seem to have developed from earlier archival genres written on wood or ivory tablets during the Proto-Dynastic period. We have exemplars of the tablet genre (see Petrie) but only descriptions of the *gnwt* (see Redford). Nevertheless, when we read these *gnwt* descriptions in light of the archaic tablets and the Palermo Stone (see next entry), the combined evidence gives us a pretty good idea of what the *gnwt* were like. The purpose of the *gnwt* appears to have been twofold: to record the major events of each year, and to provide year names that could be used for dating purposes. In this venue, "major events" included important cultic occasions, military action, construction projects, acts of taxation, and the annual inundation heights of the Nile. The *gnwt* seem to have ceased their primary recordkeeping function during the Middle Kingdom (ca. 2040–1650 B.C.E.), so that by the New Kingdom the semantic range of *gnwt* had broadened enough to include most any text that presented the past, even mythological texts (partly because, for the ancients, myths were history; Redford, 95).

One reason for the functional obsolescence and disappearance of the *gnwt* during the Middle Kingdom was the gradual development of a substitute archival genre, the daybook (*hrwyt*). Daybooks were utilized by several key institutions, including the temple, the king's residence, the necropolis, the ancestral archives, and the treasury. Their content was therefore heterogeneous and varied with the institutions that produced them (for examples, see Gardiner; Griffith; Redford, 103–26; Smither). Entries in these documents covered various kinds of information—dates, copies of official correspondence, itemized lists of military provisions, payments received by the institutions, official edicts, cultic activities, military activities, and so on. Daybook records were deposited according to need and convenience. For example, the New Kingdom military records of Thutmose III's campaigns were kept on a leather scroll in the temple of Amun. In the terminology of this volume, these daybooks are best described as historical records rather than works of historiography. Both the *gnwt* and the daybooks were consulted later by those who wrote historiographic works, such as the Palermo Stone and Annals of Thutmose III.

Texts and translations: A. H. GARDINER, *Late-Egyptian Miscellanies* (BAeg 1; Brussels: Fondation Égyptologique Reine Élisabeth, 1937), 31–32 [Daybook of an Official on the Eastern Frontier]; F. L. GRIFFITH, *The Petrie Papyri: Hieratic Papyri from Kahun and Gurob* (London: B. Quaritch, 1898), vol 2., 55–59, pls. xxii–xxiii [The Kahun Daybook]; W. M. F. PETRIE, *The Royal Tombs of the First Dynasty* (2 vols.; London: Egypt Exploration Fund, 1900–01), vol. 1: 21–24, pls., X–XVII; vol. 2: pls., I.1, III.2, III.4, III.6, V.1, VIII.1–5, XI.1–3 [archaic tablets]; A. SCHARFF, "Ein Rechnungsbuch des Königlichen Hofes aus der 13. Dynastie (Papyrus Boulaq Nr. 18)," *ZÄS* 57 (1922): 51–68; P. C. SMITHER, "A Tax Assessors Journal of Middle Kingdom," *JEA* 27 (1941): 74–76 [Tax Assessor's Daybook]; IDEM, "The Semnah Dispatches," *JEA* 31 (1934): 3–10 [Semna Dispatches]. *Translations:* ANET 258–59; R. A. CAMINOS, *Late-Egyptian Miscellanies* (London: Oxford University Press, 1954), 108–13. *Bibliography:* REDFORD, Pharaonic King-Lists, Annals, and Day-Books, 65–126.

The Palermo Stone. Ancient Egypt has given us the oldest known example of historical research, the Fifth Dynasty Palermo Stone (ca. 2350 B.C.E.). The text is fragmentarily preserved on a broken stela and originally covered the period from the predynastic kings down to the Fifth Dynasty. The arrangement marked each reign by placing the king's name above a line, under which was placed a row of horizontal rectangles. Each rectangle contained the events associated with a year in the king's reign, including the annual height of the Nile; military, religious, and building activities; and other information. Entries for the early kings are much shorter than those preserved for the later kings because of the development of daybook sources, which appeared toward the end of the period covered by the document. In lieu of these daybooks, the primary sources for the early periods appear to have been date lists and a record of Nile inundations. Although the text of the Palermo Stone superficially resembles an annal, it is more like a chronicle because it was composed all at once by culling information from various kinds of sources. The publication history of the text (which resides in Palermo, Italy) and its additional fragments (now in Cairo and London) is complex. For a more detailed explanation and bibliography, see Clagett and Wilkinson.

Texts and translations: H. SCHÄFER, *Ein Bruchstück altägyptischer Annalen* (AKPAW; Berlin: Verlag der Königlichen Akademie der Wissenschaften, 1902); K. SETHE, *Urkunden des Alten Reichs* (1 vol. in 4 parts; 2d ed.; Leipzig: Hinrichs, 1932–1933), 235–49. *Translations:* BREASTED, *Ancient Records of Egypt*, 1:51–72; M. CLAGETT, *Ancient Egyptian Science: A Source Book* (3 vols. in 4; Philadelphia: American Philosophical Society, 1989–1999), vol. 1, part 1, pp. 47–141. *Bibliography:* P. F. O'MARA, *The Palermo Stone and the Archaic Kings of Egypt* (Studies in the Structural Archaeology of Ancient Egypt; La Canada, Calif.: Paulette, 1979); R. T. RIDLEY, "The World's Earliest Annals: A Modern Journey in Comprehension," *AcAntHung* 27 (1979): 39–48; T. A. H. WILKINSON, *Royal Annals of Ancient Egypt: The Palermo Stone and Its Associated Fragments* (New York: Kegan Paul, 2000).

The Annals of Thutmose III. The New Kingdom Annals of Thutmose III (1479–1425 B.C.E.) represent Egyptian historiography par excellence and are similar in some respects to biblical history writing. These annals include a prologue and an epilogue and cover sixteen military campaigns that Thutmose undertook during a twenty-year period. They were carved on the hallway walls of the temple complex at Karnak. The sources used to compose the annals were the military daybooks kept by the king's official, Thaneni, whose biographical tomb inscription reads, "I followed the Good God, Sovereign of Truth, King of Upper and Lower Egypt, Menkheperre (Thutmose III); I beheld the victories of the king ... I recorded the victories which he won in every land, putting (them) into writing according to the facts" (Breasted, 2:165). The account of the Battle of Megiddo is especially reminiscent of biblical historiography because it includes both an extended narrative and a clear plot line: the Asiatics rebel and meet in Megiddo; the king travels toward Megiddo following a dated itinerary; the king confers with his officers about military strategy; the battle plan is finalized and implemented; the victory is realized; the collected booty is listed (see Younger). The source citations in the annals are also similar to those in the Hebrew Bible, as this comparison shows:

> Now, all that his majesty did to this city, to that wretched foe and his wretched army, was recorded on (each) day by its (the day's) name, under the title [unclear] ... Then it was recorded upon a roll of leather in the temple of Amon this day. (Breasted, vol. 2, 186)

> The rest of the deeds of Hezekiah, and all his power, and how he made the pool and the conduit and brought water into the city, are they not written in the Book of the Annals of the Kings of Judah? (2 Kgs 20:20)

The annals refer to other sources as well, particularly to the palace daybook and its economic records of income and expenses. That these sources were indeed consulted is proved, says Redford, by the fact that the annals often reflect the same laconic style and grammatical preferences as the daybooks. So it appears that in form and content these annals are similar in certain respects to the biblical materials. The biblical materials are perhaps distinguished from these annals in that the biblical histories are more integrated as narrative plots, less episodic, more serious in their development of characters, and more thematically diverse.

The historiographic tone and character of the Annals of Thutmose differ substantially from his other royal inscriptions. For instance, the account of his feats in the Gebel Barkal Stela alternates between "sober historical statements," such as appear in the annals, and "grandiose claims," such as the appearance of a shooting star that overwhelmed his enemies and resulted in military victory. Why were two historiographic texts from the same time period and scribal tradition so different? Although both texts are works of royal propaganda, the annals were content with the real accomplishments of the king whereas the stela chose fictive elaboration as a means of heightening the king's image in the text. But this difference aside, the texts are functionally and generically very similar.

Text and translation: K. SETHE and W. HELCK, *Urkunden der 18. Dynastie* (5 vols.; Urk 4; Leipzig: Hinrichs, 1906–1909 [vols. 1–4, Sethe]; Berlin: Akademie, 1958 [vol. 5, Helck]), 3:645–734. *Translations: AEL* 2:29–35 (partial); *ANET* 234–41 (partial); BREASTED, *Ancient Records of Egypt,* 2:163–217; *COS* 2.2A: 7.13 (partial); 2.2B: 14–18 (Gebel Barkal Stela). *Bibliography:* H. GOEDICKE, *The Battle of Megiddo* (Baltimore: Halgo, 2000); H. GRAPOW, *Studien zu den Annalen Thutmosis des Dritten und zu ihnen verwandten historischen Berichten des Neuen Reiches* (Berlin: Akademie, 1949); J. K. HOFFMEIER, "The Structure of Joshua 1–11 and the Annals of Thutmose III," in *Faith, Tradition, and History* (ed. Millard et al.), 165–79; W. J. MURNANE, "Rhetorical History? The Beginning of Thutmose III's First Campaign in Western Asia," *JARCE* 26 (1989): 183–89; M. NOTH, "Die Annalen Thutmosis III als Geschichtsquelle," *ZDPV* 66 (1943): 156–74; P. F. O'MARA, "The Birth of Egyptian Historiography," *DE* 46 (2000): 49–64; D. B. REDFORD, "The Historical Retrospective at the Beginning of Thutmose III's Annals," in *Festschrift Elmar Edel: 12. März 1979* (ed. M. Görg and E. Pusch; AAT 1; Bamberg: Görg, 1979), 338–42; A. J. SPALINGER, "A Critical Analysis of the 'Annals' of Thutmose III (Stücke V–VI)," *JARCE* 14 (1977): 41–54; IDEM, "Some Additional Remarks on the Battle of Megiddo," *GM* 33 (1979): 46–54; IDEM, "Some Notes on the Battle of Megiddo and Reflections on Egyptian Military Writing," *MDAIK* 30 (1974): 221–29; K. L. YOUNGER JR., *Ancient Conquest Accounts: A Study in Ancient Near Eastern and Biblical History Writing* (JSOTSup 98; Sheffield, England: Sheffield Academic Press, 1990).

The Annals of Amenophis II. The recently published Annals of Amenophis II (1427–1401) were inscribed in the Ptah temple in Memphis. Although they are fragmentary, their general character can be surmised. Unlike the Annals of Thutmose III, the Annals of Amenophis do not provide a historical narrative but rather a list of important events in the king's reign, including donations to the temple and cult, dispatches of troops and military operations, lists of tribute received, and booty lists. This information must have been culled from archival sources. Each year's records were collected into a single section of the text, and each annual section was further subdivided into three seasons, that is, "inundations," "winter," and "summer." Altenmüller and Moussa believe that these entries were probably dated, but the text is broken at the point where dates would have been inserted. From a generic perspective, this text shares many features with the much earlier Palermo Stone.

Texts and translations: H. ALTENMÜLLER and A. M. MOUSSA, "Die Inschrift Amememhets II. aus dem Ptah-Temple von Memphis: Ein Vorbericht," *SAK* 18 (1992): 1–48; J. MÁLEK and S. QUIRKE, "Memphis, 1991: Epigraphy," *JEA* 78 (1992): 13–18. *Translations:* ANET 245–47 (related inscription of Amenophis II); COS 2.3: 19–23 (related inscription of Amenophis II). *Bibliography:* J. MÁLEK, "The Annals of Amenemhet II," *Egyptian Archaeology* 2 (1982): 18.

The Victory Stela of King Piye. During the eighth century B.C.E. King Piye of Nubia conquered the land of Egypt. After his conquest, Piye entrusted the land to his vassals and immediately returned to Nubia. Although, so far as we know, he never again traveled to Egypt, Piye did commemorate his victories there with a stela at Napata. The stela begins and ends with poetic hymns in praise of the king, between which lies its narrative plot. The story commences with the advance of enemy troops (tribal chiefs and others from Egypt) and with Piye's subsequent order to have his Nubian troops repulse them at Heracleopolis. Piye then resolved to go to Egypt himself, where various battles ensued at Hermopolis, Heracleopolis, Memphis, and elsewhere; the result in every case was a complete victory for Piye. The narrative portion of the inscription concludes with a list of defeated rulers and of the tribute that they paid to Piye. The level of detail in the narrative gives the impression that it was derived from accurate historical sources, and this has resulted in a rather high view of the text's historical value. Recent studies, however, have identified numerous allusions in the stela to earlier texts, such as the Westcar Papyrus, the Tale of Sinuhe, Eloquent Peasant, the Tale of Two Brothers, the Admonitions of an Egyptian Sage, the Instructions of Merikare, the Dispute of a Man with His Ba, Ptahhotep, the Prophecy of Neferti, the Satire on the Trades, and the Book of the Dead (Grimal). So, although the information in Piye's inscription may well have been derived from historical sources, the narrative itself has been profoundly shaped by the literary sources that its author mimicked in his effort to improve the text's style and appeal. This makes the Stela of Piye an important generic innovation, since it combined the features of royal inscriptions with those of literary texts.

Texts and translations: N.-C. GRIMAL, *La stèle triomphale de Pi('ankh)y au Musée du Caire* (MIFAO 105; Études sur la propagande royale égyptienne 1; Paris: Institut Français d'Archéologie Orientale, 1981); H. SCHÄFER, ed., *Urkunden der älteren Äthiopenkönige* (2 vols.; Urkunden des ägyptischen Altertums 3; Leipzig: Hinrichs, 1905–1908), 1:1–56. *Translations:* AEL 3:66–84; COS 2.7: 42–51; LAE 367–85. *Bibliography:* J. HUDDLESTUN, "Legitimation, Usurpation, and Celebration: Ancient Egyptian Concepts and Uses of the Past" (paper delivered at the annual meeting of the Society of Biblical Literature, Chicago, November, 1994).

The Annals of Osorkon. This text preserves an annal-like account of the life of Osorkon, the high priest of Amun during the ninth century B.C.E. It was inscribed in the great temple at Karnak. Most of the inscription is cast biographically as a third-person narrative, but the conclusion is autobiographical. Among other things, the text highlights Osorkon's important role in bringing peace to Egypt during a troubled time in its history. Unfortunately, the inscription is fragmentary and difficult to evaluate in any detail, but it is remarkable insofar as its annalistic genre treats a priest rather than a king.

Text: H. H. NELSON, *Reliefs and Inscriptions at Karnak III: The Bubastite Portal* (Chicago: University of Chicago, 1954), pls. 16–22. *Translations:* BREASTED, *Ancient Records of Egypt,* 4:377–86; R. A. CAMINOS, *The Chronicle of Prince Osorkon* (AnOr 37; Rome: Pontificium Institutum Biblicum, 1958).

Egyptian Funerary Autobiographies. Autobiographies developed during the Old Kingdom as commemorative tomb inscriptions that addressed the gods and passersby with a flattering self-portrait of the entombed. The purpose of the genre was twofold: to promote the deceased's reputation and to secure regular offerings that would preserve his life in the hereafter. Early exemplars of the genre were inscribed on the tombs themselves, but in later periods the autobiographies were written on small stelae that could be placed closer to Abydos, holy city of the god Osiris (god of the dead). The private nature of the tomb autobiographies distinguishes them from the autobiographical texts of Asia, where the subjects treated were usually kings. Funerary autobiographies represent the longest-lived of Egypt's genres, flourishing uninterrupted from the Old Kingdom down into the Roman period. Consequently, the funerary autobiographies are too numerous to list exhaustively.

There are numerous similarities between the Egyptian autobiographies and the autobiographical account of Nehemiah in the Hebrew Bible. According to von Rad and Van Seters, the degree of similarity cannot be a coincidence but is better explained by assuming that the Egyptian autobiographical tradition in some degree influenced the development of Hebrew autobiography.

Translations: AEL 1:15–27, 83–93; 2:12–15; 3:13–65; *ANET* 233–34; M. CLAGETT, *Ancient Egyptian Science: A Source Book* (3 vols. in 4; Philadelphia: American Philosophical Society, 1989–1999), vol. 1, part 1, pp. 143–75; *COS* 2.1: 5–7; *LAE* 401–24; M. LICHTHEIM, *Ancient Egyptian Autobiographies Chiefly of the Middle Kingdom: A Study and an Anthology* (OBO 84; Freiburg, Switz.: Universitätsverlag, 1988). *Bibliography:* A. M. GNIRS, "Die ägyptische Autobiographie," in *Ancient Egyptian Literature: History and Forms* (ed. A. Loprieno; PA 10; New York: Brill, 1996), 191–241; H. GOEDICKE, "Some Remarks Concerning the Inscription of Ahmose, Son of Ebana," *JARCE* 11 (1974): 31–41; H. W. MÜLLER, "Die Totendenksteine des Mittleren Reich, ihre Genesis, ihre Darstellungen, und ihre Komposition," *MDAIK* 4 (1933): 165–206; G. VON RAD, "Die Nehemia-Denkschrift," *ZAW* 76 (1964): 176–87; J. VAN SETERS, *In Search of History,* 181–87.

Manetho's History of Egypt. Manetho was an Egyptian priest—perhaps the chief priest—who served in the temple of the god Re at Heliopolis. He composed his history of Egypt in Greek during the third century B.C.E. Although no copies of the history itself survive, modern scholars have been reasonably successful in their attempt to reconstruct portions of the work from fragments quoted by other Greek writers. Unfortunately, the Greek writers who quoted Manetho often did so for polemical reasons, so our sources for Manetho cannot be taken at face value. Nevertheless, a comparison of our Manetho fragments with older Egyptian traditions, such as the Turin Canon (see 11.2), shows that his work provides a reliable window into Egypt's past.

Manetho's history was essentially a long king list that began with the gods and ended with Darius, a Persian king who ruled Egypt during the fourth century B.C.E. In this list, Manetho was the first Greek author to use the word *dynasteia* to identify sequences of kings from the same family. Since this term meant "governmental power" before Manetho, he should be credited for the innovation that led to our modern concept of dynasty. Manetho interspersed his list with a variety of brief anecdotes and longer narrative episodes. His motivations for composing the history are not clear, but he expresses his desire to correct some of the mistakes in Herodotus's description of Egypt. Although Manetho's history did not supplant the popularity of Herodotus in the Hellenistic world, the preservation of Manetho's history in the sources shows that his work was widely known.

Manetho clearly has much in common with the Mesopotamian historian Berossus, since both were priests who composed their native histories in Greek during the third century B.C.E. If biblical scholars are right, the P narrative of Genesis was also written by a priest, in this case a Jewish priest who lived not long before Manetho and Berossus.

Texts and translations: JACOBY, *Die Fragmente der griechischen Historiker*, 3:5–112; W. G. WADDELL, *Manetho* (LCL; Cambridge: Harvard University Press, 1940). *Translation:* VERBRUGGHE and WICKERSHAM, *Berossos and Manetho, Introduced and Translated*, 93–212. *Bibliography:* W. HELCK, "Manethon (1)," in *DNP* 7:804–5; IDEM, *Untersuchungen zu Manetho und den ägyptischen Königslisten* (Untersuchungen zur Geschichte und Altertumskunde Ägyptens 18; Berlin: Akademie, 1956); REDFORD, *Pharaonic King-Lists, Annals, and DayBooks*.

12.2.2. Other Egyptian Texts and Sources

The Defeat and Expulsion of the Hyksos. During the 18th and 17th centuries B.C.E., dramatic increases in Egypt's Asiatic population led to the emergence of these Asiatics as a political and social force in Egypt's complex cultural matrix. Eventually, these foreigners—known as the Hyksos—solidified their hold on power and established their capital in Avaris, in the northeastern Nile Delta. The height of their power was during the 15th–17th dynasties (ca. 1650–1550 B.C.E.). Native resistance to the Hyksos emerged from the Theban south of Egypt. Seknenre of Thebes was killed in battle against the Hyksos (see Redford/Weinstein), and then his son Kamose (1555–1550) invaded Hyksos territories and made it as far as Avaris (see the Kamose inscriptions). Kamose was succeeded by his brother

Ahmose, who completed the conquest of the Hyksos and drove them back into Asia. The victory of Ahmose is commemorated in the funerary stela of one of his officers, whose name was also Ahmose (see Ahmose inscription). In the years that followed the Hyksos expulsion, nervous pharaohs of the New Kingdom secured their eastern perimeter through an aggressive imperial policy in Asia.

Struggles between the Egyptians and Hyksos eventually became the subject of legend and lore, as a fanciful New Kingdom tale about the origins of the conflict shows (see *LAE* 69–71). Although these Egyptian materials suggest that the Asiatics invaded the land in one fell swoop (see Waddell), archaeological evidence suggests that the foreigners entered Egypt in a long process of peaceful infiltration (Redford/Weinstein). Some biblical scholars suspect that peaceful infiltration played a similar role in the Israelite "conquest" (e.g., Alt; Weippert).

In a related matter, many scholars believe that the story of Israel's trek into Egypt, Joseph's rise to power in Pharaoh's court, and the final expulsion of Israel from Egypt is a distorted variation of events during the Hyksos period (Halpern; Redford). However, this historical equation between the Hyksos and the Israelites is not modern only. Josephus, the ancient Jewish historian, also identified the Hyksos with his Israelite ancestors (see Thackery; Waddell).

Texts: J. P. ALLEN, "The Speos Artemidos Inscription of Hatshepsut," *Bulletin of the Egyptological Seminar* 16 (2002): 1–17, pls. 1–2 (Hatshepsut inscriptions); A. H. GARDINER, *Late-Egyptian Stories* (BAeg 1; Brussels: Fondation Égyptologique Reine Élisabeth, 1932), xiii, 85–89 (Quarrel of Apophis and Seknenre); W. HELCK, *Historisch-Biographische Texte der 2. Zwischenzeit und Neue Texte der 18. Dynastie,* 2 (Wiesbaden: Harrassowitz, 1983), 82–98 (Kamose inscriptions); SETHE, *Urk* 4:1–11 (Ahmose inscriptions). *Translations: AEL,* 2.12–15 (Ahmose inscription); *ANET* 230–34 (Hatshepsut inscriptions; Kamose inscription 1; Ahmose inscription); *COS* 2.1: 5–7 (Ahmose inscription); *LAE* 69–71, (Quarrel of Apophis and Seknenre) 345–50 (Kamose stelae). *Bibliography:* A. ALT, *Essays on Old Testament History and Religion* (Garden City, N.Y.: Doubleday, 1968), 175–221; B. HALPERN, "The Exodus from Egypt: Myth and Reality," in *The Rise of Ancient Israel* (ed. H. Shanks; Washington: Biblical Archaeology Society, 1992), 86–117; D. B. REDFORD, *Egypt, Canaan, and Israel in Ancient Times* (Princeton: University Press, 1992), 98–122; D. B. REDFORD and J. M. WEINSTEIN, "Hyksos," *ABD* 3: 341–48; H. ST. J. THACKERAY, trans., *Josephus: The Life Against Apion* (LCL; Cambridge: Harvard University, 1976), 193–201; W. G. WADDELL, trans., *Manetho* (LCL; Cambridge: Harvard University, 1980), 77–99; M. WEIPPERT, *The Settlement of the Israelite Tribes* (SBT 21; Naperville, Ill.: Allenson, 1971).

The Shasu and Yahweh. When Egyptian pharaohs commemorated their military victories in royal inscriptions, they often included lists of those they defeated or conquered. Among the enemies listed in these inscriptions are the Shasu, wandering nomadic groups akin to what we would call Bedouin, excepting that they did not have camels, which were not yet domesticated during this period (Redford). Because the Shasu are often mentioned in connection with certain toponyms, scholars have been able to isolate their general territory to the regions around Moab and Edom, south and east of the Dead Sea. Particularly interesting is that two texts from the fourteenth and thirteenth centuries mention a place known as

"Ywh in the land of Shasu." Some scholars read this as "Yahweh in the land of Shasu" because the evidence seems to dovetail nicely with the biblical portrait of early Israel. Not only does the Bible associate Yahweh with the region of Edom (Deut 33:2; Judg 5:4; Hab 3:3); it also depicts Israel as a nomadic people who moved into Palestine from Transjordan. Moreover, the presumed date of Israel's entry into the land, about 1200 B.C.E., fits well with the date of the Shasu people. Some scholars are therefore confident that the origins of ancient Israel and its god, Yahweh, can be traced back to the Shasu (Redford); other scholars are much more skeptical (Ahlström).

Text and translation: R. GIVEON, *Les bédouins Shosou des documents égyptiens* (Leiden: Brill, 1971), 26–28 (Amenophis III), 74–77 (Rameses II). *Bibliography:* G. AHLSTRÖM, *Who Were the Israelites?* (Winona Lake, Ind.: Eisenbrauns, 1986); D. B. REDFORD, *Egypt, Canaan, and Israel in Ancient Times* (Princeton: Princeton University Press, 1992), 269–80; H. N. RÖSEL, *Israel in Kanaan: Zum Problem der Entstehung Israels* (BEATAJ 11; Frankfurt am Main: Lang, 1992).

Merenptah's "Israel" Stela. The victory stela of Merenptah dates to the end of the thirteenth century B.C.E. The text was inscribed in two different places, on a stela in Merenptah's mortuary temple and on a stela in the temple at Karnak. The poetic text is concerned largely with Merenptah's victory over the Libyans, but near its end the author mentions a number of other regions, peoples, and cities that he conquered—including "Israel" (*ysry'l*). The relevant portion of the stela reads, "The princes are prostrate, saying, 'Peace!' No one is raising his head among the Nine Bows. Now the Tehenu (Libya) has come to ruin, Hatti is pacified; The Canaan has been plundered into every sort of woe: Ashkelon has been overcome; Gezer has been captured; Yano'am is made nonexistent. Israel is laid waste and his seed is not; Hurru is become a widow because of Egypt" (Lichtheim, *AEL*). This is the first attestation of Israel in the ancient record as well as the first instance in which Israel is juxtaposed with its traditional enemy, the Canaanites. Although most scholars would concede that the Israel mentioned in this text is in some way related to biblical Israel, there is an ongoing debate about two related issues: (1) What is the nature of the Israel mentioned in the stela? (2) To what extent does the Israel depicted in the stela cohere, or not cohere, with biblical images of early Israel? A frequently discussed point is that Israel is the only name mentioned in the text that bears an Egyptian determinative for "people" rather than "land," which would seem to comport with the image of early Israel found in biblical book of Judges.

Text and translation: K. A. KITCHEN, *Ramesside Inscriptions, Historical and Biographical* (8 vols.; Oxford: Blackwell, 1975–1990), 4:12–19. *Translations: AEL* 2:73–77; *ANET* 376–78; *COS* 2.6: 40–41 (partial); *LAE* 356–60. *Bibliography:* G. AHLSTRÖM and E. EDELMAN, "Merenptah's Israel," *JNES* 44 (1985): 59–61; J. BIMSON, "Merenptah's Israel and Recent Theories of Israelite Origins," *JSOT* 49 (1991): 20–23; M. G. HASEL, "Israel in the Merneptah Stela," *BASOR* 296 (1994): 45–61; J. K. HOFFMEIER, *Egypt in Israel: The Evidence for the Authenticity of the Exodus Tradition* (New York: Oxford University Press, 1997), 27–31; A. NICCACCI, "La stèle d'Israël: Grammaire et stratégie de communication," in *Études égyptologiques et bibliques: À la mémoire du père B. Couroyer* (ed. M. Sigrist; CahRB 36; Paris: Gabalda, 1997), 43–107; L. E. STAGER, "Merneptah, Israel, and the Sea Peoples: New Light on an Old Relief," *ErIsr* 18 (1985): 56–64; SPARKS, *Ethnicity and Identity in Ancient Israel*, 94–109; F. YURCO, "Merneptah's Canaanite Campaign," *JARCE* 23 (1986): 189–215.

The Asiatic Campaign of Pharaoh Sheshonq I. During the second half of the tenth century B.C.E., Sheshonq I undertook a campaign in Syria and Palestine. Fortunately, a list of the towns and localities plundered by Sheshonq accompanies the relief at Karnak that depicts this campaign; several of the towns were Israelite. The campaign is mentioned in 1 Kgs 14:25–28, where Rehoboam of Judah halts Pharaoh Shishak's attack against Jerusalem by paying tribute to the king. This evidence confirms that the author of 1 Kings (seventh–sixth century B.C.E.) had access to relatively accurate sources covering the period of the early Judean monarchy. If this is the case, however, it is indeed odd that Jerusalem is not mentioned in Sheshonq's toponym list.

Text and translation: J. LAMMEYER, *Das Siegesdenkmal des Königs Scheschonk I. zu Karnak* (Neuss am Rhein, Germany: H. Goder, 1907), 29. *Translations: ANET* 242–43, 263–64 (partial); BREASTED, *Ancient Records of Egypt*, 4:348–57. *Bibliography:* J. SIMONS, *Handbook for the Study of Egyptian Topographical Lists Relating to Western Asia* (Leiden: Brill, 1937).

12.3. Hittite Historiography

Annalistic compositions appeared very early in the Hittite traditions, prompting H. Cancik and some others to stress that the Hittites played an important role in the origins and development of later historiography in Greece and Israel (Cancik 1976). But Hittite literature is probably too early to have served this key role. Although the best-known and most celebrated Hittite examplars are the fourteenth-century Annals of Muršili II, his annals had at least three important forerunners: the Anitta Text, the Annals of Ḥattušili I (ca. 1650–1620 B.C.E.), and the Ammuna Chronicle. Taken together, this sequence of documents reveals that the development of historiography in Hatti followed the same path as in Assyria, which began with royal inscriptions and ended with annalistic historiography.

The entries in this section are arranged chronologically. In addition to the texts treated below, readers may want to note the fifteenth-century Annals of Arnuwanda I (*CTH* 413) and Tudhaliya II (*CTH* 142), as well as the complete list of historiographical texts and fragments in *CTH* 1–218.

The Anitta Text (CTH 1). Like the Assyrian Annals, the Annita Text furnishes an autobiographical narrative of the king's military exploits and other details befitting royal propaganda. Still, it is not so much an annal as a simple compilation of royal inscriptions. This may be deduced not only from the style of the text but also from the author's explicit testimony, which at one point indicates that his content was derived from a monumental inscription on the city gate. Anitta, king of Kuššar, seems to have lived during the eighteenth century B.C.E., but we do not know his ethnic background or language. Nonetheless, the present text, which dates no later than the Hittite Old Kingdom, was written in Hittite and seems not to be a translation. Thus we likely have the later version of a Hittite text composed earlier during the time of Anitta.

Text and translation: E. NEU, *Der Anitta-Text* (StBoT 18; Wiesbaden: Harrassowitz, 1974). *Translations:* BRYCE, *The Major Historical Texts of Early Hittite History*, 21–48; COS 1.72: 182–84. *Bibliography:* GÜTERBOCK, "Die historische Tradition und ihre literarische Gestaltung bei Babyloniern und Hethitern bis 1200" (1938), 139–45; IDEM, "Hittite Historiography," 22–25; HOFFNER, "Histories and Historians of the Ancient Near East," 291–93.

The Annals of Ḫattušili I (CTH 4). In comparison with the earlier Anitta Text, the Annals of Ḫattušili (seventeenth century B.C.E.) represent a step forward in the development of Hittite historiography. The text is labeled in Hittite as *pišnadar,* an account of the king's "manly deeds." It provides a year-by-year narrative of the king's exploits on the basis of annual reports from the royal chancellery. The first five years of the king's reign are so treated, but the subject matter includes only the king's military successes and his subsequent offerings of booty to various gods and their temples. The Annals of Ḫattušili are also preserved in a third-person Akkadian version, suggesting that the authors may have envisioned foreign readers for the annals. In its concluding paragraph, which is, from a literary point of view, more elaborate than the rest of the piece, Ḫattušili states that his deeds compare favorably with Sargon of Akkad, the famous king of Assyria: "No one had crossed the Euphrates, but I, the Great King Tabarna, crossed it on foot, and my army crossed it [after me] on foot. Sargon [(also) crossed it]; he defeated the troops of Ḫaḫḫum [but] did nothing to [Ḫaḫḫum] and [did not] burn it down, nor did he show the smoke to the Storm-god of Heaven. I, the Great King Tabarna, destroyed Ḫaššuwa and Ḫaḫḫum and burned them down with fire and [showed] the smoke to the [Storm]god of Heaven. And the king of Ḫaššuwa and the king of Ḫaḫḫum I harnessed to a wagon" (trans. Güterbock, "Hittite Historiography"). This allusion to Sargon shows that the heroic depiction of Ḫattušili in his annals was in some measure inspired by the epic tradition of Mesopotamia (see 9.1.1 and 9.1.2 for Hittite copies of the Mesopotamian epics).

Text and translation: H. OTTEN, "Keilschrifttexte," *MDOG* 91 (1958): 73–83. *Translation:* BRYCE, *The Major Historical Texts of Early Hittite History,* 49–98. *Bibliography:* H. G. GÜTERBOCK, "Hittite Historiography," 25–28; IDEM, "Sargon of Akkad Mentioned by Ḫattušili of Ḫatti," *JCS* 18 (1964): 1–6; H. C. MELCHERT, "The Acts of Ḫattušili I," *JNES* 37 (1978): 1–22.

The Testament of Ḫattušili I (CTH 6). The testament is preserved in Hittite and Akkadian versions that are late copies of a text that was composed during the seventeenth-century reign of Ḫattušili I. It preserves a decree in which the dying Ḫattušili installs his adopted son Muršili I as his successor to the throne. The king believes that various episodes inserted into the body of the testament provide historical justification for his choice. The text repudiates the claims of his sister's son to the throne, primarily because the latter's past behaviors reflected a strong inclination to follow the advice of his evil mother, who was, according to Ḫattušili, "a serpent." Other would-be rulers are excluded because, excepting Muršili, "no member of my family has obeyed my will." Ḫattušili calls upon the entire assembly of warriors and dignitaries to lend their support to Muršili, concluding his edict with directives for Muršili and for Hastaya, the wife of Ḫattušili.

Text and translation: F. SOMMER and A. FALKENSTEIN, *Die hethitisch-akkadische Bilingue des Ḫattušili I (Labarna II)* (Munich: Verlag der Bayerischen Akademie der Wissenschaften, 1938) (does not include a joining fragment of the text, published in KUB 40.65). *Translations:* BRYCE, *The Major Historical Texts of Early Hittite History,* 99–131; COS 2.15: 79–81. *Bibliography:* G. M. BECKMAN, "The Hittite Assembly," *JAOS* 102 (1982): 435–42; HOFFNER, "Histories and Historians of the Ancient Near East," 300–302; P. H. J. HOUWINK TEN CATE, "The History of Warfare according to Hittite Sources: The Annals of Ḫattušilis I," *Anatolia* 11 (1984): 47–83; I. KLOCK-FONTANILLE, "Le testament politique de Ḫattušili Ier ou les conditions d'exercise de la royauté dans l'ancien royaume hittite," *Anatolia antiqua* 4 (1996): 33–66; M. MARAZZI, "Überlegunen zur Bedeutung von *pankuš* in der hethitisch-akkadischen Bilinguis Ḫattušilis I," *WO* 15 (1984): 96–102; H. M. WOLF, "The Historical Reliability of the Hittite Annals," in *Faith, Tradition, and History* (ed. Millard et al.), 159–64.

The Ammuna Chronicle (CTH 18).

In comparison with the earlier Annals of Ḫattušili, the Ammuna Chronicle (sixteenth century B.C.E.) represents a new stage in the development of Hittite historiography. Its author provides more chronographic detail than does Ḫattušili's text, and he eschews heavy-handed propaganda in favor of more sober historical reports. Bombastic descriptions of the king are therefore replaced by the military itineraries of Ammuna and his officials and by pertinent details concerning the activities of his royal lieutenants. In light of these features, Hoffner has suggested that the Ammuna Chronicle "long anticipated much of the best in the annals style of Muršili II." On the other hand, we should note the dissenting voice of Kammenhuber, who does not believe that the Ammuna Chronicle was a true predecessor of the later annalistic texts.

Text and translation: E. VON SCHULER, *Die Kaskäer: Ein Beitrag zur Ethnographie des alten Kleinasien* (Berlin: de Gruyter, 1965), 185–87 (partial). *Bibliography:* HOFFNER, "Histories and Historians of the ancient Near East," 305–6; KAMMENHUBER, "Die hethitische Geschichtsschreibung"; VAN SETERS, *In Search of History,* 108.

The Telipinu Edict (CTH 19).

This decree of King Telipinu (ca. 1500 B.C.E.) is preserved in Hittite and Akkadian copies. It was intended to bring an end to the intradynastic turmoil that for many years had plagued the Hittite Empire. Telipinu introduces his edict with a historical review that covers seven kings from Labarna down to Telipinu's predecessor, Huzziya I. According to this history, peace reigned within the royal family of the first king, Labarna, and as a result, "the great cities made progress." A desire for power, however, corrupted the remaining six regimes, and as a result, internecine strife and bloodshed reigned as members of the royal family eliminated each other. Telipinu's historical review ends with a brief account of his own rise to power; in it he claims to have seized the throne only after his predecessor, Hazziya, sought to kill Telipinu and his family. Telipinu goes on to assert that he did not respond to Hazziya by putting him to death but instead sent him away without injury. As for the subsequent murder of Hazziya and his brothers, Telipinu claims to have had no involvement in this. He further explains that he did not execute the killers because he thought it a useless response, although he did punish them by making them agricultural servants. The remainder of the decree is a list of detailed succession rules and other administrative reforms that would bring an end to the cycle of violence in the royal family.

Telipinu clearly authored this text in order to justify his usurpation of the Hittite throne. According to Telipinu, his action was nothing but a good-faith effort to bring an end to the troubling pattern of evil and violence that had reigned in the Hittite royal family. The decree is comparable to other texts that used history to justify usurpation of a throne, such as the Hittite Apology of Ḫattušili III (see below) and the Israelite apologies of David and Solomon in 1 and 2 Samuel (see Sparks).

Texts and translations: I. HOFFMANN, *Der Erlass Telipinus* (TH 11; Heidelberg: Winter, 1984); E. H. STURTEVANT and G. BECHTEL, *A Hittite Chrestomathy* (Philadelphia: University of Pennsylvania Press, 1935), 175–200. *Translations:* BRYCE, *The Major Historical Texts of Early Hittite History,* 132–61; COS 1.76: 194–98. *Bibliography:* H. G. GÜTERBOCK, "Hittite Historiography," 28–29; HOFFNER, "Histories and Historians of the Ancient Near East," 306–8; IDEM, "Propaganda and Political Justification in Hittite Historiography"; K. L. SPARKS, "Propaganda (Apology of David)"; VAN SETERS, *In Search of History,* 115–16.

The Annals of Muršili II (CTH 61). Hittite historiography came into its own with the Annals of Muršili II (fourteenth century B.C.E.), which survive in two different editions, the so-called Ten-Year Annals (*CTH* 61.1) and the Comprehensive Annals (*CTH* 61.2).

As the title implies, *CTH* 61.1 commemorates the first ten years of Muršili's reign with a year-by-year summary of his "manly deeds" (*pišnadar*), especially his military victories over foreign lands. The text answers objections to Muršili's young age at ascending the throne by highlighting his first ten years of military success. Credit for his success is given mainly to the sun goddess, Arinna, who responded to the king's petitions for help. This description of the events speaks well not only of Arinna but also of the king's piety. The Ten-Year Annals were carefully organized. Horizontal lines divide each entry, and a summary formula is provided at the end of each year: "and I carried this out in one year." The source materials for the Ten-Year Annals seem to have been a combination of earlier annals (such the Comprehensive Annals), terse military reports of Muršili's Kaška campaigns, and more refined literary accounts of the protracted Arzawa war and other matters (Hoffner, 312). In his epilogue, the author explicitly confesses that there were additional sources he did not use: "The enemy lands which the king's sons and lords conquered are not included." The propagandistic purpose of the Ten-Year Annals distinguishes it somewhat from the longer edition of the annals. Muršili's Comprehensive Annals (*CTH* 61.2) are preserved in three series editions on small, medium, and large tablets, respectively. Although the texts are somewhat fragmentary, it is clear that they are significantly more detailed and stylistically more intricate than the Ten-Year Annals. Whereas the Ten-Year Annals are obviously a single work composed by one author, the Comprehensive Annals were probably compiled, like the Assyrian Annals, as a connected series of separate compositions based on campaign reports. For a number of reasons, the comprehensive version of the Annals of Muršili has come to represent the zenith of Hittite historiography. Its scope covers the military activities not only of the king but also of his princes and generals. In some cases even veiled references to military setbacks are included. The annalist was contextually sensitive to geographical and historical details. Battle site terrain is described in some detail, and the causes of military conflicts are also considered. Although the theories of historical causation in such cases are not so complex as those offered by later Greek historians such as Herodotus and Thucydides, the Annals of Muršili reflect a sophisticated level of historical reflection. Alongside the primary theme of military action, the annals emphasize the king's religious piety. This theme was accentuated by including accounts of Muršili's festival celebrations, his observance of funeral rites, and the miraculous interventions in which the gods granted the king victory over his enemies.

Although the Annals of Muršili are not as propagandistic as the Neo-Assyrian Annals, their chronographic features and emphasis on the king's military activities are very similar to the later Assyrian exemplars. These similarities lend credence to the hypothesis that the Hittite annalistic tradition exerted some influence on the later Assyrian tradition, a conclusion supported by the frequent cultural and material contact between the Hittites and Assyrians during the Old and Middle Assyrian periods.

Texts and translations: A. GOETZE, *Die Annalen des Muršiliš* (Darmstadt: Wissenschaftliche Buchgesellschaft, 1967) (*CTH* 61.1; 61.2); J.-P. GRÉLOIS, "Les Annales décennales de Mursili II (*CTH* 61, 1)," *Hethitica* 9 (1988): 17–145 (*CTH* 61.1); P. H. J. HOUWINK TEN CATE, "Mursilis' Northwest Campaigns—Additional Fragments of his Comprehensive Annals," *JNES* 25 (1966): 162–91 (*CTH* 61.2, partial); IDEM, "Mursilis' Northwestern Campaigns—Additional Fragments of His Comprehensive Annals Concerning the Nerik Region," in *Florilegium anatolicum: Mélanges offerts à Emmanuel Laroche* (ed. E. Masson; Paris: Éditions E. de Boccard, 1979), 157–67 (*CTH* 61.2, partial). *Translation:* COS 2.16: 76–84 (*CTH* 61.1). *Bibliography:* H. CANCIK, *Grundzüge der hethitischen und alttestamentlichen Geschichtsschreibung* (Wiesbaden: Harrassowitz, 1976), 101–84; GÜTERBOCK, "Hittite Historiography," 32–35; HOFFNER, "Histories and Historians of the Ancient Near East," 311–15; IDEM, "Propaganda and Political Justification in Hittite Historiography," 50–51; P. H. J. HOUWINK TEN CATE, "Mursilis' Northwestern Campaigns—a Commentary," *Anatolica* 1 (1967): 44–61; VAN SETERS, *In Search of History*, 108–11; H. M. WOLF, "The Historical Reliability of the Hittite Annals," in *Faith, Tradition, and History* (ed. Millard et al.), 159–64.

The Deeds of Šuppiluliuma I (CTH 40). This account of Šuppiluliuma's "manly deeds" (*pišnadar*) was composed during the fourteenth century by his son Muršili II. Its author also composed the Annals of Muršili, so the two pieces share many stylistic and literary similarities. Šuppiluliuma (1380–1340 B.C.E.) is presented in the text always through the eyes of Muršili, who refers to him as "my father." Our fragments of the text pick up the story with Šuppiluliuma's service as a battlefield commander during the reign of Muršili's grandfather Tudhaliya and then progress chronologically forward into the reign of Šuppiluliuma himself. The primary themes of the history are the military prowess and conquests of Šuppiluliuma, but the activities of his military commanders also gain mention. Other notable features in the text include an extended account of Šuppiluliuma's diplomatic relationship with Egypt, an emphasis on the role of divine aid in his military victories, detailed accounts of his military maneuvers (such as his ambushes), and even a reference to one setback—a plague that struck his army while on campaign. In most of these respects, the text is like the Annals of Muršili, but unlike the latter, the account of Šuppiluliuma's deeds lacks chronological information. Neither the introduction nor the conclusion of the multitablet composition are preserved in our textual evidence. The purpose of the text was clearly to honor Šuppiluliuma, but the account of his life would have caste a favorable light on his son as well.

Texts and translations: H. G. GÜTERBOCK, "The Deeds of Suppiluliuma as Told by His Son, Mursili III," *JCS* 10 (1956): 41–68, 75–98, 107–30; P. H. J. HOUWINK TEN CATE. "A New Fragment of the 'Deeds of Šuppiluliuma as Told by His Son Muršili III,'" *JNES* 25 (1966): 27–31. **Translations:** *ANET* 319 (partial); *COS* 1.74: 185–92. **Bibliography:** T. R. BRYCE, "Some Observations on the Chronology of Šuppiluliuma's Reign." *AnSt* 39 (1989): 19–30; GÜTERBOCK, "Hittite Historiography," 31–32; HOFFNER, "Histories and Historians of the Ancient Near East," 311–13; A. MALAMAT, "Doctrines of Causality in Hittite and Biblical Historiography: A Parallel," *VT* 5 (1955): 1–12; VAN SETERS, *In Search of History,* 111.

The Apology of Ḫattušili III (CTH 81). The chief function of this thirteenth-century text was to justify Ḫattušili's usurpation of the Hittite throne from his nephew Urḫitešub. The two men had competing claims to the throne after the death of King Muwatalli because Urḫitešub was the son of Muwatalli and Ḫattušili was Muwatalli's brother (Ḫattušili and Muwatalli were both sons of Muršili II). Technically speaking, however, Urḫitešub was the preferred choice of Muwatalli, and so, according to the earlier Telipinu Edict (see above), he was the appropriate heir to the throne. How did Ḫattušili stake out his own claims in this circumstance?

The Apology is cast in the form of a royal decree instituting the cult of the goddess Ištar. Ḫattušili's son Tuthaliya and his descendants were appointed priests of Ištar, and her temple was freed from tax obligations. This short decree appears only at the end of the text, however, after a rather long historical review in which Ḫattušili defends himself. He bases his primary claim to the throne on divine election. From beginning to end, Ḫattušili's story asserts that his rise to prominence and power was guided by the providential hand of the goddess Ištar, who foretold the rise of Ḫattušili through dream visions. Ḫattušili also highlights his royal pedigree, his service as chief of the royal bodyguard, and his military victories in the service of Muwatalli. But most important, Ḫattušili claims that he never wished the throne for himelf but instead played an active role in securing his nephew's succession to the throne. Ḫattušili explains his subsequent usurpation of the throne in this way: "If someone should say: Why did you formerly establish him [Urḫitešub] in kingship? And why now are you declaring war on him? I answer: If he had not started the hostilities with me, would the gods truly have subjected a 'Great King' to a petty king." Nevertheless, Ḫattušili points out that he did not have Urḫitešub killed but only exiled him to distant lands. It is easy to detect that this text is very close to the earlier Telipinu Edict in structure, content, and function. According to Hoffner (1975), both texts use the following pattern to justify usurpation of the throne: (1) an introduction; (2) a historical survey (royal heritage); (3) a historical survey (the unworthy predecessor); (4) the coup; (5) the merciful victor; (6) the edict. Many of these themes are also prominent in the Neo-Assyrian apologies and in the apologies of David and Solomon in 1–2 Samuel.

Our tablets and fragments of the Apology of Ḫattušili imply that at least eight different copies must have existed, suggesting that this text was very important in the eyes of the Hittites. All of the texts were unearthed in the great temple of Ḫattuša. This find location suits the Hittite practice whereby historical texts were deposited before the deity: "Which enemy countries I conquered one after the other, while still young, these I will describe separately on a tablet and I will lay it down before the goddess" (Apology of Ḫattušili 1.61–74).

Texts and translations: H. OTTEN, *Die Apologie Hattusilis III: Das Bild der Überlieferung* (StBoT 24; Wiesbaden: Harrassowitz, 1981); E. H. STURTEVANT and G. BECHTEL, *A Hittite Chrestomathy* (Philadelphia: University of Pennsylvania Press, 1935), 42–99. *Translation:* COS 1.77: 199–204. *Bibliography:* GÜTERBOCK, "Hittite Historiography," 30–31; HOFFNER, "Histories and Historians of the Ancient Near East," 315–17; IDEM, "Propaganda and Political Justification in Hittite Historiography," 49–61; T. P. J. VAN DEN HOUT, "Khattushili III, King of the Hittites," *CANE* 2:1107–20; H. NOWICKI, "Ein Deutungsvorschlag zum 'Grossen Text' des Ḫattušili III," *KZ* 98 (1985): 23–35; VAN SETERS, *In Search of History,* 118–22; H. M. WOLF, "The Apology of Hattusilis Compared with Other Political Self-Justifications of the Ancient Near East" (PhD diss., Brandeis University, 1967).

Other Hittite Historiographic Texts. Scholars have frequently mentioned four other texts from the Old Kingdom in connection with the development of Hittite historiography. Our discussion proceeds from the texts that are more historical to those that appear to be more legendary. First is the so-called Palace Chronicle (*CTH* 8). This text is actually a royal decree containing a loosely arranged collection of anecdotes about high officials from the time of Ḫattušili I (seventeenth century B.C.E.). The admonitory character of the work is reflected in its retributive pattern, whereby evil officials were justly punished and those devoted to the king were rewarded. A better name for the text would be the Palace Decree.

The second text is the Siege of Urša (*CTH* 7). Composed in Akkadian, it comes down to us only in Akkadian copies. As its name partly implies, the work extols the valor and military success of King Ḫattušili I and his generals as displayed in their siege of the city of Urša. Although the text is thematically similar to the Hittite royal annals, in the final analysis it should not be considered an annal. Its author provides a snapshot of courage, wisdom, and power rather than chronological movement, and the level of fictional embellishment in the narrative is more pronounced than in the annals (so Hoffner).

The two other relevant texts are more legendary than historical. The exemplars include the Zalpa Text (*CTH* 3) and the Cannibal Text (*CTH* 17). Both have the distinction of beginning as legendary compositions before transitioning to narratives of historical people and events. The Zalpa Text was already treated in 9.3. The very fragmentary exemplar of the Cannibal Text takes its name from a motif whereby the Hittite protagonists distinguished between human enemies and supernatural enemies on the basis of what their enemies ate: human flesh or animal flesh. Little else can be said about the story.

Text and translation: H. G. GÜTERBOCK, "Die historische Tradition und ihre literarische Gestaltung bei Babyloniern und Hethitern bis 1200" (1938), 105–13 (Cannibal Text), 113–39 (Urša Text). *Translation:* G. M. BECKMAN, "The Siege of Uršu Text (*CTH* 7) and Old Hittite Historiography," *JCS* 47 (1995): 23–34. *Bibliography:* H. G. GÜTERBOCK, "Die historische Tradition und ihre literarische Gestaltung bei Babyloniern und Hethitern bis 1200" (1938), 100–101 (Palace Chronicle), 101–5 (Zalpa Text); HOFFNER, "Histories and Historians of the Ancient Near East," 289–91 (Zalpa Text), 299–300 (Siege of Uršu), 303 (Palace Chronicle); KAMMENHUBER, "Die hethitische Geschichtsschreibung"; VAN SETERS, *In Search of History,* 114–15.

12.4. Persian Historiography

A large corpus of Persian royal inscriptions has been recovered from the ancient Near East, much of it preserved trilingually in Old Persian, Elamite, and Akkadian. Although the city of Susa seems to have been one of the main residences of the Persian king, most of the inscriptions are preserved in the palaces, royal tombs, structures, and building foundations of Persepolis. The texts treated below include one of these Persepolis texts and two other inscriptions that are of particular interest for the study of the Hebrew Bible.

The Cyrus Cylinder. This Akkadian text praises Cyrus of Persia as the deliverer and restorer of Babylon. It begins with a third-person account of the last Babylonian king, Nabonidus, in which the former king is depicted as an evil and irreverent oppressor of the city. Marduk, the chief god of Babylon, responded to this difficulty by sending Cyrus of Persia to deliver Babylon and to restore its temple and cult. At this point the inscription transitions into an autobiographical address in which Cyrus outlines his many acts of kindness and support on behalf of Babylon and on behalf of various cities, gods, and peoples of the land. His most important acts concerned the divine statues formerly seized by the Babylonians during their imperial conquests. According to the inscription, Cyrus returned the gods to their native temples, along with any people associated with these deities. There follows a prayer that entreats the restored deities to speak daily to the gods Marduk and Nabu on behalf of Cyrus and his son Cambyses. A new fragment of the cylinder, recently published by Berger, suggests how the text then ended. During his renovations of Marduk's temple, Cyrus discovered a foundation inscription belonging to King Assurbanipal of Assyria. Since Assurbanipal's inscription almost certainly commemorated earlier Assyrian restorations in Babylon, we may surmise that the Cyrus Cylinder itself was composed as a Persian effort to mimic the earlier text of Assurbanipal. The close stylistic parallels between the Cyrus Cylinder and Assurbanipal's royal inscriptions confirm this thesis (Harmatta). So, although we do not know where Cyrus's clay cylinder was discovered, scholars surmise that it was originally deposited in the foundation of Marduk's temple in Babylon, where it commemorated Cyrus's restoration projects at the temple and elsewhere in the city of Babylon.

Several features in the Cyrus Cylinder make it an important text for students of the Hebrew Bible. First, Cyrus claims divine sanction for his conquest of Babylon by citing the blessing of Marduk, the chief deity of his new subjects. Indeed, at least one Babylonian text suggests that the Babylonians adopted this view as their own (see the Verse Account of Nabonidus in 12.1.2). In this light, one wonders how much the Hebrew view of Cyrus as Yahweh's "messiah" was influenced by Persian propaganda (see Isa 44:24–45:1). Second, in a related matter, there seems to be some connection between Cyrus's claim to have restored gods and peoples to their lands and the biblical texts that record a decree by Cyrus whereby he allowed exiled Jews in Babylon to return home (Ezra 1:2–4). As Kuhrt points out, the Cyrus Cylinder does not describe a general return of exiled refugees such as appears in the book of Ezra; nevertheless, the inscription certainly makes the account in Ezra appear more plausible. Third and finally, the Cyrus Cylinder lends support to the generally accepted view of Persian imperialism, that the Persians garnered support from their new subjects by restoring and supporting native religious institutions. Cyrus claims to have done so in Babylon, and the Hebrew Bible claims that the Persians did this for the Jews (Ezra 6:2–5; 7:1–28; Neh 2:1–8).

Texts and translations: P. R. BERGER, "Der Kyros Zylinder mit Zusatzfragment BIN II Nr. 32 und die akkadischen Personennamen in Danielbuch," *ZA* 64 (1975): 192–234; H. SCHAUDIG, *Die Inschriften Nabonids von Babylon und Kyros' des Grossen, samt den in ihrem Umfeld entstandenen Tendenzschriften: Textausgabe und Grammatik* (AOAT 256; Münster: Ugarit, 2001), 550–56; F. H. WEISSBACH, *Die Keilinschriften der Achämeniden* (Leipzig: J. C. Hinrichs, 1911). *Translations:* ANET 315–16; COS 2.124: 314–16. *Bibliography:* E. BICKERMAN, "The Edict of Cyrus in Ezra I," *JBL* 65 (1946): 247–75; J. HARMATTA, "The Literary Patterns of the Babylonian Edict of Cyrus," *AcAntHung* 19 (1971): 217–32; A. KUHRT, "The Cyrus Cylinder and Achaemenid Imperial Policy," *JSOT* 25 (1983): 83–97.

The Bisitun Inscription of Darius. Also known as the Behistun Inscription, this text was engraved about a hundred meters above the ground on the rock face of

Bisitun Mount, a site near the modern town of Bisitun on a road that ran between the ancient cities of Ecbatana and Babylon. A large panel depicting the scene of a victory by Darius of Persia (521–486 B.C.E.) accompanies the text, which appears in three languages: Old Persian, Akkadian, and Elamite. The inscription survives to this day because Darius had the ledge beneath it knocked out after the inscription was completed. In the text Darius describes how the god Ahuramazda helped him seize the throne from a certain Gaumata. Darius bases his claim to the throne on his royal lineage and divine legitimacy, but he also asserts that Gaumata had illegitimately seized the throne by pretending to be the brother of the previous king, Cambyses. The remainder of the text enumerates a long list of other "liars" whose rebellions were quelled during Darius's first year as king. In spite of Darius's claims, modern scholars suspect that Gaumata was indeed the brother of Cambyses, in which case it was Darius, not Gaumata, who was the real usurper (Briant). The text is similar to other examples of Near Eastern propaganda in which kings defended their disputed claims to the throne. Although the text is a parade example of royal propaganda, the inscription at Bisitun is not legible from the ground below. Darius tells us that he disseminated the text throughout the empire by means of hand copies that were prepared on clay tablets, parchments, and papyrus. Such a papyrus copy was discovered in the Jewish archive of Elephantine, in the far south of Egypt (see 1.3). So there is no question that Persian kings were adept at spreading their propaganda.

Although the Bisitun text is interesting for its own sake, the inscription is most famous for the key role that it played in the deciphering of Akkadian. Once the simpler alphabetic Old Persian text was understood, the more complicated Akkadian cuneiform soon followed. This linguistic feat was in fact so great that many leading scholars, such as J. E. Renan in France and G. C. Lewis in England, did not believe it. The matter was put to a test in 1855 at the suggestion of W. H. Fox-Talbot. Four scholars—Talbot, H. C. Rawlinson, E. Hincks, and J. Oppert—presented the Royal Asiatic Society with their independent translations of a previously untranslated Akkadian text. A committee of the society compared the translations and found that they agreed tolerably well. Assyriology was born. For the whole story, see Rawlinson; Rogers.

Texts and translations: J. C. GREENFIELD and B. PORTEN, *The Bisitun Inscription of Darius the Great, Aramaic Version* (Corpus inscriptionum iranicarum, 1: Inscriptions of Ancient Iran; London: Lund Humphries, 1982); R. O. KENT, *Old Persian: Grammar, Texts, Lexicon* (AOS 33; New Haven: American Oriental Society, 1950), 107–8, 116–35; R. SCHMITT, *The Bisitun Inscriptions of Darius the Great, Old Persian Text* (Corpus inscriptionum iranicarum, 1: Inscriptions of Ancient Iran; London: Lund Humphries, 1991); E. VON VOIGHTLANDER, *The Bisitun Inscription of Darius the Great, Babylonian Version* (Corpus inscriptionum iranicarum, 1: Inscriptions of Ancient Iran; London: Lund Humphries, 1978). *Bibliography:* Ch.-H. BAE, *Comparative Studies of King Darius's Bisitun Inscription* (PhD diss., Harvard, 2001); BALCER, *Herodotus and Bisitun;* P. BRIANT, "Persian Empire," *ABD* 5:236–44; G. G. CAMERON, "A Photograph of Darius' Sculptures at Behistan," *JNES* 2 (1943): 115–16; A. FAWKERS, "The Behistun Relief," in *The Median and Achaemenian Periods* (ed. Ilya Gershevitch; vol. 2 of *The Cambridge History of Iran;* Cambridge: Cambridge

University Press, 1985), 828–31; H. C. RAWLINSON, *Persian Cuneiform Inscription at Behistun Decyphered and Translated* (London: J. W. Parker, 1847); R. W. ROGERS, *A History of Babylonia and Assyria* (6th ed.; New York: Abingdon, 1915).

A Persepolis Inscription of Xerxes. Xerxes I (485–465 B.C.E.) left us several royal inscriptions in Persepolis, among them a trilingual foundation tablet that bears a text in Old Persian, Elamite, and Akkadian versions. The inscription is a religious text insofar as it praises the Persian god Ahuramazda and recounts to the deity how Xerxes responded to rebel nations in the empire. After defeating the rebels, Xerxes claims to have uncovered among them religious services that were regularly performed for "evil gods." Says Xerxes, "Wherever formerly service was performed to the evil gods, I myself performed a service to Ahuramazda and the *arta* [cosmic order] reverently." Knowing that his foundation text would one day be discovered by others, Xerxes adds, "Whosoever you are, in future days who thinks as follows: 'May I be prosperous in this life and blessed after my death'—do live according to this law which Ahuramazda has promulgated: 'Perform service for Ahuramazda and act reverently.'" The text concludes with a prayer that Ahuramazda might protect the royal family and all nations from evil. (The court of Xerxes I provides the ostensible setting for the biblical story of Esther, where Xerxes is known as Ahasuerus [Shea].)

Texts: R. O. KENT, *Old Persian: Grammar, Texts, Lexicon* (AOS 33; New Haven: American Oriental Society, 1950), 112, 150–52 (Old Persian); E. F. SCHMIDT, *Persepolis II: Contents of the Treasury and Other Discoveries* (OIP 69; Chicago: University of Chicago Press, 1957), pls. 21a (Old Persian), 22a (Akkadian), 22b (Elamite). ***Translation:*** *ANET* 316–17. ***Bibliography:*** W. H. SHEA, "Esther and History," *AUSS* 14 (1976): 227–46.

12.5. Ancient Phoenician Historiography

The Phoenician History of Philo Biblius. Scholars have reconstructed only a small portion of this Greek text by editorially joining quotations of it found in Eusebius's *Praeparatio evangelica* and in a few other classical sources. The little that has been recovered reveals that Philo presented his work as a Greek translation and adaptation of an earlier Phoenician history composed by a certain Sanchuniathon, whose history was supposedly based on a still more ancient text written by Taautos (the Egyptian god Thoth). Philo's history appears to have included a mythological cosmogony (the origins of the cosmos), a technogony (the origins of human civilization and technology), and a history of the reign of Kronos and his successors, whom Philo euhemeristically understood to be humans who were inadvertently remembered as gods. Interpretation of the text must contend with the problem of sorting out the views of Sanchuniathon from those of Philo himself. This problem becomes still more complicated because of the possibility that Sanchuniathon's history never really existed. Many scholars suspect that Philo's reference to Sanchuniathon is a topos, common in Hellenistic histories, in which the historian buttressed the authority of his account by fictionally claiming access to ancient sources (Barr; see discussion in Attridge/ Oden). Those who accept the authenticity of Sanchuniathon's history usually cite as evidence that his name is Phoenician and that Philo's text reflects familiarity with ancient mythological material.

Regardless of where one stands on the question of Sanchuniathon, there is no doubt that Philo's work is typical of the Hellenistic histories composed by non-Greeks during the Greco-Roman period. According to Oden, the common features in this genre included the following: (1) the author claims to have access to ancient or esoteric sources for his history; (2) the gods are euhemeristically interpreted to be vague memories of human kings and cultural heroes; (3) the scope of the history tends to be universal rather than merely local; (4) the author expresses his patriotism by emphasizing the antiquity and accomplishments of his native culture; (5) the texts reflect a general antagonism toward Greek culture and Greek authors. Philo's history dates to the Hellenistic or early Roman period, but a more definite date cannot be ascertained. Other exemplars of this genre include the Babylonian history of Berossus and the Egyptian history of Manetho.

Readers may also wish to note the Annals of Tyre, a Phoenician history that is no longer preserved but is mentioned by the Jewish author Josephus. For a brief discussion of this text, see Van Seters, 195–99.

Text and translation: H. W. ATTRIDGE and R. A. ODEN JR., *Philo of Byblos, The Phoenician History: Introduction, Critical Text, Translation, Notes* (CBQMS 9; Washington: Catholic Biblical Association, 1981). *Bibliography:* J. BARR, "Philo of Byblos and His Phoenician History," *BJRL* 57 (1974): 17–68; A. I. BAUMGARTEN, *The Phoenician History of Philo of Byblos: A Commentary* (Leiden: Brill, 1981); J. CORS I MEYA, *A Concordance of the Phoenician History of Philo of Byblos* (Barcelona: Editorial AUSA, 1995); O. EISSFELDT, *Sanchunjaton von Berut und Ilumilku von Ugarit* (Halle: Niemeyer, 1952); R. A. ODEN, "Philo of Byblos and Hellenistic Historiography," *PEQ* 110 (1978): 115–26; J. VAN SETERS, *In Search of History,* 205–8.

12.6. Ancient Greek Historiography

Although scholars commonly attribute the best of ancient history writing to Greece and Israel, the two historiographic traditions differ from each other substantially. Before we turn to the relevant Greek entries, a few introductory comments are in order. The development of Greek historiography is of special comparative importance because we know somewhat more about it than about the development of Israelite historiography. In a simplified chronology, the process that led to the prose histories of Herodotus and Thucydides can be represented as four phases. The first phase began in hoary antiquity as the Greek bards composed and preserved a large corpus of oral tales, epics, legends, and myths. This phase continued until the eighth century B.C.E., when these oral traditions were arranged by Homer into coherent literary compositions (the *Odyssey* and the *Iliad;* see Whallon). Near the end of this second phase, Hesiod composed his *Theogony.* This work reflected Homer's epic style but was not, strictly speaking, an epic. Hesiod attempted to make sense of the divine realm by constructing a genealogy of the gods into which he fitted various mythological stories (see Evelyn-White). The Greek genealogical tradition subsequently undertook similar efforts with human genealogies. Both Homer and Hesiod therefore seem to have exerted a considerable influence on the awakening and development of the Greek historical perspective (see Starr).

During the third phase (700–450 B.C.E.), the so-called logographic period, the logographers discarded the poetic form of the epic and produced a variety of prose narrative texts that covered mythological, legendary, genealogical, geographical, ethnographical, and historical topics (see Pearson/Hornblower). The logographers were in many respects antiquarianists (captivated with traditions of the past), who drew heavily upon materials and themes from the earlier periods—particularly from myths, epics, legends, and genealogies (see Momigliano 1978). These authors systematically collected and organized the earlier traditions into more orderly narratives with varied degrees of success. Classical scholars have classified the logographic works under five headings: mythographic treatises, geographical works, ethnography, chronological works (king lists, etc.), and local histories about the founding of cities (Pearson/Hornblower). These works were orally recited before audiences—in this early period, the usual way of exposing people to a work (see Harris). It is unfortunate that the logographic works are so fragmentary because their contents were probably more reminiscent of Hebrew historiography than are either Herodotus or Thucydides. The transitional figure between these early logographic works and Herodotus was Hecataeus of Miletus (ca. 520–500 B.C.E.). His *Genealogiae* was characterized by investigation (*historia*) and also by a rationalistic tendency to make the heroic legends adhere more closely to the world of common experience (Momigliano 1978). Hecataeus used the genealogies to produce a kind of chronological framework going back to the heroic age and then filled in this framework with various hero stories and traditions that were subjected to his rationalistic critique. Hecataeus also composed an influential geographical and ethnographic work entitled *Periēgēsis*. The Pseudo-Hesiodic Catalogue of Women, which will be treated below, fits into this phase in the development of Greek historiography.

According to Van Seters 1983, the fourth phase, the age of early Greek historiography, exhibited two different rationalizing tendencies. The first, exemplified by Herodotus (ca. 490–425 B.C.E.), was to focus one's historiographic effort on recent and therefore accessible topics such as the Persian War. The other tendency, represented by Hellanicus of Lesbos (480–395 B.C.E.), attempted to make history out of ancient myths and legends and to connect this history, via genealogy and chronology, to the historian's contemporary milieu. In both cases, it is of particular interest to classicists that most of these early historians lived in the Ionian regions of Asia Minor. Thus it has become customary to speak of an "Ionian Enlightenment" that gave rise to Greek historiography. Although this intellectual movement is difficult to explain, Momigliano has speculated that contacts with the Orient and the pressures of life under the Persians may have been deciding factors (Momigliano 1978; 1983).

The three texts treated below represent the nascent stages of Greek historiography as it transitioned from the antiquarian works of the third phase—here represented by the Catalogue of Women—to the earliest histories of Herodotus and Thucydides. For good introductions to Greek historiography, see Fornara 1983 and Marincola 1997 and 2001.

The Pseudo-Hesiodic Catalogue of Women. The Catalogue (sixth century B.C.E.) is a five-book continuation of Hesiod's Theogony, but Hesiod himself certainly is not the author, since it clearly dates one or two centuries after him. The work presents a series of narratives that have been placed within a genealogical framework, a structure that was created by joining disparate genealogies into a coherent whole by postulating and inventing connections between them. The goals of this effort were etiological (explaining the origins of various groups) and sociological (giving expression to the relationships between these groups). The narrative traditions inserted into this genealogical framework reflect an epiclike poetic form, so that the unique combination of genealogy and narrative represents a transitional phase between the Homeric/Hesiodic epic traditions and the rise of the Greek logographers. The content of the narratives would strike modern readers as legendary and fanciful in many instances. This feature may have stemmed in part from the author's naïve view of history, but it appears that he was more interested in preserving tradition than in getting the story right. In this respect, the Catalogue reflects antiquarian interests that historians such as Thucydides would eventually set aside. The author's compositional strategy, which used genealogies as the framework for holding the narratives together, can be fruitfully compared to the biblical book of Genesis (Van Seters 1988; 1992). For more on the genealogical aspects of the Catalogue of Women, see 11.4.

Text and translation: H. G. EVELYN-WHITE, *Hesiod: The Homeric Hymns and Homerica* (LCL; Cambridge: Harvard University Press, 1982), 2–65. ***Bibliography:*** R. S. HESS, "The Genealogies of Genesis 1–11 and Comparative Literature," *Bib* 70 (1989): 241–54; J. VAN SETERS, "The Primeval Histories of Greece and Israel Compared," *ZAW* 100 (1988): 1–22; IDEM, *Prologue to History: the Yahwist as Historian in Genesis* (Louisville: Westminster John Knox, 1992); M. L. WEST, *The Hesiodic Catalogue of Women: Its Nature, Structure, and Origins* (Oxford: Oxford University Press, 1985).

Herodotus's History of the Persian War. Herotodus (ca. 484–425 B.C.E.) is often remembered as the "father of history" because of his seven-book history of the Greek and Persian War. In this work he took up the dual task of writing about the war and explaining why the war took place. He sought the war's cause by using the principle of reciprocity, according to which human beings respond to each other with good for good and evil for evil. According to Herodotus, the cause of wars could be traced back to the distant past, when Coresus of Lydia began his "wrongful acts against the Greeks." Although the war itself was the explicit and ostensible purpose of the Histories, Herodotus was clearly pursuing other aims as well. This is especially visible in his propensity to digress from the main point into detailed descriptions of tradition, myth, geography, biography, cultural practices, flora and fauna, politics, and so on. According to Momigliano (1978), these digressions reflect Herodotus's threefold interest in ethnography, political and social institutions, and war history, but from a thematic standpoint, some of his material eludes even these characterizations and must be considered anecdotal (e.g., his description in book 2 of Egyptian crocodilian species). It appears that Herodotus gives us a record of his inquiries rather than a strictly thematic account of the Greek-Persian war. As Lateiner points out, "Herodotus reports even obvious errors in order to conserve knowledge about humans, their manners, beliefs, and institutions" (Lateiner, 83). He was clearly an antiquarianist whose desire to preserve tradition was at odds with modern notions of history writing.

Despite Herodotus's long-standing reputation as the father of history, in antiquity he was considered unreliable, a characterization that began with his near contemporary, Thucydides, and followed him down through history in the works of Aristotle, Cicero, Josephus, Plutarch, Manetho, and Libanius (Sparks). This characterization was prompted in part by his antiquarianism, which, as in the earlier logographers, was as interested in preserving tradition as in getting the facts straight. Modern scholars are sharply divided about the character of the *Histories,* viewed by some as serious history writing (Balcer; Lloyd; Pritchett) and by others as an imaginative product of literary invention (Fehling; Rollinger). A careful reading of Herodotus reveals that there is some truth in both views because at numerous points the history is accurate but at other points Herodotus seems to have invented sources that support his opinions. According to P. Levi, this bipolar tendency is best explained by the fact that Herodotus was as much a storyteller as an historian, which coheres nicely with Thucydides' criticism that previous historians had sought to "please the ear" rather than write histories.

Although Herodotus consulted the work of earlier logographers, particularly Hecataeus, he seems to have preferred oral sources for two reasons. At this stage in history, Greek writers generally trusted oral sources more than written sources; perhaps more important, written evidence was not abundant in the fifth century B.C.E. (Momigliano 1978; Thomas). The resulting emphasis on oral speech appears in the *Histories* as both direct speech (*oratio recta*) and indirect speech (*oratia obliqua*), the latter reflecting information drawn from oral sources and the former signaling the author's own fictive compositions. The fictiveness of the direct speech is deduced from that fact that Herodotus could not have had sound authorities for the personal and intimate conversations he sometimes included (Lateiner). He composed these conversations by combining his source materials with his own psychological and political insights. The speeches were enhanced by frequent references to nonverbal behaviors—smiles, tears, obscene gestures, and so on—and these verisimilitudes added to the persuasive and engaging style of his work. Here, as in so many ways, the literary complexity of the *Histories* sets them apart from the other ancient Near Eastern sources.

Text and translation: A. D. GODLEY, trans., *Herodotus* (4 vols.; LCL; Cambridge: Harvard University Press, 1920–1925). ***Bibliography:*** E. BADIAN, "Herodotus on Alexander I of

Macedon: A Study in Some Subtle Silences," in *Greek Historiography* (ed. Hornblower), 91–106; E. J. BAKKER, I. J. F. DE JONG, and H. VAN WEES, *Brill's Companion to Herodotus* (Boston: Brill, 2002); BALCER, *Herodotus and Bisitun;* COBET, "Herodotus and Thucydides on War"; P. DEROW and R. PARKER, *Herodotus and His World: Essays from a Conference in Memory of George Forrest* (New York: Oxford University Press, 2003); D. FEHLING, *Herodotus and His "Sources"* (ARCA Classical and Medieval Texts, Papers, and Monographs 21; Leeds, England: Francis Cairns, 1989); C. W. FORNARA, *Herodotus: An Interpretive Essay* (Oxford: Clarendon, 1971); J. GOULD, "Herodotus and Religion," in *Greek Historiography* (ed. Hornblower), 91–106; D. LATEINER, *The Historical Method of Herodotus* (Toronto: University of Toronto Press, 1989); P. LEVI, *A History of Greek Literature* (New York: Viking, 1985), 153–66; A. B. LLOYD, *Herodotus, Book II: Commentary 99–182* (3 vols.; Études préliminaires aux religions orientales dans l'Empire romain 43; Leiden: Brill, 1975–1988), 3:21–25, 185–95; J. D. MIKALSON, *Herodotus and Religion in the Persian Wars* (Chapel Hill: University of North Carolina Press, 2003); MOMIGLIANO, "Greek Historiography"; W. K. PRITCHETT, *The Liar School of Herodotus* (Amsterdam: J. C. Bieben, 1993); R. ROLLINGER, *Herodots Babylonischer Logos: Eine kritische Untersuchung der Glaubwürdigkeitsdiskussion an Hand ausgewählter Beispiele* (Innsbrucker Beiträge zur Kulturwissenschaft 84; Innsbruck: Verlag des Instituts für Sprachwissenschaft der Universität Innsbruck, 1993); SPARKS, *Ethnicity and Identity in Ancient Israel,* 57–61; R. THOMAS, *Herodotus in Context: Ethnography, Science, and the Art of Persuasion* (New York: Cambridge University Press, 2000); IDEM, *Oral Tradition and Written Record in Classical Athens* (Cambridge: Cambridge University Press, 1989); J. W. WESSELIUS, *The Origin of the History of Israel: Herodotus's Histories as the Blueprint for the First Books of the Bible* (New York: Sheffield Academic Press, 2002).

Thucydides's History of the Peloponnesian War. Like his predecessor Herodotus, Thucydides (ca. 460–399 B.C.E.) was the writer of a war history (the *Historiae*). Their works are quite different, however, because Thucydides undertook his with a new spirit of critical inquiry that left behind ancient historiography and became the root of modern historiography's quest to write history *wie es eigentlich gewesen ist* ("as it actually occurred"). Ancient and modern scholars alike have recognized that Thucydides' history of the Peloponnesian War was rigorous in its pursuit of "a true picture of the events which have happened" (Thucydides, *Historiae* 1.20–21 [see Smith]), thus producing a resource that is useful even for modern historians. His narrative adhered strictly to the war and its history, and so one does not find in it ethnographic digressions such as appear in Herodotus, nor is there antiquarianism—tradition for tradition's sake. What we might label as mythical or legendary is generally absent, with the one following exception.

Although Thucydides was primarily interested in the Peloponnesian War itself, in book 1 of the *Historiae* he found it necessary to offer as the prolegomenon a brief overview of Greece history before the war. But because his only source materials for this point in history were the old poets such as Homer, his history of the early period features legendary characters such as Deucalion, Hellen, Agamemnon, and King Minos. Thucydides understood that the Homeric sources contained at least some valuable historical information, as is generally acknowledged about such epic and legendary materials, but he also recognized the very real problems with this type of source (*Historiae* 1.21).

For the more recent periods, Thucydides utilized oral reports. This preference resulted in part from his emphasis on the importance of political speech, but it was also a consequence of his general preference for oral sources and of the paucity of written ones. Thucydides wrote at length about the problems created by these oral sources: "As to the speeches that were made by different men . . . it has been difficult to recall with strict accuracy the words actually spoken, both for me as regards that which I myself heard, and for those who from various other sources have brought me reports. Therefore the speeches are given in the language in which, as it seemed to me, the several speakers would express, on the subjects under consideration, the sentiments most befitting the occasion" (1.22). Even for a historian dedicated to the truth, when the sources were few or difficult to procure, a certain fictive element entered into the compositional equation. In such cases, Thucydides was forced to write what he thought they would have said, in the way he thought they would have said it.

The historiographic tradition of the Greeks is impressive, setting it apart from all other ancient literature, including that of ancient Israel. The transparency of the writers, their critical spirit of inquiry, their preference for oral sources, and the thematic complexity of the histories are unique among the texts that have been examined in this chapter. The momentum of this tradition ultimately spawned similar histories of Greece's ancient neighbors, including Egypt (Manetho), Israel (Josephus), Mesopotamia (Berossus), and Phoenicia (Philo of Byblos).

Text and translation: C. F. SMITH, trans., *Thucydides: History of the Peloponnesian War* (4 vols.; LCL; Cambridge: Harvard University Press, 1919–1923). **Bibliography:** COBET, "Herodotus and Thucydides on War"; W. R. CONNOR, "Narrative Discourse in Thucydides," in *The Greek Historians, Literature and History: Papers Presented to A. E. Raubitschek* (Stanford: Stanford University Press, 1985), 1–17; F. M. CORNFORD, *Thucydides mythistoricus* (London: Arnold, 1907); L. S. GUSTAFSON, *Thucydides' Theory of International Relations: A Lasting Possession* (Baton Rouge: Louisiana State University Press, 2000); S. HORNBLOWER, *A Commentary on Thucydides* (New York: Oxford University Press, 1997–); IDEM, "Narratology and Narrative Techniques in Thucydides," in *Greek Historiography* (ed. Hornblower), 131–66; R. D. LUGINBILL, *Thucydides on War and National Character* (Boulder, Colo.: Westview, 1999); C. ORWIN, *The Humanity of Thucydides* (Princeton: Princeton University Press, 1994); C. G. STARR, "Ideas of Truth in Early Greece," *La parola del passato* 23 (1968): 348–59.

12.7. Excursus: The Scandinavian Sagas

The Scandinavian sagas hail from the medieval period and hence come to us from a time and place quite distant from the world of ancient Israel. Nevertheless, modern scholars have sometimes cited these texts in their comparative endeavors to understand the nature and origins of Hebrew historiography. To the extent that the sagas are of comparative value for readers of the Hebrew Bible, the similarities are of the phenomenological sort, in that early Scandinavian historians used sources and strategies that were similar to those used in ancient Israel.

The Scandinavian Sagas and Hebrew Histories. A. Jolles first suggested that appropriate comparative materials for the study of Israelite historiography could be found in the Scandinavian sagas. The sagas offered a precritical narrative of historical events, were thematically focused on the military exploits of kings and heroes, and included a rich generic blend of legends, anecdotes, reports, genealogies, and hymns. In all of these respects, Jolles found the sagas reminiscent of Hebrew historiography. S. Mowinckel, following up on this idea, identified the earliest Israelite saga as the Book of the Acts of Solomon mentioned in 1 Kgs 11:41. This identification implies that the biblical record indeed provides access to genuine history, albeit in a literary form that is more fanciful and legendary than modern histories. C. Westermann argues that the patriarchal narratives of the Pentateuch are based on old family sagas from the early days of the Israelite people. Although such comparative uses of the sagas may be of benefit in our study of the Hebrew Bible, saga scholars, unfortunately, face the same kinds of questions about the development of their genre as do readers of Hebrew historiography (Neff).

Sample texts and translations: M. MAGNUSSON and H. PÁLSSON, trans., *King Harald's Saga: Harald Hardradi of Norway* (New York: Penguin, 1966); IDEM, *Laxdaela Saga* (Baltimore: Penguin Books, 1969); H. PÁLSSON and P. EDWARDS, *Egil's Saga* (New York: Penguin, 1976). *Bibliography:* T. M. ANDERSSON, *The Problem of Icelandic Saga Origins* (New Haven: Yale University Press, 1964); S. EINARSSON, *A History of Icelandic Literature* (New York: American-Scandinavian Foundation, 1957); A. JOLLES, *Einfache Formen* (2d ed.; Tübingen: Niemeyer, 1952), 62–90; S. MOWINCKEL, "Israelite Historiography," *ASTI* 2 (1963): 4–26; R. W. NEFF, "Saga," in *Saga, Legend, Tale, Novella, Fable* (ed. G. W. Coats; JSOTSup 35; Sheffield, England: JSOT Press, 1985), 17–32; M. I. STEBLIN-KAMENSKIJ, *The Saga Mind* (Odense, Denmark: Odense Universitetsforlag, 1973); VAN SETERS, *In Search of History*, 222–24; C. WESTERMANN, *Genesis: A Commentary* (3 vols.; Minneapolis: Augsburg, 1974–1985), 2:23–86; IDEM, *The Promises to the Fathers: Studies on the Patriarchal Narratives* (Philadelphia: Fortress, 1980), 165–86.

Concluding Observations

1. The Development of Historiography. Biblical scholars are very interested in determining how and when the first Hebrew histories were written. The comparative materials surveyed in this chapter cast considerable light on this question, and from various angles. In cases where the data are significant, it is possible to trace the emergence of ancient historiography back to simpler generic types. Such a path is visible in the development of the Babylonian Chronicles from the earlier king lists, in the development of the Assyrian Annals from earlier royal inscriptions, in the development of Greek histories from the earlier epics, and in the development of the Egyptian Palermo Stone from simpler annalistic records. In the case of the Hittites, one can trace this path of generic evolution in discrete steps proceeding from the simple Anitta Text through the more complex Annals of Ḫattušili

I and the Ammuna Chronicle to the Annals of Muršili II, which by all accounts represent the zenith of Hittite historiography. At the same time, these generic developments were never hermetically sealed from outside cultural influences. The Mesopotamian epics of Sargon and Naram-Sin inspired aspects of the Hittite royal annals, and it appears that the Hittite annals in turn influenced the Assyrian Annals. On the basis of this comparative discussion, we can expect that Hebrew historiography developed from earlier and simpler native Hebrew genres and, further, that the generic conventions of the Near East influenced this process in some degree. In light of these expectations, it is worth noting that S. B. Parker has recently demonstrated that Hebrew historiography was deeply influenced by the older inscriptional genres of its Syro-Palestinian context.

Certain genres were particularly important precursors to the development of historiography. Chronological texts, such as the king lists (Mesopotamia), genealogies (Greece), and archival records (Egypt; Mesopotamia), provided the sequential frameworks for organizing the ancient histories. Without this sequential pattern, there could be no historiography. The other important predecessors of history were the narrative genres, such as the myths, legends, epics, and folktales. These texts served two significant roles in the origins of historiography. First, ancient scribes used these genres to pioneer narrative styles that would later appear in historiography. And second, these heroic and legendary genres sometimes provided the basic source materials for the first historical narratives. The source types used by ancient historians, however, were always a function of whether they were writing proximate or nonproximate histories.

2. **Proximate and Nonproximate Histories.** The royal annals of Mesopotamia, Egypt, and Hatti were composed not long after the events they narrated. For the authors of these proximate histories, access to the information they needed would have been relatively straightforward, since eyewitnesses as well as temporary and/or archival records were readily accessible. In other cases, however, ancient historians were not so fortunate. The authors of nonproximate texts such as the Weidner Chronicle, the Synchronistic History, and certain of the Babylonian Chronicles composed their texts several centuries after the periods that they sought to narrate. In such cases, it can be demonstrated that the historians had to rely upon inferior sources—or even upon their own imaginations—when narrating the remote past. Consequently, the following pattern is generally visible in ancient histories: recent periods were narrated on the basis of relatively dependable historical records (king lists, inscriptions, annalistic sources, and archives), but more remote periods were reconstructed on the basis of less dependable traditions (myths, legends, and folktales) or on the basis of less accessible traditions (such as royal inscriptions and omen texts). This legend-to-history

pattern is especially visible in the Hittite Zalpa and Cannibal texts, and even in the Greek history of Thucydides, where it is clear that the narratives began with legendary periods of history before transitioning to more concrete events of the author's own day. The same pattern appears in Hebrew historiography. As we read the account of Israel's history from Genesis to Ezra/Nehemiah, we notice not so subtle generic shifts as we move from the mythical and legendary events of early history to the historical realities of life in monarchic Israel and early Judaism. Thus our appreciation for the early books of the Hebrew Bible requires an equally subtle appreciation for the generic sources its authors used, which included myths, legends, epics, genealogies, novellas, folktales, laws, and rituals, among others.

3. **Historiography and Mimesis.** Ancient historians often shaped their texts so that they mimicked the traditions of neighboring cultures. Mimicry of this sort took place on both micro and macro levels. At the micro level, the writers sometimes duplicated the literary styles of foreign writers. Such was the case in the victory stela of Pharaoh Piye, when the Nubian king mimicked Egyptian literary motifs in his royal inscription. Macro-level mimesis appeared especially in the Hellenistic histories as various Near Eastern authors tried to present their native traditions in the language and garb of Greek. Many other instances of mimesis could be cited. The two major narratives in the Hebrew Pentateuch, those of the Yahwist and the Priestly writer, seem to be mimetic works as well. Their basic structural shape and thematic features are very similar to Near Eastern texts such as Atrahasis, the Eridu Genesis, and the history of Berossus. A likely explanation is that the Pentateuch was composed mainly during and after the Babylonian exile, when Israelite scholars were living in close proximity to the Mesopotamian peoples.

4. **Historiography and Anachronism.** The author of the Weidner Chronicle wrote his history during a period when Marduk, the chief god of Babylon, was the highest and most prominent god in the Mesopotamian cult. Although it was natural for him to assume that Marduk had always been so important, this assumption was incorrect. Thus the author's narrative of history during the third millennium B.C.E. made Marduk appear much more important than he actually was. What accounts for this anachronism? For ancient and modern historians alike, sources of information are at best partial windows into the past. Historians therefore inevitably complete their pictures of the past by including elements—indeed, many elements—from their own world and experience. Anachronism appears whenever the world of the author is foreign to the ancient world he narrates. Biblical scholars have noted many instances in which Hebrew historians anachronistically read the viewpoints and perspectives of their own day into their narratives of Israelite antiquity. For example, the narratives in Genesis

assume that human beings were speaking Hebrew and Aramaic long before these languages appeared in the linguistic spectrum of the Near East (Gen 31:45–47). Many other examples could be cited in the Pentateuch, the Deuteronomistic History, and the Hebrew Chronicler.

5. **History, Historiography, and Antiquarianism.** Greek historians such as Herodotus, Hesiod, Pseudo-Hesiod, Hecataeus, and the logographers were often inclined to collect into their histories information about biology, geography, ethnography, cultural history, genealogies, and other interesting curiosities. Scholars call this peculiar interest in curio and ancient lore antiquarianism. One result of antiquarian historiography is that its authors often juxtaposed their "true" narratives of the past with antiquarian materials whose truth was questionable, without explicitly saying so. Antiquarianism is most visible in the texts when the author includes subject matter that has little to do with the central theme of his history or when he chooses to include two or more versions of the same story or tradition. There is good evidence that Hebrew historians were sometimes motivated by antiquarian interests. The compiler of the Pentateuch was perfectly satisfied with his two versions of the naming of Bethel (Gen 28; 35), of Jacob's name change (Gen 32; 35), and of the rebellion at Massah (Exod 17; Num 20) and with countless other duplications. Even more striking is the account, in 1 Sam 16:14–17:58, in which young David meets King Saul *twice* for the *first* time. Because of the potential presence of antiquarian lore in ancient historiography, modern scholars need to approach these works with caution if they hope to use them as sources for composing histories of the ancient world.

6. **Historiography and Fiction.** As discussed in chapter 8, above, it is not easy to draw neat and clean distinctions between history and fiction; this partial list of the possible relationships between fiction and historiography illustrates the difficulty:

a. The historian uses a fictional source but believes it is historical.

b. The historian uses a fictional source though he believes or suspects that it is not historical. He includes it in order to preserve the tradition (antiquarianism).

c. The historian uses a fictional source though he believes or suspects that it is not historical. He includes it because it suits his ideological agenda (generic ruse).

d. In the absence of sources, the historian postulates what probably or certainly must have happened in antiquity and then narrates this in his history. In this way, he creates a fictional account of the past that he really believes to be historically true (reified fiction).

e. The historian creatively composes a fictional text whose formal features mimick historiography. Although the writer knows that his readers will read his text as an accurate history, the philosophical or theological benefits of the truth the text conveys outweigh the deception itself (generic ruse).

f. In some form or fashion, the historian includes fiction in his history in order to maliciously mislead his readers (generic deception).

Other permutations of the fiction-history combination are possible, but these examples suffice to illustrate how complex the options are. Moreover, in most cases it is very difficult in practice to determine which of these categories best describes a given text. For instance, although modern scholars are fairly confident that the authors of the Weidner Chronicle and the Synchronistic History invented many aspects of their histories, it is impossible to know whether they really believed their invented stories (reified ficiton) or whether they merely used them to achieve pious aims (generic ruse or generic deception).

7. **Historiography and *Tendenz.*** As we have seen, the use of source materials in each history was guided by an ideological perspective, a *Tendenz* through which the past was interpreted. On the basis of our discussion, we can isolate four basic tools that ancient historians used to convey their distinctive view of the past. First, historians infused their *Tendenz* into the history by schematically structuring the texts so that the main themes stood out in relief. This strategy is especially visible in texts such as the Weidner Chronicle, where a distinctive pattern of retributive justice insured that those who lived well were blessed and those who did not were punished or cursed (cf. the Deuteronomistic Historian and the Hebrew Chronicler). Second, historians selected or edited their sources so that their narratives would reflect their historical viewpoints. For instance, the Synchronistic Historian seems to have included only sources that fit into the retributive historical pattern he wanted to teach. Third, in some cases, the historians resorted to fictive modes of composition. Thucydides tells us plainly that he did this in his history, and we suspect the same of certain Hebrew and Near Eastern historians. For this reason, great care must be taken when we use ancient histories as the grist for our modern historiographic mills. Finally, the fourth strategy for bringing the historian's perspective into the text is what narratologists call extranarrative intervention, which is a fancy term for the historian's use of commentary. This pattern appears primarily in the Greek histories, the only histories in which the writers periodically stepped out

from behind the curtain of the narrative in order to tell us who they were and what they hoped to accomplish with their stories.

Extranarrative intervention appears to be a unique property of the Greek histories, but the biblical histories also exhibit their own unique property. Biblical historians seem to have cast themselves as omniscient narrators who enjoyed a "God's-eye" view of all matters divine and human (Sternberg). Rhetorically speaking, this omniscient perspective becomes most visible when characters in the story know less than the narrator or when readers are able to scrutinize the invisible thoughts of biblical characters: "So Sarah laughed to herself, saying, 'After I have grown old, and my husband is old, shall I have pleasure?'" (Gen 18:12). According to some scholars, the practice of omniscient narrating may imply that the biblical historians, like the prophets, viewed themselves as composing revealed perspectives on Israel's past.

The *Tendenz* of each history was mainly a product of the author's social context. The dispassionate accounts of the Babylonian Chronicle Series and the freedom of expression in the Greek historians reflect scribal worlds in which the writers enjoyed relative independence from the demands of king and state. In contrast, narrative freedom of this sort was entirely foreign to the authors of the government-sponsored annals of Egypt, Assyria, and Hatti. In these annalistic texts and in many other palace-sponsored exemplars, royal propaganda was far and away the most common ideological aim. The sitting king thereby either consolidated his claim to the throne or justified his usurpation of it. The usual strategy for asserting political legitimacy was to accentuate the king's royal pedigree, divine election, military successes, and kindness of heart. Where usurpation was at issue, the king's opponent was vilified while the king himself was portrayed as gracious and merciful toward his defeated rival. In cases where the rival perished, the king denied a role in the murder or explained why circumstances forced the king to eliminate his adversary. In all these respects, the royal apologies of the ancient Near East are very similar to the biblical stories about the rise of David and Solomon, which lavish praise on David, vilify the house of Saul, and absolve David's household of complicity in the murder of Saul's family (see Sparks).

8. History Writing in Greece and Israel. The Greek histories clearly provide the comparative exemplars closest to the histories in the Hebrew Bible. The book of Genesis, with its genealogies, ethnographies, myths, and legends, suggests an author who was particularly close in method and viewpoint to the antiquarian writers of Greek history. Nevertheless, these important similarities should not distract from a fundamental distinction between Greek and Hebrew historiography. Greek historiography was a product not only of inquiry but of critical inquiry. This contrast between Greek and Hebrew historiography is brought out most clearly by P. Noble's useful distinction between "quotation-theoretic" and "resource-theoretic" modes of historical composition. The quotation method of historiography simply recopies blocks of material derived from the sources whereas the resource method draws information from the sources but actively transforms these into a new narrative. Israelite historiography seems to have made a more extensive use of the quotation approach, and the more critical Greek stance dictated preference for the resource method. The quotation-theoretic approach of the Hebrew authors has made it relatively easy for biblical scholars to identify and distinguish the sources and editorial layers in the Israelite histories.

9. Historiography and Redaction. If modern scholars are correct, then the Hebrew histories that run from Genesis to Nehemiah are the end result of a long and complex editorial process. Although some redactional activity is discernable in the Assyrian Annals and even in the Mesha Inscription (see ch. 15, below), this evidence does not comport with the active process of redaction that modern scholars perceive in the composition of the Hebrew histories. Why the difference? The Assyrian Annals were not submitted to thoroughgoing redactions because the texts were transmitted and copied by royal scribes who shared the same ideological perspectives and so had no strong motivation to edit the texts. Scholars are fairly confident that this situation did not hold for the Hebrew Bible. The Hebrew texts passed through many ideological communities and contexts during their historical odyssey from ancient Israel to us. The result was an active pattern of editorial emendation and revision, especially in response to the great contextual and theological crises prompted by the Babylonian exile. When we examine Near Eastern texts with similarly long transmission histories, such as the Gilgamesh Epic, we find the same editorial and compositional features as in the Hebrew histories (see ch. 9, above).

In spite of Hebrew propensities to edit their histories, the net effect was perhaps not what one might expect. In no other comparative texts do we find a *Tendenz* that is so critical of its own people as in Hebrew histories, which paint the entire history of Israel—its people and its leaders—in extremely dark shades. As Hallo has said about one of its stories, "Where but in the Bible could one find national literature preserving the materials for so scathing a self-examination?" (*COS* 1:xxvii).

10. Historicity of the Hebrew Histories. Readers of the Hebrew Bible are generally interested not only in Israel's literature but also in its social, political, and religious history. For this reason, a few comments about the value of the Hebrew narratives as historical sources are suitable. As already pointed out, the primary history of Israel, which runs from Genesis to Ezra and

Nehemiah, begins with mythical, legendary, and folklorish sources that treat the origins of the cosmos and of early Israel (Genesis to Judges). A good historical assessment of these sources should assess their historical value in light of the respective genres. Needless to say, historians would be unwise to take these sources at face value; nevertheless, our discussion in previous chapters has demonstrated that nonhistoriographical genres such as legends and epics often preserve valuable historical content. The next phase in Israelite's history, narrated in 1 and 2 Samuel, includes the rise of Saul and the origins of the Davidic monarchy. The comparative evidence suggests that this material is full of political apology, produced by David and Solomon as they defended their claims to the throne against the house of Saul. Thus the material in 1 and 2 Samuel is indeed old and provides a genuine window into the nascent monarchy of Israel, but this material must be carefully sifted to separate the propaganda from the facts. When we turn to the period of the divided monarchy onward, we find that the essential outline of Israel's history in Kings, Chronicles, Ezra, and Nehemiah is relatively close to the facts. Near Eastern evidence confirms Sheshonq's invasion of Palestine, Israel's trouble with Assyria, Judah's trouble with Assyria and Babylon, the Babylonian exile, the fate of Jehoiachin in Babylon, and the return of Jewish exiles under Cyrus of Persia. In light of this evidence, it is difficult to understand why some minimalist scholars insist so strenuously that there is no connection between the Hebrew histories of ancient Israel and ancient Israelite history.

General Bibliography

B. ALBREKTSON, *History and the Gods: An Essay on the Idea of Historical Events as Divine Manifestations in the Ancient Near East and in Israel* (ConBOT 1; Lund, Sweden: Gleerup, 1967); Y. AMIT, *History and Ideology: Introduction to Historiography in the Hebrew Bible* (Sheffield, England: Sheffield Academic Press, 1999); J. M. BALCER, *Herodotus and Bisitun: Problems in Ancient Persian Historiography* (Stuttgart: Franz Steiner, 1987); J. H. BREASTED, *Ancient Records of Egypt* (5 vols.; Chicago: University of Chicago Press, 1906–1907); E. BREISACH, *Historiography: Ancient, Medieval, and Modern* (2d ed.; Chicago: University of Chicago Press, 1994); M. Z. BRETTLER, *The Creation of History in Ancient Israel* (New York: Routledge, 1995); T. R. BRYCE, *The Major Historical Texts of Early Hittite History* (Asian Studies Monograph 1; Brisbane: University of Queensland, 1980); H. CANCIK, *Grundzüge der hethitischen und alttestamentlichen Geschichtsschreibung* (Wiesbaden: Harrassowitz, 1976); IDEM, *Mythische und historische Wahrheit: Interpretationen zu Texten der hethitischen, biblischen, und griechischen Historiographie* (SBS 48; Stuttgart: Katholisches Bibelwerk, 1970); J. COBET, "Herodotus and Thucydides on War," in *Past Perspectives: Studies in Greek and Roman Historical Writing* (ed. I. S. Moxon, J. D. Smart, and A. J. Woodman; Cambridge: Cambridge

University Press, 1986), 1–18; M. COGAN and I. EPH'AL, eds., *Ah, Assyria . . . Studies in Assyrian History and Ancient Near Eastern Historiography Presented to Hayim Tadmor* (ScrHier 33; Jerusalem: Magnes Press, 1991); I. CUNNISON, *History on the Luapula: An Essay on the Historical Notions of a Central African Tribe* (Rhodes-Livingstone Papers 21; London: Oxford University Press, 1951); R. C. DENTAN, ed., *The Idea of History in the Ancient Near East* (New Haven: Yale University Press, 1955); S. DONADONI, "On the Historiography of Ancient Egypt," *StudOr* 13 (1994): 73–86; M. DEJ. ELLIS, *Essays on the Ancient Near East in Memory of Jacob Joel Finkelstein* (Memoirs of the Connecticut Academy of Arts & Sciences 19: Hamden, Conn.: Published for the Academy by Archon Books, 1977); M. I. FINLEY, "Myth, Memory, and History," *History and Theory* 4 (1965): 281–302; C. W. FORNARA, *The Nature of History in Ancient Greece and Rome* (Berkeley: University of California Press, 1983); E. GABBA, "True History and False History in Classical Antiquity," *JRS* 71 (1981): 50–62; L. L. GRABBE, *Did Moses Speak Attic? Jewish Historiography and Scripture in the Hellenistic Period* (JSOTSup 317; Sheffield, England: Sheffield Academic Press, 2001); J.-J. GLASSNER, *Mesopotamian Chronicles* (SBLWAW 19; Atlanta: Society of Biblical Literature, 2004); A. K. GRAYSON, *Assyrian and Babylonian Chronicles* (Locust Valley, N.Y.: J. J. Augustin, 1975; repr., Winona Lake, Ind.: Eisenbrauns, 2000); IDEM, "Chronicles and the Akitu Festival," in *Actes de la XVIIe Rencontre assyriologique internationale* (ed. A. Finet; PCBRHEAM 1; Ham-sur-Heure, Belgium: Comité Belge de Recherches en Mésopotamie, 1970), 160–70; IDEM, "Königslisten und Chroniken, B: Akkadisch," *RlA* 6:86–134; H. G. GÜTERBOCK, "Die historische Tradition und ihre literarische Gestaltung bei Babyloniern und Hethitern bis 1200," *ZA* 42 (1934): 1–91; 44 (1938): 45–149; IDEM, "Hittite Historiography: A Survey," in *History, Historiography, and Interpretation: Studies in Biblical and Cuneiform Literature* (ed. H. Tadmor and M. Weinfeld; Jerusalem: Magnes Press, 1983), 21–35; W. V. HARRIS, *Ancient Literacy* (Cambridge: Harvard University Press, 1989); H. A. HOFFNER JR., "Histories and Historians of the Ancient Near East: The Hittites," *Or* 49 (1980): 283–332; IDEM, "Propaganda and Political Justification in Hittite Historiography," in *Unity and Diversity: Essays in the History, Literature, and Religion of the Ancient Near East* (Baltimore: Johns Hopkins University Press, 1975), 49–62; S. HORNBLOWER, ed., *Greek Historiography* (Oxford: Clarendon, 1994); F. JACOBY, *Die Fragmente der griechischen Historiker* (3 vols.; Leiden; Boston: Brill, 1998–1999); A. KAMMENHUBER, "Die hethitsche Geschichtsschreibung," *Saeculum* 9 (1958): 136–55; S. N. KRAMER, "Sumerian Historiography," *IEJ* 3 (1953): 217–32; A. B. LORD, *The Singer of Tales* (Cambridge: Harvard University Press, 1960); J. MARINCOLA, *Greek Historians* (Oxford: Oxford University Press, 2001); IDEM, *Tradition and Authority in Ancient Historiography* (Cambridge: Cambridge University Press, 1997); A. MEGILL, "Historiology / Philosophy of Historical Writing," in *Encyclopedia of Historians and Historical Writing* (ed. K. Boyd; 2 vols.; Chicago: Fitzroy Dearborn, 1999), 2:539–43; A. R. MILLARD et al., eds., *Faith, Tradition, and History: Old Testament Historiography in Its Near Eastern Context* (Winona Lake, Ind.: Eisenbrauns, 1994); A. MOMIGLIANO, *Classical Foundations of Modern Historiography* (Sather Classical Lectures 54; Berkeley: University of

California Press, 1990); IDEM, *The Development of Greek Biography* (exp. ed.; Carl Newell Jackson Lectures 1968; Cambridge: Harvard University Press, 1993); IDEM, *Essays in Ancient and Modern Historiography* (Oxford: Blackwell, 1977); IDEM, "Greek Historiography," *History and Theory* 17 (1978): 1–27; IDEM, "The Origins of Universal History," in *The Poet and the Historian* (ed. R. E. Friedman; HSS 26; Atlanta: Scholars Press, 1983), 133–48; IDEM, *Studies in Historiography* (New York: Harper & Row, 1966); A. T. MURRAY, ed., *The Iliad* (2 vols.; LCL; Cambridge: Harvard University Press, 1924–1925); IDEM, *The Odyssey* (2 vols.; LCL; Cambridge: Harvard University Press, 1919); P. NOBLE, "Synchronic and Diachronic Approaches to Biblical Interpretation," *Literature and Theology* 7 (1993): 130–48; S. B. PARKER, *Stories in Scripture and Inscriptions: Comparative Studies on Narratives in Northwest Semitic Inscriptions and the Hebrew Bible* (Oxford: Oxford University Press, 1997); L. PEARSON and S. HORNBLOWER, "Logographers," *OCD* 882; D. B. REDFORD, *Pharaonic King-Lists, Annals, and Day-Books: A Contribution to the Egyptian Sense of History* (SSEA Publication 4; Mississauga, Ont.: Benben, 1986), 65–126; K. L. SPARKS, *Ethnicity and Identity in Ancient Israel* (Winona Lake, Ind.: Eisenbrauns, 1998); IDEM, "Propaganda (Apology of David)," in *Dictionary of the Old Testament Historical Books* (Downer's Grove, Ill.: InterVarsity, forthcoming); C. G. STARR, *The Awakening of the Greek Historical Spirit* (New York: Knopf, 1968), 12–36; M. STERNBERG, *The Poetics of Biblical Narrative* (Bloomington: Indiana University Press, 1985); H. TADMOR and M. WEINFELD, eds., *History, Historiography, and Interpretation: Studies in Biblical and Cuneiform Literatures* (Jerusalem: Magnes Press, 1983); J. VAN SETERS, *In Search of History: Historiography in the Ancient World and the Origins of Biblical History* (New Haven: Yale University Press, 1983); IDEM, *Prologue to History: The Yahwist as Historian in Genesis* (Louisville: Westminster John Knox, 1992); G. P. VERBRUGGHE and J. M. WICKERSHAM, *Berossos and Manetho, Introduced and Translated: Native Traditions in Ancient Mesopotamia and Egypt* (Ann Arbor: University of Michigan Press, 2001); M. WEINFELD, "Divine Intervention in War in Ancient Israel and in the Ancient Near East," in *History, Historiography, and Interpretation* (ed. Tadmor and Weinfeld), 121–47; W. WHALLON, *Formula, Character, and Context: Studies in Homeric, Old English, and Old Testament Poetry* (Cambridge: Harvard Unversity Press, 1969).

CHAPTER THIRTEEN

Law Codes

Introduction

Law is an important cultural convention that counters threats to social order. Its regulations and procedures establish both the rules for proper conduct and the means of enforcing them. Ancient Near Eastern cultures produced many kinds of legal genres, including loans, leases, contracts, pledges, marriage agreements, adoptions, real-estate transactions, lawsuits, royal edicts, and law codes, among others. Although the biblical materials allude to many of these types of materials, the major legal genre that has been preserved in the Hebrew Bible is the law code, and this genre is the focus here.

Near Eastern law codes were collections of legal stipulations along with their corresponding sentences or remedies. The form of the laws was usually *casuistic;* that is, they established the case to be treated with a protasis, "*If* a man commits a homicide," then followed this with an apodosis that pronounced the penalty, "then they shall kill that man." Scholars often contrast these casuistic forms with the so-called *apodictic* laws, which take the form of an assertion: "Thou shalt" or "Thou shalt not" do such and such. The apodictic form is unusual in Near Eastern law codes, but it appears frequently in the Hebrew Bible. Another law form, which begins with a relative clause, also appears in the ancient laws. These laws generally follow the pattern "A man who does this or that shall receive such and such punishment." Some scholars understand this as an apodictic form, but it is more common to view it as variation of the casuistic formulation (e.g., "In the case of the man who . . ."). Like their modern counterparts, the ancient scribes were sometimes explicitly aware of these legal forms, as is illustrated by the Sumerian Handbook of Legal Forms, a compendium of legal clauses, phrases, and case laws used as a reference tome for training legal scribes. The text is functionally comparable to other scribal instruction texts, such as the model contracts (see Landsberger 1937). In the case of law, as in other genres, the ancients had to master a range of forms as they prepared for their scribal duties.

Before turning to the laws themselves, let us briefly consider the nuts and bolts of administering ancient law. Near Eastern law was generally administered in three different contexts: the royal court system, the temples, and among the local elders. The royal courts were managed on a day-to-day basis by the king's appointed magistrates. These officials could be consulted at many locations in the kingdom, and most large cities had a "chief justice" that presided over the legal process. The king seems to have been involved only when monarchic interests were at stake or when the case was considered an especially serious one. Although there was no formal court of appeal in antiquity, many letters addressed to the king show that he was constantly asked to investigate or overturn decisions in the lower courts. In light of these facts, it is not surprising that the king's judicial role was frequently accentuated in the prologues and epilogues of law codes, which sought to convince both men and the gods that the king was a just, fair, and equitable ruler for the land. In many cases—perhaps most—royal appointees were able to work out terms between litigants without a formal trial. But when trials could not be avoided, the general pattern was as follows.

A plaintiff filed a case, and the named defendant was then summoned to the court. The defendant was expected to present evidence in support of his or her alternative point of view. Although documentary evidence was occasionally cited, witnesses were the testimony of choice in the courts. In the absence of witnesses and solid evidence, it was not uncommon for the defendant to be cleared on the basis of an exculpatory oath, in which the defendant swore by the gods that he or she was innocent. Refusal to take such an oath pointed to fear and hence to guilt. Barring such an oath, the trial normally proceeded with the presentation of witnesses, interrogatories, and the pronouncement of a verdict by the magistrate. Court officials were sometimes appointed to insure that the litigants complied with this verdict, and magistrates also required, on occasion, that litigants swear an oath that they considered the matter settled. Strict penalties were sometimes prescribed for the parties who raised the issue again. A record of the case was sometimes sealed in a clay envelope and placed in the archives for future consultation if the dispute resurfaced, but recent studies suggest that tablet documentation was the exception rather than the rule (Greengus). If this is so, the legal texts available to us are only the tip of an ancient judicial iceberg that was predominantly oral in nature.

Although the royal administration of justice was important in all periods of antiquity, the temple-based judicial system was prominent only in certain periods, particularly in the Old Babylonian period. The priests administered this temple system, their importance and power varying with the scope of jurisdiction granted to the temple. But no matter what the historical period, two circumstances promoted a connection between the temple and adjudication: (1) solemnly sworn oaths before gods could only be done in the temple precinct, and (2) even during periods when the temple-based system was not prominent, it often had jurisdiction in religious matters.

The local council of elders represents the third context in which ancient justice was administered. These elders—traditionally seated at the city gate—

handled much of the legal process in antiquity, especially in the smaller towns and villages that had no royal magistrates (McKenzie). In these contexts, formal suits were presented when one person publicly accused another of some trespass or personal liability. If no settlement was readily achieved, the plaintiff would suggest that the two agree on a time, perhaps a few days later, when they would meet with the council of elders at the city gate. This would provide time for each litigant to procure witnesses and to prepare for the case. At the time of the trial, the elders would take a seat at the gate, announce the suit, and request a presentation of the evidence from both sides of the argument. The case ended when the elders interrogated the parties, discussed the matter, pronounced a verdict, and then decreed a punishment or an appropriate remedy. As is now clear in the case of the monarchic system, and even more so in the local elder-based context, jurisprudence was administered predominantly on an oral basis. Whether and to what extent any written law code played a role in adjudication varied from case to case, as we will see shortly.

Our examination of these ancient law codes begins with the oldest of the exemplars—those written in Sumerian—and then goes on to consider the Akkadian samples from Ešnunna, Babylon, and Assyria, the legal collections of the Hittites, and a single sample each from Greece (the Gortyn Law Code) and Egypt (the Code of Hermopolis). For purposes of completeness, this examination includes an entry on sources that relate to the possible role of the Persians in publishing native laws in the conquered regions of their empire.

13.1. The Sumerian Laws

The Laws of Ur-Nammu. Soon after King Ur-Nammu of Ur (2112–2095 B.C.E.) unified the city-states of northern and southern Mesopotamia into what became the Third Dynasty of Ur, he sought to solidify his control over Mesopotamia by presenting himself as a divinely appointed restorer of peace and social order. One element in this propaganda was his law code. As in other ancient codes, political propaganda was conveyed through its narrative prologue, in which Ur-Nammu recounted his acts of emancipation (political/historical content), his new standards for measurement and trade (economic content), and the new securities and protections he afforded to travelers on both land and water—especially for the poor, the orphan, and the widow (ethical content). The presence of a prologue suggests that it originally had an epilogue as well, but the end of the code is missing. The fragmentary law code identified by Roth as the "Laws of X" (see Roth, 36–39; Michalowski/Walker) may actually be the end of Ur-Nammu's code, since it dates to approximately the same period and ends with an epilogue. If so, the epilogue included the standard warning that anyone who effaced or damaged the text would be subject to a curse and to punishment by the gods. Although our copies of the text are on clay tablets, the original was probably inscribed on a monumental stela in the temple, palace, or public forum. The same can be said of

some other Mesopotamian law codes. The collection includes almost forty casuistic legal statutes, but because it is broken, the original number is unknown.
Generally speaking, the laws are arranged topically. The first law penalizes murder with death, and the laws that follow treat personal injuries, slave issues, sexual
offenses, marital problems, agricultural disputes, and perjury. Laws 13–14 refer to
the divine "river ordeal," in which an accused person (or his accuser) was placed
in the river under the presumption that the river god would drown the guilty
party (see Lafont). This procedure was used only in certain types of cases, particularly when the evidence was unclear or when witnesses were unavailable. The
practice commonly appears in ancient Near Eastern law (cf. Code of Hammurabi
§132), but apart from possible allusions to it in the Hebrew Bible, river ordeals
were not used in ancient Israel (McCarter). A different type of ordeal procedure is
prescribed in the biblical law of Num 5:11–31, which addresses the case of a husband who suspected his wife of adultery. Ur-Nammu's laws eventually became an
object of scholarly study; scribes were still copying the laws several centuries later,
during the days of Hammurabi (Kramer/Falkenstein).

Although the laws in this code were presented as those of Ur-Nammu,
some scholars suspect that the code was actually composed by his son, Šulgi
(2094–2047). If this thesis is correct, we may surmise that Šulgi did so in order to
honor his father and perhaps to lend authority to his own reform efforts.

Texts and translations: J. J. FINKELSTEIN, "The Laws of Ur-Nammu," *JCS* 22 (1969):
66–82; P. MICHALOWSKI and C. B. F. WALKER, "A New Sumerian 'Law Code,'" in *DUMU-
E2–DUB-BA-A: Studies in Honor of Åke Sjöberg* (ed. H. Behrens, D. T. Loding, and M. Roth;
OPSNKF 11; Philadelphia: University Museum, 1989), 383–96; ROTH, *Law Collections
from Mesopotamia and Asia Minor,* 13–22. *Translations:* ANET 523–25; COS 2.153:
408–10. *Bibliography:* BOECKER, *Law and the Administration of Justice in the Old Testament and Ancient East,* 57–58; S. N. KRAMER and A. FALKENSTEIN, "Ur-Nammu's Law
Code," *Or* 23 (1954): 40–51; IDEM, "The Ur-Nammu Code: Who Was Its Author?" *Or* 52
(1983): 453–56; B. LAFONT, "The Ordeal," in J. BOTTÉRO, *Everyday Life in Ancient Mesopotamia* (Baltimore: Johns Hopkins University Press, 1992), 199–209.

The Laws of Lipit-Ištar. If we assume that Ur-Nammu's laws were concluded
with an epilogue like that found in the "Laws of X," then the other Sumerian law
code, composed by Lipit-Ištar of Isin (1934–1924 B.C.E.), is similar to Ur-
Nammu's laws. The similarities, which include the tripartite form (prologue, casuistic law collection, epilogue), the general content of these three sections, and
the emphasis on the great gods, Anu and Enlil, are visible in spite of the broken
state of the text, which preserves only about four hundred of twelve hundred
original lines. Perhaps the most important difference between the two codes is
breadth of subject matter. Lipit-Ištar's laws cover five major categories of civil law
(marriage/family, inheritance, property, slaves, debts, and wages) whereas Ur-
Nammu's laws cover three categories of civil law but add criminal laws that address adultery/rape, assault, and perjury.

Text and translation: ROTH, *Law Collections from Mesopotamia and Asia Minor,* 23–35.
Translations: ANET 159–61; COS 2.154: 410–14. *Bibliography:* BOECKER, *Law and the*

Administration of Justice in the Old Testament and Ancient East, 58–60; A. FALKENSTEIN and M. SAN NICOLÒ, "Das Gesetzbuch Lipit-Istars von Isin," *Or* 19 (1950): 103–18.

Sumerian Scholastic Legal Texts. Our corpus of Near Eastern legal material contains several scholastic inscriptions, including model texts and exercise tablets. One of the most important model texts, the Sumerian Handbook of Legal Forms, is a clay prism inscribed with components of the laws that scribes needed to master (e.g., protoses without apodoses and vice versa). Students apparently consulted this text during their training. Among the exercise tablets is an interesting collection of laws, concerning oxen, that have parallels in numerous ancient law codes and in the Hebrew Bible (Lipit-Ištar, Hammurabi, Ešnunna, Hatti; Exod 21:28–36). The peculiar interest in laws on oxen suggests that these laws were highly valued as a subject of legal contemplation.

Text and translation: ROTH, *Law Collections from Mesopotamia and Asia Minor,* 40–54. *Translations:* ANET 525–26 (exercise tablet [Roth, text 5]); *COS* 3.140–42: 311–12. *Bibliography:* M. CIVIL, "New Sumerian Law Fragments," in *Studies in Honor of Benno Landsberger on His Seventy-Fifth Birthday* (ed. Güterbock and Jacobsen), 1–12; M. T. ROTH, "The Scholastic Exercise 'Laws about Rented Oxen,'" *JCS* 32 (1980): 127–46.

13.2. The Akkadian Laws and *Mīšaru* Edicts

The Laws of Ešnunna. This code is now generally attributed to Dadusha (ca. 1770 B.C.E.), but the text is, unfortunately, broken at the point where the ruler who promulgated the laws was named. Still, nearly the entire law code of sixty provisions is preserved. Some of these provisions deal with wage and price standards, but most of them address civil and criminal concerns in the casuistic form. The code is unusual in comparison with the earlier Sumerian laws and the Code of Hammurabi (see next entry) because it lacks both prologue and epilogue. The only introduction to the Laws of Ešnunna is a dated superscription that originally included the king's name. This use of the date formula is a clue to the text's function. Date formulas were used to introduce Old Babylonian *mīšaru* reform edicts (see below), suggesting that Dadusha's code was similarly promulgated to support a reform effort. Confirmation of this conclusion is found in the code itself, which addresses matters of economic reform (weights, measures, and prices) but lacks the prologue and epilogue through which kings normally added propaganda to their codes. Although this does not preclude the reform's propagandistic value for Dadusha, it suggests that the reform effort itself was a serious one. It is not clear how the laws were implemented in support of this reform. Perhaps they served as admonitions to magistrates, judges, and other officials, or perhaps they served a more direct role as the statutes by which cases were adjudicated.

Texts and translations: A. GOETZE, *The Laws of Eshnunna* (AASOR 31; New Haven: American Schools of Oriental Research, 1956); ROTH, *Law Collections from Mesopotamia and Asia Minor,* 57–70. *Translations:* ANET 161–63; *COS* 2.130: 332–35. *Bibliography:*

BOECKER, *Law and the Administration of Justice in the Old Testament and Ancient East,* 60–65; B. EICHLER, "Literary Structure in the Laws of Eshnunna," in *Language, Literature, and History: Philological and Historical Studies Presented to Erica Reiner* (ed. F. Rochberg-Halton; New Haven: American Oriental Society, 1987), 71–84; E. OTTO, *Rechtsgeschichte der Redaktionen im Kodex Esnunna und im "Bundesbuch,"* (OBO 85; Freiburg, Switz.: Universitätsverlag, 1989); H. PETSCHOW, "Zur 'Systematik' in den Gesetzen von Eschnunna," in *Symbolae iuridicae et historicae Martino David dedicatae* (ed. J. A. Ankum, R. Feenstra, and W. F. Leemans; 2 vols.; Leiden: Brill, 1968), 2:131–43.

The Code of Hammurabi. This law code has generated more interest than any other because it was the first ancient law code to be discovered and because it remains the largest and most extensive code from antiquity. The text includes almost three hundred provisions, but the precise number is unknown because there are several gaps in the laws. Hammurabi's provisions were carefully organized into the following subject areas: (1) the administration of justice, 5 laws; (2) offenses against property, 20 laws; (3) land tenure, about 50 laws; (4) trade and commerce, about 40 laws; (5) family and social institutions, 68 laws; (6) penalties for assault, 20 laws; (7) regulations for professional services, 26 laws; (8) oxen, 16 laws; (9) agriculture, 11 laws; (10) employment wages, 10 laws; (11) slaves, 5 laws. Included among these provisions are numerous instances of *lex talionis* ("law of retribution"), the eye-for-an-eye justice that appears in the Hebrew Bible, as well as other close parallels to biblical law (the slave laws in HL §117; Deut 15:12; the ox laws in HL §§250–51; Exod 21:28–29).

The Code of Hammurabi is framed by a prologue and an epilogue whose propagandistic content corresponded to the impressive physical features of the text, which was originally published on numerous large public stelae, the most famous and complete being the nine-foot black basalt stone discovered during excavations at Susa in 1901–1902. The choice of black basalt made the stela particularly attractive, as did other aesthetic features, especially the picture at its top. Hammurabi is depicted receiving a royal scepter from Šamaš, the sun god and divine patron of justice, who appears to be on a mountain and flanked by fire. Although the significance of this scene is a matter of debate, in broad strokes it is safe to say that the laws are presented as having divine rather than merely human origins. The text's stately appeal was further enhanced by its use of an archaic ductus (script) and by the direction of the writing, which followed an old pattern turned ninety degrees counterclockwise. In a comparative context, the Code of Hammurabi probably shared a reform function with the laws of Ešnunna but differed from them by expressing its political aims more overtly.

When the Code of Hammurabi and similar codes were first discovered, they were imagined to be codes of substantive law akin to our like modern legal codes. As we have seen, however, the propagandistic purposes of the ancient laws make this reading shy of that mark. Nevertheless, even if the codes such as Hammurabi's were not published as substantive law, their provisions undoubtedly exerted some influences on both the judicial processes and socioeconomic conditions (Finkelstein 1981). Hammurabi's laws eventually attracted the attention of ancient scholars and so became an object of scribal study for more than a millennium after their promulgation (Boecker, 57). In no instance is this scholastic interest more apparent than in some of our first-millennium copies, which dropped the propagandistic prologue and epilogue from the manuscript (Finkelstein 1967). This generic process, in which the propagandistic laws became a scholarly legal text, illustrates the multivalence of the ancient codes in regard to function.

It has long been recognized that the form and content of the Code of Hammurabi are particularly close to the book of the covenant in Exod 20:22–23:33. This applies not only to the content and order of the laws (see Wright) but also to matters of iconography, since Hammurabi, like Moses, is depicted receiving his laws directly from the deity atop a fire- and smoke-enshrouded mountain (Van Seters). The best explanation for this similarity is that the biblical author knew the Code of Hammurabi and intentionally shaped his work so as to mimic the older, more venerated text.

Texts and translations: DRIVER and MILES, *The Babylonian Laws;* ROTH, *Law Collections from Mesopotamia and Asia Minor,* 71–142. *Translations: ANET* 163–80; *COS* 2.131: 335–53. *Bibliography:* BOECKER, *Law and the Administration of Justice in the Old Testament and Ancient East,* 67–133; J. BOTTÉRO, *Mesopotamia: Writing, Reasoning, and the God* (Chicago: University of Chicago Press, 1992), 156–84; C. EDWARDS, *The Hammurabi Code and the Sinaitic Legislation* (Port Washington, N.Y.: Kennikat, 1971); A. FINET, *Le Code de Ḥammurapi* (2d ed.; Paris: Cerf, 1983); J. J. FINKELSTEIN, "A Late Old Babylonian Copy of the Laws of Hammurapi," *JCS* 21 (1967): 39–48; V. A. HUROWITZ, *Inu Anum ṣīrum: Literary Structures in the Non-juridical sections of Codex Hammurabi* (OPSNKF 15; Philadelphia: University Museum, 1994); F. R. KRAUS, "Ein zentrales Problem des altmesopotamischen Rechtes: Was ist der Codex Hammurabi?" *Geneva* NS 8 (1960): 283–96; B. LANDSBERGER, "Die babylonischen Termini für Gesetz und Recht," in *Festschrift Paul Koschaker* (3 vols.; Weimar: Hermann Böhlaus, 1939), 2:218–34; H. PETSCHOW, "Zur Systematik und Gesetzestechnik im Codex Hammurabi," *ZA* 57 (1965): 146–72; J. VAN SETERS, *A Law Book for the Diaspora: Revision in the Study of the Covenant Code* (Oxford: Oxford University Press, 2003), 56–57; H.-D. VIEL, *The Code of Hammurabi* (Munich: Lincom Europa, 2003); D. P. WRIGHT, "The Laws of Hammurabi as a Source for the Covenant Collection (Exodus 20:23–23:19)," *Maarav* 10 (2003): 11–88.

The Old Babylonian Mīšaru *Edicts.* Kings in the dynasty of Hammurabi did not wish to sponsor new law codes that might be viewed as challenging the laws of the dynastic founder. As a result, they customarily published new laws in the form of royal edicts, which were proffered as acts of "justice" or "equity" (*mīšaru*). The edicts were published at the beginning of the king's reign and at other times, although probably not at regular intervals, as some scholars have maintained. Our primary exemplars are the edicts of Samsuiluna (1749–1712 B.C.E.) and Ammiṣaduqa (1646–1626), but we may also have a fragmentary edict of Ammiditana (1683–1647) (see Kraus 1984). The basic purpose of the edicts was to promote social order and secure popular support for the regime by initiating economic reforms and canceling private debts. Some of the law codes probably served similar functions. Although the *mīšaru* practice seems to have died out with the Old Babylonian period, some of its features continued in the institutions of the *kidinnūtu* (Leemans) and in the Neo-Assyrian *andurāru* (Lemche). Similar features in the biblical laws would include the Sabbath year (Deut 15; Lev 25), the priestly Jubilee (Lev 25), and edicts of emancipation (Jer 34:8–22).

Texts and translations: F. R. KRAUS, *Ein Edikt des Königs Ammiṣaduqa von Babylon* (Studia et documenta 5; Leiden: Brill, 1958); IDEM, "Ein Edikt des Königs Samsu-iluna von Babylon," in *Studies in Honor of Benno Landsberger on His Seventy-Fifth Birthday* (ed. Güterbock and Jacobsen), 225–31. *Translations:* ANET 526–28 (Ammiṣaduqa); COS 2.134: 362–64 (Samsuiluna). *Bibliography:* D. CHARPIN, "Les décrets royaux à l'époque paléo-babylonienne, à propos d'un ouvrage récent," *AfO* 34 (1987): 36–41; J. J. FINKEL-STEIN, "Ammiṣaduqa's Edict and the Babylonian 'Law Codes,'" *JCS* 15 (1961): 91–104; W. W. HALLO, "Sharecropping in the Edict of Ammisaduqa," in *Hesed ve-Emet: Studies in Honor of Ernest S. Frerichs* (ed. J. Magness and S. Gitin; BJS 320; Atlanta: Scholars Press, 1998), 205–16; F. R. KRAUS, *Königliche Verfügungen in altbabylonischer Zeit* (Studia et documenta 11; Leiden: Brill, 1984); W. F. LEEMANS, "*Kidinnu*, un symbole de droit divin babylonien," in *Symbolae ad jus et historiam antiquitatis pertinentes Julio Christiano Van Oven dedicatae* (ed. M. David et al.; Leiden: Brill, 1946), 36–61; N. P. LEMCHE, "*Andurarum* and *Mišarum:* Comments on the Problem of Social Edicts and Their Application in the Ancient Near East," *JNES* 38 (1979): 11–22; IDEM, "Manumission of Slaves–Fallow Year–the Sabbatical Year–the Jobel Year," *VT* 26 (1976): 38–59; S. J. LIEBERMAN, "Royal 'Reforms' of the Amurrite Dynasty," *BO* 46 (1989): 241–59; H. OLIVIER, "The Effectiveness of the Old Babylonian Mešarum Decree," *JNSL* 12 (1984): 107–13; IDEM, "The Periodicity of the Mešarum Again," in *Text and Context: Old Testament and Semitic Studies for F. C. Fensham* (ed. W. Claassen; JSOTSup 48; Sheffield, England: JSOT Press, 1988), 227–35; E. OTTO, "Soziale Restitution und Vertragsrecht: *Mischaru(m), (an)-durarum, kirenzi, para tarnumar, schemitta,* und *derôr* in der hebräischen Bibel und die Frage des Rechtstransfers im alten Orient," *RA* 92 (1998): 125–60; R. F. G. SWEET, "Some Observations on the Edict of Ammiṣaduqa Prompted by Text C," in *The Archaeology of Jordan and Other Studies Presented to Siegried H. Horn* (ed. L. T. Geraty and L. G. Herr; Berrien Springs, Mich.: Andrews University Press, 1986), 579–600; M. WEINFELD, "'Justice and Righteousness' in Ancient Israel against the Background of 'Social Reforms' in the Ancient Near East," in *Mesopotamien und seine Nachbarn: Politische und kulturelle Wechselbeziehungen im alten Vorderasien von 4. bis 1. Jahrtausend v. Chr.: XXV. Rencontre assyriologique internationale* (ed. H.-J. Nissen and J. Renger; BBVO 1; Berlin: D. Reimer, 1982).

The Middle Assyrian Laws. These fifteen legal texts, which are copies of earlier fourteenth-century B.C.E. originals, have been labeled by scholars tablets A–O, with A being the largest of the collections (with fifty-nine provisions). Like most of the codes, their provisions distinguish various social classes from each other, but it has been frequently noted that the Middle Assyrian Laws allow for rather harsh treatment of women. The casuistic laws cover a variety of topics, among them theft, personal injury, sexual assault, homicide, inheritance, marriage, and business transactions. Some tablets include a breadth of subject matter (tablet A) whereas others seem focused on particular issues (e.g., pledges and deposits in tablets C and G). Despite their similarities to earlier laws, the Middle Assyrian

Laws differ from them on several points. They include no political prologue or epilogue, nor do they include a promulgation date like the Ešnunna law code. The collection is also less orderly and structured than many other codes, containing legal provisions that are often lengthy, convoluted, and detailed. How might these divergent tendencies be explained? According to Driver and Miles (following Koschaker), a closer examination of the laws reveals several telling patterns. The apparently heterogeneous set of laws in text A actually reflects a coherent effort to collect law provisions that address women, especially married women. The length and detail of these laws attest furthermore to a tradition of legal interpolation that included explanatory glosses, textual additions, and alterations to older editions of the laws. This editorial process is best understood as the work of learned legists who apparently preserved and edited the legal tradition to support jurists and magistrates in the adjudication of law. The Middle Assyrian Laws therefore served a much more direct function within the courts than was the case in most ancient codes.

Texts and translations: DRIVER and MILES, *The Assyrian Laws;* ROTH, *Law Collections from Mesopotamia and Asia Minor,* 153–94. *Translations: ANET* 180–88; *COS* 2.132: 353–60. *Bibliography:* CARDASCIA, *Les lois assyriennes;* P. KOSCHAKER, *Quellenkritische Untersuchungen zu den "altassyrischen Gesetzen"* (MVAG 26.3; Leipzig: J. C. Hinrichs, 1921), 79–84.

The Middle Assyrian Harem Edicts. Also known as the Middle Assyrian Palace Decrees, these edicts governed behavior within the royal household, especially regarding the king's harem. The decrees were assembled during the reign of Tiglath-pileser I (1114–1076 B.C.E.), but they include royal edicts from as far back as the fourteenth century B.C.E. The text reflects the same ongoing editorial process visible in the Middle Assyrian Laws.

Texts and translations: ROTH, *Law Collections from Mesopotamia and Asia Minor,* 195–209. *Bibliography:* CARDASCIA, *Les lois assyriennes;* DRIVER and MILES, *The Assyrian Laws.*

The Neo-Babylonian Laws. Chronologically speaking, the last of the Akkadian law codes is Neo-Babylonian (ca. 700 B.C.E.). A single tablet preserves fifteen of approximately eighteen original laws in the text. Although these laws are similar at points to earlier laws, the differences accent their unique Neo-Babylonian origin. There is no prologue or epilogue, and the protasis of these casuistic laws is introduced with the relative form, *amēlu ša* ("[in the case of] a man who . . ."), rather than with *šumma* ("if"). The tablet has more than its fair share of scribal mistakes, which has prompted Driver and Miles to suggest that it was a scholastic exercise for scribal students.

Texts and translations: DRIVER and MILES, *The Babylonian Laws;* ROTH, *Law Collections from Mesopotamia and Asia Minor,* 71–142. *Translations: ANET* 197–98; *COS* 2.133: 360–61. *Bibliography:* H. PETSCHOW, "Das neubabylonische Gesetzesfragment," *Zeitschrift der Savigny-Stiftung für Rechtsgeschichte* 76 (1959): 36–96.

13.3. Other Codes and Texts

The Hittite Laws. The Hittite documents attest to a long legal tradition extending
from the Old Kingdom down to the end of the New Kingdom (i.e., seventeenth–twelfth centuries B.C.E.). The standard text edition contains two hundred
casuistic laws in two series of one hundred, each series designated by the initial
statute within it (series 1, "If a man . . ."; series 2, "If a vine . . ."). As Hoffner has
emphasized, the organization of the laws reflects an effort to arrange them topically: homicide (§§1–6, 42–44), assault (§§7–18), slaves (§§19–24), marriage
(§§26–36), land tenure (§§39–41, 46–56), theft of or injury to animals (§§57–92),
unlawful entry (§§93–97), arson (§§98–100), theft of or damage to plants
(§§101–120), theft of or damage to implements (§§121–144), wages and fees
(§§150–161), prices (§§176–186), and sexual offenses (§§187–200). Although
there is no prologue or epilogue, the code is otherwise similar to the other ancient
Near Eastern codes. It differs from the others primarily in its jurisprudence,
which recognizes the legitimacy of local elder courts, and in certain legal peculiarities that are comparable to those in Hebrew laws. This is true of the laws
about sexual pairings with humans and animals in §§187–200, the law of the
"Levirate marriage" (§193), and the scapegoat laws that allowed animals to be
killed in lieu of human beings (§199). In these respects, the Hittite Laws represent
a legal tradition that stands apart from the other texts that have been examined.

The Hittite Laws contain a number of irrelevant details that appear to be
the remnants of precedent cases, so these laws are not the products of scholastic
legal speculation but the results of actual adjudication. Two lines of evidence
show that this legal function did not end with the code's composition. First, the
laws were apparently updated to adjust prescribed penalties for changes in economic and social conditions. As a result, large fines became smaller ones, and
corporal punishments were replaced with fines. These editorial changes were
often introduced with the word *karū* ("formerly" or "long ago") and took the following form: "Long ago, such and such was done, but now such and such will be
done." Second, efforts to edit the laws went beyond these minor editorial changes
to a fuller revision of the laws, called the Late Parallel Version.

Although it is not entirely clear how the Hittite Laws were utilized, the editorial process itself suggests that ancient jurists consulted the laws. The Hittite
Laws were therefore canonical texts rather than monumental for propaganda.
Another peculiar feature of the Hittite Laws are the legal concessions. For instance, §190 states, "If a man has sexual relations with his stepmother, *it is not an
offense.* But if his father is still living, it is an unpermitted sexual pairing" (italics
added). Why was it necessary to promulgate laws that *permit* a behavior? The answer lies in the previous law (§189), which states, "If a man has sexual relations
with his mother, it is an unpermitted sexual pairing." This raised the question,
Does this ruling also apply to stepmothers? Law 190 was composed to answer this
question with a "no" (in the sense that the stepmother is not like a mother) but
also with a "yes" (in the sense that one should not copulate with the wife of one's

father). Laws of concession were enacted when the principles of analogy or implication might lead to judgments that were considered undesirable by jurists and
magistrates.

Text and translation: H. A. HOFFNER JR., *The Laws of the Hittites: A Critical Edition*
(DMOA 23; New York: Brill, 1997). *Translations: ANET* 188–97; *COS* 2.19: 100–13; ROTH,
Law Collections from Mesopotamia and Asia Minor, 213–47. *Bibliography:* T. R. BRYCE, *Life
and Society in the Hittite World* (Oxford: Oxford University Press, 2002), 32–55; R. HAASE,
"Some Problems of Hittite Law and Jurisdiction," in *Society and Economy in the Eastern
Mediterranean (c. 1500–1000 B.C.)* (ed. M. Heltzer and E. Lipinski; OLA 23; Leuven:
Peeters, 1988), 69–77; H. A. HOFFNER JR., "On Homocide in Hittite Law," in *Crossing
Boundaries and Linking Horizons: Studies in Honor of Michael C. Astour on His 80th Birthday*
(Bethesda, Md.: CDL Press, 1997), 293–314; E. OTTO, "Körperverletzung im hethitischen
und israelitischen Recht: Rechts-und religionshistorische Askpekte," in *Religionsgeschicht-
liche Beziehungen zwischen Kleinasien, Nordsyrien, und dem Alten Testament* (ed. B. Janowski et al.; Freiburg, Switz.: Universitätsverlag, 1993), 391–425.

The Greek Gortyn Law Code. The fifth-century B.C.E. laws found at Gortyn, on
the island of Crete, are among the oldest Greek legal inscriptions. These were
written on a circular stone wall that may have served as the foundation of a law
court building. The topics treated include property, marriage, kinship, inheritance, adultery, divorce, adoption, and rules for the administration of justice. As
with the Near Eastern laws, the cases addressed by the casuistic provisions are too
few and limited to provide the legal breadth one expects of a true law code. A
careful examination of the text within its ancient context, however, shows that it
nonetheless served a role within the Cretan legal system. The Gortyn text reflects
signs of supplementation and emendation in its last two columns (cols. XI–XII),
and it also refers to other written laws. Although this confirms that the text was
used judicially, how does this judicial function square with the obviously narrow
breadth of subject matter in the code?

Legal processes in Greece were usually oral, as reflected in the absence of
legal records such as appear in the Near East, and in the special office of the
mnēmōn, whose role was to remember the outcomes of court proceedings and
rulings. Oral adjudication in other Greek communities necessitated the preservation of laws by means of recitation, chanting, and singing. In such contexts, the
best way to understand a code like this one is as supplemental to other written
and oral laws that provided the fundamental basis for judicial activity.

Text and translation: R. F. WILLETTS, *The Law Code of Gortyn* (Kadmos Supplement 1;
Berlin: de Gruyter, 1967). *Bibliography:* J. K. DAVIES, "Deconstructing Gortyn: When Is a
Code a Code?" in *Greek Law in Its Political Setting* (ed. Foxhall and Lewis), 33–56;
R. THOMAS, "Written in Stone? Liberty, Orality, and Codification of Law," in *Greek Law in
Its Political Setting* (ed. Foxhall and Lewis), 9–31.

Persian Authorization of Native Law. Although we do not possess copies of any
Persian law codes, several texts from Egypt and Asia Minor suggest that the Persians played a role in the promulgation of local laws in those regions. These texts

include the following: (1) a report, preserved in Aramaic and Egyptian demotic, on the reverse of the papyrus that bears the Demotic Chronicle (see 7.2), that Darius I (519–503 B.C.E.) commissioned a group of Egyptian soldiers, priests, and scribes to produce a code of extant Egyptian law (see Spiegelberg); (2) a fifth-century Aramaic letter, discovered in the Jewish archive at Elephantine (Egypt), in which King Darius II played a role in regulating observation of the Passover festival among Jews in Egypt (see Porten and Yardeni; also the entry on Elephantine in 1.3); (3) a Greek inscription in which the Persians played a role in resolving a border dispute between Miletus and Myus in Asia Minor; (4) a trilingual stela inscription, in Greek, Lycian, and Aramaic, in which the Persians regulated cult practices for the goddess Leto in Lycia, the southwestern peninsula of Asia Minor. The use of Persia's Imperial Aramaic reflects the official nature of the proceedings behind these texts. In recent years, these exemplars have prompted some biblical scholars to conclude that the Persians also played an important role in promulgating Ezra's laws (i.e, the Pentateuch) and in sponsoring Nehemiah's reforms (see bibliography). A pertinent question is whether this Persian role significantly influenced the content of the biblical laws.

Texts and translations: H. METZGER et al., eds., *La stèle trilingue du Létôon* (vol. 6 of *Fouilles de Xanthos;* Paris: Klincksieck, 1979); B. PORTEN and A. YARDENI, *Textbook of Aramaic Documents from Ancient Egypt* (4 vols.; Jerusalem: Hebrew University Press, 1986–1999), 1:54–55; W. SPIEGELBERG, *Die sogenannte demotische Chronik des Pap. 215 der Bibliothèque nationale zu Paris* (Demotische Studien 7; Leipzig: Hinrichs, 1914); N. TOD, *A Selection of Greek Historical Inscriptions* (2 vols; Oxford: Oxford University Press, 1946), 2:36–39. *Bibliography:* J. BLENKINSOPP, "The Mission of Udjahorresnet and Those of Ezra and Nehemiah," *JBL* 106 (1987): 409–21; P. FREI and K. KOCH, *Reichsidee und Reichsorganisation im Perserreich* (OBO 55; Freiburg, Switz.: Universitätsverlag, 1984); K. G. HOGLAND, *Achaemenid Imperial Administration in Syria-Palestine and the Missions of Ezra and Nehemiah* (SBLDS 125; Atlanta: Scholars Press, 1992); E. SEIDL, *Ägyptische Rechtsgeschichte der Saiten-und Perserzeit* (2d ed.; ÄF 20; Glückstadt, Germany: J. J. Augustin, 1968); WATTS, *Persia and Torah.*

The Demotic Law Code of Hermopolis. This fragmentary Egyptian papyrus contains our earliest collection of Egyptian laws. The text dates to the third century B.C.E. and is commonly understood as a later development of the legal codification begun under Darius (see previous entry). According to Redford, however, the contents of the text are too local and parochial to suit this reading. The topics include land and property leases, annuity laws, house ownership, building codes, inheritance laws, and cemetery regulations. Thus the text is perhaps best understood as a legal manual that governed life in a rural, medium-sized Egyptian community.

Text and translation: G. MATTHA and G. R. HUGHES, *The Demotic Legal Code of Hermopolis West* (Cairo: Institut Français d'Archéologie Orientale, 1975). *Bibliography:* K. DONKER VAN HEEL, *The Legal Manual of Hermopolis* (Uitgaven vanwege de stichting "Het Leids Papyrologisch Instituut" 11; Leiden: Papyrologisch Instituut, 1990); S. GRUNERT, Der Kodex Hermopolis und ausgewählte private Rechtsurkunden aus dem ptolemäischen Ägypten (Leipzig: Phillip Reclam, 1982); D. B. REDFORD, "The So-Called

'Codification' of Egyptian Law under Darius I," in *Persia and Torah* (ed. Watts), 135–59; A. THÉODORIDÈS, "The Concept of Law in Ancient Egypt," in *The Legacy of Egypt* (2d ed.; ed. J. R. Harris; Oxford: Clarendon, 1971), 291–322.

Concluding Observations

The insights gleaned from our survey of Near Eastern laws can be distilled under four headings, beginning with the function of the ancient law.

1. Function. Near Eastern law codes filled a variety of functional roles, in some cases serving as substantive laws but in others as political apologia, socio-economic reform texts, and even scholastic texts. A single law code could serve several functions, since political propaganda, for instance, did not preclude concerns about substantive law or economic reform. Nevertheless, true judicial texts distinguish themselves from the rest by the fact that they are written on tablets rather than on public stelae, lack prologues or epilogues, and display many signs of editorial emendation. The editorial revisions were a simple consequence of the need to adjust the legislation for changing social, economic, and political circumstances (cf. the law codes from Gortyn, Hatti, and Middle Assyria). None of these judicial texts were codes in the modern sense of coherent and systematic expressions of law. They are better understood as texts that supplemented the larger oral context of ancient jurisprudence. In contrast, the reform and apologetic codes, such as the laws of Ur-Nammu, Lipit-Ištar, and Hammurabi, are inscribed on public stelae, include prologues and epilogues, and do not reflect the editorial amendments visible in their judicial cousins. This does not mean that the authors of these reform texts were uninterested in initiating changes in society and law—they probably were—rather, it means that the concerns of propaganda were primary and that these texts were not designed to provide substantive laws for jurisprudence.

The functional boundaries highlighted here were rather permeable. The Code of Hammurabi was eventually adopted as a scholastic text, and the oxen laws of the Near East appeared in a variety of law code types, including reform documents, substantive laws, and scribal exercises. The same laws, then, could pass from one sphere to another rather easily: precedent laws became substantive laws, substantive laws became reform laws, reform laws became scribal traditions, and so on. Exchanges of tradition seem to have been especially prominent between the judicial processes and the scribal legal tradition, perhaps because the scribal tradition served as a corpus of judicial reflection for ancient legists and jurists. This exchange of legal tradition is explicitly confirmed in the Code of Hammurabi, which reflects influences from adjudication and "scholastic law," as well as from the concerns of political and socioeconomic reform.

The potential implications for the function of biblical law are twofold:
(1) biblical law codes may include statutes that come from a variety of
functional contexts, and (2) the functions of biblical law had the potential
to change over time.

2. Form, Content, and the Near Eastern Legal Tradition. Most of the Near Eastern legal stipulations were of the casuistic type and addressed matters of
civil and criminal law. The form and content of Hebrew laws are similar
and sometimes include provisions that are nearly identical to their Near
Eastern counterparts (cf. Deut 15:12//Code of Hammurabi §117 [slave
laws]; Exod 21:28–29//Code of Hammurabi §§250–251 [ox laws]). Although some scholars attribute the similarities in biblical and Near Eastern
law to the similar social and economic circumstances that produced them
(the evolutionist/phenomenological approach; see Jackson; Otto 1991;
Yaron), the similarities are so pronounced that most scholars believe there
must be a more direct cultural link (the diffusionist approach). Some
diffusionists understand this link as an indirect path that followed the
common-law tradition of antiquity (Paul; Boecker), whereas others argue
for a more straightforward literary link, suggesting that the laws were products of an ongoing scholastic legal tradition that was widely disseminated
in the Near East (Bottéro; Finkelstein; Kraus; Malul 1990). My own view is
that there is some truth in both the phenomenological and diffusionist positions on this question, but in the end, there can be no doubt that the biblical authors were directly influenced by Near Eastern law in some cases, the
parade example being the influence of the Code of Hammurabi on the
book of the covenant in Exod 20:22–23:33.

Despite the similarities just noted, readers of Hebrew law find that the biblical laws differ from their Near Eastern counterparts on two counts. The
biblical laws include a broader range of forms, especially of the apodictic
variety, and they also address a much broader range of topics, including not
only humanitarian statutes but also many cultic and religious regulations.
The prominence of these cultic and religious laws in the Hebrew Bible requires an explanation. One promising possibility is that the biblical laws
were influenced by Israel's wisdom tradition in ways that Near Eastern texts
were not (Gerstenberger, *Wesen;* Richter; Blenkinsopp; cf. Prov 22:28//Deut
19:14a; Prov 3:30//Exod 23:1a; Prov 4:14//Exod 23:21). The other, related
explanation is that the Pentateuch is an anthological compendium of ancient Israelite tradition, in which case we should not be surprised to find
that it includes not only laws and wisdom but also ritual and cultic
regulations.

The influence of legal motifs and language also appears in many other parts
of the Hebrew Bible. This is particularly true of the book of Job, where the

protagonist wishes for his day in court (24:1; 27:1–6) and takes an exculpatory oath (ch. 31), but it is also true of various narrative pericopes (e.g., Ruth 4; Jer 26) and especially of the prophets, who confronted sinful Israelites with their so-called "covenant lawsuit" (see ch. 14).

3. Orality and Law. Unlike modern law, ancient law was largely an oral procedure. Rules and standards of adjudication were hardly addressed by the written laws, and many aspects of civil and criminal law were slighted or ignored. Prescribed verdicts were often replaced by the discretion of judges ("as the judges determine," cf. Exod 21:22; Lev 13:59; Deut 25:1). These codes therefore placed the onus both of forming law and of adjudication squarely in the hands of elders, judges, priests, or royal functionaries. If, as argued here, the Near Eastern laws should be understood as part of a larger oral context, then from the outset we must realize that the biblical laws, as products of less complex societies, were dependent upon oral processes in an even more profound way (Morrow; Patrick).

4. Authorship and Publication. Jews and Christians have for centuries ascribed the laws of the Pentateuch to Israel's traditional lawgiver, Moses. Modern scholarship, however, has raised questions about this uncomplicated viewpoint because of comparative data from the Near East and because three basic features in the biblical laws point not to a single author but to several. First, unlike the Near Eastern codes, the laws in the Pentateuch are not collected into a single code but are instead nested in several separate collections, namely, the book of the covenant (Exod 20:22–23:33), the Deuteronomic Code (Deut 12–26), the Holiness Code (Lev 17–26), and the Priestly Code (primarily Exod 25–40; Lev 1–16; Numbers). On analogy with the Near Eastern codes, this suggests that we have not one but several codes stemming from different contexts and authors. This impression is reinforced by repetitions of the same laws in the various legal collections, such as the festival laws (Exod 23:14–19; 34:18–26; Lev 23:1–44; Num 28–29; Deut 16:1–17), Sabbath rules (Exod 20:8–11; 31:12–17; 35:1–3; Lev 23:3; Deut 5:12–15), and the enigmatic command "You shall not boil a kid in its mother's milk" (Exod 23:19; 34:26; Deut 14:21). Such repetitions would be unnecessary in a single code, but they make good sense if we imagine that the Pentateuch in fact contains several law codes that originated in different situations. The third feature suggesting that various authors have written the Hebrew laws is the presence of significant differences between the law collections. The laws for the altar for burnt offering (Exod 20:24–26; 27:1–2) differ significantly, as do the Passover regulations given in Deut 16:7 (boil the meat) and Exod 12:8–9 (roast the meat, do not boil it). The repetitions, tensions, and differences within the laws of the Pentateuch imply that they are the work of several authors and redactors who have contributed to the Hebrew laws in quite different situations. This is commensurate with the evidence from certain Near Eastern law codes that reflect a lively process of editorial emendation (Hittite Laws; Middle Assyrian Laws; the Gortyn Law Code). From this one could deduce that the pentateuchal laws were traditionally "Mosaic," in the same way that Israel's wisdom was "Solomonic" and its hymnic literature "Davidic." In Jewish tradition, this *topos* of Mosaic authorship extended far beyond the Hebrew canon to include even rabbinic law (the so-called oral Torah).

On the publication of Hebrew law, another development in recent years is the increasing suspicion that the Persians played a role, perhaps a prominent role, in either supporting or sponsoring the codification of Hebrew law as it appears in the final form of the Pentateuch. If this is so, then our canonical edition of Hebrew law should be read with an awareness that its contents were perhaps shaped not only by the Jews of Palestine but also by Diaspora Jews in Mesopotamia and by the Persians themselves.

General Bibliography

J. BLENKINSOPP, *Wisdom and Law in the Old Testament: The Ordering of Life in Israel and Early Judaism* (Oxford: Oxford University Press, 1995); J. J. BOECKER, *Law and the Administration of Justice in the Old Testament and Ancient East* (Minneapolis: Augsburg, 1980); J. BOTTÉRO, "The 'Code' of Hammurabi," *Mesopotamia: Writing, Reasoning, and the Gods* (Chicago: University of Chicago Press, 1992); G. CARDASCIA, "Égalité et inégalité des sexes en matière d'atteinte aux moeurs dans le Proche-Orient ancien," *WO* 11 (1980): 7–16; IDEM, *Les lois assyriennes* (Paris: Cerf, 1969); G. R. DRIVER and J. C. MILES, *The Assyrian Laws* (Ancient Codes of the Near East 2; Oxford: Clarendon, 1935); IDEM, *The Babylonian Laws* (2 vols.; Ancient Codes of the Near East 1; Oxford: Clarendon, 1952–1955); F. C. FENSHAM, "Widow, Orphan, and the Poor in Ancient Near Eastern Legal and Wisdom Literature," *JNES* 21 (1962): 129–39; J. J. FINKELSTEIN, *The Ox That Gored* (TAPS 71.2; Philadelphia: American Philosophical Society, 1981); L. FOXHALL and A. D. E. LEWIS, eds., *Greek Law in Its Political Setting: Justifications, Not Justice* (Oxford: Clarendon, 1996); E. GERSTENBERGER, "Covenant and Commandment," *JBL* 84 (1965): 38–51; IDEM, *Wesen und Herkunft des "apodiktischen Rechts"* (WMANT 20; Neukirchen: Neukirchener Verlag, 1965); S. GREENGUS, "Some Issues Relating to the Comparability of Laws and the Coherence of the Legal Tradition," in *Theory and Method in Biblical and Cuneiform Law* (ed. Levinson), 60–87; H. G. GÜTERBOCK and T. JACOBSEN, eds., *Studies in Honor of Benno Landsberger on His Seventy-Fifth Birthday* (AS 16; Chicago: University of Chicago Press, 1965); B. HALPERN and D. W. HOBSON, *Law, Politics, and Society in the Ancient Mediterranean World* (Sheffield, England: Sheffield Academic Press, 1993); M. HARAN, *Temples and Temple Service in Ancient Israel* (Oxford: Oxford University Press, 1978); B. S. JACKSON, Essays in Jewish and Comparative Legal History (SJLA 10; Leiden: Brill, 1975); R. JAS, *Neo-Assyrian Judicial Procedures*

(SAAS 5; Helsinki: Helsinki University Press, 1996); L. KATAJA, "A Neo-Assyrian Document on Two Cases of River Ordeal," *SAAB* 1 (1987): 65–68; I. KNOHL, *The Sanctuary of Silence: The Priestly Torah and the Holiness School* (Minneapolis: Fortress, 1995); F. R. KRAUS, "Ein zentrales Problem des altmesopotamischen Rechtes: Was ist der Codex Hammu-rabi?" *Genava* 8 (1960): 283–96; B. LANDS-BERGER, *Die Serie ana ittišu* (vol. 1 of *Materialien zum sumerischen Lexikon*, ed. B. Landsberger; Rome: Sumptibus Pontificii Instituti Biblici, 1937); S. LANGDON, *The Sumerian Law Code compared with the Code of Hammurabi* ([s.l.]: [s.n.], 1920); B. M. LEVINSON, ed., *Theory and Method in Biblical and Cuneiform Law: Revision, Interpolation, and Development* (JSOTSup 181; Sheffield, England: Sheffield Academic Press, 1994); M. MALUL, *The Comparative Method in Ancient Near Eastern and Biblical Legal Studies* (AOAT 227; Neukirchen-Vluyn: Neukirchener Verlag, 1990); IDEM, *Studies in Mesopotamian Legal Symbolism* (AOAT 221; Kevelaer, Germany: Butzon & Bercker, 1988); P. K. MCCARTER, "The River Ordeal in Israelite Literature," *HTR* 66 (1973): 403–12; D. A. MCKENZIE, "Judicial Procedure at the Town Gate," *VT* 14 (1964): 100–104; J. MILGROM, *Leviticus 1–16* (AB 3; New York: Doubleday, 1991); W. S. MORROW, *Scribing the Center* (SBLMS 49; Atlanta: Scholars Press, 1995); E. OTTO, *Das Deuteronomium: Politische Theologie und Rechtsreform in Juda und Assyrien* (BZAW 284; New York: de Gruyter, 1999); IDEM, "Die Geschichte der Talion im Alten Orient und Israel," in *Ernten, was man sät: Festschrift für Klaus Koch zu seiner 65. Geburtstag* (ed. D. R. Daniels, W. Glessmer, and M. Rösel; Neukirchen-Vluyn: Neukirchener Verlag, 1991), 101–30; IDEM, *Körperverletzungen in den Keilschriften und im Alten Testament* (AOAT 226; Neukirchen-Vluyn: Neukirchener Verlag, 1991); IDEM, "Town and Rural Countryside in Ancient Israelite Law: Reception and Redaction in Cuneiform and Israelite Law," *JSOT* 57 (1993): 3–22; D. I. OWEN, "A Unique Late Sargonic River Ordeal in the John Frederick Lewis Collection," in *A Scientific Humanist: Studies in Memory of Abraham Sachs* (ed. E. Leichty, M. deJ. Ellis, and P. Gerardi; OPSNKF 9; Philadelphia: University Museum, 1988), 305–11; D. PATRICK, *Old Testament Law* (Atlanta: John Knox, 1985); S. M. PAUL, *Studies in the Book of the Covenant in the Light of Cuneiform and Biblical Law* (VTSup 18; Leiden: E. J. Brill, 1970); W. RICHTER, *Recht und Ethos* (SANT 15; Munich: Kösel, 1966); G. RIES, *Prolog und Epilog in Gesetzen des Altertums* (Munich: Beck, 1983); A. ROFÉ, *Introduction to the Composition of the Pentateuch* (Biblical Seminar 58; Sheffield, England: Sheffield Academic Press, 1999); M. T. ROTH, "A Case of Contested Status," in *DUMU-E2–DUB-BA-A: Studies in Honor of Åke Sjöberg* (ed. H. Behrens, D. T. Loding, and M. Roth; OPSNKF 11; Philadelphia: University Museum, 1989), 481–89; IDEM, *Law Collections from Mesopotamia and Asia Minor* (2d ed.; SBLWAW 6; Atlanta: Society of Biblical Literature, 1997); I. M. ROWE, "The Legal Texts from Ugarit," in *Handbook of Ugaritic Studies* (ed. W. G. E. Watson and N. Wyatt; Leiden: Brill, 1999), 390–422; A. SCHAFIK, "Réflexions sur le 'code legal' d'Hermopolis dans l'Égypt ancienne," *ChrEg* 61 (1986): 50–75; IDEM, "Traces de 'codification' en Égypte ancienne (à la basse époque)," *RIDA* 40 (1993): 11–26; A. THÉODORIDÈS, "The Concept of Law in Ancient Egypt," in *The Legacy of Egypt* (ed. J. R. Harris; 2d ed.; Oxford: Clarendon, 1971), 291–322; J. VAN SETERS, *A Law*

Book for the Diaspora: Revision in the Study of the Covenant Code (Oxford: Oxford University Press, 2003); J. W. WATTS, ed., *Persia and Torah: The Theory of Imperial Authorization of the Pentateuch* (SBLSymS 17; Atlanta: Society of Biblical Literature, 2001); R. WESTBROOK, *Studies in Biblical and Cuneiform Law* (CahRB 26; Paris: J. Gabalda, 1988); C. WILCKE, *Early Ancient Near Eastern Law—a History of Its Beginnings: The Early Dynastic and Sargonic Periods* (SBAW 2003.2; Munich: Verlag der Bayerischen Akademie der Wissenschaften. In Kommission beim Verlag C. H. Beck, 2003); R. YARON, "The Goring Ox in Near Eastern Law," in H. H. Cohn, *Jewish Law in Ancient and Modern Israel* (New York: Ktav, 1971), 50–60.

CHAPTER FOURTEEN

Treaty and Covenant

Introduction

Although their meanings overlap, the terms *treaty* and *covenant* differ because the first generally refers to political agreements whereas the second is semantically broader and includes a wider range of agreements and pacts. Nevertheless, the two concepts share a common status as *agreements enacted between two parties in which one or both make promises under oath to perform certain actions while avoiding others* (cf. *ABD* 1:1179–1202). The international treaties that have figured most prominently in this comparative discussion are the Hittite treaties, the Neo-Assyrian treaties, and the Aramaic treaties from Sefire. Political treaties were a fact of life for the modest states of ancient Palestine and Syria, primarily because as peripheral nations they were much smaller than the core empires of Egypt, Mesopotamia, and Asia Minor. The survival of these smaller nations therefore depended on their ability to forge protective relationships with one of the major powers in the region or with each other. Israel sometimes benefited from treaties with the powerful empires, but at certain points it also resisted these empires in concert with the surrounding petty nations. For obvious reasons, such acts of rebellion were the exception rather than the rule. There were two kinds of ancient treaty: the *vassal treaty* between a powerful king (the suzerain) and his vassal states, and the *parity treaty* between nations of equal stature. Each kind had a particular role in the context of international politics.

Vassal treaties—not military conquest—accounted for much of the growth and expansion of the great empires. This was simply because smaller nations generally knew better than to resist the Near Eastern powers and therefore accepted terms of peace before resorting to futile bloodshed. Parity treaties also contributed to stability in international relations because they enacted agreements of mutual assistance and nonaggression between the major power brokers. One of the most famous of these parity treaties, the thirteenth-century B.C.E. treaty between the Hittites and the Egyptians, established a peace that lasted more than fifty years.

Loyalty oaths stand alongside the treaties as an important, related genre. Ancient kings required these oaths of their subjects at key historical junctures, usually when their regime was threatened by a coup or when a new king ascended the throne. Although the oaths and treaties share a similar form, they differ in that the oaths address not those outside the empire but especially those within it. Most of our loyalty oaths come from the Sargonid dynasty of Neo-Assyria.

Readers should also note the Ugaritic purgation ritual treated in 5.2 (RS 1.002/*KTU* 1.40), which accentuates national unity and hence is comparable in certain respects to the treaty/covenant texts treated in the present chapter. A fragmentary Akkadian treaty was also discovered at Ugarit (see Bordreuil, 15–16).

Treaties, Oaths, and Grants

The Early Treaties. Although the best-known treaty exemplars from the ancient world are those of the Hittites and Neo-Assyrians, the genre was in use long before these cultures employed it. The earlier texts include three from the third millennium B.C.E. (see Cooper; Edzard; König), a number of second-millennium texts from the Old Babylonian period (Ischcali, Mari, Leilan) and Alalakh, and many treaty fragments and unpublished texts. Treaties are international documents, so there is a corresponding tendency for the genre to be shared cross-culturally. Consequently, in spite of their idiosyncrasies, common generic patterns are readily visible in the various texts. In every case, treaties were ratified in a ceremony that included rituals and sworn oaths by the treaty's parties. The treaty text itself defined both the contours of loyalty and the consequences of disloyalty by using at least three fundamental elements: stipulations (what the treaty partners must do or refrain from doing), lists of divine witnesses (the gods who would ensure obedience to the treaty), and curse formulas (punishments that would be received by treaty breakers). Several other features should be noted. First, the physical document itself was very important. This was reflected in the practice of depositing the text in the temple, where the gods could read and thereby enforce the treaty, and in the opposite practice of removing the text from the temple and either erasing or destroying it (see Cooper, 39–40). This last act nullified the treaty and is reminiscent of Moses' actions in Exod 32:19. Second, Near Eastern treaties generally had their eyes on future generations. The eighteenth-century B.C.E. treaty between Abban-AN and Yarimlim is an early reflection of this concern: "If a successor of Yarimlim should sin against Abba-AN or if a successor of Abba-AN should do the same . . . then he shall forfeit his city and his territories" (Wiseman 1958). This theme figures prominently in the later treaties from Hatti, Assyria, and Sefire as well. Third, it is clear that ancient treaties cannot always be taken at face value. Although Mari's nineteenth-century B.C.E. treaty with Ešnunna suggests that Mari was the treaty's suzerain, Ešnunna's copy of the treaty claims the same for Ešnunna (Charpin 1991). Because the concerns of propaganda obviously influenced the composition of the treaties, a more complete understanding of the documents and their history must be pursued through other sources, such as the letters and archival materials from the two sites.

Third millennium—texts, translations, and studies: J. S. COOPER, *Presargonic Inscriptions* (Sumerian and Akkadian Royal Inscriptions 1; New Haven: American Oriental Society, 1986), 33–39; D. O. EDZARD, "Der Vertrag von Ebla mit A-Bar-Qa," in *Literature and Literary Language at Ebla* (ed. P. Fronzaroli; QS 18; Florence: Dipartimento di Linguistica, Università di Firenze, 1992), 187–217; B. KIENAST, "Der Vertrag Ebla-Assur in rechtshistorischer Sicht," in *Wirtschaft und Gesellschaft von Ebla* (ed. H. Waetzoldt and H. Hauptmann; Heidelberg: Heidelberger Orientverlag, 1988), 231–43; F. W. KÖNIG, *Die elamischen Königsinschriften* (AfOB 16; Graz: Im Selbstverlage des Herausgebers, 1965); W. G. LAMBERT, "The Treaty of Ebla," in *Ebla, 1975–1985—dieci anni di studi linguistici e filologici: Atti del Convegno internazionale* (ed. L. Cagni; Naples: Istituto Universitario Orientale, Dipartimento di Studi Asiatici, 1987), 353–64; E. SOLLBERGER, "The So-Called 'Treaty between Ebla and Ashur,'" *Studi eblaiti* 3 (1980): 129–55; F. THUREAU-DANGIN, *Die sumerischen und akkadischen Königsinschriften* (VAB 1.1; Leipzig: J. C. Hinrichs, 1907), 10.4a.

Ischcali—texts, translations, and studies: S. GREENGUS, *Old Babylonian Tablets from Ischali and Vicinity* (Istanbul: Nederlands Historisch-Archaeologisch Instituut, 1979), 74–77, pls. cxi–cxii; LAFONT, "Relations internationales, alliances et diplomatie au temps des royaumes amorrites"; W. YUHONG, "The Treaty between Shadlash (Sumu-Numhim) and Neribtum (Hammi-Dushur)," *Journal of Ancient Civilizations* 9 (1994): 124–36.

Mari—texts, translations, and studies: M. ANBAR, "Let the Gods Come for the Treaty (Ceremony)," *ErIsr* 27 (2003): 185–88 [Hebrew]; D. CHARPIN, "Une alliance contre l'Elam et le ritual du *Lipit Napištim*," in *Contribution à l'histoire de l'Iran: Mélanges offerts à Jean Perrot* (ed. François Vallet; Paris: Éditions Recherche sur les Civilisations, 1990), 109–18; IDEM, "Le traité entre Zimri-Lim de Mari et Ibâl-pî-El II d'Ešnunna," in *Marchands, diplomates, et empereurs* (ed. Charpin and Joannès), 139–66; M. HELD, "Philological Notes on the Mari Covenant Rituals," *BASOR* 200 (1970): 32–40; F. JOANNÈS, "Le traité de vassalité d'Atarum d'Andarig envers Zimri-Lim de Mari," in *Marchands, diplomates, et empereurs* (ed. Charpin and Joannès), 167–78; J.-R. KUPPER, "Zimri-Lim et ses vassaux," in *Marchands, diplomates, et empereurs* (ed. Charpin and Joannès), 179–84; LAFONT, "Relations internationales, alliances et diplomatie au temps des royaumes amorrites."

Leilan—texts, translations, and studies: J. EIDEM, "An Old Assyrian Treaty from Tell Leilan," in *Marchands, diplomates, et empereurs* (ed. Charpin and Joannès), 185–208; IDEM, "Tell Leilan Archives 1987," *RA* 85 (1991): 109–35; LAFONT, "Relations internationales, alliances et diplomatie au temps des royaumes amorrites."

Alalakh—texts, translations, and studies: ANET 531–32; COS 2.127–29: 329–32; MCCARTHY, *Treaty and Covenant*; D. J. WISEMAN, "Abban and Alalaḫ," *JCS* 12 (1958): 124–29; IDEM, *The Alalakh Tablets* (OPBIAA 2; London: British Institute of Archaeology at Ankara, 1953), 25–32.

The Hittite Treaties. Between 1700 and 1200 B.C.E. a powerful empire emerged in the region of Anatolia (modern Turkey), centered at its capital city of Ḫattuša (modern Boğazköy). As this empire grew and expanded south and east into Syria, Palestine, and upper Mesopotamia, it concluded many treaties with the smaller states in the region. Most of these were unilateral vassal treaties in which the Hittite king was the suzerain. Submission to the terms of these treaties was guaranteed in part by a fear of Hittite strength and of the gods who witnessed the treaties, but the Hittites made every effort to create an atmosphere of mutual brotherhood through words of friendship and diplomatic marriages. More than thirty-five treaties have been preserved in whole or in part, and many others are mentioned in Hittite correspondence. The texts were originally composed in two languages, Hittite and Akkadian, for the obvious reason that Hittite was the national language and Akkadian the international diplomatic language. The treaties that are preserved in both languages show us not only that they were different translations but also that, on occasion, different versions were composed to suit political exigencies. One Hittite treaty, for instance, preserved the fiction of Mittanni's independence by preparing a vassal copy that eliminated the treaty's stipulations and presented the treaty as an overture of Mittanni's king rather than as a demand of the Hittite king. Official copies of the treaties were inscribed on silver tablets rather than on clay.

Although there is some variation, the many preserved texts allow us to describe the basic form of the Hittite treaty genre. The much-discussed pattern includes six components presented in a standard order: (1) the *preamble* provides the names and titles of the kings involved in the treaty; (2) the *historical prologue* recounts the previous history of relations between the parties of the treaty; (3) the *stipulations* specify the provisions imposed upon the vassal by the Hittite king, including the payment of tribute, the promise of military assistance, the renunciation of previous diplomatic relationships, the extradition of Hittite fugitives, and support for the Hittite king in the event of revolts or during times of succession; (4) the *deposition* dictates that the treaty tablet be placed in the temple of the vassal's chief deity, where it is to be read aloud before the vassal at stated intervals; (5) the *list of divine witnesses* names the deities (of both kings) who served as witnesses of the treaty oaths; (6) the *curses and blessing* enumerate the punishments for breaking the stipulations of the treaty as well as the blessings that result from keeping them. The stipulations include a variety of apodictic formulations ("Let him do this," "Let him not do that," "Thou shalt not . . .") and casuistic forms ("If such and such is the case . . ."). These are similar to law code stipulations and create a blend of treaty and law that is reminiscent of the blend of covenant and law found in the Hebrew Pentateuch.

Although most of the Hittite treaties were of the vassal type, the Hittites also concluded several bilateral parity treaties, the best known being the thirteenth-century treaty between Hattušili III and Rameses II of Egypt (Beckman, 90–95). The treaty is preserved on clay Akkadian tablets found in Hatti and also on the walls of the Egyptian temple of Amon at Karnak. These are copies of metal texts that were exchanged between the two parties. The Egyptians composed a version of the text on silver tablets that were transmitted by envoy to Hatti, and the Hittites did the same. The Egyptian version is therefore a translation of the Akkadian copy sent to them from Hatti. This unusual exchange of texts was dictated by the bilateral nature of the agreement. The treaty established peace between the two nations and divided the Levantine region between them, with Hatti taking jurisdiction of Syria, and Egypt of Palestine.

The Hittite treaties adhered to the more general Near Eastern treaty pattern, but they also had their own peculiarities. Scholars have often commented that the lengthy historical prologues of the Hittite treaties were exceptional in their ancient context. Only in the third-millennium Vulture Stela and in some first-millennium Neo-Assyrian treaties did similar prologues appear, but these were much shorter. The uniqueness of the Hittite prologues is not entirely surprising. Historiographic narratives developed early in the Hittite traditions (see 12.3), and historiographic recapitulations like those in the treaties also appear in other Hittite genres, such as the Telipinu Edict (see 12.3) and the Indictment of Madduwatta (see Beckman). In these and other cases, the Hittites clearly appreciated the importance of historical precedent in interpreting present circumstances, and this perspective gave rise to the inclusion of historical prologues in their treaties.

Another distinctive feature in the Hittite treaties is their emphasis on public readings of the document. Duplicate tablets were to be placed in the chief temples of both Hatti and the vassal, and the text was to be read to the vassal king and his people "repeatedly, forever and ever" (Beckman, 42). Since the stipulation to read the text required an intact copy of the treaty, the Hittite treaties also prescribed that the treaty tablets not be broken, altered, or hidden. Similar efforts to preserve the text appear in many other Near Eastern treaties. The Hittite emphasis on reading and rereading the text must be understood as part of a larger strategy to protect the exclusive relationship the treaty sought to establish: "You, Huqqana (King of Hayasa), benevolently protect My Majesty (Suppiluliuma I of Hatti), and stand behind only My Majesty. You shall not recognize anyone else beyond that. And I, My Majesty, will benevolently protect you. Later, I will protect your sons, and my son will protect your sons" (Beckman, 24).

Formal enactment of some Hittite treaties included the exchange of family members in royal marriages. This prompted the inclusion of a unique feature in these treaties, namely, directions about proper sexual conduct. The stipulations prohibited certain kinds of sexual activity (e.g., "A brother does not take his sister or female cousin sexually") and also warned against fraternizing with palace women ("Who was Mariya, and for what reasons did he die? . . . That man perished just for looking from afar [at a palace woman]"). A similar emphasis on sexual conduct also appears in the Hittite law codes and in the laws of the Hebrew Bible. Until recently scholars often noted the close similarities between the Hittite treaties and the covenants of the Hebrew Bible, particularly the covenant as expressed in the book of Deuteronomy. Although these similarities remain important, there is now a greater interest in the features that Deuteronomy shares with the Neo-Assyrian treaties.

Texts and translations: For the various texts, see *CTH* 2–29; J. FRIEDRICH, *Staatsverträge des Hatti-Reichs in hethitischer Sprache* (2 vols.; MVAG 31, 34; Leipzig: Hinrichs, 1926–1930); H. OTTEN, *Die Bronzetafel aus Boğazköy: Ein Staatsvertrag Tuthalijas IV* (StBoT 1;

Wiesbaden: Otto Harrassowitz, 1988); E. F. WEIDNER, *Politische Dokumente aus Kleinasien* (BoSt 8–9; Leipzig: Hinrichs, 1923). ***Translations:*** *ANET* 201–6, 529–30; G. BECKMAN, *Hittite Diplomatic Texts* (ed. H. A. Hoffner Jr.; SBLWAW 7; Atlanta: Scholars Press, 1996) (includes all the major texts and a catalogue of publications); *COS* 2.17–18: 87–100. ***Bibliography:*** A. ALTMAN, "The 'Deliverance Motif' in the 'Historical Prologues' of Šuppiluliuma I's Vassal Treaties," in *Confrontation and Co-existence* (ed. P. Artzi; Bar-Ilan Studies in History 2; Ramat Gan, Israel: Bar-Ilan University Press, 1984), 41–76; IDEM, *The Historical Prologue of the Hittite Vassal Treaties: An Inquiry into the Concepts of Hittite Interstate Law* (Bar-Ilan Studies in Near Eastern Languages and Culture; Ramat Gan: Bar-Ilan University, 2004); IDEM, "On the Legal Meaning of Some of the Assertions in the 'Historical Prologue' of the Kizzuwatna Treaty (KBo I, 5)," in *Bar-Ilan Studies in Assyriology Dedicated to Pinhas Artzi* (ed. J. Klein and A. Skaist; Ramat Gan, Israel: Bar-Ilan University Press, 1990), 177–206; R. H. BEAL, "The History of Kizzuwatna and the Date of the Šunaššura Treaty," *Or* 55 (1986): 425–45; G. BECKMAN, "Some Observations on the Šuppiluliuma-Šattiwaza Treaties," in *The Tablet and the Scroll: Near Eastern Studies in Honor of William W. Hallo* (ed. M. E. Cohen; Bethesda, Md.: CDL Press, 1993), 53–57; O. CARRUBA, "Die Hajasa-Verträge Hattis," in *Documentum Asiae Minoris antiquae: Festschrift fur Heinrich Otten zum 75. Geburtstag* (ed. E. Neu and C. Ruster; Wiesbaden: Harrassowitz, 1988), 59–75; M. DIETRICH and O. LORETZ, "Der Vertrag zwischen Šuppiluliuma und Niqmandu: Eine philologische und kulturhistorische Studie," *WO* 3 (1964–1966): 206–45; F. C. FENSHAM, "Clauses of Protection in Hittite Vassal-Treaties and the Old Testament," *VT* 13 (1963): 133–43; J. B. GEYER, "Ezekiel 18 and a Hittite Treaty of Muršiliš II," *JSOT* 12 (1979): 31–46; O. R. GURNEY, "Schutz-und Loyalitätsverpflichtungen in hethitischen Staatsverträgen," in *Essays on Anatolian Archaeology* (ed. H. I. H. Prince Takahito Mikasa; BMECCJ 7; Wiesbaden: Otto Harrassowitz, 1993), 99–118; IDEM, "The Treaty with Ulmi-Tešub," *AnSt* 43 (1993): 13–28; F. IMPARATI, "A propos des témoins du traité avec Kurunta de Tartuntassa," in *Hittite and Other Anatolian and Near Eastern Studies in Honour of Sedat Alp* (ed. H. Otten et al; Ankara: Türk Tarih Kurumu, 1992), 305–22; V. KOROŠEC, *Hethitische Staatsverträge: Ein Beitrag zu ihrer juristischen Wertung* (Leipziger rechtswissenschaftliche Studien 60; Leipzig: T. Weicher, 1931); IDEM, "Über den nichtparitätischen Charakter des Šunaššura-Vertrages (KBo I, 5)," in *Vorträge gehalten auf der 28. Rencontre assyriologique internationale* (ed. H. Hunger and H. Hirsch; AfOB 19; RAI 28; Horn, Austria: F. Berger, 1982), 168–72; C. KÜHNE and H. OTTEN, *Der Šaušgamuwa-Vertrag. Eine Untersuchung zu Sprache und Graphik* (StBoT 16; Wiesbaden: Harrassowitz, 1971); MCCARTHY, *Treaty and Covenant*; N. NA'AMAN, "The Historical Introduction of the Aleppo Treaty Reconsidered," *JCS* 32 (1980): 34–42; H. OTTEN, *Die 1986 in Boğazköy gefundene Bronzetafel: Zwei Vorträge* (Innsbrucker Beiträge zur Sprachwissenschaft, Vorträge und kleinere Schriften 42; Innsbruck: Institut für Sprachwissenschaft der Universität Innsbruck, 1989); A. RAINEY and Z. COCHAVI-RAINEY, "Comparative Grammatical Notes on the Treaty between Ramses II and Hattusili III," in *Studies in Egyptology Presented to Miriam Lichtheim* (2 vols; ed. S. Israelit-Groll; Jerusalem: Magnes Press, 1990), 2:796–823; M. B. ROWTON, "The Background of the Treaty between Ramses II and Ḥattušiliš III," *JCS* 13 (1959): 1–7; I. SINGER, "The Kuruštama Treaty Revisited," in *Šarnikzel: Hethitologische Studien zum Gedankenan Emil Orgetorix Forrer* (ed. D. Groddek and S. Röile; Dresden: Technische Universität, 2004), 591–607; IDEM, "The 'Land of Amurru' and the 'Lands of Amurru' in the Šaušgamuwa Treaty," *Iraq* 53 (1991): 69–74; A. SPALINGER, "Considerations on the Hittite Treaty between Egypt and Hatti," *SAK* 9 (1981): 299–358; D. SÜRENHAGEN, *Paritätische Staatsverträge aus hethitischer Sicht* (Pavia, Italy: Gianni Iuculano Editore, 1985).

Hittite Military Oaths. Military conscripts of the Hittite army took solemn oaths to support the king and his regime. The oaths were administered by diviners, whose work was aided by consulting prescriptive texts (see *CTH* 427) that provided both the oaths to be recited and the rituals that were to be performed. The rituals symbolized the divine punishments that would result from infractions of the oath and illustrate for modern readers the kinds of treaty ritual used elsewhere in the ancient Near East.

Text and translation: N. OETTINGER, *Die militärischen Eide der Hethiter* (StBoT 22; Wiesbaden: Harrassowitz, 1976). *Translations: ANET* 353–54; *COS* 1.66–67: 165–68.

The Neo-Assyrian Treaties and Loyalty Oaths. Although the Assyrians seem to have utilized treaty forms much earlier, our oldest exemplars are Neo-Assyrian and were composed in the ninth century B.C.E. The genre continued in use until the end of the Neo-Assyrian period (seventh century B.C.E.). There is some variation in the format of our fourteen Neo-Assyrian exemplars, but they share fundamental similarities with each other and with other Near Eastern treaties. Two text types belong to this Assyrian generic family: the treaties and the loyalty oaths. Loyalty oaths were established between the royal family and Assyrian citizens. The most famous examples are the loyalty oaths of Esarhaddon, which he enacted to support the succession of his son, Assurbanipal, to the throne. Before Esarhaddon's death, Assurbanipal's grandmother, Queen Zakutu, enacted a similar loyalty oath with the royal household and with the citizens of Assyria. Although we know from Assurbanipal's inscriptions that Esarhaddon enacted loyalty oaths with Assyrians on behalf of his son, the texts in our possession are his international treaty agreements with non-Assyrians, such as the vassal Median chieftains. From this, scholars have concluded that Esarhaddon contracted many treaties with both Assyrians and non-Assyrians and that, furthermore, the same basic genre could function as both a loyalty oath for Assyrians and as a vassal treaty for non-Assyrians.

Although the formal order of the elements in Assyrian treaties does not vary much, they contain great variation in whether and to what extent all of the elements are included. When the entire form is present, it yields the following treaty structure: (1) the *preamble* provides the names and titles of the kings participating in the treaty; (2) the *seal impression* is that belonging to the Assyrian king enacting the treaty; (3) the *list of divine witnesses* includes the treaty parties' deities, who serve as witnesses of the treaty oaths and enforcers of its curses; (4) the *oath/adjuration* calls vassals to the treaty oath, taking the form "Swear by the god . . . !"; (5) the *stipulations* specify the provisions imposed by the treaty, including payment of tribute, promise of military assistance, extradition of fugitives, commercial regulations, accepting Assur as god, and loyalty to the Assyrian king at all times; (6) the *violation clause* warns against changing the treaty text or transgressing its stipulations; (7) the *curses* enumerate the punishments for breaking the stipulations of the treaty; (8) the *colophon and date* confirm the date that the text was written and identify it as a treaty of the Assyrian king. In only one set of the treaties (Esarhaddon's vassal treaties) are all of the elements present, but with the exception of the seal impression, each feature can be found in at least one other treaty.

Several idiosyncrasies distinguish the Assyrian genre from its ancient Near Eastern counterparts. First, the historical prologues and blessing lists so common in the Hittite treaties are generally absent from the Assyrian documents. This distinction probably stems from the differing strategies adopted by the two empires to secure covenant fidelity. Among the Hittites, it was hoped that the vassal's gratitude and faithfulness might be secured by the king's acts of kindness toward him. The treaty's historical prologue therefore enumerated these acts of friendship and the blessing list promised benefits to faithful vassals. In contrast, the primary motivation for vassal fidelity in the Assyrian documents was fear. Vassals were not promised blessings (although these may be implied), but they were warned instead that acts of infidelity would result in a curse from the gods and the wrath of the Assyrian army. This distinctive strategy gave rise to lengthy and gruesome curse lists in the Assyrian texts. A second peculiarity of the Assyrian treaties is their emphasis on the internal disposition of the vassal. When Esarhaddon commanded that a loyalty oath be recited, he prescribed not only the content of the oath but also its sincerity: "While you stand on the place of this oath, you shall not swear the oath with your lips only but shall swear it *wholeheartedly;* you shall teach it to your sons to be born after this treaty; you shall not feign incurable illness but take part in this treaty of Esarhaddon, king of Assyria, concerning Assurbanipal, the great crown prince designate. In the future and forever Aššur will be your god, and Assurbanipal, the great crown prince designate, will be your lord. May your sons and your grandsons fear him" (Parpola/Watanabe, italics added). As this illustrates, the Assyrians aimed not only at proper behavior among vassals but also at the higher objective of genuine loyalty. Although this theme of wholehearted devotion appears in some other Near Eastern treaties, particularly the Sefire treaties, it is most prominent in those from Neo-Assyria.

In modern times, biblical scholars have paid close attention to the striking similarities between these Neo-Assyrian treaties and the book of Deuteronomy. These similarities include not only structure and important themes—such as wholehearted fidelity—but also word-for-word parallels in the curse sections of the two sources, which in Deuteronomy reflect the order of the Neo-Assyrian pantheon (see Frankena; Otto 1996, 1999; Steymans; Weinfeld 1972). If the treaty edition of Deuteronomy dates to the time of Josiah, as many scholars suppose, then the author would have had easy access to Neo-Assyrian treaties; one of them, written in Hebrew, was probably resting in the Jerusalem temple (Frankena). Without doubt, the purpose of Deuteronomy would have been to state in the strongest possible terms that Israel's suzerain was not the king of Assyria but rather Yahweh himself.

Texts and translations: PARPOLA and WATANABE, *Neo-Assyrian Treaties and Loyalty Oaths;* D. J. WISEMAN, *The Vassal-Treaties of Esarhaddon* (London: British School of Archaeology in Iraq, 1958). ***Translations:*** *ANET* 532–41. ***Bibliography:*** M. COGAN, *Imperialism and*

Religion: Assyria, Judah, and Israel in the Eighth and Seventh Centuries B.C.E. (Missoula, Mont.: Scholars Press, 1974); R. FRANKENA, "The Vassal-Treaties of Esarhaddon and the Dating of Deuteronomy," *OtSt* 14 (1965): 122–54; A. K. GRAYSON, "Akkadian Treaties of the Seventh Century B.C.," *JCS* 39 (1987): 127–60; MCCARTHY, *Treaty and Covenant;* N. NA'AMAN, "Forced Participation in Alliances in the Course of the Assyrian Campaigns to the West," in *Ah, Assyria . . . Studies in Assyrian History and Ancient Near Eastern Historiography Presented to Hayim Tadmor* (ed. M. Cogan and I. Eph'al; ScrHier 33; Jerusalem: Magnes Press, 1991), 80–98; E. OTTO, *Das Deuteronomium: Politische Theologie und Rechtsreform in Juda und Assyrien* (BZAW 284; New York: de Gruyter, 1999); IDEM, "Treueid und Gesetz: Die Ursprünge des Deuteronomiums im Horizont neuassyrischen Vertragsrechts," *ZABR* 2 (1996): 1–52; S. L. RICHTER, *The Deuteronomistic History and the Name Theology:* lĕšakkēn šĕmô šām *in the Bible and the Ancient Near East* (BZAW 318; Berlin: de Gruyter, 2002); H. U. STEYMANS, *Deuteronomium 28 und die adê zur Thronfolgeregelung Asarhaddons: Segen und Fluch im Alten Orient und in Israel* (OBO 145; Freiburg, Switz.: Universitätsverlag, 1995); M. WEINFELD, *Deuteronomy and the Deuteronomic School* (Oxford: Oxford University Press, 1972), 116–29; IDEM, "The Loyalty Oath in the Ancient Near East," *UF* 8 (1976): 392–93.

The Aramaic Treaties from Sefire. These inscriptions preserve the texts of three treaties concluded between a northern Syrian ruler of Arpad named Matî'el and a Mesopotamian ruler named Bir-Ga'yah of KTK. The Aramaic texts, named AIS I, II, and III, were inscribed on stone (AIS I and II on pyramid-shaped stelae and AIS III on a flat slab). Because of its fragmentary nature, it is not entirely clear whether AIS III is an Arpad-KTK treaty, but the evidence suggests that this is the correct conclusion. Although Matî'el of Arpad is known from other ancient documents, there has been considerable debate about the identity of Bir-Ga'yah and about the location of KTK. In recent years it has become fashionable to suggest that Bir-Ga'yah was none other than Aššur-nerari V of Assyria (754–745 B.C.E.), who also concluded a treaty with Matî'el (see Parpola/Watanabe, 8–13). This would answer many questions and make the Sefire treaties Arpad's version of that Neo-Assyrian treaty. AIS I is the most complete of the Sefire texts; AIS II and III are more fragmentary. Nonetheless, is appears that AIS I and II are closely related and should be considered variants of the same treaty, with one or the other being a later recension or edition of the treaty.

The basic structure of AIS I is as follows: (1) the *preamble* provides the names and titles of the kings participating in the treaty; (2) the *list of divine witnesses* includes the treaty parties' deities, who serve as witnesses of the treaty oaths and enforcers of its curses; (3) the *curses* enumerate the punishments for breaking the stipulations of the treaty; (4) the *curse rituals*, which illustrate the curses, are described and explained (see below); (5) the *statement of sacrality* identifies the treaty as one that the gods have concluded; (6) the *stipulations* specify the provisions imposed by the treaty, including general obedience to the suzerain, the promise of military assistance and loyalty, and faithfulness among the king's progeny (AIS III adds fugitive agreements); (7) the *blessings* spell out the rewards for faithfulness to the treaty; (8) the *violation clause* warns against changing the treaty text or transgressing its stipulations. This eightfold order deviates somewhat from the other Near Eastern treaties, but in most respects it mirrors them.

Among the most notable features in AIS is its concise description of treaty rituals and their meaning: "Just as this wax is burned by fire, so may Arpad be burned. . . . Just as this wax is burned by fire, so may Matiᶜel be burned by fire. . . . Just as this bow and these arrows are broken, so may ʾInurta and Hadad break the bow of Matiᶜel, and the bow of his nobles. . . . And just as a man of wax is blinded, so may Matiᶜel be blinded. . . . Just as this calf is cut in two, so may Matiᶜel be cut in two, and may his nobles be cut in two. . . . And just as this wax woman is taken and one strikes her on the face, so may the wives of Matiᶜel be taken" (AIS I A.36–42). This ritual symbolism is characteristic of the Neo-Assyrian treaties, particularly the butchered livestock, the broken bow, and the use of wax figures to threaten the king's harem (cf. Gen 15; Jer 34:12–20; 1 Sam 11:7; Judg 19:29–30). Rituals served not only as powerful illustrations of the curse-threat but also the more immediate function of "sympathetic magic," in which symbolic acts were thought to bring about the actual circumstance if the treaty were broken. It is for this reason that the treaty says of the wax figure of Matiᶜel, "It is his person."

As already mentioned, it appears that AIS I and II are so similar that one must be understood as a recension of the other. If we judge from changes in content, the likely order of development was AIS I, AIS II, then AIS III. The Sefire treaties provide ideal comparative materials for our study of the covenants and treaties in the Hebrew Bible. They are written in a West Semitic tongue (Aramaic) that is similar to Hebrew and stem from a cultural milieu and time frame that is much closer to Israel than the Mesopotamian and Hittite exemplars. Note that the treaty stelae in AIS are called *bty ʾlhyʾ*, literally, "houses of the gods." These are comparable to the stelae upon which the books of the law were to be displayed (Deut 27:1–8) and also to the incident in Gen 28 where Jacob anoints a sacred stone: "and this stone, which I have set up for a pillar, shall be God's house [*bt ʾl*]."

Texts and translations: J. A. FITZMEYER, *The Aramaic Inscriptions of Sefire* (BibOr 19; Rome: Pontifical Biblical Institute, 1967; rev. ed., BibOr 19/A; Editrice Pontificio Istituto Biblico, 1995); KAI #222–24. *Translations:* ANET 659–61; COS 2.82: 213–17). *Bibliography:* McCARTHY, *Treaty and Covenant;* SPARKS, *Ethnicity and Identity in Ancient Israel,* 154–55.

Near Eastern Royal Grants. In addition to the treaty form, several covenants in the Hebrew Bible have been compared to the ancient Near Eastern genre of the royal grant, in which a benevolent king bestowed property, promises, and blessings upon his loyal servants and their descendants. Many of the texts in this corpus are Neo-Assyrian, but we possess others as well (e.g, from Middle Bronze Alalakh; see Wiseman). Parallels from the Bible would include the covenant promises bestowed upon Abraham in Genesis (the Abrahamic covenant) and those given to King David in 2 Sam 7 (the Davidic covenant). Scholars continue to debate, however, the extent to which these biblical covenants reflect a direct dependence on the royal grant genre.

Texts and translations: L. KATAJA and R. WHITING, *Grants, Decrees, and Gifts of the Neo-Assyrian Period* (SAA 12; Helsinki: Helsinki University Press, 1995); D. J. WISEMAN, *The Alalakh Texts* (OPBIAA 2; London: British Institute of Archaeology at Ankara, 1953), 33–34, 125–29. *Translation:* COS 2.136–137: 368–70. **Bibliography:** G. N. KNOPPERS, "Ancient Near Eastern Royal Grants and the Davidic Covenant: A Parallel?" *JAOS* 116 (1996): 670–97; S. E. LOEWENSTAMM, "The Divine Grants of Land to the Patriarchs," *JAOS* 91 (1971): 509–10; J. N. POSTGATE, *Neo-Assyrian Royal Grants and Decrees* (Rome: Pontifical Biblical Institute, 1969); M. WEINFELD, "The Covenant of Grant in the Old Testament and the Ancient Near East," *JAOS* 90 (1970): 184–203; IDEM, "Covenant Terminology in the Ancient Near East and Its Influence on the West," 194–96; IDEM, "The Davidic Covenant," *IDBSup* 189; IDEM, *The Promise of the Land: The Inheritance of the Land of Canaan by the Israelites* (Taubman Lectures in Jewish Studies 3; Berkeley: University of California Press, 1993).

Concluding Observations

Numerous texts in the Hebrew Bible either describe treaties or reflect the treaty/covenant genre. Important examples include Exod 19–24 (the Decalogue and the Sinai pericope), Gen 21:22–34 (Abraham's covenant with Abimelech), Gen 26:26–31 (Isaac's covenant with Abimelech), Gen 31 (Jacob's covenant with Laban), Josh 24 (the covenant renewal at Shechem), and Jer 34:12–20 (Judah's covenant renewal). Nevertheless, no biblical book seems so closely linked to the treaty genre as Deuteronomy. The following features in Deuteronomy have parallels in the Near Eastern treaties:

1. the structure: a historical prologue (Deut 1–11), stipulations (Deut 12–26), blessings, curses, ratification rituals (Deut 27–28), an epilogue (Deut 29–30), witnesses, and provisions for the deposit and public reading of the text (27:1–8; 31:9–13, 26; cf. 10:1–5)

2. the historical prologue and blessing formulas (cf. Hittite treaties)

3. clauses that stipulate the deposit and reading of the document (cf. Hittite treaties)

4. the focus on affection between the treaty participants (cf. Neo-Assyrian treaties)

5. the long and detailed curse list (cf. Neo-Assyrian treaties; Sefire treaties)

6. the text deposited in the temple (cf. the standard treaty pattern)

As we have noted, the similarities between Deuteronomy and the Neo-Assyrian treaties are particularly close, including very specific features in the order and phrases of the curses in Deuteronomy. This demands an explanation.

There is a strong consensus among biblical scholars that the "book of the law" discovered in the temple during the seventh-century reign of King Josiah of Judah was a version of the book of Deuteronomy (2 Kgs 22–23). This conclusion is based upon three points: Deuteronomy calls itself the "book of the law"; Josiah's actions after reading the document parallel exactly the commands of Deuteronomy; and the prophet Jeremiah, living during approximately the same period, cites only laws from the book of Deuteronomy in his preaching about Torah obedience (see Davidson; Holladay, 1:1–10; Hyatt; Weinfeld 1972, 140–46). The appearance of Deuteronomy in the form of a treaty at this historical juncture cannot be a coincidence. Up until the reign of Josiah, Judah had been a vassal state of the Neo-Assyrian Empire. Both the Assyrian Annals and the Bible itself mention that Josiah's grandfather, Manasseh, had sworn an oath of loyalty to Assyria (ANET 294–95; 2 Chron 33:11), and we should assume that a copy of this treaty—probably in Hebrew—would have been resting in the Jerusalem temple at the time of Josiah. The publication of Deuteronomy in the form of a Neo-Assyrian treaty and the pious ruse of depositing this new text in the temple would have been an effective way of making the religious point that Judah's covenant relationship with Yahweh was older and more important than its treaty with Assyria. Thus the treaty form of the book of Deuteronomy is best understood as polemic against Neo-Assyrian oppression.

On the other hand, Deuteronomy has several elements distinguishing it from the Near Eastern treaties. Its historical prologue is much longer than even the longest in the Hittite treaties, and its content serves not merely to induce feelings of Israelite gratitude (as in the Near Eastern treaties) but also to recount Israel's deeds of rebellion. Deuteronomy's paraenesis is much more pronounced than in the Near Eastern treaties and takes the form of three hortatory speeches given by Moses before his death (Deut 1:1–4:43; 4:44–28:68; 29:1–30:20). This speech form, which inspired the "ethical wills" of medieval Judaism, is characteristic of neither laws nor treaties and has been variously identified as priestly sermon, prophetic oracle, or wisdom teaching. The fact that these speeches were delivered at the end of Moses' life corresponds to the Neo-Assyrian loyalty oaths, which were also administered upon the death of the king.

Another distinctive feature of Deuteronomy in comparison with Near Eastern treaties is the breadth of its thematic concern. Its stipulations include not only a wide range of legal traditions (scholastic, substantive, economic, etc.) but also religious, ceremonial, and ritual statutes. Much of this distinctiveness stems, no doubt, from Deuteronomy's chief departures from the treaty genre: it originated as a lawbook, and insofar as it became an Israelite treaty, Israel's suzerain was a God. This reminds us that Deuteronomy is not a treaty per se so much as a religious lawbook that has been cast in treaty form. Whereas the Near Eastern treaties were essentially archival texts serving a role in international law, Deuteronomy was a canonical text that was preserved and transmitted by Israelite religious tradition for many years.

Because of the conceptual influence of covenant/treaty ideas on Israelite theology, the nation's military, social, and agricultural difficulties were often interpreted as "curses" sent by Yahweh because of Israel's covenant infidelity. The prophets Hosea and Jeremiah are best known for this feature (esp. Jer 2; Hos 4; see Huffmon; Sparks, 146–58), but it also appears in other prophetic books. Jeremiah and Hosea combined their covenant emphasis with legal language, creating the so-called "covenant lawsuit," a metaphorical court in which Israel had been judged guilty of breaking its covenant with Yahweh. As a result, prophets like Jeremiah and Ezekiel found it necessary to postulate a New Covenant, which would secure once and for all Israel's relationship with Yahweh (see Jer chs. 31–32; Ezek ch. 34). This theological innovation was later radicalized in certain Jewish traditions, giving rise to the community at Qumran and to Christianity.

For an overview of the present state of biblical studies regarding treaty and covenant, see Mendenhall/Herion.

General Bibliography

P. BORDREUIL, *Une bibliothèque au sud de la ville* (Ras Shamra-Ougarit VIII; Paris: Éditions Recherche sur le Civilisations, 1991); J. P. BROWN, "Treaty and Loyalty-Oath," in *Israel and Hellas* (BZAW 231; Berlin: de Gruyter, 1995), 253–89; D. CHARPIN and F. JOANNÈS, *Marchands, diplomates, et empereurs: Études sur la civilisation mésopotamienne offertes à Paul Garelli* (Paris: Éditions Recherche sur les Civilisations, 1991); R. DAVIDSON, "Orthodoxy and the Prophetic Word: A Study of the Relationship of Jeremiah and Deuteronomy," *VT* 14 (1964): 407–16; V. DONBAZ, "Some Observations on the Treaty Documents of Qadesh," *IstMitt* 43 (1993): 27–37; M. HARAN, "The 'Covenant': Its Nature and Ceremonial Background," in *Tehillah le-Moshe: Biblical and Judaic Studies in Honor of Moshe Greenberg* (ed. M. Cogan et al; Winona Lake, Ind.: Eisenbrauns, 1997), 203–19; D. R. HILLERS, "Rite: Ceremonies of Law and Treaty in the Ancient Near East," in *Religion and Law: Biblical-Judaic and Islamic Perspectives* (ed. E. B. Firmage et al.; Winona Lake, Ind.: Eisenbrauns, 1990), 351–64; W. L. HOLLADAY, *Jeremiah* (2 vols.; Hermeneia; Philadelphia: Fortress, 1986–1989); H. B. HUFFMON, "The Covenant Lawsuit in the Prophets," *JBL* 78 (1959): 285–95; J. P. HYATT, "Jeremiah and Deuteronomy," *JNES* 1 (1942): 166; P. KALLUVEETTIL, *Declaration and Covenant: A Comprehensive Review of Covenant Formulae from the Old Testament and the Ancient Near East* (AnBib 88; Rome: Biblical Institute Press, 1982); M. KLINE, *Treaty of the Great King* (Grand Rapids: Eerdmans, 1963); F. B. KNUTSON, "Literary Genres in PRU VI," in *Ras Shamra Parallels II* (ed. L. R. Fisher; AnOr 50; Rome: Pontificium Institutum Biblicum, 1975), 180–94; B. LAFONT, "Relations internationales, alliances et diplomatie au temps des royaumes amorrites. Essai de synthèse," *Amurru* 2 (2001): 213–328; D. J. MCCARTHY, *Treaty and Covenant* (AnBib 21; Rome: Pontifical Biblical Institute, 1963; 2d ed.; AnBib 21a; Rome: Pontifical Biblical Institute, 1978); G. E. MENDENHALL, "Ancient Oriental and Biblical Law" and "Covenant Forms in Israelite Tradition," *BA* 17 (1954): 26–46, 50–76; IDEM, "The Conflict between Value Systems and Social Control," in *Unity and Diversity: Essays in the History, Literature, and Religion of the Ancient Near East* (ed. H. Goedicke and J. J. M. Roberts; Baltimore: Johns Hopkins University Press, 1975), 169–81; IDEM, "The Suzerainty Treaty Structure: Thirty Years Later," in *Religion and Law: Biblical-Judaic and Islamic Perspectives* (ed. E. B. Firmage et al.; Winona Lake, Ind.: Eisenbrauns, 1990), 85–100; G. E. MENDENHALL and G. A. HERION, "Covenant," *ABD* 1:1179–1202; W. L. MORAN, "The Ancient Near Eastern Background of the Love of God in Deuteronomy," *CBQ* 25 (1963): 77–87; S. PARPOLA and K. WATANABE, *Neo-Assyrian Treaties and Loyalty Oaths* (SAA 2; Helsinki: Helsinki University Press, 1988); K. L. SPARKS, *Ethnicity and Identity in Ancient Israel* (Winona Lake, Ind.: Eisenbrauns, 1998); M. WEINFELD, "The Common Heritage of Covenantal Traditions in the Ancient World," in *I trattati nel mondo antico: Forma, ideologia, funzione* (ed. O. Canfora et al; Rome: "L'ERMA" di Bretschneider, 1990), 175–91; IDEM, "Covenant Terminology in the Ancient Near East and Its Influence on the West," *JAOS* 93 (1973): 190–99; IDEM, *Deuteronomy and the Deuteronomic School* (Oxford: Oxford University Press, 1972); Z. ZEVIT, "A Phoenician Inscription and Biblical Covenant Theology," *IEJ* 27 (1977): 110–18.

CHAPTER FIFTEEN

Epigraphic Sources from Syria-Palestine and Its Environs

Introduction

The material outlined in this chapter provides an important supplement to the texts discussed in chapters 1–14. These epigraphic sources are invaluable for reconstructing the social and political history of ancient Israel and are essential to our understanding of the origins and development of the language and genres of the Hebrew Bible (see Rösel). The entries in this chapter are divided into two sections, one covering the native Hebrew inscriptions and the other the West Semitic inscriptions. Insofar as possible, each section is in chronological order. These entries, though important, represent only a fraction of the thousands of inscriptions from Israel's ancient milieu. Many closely related entries are found elsewhere in this volume.

Unfortunately, we cannot assume that all of these inscriptions are authentic. Modern forgeries are increasingly easy to produce and can often fool even very seasoned epigraphers. Even as I write, a forgery ring has just been uncovered in Israel, revealing that a number of the best-known inscriptions are almost certainly fakes (as many scholars had already suspected). As a result, the growing trend in scholarship is to regard unprovenanced inscriptions with suspicion. Where serious questions have been raised concerning the authenticity of any text, this is noted in the corresponding entry, which is marked with an asterisk (*) or a double asterisk (**). A single asterisk marks the inscriptions whose authenticity is in doubt, while the double asterisk marks those that are almost certainly forgeries, such as the Jerusalem Pomegranate, the Temple of the Lord Ostracon, and the Widow's Plea Ostracon. Texts that are obvious forgeries have not been included at all, such as the so-called Joash Inscription that recently surfaced in the antiquities market. For an overview of the issues regarding the authenticity of ancient inscriptions, see Rollston's articles on non-provenanced epigraphs.

15.1. Hebrew Inscriptions

The Gezer Calendar. Our oldest substantive Hebrew inscription (tenth–ninth century B.C.E.) is a little limestone tablet, a calendar that identifies the months of the year according to the agricultural activities that each included (e.g., "month of sowing"). The first two months are associated with the autumnal harvest, which probably reflects the Hebrew concept of an autumnal New Year. Some scholars view the calendar as a votive tablet, others as a school exercise tablet, and still others as an expression of basic agricultural wisdom. The last two options seem more probable and are perhaps compatible. A similar example of agricultural wisdom would be the so-called Sumerian Farmer's Almanac (see 2.1.3).

Texts and translations: KAI #182; SSI 1.1–4. Translations: COS 2.85: 222; ANET 320. **Bibliography:** N. AVIGAD, "Hebrew Epigraphic Sources," 21; O. BOROWSKI, *Agriculture in Iron Age Israel* (Boston: American Schools of Oriental Research, 2002), 31–44; CROSS and FREEDMAN, *Early Hebrew Orthography,* 45–47; D. C. HOPKINS, "Life on the Land: the Subsistence Struggles of Early Israel," *BA* 50 (1987): 178–91; J. B.-Z. SEGAL, "Yrch in the Gezer 'Calendar,'" *JSS* 7 (1962): 212–21; D. SIVAN, "The Gezer Calendar and Northwest Semitic Linguistics," *IEJ* 48 (1998): 101–5; W. WIRGIN, "The Calendar Tablet from Gezer," *ErIsr* 6 (1960): 9–12; I. M. YOUNG, "The Style of the Gezer Calendar and some 'Archaic Biblical Hebrew' Passages," *VT* 42 (1992): 362–75.

Lamed-PN Inscriptions. One of our oldest Hebrew (tenth century B.C.E.) inscriptions comes from the shoulder of a storage jar found at Tel ʿAmal (or Tel el-ʿAṣī just west of Beth Shean). It reads *lnmš,* meaning "[belonging] to Nimši." This is the earliest of many such inscriptions that use the formula l + PN (i.e., the Hebrew preposition *lamed* plus the personal name) to identify the owners of pottery and other items. We possess numerous exemplars dating from periods throughout Israel's history. Although many of these inscriptions were engraved into the hard surface of the pottery, we should note that some l + PN formulas appear on seal stamps or on impressions made by using them. In such cases the stamp was applied to the vessel before it was properly fired. Among these are the very important *lmlk* seal impressions ("[belonging] to the king"). Stamps could also be used to seal letters by impressing small lumps of clay onto a string tied around the papyrus document. The resulting impression is called a bulla (pl., bullae). The stamp seals, as well as the *lmlk* and bullae inscriptions, are discussed below.

Text and translation: HAE I.29–30. **Bibliography:** A. LEMAIRE, "A propos d'une inscription de Tel ʿAmal," *RB* 80 (1973): 559; S. LEVY and G. EDELSTEIN, "Cinq années de fouilles à Tel ʿAmal: Nir David," *RB* 79 (1972): 325–67.

The Pithoi from Kuntillet ʿAjrud. Eleven inscriptions from the ninth–eighth centuries B.C.E. were found in a ruined building at this site, an important crossroads in northeastern Sinai. Several of the texts were inscribed on two pithoi (large storage jars). Although the texts reflect epistolary forms, their content suggests that they are votive inscriptions that request or pronounce blessings from Yahweh. The first pithos (A) is an utterance of King Joash of Israel (ca. 802–787 B.C.E.) that blesses two men "by Yahweh of Samaria and his asherah." The second pithos (B) contains two blessings, one fragmentary and the other complete, that pronounce blessings "by Yahweh of Teman and his asherah." Our generic assessment of pithos B is complicated, however, by an abecedary (alphabetic text) that appears on the jar. The presence of an abecedary exercise and the brief formulaic nature of the epistolary inscription suggest that this is a student's scribal exercise, a judgment that is reinforced by other scribal exercises found at the site (see *HAE* I.47–66; for additional Hebrew scribal exercises, see *HAE* II/1.22–25). This has prompted some scholars to identify the ruined building as a scribal school and/or as a religious center (see Lemaire and Meshel, respectively). At any rate, most scholars take the pithoi as evidence that some ancient Israelites believed in multiple manifestations of Yahweh (e.g, "of Samaria," "of Teman" [cf. Hab 3:3: "God came from Teman, the Holy One from Mount Paran"]) and that the goddess Asherah was the consort of Yahweh (just as she was the consort of El at Ugarit). Regarding Asherah, there are various pictographic images on pithos A, one or more of which may depict the goddess. These include two bovine figures (perhaps Yahweh and Asherah), a seated lyre player (perhaps Asherah), and a stylized tree flanked by ibexes (perhaps a representation of Asherah). The early Canaanite inscription on the thirteenth-century B.C.E. Lachish Ewer (a type of pitcher with a handle) is an important source to consider for interpreting Asherah in the Kuntillet ʿAjrud evidence (see Hestrin 1991). Asherah is mentioned in the Hebrew Bible about forty times, in some cases appearing as a goddess and in others as a cult pole (cf. Deut 16:21; Judg 6:25; 1 Kgs 15:13; 1 Kgs 18:19). Pithos B also includes pictographic images, in this case, of a cow, of an archer, and of supplicants with their hands lifted into the air.

Texts and translations of pithos A: *HAE* I.59–61; DEVER, "Asherah, Consort of Yahweh?"; LINDENBERGER, *Ancient Aramaic and Hebrew Letters,* 136. *Translation of pithos A:* COS 2.47A: 171. *Texts and translations of pithos B:* *HAE* I.62–64; DEVER, "Asherah, Consort of Yahweh?" (partial). *Translation of pithos B:* COS 2.47B: 171–72. *Bibliography:* J. A. EMERTON, "New Light on Israelite Religion: The Implications of the Inscriptions from Kuntillet Ajrud," *ZAW* 94 (1982): 2–20; J. M. HADLEY, *The Cult of Asherah in Ancient Israel and Judah: Evidence for a Hebrew Goddess* (Cambridge: Cambridge University Press, 2000); R. HESTRIN, "The Lachish Ewer and the ʾAsherah," *IEJ* 37 (1987): 212–23; IDEM, "Understanding Asherah: Exploring Semitic Iconography," *BAR* 17, no. 5 (1991): 50–59; R. KLETTER, "Asherah and the Judean Pillar Figurines Engendered," in *Sex and Gender in the Ancient Near East* (2 vols.; ed. S. Parpola and R. M. Whiting; RAI 47; Helsinki: Neo-Assyrian Text Corpus Project, 2002), 1:289–300; A. LEMAIRE, *Les écoles et la formation de la Bible dans l'ancien Israël* (OBO 39; Göttingen: Vandenhoeck & Ruprecht, 1981), 25–32; W. A. MAIER III, *Asherah: Extrabiblical Evidence* (HSM 37; Atlanta: Scholars Press, 1986); B. MARGALIT, "The Meaning and Significance of Asherah," *VT* 40 (1990): 264–97; Z. MESHEL, "Did Yahweh Have a Consort?" *BAR* 5, no. 2 (1979): 24–35; S. OLYAN, *Asherah and the Cult of Yahweh in Israel* (SBLMS 3; Atlanta: Scholars Press, 1988); M. S. SMITH, *The Early History of God* (San Francisco: Harper, 1990), 89–114; V. WILSON, "The Iconography of Bes with Particular Reference to the Cypriot Evidence," *Journal of the British School of*

Archaeology in Jerusalem 7 (1975): 77–103. See also the bibliographies for the plaster inscriptions from Kuntillet ʿAjrud and the mortuary inscriptions from Khirbet el-Qôm.

The Plaster Inscriptions from Kuntillet ʿAjrud. Three plaster inscriptions were discovered at this site, the first illegible and the other two fragmentary. Inscription 2 contains a votive text similar to that on the Kuntillet ʿAjrud pithoi (apparently a blessing pronounced in the name of Yahweh of Teman). The very fragmented third inscription is a poetic text that describes the god El arriving for battle, that he "shone forth" and that "mountains melted and peaks grew weak." This is comparable to the introduction found in Moses' blessing upon the tribes in Deut 33:2 and to texts related to the motif of the divine warrior (Judg 5; Hab 3; Ps 97:5). Like the pithoi from this site, the date of the plaster inscriptions is the end of the ninth or beginning of the eighth century B.C.E.

Text and translation of inscription 2: HAE I.58. *Translation of inscription 2:* COS 2.47C: 172. *Text and translation of inscription 3:* HAE I.59. *Translation of inscription 3:* COS 2.47D: 173. *Bibliography:* Z. MESHEL, *A Religious Centre from the Time of the Judaean Monarchy on the Border of Sinai* (Jerusalem: Israel Museum, 1987); M. WEINFELD, "Kuntillet ʿAjrud Inscriptions and Their Significance," *SEL* 1 (1984): 121–30. See also the bibliographies for the pithoi from Kuntillet ʿAjrud and the mortuary inscriptions from Khirbet el-Qôm.

The Mortuary Inscriptions from Khirbet el-Qôm. Three eighth-century grave inscriptions were discovered at this site in the hills eight miles west of Hebron. The most important (no. 3) was inscribed on a pillar near one of the burial chambers. In it a certain "Uriyahu, the rich" claims that he was "blessed to Yahweh," who had saved him from his enemies "by his [Yahweh's] asherah." The text is inscribed around an inverted hand image incised in the rock. Although it is generally believed that the hand image was already there when the inscription was made (see *COS* 2.52), some scholars have suggested that the hand represents Yahweh's blessing and protection upon the dead (Spronk; Niehr).

Texts and translations: HAE I.199–211; Z. ZEVIT, "The Khirbet el-Qôm Inscription Mentioning a Goddess," *BASOR* 225 (1984): 39–47. *Translation:* COS 2.52: 179. *Bibliography:* A. LEMAIRE, "Les inscriptions de Khirbet el-Qôm et l'Ashérah de Yhwh," *RB* 84 (1977): 595–608; S. MITTMANN, "Das Symbol der Hand in her altorientalischen Ikonographie," in *La main de Dieu: Die Hand Gottes* (ed. R. Kieffer and J. Bergmann; Tübingen: Mohr Siebeck, 1994), 19–47; H. NIEHR, "The Changed Status of the Dead in Yehud"; K. SPONK, "Ideeën over de doden en het leven na de dood in het bijbelse Israel," *Phoenix* 42 (1996): 78–90. See also the bibliographies for the pithoi from Kuntillet ʿAjrud and the plaster inscriptions from Kuntillet ʿAjrud.

The Jerusalem Pomegranate.✱✱ Although this inscription was purchased by the Israel Museum for $550,000, new evidence suggests that it is almost certainly a forgery, as was long suspected by some scholars. The text is inscribed on a small ivory pomegranate and reads, "Belonging to the tem[ple of Yahw]eh, holy to the priests." Epigraphically, the text appears to be from the eighth century B.C.E. Although this inscription is probably not genuine, the pomegranate itself is very old—dating to the Late Bronze Period—and may have served as the headpiece for a scepter. The artifact reminds us of the decorative pomegranates mentioned in connection with the Israelite tabernacle (see Exod 28:33–34; 39:24–26) and Solomon's Temple (1 Kgs 7).

Text and translation: HAE I.192–93. *Translation:* COS 2.48: 173. *Bibliography:* N. AVIGAD, "The Inscribed Pomegranate from the 'House of the Lord,'" BA 53 (1990): 157–66; A. LEMAIRE, "Une inscription paléo-hébraïque sur grenade en ivoire," RB 88 (1981): 236–39; IDEM, "Probable Head of Priestly Scepter from Solomon's Temple Surfaces in Jerusalem," BAR 10, no. 1 (1984) 24–29.

A Stela Fragment from Samaria. This fragmentary inscription yields just one legible word, but because of the material used (part of a limestone stela) and the location of the text's discovery (the rubble of Samaria's east gate) scholars presume that it was a royal inscription. Though otherwise illegible, it provides evidence that Israelite kings—like their foreign counterparts—produced royal inscriptions. Additional evidence for this practice in ancient Israel may appear in 2 Sam 18:18, where Absalom erects a memorial stela in his own honor.

Text and translation: HAE I.135. *Bibliography:* HAE II/1.3.

The Samaria Ostraca. These ostraca come from two sites. The largest find was an administrative archive from the palace containing over one hundred eighth-century ostraca, including about sixty legible receipts for deliveries or disbursements of wine and oil. These records clearly concern central administration in the northern kingdom of Israel and may record taxes paid to the royal palace, but the latter is not certain. The texts are dated and include the names of those involved in the transactions as well as the administrative districts in which they lived. In many cases these districts match precisely the male and female progeny in Manassah's genealogies from Num 26:29–34 and Josh 17:1–3, suggesting that the biblical genealogies provide the eponyms for districts in the region. It is possible that the ostraca were not permanent records but instead temporary "scratch pad" notes that were discarded after their contents were added to a papyrus ledger. Eleven other ostraca were found at a site just east of the city. The Hebrew dialect of the texts reflects their northern provenance.

Texts and translations: HAE I.79–110, 135–44; KAI #183–88 (partial); SSI 1.5–15 (partial). *Translation:* ANET 321 (partial). *Bibliography:* AVIGAD, "Hebrew Epigraphic Sources," 26–32; F. M. CROSS JR., *Leaves from an Epigrapher's Notebook: Collected Papers in Hebrew and West Semitic Epigraphy* (HSS 51; Winona Lake, Ind.: Eisenbrauns, 2003); CROSS and FREEDMAN, *Early Hebrew Orthography,* 48–49; N. NA'AMAN, *Borders and Districts in Biblical Historiography* (Jerusalem Biblical Studies 4; Jerusalem: Simor, 1986); A. F. RAINEY, "The Samaria Ostraca in the Light of Fresh Evidence," PEQ 99 (1967): 32–41; IDEM, "The *Sitz im Leben* of the Samaria Ostraca," TA 6 (1979): 91–94. For additional bibliography on the large corpus, see the individual entries in HAE.

The Nimrud Ivories. These three inscribed ivory fragments were discovered in the Neo-Assyrian city of Kalḫu. The best explanation for Hebrew inscriptions so far removed from Palestine is that these were part of the plunder seized by Shalmaneser V when he took control of Samaria in 722 B.C.E. The ivories likely were votive plaques originally placed in an Israelite temple, as is suggested by the curse formula on Nimrud 1, which was presumably intended for anyone who might damage or remove the inscription. The other two texts are *lamed*-PN inscriptions (i.e., "belonging to [personal name]").

Texts and translations: HAE I.129–132; A. R. Millard, "Alphabetic Inscriptions on Ivories from Nimrud," *Iraq* 24 (1962): 41–51. *Translation: COS* 2.88: 224 (partial). ***Bibliography:*** A. LEMAIRE, "Notes sur quelques inscriptions sur ivoire provenant de Nimrud," *Semitica* 26 (1976): 66–70.

The Susa Alabaster Inscriptions. Two small alabaster containers were found in the Persian city of Susa, each inscribed with units of liquid measure that are also used in the Hebrew Bible (e.g., "One hin and a half log and a quarter log"). The inscriptions date to the end of the eighth century but were found in the destruction level left by Assurbanipal when he leveled Susa during the seventh century. It is not clear how the pieces came to be in Susa. Perhaps they were seized by Assyrians when the northern kingdom fell and then found their way to Persia, or perhaps they were brought there by Israelite conscripts in Assurbanipal's army, or perhaps they were manufactured by Israelites exiled to the region.

Text and translation: HAE I.240–41. ***Bibliography:*** C. CLERMONT-GANNEAU, "Note sur deux alabastra israélites archaïques découvertes à Suse (mission de Moran)," *CRAI* (1906): 237–48; M. A. POWELL, "Weights and Measures," *ABD* 6:897–908; IDEM, "Weights and Measures," *OEANE* 5:339–42.

The Creator of the Earth Ostracon. This brief text was inscribed upon the shoulder of a storage jar found in Jerusalem in 1971. It dates to the late eighth century B.C.E. and includes several personal names and what may be a reference to the "creator of the earth."

Text and translation: HAE I.197–98. *Translation: COS* 2.49: 174. ***Bibliography:*** P. D. MILLER JR., "El, Creator of the Earth," *BASOR* 239 (1980): 43–46.

The Royal Steward Burial Inscription. This inscription from the late eighth century B.C.E. was found in an impressive burial chamber on the eastern side of the Kidron Valley. The text is damaged, but the restored reading suggests that it may be the tomb of Shebna, Hezekiah's royal steward, who was criticized by Isaiah for his extravagant burial preparations (see Isa 22:15–19).

Text, translation, and discussion: N. AVIGAD, "The Epitaph of a Royal Steward from Siloam Village," *IEJ* 3 (1953): 137–52. *Translation: COS* 2.54: 180. ***Bibliography:*** R. M. GOOD, "The Israelite Royal Steward in the Light of Ugaritic *'l bt*," *RB* 36 (1979): 580–82.

The lmlk *Seals.* Our corpus of Hebrew seals includes the actual seals as well as seal impressions on bullae and on pottery. Here our interest is the nearly two thousand jar handles that carry *lmlk* impressions ("belonging to the king") that were produced when stamp seals were applied to clay storage jars before they were fired. These have been discovered at numerous sites, with the largest collections coming from Lachish, Jerusalem, Ramat Rahel, Gibeon, and Mizpah. The Lachish exemplars were found in destruction layers associated with Sennacherib's attack in 701 B.C.E., and it is now almost certain that the *lmlk* impressions are associated with the Judean king who reigned at the time, Hezekiah. This conclusion is reinforced by evidence from other sites and by the presence of scarab figures on the jar seals that are similar to the scarabs on Hezekiah's personal stamp seals (if these are genuine; see below, "Hebrew Bullae from Jerusalem"). The jars bearing the seals were for storing liquids, most likely wine, and it is believed that they were distributed about the country as Hezekiah prepared for an eventual attack from Sennacherib. The royal stamps on the jars refer to four different cities (Hebron, Ziph, Sokoh, Mamshit) that probably correspond to Hezekiah's administrative centers or to the regions from which the wine came. Some of the *lmlk* jars also bear a private seal impression, a matter of considerable discussion (see Avigad and Sass). All of the royal jars were apparently manufactured at the same site (somewhere in the Judean Shephelah), and only twenty seals seem to account for the many impressions (see Mommsen, Perlman, and Yellin; *COS* 2.77: 202–3). Related biblical texts include: 1 Sam 8:14–15; 1 Chron 4:23; 27:25–31; 2 Chron 31:4–20.

Texts and translations: AVIGAD and SASS, *Corpus of West Semitic Stamp Seals; HAE* II/2 (forthcoming). *Bibliography: COS* 2.77: 202–3; A. LEMAIRE, "Classification des estampilles royales judéennes," *ErIsr* 15 (1981): 54–60; H. MOMMSEN, I. PERLMAN, and J. YELLIN, "The Provenience of the LMLK Jars," *IEJ* 34 (1984): 89–113; N. NA'AMAN, "Hezekiah's Fortified Cities and the LMLK Stamps," *BASOR* 261 (1986): 5–21; IDEM, "Sennacherib's Campaign to Judah and the Date of the LMLK Stamps," *VT* 29 (1979): 61–86; D. USSISHKIN, "The Assyrian Attack on Lachish: The Archaeological Evidence from the Southwest Corner of the Site," *TA* 17 (1990): 53–86; IDEM, "The Destruction of Lachish by Sennacherib and the Dating of the Royal Judean Storage Jars," *TA* 4 (1977): 28–60; IDEM, "Royal Judean Storage Jars and Private Seal Impressions," *BASOR* 223 (1976): 1–13; A. G. VAUGHN, "Palaeographic Dating of Judean Seals and Its Significance for Biblical Reseach," *BASOR* 313 (1999): 43–64; IDEM, *Theology, History, and Archaeology in the Chronicler's Account of Hezekiah* (SBLABS 4; Atlanta: Scholars Press, 1999).

Siloam Tunnel Inscription. According to biblical sources, King Hezekiah of Judah commissioned workers in Jerusalem to bore a tunnel that would bring water from the Gihon spring to the pool of Siloam (2 Kgs 20:20; 2 Chron 32:2–8). The purpose of this work was to provide a secure water supply in the event of an Assyrian siege. The Hebrew inscription commemorates the successful completion of the task by providing a brief description of how the nearly 550–meter tunnel was built. If the tunnel is indeed that of Hezekiah—as most scholars presume—then the inscription would date to about 701 B.C.E. (see Frumkin,

Shimron, and Rosenbaum). This would also make it the earliest use of *matres lectionis* in Hebrew (e.g., ʾārûr ["cursed"] is spelled ʾrwr rather than ʾrr, where w marks the *u* vowel).

Texts and translations: KAI #189; *HAE* I.178–89; *SSI* 1.21–23. *Translations: COS* 2.28: 145–46; *ANET* 321. *Bibliography:* Z. ABELLS and A. ARBIT, "Some New Thoughts on Jerusalem's Ancient Water Systems," *PEQ* 127 (1995): 2–7; CROSS and FREEDMAN, *Early Hebrew Orthography*, 49–51; A. FRUMKIN, A. SHIMRON, and J. ROSENBAUM, "Radiometric Dating of the Siloam Tunnel, Jerusalem," *Nature* 425 (Sept 2003): 169–71; D. GILL, "How They Met," *BAR* 20, no. 4 (1994): 20–33; J. A. HACKETT et al., "Defusing Pseudo-scholarship: The Siloam Inscription Ain't Hasmonean," *BAR* 23, no. 2 (1997): 41–50, 68–69; PARKER, *Stories in Scripture and Inscriptions*, 36–42; J. W. ROGERSON and P. R. DAVIES, "Was the Siloam Tunnel Built by Hezekiah?" *BA* 59, no. 3 (1996): 138–49; V. SASSON, "The Siloam Tunnel Inscription," *PEQ* 114 (1982): 111–17; K. L. YOUNGER JR., "The Siloam Tunnel Inscription—an Integrated Reading," *UF* 26 (1994): 543–56.

The Census Ostracon from Tell ʿIra. In 1979, a small ostracon bearing a census inscription was discovered in the court of a building at Tel ʿIra (Ḥorvat el-Garra), just east of Beersheba. Paleographically and archaeologically, this Hebrew inscription appears to come from the first half of the 7th century B.C.E. The inscription is introduced with the rubric *mpqd brkyhw*, "Census of Berekyahu," and then follows with a list of three personal names. It has been suggested that the term *mpqd* might mean "muster" (Garfinkel), in which case the census has to do with military conscription rather than taxation. Regardless, this little text gives us some idea about how the ancients gathered census information. For related texts in the Hebrew Bible, see the census lists in the books of Numbers (chs. 1–4, 26), Ezra (chs. 2, 8), and Nehemiah (chs. 7, 11–12). Readers should also note the Ophel Ostracon (see below in this section), which is probably a census or registration list from the late 7th century.

Text and translation: HAE I.251–52. *Bibliography:* I. BEIT-ARIEH, "A First Temple Period Census Document," *PEQ* 115 (1983): 105–8; IDEM, *Tel ʿIra: A Stronghold in the Biblical Negev* (Tel Aviv: Institute of Archaeology, Tel Aviv University, 1999); Y. GARFINKEL, "The Meaning of the Word MPQD in the Tel ʿIra Ostracon," *PEQ* 119 (1987): 19–23; V. A. HUROWITZ, "How Were the Israelites Counted? Numbers 1:2 and the Like in Light of a New Ostracon from Tel ʿIra," *Beer-Sheva* 3 (1988): 53–62 [Hebrew].

Meṣad Ḥashavyahu Letter. This Hebrew letter, written on an ostracon, was one of seven inscriptions discovered in 1960 at the guardroom of a small fortress called Meṣad Ḥashavyahu (near Yavneh Yam, on the Judean coast between Joppa and Ashdod). In it a field worker asks the district governor to reverse a sentence imposed upon him by a lower official. The official had ordered that one of the worker's garments be confiscated, probably because the worker had failed to achieve his quota of grain (cf. Exod 22:25–26 [Eng. 22:26–27]; Deut 24:10–15, 17). In response the worker asserts his innocence and cites his fellow workers as witnesses to his claim. The text is an important source for the study of ancient Israelite law and for the study of Judah's administrative system. Most scholars date the letter to the seventh century B.C.E.

Texts and translations: HAE I.315–34 (all Meṣad Ḥashavyahu inscriptions); *KAI* #200; *SSI* 1.26–30; LINDENBERGER, *Ancient Aramaic and Hebrew Letters*, 109–10. *Translation: ANET* 568; *COS* 3:41: 77–78. *Bibliography:* AVIGAD, "Hebrew Epigraphic Sources," 32; CROSS, "Epigraphic Notes on Hebrew Documents of the Eighth–Sixth Centuries B.C.," 34–46; J. NAVEH, "A Hebrew Letter from the Seventh Century BC," *IEJ* 10 (1960): 129–39; IDEM, "Some Notes on Reading the Meṣad Ḥashavyahu Letter," *IEJ* 14 (1964): 158–59; D. PARDEE, "The Judicial Plea from Meṣad Ḥashavyahu (Yavneh-Yam): A New Philological Study," *Maarav* 1 (1978): 33–66; PARKER, *Stories in Scripture and Inscriptions*, 13–35.

The Wadi Murabba'at Papyrus. This text, discovered in a cave in Wadi Murabba'at (about ten miles south of Qumran near the Dead Sea), is our only Hebrew papyrus from preexilic times. In antiquity the caves in the region provided a safe haven for refugees. This explains the presence of a text in such a desolate area. Two texts are on the papyrus, one a fragmentary letter and the other an inventory list of some sort. The papyrus dates to the seventh century B.C.E.

Texts and translations: HAE I.283–86; *SSI* 1.31–32; P. BENOÎT, J. T. MILIK, R. DE VAUX et al., *Les grottes de Murabba'ât* (2 vols.; DJD 2; Oxford: Clarendon, 1961), 2.93–100. *Bibliography:* CROSS, "Epigraphic Notes on Hebrew Documents of the Eighth–Sixth Centuries B.C.," 34–42.

The Temple of the Lord Ostracon.★★ This text appears to be the archival record for a three-shekel silver contribution made by a certain king 'Ashyahu to the Jerusalem temple. Paleographically, the text appears to be from the late seventh century, suggesting that 'Ashyahu (a variant of the name Josiah) should be identified with king Josiah of Judah (640–609 B.C.E.). Questions about the authenticity of this text have been in the air for some time, and recent legal developments in the antiquities market are casting a yet darker shadow on its genuineness (Eph'al/Naveh; Rollston). If this text is a forgery, it is one of two famous ones from the private Shlomo Moussaieff collection.

Texts and translations: BORDREUIL, ISRAEL, and PARDEE, "Deux ostraca paléo-hébreux de la collection Sh. Moussaïeff"; LINDENBERGER, *Ancient Aramaic and Hebrew Letters,* 111. *Translation: COS* 2.50: 174–75. *Bibliography:* B. BECKING, "Does a Recently Published Paleo-Hebrew Inscription Refer to the Solomonic Temple?" *BN* 92 (1998): 5–11; I. EPH'AL and J. NAVEH, "Remarks on the Recently Published Moussieff Ostraca," *IEJ* 48 (1998): 269–73; ROLLSTON, "Non-provenanced Epigraphs."

The Widow's Plea Ostracon.★★ Like the Temple of Lord Ostracon treated in the previous entry, this one is from the private collection of Shlomo Moussaieff. It purports to be a widow's legal petition to a public official. She had no sons and so asked to receive the inheritance from her deceased husband, a claim that she based partially on previous oral conversations between the official in question and her deceased husband. She concludes her letter by reminding the official that he has already distributed her husband's wheat field to her brother-in-law. Obviously, if this text is not genuine, its verisimilitude is the product of a very imaginative forger. Although the text appears to date to the seventh century B.C.E., certain unusual epigraphic features, and its lack of provenance, have long cast doubt on its authenticity. It is instructive to compare the grave doubts that some scholars have about the text's authenticity (see Eph'al/Naveh; Rollston) with the confidence that some others have in its genuineness (see *COS*).

Texts and translations: BORDREUIL, ISRAEL, and PARDEE, "Deux ostraca paléo-hébreux de la collection Sh. Moussaïeff"; LINDENBERGER, *Ancient Aramaic and Hebrew Letters,* 110–11. *Translation: COS* 3.44: 86–87. *Bibliography:* A. BERLEJUNG and A. SCHÜLE, "Erwängungen zu den neuen Ostraka aus der Sammlung Moussaïeff," *ZAH* 11 (1998): 68–73; I. EPH'AL and J. NAVEH, "Remarks on the Recently Published Moussieff Ostraca," *IEJ* 48 (1998): 269–73; A. LAMAIRE, "Veuve sans enfants dans le royaume de Juda," *ZABR* 5 (1999): 1–14; B. LANG, "The Decalogue in the Light of a Newly Published Palaeo-Hebrew Inscription (Hebrew Ostracon Moussaieff No. 1)," *JSOT* 77 (1998): 21–25; ROLLSTON, "Non-provenanced Epigraphs."

The Ophel Ostracon. This late-seventh-century ostracon was discovered on the hill of Ophel, in the vicinity of the temple and palace area of Jerusalem. It is a census or registration list that mentions personal names by clan: "Jehizkiah son of the Partridge clan from the stock of Bukkiah," "Ahijah son of the Sorrel horse from the valley of Jeho(shaphat)," ". . .–iah son of the Gadfly clan from the valley of Jeho[shaphat]" (here following roughly Gibson's translation). Avigad has demonstrated, from a seal impression and from the biblical census lists (Numbers, Chronicles, Ezra, and Nehemiah), that Judeans sometimes expressed their family identity through the names and images of various insects, animals, plants, and so on, an ancient equivalent of "family crests." Although this might suggest that our ostracon coheres nicely with other biblical and epigraphic evidence, not all scholars are so convinced by this reading of the text. For instance, in *COS* 3.86 Younger is content to read "son of Qōr'ēh" rather than "son of Partridge."

Texts and translations: KAI #190; *HAE* I.310–11; *SSI* 1.25–26. *Translation: COS* 3.86: 203–4. *Bibliography:* N. AVIGAD, "A Hebrew Seal with a Family Emblem," *IEJ* 16 (1966): 50–53; R. HESTRIN, *Inscriptions Reveal: Documents from the Time of the Bible, the Mishna, and the Talmud* (Jerusalem: Israel Museum, 1973).

Hebrew Seals and Bullae from Jerusalem and Elsewhere.★ Papyrus letters and documents were often sealed by impressing lumps of clay with a stamp that bore the owner's name (as mentioned earlier, the stamp impression is called a bulla).We are fortunate to have recovered many such seals and bullae, the largest troves coming from Jerusalem. One important source of these artifacts was a hoard of more than fifty bullae from a private household archive in the city of David; this is particularly fascinating because it attests to the existence of many Hebrew documents now lost to us. Our other major source of bullae is the antiquities market. Unfortunately, these unprovenanced exemplars include not only

genuine articles but also modern forgeries, as is probably the case with the famous bulla that purportedly belonged to Jeremiah's scribe, Baruch (see Fox;
Joffee; Rollston 2003; 2004; Sass 1993). Some of the unprovenanced seals bear the
names of biblical figures, such as kings Ahaz and Hezekiah of Judah. The only
provenanced bulla that may bear the name of a biblical character is no. 405 in
Avigad/Sass, a bulla found at Lachish that reads, "Belonging to Gedalyahu, who is
over the House." This may have been the Gedaliah whom the Babylonians placed
in charge of Jerusalem after the fall of the city (2 Kgs 25:22).

The total corpus of seals and seal impressions from Israel and its ancient
environs is now quite large (see Avigad/Sass). Although most of our samples appear to come from Jerusalem during the late Judean monarchy, some of them
come from the eighth century and from other sites in Israel, among them an authentic seal from Megiddo that belonged to a servant of Jeroboam II, king of the
northern kingdom from 784 to 748 B.C.E. A few of the seals belonged to women
(13 out of more than 700 in Avigad/Sass), and many belonged to men without
formal titles (e.g., "Belonging to Malkiyahu son of Shallum"). At present, the
great need is to submit all of these finds to epigraphic study and laboratory testing so that their authenticity—or inauthenticity—can be more confidently
established (see Rollston 2003; 2004).

Texts and translations: HAE II/2 (forthcoming); N. AVIGAD, *Hebrew Bullae from the Time
of Jeremiah: Remnants of a Burnt Archive* (Jerusalem: Israel Exploration Society, 1986);
AVIGAD and SASS, *Corpus of West Semitic Stamp Seals;* R. DEUTSCH, *Biblical Period Personal Seals in the Shlomo Moussaieff Collection* (Tel Aviv: Archaeological Center Publication, 2000); IDEM, *Messages from the Past: Hebrew Bullae from the Time of Isaiah through the
Destruction of the First Temple* (Tel Aviv: Archaeological Center Publication, 1999);
DEUTSCH and HELTZER, *Forty New Ancient West Semitic Inscriptions.* **Translation:** *COS*
2.70: 197–201 (partial). **Bibliography:** R. DEUTSCH, "Lasting Impressions: New Bullae Reveal Egyptian-Style Emblems on Judah's Royal Seals," *BAR* 28, no. 4 (2002): 42–51, 60–62;
N. S. FOX, *In the Service of the King: Officialdom in Ancient Israel and Judah* (Cincinnati:
Hebrew Union College, 2000), 23–32; L. G. HERR, "The Palaeography of West Semitic
Stamp Seals," *BASOR* 312 (1998): 45–77; A. H. JOFFEE, review of R. Deutsch, *Messages from
the Past: Hebrew Bullae from the Time of Isaiah through the Destruction of the First Temple,*
and R. Deutsch, *Biblical Period Personal Seals in the Shlomo Moussaieff Collection, JNES* 62
(2003): 119–25; B. SASS, "The Pre-exilic Hebrew Seals: Iconism vs. Aniconism," in *Studies
in the Iconography of Northwest Semitic Inscribed Seals* (ed. B. Sass and C. Uehlinger; OBO
125; Freiburg, Switz.: University Press, 1993), 194–256; A. G. VAUGHN, "Palaeographic
Dating of Judaean Seals," *BASOR* 313 (1999): 43–64.

The Arad Ostraca. More than one hundred ostraca, dating from the ninth to the
sixth centuries and found at Arad, reflect various stages of archival bookkeeping
at the citadel. An additional archive of eighty-five ostraca recording barley deliveries has been dated to the Persian period. Among the sixth-century texts are letters or orders to a certain Elyashib regarding dispersals of wine, bread, and oil
from storehouses to the citadel and to others. Some of these dispersals were perhaps to Greek mercenaries (e.g., Kittim in Arad 1), and some perhaps to a class of

temple servants known as the Qerosites (Arad 18; cf. Ezra 2:44; Neh 7:47). One of the seventh-century inscriptions seems to announce the coronation of a new king in Judah (Arad 88), and there are references to commands from the king and to the Jerusalem temple (Arad 18; 24). This illustrates the level of centralization in late-kingdom Judah. The archive indicates that Judah had ongoing trouble with the Edomites during the seventh and early sixth centuries (Arad 24; 40).

Texts and translations: HAE I.40–47, 67–74, 111–21, 145–64, 290–306, 347–403, 441; *SSI* 49–56 (partial); LINDENBERGER, *Ancient Aramaic and Hebrew Letters,* 113–24 (partial). **Translation:** *ANET* 568–69; *COS* 3.43: 81–85 (partial). **Bibliography:** AVIGAD, "Hebrew Epigraphic Sources," 29–30; D. PARDEE, "Letters from Tel Arad," *UF* 10 (1978): 289–336; Z. HERZOG et al. "The Israelite Fortress at Arad," *BASOR* 254 (1984): 1–34; Z. HERZOG, M. AHARONI, and A. RAINEY, "Arad: An Ancient Israelite Fortress with a Temple to Yahweh," *BAR* 13, no. 2 (1987): 16–35. For additional bibliography, see *HAE.*

The Ketef Hinnom Amulets. These two tiny silver scrolls, which were discovered on the hillside of the Hinnom Valley in Jerusalem, have been dated to the seventh–sixth century B.C.E. Each amulet contains a text that is very similar to the priestly blessing in Num 6:24–26. This evidence may seem to create problems for the common scholarly view that the Pentateuch's priestly material is late (so Waaler), but pentateuchal scholars have long presumed that the priestly blessing is older than the surrounding priestly material (see G. B. Gray, *Critical and Exegetical Commentary on Numbers* [ICC; Edinburgh: T&T Clark, 1903]).

Texts and translations: AHI 4.301–302; *HAE* I.447–56. **Translation:** *COS* 2.83: 221. **Bibliography:** A. BARKAY, "The Priestly Benediction on Silver Plaques from Ketef Hinnom in Jerusalem," *TA* 19 (1992): 139–94; B. A. LEVINE, *Numbers 1–20* (AB 4A; New York: Doubleday, 1993), 236–44; E. WAALER, "A Revised Date for Pentateuchal Texts? Evidence from Ketef Hinnom," *TynBul* 53 (2002): 29–55; A. YARDENI, "Remarks on the Priestly Blessing on Two Ancient Amulets from Jerusalem," *VT* 41 (1991): 176–85.

The Lachish Letters. This sixth-century B.C.E. administrative archive contained several letters kept in the city's gate area. About twenty ostraca were found, yielding about ten readable letters that were apparently written by Hoshiah, an outpost commander, to the governor of Lachish (Jaush). In one of the letters (Lachish 4) Hoshiah claims that he is watching for "signals" from Lachish but no longer sees any signals from Azekah. The disappearance of Azekah's signals probably reflects the town's fall to Babylon during the invasion of about 589–586 B.C.E. Two texts mention prophets who were apparently spreading discouraging messages by means of letters, which royal functionaries attempted to intercept and confiscate (see Lachish 3; 6; cf. 16). The pessimistic prophetic message expressed in these texts—"Watch out!"—is reminiscent of Jeremiah's ministry. Indeed, the broken end of the prophet's name mentioned in Lachish 16:5, "-yahu the prophet," could fit Jeremiah.

One of the ostraca, Lachish 3, has important implications for literacy during the late Judean monarchy. In it, Hoshiah—a junior officer who was not from the scribal class—defended himself against the charge that he could not read. Clearly, the text presupposes that illiteracy carried a negative social stigma for leaders in the Judean military (Schniedewind).

Texts and translations: HAE I.405–440; *SSI* 32–49 (partial); *KAI* #192–99; LINDEN-BERGER, *Ancient Aramaic and Hebrew Letters,* 113–18, 124–31 (partial). *Translations:* ANET 321–22; *COS* 3:42: 78–81 (partial). *Bibliography:* AVIGAD, "Hebrew Epigraphic Sources," 30–32; CROSS and FREEDMAN, *Early Hebrew Orthography,* 51–57; N. R. GANOR, "The Lachish Letters," *PEQ* 99 (1967): 74–77; D. PARDEE, "An Overview of Ancient Hebrew Epistolography," *JBL* 97 (1978): 321–46; J. REIDER, "The Lachish Letters," *JQR* 29 (1939): 225–39; W. M. SCHNIEDEWIND, *How the Bible Became a Book: The Textualization of Ancient Israel* (Cambridge: University Press, 2004), 101–3. For a more extensive bibliography, see the individual entries in *HAE*.

Inscriptions from Khirbet Beit Lei. A burial cave about five miles east of Lachish has yielded several short inscriptions and grafitti as well as two somewhat longer inscriptions that do not appear to be burial inscriptions at all. Our present interest is in the two longer inscriptions. Because both texts praise Yahweh and request his assistance (in a manner reminiscent of Psalms), we can imagine that the texts were inscribed by troubled refugees who sought shelter in the cave. If Israelite literacy was as limited as it seems, these refugees were certainly not from the peasant classes. Recently some scholars have elected to read these texts as burial inscriptions, in which case we are no longer dealing with living sufferers but rather with the dead, who were appealing to Yahweh for salvation in the afterlife (Niehr; Särkiö). At any rate, the inscribing of prayers is an interesting religious phenomenon, for it suggests that the ancients deemed their written expressions of praise and prayer as somehow superior to oral petitions. The date of the inscriptions has been a matter of some debate, but a date around the end of the Judean monarchy is most likely (early sixth century). For a discussion of these and similar inscriptions see Naveh 2001.

Texts and translations: HAE I.245–51; *SSI* 57–58. *Translation:* COS 2.53: 180–81. *Bibliography:* F. M. CROSS JR., "The Cave Inscriptions from Khirbet Beit Lei," in *Near Eastern Archaeology in the Twentieth Century: Essays in Honor of Nelson Glueck* (ed. J. A. Sanders; Garden City, N.Y.: Doubleday, 1970), 299–306; P. D. MILLER JR., "Psalms and Inscriptions," in *Congress Volume: Vienna, 1980* (VTSup 32; Leiden: Brill, 1981), 311–32; J. NAVEH, "Hebrew Graffiti from the First Temple Period," *IEJ* 51 (2001): 226–32; IDEM, "Old Hebrew Inscriptions in a Burial Cave," *IEJ* 13 (1963): 74–92; H. NIEHR, "The Changed Status of the Dead in Yehud"; P. SÄRKIÖ, "Hilferuf zu Jahwe aus dem Versteck," *ZDPV* 113 (1997): 39–60.

The M(w)ṣh Stamp Impressions. Archaeologists have recovered a corpus of forty-three stamp impressions that bear the word *mṣh* or *mwṣh.* The stamps appear on large storage jars that may be tentatively dated to the sixth century B.C.E. The vast majority of the stamp impressions (30) were unearthed at Tell en-Naṣbah (Mizpah), while others were recovered at Gibeon (4), Jerusalem (4), Jericho (2), Ramat Raḥel (1), and in the debris of a Crusader castle in Ṣuba (1). Another unprovenanced exemplar is in the Bible Lands Museum, Jerusalem. All of these sites are essentially from the region of Benjamin, a region that the Babylonians did not destroy when they invaded Judah in the sixth century (see Lipschits). This is also the area in which the Babylonians set up some sort of administrative center at Mizpah (see 2 Kgs 25:23–25). From this and other evidence, we may tentatively conclude that these storage jars were manufactured at the Benjaminite town of Moṣah (*mṣh;* see Josh 18:26), probably for storing wine manufactured in the region. The relative prominence of these stamp impressions at Mizpah suggests that the city was used by the Babylonian-era administration as a distribution or storage center for Moṣah's products.

Texts and translations: Y. AHARONI, *Excavations at Ramat Rahel: Seasons 1961 and 1962.* (Serie Archeologica 6; Roma: Centro di studi semitici, 1964), 18, 23, pl. 20:8; R. BARLETT, "Appendix A: Iron Age and Hellenistic Stamped Jar Handles from Tell es-Sultan," in K. M. Kenyon and T. A. Holland, *Excavations at Jericho* (5 vols.; London: British School of Archaeology in Jerusalem, 1960–1983), 4:537–45, pl. III.b; C. C. MCCOWN, *Tell en-Nasbeh, I: Archaeological and Historical Results* (Berkeley; New Haven: Yale, 1947), 165–67, pls. 56:15–28, 57:15–16; A. R. MILLARD, "Note on Two Seal Impressions on Pottery," *Levant* 21 (1989): 60–61; J. B. PRITCHARD, *Hebrew Inscriptions and Stamps from Gibeon* (Philadelphia: University Museum, University of Pennsylvania, 1959), 27, figs. 10:1, 11:1; IDEM, *Winery, Defenses and Soundings at Gibeon* (Philadelphia: University Museum, University of Pennsylvania, 1964), 4, 210, figs. 50:4, 50:7, 51:6; E. SELLIN and K. WATZINGER, *Jericho* (MVDOG 22; Leipzig: Hinrichs, 1913), 158, pl. 42:K. ***Bibliography:*** O. LIPSCHITS, "Demographic Changes in Judah between the Seventh and the Fifth Centuries B.C.E." in *Judah and the Judeans in the Neo-Babylonian Period* (ed. O. Lipschits and J. Blenkinsopp; Winona Lake, Ind.: Eisenbrauns, 2003), 323–76; D. VANDERHOOFT, "Babylonian Strategies of Imperial Control in the West," in *Judah and the Judeans in the Neo-Babylonian Period* (ed. O. Lipschits and J. Blenkinsopp; Winona Lake, Ind.: Eisenbrauns, 2003), 235–62; J. ZORN, "Tell en-Nasbeh and the Problem of the Material Culture of the Sixth Century," in *Judah and the Judeans in the Neo-Babylonian Period* (ed. O. Lipschits and J. Blenkinsopp; Winona Lake, Ind.: Eisenbrauns, 2003), 413–47; J. ZORN, J. YELLIN, and J. HAYES, "The *m(w)ṣh* Stamp Impressions and the Neo-Babylonian Period," *IEJ* 44 (1994): 161–83.

Persian-Era Stamp Impressions and Coins. Several hundred jar handles from the sixth–fourth centuries B.C.E. bear the word *yhwd/yhd* ("Yehud"), the name of the Persian province of Judah. These come from various sites and attest to imperial administration in the region during the postexilic period, as do stamps that refer to governors (*pḥwʾ*) and officials (*pqd*). Silver coins from the period also bear the "Yehud" label.

Texts and translations: *AHI* 250–56; *HAE* II/2 (forthcoming); N. AVIGAD, *Bullae and Seals from a Post-exilic Judean Archive* (Qedem 4; Jerusalem: Institute of Archaeology, Hebrew University, 1976); AVIGAD and SASS, *Corpus of West Semitic Stamp Seals.* ***Translation:*** *COS* 2.78: 203–4 (partial).

Inscribed Weights. Like their neighbors, the Israelites used scales and weights to facilitate equitable trade in their products, but they were not able to achieve anything like the precision and standardization of modern measures. Our understanding of the units of measure used in these transactions has been greatly enhanced by the discovery of more than four hundred weights bearing inscribed units of measures. Most of these weights are stone, but a few are bronze. Although they vary in date and are often unprovenanced, most of them come from eighth-to-seventh-century Judah. Many of the weights bear a sign in the shape of a loop, which scholars surmise to represent the shekel. From this evidence scholars have been able to determine that the Hebrew shekel equaled about 11.33 grams. The inscriptions are sometimes in Hebrew, but most were derived from the Egyptian hieratic writing system. Other units of weight among the samples are the *pym* (see 1 Sam 13:31), the *bq'* (see Gen 24:22), and the *grh* (see Exod 30:13; Lev 27:25).

Texts and translations: AHI 257–62; DEUTSCH and HELTZER, *Forty New Ancient West Semitic Inscriptions,* 63–68 (partial); *HAE* II/2 (forthcoming); R. KLETTER, "The Inscribed Weights of the Kingdom of Judah," *TA* 18 (1991): 121–63. **Translation:** *COS* 2.81: 210. ***Bibliography:*** R. KLETTER, *Economic Keystones: The Weight System of the Kingdom of Judah* (JSOTSup 276; Sheffield, England: Sheffield Academic Press, 1998); M. A. POWELL, "Weights and Measures," *ABD* 6:897–908.

15.2. Other West Semitic Inscriptions

The Semitic Graffiti from Wadi el-Hol. These two texts were inscribed in stone along a military road in a desolate part of southern Egypt, in the relative vicinity of Thebes. The inscriptions date between 2000–1800 B.C.E. and represent our earliest examples of an alphabetic script. So far as can be determined, Semitic peoples working for the Egyptians invented the script. Its alphabetic characters were adapted from Egyptian hieroglyphs, as was also the case for the better-known Proto-Sinaitic Inscriptions treated in the following entry. It is possible, perhaps likely, that the Proto-Sinaitic Inscriptions represent a later development of these inscriptions. At any rate, Semitic speakers probably invented the script because of the complexities of learning and using the much more complex system of Egyptian hieroglyphs. Although the inscriptions were announced about ten years ago (see J. C. Darnell's 1994–95 annual report of the Oriental Institute, University of Chicago), they have not yet to been officially published, nor have any convincing translations been worked out. The delay in publication stems in part from Darnell's effort to publish a much larger corpus of Egyptian graffiti from the region. In spite of the present uncertainties, the alphabetic texts provide good evidence that Semitic speakers lived and worked in Egypt as early as the Egyptian Middle Kingdom.

Bibliography: S. FELDMAND, "Not as Simple as A-B-C: Earliest Use of Alphabet Found in Egypt," *BAR* 26, no. 1 (2000): 12; W. M. SCHNIEDEWIND, *How the Bible Became a Book: The Textualization of Ancient Israel* (Cambridge: University Press, 2004), 38–39; S. J. WIMMER and S. WIMMER-DWEIKAT, "The Alphabet from Wadi el-Hol: A First Try," *GM* 180 (2001): 107–12.

The Proto-Sinaitic Inscriptions. Excavations in Sinai during the late nineteenth and the twentieth centuries uncovered a corpus of inscriptions that were later determined to reflect a pictographic West Semitic alphabet dating from about 1500 B.C.E. The texts were mainly votive offerings to the goddess Baalat and the god El, apparently written by Semitic-speaking people employed by Egypt in the region. For some time it was thought that these miners invented the alphabetic script, but several older inscriptions prove that this judgment was incorrect. These older inscriptions include the Wadi el-Hol inscriptions discussed in the previous entry, as well as three cuneiform alphabetic inscriptions Late Bronze Palestine (for these brief inscriptions, see the following entry).

Text and translation: W. F. ALBRIGHT, *The Proto-Sinaitic Inscriptions and Their Decipherment* (HTS 22; Cambridge: Harvard University Press, 1969). *Bibliography:* NAVEH, *Early History of the Alphabet,* 23–42.

Cuneiform Texts from Ancient Palestine. To date, eighty-nine cuneiform texts have been discovered in the land of Israel. The corpus includes letters, literary texts, royal inscriptions, cylinder seals, lexical texts, mathematical texts, omens, and medical texts. Almost all of these texts are small and fragmentary, and most are in Akkadian. The remaining texts are in Sumerian (a few cylinder seals), in Elamite (a Persian royal inscription), and in a West Semitic language akin to Ugaritic (three texts). The richest finds come from the Late Bronze levels of Taanach (17 texts), Hazor (15 texts), Aphek (8 texts), Samaria (6 texts), and Megiddo (5 texts). Undoubtedly, the texts that have attracted the most attention have been the fragment of the Gilgamesh Epic from Megiddo (see Goetze/ Levy) and the three small alphabetic texts from Beth Shemesh (Sass), Taanach (Cross), and Nahal Tabor (Dietrich/Loretz). The alphabetic texts, which date to the Late Bronze era, are West Semitic and were written in a cuneiform alphabet similar to the alphabet used in Ugarit. A complete catalogue of the cuneiform texts from ancient Palestine has been published by Horowitz, Oshima, and Sanders, and a new edition of the texts is forthcoming from the same scholars.

Texts and translations: F. M. CROSS JR., "The Canaanite Cuneiform Tablet from Taanach," *BASOR* 190 (1968): 41–46; A. GOETZE AND S. LEVY, "Fragment of the Gilgamesh Epic from Megiddo," *Atiqot* 2 (1959): 121–28; M. DIETRICH AND O. LORETZ, *Die Keilalphabete* (Münster: Ugarit-Verlag, 1988), 239–42; B. SASS, "The Beth Shemesh Tablet and the Early History of the Proto-Canaanite, Cuneiform and South Semitic Alphabets," *UF* 23 (1991): 315–26. *Bibliography:* W. HOROWITZ, T. OSHIMA, AND S. SANDERS, "A Bibliographical

List of Cuneiform Inscriptions from Canaan, Palestine/Philistia, and the Land of Israel," *JAOS* 122 (2002): 753–766; NAVEH, *Early History of the Alphabet*, 28–30.

The Izbet Ṣarṭah Abecedary. This twelfth-century ostracon bears our largest Proto-Canaanite inscription, which a few scholars are willing to label "early Hebrew." An unskilled hand wrote out a twenty-two-letter West Semitic alphabet (cf. the twenty-seven letters at Ugarit) and then proceeded to inscribe several lines of random letters. Izbet Ṣarṭah lies in the western margin of the hill country, about one mile east of Tell Aphek. For more on Hebrew abecedaries and scribal exercises, see "The Pithoi from Kuntillet 'Ajrud," above.

Texts and translations: F. M. CROSS JR., "Newly Found Inscriptions in Old Canaanite and Early Phoenician Script," *BASOR* 238 (1980): 1–21; J. NAVEH, "Some Considerations on the Ostracon from Izbet Sartah," *IEJ* 28 (1978): 31–35. *Translation: COS* 1.107: 362–65. *Bibliography:* M. D. COOGAN, "Alphabets and Elements," *BASOR* 216 (1974): 61–63; F. M. CROSS JR. and T. O. LAMBDIN, "A Ugaritic Abecedary and the Origins of the Proto-Canaanite Alphabet," *BASOR* 160 (1960): 21–26; A. DEMSKY, "The 'Izbet Sartah Ostracon—Ten Years Later," in *'Izbet Sartah: An Early Iron Age Site near Rosh Ha'ayin, Israel* (ed. I. Finkelstein; Oxford: Oxford University Press, 1986), 186–97; IDEM, "A Proto-Canaanite Abecedary Dating from the Period of the Judges and Its Implications for the History of the Alphabet," *TA* 4 (1977): 14–27; NAVEH, *Early History of the Alphabet*, 36–37; E. PUECH, "Abécédaire et liste alphabétique de noms hébreux du début du 2e siècle A. D.," *RB* 87 (1980): 118–26.

The El Khadr Arrowheads. These five bronze arrowheads bear the Old Canaanite inscription of their owner, a certain 'Abd-Labi't. Because the artifacts date to the eleventh century B.C.E. and were found near Bethlehem, they are properly related to the so-called Judges period. The owner's name translates as "servant of the lioness," suggesting that he was a goddess devotee. 'Abd-Labi't's arrowheads should be compared to the larger corpus of similar tenth-and eleventh-century Phoenician arrowheads discovered in Lebanon (see Deutsch/Heltzer). Many of the figures mentioned on the Phoenician arrowheads were prominent military leaders, and in one exemplar a "king of Amurru." From this we may cautiously conclude that our Phoenician arrowheads belonged to warriors and commanders in the service of this king. All tallied, we now possess forty-three inscribed bronze arrowheads from Syria-Palestine.

Texts, translations, and bibliography: F. M. CROSS JR., "New Found Inscriptions in Old Canaanite and Early Phoenician Inscriptions," *BASOR* 238 (1980): 1–20; DEUTSCH and HELTZER, *Forty New Ancient West Semitic Inscriptions*, 11–21; IDEM, *New Epigraphic Evidence from the Biblical Period* (Tel Aviv–Jaffa: Archaeological Center Publication, 1995), 11–38; J. T. MILIK and F. M. CROSS JR., "Inscribed Javelin Heads from the Period of the Judges: A Recent Discovery in Palestine," *BASOR* 134 (1954): 5–15. *Translation: COS* 2.84: 221–22.

The Bilingual Tell Fekherye Statue. This ninth-century statue was discovered at Tell Fekherye (ancient Sikanu?), where it was originally set up by Hadad-yis'i, the ruler of nearby Gozan (biblical Gozan, modern Tell Halaf). A bilingual Aramaic/ Akkadian dedicatory inscription on the statue asked for blessing from the god Hadad/Adad and pronounced curses upon anyone who might destroy or otherwise deface the piece. The statue's aesthetic form is Neo-Assyrian, which is not a surprise given Assyria's dominance in the region during this period. The use of Aramaic and Akkadian reflects not only linguistic realities in the region but also the increasing prominence of Aramaic during the first millennium (on the role of Aramaic during the Neo-Assyrian period, see Dalley).

Texts and translations: A. ABOU-ASSAF, P. BORDREUIL, and A. R. MILLARD, *La statue de Tell Fekherye et son inscription bilingue assyro-araméenne* (Paris: Éditions Recherche sur les Civilisations, 1982); *KAI* #309. *Translation: COS* 2.34: 153–54. *Bibliography:* P. BORDREUIL and A. R. MILLARD, "A Statue from Syria with Assyrian and Aramic Inscriptions," *BA* (1982): 135–41; S. DALLEY, "Assyrian Court Narratives in Aramaic and Egyptian: Historical Fiction," in *Proceedings of the XLV Rencontre assyriologique internationale: History and Historiography in the Cuneiform World* (ed. Tz. Abusch et al.; 2 vols.; Bethesda, Md.: CDL Press, 2001), 1:149–61; V. J. J. DE CAEN, *A Revised Bibliography for the Samalian Dialect of Old Aramaic* (Newsletter for Targumic and Cognate Studies, Sup. 6; Toronto: University of Toronto, 1996); J. C. GREENFIELD and A. SHAFFER, "Notes on the Curse Formulae of the Tell Fekherye Inscription," *RB* 92 (1985): 47–59; S. A. KAUFMAN, "Reflections on the Assyrian-Aramaic Bilingual from Tell Fakhariyeh," *Maarav* 3 (1982): 137–75; T. MURAOKA, "The Tell-Fekherye Bilingual Inscription and Early Aramaic," *Abr-Nabrain* 22 (1983–84): 79–117.

The Mesha Inscription. Also called the Moabite Stone, this ninth-century stela from Diban provides a brief outline of the deeds of King Mesha and the events leading up to his reign in Moab. In this autobiographical text, Mesha refers both to defeats suffered by his forerunners and to his own subsequent victories and accomplishments. He placed the stela in a recently completed temple to memorialize these achievements before the chief deity of Moab, Chemosh. In this sense, the Mesha Inscription is a royal memorial inscription as well as a dedicatory inscription given to Chemosh because the deity had granted Mesha success. The narrative style and content of the text have often been compared to the books of Kings in the Hebrew Bible, which also narrate royal history using the so-called *waw*-consecutive verbal form (see Niccacci). The two works also share common theological ideas, attributing military defeats to the anger and displeasure of the deity and victories to blessings from the same. Another point of comparison with the Hebrew Bible is found in the notion of *ḥērem,* which in Israelite tradition was an act of devotion in which conquered enemies were slaughtered as a kind of offering to the deity (see Deut 7:26; Josh 6:17). The same term, used in the same way, also appears in the Mesha Inscription.

There is evidence that the composer of the inscription consulted and edited sources to write his work. According to S. Parker's study, differences of style and narrative form in the text suggest that the writer took up an earlier memorial inscription that recounted Mesha's building activities, added an introduction to commemorate the occasion of the temple's construction, and then filled out the text with accounts of recent construction and military activity. Thus, through redactional activities the generic character of the text was extended from that of a memorial inscription in honor of Mesha to a commemorative inscription in honor of the deity. But in either case, a primary function of the text remained royal apologia.

Texts and translations: KAI #181; SSI 1.71–84. *Translations:* COS 2.23: 137–38; ANET 320–21. *Bibliography:* A. DEARMAN, *Studies in the Mesha Inscription and Moab* (Atlanta: Scholars Press, 1989); J. M. MILLER, "The Moabite Stone as Memorial Stela," *PEQ* 106 (1974): 9–18; A. NICCACCI, "The Stela of Mesha and the Bible: Verbal System and Narrativity," *Or* 63 (1994): 226–48; PARKER, *Stories in Scripture and Inscriptions,* 44–58; K. A. D. SMELIK, "Some Literary Features of King Mesha's Inscription," *JSOT* 46 (1990): 21–30.

The Marzeaḥ *Papyrus.** Dating to the ninth century, this Moabite text records a divine decision on a court case concerning the property of a *marzeaḥ*, i.e., a voluntary association with its own building, millstones, and house. Similar cases of divine legal judgment appear in Exod 22:6–8 and 1 Kgs 8:31–32. This papyrus, however, is yet another unprovenanced text, whose authenticity has been correspondingly questioned.

Text and translation: P. BORDREUIL and D. PARDEE, "Le papyrus du marzeaḥ," *Sem* 38 (1990): 49–68.

The Tel Dan Inscription. Discovered during excavations in the 1993–1994 seasons at Tel Dan, this Aramaic text was apparently sponsored by an Aramean king who wished to commemorate his victories over the "house of David," that is, Judah. The text begins with a historical review of Israel's previous triumphs over the king's father, then turns to his own divine election by the god Hadad, after which he defeated Judah and exacted tribute from it. The basalt monument dates to the ninth century B.C.E. Some minimalist scholars, who seriously doubt the existence of a Davidic kingdom so early, have challenged the reading "house of David," but it is a marginal view. When considered judiciously, the text sheds considerable light on the coup of Jehu described in 1 Kgs 19:16–17, 2 Kgs 9–10, and Hosea 1:4 (see Schniedewind).

Texts and translations: A. BIRAN and J. NAVEH, "An Aramaic Stele Fragment from Tel Dan," *IEJ* 43 (1993): 81–98; IDEM, "The Tel Dan Inscription: A New Fragment," *IEJ* 45 (1995): 1–18; *KAI* #310. *Translation:* COS 2.39: 161–62 (with bibliography). *Bibliography:* G. ATHAS, *The Tel Dan Inscription: A Reappraisal and a New Interpretation* (JSOTSup 360; New York: Sheffield Academic Press, 2003); P. R. DAVIES, " 'House of David' Built on Sand: The Sins of the Biblical Maximizers," *BAR* 20, no. 4 (1994): 54–55; P.-E. DION, "The Tel Dan Stele and Its Historical Significance," in *Michael: Historical, Epigraphical and Biblical Studies in Honor of Prof. Michael Heltzer* (ed. Y. Avishur and R. Deutsch; Jaffa: Archaeological Center Publications, 1999), 145–56; J. A. EMERTON, "Two Issues in the Interpretation of the Tel Dan Inscription," *VT* 50 (2000): 27–37; K. A. KITCHEN, "A Possible Mention of David in the Late Tenth Century B.C.E. and Deity *Dod as Dead as the Dodo?" *JSOT* 76 (1997): 29–44; I. KOTTSIEPER, "Die Inschrift von Tell Dan und die politischen

Beziehungen zwischen Aram-Damaskus und Israel in der 1. Hälfte des 1. Jahrtausends vor Christus," in *Und Mose schrieb dieses Lied auf* (ed. Dietrich and Kottsieper), 475–500; PARKER, *Stories in Scripture and Inscriptions,* 58; G. A. RENDSBURG, "On the Writing *bt-dwd* in the Aramaic Inscription from Tel Dan," *IEJ* 45 (1995): 22–25; W. M. SCHNIE-DEWIND, "Tel Dan Stela: New Light on Aramaic and Jehu's Revolt," *BASOR* 302 (1996): 75–90.

The Amman Citadel Inscription. Inscribed on white limestone, this short fragmentary Ammonite inscription was discovered on the citadel mound of ancient Rabbath-ammon (Amman, Jordan). It dates to the ninth century B.C.E. and appears to commemorate work on a temple or on the citadel itself. Its "author"—an Ammonite king, no doubt—claims that Milkom, the national deity of Ammon, requested that the work be done. The inscription appears to be in the form of an oracle delivered in the name of Milkom (Seow), making it comparable in certain respects to Israelite prophecy (see Margalit).

Texts and translations: CAI 154–63; KAI #307. **Translation:** COS 2.24: 139. **Bibliography:** AVIGAD, "Hebrew Epigraphic Sources," 41–42; U. HÜBNER, *Der Ammoniter: Untersuchungen zur Geschichte, Kultur, und Religion eines transjordanischen Volkes in 1. Jahrtausend v. Chr.* (Wiesbaden: Harrassowitz, 1992), 17–21; B. MARGALIT, "Ninth-Century Israelite Prophecy in the Light of Contemporary NWSemitic Epigraphs," in *Und Mose schrieb dieses Lied auf* (ed. Dietrich and Kottsieper), 515–32; C.-L. SEOW, "West Semitic Sources," in *Prophets and Prophecy in the Ancient Near East* (ed. M. Nissinen; SBLWAW 13; Atlanta: Scholars Press, 2003), 201–18; W. H. SHEA, "The Architectural Layout of the Amman Citadel Inscription Temple," *PEQ* 123 (1991): 62–66.

Kilamuwa Inscription. Although composed as a memorial stela for the king of an Aramean city called Sam'al (modern Zincirli, Turkey), this ninth-century text is written in a Phoenician dialect that reflects Aramaic influence. The text is divided into two sections and features a relief of Kilamuwa pointing to divine symbols of his authority. The king's accomplishments are memorialized by comparing them with his predecessors (part 1) and by describing the prosperity that he has brought to Sam'al (part 2). The inscription concludes with a list of curses that would befall anyone who destroyed the stela.

Texts and translations: KAI #24; SSI 3.30–39; TROPPER, *Die Inschriften von Zincirli,* 27–46. *Translations:* ANET 654–55; COS 2.30: 147–48. **Bibliography:** T. COLLINS, "The Kilamua Inscription—A Phoenician Poem," WO 6 (1971): 183–98; P.-E. DION, *La langue de Ya'udi: Description et classement de l'ancien parler de Zencirli dans le cadre des langues sémitiques du nord-ouest* (Waterloo, Ont.: Corporation pour la Publication des Études Académiques en Religion au Canada, 1974); F. M. FALES, "Kilamuwa and the Foreign Kings: Propaganda vs. Power," WO 10 (1979): 6–22; M. O'CONNOR, "The Rhetoric of the Kilamuwa Inscription," *BASOR* 226 (1977): 15–29; PARKER, *Stories in Scripture and Inscriptions,* 76–83; P. SWIGGERS, "Notes on the Phoenician Inscription of Kilamuwa," *RSO* 55 (1981): 1–4.

The Melqart Stela. This basalt stela carries an inscription in which Bir-Hadad, a king of Aram, honors his vow to the god Melqart after the god responded to his pleas. Some scholars believe that this Bir-Hadad was one of the kings mentioned in the Hebrew Bible (cf. 1 Kgs 15:18; 2 Kgs 8:7–15), but this is a matter of some debate. The stela was found near Aleppo, Syria, and dates to the ninth or eighth century B.C.E.

Texts and translations: KAI #201; *SSI* 2.1–4. *Translations: ANET* 655; *COS* 2.33: 152–53.
Bibliography: W. F. ALBRIGHT, "A Votive Stele Erected by Ben Hadad I of Damascus to the God Melcarth," *BASOR* 87 (1942): 23–29; P. BORDREUIL and J. TEIXIDOR, "Nouvel examen de l'inscription de Bar-Hadad," *AO* (1983): 271–76; F. M. CROSS JR., "The Stele Dedicated to Melcarth by Ben-Hadad," *BASOR* 205 (1972): 36–42; A. LEMAIRE, "La stèle araméenne de Bar-Hadad," *Or* 53 (1984): 337–49; W. T. PITARD, "The Identity of the Bir-Hadad of the Melqart Stela," *BASOR* 1988 (272): 3–21; E. PUECH, "La stèle de Bar-Hadad à Melqart et les rois d'Arpad," *RB* 99 (1992): 311–34.

Zakkur Inscription. This basalt stela memorializes the reign of Zakkur, king of Hamath (ca. 800 B.C.E.). The bulk of the Aramaic text enumerates an episode in which the gods delivered Zakkur from a coalition of seventeen kings who were besieging his city. Particularly interesting is that the god responded to Zakkur's prayers with prophetic messages: "Do not be afraid! Since I have made you king, I will stand beside you. I will save you from all these kings who have besieged you." Following this episode is a brief list of Zakkur's achievements and a series of curses that would befall anyone who removed his monument stela. Some scholars have noted that there are interesting similarities between the prayers on the Zakkur inscription and those in the Davidic *miktām* psalms (see the superscription in Pss 16 and 56–60). This suggests that the *miktām* psalms may have originated as royal inscriptions, a possibility reinforced by the Septuagint, which translates the term *miktām* as *stēlographia* ("stela inscription"). The Zakkur psalms are also comparable to the biblical laments (see Zobel) and thanksgiving psalms (see Greenfield).

Texts and translations: KAI #202; *SSI* 2.6–17. *Translations: ANET* 655–56; *COS* 2.35: 155.
Bibliography: J. C. GREENFIELD, "The Zakir Inscription and the Danklied," in *Proceedings of the Fifth World Congress of Jewish Studies* (5 vols.; Jerusalem: World Union of Jewish Studies, 1972), 1:174–91; A. R. MILLARD, "The Homeland of Zakkur," *Sem* 39 (1990): 47–52; B. OTZEN, "The Aramaic Inscriptions," in *Les objets de la période dite syro-hittite (Âge du fer)* (ed. P. J. Riis and M.-L. Buhl; Copenhagen: Nationalmuseet, 1990), 267–318; PARKER, *Stories in Scripture and Inscriptions*, 105–30; H.-J. ZOBEL, "Das Gebet um Abwendung der Not und seine Erhörung in den Klageliedern des Alten Testaments und in der Inschrift des Königs Zakir von Hamath," *VT* 21 (1971): 91–99.

Panamuwa's Hadad Inscription. This eighth-century Aramaic text was inscribed on a large statue of the god Hadad. It commemorates not only the reign of Panamuwa, king of Y'dy (= Sam'al) but also the building of his burial chamber, in which the statue was placed. The text narrates how the gods blessed Panamuwa and his people with peace during his reign and how he returned the favor with religious piety. Although Panamuwa's building projects are briefly described, a primary purpose of the text was to command future kings to pray this prayer on his behalf: "May the dead spirit of Panamuwa eat with Hadad, and may the dead spirit of Panamuwa drink with Hadad." The text concludes by promising that blessings awaited future kings who did this faithfully whereas a long list of curses awaited those who did not. Ritual meals for the deceased were called *kispum* in Mesopotamian and *marzeaḥ* in West Semitic culture (see Jer 16:6).

Texts and translations: KAI #214; *SSI* 60–76; TROPPER, *Die Inschriften von Zincirli*, 54–97. *Translation: COS* 2.36: 156–58. *Bibliography:* J. GREENFIELD, "Un rite religieux araméen et ses parallèles," *RB* 80 (1973): 46–52; W. W. HALLO, "Royal Ancestor Worship in the Biblical World," in *'Sha^carei Talmon': Studies in the Bible, Qumran, and the Ancient Near East Presented to Shemaryahu Talmon* (ed. M. Fishbane and E. Tov; Winona Lake, Ind.: Eisenbrauns, 1992), 381–401; B. SCHMIDT, *Israel's Beneficent Dead: Ancestor Cult and Necromancy in Ancient Israelite Religion and Tradition* (FAT 11; Tübingen: J. C. B. Mohr, 1994).

Bar-Rakib's Panamuwa Inscription. This eighth-century Aramaic text appears on a statue of Panamuwa that Bar-Rakib king of Sam'al erected to honor his father, a memorial that was likely linked to the cult of the royal ancestors. The inscription combines features of both the dedicatory and the memorial genres, but it appears that more was at stake than honoring Panamuwa. The first half of the text describes in some detail how the gods protected Panamuwa from troubles in his household and made him a successful king who was much loved by his overlord, Tiglath-pileser of Assyria. Because the second half of the text depicts Bar-Rakib in a similar fashion—as a lover of the gods, his father, and Tiglath-pileser—the author's primary aim clearly was to secure Bar-Rakib's claim to his father's throne.

Texts and translations: KAI #215; *SSI* 2.76–86; TROPPER, *Die Inschriften von Zincirli*, 98–139. *Translation: COS* 2.37:158–60. *Bibliography:* B. MARGALIT, "Studies in NWSemitic Inscriptions," *UF* 26 (1994): 271–315; H. NIEHR, "Zum Totenkult der Könige von Sam'al im 9. und 8. Jh. v. Chr.," *SEL* 11 (1994): 58–73; PARKER, *Stories in Scripture and Inscriptions*, 83–89; YOUNGER, "Panammuwa and Bar-Rakib."

Bar-Rakib's Palace Inscription. With this inscription Bar-Rakib, king of Sam'al (eighth century B.C.E.), celebrated the construction of his new royal palace. Written on a large block of stone, the text accentuates the king's success but also expresses loyalty to Tiglath-pileser III, the Assyrian overlord who permitted Bar-Rakib to succeed his father to the throne.

Texts and translations: KAI #216; *SSI* 2.87–93; TROPPER, *Die Inschriften von Zincirli*, 132–39. *Translations: ANET* 655; *COS* 2.38: 160–61. *Bibliography:* YOUNGER, "Panammuwa and Bar-Rakib."

Azatiwada Inscription. Archaeologists have discovered three copies of this bilingual inscription in the fortifications of Karatepe (in southeast Turkey), two on stelae and the other on a divine statue. They are the longest of our Phoenician and Luwian inscriptions and were instrumental in solidifying our knowledge of the Luwian hieroglyphs. In these texts Azatiwada, a subordinate ruler to the kingdom of Adana, memorializes himself with an account of his successes, including his geographical expansion of the kingdom, his fortifications and building projects, and his religious reforms. The text concludes by pronouncing blessings upon future kings but adds that curses await anyone who defaces the inscriptions. The last few lines of the text express the king's motive for its composition: "Only may the name of Azatiwada be forever like the name of the sun and the moon!" Orthographic and historical data suggest that the text dates to the late eighth or early seventh century B.C.E.

Texts and translations: Phoenician edition: *KAI,* #26; W. RÖLLIG, "Appendix I: The Phoenician Inscriptions," *CHLI* 2:50–81; *SSI* 3.41–64; Luwian edition: *CHLI* 2:35–36, 108–10. *Translations COS* 2.21: 124–26; 2.31: 148–50. *Bibliography:* M. L. BARRÉ, "An Analysis of the Royal Blessing in the Karatepe Inscription," *Maarav* 3, no. 2 (1982): 177–94; IDEM, "A Note on *rš't* in the Karatepe Inscription," *JANES* 13 (1981): 1–3; S. GERVITZ, "Phoenician *wšbrt mlṣm* and Job 33:23," *Maarav* 5–6 (1990): 145–58; J. C. GREENFIELD, "Scripture and Inscription: The Literary and Rhetorical Element in Some Early Phoenician Inscriptions," in *Near Eastern Studies in Honor of W. F. Albright* (ed. H. Goedicke; Baltimore: Johns Hopkins University Press, 1971), 253–68; K. L. YOUNGER JR., "The Phoenician Inscription of Azatiwada: An Integrated Reading," *JSS* 43 (1998): 11–47.

Ikausu's Temple Inscription. This brief seventh-century dedicatory inscription, written on stone in the Philistine-Canaanite dialect, commemorates Ikausu's construction of a temple for the goddess Ptygyh. It concludes with royal prayers for blessing, protection, and long life. Ikausu was the son of Padi and a king of the Philistine city of Ekron. Both figures are mentioned in the Assyrian Annals, and the consonantal spelling of Ikausu (*'kyš*) matches exactly the Hebrew spelling for the Philistine king Achish (*'kyš*), who figures prominently in the biblical accounts of Saul and Solomon (1 Sam 21:11–26; 1 Sam 27–29; 1 Kgs 2:39–40).

Texts and translations: S. GITIN, T. DOTHAN, and J. NAVEH, "A Royal Dedicatory Inscription from Ekron," *IEJ* 47 (1997): 1–16; *KAI* #286. *Translation: COS* 2.42: 164. *Bibliography:* A. DEMSKY, "Discovering a Goddess: A New Look at the Ekron Inscription Identifies a Mysterious Deity," *BAR* 24, no. 5 (1998): 53–58; J. NAVEH, "Achish-Ikausu in the Light of the Ekron Dedication," *BASOR* 310 (1998): 35–37; V. SASSON, "The Inscription of Achish, Governor of Ekron, and Philistine Dialect, Cult, and Culture," *UF* 29 (1997): 627–39.

An Aramaic Report from an Assyrian Officer. This lengthy but fragmentary text was discovered on a seventh-century B.C.E. ostracon recovered at Aššur. It preserves an intelligence report from an Assyrian officer to King Assurbanipal in which the first inklings of the rebellion of Šamaš-šum-ukin in Babylon are reported (for more on this historical milieu, see the discussion of the Tale of Sarbanapal and Sarmuge in 9.1.3). The most significant feature of the letter is not its content but the fact that it is our only Aramaic letter from the Neo-Assyrian period. All other surviving Neo-Assyrian letters, of which there are thousands, were composed in Akkadian. This single Aramaic text represents the many

Aramaic texts from the period that are now lost to us because they were composed on perishable papyrus rather than on ostraca.

Texts and translations: KAI #233; LINDENBERGER, *Ancient Aramaic and Hebrew Letters,*
17–23; *SSI* 2.98–110. *Bibliography:* F. M. FALES, "Aramaic Letters and Neo-Assyrian Letters: Philological and Methodological Notes," *JAOS* 107 (1997): 451–69; S. A. KAUFMAN,
Aramaic Influences on Akkadian (Chicago: University of Chicago Press, 1974).

The Aramaic Letter from Adon of Ekron. In 598/597 B.C.E., Nebuchadnezzar of
Babylon advanced on the coastal states of Palestine, including Philistia and Judah.
The circumstances of this campaign are reported in 2 Kgs 24:1–7 and Jer 46–47.
In this Aramaic letter, King Adon of the Philistine city-state of Ekron appeals to
Pharaoh Neco II of Egypt (610–594) for help against the Babylonian invaders.
Because the papyrus was discovered in Saqqara, we know that the letter eventu-
ally reached its addressee in Egypt, but Neco was in no position to help the
troubled Philistine city.

Texts and translations: KAI #266; LINDENBERGER, *Ancient Aramaic and Hebrew Letters,*
23–24; B. PORTEN and A. YARDENI, *Textbook of Aramaic Documents from Ancient Egypt*
(4 vols.; Winona Lake, Ind.: Eisenbrauns, 1986–1999), #1.1; *SSI* 2.110–16.

The Amminadab Inscription from Tel Siran. This Ammonite inscription was
placed on a small metal bottle (copper, tin, and lead) that contained barley,
wheat, and nonprecious metals. Because the inscription requests divine blessings
upon the "produce" of Ammon ("May the produce of Amminadab . . . cause re-
joicing and gladness for many days and in years far off"), the bottle's content may
have been a votive offering. The term here translated as "produce," however, has
also been interpreted to mean "building" or "poem." Scholars date the find to
about 600 B.C.E.

Text and translations: CAI 203–11; KAI #308. *Translation:* COS 2.25: 139–40. *Bibliography:* R. B. COOTE, "The Tel Siran Bottle Inscripton," *BASOR* 240 (1980): 93.

The Sarcophagus Inscription of Eshmunazor. This basalt sarcophagus of Egyptian
make was imported to Phoenicia, where it became the final resting place for Eshmunazor, king of Sidon. The Phoenician inscription includes: (1) the king's lament
that he lived to be only fourteen years old; (2) curses to dissuade would-be
desecrators of his grave; (3) a list of pious and military achievements, jointly attributed to both Eshmunazor and his mother; and (4) a final warning against
desecration of the grave. The inscription implies that Eshmunazor's relative youth
forced his mother to take an active role in ruling Sidon. This political feature may
be compared to the Hebrew institution of the Queen mother (*gᵉbîrâ*), who played a
significant political role, especially when the new king was young (e.g., see 1 Kgs
15:13; 2 Kgs 10:13). For similar Phoenician exemplars, see *COS* 2.55–56, *ANET* 661.

Texts and translations: KAI #14; *SSI* 3.105–14. *Translations:* ANET 662; COS 2.57:
182–83. *Bibliography:* K. GALLING, "Eshmunazar und der Herr der Könige," *ZDPV* 79

(1963): 140–51; J. C. GREENFIELD, "Scripture and Inscription: The Literary and Rhetorical Element in Some Early Phoenician Inscriptions," in *Near Eastern Studies in Honor of W. F. Albright* (ed. H. Goedicke; Baltimore: Johns Hopkins, 1971), 253–68; R. S. TOMBACK, *A Comparative Semitic Lexicon of the Phoenician and Punic Languages* (SBLDS 32; Missoula, Mont.: Scholars Press, 1978).

The Yeḥawmilk Inscription. This combination memorial-votive inscription was originally placed by Yeḥawmilk, king of Byblos, in the sanctuary of the city's goddess (fifth–fourth century B.C.E.). The king alerts the goddess to the works of art that he has prepared for her and then requests the blessing of a long life. Like most royal inscriptions, this ends with a curse upon anyone who would deface the text. Yeḥawmilk, however, goes one step further; he demands that any future work done to the temple should be commemorated by adding his name to the list of those performing the renovations.

Texts and translations: KAI #10; *SSI* 3.93–99. *Translations:* ANET 656; COS 2.32: 151–52. *Bibliography:* M. DUNAND, "Encore la stèle de Yahvmilk roi de Byblos," *Bulletin du Musée Beyrouth* 5 (1941): 57–85; A. DUPONT-SOMMER, "L'Inscription de Yehawmilk roi de Byblos," *Sem* 3 (1950): 35–44.

West Semitic Seals and Seal Impressions. We now possess a large corpus of seals and seal impressions from the West Semitic world of Edom, Moab, Ammon, Aram, Phoenicia, and their environs. These are comparable to the Hebrew seals discussed in 15.1. This large corpus of texts, however, probably includes some, perhaps many, forgeries. For this reason, the authenticity of unprovenanced inscriptions should not be assumed.

Texts, translations, and bibliography: AVIGAD and SASS, *Corpus of West Semitic Stamp Seals; CAI* 1–333 (partial); *HAE* II/2 (forthcoming); U. HÜBNER, *Der Ammoniter: Untersuchungen zur Geschichte, Kultur, und Religion eines transjordanischen Volkes in 1. Jahrtausend v. Chr.* (Wiesbaden: Harrassowitz, 1992); B. MACDONALD and R. W. YOUNKER, *Ancient Ammon* (Boston: Brill, 1999). *Translation:* COS 2.71–76: 201–2 (partial).

The Samaria Papyri. These fourth-century fragmentary papyri were discovered in a wadi cave about 8.5 miles north of Jericho. The Aramaic texts are apparently title deeds belonging to Persian-era officials of Samaria who fled the forces of Alexander the Great in 331 B.C.E. Although the officials and their families were killed in the cave, their bones and their texts were partially preserved. Most of the legal documentation relates to the slave trade, but a few exemplars refer to other transactions. The names in the texts are uniformly Yahwistic and feature in one case the family of Sanballat, the governor of Samaria (so the Aramaic Elephantine archive) who resisted Nehemiah's construction and reform efforts in fifth-century Jerusalem.

Texts and translations: F. M. CROSS JR., "The Discovery of the Samaria Papyri," *BA* 26 (1963): 110–21; D. M. GROPP, *Wadi Daliyeh, II: The Samaria Papyri from Wadi Daliyeh* (DJD 28; Oxford: Clarendon 2001). *Bibliography:* F. M. CROSS JR., "A Report on the

Samaria Papyri," in *Congress Volume: Jerusalem, 1986* (ed. J. A. Emerton; VTSup 40; Leiden: Brill, 1988), 17–26; D. M. GROPP, "Samaria (Papyri)," *ABD* 5:931–32; P. W. LAPP and N. L. LAPP, eds., *Discoveries in the Wâdi ed-Dâliyeh* (AASOR 41; Cambridge, Mass.: American Schools of Oriental Research, 1974).

Punic Mulk Inscriptions. Although these sources do not come from Syria-Palestine, they are included here for reasons that will become clear. The Phoenicians who immigrated to various sites in the Mediterranean basin during the first millennium B.C.E. are known as the Punic peoples. Their language was West Semitic, similar to Hebrew. At the chief Punic city, Carthage, and at several other Punic sites, sacrificial precincts have been unearthed that hold urns containing the charred bones of sacrificed animals and human infants. These were votive offerings granted to the god Baal Hammon or to the goddess Tanit in exchange for divine blessing. Accompanying the urns are stelae that often bear inscriptions such as this: "To the Lord, to Baal Hammon, the vow which was vowed by 'DNBL'L, son of 'BD'ŠMN: an offering of a man, his own son in completeness. He [the god] heard his [the offerer's] voice and blessed him" (*KAI* #107). The burnt offerings were called *mlk* offerings, and the formulas appearing on the stelae included *mlk 'mr* (sacrifice of a lamb), *mlk b'l* (sacrifice of a lord [a wealthy family's child?]), and *mlk 'dm* (sacrifice of man [a commoner's child]), among others. The substitutionary purpose of the animal sacrifices is clearly spelled out in one Latin stela: "Life for life, blood for blood, a lamb as a substitute" (see comments in *KAI* #61).

The textual and archaeological evidence suggests that *mlk* sacrifices were offered from about 800 B.C.E. until the fall of Carthage in 146 B.C.E. These Punic texts are of interest to biblical scholars because Jer 32:35 and 2 Kgs 23:10 describe human sacrifices in ancient Israel and especially because Lev 18:21 and 20:1–5 forbade the sacrificing of children "to" or "for" *mlk* (*lmlk*). Although these texts in Leviticus have often been interpreted as forbidding sacrifices to the god Molech, on the basis of the Punic evidence many scholars now read these texts as prohibiting *mulk* offerings, that is, burnt offerings of human infants. Although the Punic inscriptions present the sacrifices as acts of devotion, some scholars believe that this was a means of population control (Stager), and a few others believe that the infants offered were stillborn fetuses (Moscati).

Texts and translations: For a few of the many samples, see *KAI* # 61, 98, 99, 103, 105–7, 109–10, 167. **Bibliography:** S. S. BROWN, *Late Carthaginian Child Sacrifice and Sacrificial Monuments in Their Mediterranean Context* (JSOT/ASOR Monograph Series 3; Sheffield, England: JSOT Press, 1991); F. M. CROSS JR., "A Phoenician Inscription from Idalion: Some Old and New Tests Relating to Child Sacrifice," in *Scripture and Other Artifacts* (ed. J. A. Greene; Louisville: Westminster John Knox, 1994), 93–107; CROSS and FREEDMAN, *Early Hebrew Orthography;* J. DAY, *Molech: A God of Human Sacrifice in the Old Testament* (University of Cambridge Oriental Publications 4; Cambridge: Cambridge University Press, 1989); O. EISSFELDT, *Molk als Opferbegriff im Punischen und Hebräischen und das Ende des Gottes Moloch* (Halle, Germany: Niemeyer, 1935); G. C. HEIDER, *The Cult of Molek: A Reassessment* (JSOTSup 43; Sheffield, England: JSOT Press, 1986); K. MANSELL,

"Zeremonielle und rituelle Handlungen bei Baumassnahmen: Zu phönizisch-punischen Bauopfern," in *Rituale in der Vorgeschichte, Antike, und Gegenwart: Studien zur vorderasiatischen, prähistorischen, und klassischen Archäologie, Ägyptologie, alten Geschichte, Theologie, und Religionswissenschaft* (ed. C. Metzner-Nebelsick et al.; Rahden, Germany: Marie Leidorf, 2004), 129–48; S. MOSCATI, "Il sacrificio punico dei fanciulli: Realtà o invenzione?" *Problemi atuali di scienza e di cultura: Accademia Nazionale die Lincei* 261 (1987): 3–15; L. E. STAGER, "Child Sacrifice at Carthage: Religious Rite or Population Control?" *BAR* 10, no. 1 (1984): 31–51; IDEM, "The Rite of Child Sacrifice at Carthage," in *New Light on Ancient Carthage* (ed. J. G. Pedley; Ann Arbor: University of Michigan Press, 1980), 1–11; M. WEINFELD, "The Worship of Molech and the Queen of Heaven and Its Background," *UF* 4 (1972): 133–54.

General Bibliography

W. E. AUFFRECHT, *A Corpus of Ammonite Inscriptions* (Ancient Near Eastern Texts and Studies 4; Lewiston, N.Y.: Mellen, 1989); N. AVIGAD, "Hebrew Epigraphic Sources," in *The Age of the Monarchies: Political History* (ed. A. Malamat; WHJP 4.1; Jerusalem: Massada, 1979), 20–43; N. AVIGAD and B. SASS, *Corpus of West Semitic Stamp Seals* (rev. ed.; Jerusalem: Israel Academy of Sciences and Humanities, Israel Exploration Society, and Institute of Archaeology, Hebrew University, 1997); P. BORDREUIL, F. ISRAEL, and D. PARDEE, "Deux ostraca paléo-hébreux de la collection Sh. Moussaïeff," *Sem* 46 (1996): 49–76; F. M. CROSS JR., "Epigraphic Notes on Hebrew Documents of the Eighth–Sixth Centuries B.C., II: Murabba'ât Papyrus and the Letter Found Near Yabneh-Yam," *BASOR* 165 (1962): 34–46; F. M. CROSS JR. and D. N. FREEDMAN, *Early Hebrew Orthography* (New Haven: American Oriental Society, 1952); G. I. DAVIES, *Ancient Hebrew Inscriptions: Corpus and Concordance* (Cambridge: Cambridge University Press, 1991); M. DIETRICH and I. KOTTSIEPER, eds., *Und Mose schrieb dieses Lied auf—Studien zum Alten Testament und zum alten Orient: Festschrift für Oswald Loretz* (AOAT 250; Münster: Ugarit, 1998); R. DEUTSCH and M. HELTZER, *Forty New Ancient West Semitic Inscriptions* (Tel Aviv: Archaeological Center Publication, 1994); W. G. DEVER, "Asherah, Consort of Yahweh? New Evidence from Kuntillet 'Ajrûd," *BASOR* 255 (1984): 21–37; H. DONNER and W. RÖLLIG, *Kanaanäische und aramäische Inschriften* (3 vols.; 3d ed.; Wiesbaden: Harrassowitz, 1971–1976); J. C. L. GIBSON, *Textbook of Syrian Semitic Inscriptions* (3 vols.; Oxford: Clarendon, 1971–1982); F. E. GREENSPAHN, "Aramaic," in *Beyond Babel: A Handbook for Biblical Hebrew and Related Languages* (ed. J. Kaltner and S. L. McKenzie; Atlanta: Society of Biblical Literature, 2002), 93–108; J. A. HACKETT, "Hebrew (Biblical and Epigraphic)," in *Beyond Babel: A Handbook for Biblical Hebrew and Related Languages* (ed. J. Kaltner and S. L. McKenzie; Atlanta: Society of Biblical Literature, 2002), 139–56; J. D. HAWKINS and H. ÇAMBEL, *Corpus of Hieroglyphic Luwian Inscriptions* (2 vols. in 4; New York: de Gruyter, 1999–2000); C. R. KRAHMALKOV, "Phoenician," in *Beyond Babel: A Handbook for Biblical Hebrew and Related Languages* (ed. J. Kaltner and S. L. McKenzie; Atlanta: Society of

Biblical Literature, 2002), 207–22; J. M. LINDENBERGER, *Ancient Aramaic and Hebrew Letters* (2d ed.; SBLWAW 14; Atlanta: Society of Biblical Literature, 2003); J. NAVEH, *Early History of the Alphabet: An Introduction to West Semitic Epigraphy and Palaeography* (2d rev. ed.; Jerusalem: Magnes Press, 1987); H. NIEHR, "The Changed Status of the Dead in Yehud," in *Yahwism after the Exile: Perspectives on Israelite Religion in the Persian Era* (ed. R. Albertz and B. Becking; Assen, Neth.: Van Gorcum, 2003), 136–55; S. B. PARKER, "Ammonite, Edomite, and Moabite," in *Beyond Babel: A Handbook for Biblical Hebrew and Related Languages* (ed. J. Kaltner and S. L. McKenzie; Atlanta: Society of Biblical Literature, 2002), 43–60; IDEM, *Stories in Scripture and Inscriptions: Comparative Studies on Narratives in Northwest Semitic Inscriptions and the Hebrew Bible* (Oxford: Oxford University Press, 1997); J. RENZ and W. RÖLLIG, *Handbuch der althebräischen Epigrafik* (Darmstadt: Wissenschaftliche Buchgesellschaft, 1995–); C. A. ROLLSTON, "Non-provenanced Epigraphs, I: Pillaged Antiquities, Northwest Semitic Forgeries, and Protocols for Laboratory Tests," *Maarav* 10 (2003): 135–94; IDEM, "Non-provenanced Epigraphs, II: The Status of Non-Provenanced Epigraphs within the Broader Corpus of Northwest Semitic," *Maarav* 11 (2004): forthcoming; M. RÖSEL, "Inscriptional Evidence and the Question of Genre," in *The Changing Face of Form Criticism for the Twenty-First Century* (ed. M. A. Sweeney and E. Ben Zvi; Grand Rapids: Eerdmans, 2003), 107–21; A. SÁNZ-BADILLOS, *A History of the Hebrew Language* (Cambridge: Cambridge University Press, 1993); J. H. TIGAY, *You Shall Have No Other Gods: Israelite Religion in the Light of Hebrew Inscriptions* (HSS 31; Atlanta: Scholars Press, 1986); J. TROPPER, *Die Inschriften von Zincirli* (ALASP 6; Münster: Ugarit, 1993); K. L. YOUNGER JR., "Panammuwa and Bar-Rakib: Two Structural Analyses," *JANES* 18 (1986): 91–103.

Index of Modern Authors

Baines, J., 255, 258, 341
Baker, D. W., 175
Baker, H. D., 38
Bakir, A. el-Mohsen, 232
Bakker, E. J., 405
Bal, M., 268
Balcer, J. M., 399, 404, 405, 414
Barguet, P., 297
Barkay, A., 460
Barkay, G., 92, 200
Barlett, R., 462
Barnes, J. A., 354, 359
Barnes, J. W. B., 255
Barnett, R. D., 125, 212
Barns, J., 108
Barr, J., 1, 21, 401
Barré, M. L., 234, 471
Barstad, H. M., 238
Barta, M., 46, 255
Barta, W., 74, 75
Bartlett, J. R., 359
Barton, G. A., 282
Barton, J., 12, 21
Baruq, A., 122
Bascom, W. R., 11, 15, 21, 268
Batto, B. F., 307, 308, 316, 318
Bauer, J., 40, 198
Baumgarten, A. I., 401
Bayer, B., 125
Bayliss, M., 104, 198
Beal, R. H., 77, 440
Beaulieu, P.-A., 89, 181, 243, 380
Bechtel, G., 393, 396
Becking, B., 457
Beckman, G. M., 51, 77, 171, 190, 278, 330, 392, 397, 438, 439, 440
Beebee, T. O., 21
Begrich, J., 122
Behlmer, H., 29, 52
Behrens, H., 303
Beit-Arieh, I., 456
Beld, S. G., 34
Bell, C., 145, 212
Ben Zvi, E., 7, 24, 238
Ben-Amos, D., 11, 22, 268, 303
Benito, C. A., 309, 310, 341
Benoît, P., 457
Bentzen, A., 185
Berchman, R., 238
Berg, S. B., 269
Berger, P. R., 99, 398
Bergman, J., 247, 251
Bergmann, E., 84
Berhardt, K. H., 106

Berlejung, A., 148, 458
Berlin, A., 22, 269, 275
Bernabé, A., 331, 332, 341
Bickerman, E., 381, 398
Biggs, R. D., 37, 58, 84, 125, 184, 219, 243
Bilgiç, E., 52
Bimson, J., 389
Bing, J. D., 278, 318
Bin-Nun, S. R., 233, 359, 360
Binsbergen, W. van, 212
Biran, A., 467
Birot, M., 196, 197, 349
Bittel, K., 171
Bjerke, S., 149
Black, J. A., 52, 95, 127, 134, 142, 168, 275, 312
Black, J. R., 68
Blacker, C., 322, 341
Blackman, A. M., 70, 122, 142, 149, 231, 254, 255, 258, 328
Blasius, A., 251
Blenkinsopp, J., 278, 428, 432
Block, D. I., 290
Blome, F., 150
Blumenthal, E., 68, 255
Böck, B., 97, 223
Bodi, D., 200
Boecker, J. J., 420, 422, 423, 430, 432
Boehmer, R. M., 45
Boeser, P., 75
Bohannan, L., 360
Bohannan, P., 360
Böhl, F. M. T., 60, 125
Bolle, K. W., 57, 306, 341
Bolle, S. D., 82
Bonechi, M., 223
Bongenaar, A. C. V. M., 44
Bonhême, M.-A., 108
Borchardt, L., 356
Bordreuil, P., 37, 200, 436, 447, 457, 458, 466, 467, 469, 475
Borger, R., 97, 130, 173, 179, 181, 182, 184, 242, 290, 346, 347, 352, 364, 367
Borghouts, J. F., 186, 187
Borowski, O., 450
Bottéro, J., 45, 62, 64, 104, 122, 142, 177, 179, 181, 198, 212, 223, 224, 311, 312, 420, 423, 430, 432
Bounni, A., 37
Bowker, J., 213
Bowman, R. A., 52, 112
Braidwood, L. S., 203
Braidwood, R. J., 203
Braun, J., 125

Index of Hebrew Bible and Early Jewish Literature

Index of Ancient Near
Eastern Sources

Index to English Translations
found in *ANET*

This specialized index is provided for those wishing to find where a given article in *ANET* is referenced in the bibliographies of *Ancient Texts for the Study of the Hebrew Bible.*

Index to English Translations found in *COS*

This specialized index is provided for those wishing to find where a given article in *COS* is referenced in the bibliographies of *Ancient Texts for the Study of the Hebrew Bible.*

Index of Museum Numbers, Textual Realia, and Standard Text Publications